ARCHIBALD PITCAIRNE
THE LATIN POEMS

BIBLIOTHECA LATINITATIS NOVAE

Editors
Jan Waszink • Yasmin Haskell • David Money
Liesbeth de Wreede • Wouter Kool

Advisory Board
Philip Ford • Fokke Akkerman • Chris Heesakkers
Karl Enenkel • Andreas Kinneging

IN THE UNITED STATES AND CANADA, THIS VOLUME IS
PUBLISHED AS PART OF:

MEDIEVAL AND RENAISSANCE
TEXTS AND STUDIES
VOLUME 359

IN THE SERIES:

NEO-LATIN TEXTS AND TRANSLATIONS

Editors
Philip Ford • David Money
Yasmin Haskell • Craig Kallendorf

BLN aims to make available a wide range of Latin texts from the
Renaissance and early modern period.
The series will serve Latinists as well as modern linguists, Renaissance
and early modern historians, historians of art, science and law, and all other
students of the Classical Tradition.

Archibald Pitcairne
THE LATIN POEMS

edited and translated

by

John & Winifred MacQueen

royal van gorcum
acmrs (arizona center for medieval and renaissance studies), tempe, az

2009

© 2009 Koninklijke Van Gorcum BV, PO Box 43, 9400 AA Assen, The Netherlands

All rights reserved. No part of this publication may be reproduced, stored in a retrieval system, or transmitted, in any form or by any means, electronic, mechanical, photocopying, recording, or otherwise, without the prior permission of the publisher.

ISBN 978 90 232 4599 5 (Royal Van Gorcum)
      978 0 86698 407 2 (MRTS)

Printed in The Netherlands by Royal Van Gorcum, Assen

CONTENTS

Preface xi
Abbreviations xiii

Introduction

Archibald Pitcairne (1652–1713) 1
The Political and Religious Background 2
Life 5
    Medical studies. Journeys to France. Pitcairne's rise in medical science 5
    On the Losing side: Pitcairne and the Glorious Revolution. Appointment to Leiden 7
    Unexpected return to Scotland 9
    Promoting Anatomy. A war of pamphlets 11
    Pitcairne's expulsion from the Royal College of Physicians 13
    Jacobites and the Scottish colonial enterprise; Pitcairne arrested 15
    Events in Europe 17
    Pitcairne's later life 19
    Pitcairne's private life. Books and conviviality 27
The Poems 34
The Texts 42
This Edition 46

Bibliography 53

Texts, Translations and Commentaries

1. The *Poemata Selecta* 65
    1. *Ad Rob. Lindesium, 1689.* 66
    2. [*Scotia Martio, 1689.*] 68
    3. *In Geo. Locartum.* 70
    4. *In mortem Vicecomitis Taodunensis* 72
    5. *In Geo. Makinnium* 74
    6. *Ad ★★★* 76
    7. *Ad Marcum Lermontium* 78
    8. *Ad Greppam* 80

CONTENTS

    9. *Ad Dannistonum* 82
  10. *[Ad Jacobum VII]* 84
  11. *Ad Carolum II* 86
  12. *Fabulæ 2. Lib. 1 Phædri Metaphrasis* 88
  13. *In 30. Januarii 1708* 92
  14. *In 30. Januarii 1709* 92
  15. *Ad Janum. 1709* 94
  16. *In Johannem Belhavenium* 98
  17. *In Geo. Makinnium Georgii filium* 98

2. Longer Satiric and Philosophical Poems in Elegiac Couplets 101
  18. *David and Venus* 102
  19. *Edinburgh Taverns* 108
    (a) *To M^r. B. Stote concerning the Edenburgh Taverns* 108
    (b) *Poema Pitcarnii M.D.* 112
  20. *Gualteri Dannistoni ad Georgium Buchananum Epistola et Buchanani Responsum* 118
  21. *Joanni Duci Roxburgi, Archibaldus Pitcarnius S.D.* 132
  22. *Archibaldi Pitcarnii Scoti. Carmen. Anno Aetatis suae LX* 134

3. Wives and Daughters 139
  23. *Ad Annam Pitcarniam* 140
  24. *In Uxorem suam* 140
  25. *Ad Elisam Pitcarniam 10 Junii. 1710* 142
  26. *Ad Joanetam Pitcarniam Decimo Junii Natam* 142
  27. *Ad Margaritam Pitcarniam* 142
  28. *Ad Janum* 144

4. Physicians and Surgeons 147
  29. *Balfoureus moriens loquitur* 148
  30. *In Robertum Sibaldum M.D.* 148
  31. *Q. Horatio Flacco Archibaldus Pitcarnius Caledonius* 150
  32. *[Ad Robertum Morisonum. M.D. et Botanices Professorem Oxoniensem]* 152
  33. *Ad Phoebum Apollinem* 154
  34. *In Davidem Haium Medicum* 154
  35. *[Ad Kirktonum Chirurgum]* 156
  36. (a) *Ad Georgium Kirtonum, Proserpinæ a Potione* 156
    (b) *Ad eundem* 158
  37. *Pitcarnius rogat Tho. Kinkadium ut ad se veniat Decima Junii, quæ sacra est Divæ Margaritæ Scotorum Reginæ* 158
  38. *Thomæ Kinkadio Chirurgo, Archibaldus Pitcarnius Chirurgus, S.D.* 160
  39. *Roberto Graio Scoto Londini Medicinam Profitenti Archibaldus Pitcarnius Scotus S.* 160

CONTENTS

40. (a) *In obitum Archibaldi Stevensoni, Medicorum sui seculi facile principis* 164
    (b) *In obitum Archibaldi Stevensoni, Medici Regii* 164
    (c) *Archibaldo Stevensono Equiti, Scotorum Archiatrorum Comiti, Octogenario, Socero suo, Archibaldus Pitcarnius S.* 166
    (d,1) *In undecimum Martii, quo ante annos octaginta natus est Archibaldus Stevensonus Medicorum apud Scotos facile Princeps* 166
    (d,2) *On the Chief Physitian Sir Archibald Stevenson* 168
41. *Ad Elisam Ramisaeam Archibaldi Stevensoni Medicorum Principis Conjugem Archibaldus Pitcarnius* 168
42. *[Ad Gulielmum Kethum Magnum Scotiæ Mariscallum,* Anno MDCCXII*]* 170
43. *Heriotus Senatui a se constituto sapere* 170
44. *In obitum Alexandri Monteith Chirurgi* 172

5. Friends and Opponents 175

   45. *Ad Robertum Lindesium* 176
   46. *In Joannem Patersonum* 176
   47. *Pythagoras Samius et Isaacus Neutonus Anglus* 178
   48. *D. Atkins Episcopus Orcadensis* 180
   49. *Ad Walterum Dennistonum Ludi Magistrum Mussilburgensem* 180
   50. *Gualterus Danistonus Scotus Sannazario Veneto Propriam quietem Gratulatur* 182
   51. *Vice-Comes de Stairs* 184
   52. *Ad D. Davidem Dalrymplium Equitem &c.* 184
   53. *Ad Hugonem Dalrimplium Supremi Senatus Juridici in Scotia Præsulem* 186
   54. *Ad Gulielmum Carmichael* 186
   55. *Monopennius J.C.* 186
   56. *In Carolum Wilson* 188
   57. *Georg: Ferquhard ad uxorem demortuam* 188
   58. *Thomæ Boero Scoto, Matheseos & Medicinæ Professori, Arch. Pitcarnius Scotus S.* 190
   59. (a) *Ad Andream Tenant* 190
       (b) *Ad Thomam Kinkadium* 192
   60. *Ad Bertramum Stotum Equitem Anglum* 194
   61. *Ad Jovem* 194
   62. *In Barbaram & Margaritam Caroli Stuarti Comitis Traquarij Filias Gemellas* 196
   63. *In Davidem Drummondum in certamine Sagittariorum Edinburgensi Victorem Anno ------* 196
   64. *Davidi Dromondio Jurisconsulto Archibaldus Pitcarnius S.* 196
   65. *Ad Gulielmum Benedictum Equitem Auratum Grubetii Agri Dominum* 200
   66. *Ad Gul. Benedictum de Grubbet, Equitem ----- A.P.* 200
   67. *Andraeae Flechero Regulo Saltonio Archibaldus Pitcarnius S.D.* 202

CONTENTS

68. Viscount Dupplin, his Wife, and his Father 202
    (a) *Dannistonus Pitcarnio S.D.* 202
    (b) *Pitcarnius Dannistono S.D.* 204
    (c) *Maecenati Duplinio Robertus Fribarnus S.D.* 204
    (d) *Archibaldo Pitcarnio Gualterus Dannistonus Ευχαιρειν* 204
    (e) *Ad Haium Comitem Kinulium* 206
69. *Ad Annam Sexto Februarij, Anni 1711* 206
70. *Roberto Fribarnio, Typographo Regio, Et in certamine Sagittariorum Regiorum Victori, A.P.S.D.* 208
71. *Ad Archibaldum Reidium Joannis Reidij Typographi Optimi Filium* 208

6. Political, mainly Jacobite 211
    72. *Lauderdaliæ Dux* 212
    73. *Jacobo Septimo Ejus Nominis, Scotiæ Regi, Die Octobris Decimo quarto* 212
    74. *Ad Phoebum* 212
    75. (a) *Ad G.B.* 214
        (b) *Ad Gilb. Burnet. Scotum, A.P. Scotus* 214
    76. (a) *Proceres Scotorum Anno* MDCXC 216
        (b) *Aliter* 218
    77. *In Nuptias Comitis Levinii* 222
    78. *Ad --------- Malavillam* 222
    79. *Hectoris exuvias indutum cernite Mosen* 224
    80. *[In Jacobum II. Britanniæ Regem]* 224
    81. *In mortem Gulielmi Aurasionensis* 224
    82. *Horatius ad Luciferum* 226
    83. *Hac Jovis Hammonis cineres conduntur in urna* 226
    84. *In Marchionem Montis Rosarum* 228
    85. *Gualteri Dannistoni Epistola ad Joannem Cuningamium Juris Antecessorem, ut maturet reditum ad Inferos* 228
    86. *Ad Cyclopas Alpinos. Virgilius Aeneidos Libro Octavo* 228
    87. *Ad Comitem Cromarteum* 230
    88. *Ad Jacobum Gallovidium Equitem Caledonium* 230
    89. *Elisae Havartae Principi Gordoniae A.P. Scotus S.D.* 230
    90. *Ad Homerum, Catulli carmen ex Græco Sapphûs versum, & Albæ Græcæ repertum, Anno vulgaris Æræ 1711* 232
    91. *[Ad Annam R. Anno* MDCCXI*]* 234
    92. *Goddolphine Stygem potas et Averna fluenta* 234
    93. *Ad Jonathenem ------- Novembris Anni* MDCCXII 236
    94. *In Jacobum Principem Hamiltonium Virum Fortissimum, Parricidio foedissimo trucidatum, Londini Die quindecimo Novembris Anni* MDCCXII 236
    95. *Delphinis quanto Balaena Britannica fertur* 238
    96. *Harlaio* 238
    97. *Arbiter Europae, mandata Brittonis Annae* 238

CONTENTS

- 98. *Ad Annam Britannam* 238
- 99. *Saxonas ac Anglos olim Germania fudit* 240
- 100. *Annae Reginae Archibaldus Pitcarnus Scotus S.D.* 240
- 101. *Multa tulere sacrae, Te, Rex, absente columbae* 240
- 102. *Ad Jacobum Dromondum, Dominus Stobhallum, Archibaldus Pitcarnius Scotus* 242

7. Calendar and Church Year 245
   - 103. *Ad Josephum Scaligerum 29 Maij 1710* 246
   - 104. (a) *In Maij vigesimam nonam, Anno MDCCXII* 246
     - (b) *In Maii XXIX, Sive Juni X, Anni MDCCXII* 248
     - (c) *In Maij vigesimam nonam, Anno MDCCXII* 248
   - 105. (a) *Ad Junium* 248
     - (b) *Ad Junium Anni MDCCXII* 248
   - 106. *IV. Nov. MDCC.XII Ad Calvini Discipulos* 250
   - 107. *Ad Jacobum Magnum* 250
   - 108. *Die XXX Novembris, Anni MDCCXII. Ad Andream Christi Apostolum. Qui Scotis dedit esse Christianis. A.P.* 252
   - 109. (a) *Die XXV. Decembris, Anni MDCCXII* 252
     - (b) *Davidi Drummondo, Edinburgi, XXV Decembris MDCCXIII* 254
   - 110. *Ad Jesum Christum Dei Filium Archibaldus Pitcarnius Scotus* 256
   - 111. *Cur Tibi Natalem felix Heriote quotannis* 258
   - 112. *Ad Januarium Anni MDCCXIII, Archibaldus Pitcarnius Anno Aetatis suae LXI* 258
   - 113. *Dum Tibi laudatur Maij Vigesima Nona* 260
   - 114. *Margarita Regina et Diva Scotorum, Ad Maij Vigesimam Nonam Anni MDCCXIII* 260
   - 115. *Presbyteri Scoti Petro* 260
   - 116. *XXV Julii MDCCXIII* 262
   - 117. *Calderus Visharto, qui se Moderatorem, hoc est, vel Deum aut Regem vocat: sacerdos spurius ex infima Fanatiquaque Plebe* 262

8. European 265
   - 118. (a) *Vaticinium* 266
     - (b) *Vaticinium in Sepulcro Caroli Quinti repertum 1710* 266
   - 119. *Carole, si similis Fratris, similisque Parentis* 266
   - 120. (a) *[Ad Carolum XII. Suecorum Regem.]* 268
     - (b) *Carole Gothorum Ductor fortissime, solus* 270
   - 121. *Lodoix Maria Stuarta* 270
   - 122. (a) *Maria Lodoix Britanna ad Alaricam Suecam* 270
     - (b) *Maria Lodoix Stuarta, ad Alaricam Suecam* 272

CONTENTS

  9. Translations 275
     123. *ΜΟΡΜΟΝΟΣΤΟΛΙΣΜΟΣ sive Lamiarum Vestitus* 276
     124. *An Inscription on John Bell* 288

10. Dubia. Poems probably by Walter Dennistoun and Robert Hepburn 293
     125. *In Annum Millesimum Septingentesimum* 294
     126. *Ricardio Stilio Anglo, Viro hujus Sæculi Maximo, Robertus Hepburnius Scotus. S.D.* 294
     127. *Ad Georgium Makenzium, Regium, olim, apud Scotos, Advocatum, Roberti Hepburnii, Scoti, Carmen Sapphicum* 298

Commentary 301

Index of Titles 459
Index of First Lines 463
Index of Poems Referred to in the Introduction 469
Index 471

PREFACE

Archibald Pitcairne (1652–1713) is the latest, the liveliest and, in some ways, the most original Scottish writer of neo-Latin verse. His poems are still worth reading for their quality and originality, and for the vivid image they present of an intellectual universe, historical certainly, but by now almost wholly unfamiliar, which combines the new world of science and medicine with the old world in which the Divine Right of Kings and the authority of the classical past predominated. Pitcairne's poetry was much appreciated in his own time, but there is to date no complete edition of his poems. 'There is a design of collecting his poems, and printing them altogether.' So wrote Dr John Drummond immediately after Pitcairne's death. *Selecta Poemata Archibaldi Pitcarnii Med. Doctoris ... et Aliorum* was published in 1727, but, as the title indicates, contained no more than a selection and gave only the Latin text of the poems included. Quite apart from this, an amount of early printed and MS material sufficient to surprise us has survived in Scottish, English and American libraries. In this volume we have attempted to bring together the entire corpus of Pitcairne's Latin verse, together with introduction, translation and commentary. The range is considerably wider than might be suspected by a reader who confined himself to *Selecta Poemata*.

We must acknowledge the great help which a number of libraries and their staffs have cheerfully provided: the Librarian and staff of the National Library of Scotland; the Edinburgh Room, Edinburgh Central Library; Special Collections, Edinburgh University Library; Special Collections, Glasgow University Library; the Bodleian Library; the British Library; the Brotherton Library, University of Leeds and the Rosenbach Museum and Library, Philadelphia. We have also received assistance, for which we are grateful, from the Director and staff of the Harry Ransom Humanities Research Center, University of Texas at Austin, and the Curator and staff of the Beinecke Rare Book and Manuscript Library at Yale.

We owe special thanks to John Dallas, Rare Books Librarian of the Royal College of Physicians, Edinburgh, Dr Anita Guerrini of the Centre Alexandre Koyré, Paris, Dr David Money of Cambridge University, and Dr Jan Waszink of the University of Utrecht, all of whom have given us useful, sometimes salutary, information, commentary and advice. For much detailed help we also thank Tricia Boyd, Geoffrey Carnall, Khumo Fisher, Professor R.D.S. Jack, Steve Kerr, Najia Khan, Professor H.L. MacQueen, Professor M. Pittock, Fred Robertson, Sheriff J. Irvine Smith, and Dr Corinna Vermeulen.

We gratefully acknowledge permission to reproduce illustrations granted by the Royal College of Physicians, Edinburgh, for the portrait of Archibald Pitcairne; the National Galleries of Scotland for the portrait of James VII and II; the National

PREFACE

Portrait Gallery for the portraits of Prince James Francis Edward Stuart and Princess Louisa Maria Theresa Stuart, and to the Bodleian Library, University of Oxford for permission to reproduce a page from their copy of *Poemata Selecta*.

For financial support towards the publication of this volume we are grateful to the Royal Society of Edinburgh, the Strathmartine Trust, and the Carnegie Trust for the Universities of Scotland.

We are, of course, ourselves solely responsible for any errors or omissions.

John and Winifred MacQueen

ABBREVIATIONS

A. Sigla

A   *Ad Haium Comitem Kinulium* (Robert Freebairn: Edinburgh, n.d.).

APP   EUL MS, *Archibaldi Pitcarnii M.D. Poemata. Oct^{ri} An. 1703*, bound in with printed *Catalogus Librorum Archibald Pitcairne*, shelf-mark La.III.629.

BA(4)   Oxford, Bodleian Library, *Antiq.d.x.7(4)* [MS].

BA(4a)   Oxford, Bodleian Library, *Antiq.d.x.7(4)* [Broadsides].

BD   Oxford, Bodleian Library, MS *Don.c.58*.

D   *Die XXV Decembri; Anni MDCCXII* ([Edinburgh]: Robert Freebairn, 1712).

E   *Gualteri Dannistoni ad Georgium Buchananum Epistola et Buchanani Responsum* (Edinburgh: James Watson, 1700).

F   GUL MS, *Ferguson 108*.

HRHRC   Harry Ransom Humanities Research Center, University of Texas at Austin.

N   NLS, *H.23.a.16* (broadside and MS content).

PS   *Poemata Selecta 9ab5c2d8eg2h14i3l8m10n5o4p7r6s7t6v* (?Edinburgh: s.n., ?1709)

R^1, R^2   *Reliquiae Pitcairnianae*, Edinburgh Room, Edinburgh Central Library, ref. qyR489P68, accession nos., 13817, 36553 (broadside content).

S   BL, MS *Sloane 3198*.

SP   *Selecta Poemata Archibaldi Pitcarnii Med. Doctoris, Gulielmi Scot a Thirlestane, Equitis, Thomæ Kincadii, Civis Edinburgensis, et Aliorum* (Edinburgh: Robert Freebairn, 1727).

SRO, MK.GD.124.15   Mar and Kellie Papers in Scottish Record Office

YB   Beinecke Rare Book and Manuscript Library, Yale University.

The *apparatus criticus* to this edition is set up as follows. It is organised by source (not verse line). First the apparatus gives the sources (manuscripts or printed books) of the *Title*(s) and *Text* of the poem in question (e.g. *BA(4)*), subdivided into different versions where applicable by (a), (b) etc, and followed by the relevant location in it. The source indications are explained in the *Sigla*. The apparatus then gives the significant textual differences from the printed text; organised by source, followed by line number in the poem. The location of the poem in the source is now omitted (see e.g. p. 176: BA(4): 1 or BA(4), 1 = *BA(4)*, f.7^r, line 1).

ABBREVIATIONS

B. General

ASLS	Association for Scottish Literary Studies
Assembly	see Tobin, *Assembly*
AV	Authorised Version
b.	born
BL	British Library
Black, *Surnames*	George F. Black, *The Surnames of Scotland*
Bond Book	*Bond Book of the Royal Company of Archers*
c.	around, about
Cf., cf.	compare
Chambers, *Traditions*	Robert Chambers, *Traditions of Edinburgh*
Craig, *History*	W.S. Craig, *History of the Royal College of Physicians of Edinburgh*
CUP	Cambridge University Press
Curtius, *Latin Middle Ages*	E.R. Curtius, *European Literature and the Latin Middle Ages*
d.	died
Devine, *Scottish Nation*	T.M. Devine, *The Scottish Nation 1700–2000*
Dickinson, *Reformation in Scotland*	*John Knox's History of the Reformation in Scotland*
DNB	*Dictionary of National Biography*
ed.	editor, edited (by)
e.g.	for example
edn.	edition
EUL	Edinburgh University Library
EUP	Edinburgh University Press
f., ff.	folio(s)
Figgis, *Divine Right*	John Neville Figgis, *The Divine Right of Kings*
Foxon, *Verse*	David F. Foxon, *English Verse 1701–1750* (2 vols.)
Goldie, *Episcopal Church*	Frederick Goldie, *A Short History of the Episcopal Church in Scotland from the Restoration to the Present Time*
Grant, *Faculty of Advocates*	F.J. Grant, *The Faculty of Advocates in Scotland 1532–1943*
Hiscock, *Gregory*	David Gregory, *Isaac Newton and their circle. Extracts from David Gregory's memoranda, 1677–1708*, ed. W.G. Hiscock
HMSO	Her (or His) Majesty's Stationery Office
Hoppit, *Land of Liberty?*	Julian Hoppit, *A Land of Liberty? England 1689–1727*
Ibid., ibid.	in the same place
i.e.	that is
Johnston, *Best of our owne*	*The best of our owne: letters of Archibald Pitcairne 1652–1713*, ed. W.T. Johnston

ABBREVIATIONS

Kinloch, *Babell*	*Babell; or The Assembly, a Poem* MDCXCII, ed. George R. Kinloch
l., ll.	line(s)
leg.	read
Lenman, *Jacobite Risings*	Bruce Lenman, *The Jacobite Risings in Britain 1689–1746*
Lewis and Short	C.T. Lewis and C. Short, *A Latin Dictionary*
loc. cit.	in the place already cited
Minute Book	*Minute Book of the Faculty of Advocates*, ed. J.M. Pinkerton
MLA	*Musa Latina Aberdonensis*, ed. Sir William Duguid Geddes and William Keith Leisk
Molhuysen, *Bronnen*	*Bronnen tot de Geschiedenis der Leidsche universiteit. 1574–1811* IV, ed. P.C. Molhuysen
Money, *English Horace*	D.K. Money, *The English Horace: Anthony Alsop and the Tradition of British Latin Verse*
MS, MSS	manuscript(s)
NAS	National Archives of Scotland
n.d.	no date (of publication)
NLS	National Library of Scotland
n.p.	no place (of publication)
N.S.	New Style (of dating)
OBGV	*Oxford Book of Greek Verse*
OBLV	*Oxford Book of Latin Verse*
OCD	*Oxford Classical Dictionary*
OCL	*Oxford Companion to Law*
OCT	Oxford Classical Texts
ODCC	*Oxford Dictionary of the Christian Church*
ODS	*Oxford Dictionary of Saints*
op.cit.	in the work already cited
O.S.	Old Style (of dating)
OUP	Oxford University Press
OxfDNB	*Oxford Dictionary of National Biography* (online edn.)
p., pp.	page(s)
PBGV	*Penguin Book of Greek Verse*
Pittock, *Poetry and Politics*	Murray G.H. Pittock, *Poetry and Jacobite Politics in Eighteenth-Century Britain and Ireland*
Quintilian, *Inst.*	Marcus Fabius Quintilianus, *Institutio Oratoria*
q. v.	which see
RCPE	Royal College of Physicians of Edinburgh
Ritchie, *Early Days*	Robert Peel Ritchie, *The Early Days of the Royall Colledge of Phisitians, Edinburgh*
Scotland's Ruine	George Lockhart of Carnwath, *Scotland's Ruine*

ABBREVIATIONS

Shirlaw, 'Black Years'	Leslie Shirlaw, 'Dr Archibald Pitcairne and Sir Isaac Newton's "Black Years" (1692–1694)'
SHS	Scottish History Society
s.n.	without name (of publisher)
SRS	Scottish Record Society
Stair, *Institutes*	James Dalrymple, 1st Viscount Stair, *Institutions of the Law of Scotland*
STS	Scottish Text Society
s.v.	under the title
Tobin, *Assembly*	*The Assembly by Archibald Pitcairne*, ed. Terence Tobin
trs.	translator, translated (by)
ut cit.	as cited
v.	see

INTRODUCTION[1]

ARCHIBALD PITCAIRNE (1652–1713)

Pitcairne was a politically motivated physician who left a substantial legacy of Latin verse, mostly of remarkable quality. His poems are intensely personal; they are terse (sometimes to a fault) and even the longest retains something of the flavour of the epigram. Politically he was on the losing side and, partly as a consequence, he saw and judged the world of late seventeenth- and early eighteenth-century Europe in terms of the later Roman Empire. His poems frequently echo Horace and Virgil, but their closer kinship with Martial, Juvenal, even Claudian, soon becomes evident. Pitcairne assumes that the natural state, from which Britain, and more particularly Scotland, has fallen, is Augustan, as it had been during the golden reign of Charles II (1660–1685). Despite its subsequent occupation by the barbarians, Edinburgh remains *Augusta*. Abused Scottish institutions he continues to see in terms of their Roman counterparts – *Jura silent, torpent classica, Rostra vacant*.

Paradoxically (to us), Pitcairne was also an exponent of the new science which established itself during the seventeenth century. He was a friend and disciple of Sir Isaac Newton and an exponent of medical and surgical treatment based on experiment – dissection, measurement and mathematical analysis. This brought him into conflict with more old-fashioned practitioners, a conflict reflected in a number of satirical mock-epitaphs as well as in poems of direct denunciation. Correspondingly, some of his odes and addresses are poems in praise of the more enlightened members of his profession. As many poems show, Pitcairne was a convivial man. He enjoyed the company of his friends even more than

---

[1] For events and movements during the period, we have mainly relied on Gordon Donaldson, *Scotland James V to James VII* (Edinburgh and London, 1965), Frances Dow, *Cromwellian Scotland 1651–1660* (Edinburgh, 1979, reprinted 1999); William Ferguson, *Scotland 1689 to the Present* (Edinburgh, 1968 and later reprints); A. Goldie, *A Short History of the Episcopal Church in Scotland*, 2nd edn. (Edinburgh, 1976), Ian B. Cowan, *The Scottish Covenanters 1660–1688* (London, 1976), Julian Hoppit, *A Land of Liberty? England 1689–1727* (Oxford, 2000); Bruce Lenman, *The Jacobite Risings in Britain 1689–1746* (London, 1980, new edn. Aberdeen, 1995); Murray G.H. Pittock, *Poetry and Jacobite Politics in Eighteenth-Century Britain and Ireland* (Cambridge, 1994); *Jacobitism* (London, 1998), D.K. Money, *The English Horace: Anthony Alsop and the Tradition of British Latin Verse* (Oxford, 1998), and John Prebble, *Darien. The Scottish Dream of Empire* (reprint, Edinburgh, 2000). For Pitcairne's life, we are particularly indebted to Dr Anita Guerrini's account in *OxfordDNB*; we have used the online edn. which lacks pagination. T.F. Henderson's article in the old *DNB* (London, 1908–1909, XV, 1222–1223) still has some useful material. See too Charles Webster, *An Account of the Life and Writings of Dr. Pitcairne* (Edinburgh, 1781). Pitcairne habitually wrote little personal memoirs for himself or his friends. These sometimes produce illuminating detail. For help with material relating to the Netherlands we are much indebted to Dr Jan H. Waszink of the University of Utrecht.

the discomfort of his enemies. Obviously he took pleasure in the mere act of composition, but his poetry also served, or at least was intended to serve, as an instrument of scientific and political advance. It is thus almost wholly occasional.

The Political and Religious Background

During most of Pitcairne's life his native Scotland was a kingdom with its own parliamentary, church and legal systems. Scottish events and institutions helped to shape his mind and outlook. Because much of this may be unfamiliar to some readers, it seems best to begin with an outline of the more relevant details.

In 1603 King James VI of Scotland (reigned 1567–1625) succeeded to the throne of England as James I, but, until the incorporating Union of the Scottish and English Parliaments in 1707, he and his successors ruled over what were still two separate countries. His successors were Charles I (1625–1649), Charles II (1651–1685 in Scotland, 1660–1685 in England), James VII of Scotland, II of England (1685–1689), William II and III (1689–1702), for a time joint ruler with his wife, Mary II (1689–1694), daughter of James VII and II, and finally Anne (1702–1714), also a daughter of James, during whose reign the incorporating Union took place. With the exception of William, all belonged to the House of Stuart, the Scottish royal house since 1371. The reigns of Charles I and II were separated by the republican interlude of the Commonwealth and the rule of Oliver Cromwell. The English Civil War (1642–1649) ended with the execution of Charles I on 30 January 1649, an act which roused almost universal horror, after which Cromwell's forces invaded and conquered Scotland, which was then (October 1651) made part of the Commonwealth. The death of Cromwell on 3 September 1658 led fairly quickly to the restoration of the monarchy, symbolised by the meeting in Whitehall of Charles II and the English Parliament on 29 May 1660, a day which was also the King's birthday. In general, it was regarded as an occasion for rejoicing. With the Restoration Scotland recovered the status of a separate kingdom.

During this period, two forms of church government played an important, if disruptive, role in Scottish affairs. One was the Episcopalian system according to which the supreme head of the church was the monarch, who delegated authority to archbishops and bishops whom he appointed. There were two Scottish archbishoprics, St Andrews and Glasgow, and thirteen diocesan bishoprics. The form of service to be used in churches was set out in the printed Prayer Book. Vestments were worn by the clergy. The festivals of the Christian Year, in particular Christmas, Easter and some saint's days, were observed. Theology was in general somewhat less rigid than that of their rivals, the Presbyterians. Episcopalians held to the doctrine of the Divine Right of Kings and the Passive Obedience of subjects; they were firm believers in a hereditary monarchy.[2] In the view of extreme Presbyterians, much of this was heresy.

---

[2] See especially John Neville Figgis, *The Divine Right of Kings*, 2nd edn. (Cambridge, 1922).

INTRODUCTION

Episcopalianism predominated in Scotland during the reigns of Charles II and James VII.

In the Presbyterian system, individual churches were controlled by the parish minister and his ruling elders. Parishes were grouped into local presbyteries; over all was the General Assembly which, in theory at least, met annually to legislate for the entire church. (In fact, there was no Assembly between 1653 and 1690. Neither Cromwell, Charles II nor James VII approved of the institution.) A Moderator, elected annually by the Assembly, presided. The monarch nominated a Commissioner to the Assembly, but otherwise had no special position or authority. Services kept to no prescribed form. The most important feature was the sermon, in which the preacher expounded the Word and its implications, as he saw them. No Church festivals were observed. Ministers were distinguished only by the Geneva gown and bands. The theology was that of John Calvin (1509–1564), with a heavy emphasis on predestination (to damnation as well as salvation) and consequently on the Elect.

Most Presbyterians held to the National Covenant (1638) and the Solemn League and Covenant (1643). The first was a manifesto against the Episcopalian High Church rituals encouraged by Charles I; the second an agreement on the part of the Presbyterians to assist the English Parliament against Charles I during the English Civil War, on condition that Parliament would impose Presbyterianism on England. The aid was given, but the condition systematically ignored.

Presbyterians dominated Scottish affairs between 1638 and 1651. After the execution of Charles I, however, they split into two parties, the extremist Protesters or Remonstrants who were in favour of the execution, and the Resolutioners, who were not. The Protesters adhered strictly to the Covenants and became known as Covenanters. Under the Commonwealth they lost power (Cromwell and most of his English supporters were neither Presbyterian nor Episcopalian, but Congregationalist) and, after the Restoration, in 1662 some 250 ministers, for the most part Protesters, were deprived from their parishes. They took to field-preaching, which the government attempted to stamp out, only to meet armed resistance. The main encounters were at Rullion Green (1666), Drumclog (1 June 1679), Bothwell Brig (22 June 1679) and Airds Moss (22 July 1680). The Protesters or Covenanters were victorious only at Drumclog. Many who were captured were executed or shipped off to slavery overseas. To the government they were rebels and anarchists; to the faithful they were saints and martyrs.

Both denominations, but especially the Presbyterians, disliked, many actively feared, the Roman Catholicism, to which James VII had been converted when he was still Duke of York. For most Episcopalians, however, loyalty to the royal line remained predominant. During James's reign many Protesters together with a few Resolutioners and Episcopalians emigrated from Scotland to the Netherlands, where the Stadholder was James's Protestant son-in-law, William of Orange-Nassau (1650–1702). Meanwhile, in England and Scotland, religious and political discomfort culminated with the birth of a royal son and heir, James Francis (1688–1766), on 10 June 1688, and the consequent prospect of a continuance of Catholic sovereignty. On 5 November William landed at Torbay in Devon and rapidly made a bloodless conquest of England. One of James's leading officers, John Churchill (1650–1722), went over to William. He became Earl of Marlborough and Commander-in-Chief of the English army. In Scotland, John Graham of Claverhouse, Viscount Dundee (1648–1689) offered armed resistance; he defeated William's forces at Killiecrankie, 27 July 1689, but was himself mortally wounded. For a time thereafter active resistance petered out. Rather to William's discomfort, the Protesters seized their opportunity. Between 1689 and 1702, at a time when the total number of Scottish parishes was about 900, some 664 Episcopalian ministers either left or were driven out of their parishes. The Scottish Universities were 'purged' of their teachers in the same way.

Episcopalian loyalists, together with others of a like mind, became known as 'Tories' or 'Jacobites' (Latin *Jacobus*, 'James'). Supporters of William were 'Whigs'.

Much of William's reign was occupied with the Nine Years War (1689–1697) against the French king, Louis XIV, who extended his protection to the fugitive James VII. Churchill was dismissed from his command in 1692, almost certainly for Jacobitical activities. Most Jacobites at least passively supported Louis, as they also did during the War of the Spanish Succession (1702–1713), which soon followed.

Jacobitism remained a living force in Scotland, and also, to a more limited extent, in England. In 1708 there was an abortive attempt at a Scottish rising in favour of James Francis, 'James VIII and III', the Old Pretender. When Queen Anne died in 1714, leaving no surviving child, swift action on the part of the Whigs ensured the succession of the Protestant Hanoverian, George I (1714–1727); the unsuccessful rising of 1715 followed. That of 1745, under the Young Pretender, Prince Charles Edward Stuart (1720–1788), son of James Francis, was a much more serious affair. Indeed, even as late as 1777, more than ten years after the death of the Old Pretender, Dr Johnson could remark: 'If England were fairly polled, the present King [George III] would be sent away tonight, and his adherents hanged tomorrow ... The state of the country is this: the people knowing it to be agreed on all hands that this King has not the hereditary right to the crown, and there being no hope that he who has it can be restored, have grown cold and indifferent upon the subject of loyalty, and have no warm attachment to any King. They would not, therefore, risk anything to restore the exiled family. They would not give twenty shillings a piece to bring it about. But if a mere vote could do it, there would be twenty to one; at least, there would be a very great majority for it.'[3]

By then, much the same, probably, was true of Scotland. Earlier, at the turn of the eighteenth century, Jacobitism, usually combined with Episcopalianism, was

---

[3] *Boswell's Life of Johnson*, 2 vols. (Everyman's Library, London, 1960), ii, 115–116.

INTRODUCTION

more active and more vocal. The distrust of Roman Catholicism felt by most Episcopalians was insufficient to outweigh hereditary loyalty and moreover was tempered by unrealistic hopes that James, with his son, might yet return to the religion of his earlier days.

Life

Archibald Pitcairne was born in Edinburgh on Christmas Day, 1652, the son of Alexander Pitcairne, merchant and magistrate, and Janet Sydserff (d. 1698). The family were Episcopalian and had a long history of loyalty to the Stuart royal family. His mother was probably related to Thomas Sydserf (1587–1663), Bishop of Brechin (1634) and of Galloway (1635), deposed in 1638, but restored as Bishop of Orkney in 1661. Pitcairne, from which the family took its name, is, or was, a hamlet near Leslie in Fife. Pitcairnegreen, a small estate near Perth, belonged to Alexander Pitcairne.

Archibald attended the High School of Dalkeith, Midlothian, not far from Edinburgh. There he acquired the skill in Latin prose, verse and conversation necessary for entrance to the four-year course, leading to the degree of MA, in the Tounis College, the University of Edinburgh. He entered the College in 1668. The undergraduate course was general, 'including both classics and exact sciences, and culminating in compulsory philosophy'.[4] As was usual at the time, Latin was the main language used in teaching. Within the College, the use of any other, save Greek and Hebrew, was forbidden.

Pitcairne's closest friend in the College was Robert Lindsay, eldest son of James Lindsay of the Mount, Fife, whom he had known from childhood. Another contemporary was Walter Dennistoun, afterwards schoolmaster of Musselburgh, Midlothian, who had aspirations as a Latin poet, aspirations which led to his becoming the butt of much of Pitcairne's own Latin verse.[5]

Medical studies. Journeys to France. Pitcairne's rise in medical science

Pitcairne graduated on 20 May 1671. His first intention thereafter was to qualify as an advocate, a lawyer entitled to plead in the highest Scottish courts. The intensity of his legal studies, however, made him ill. To recover he was sent to France. In Paris he met with some Scottish medical students and began to develop an interest in their subject. A few months later, his father summoned him home. There he returned to mathematics, in which he rapidly gained considerable expertise. His contribution to the method of infinite series, important for the new discipline of calculus, was later recognised in the third volume of the *Opera Mathematica* (1693–1699) of the English mathematician and cryptologist John Wallis (1616–1703).

---

[4] George Elder Davie, *The Democratic Intellect*, 2nd edn. (Edinburgh, 1964), 4.
[5] See below.

Pitcairne thus gained the instrument for much of his later work in medicine and anatomy and for his interest in Newtonian physics and problems of the calendar.

In 1675 Pitcairne returned to Paris to pursue medical studies. Shortly after his arrival, Robert Lindsay died in Edinburgh. His death and subsequent apparition had a lasting affect on Pitcairne.[6] Little is known of Pitcairne's medical studies, but on 13 August 1680 he obtained his MD from the University of Rheims. He returned to Edinburgh, where, so far as he was concerned, the great event was the establishment in 1681 of the Royal College of Physicians. Pitcairne was the youngest among the twenty-one original Fellows, probably also the most advanced in terms of medical theory and practice. From 1683 to 1685 he was Depute Honorary Librarian, and from 1684 to 1695 Secretary of the College. In 1685 he became one of three professors of medicine in the University. The Town Council gave no support and none of the three seems ever to have lectured in University precincts. Notes by students, however, on lectures undoubtedly given by Pitcairne are preserved in the Library of the Royal College of Physicians of Edinburgh.[7]

It seems likely that by 1680 Pitcairne had met David Gregory (1661–1708), nephew of James Gregorie (1638–1675), Professor of Mathematics at St Andrews from 1668 to 1674, and at Edinburgh from 1674 to his premature death. Gregorie's unpublished papers were left to his nephew. Together with Pitcairne, he set to work on them. 'Amongst the Gregory MSS in Edinburgh University Library are innumerable sheets of calculations, some begun in Pitcairne's writing and finished in Gregory's, others the other way about'.[8] In 1683 Pitcairne issued a public challenge to the incumbent of the Edinburgh chair of mathematics, John Young, to solve a problem.[9] Young's failure led to his dismissal, and although David Gregory had not yet completed his degree, he was elected to the chair. Pitcairne may have issued his challenge with such an outcome in mind.

In 1687 the two briefly shared lodgings. They were together when Gregory received a copy of Newton's *Principia* shortly after its publication in July of that year. Pitcairne shared Gregory's excitement.

Earlier, in 1683, Pitcairne had delivered the oration at the funeral of the Scot, Robert Morison (1620–1683), physician and Professor of Botany at Oxford. He may have been invited to do so by his London-based friend, Dr Robert Gray,

[6] See 1 and introductory note.

[7] *Praxis medica Pitcarniana*, 2 vols., one quarto, one folio [c. 1700?]. *Collegium medicinae practicum secundum methodum Riverianum ordinatum Edinburgh* [c. 1700?] is bound with the *Praxis* in the quarto volume.

[8] Leslie Shirlaw, 'Dr. Archibald Pitcairne and Sir Isaac Newton's "Black Years" (1692–1694)', *Royal College of Physicians, Edinburgh, Chronicle*, 5 (Jan. 1975), 24.

[9] *Exempla additionis, subtractionis, multiplicationis, divisionis, involutionis et evolutionis, ad quorum reflectionem Joannem Young invitat Archibald Pitcairne* (Edinburgh, March 1, 1683); *Quamvis Johannes Young publice fuerit ab Archibaldo Pitcairne invitatus ut problemata duo solveret* ... (Edinburgh, March 20, 1683). Both brief pamphlets are in EUL, Special Collections, ref. *Dc.1.61/187*.

INTRODUCTION

who appears to have been related to Morison. The invitation reflects the scientific esteem in which he was already held.

In or about 1685 Pitcairne married Margaret Hay, daughter of Colonel James Hay of Pitfour, Aberdeenshire. They had a daughter, Anne, and a son, who died in infancy. Margaret herself died in 1690 and was buried in Greyfriars churchyard, Edinburgh. Anne was still alive in 1694; how long she lived is uncertain.

In 1688 Pitcairne published in Edinburgh a pamphlet, *Solutio problematis de historicis; seu de inventoribus dissertatio*, primarily a vindication of the Englishman, William Harvey's claim (1628) to the discovery that blood circulates through the arteries and veins of the body. At much the same time he wrote a satire, *Epistola Archimedis ad Regem Gelonem*, in form a reply by the Greek mathematician Archimedes (c. 287–212 BC) to the query whether geometrical methods might be applied to religious matters, but in fact directed predominantly against Roman Catholic and Presbyterian beliefs and practices. At first this probably circulated in MS; it was not actually printed until 1710,[10] with no indication of authorship.

On the Losing side: Pitcairne and the Glorious Revolution. Appointment to Leiden

On 10 June 1688 a son and heir, James Francis, was born to the reigning monarch, the Catholic James VII and II, an event which, as has been noted, led directly to the so-called Glorious Revolution of 1688–1689. Pitcairne and his friends remained committed, politically and ecclesiastically, to the old regime. His own position is clearly demonstrated by his play, *The Assembly*,[11] a brilliant satirical portrait of life in Edinburgh during the unrepresentative 1690 meeting of the General Assembly of the Church of Scotland (the first since 1653), which took place as a consequence of the Revolution. The play was begun 'just after the king of France took Mons' (on 9 April 1691), but not completed until some four-and-a-half months later. It may or may not have been performed, and was first published anonymously in 1722, several years after Pitcairne' death.

Circumstances at home became awkward. The Acts of the 1690 Assembly led to a 'purgation' of the Scottish universities, David Gregory did not lose his post, but left the country in disgust, soon to become (on Newton's recommendation) Savilian Professor of Astronomy at Oxford (December 1691). Pitcairne shared his disgust.

On 8 September 1691 (*n.s.*; *o.s.*, 30 August) the Senatus of the University of Leiden in Holland resolved to obtain particulars of Pitcairne with a view to appointing him Professor of Medicine in succession to Lucas Schacht, who had died on 10 March. On 18 October the Curators of the University received a letter from the Scot, Gilbert Burnet, Bishop of Salisbury, commending Pitcairne.

---

[10] An edition may have appeared at Amsterdam in 1706. See S.M. Simpson, 'An Anonymous and Undated Edinburgh Tract', *The Book Collector* (1966), 67.

[11] Ed. Terence Tobin (Lafayette, Indiana, 1972).

INTRODUCTION

On 28 November they received another from James Dalrymple, 1st Viscount Stair (1619–1695). They offered the chair to Pitcairne, using Dalrymple as their intermediary.[12] On 26 December (*o.s.*), Pitcairne wrote, accepting the offer.[13]

It is somewhat surprising to find in Burnet and Dalrymple, both adherents of King William, the patrons of a man who belonged to a party opposed to their own. Almost equally surprising is the fact that Pitcairne accepted an appointment in a country the Stadholder of which he so much abhorred.

In April 1692 Pitcairne took up the appointment. On his way to Holland he and Gregory stayed with Newton in Cambridge from 2 to 3 March. Newton 'was in the middle of writing a short paper, "De Natura Acidorum", but seemed unable to finish it. Pitcairne completed it, adding two explanatory phrases, the last five lines of the essay, and two short notes that follow. The original MS, with the additions in Pitcairne's handwriting, still exists, and most of Pitcairne's completion was incorporated in the printed edition. Thereafter, Pitcairne wrote several letters in Latin to Newton, mostly on physical and chemical subjects. The correspondence, however, gradually petered out.'[14]

Pitcairne's inaugural lecture on 26 April 1692 was printed (Leiden, 1692; Edinburgh, 1696) as *Archibaldi Pitcarnii oratio qua ostenditur medicinam ab omni philosophorum sectâ esse liberam; et exemplo docetur quantam utilitatem medicis afferre possit mathesis.* A brief extract illustrates his main thesis, that medicine should abandon all metaphysical elements and instead, like Newtonian astronomy and physics, base itself on mathematics: *Astronomi paucis contenti postulatis facile ostendunt nihil sibi officere sectarum opiniones neque demonstrationes suas turbari sive extent formæ substantiales sive non extent, & sive extet materia subtilis, sive non extet. Et nos adhuc dubitamus iisdem artibus Medicinam extendere?*[15]

The inaugural lecture, together with the subsequent lecture-course, was later published as *Dissertationes medicæ* (Rotterdam, 1701). His Leiden students included men of some future distinction – the physicians William Cockburn (1669–1739) and Richard Mead (1673–1754), the surgeons John Monro (1670–1740) and Robert Elliot (d. 1714). Mead subsequently interceded for Pitcairne's son, Andrew, who had been condemned to death for his involvement in the 1715 Jacobite rising, and succeeded in obtaining his release from the Tower of London.

The great Dutch teacher of medicine, Herman Boerhaave (1668–1738), may have been another who attended Pitcairne's lectures,[16] although there is no positive proof that he did. Otherwise the students mentioned are all Scots or English. Those

---

[12] P.C. Molhuysen, *Bronnen*, IV (Den Haag, 1920), 96.
[13] W.T. Johnston (ed.), *The best of our owne: letters of Archibald Pitcairne, 1652–1713* (Edinburgh, 1979), 15, letter 1.
[14] Shirlaw, 'Black Years', 24–25.
[15] *Oratio*, as printed in *Dissertationes medicæ*, 5.
[16] E. Ashworth Underwood, *Boerhaave's Men at Leyden and After* (Edinburgh, 1977), 90. But contrast p. 7: 'there is not a vestige of evidence that Boerhaave ever attended a formal medical lecture in the University of Leyden'.

who came from continental Europe may have had difficulties with Pitcairne's way of pronouncing Latin. In letters dated 17 and 18 December 1691, the humanist Theodoor Jansson van Almeloveen (1657–1712) criticised his appointment on two grounds; *difficile Scotis adeo lingua latina est, ut vix ulli intelligantur, dein nostrae provinciae ac terrae longe alius genius est, longe aëris constitutio, homines aliter educati*.[17] The second may be discounted; the first, however, may have some force. Almeloveen makes the final comment that it would have been better to appoint a native of Holland.

These comments may not have been entirely disinterested. Almeloveen was professor of medicine, as well as history and Greek, in the short-lived University of Harderwijk on the shores of the Zuiderzee, and may have wanted the Leiden post for himself. He was also the author of *Inventa novantiqua. Id est brevis enarratio ortus & progressus artis medicae, ac praecipue de inventis vulgo novis … in ea repertis* (Amsterdam, 1684), in which he claimed, and sought to demonstrate, that modern medical discoveries had in fact been anticipated by physicians of the ancient school of Hippocrates of Cos. In particular, chapter XXVIII (pp. 223–238) is concerned with the circulation of the blood, dismissing Harvey's claim to the discovery. This thesis was of course directly contradicted by Pitcairne in *Solutio problematis de historicis; seu de inventoribus dissertatio*, the pamphlet which appeared four years after *Inventa novantiqua*, the subtitle of which might be taken to contain a disparaging reference to Almeloveen's work. The two men stood on opposite sides in the quarrel between Ancients and Moderns which at that time split the republics of letters and science. Almeloveen may well have felt some personal hostility to Pitcairne, even to the University of Leiden as a stronghold of the 'moderns'.

Unexpected return to Scotland

Pitcairne's professorship was successful; his salary was twice substantially increased and he played a prominent part in Senatus business. However, it lasted for only three semesters. In the summer of 1693 he returned to Scotland on vacation, in full expectation, apparently, of a return to Leiden, but in a letter of 19 December (*o.s*) he resigned his post, giving no explanation other than an 'unexpected obstacle' (*insperatum mihi obicem*). He mentions enemies at Leiden, but claims that they were overmatched by his friends. Significantly, however, he claims that he is unwilling to accept the guilt of causing the University to lack a better professor by remaining longer in post (*nolui committere ut Academia meâ culpâ meliore Professore diutius careret*). This suggests that he had met and felt strong internal opposition to his appointment. It may be that his pronunciation of Latin had in fact proved something of a problem.

[17] Utrecht University Library MS 995 III 6K12, f. 68ᵛ. The letters occupy ff. 67ʳ–68ᵛ, 69ʳ–70ʳ. We owe this reference to Françoise Waquet, *Latin or the Empire of a Sign, From the Sixteenth to the Twentieth Centuries*, trs. John Howe (London, New York, 2001), 160–163.

INTRODUCTION

The likely occasion for Pitcairne's return to Scotland was his marriage on 8 August to Elizabeth Stevenson, daughter of Sir Archibald Stevenson (1630–1710), MD of Leiden (1661), a founding Fellow, and first President, of the Edinburgh Royal College of Physicians. It is often held that Pitcairne met opposition from his wife to a return to Holland, a suggestion, however, well countered by Shirlaw's remark: 'Since the couple had become engaged before ever Pitcairne left for Leyden, he would have known this already, and would not have left the University authorities expecting his return'.[18] Shirlaw, in turn, proposes that the unexpected obstacle was the mental illness suffered by Newton during the years 1692–1694, and that Pitcairne as physician and friend was called in to treat it. The hypothesis has some plausibility. As has been indicated, Newton, Pitcairne and Gregory were friends. At some time between 1592 and 1594, Pitcairne twice repeated his visit to Newton. Gregory was a qualified physician who had taken the degree of MD at Oxford on 18 February 1692. He exchanged letters with Pitcairne on medical matters and was distinguished enough as to be admitted an Honorary Fellow of the Edinburgh Royal College on 22 August 1705. It is conceivable that he was first to be consulted and that he, in turn, called on his friend, the more experienced Pitcairne. Every attempt was made to hush up the illness. Even so, it is curious that no direct evidence of Pitcairne's or Gregory's involvement has survived.

Whatever the reason for Pitcairne's failure to return, the authorities at Leiden were much displeased. On receipt of his letter, they proceeded (8 February 1694) to dismiss him from his post for improper conduct in taking his departure to Scotland without leave (*den gemelten Pitcairn [als sijnde sonder voorgaande kennisse of afscheyt nae Schotlant vertrocken] omme sijne onbehoorlyke conduite van de voors, professie sal verden gedeportiert*).[19] They also withheld part of his salary, although in 1725, long after his death, this was paid to his widow. She died in 1754.

Pitcairne resettled himself as a physician in Edinburgh. His second wife bore him five children who survived: four daughters, Elizabeth, born 10 June, 1695, died 18 March, 1718; Jane or Janet, born 10 June, perhaps in 1696, died 7 June, 1776; Margaret, born 8 March, 1702(?), died August 1777; Agnes, whose dates are uncertain, but who was born on 6 January, and a son, Andrew, who, as has been noted, was confined for a time after the 1715 Rising in the Tower of London, and who may well have been the eldest child of this second marriage. Three of the girls were born on Jacobite festal days. Two married. Janet became the wife of Alexander Erskine, 5th Earl of Kellie (died 1756), and mother of the composer Thomas Alexander Erskine, 6th Earl of Kelly (1732–1781) and the poet Andrew Erskine (1740–1793). Agnes married Colin Arthur, surgeon-apothecary in Fife.

Chambers preserves a story[20] which may show something of Pitcairne as father. 'When Mrs Siddons came to Edinburgh in 1784, the late Mr Alexander Campbell

[18] Shirlaw, 'Black Years', 25.
[19] Molhuysen, *Bronnen*, 118.
[20] Robert Chambers, *Traditions of Edinburgh*, new edn. (Edinburgh, 1847), 321–322.

INTRODUCTION

[(1764–1824)], author of the *History of Scottish Poetry*, asked Miss Pitcairne [presumably Margaret], daughter of Dr Pitcairne, to accompany him to one of the representations. The old lady refused, saying with coquettish vivacity: "Laddie, wad ye ha'e an aul lass like me to be running after the play-actors – me that hasna been at a theatre since I gaed wi' papa to the Canongate in the year *ten*?" The theatre was in those days encouraged chiefly by such Jacobites as Dr Pitcairn'. The Royal Tennis Court in the Canongate was used as a theatre at least during the Duke of York's time in Scotland (1681–1685), and possibly later. Unfortunately for the story, however, in 1784 Margaret Pitcairne had been dead for some seven years. Campbell or Chambers may have confused the 1784 visit of Mrs Siddons with some earlier occasion, or the encounter may have been apocryphal.

During his time in Holland, or (more probably) shortly after his return, Pitcairne wrote his Hudibrastic poem on the 1692 General Assembly, *Babell; or The Assembly, a Poem, MDCXCII. Written originally in the Irish Tongue and Translated into Scottish for the Benefite of the Leidges. By A.P. a Well Wisher to the Cause.*[21]

Promoting Anatomy. A war of pamphlets

Pitcairne wished to raise the standard of medical knowledge and care in Scotland. About this time he urged his friend, the surgeon Alexander Monteith (d. 1713), to petition the Town Council for the provision of bodies for dissection. In October 1694 Monteith was granted the use of 'the bodies of those who died in the Correction House, as well as infant foundlings, in exchange for free medical care for the poor'.[22] In a letter to Dr Gray in London dated 24 October of that year,[23] Pitcairne claimed a personal role: 'I am busie seeking a libertie for a comarad (a good surgeon and anatomist) to open the bodies of those poor who dye in Pauls-work & have none to owne & bury them. Wee offer to wait on those poor for nothing, bury them after dissection on our owne charges (which now the towne must doe on theirs) And yet Sir, there is vast opposition made to it, by the chief-surgeons, who neither will eat hay, nor suffer the oxen to eat it. I doe propose, if it be granted, to make better emprovements, in anatomie, than have been made at Leyden these thrittie years:[24] for I think most or all anatomists have neglected or not knowne what was most useful for a physician'. In a postscript dated 25 October he adds: 'to day the bill for the dissections is granted by the towne-council. & I hope to be this winter edified in many things, & particularly those yow spoke of in yo[r] last.' Later letters sometimes discuss the results of dissections which he performed.[25]

[21] Ed. George R. Kinloch (Edinburgh, Maitland Club, 1830).
[22] Guerrini, in *OxfDNB*.
[23] Johnston, *Best of our owne*, 19, letter 4.
[24] Note the wry reference to Leiden.
[25] Nos. 5, 13, 15, dated 20 December 1694, 27 November 1700, 27 February 1701; Johnston, *Best of our owne*, 20, 33, 36.

INTRODUCTION

The years between 1694 and 1696 were critical for Pitcairne. During 1694 he suffered a severe illness, and for amusement during his convalescence read, or re-read, the encyclopaedic *Scotia Illustrata sive Prodromus Historiæ Naturalis*,[26] published in 1684, the *opus viginti annorum* of his distinguished colleague, Sir Robert Sibbald (1641–1722), Fellow, past-President, and in many respects founder, of the Edinburgh College of Physicians. In *Dissertatio de Legibus Historiæ Naturalis* (Edinburgh, 1696), Pitcairne attacked the methods used by Sibbald to gather material for *Scotia Illustrata*, at the same time setting out what he regarded as the proper scientific way of proceeding. Relationships between Sibbald and Pitcairne were probably never very warm and the *Dissertatio* did nothing to improve them.

The treatment of fevers was at this time a matter of some medical dispute.[27] In November 1694 Pitcairne delivered his *Disputatio de curatione Febrium quæ per evacuationes instituitur* to the College of Physicians. This was printed, probably in Edinburgh, early in 1695. Soon afterwards appeared an anonymous pamphlet, almost certainly by Edward Eizat, at that time not yet a Fellow of the College, *Apollo Mathematicus, or the Art of Curing Diseases by the Mathematicks, according to the Principles of Dr Pitcairne. A work both profitable and pleasant, and never published in English before. To which is subjoined, a discourse of certainty, according to the principles of the same author* (London[?], 1695). In the final section Eizat claimed that Pitcairne's emphasis in the *Disputatio* on mathematics as the only source of scientific certainty implied a denial of biblical truth, that Pitcairne, in other words, was an atheist, or at best a deist.

A reputation for atheism clung to Pitcairne for the rest of his life. Chambers tells the story of a book-sale (undated), where a Philostratus [presumably the *Life of Apollonius of Tyana*] a philosophising pagan mystic of the 1st century AD was sold for a good price, but a copy of the Bible received no bids: 'Pitcairn said to someone who remarked the circumstance: "Not at all wonderful; for is it not written, *Verbum Dei manet in eternum*?"' Pitcairne brought a legal action against a minister of St Giles who, as a result of this jest, called him an atheist. The action ended, apparently, in a compromise.[28]

A recently-elected Fellow of the College, George Hepburn (c. 1669–1759), declared for Pitcairne in a pamphlet, *Tarrugo unmasked: or, An Answer to a late pamphlet intituled, Apollo mathematicus* (Edinburgh, 1695). Among much else, this included the suggestion that Sibbald had a major hand in the composition of *Apollo Mathematicus*: 'Whoever *Tarrugo* be, yet it's known That the papers were revised, corrected, and approven by one who twice in one year changed his Religion, upon how honest and religious principles I doe not determine: Now it may seen strange that this Gentleman has not struck out those passages about *Atheisme*

---

[26] BL MS, Sloane 3198.
[27] W.S. Craig, *History*, 409–410.
[28] Chambers, *Traditions*, 160–161.

and Irreligion, both for his own, and for his Author's sake.'[29] The reference is to Sibbald's brief, but notorious, conversion to Catholicism (1685–1686).[30]

A literal English translation of the *Disputatio* was prepared, apparently with Pitcairne's approval, but was turned against him in yet another pamphlet, *Apollo Staticus, Or, The Art of Curing Fevers by the staticks: Invented by D^r. Pitcairn and Publish'd by him in Latine: Now Made English by a Well-wisher to the* MATHEMATICKS (Edinburgh, 1695).

Pitcairne's expulsion from the Royal College of Physicians

The war of pamphlets thus begun continued for several years with several others among Pitcairne's friends rallying to his support. One of them was probably Dr John Arbuthnot (1667–1735), like David Gregory a refugee in England from the new regime in Scotland, later to become the close friend of Pope and Swift. He is the likeliest author of *A Modest Examination of a Late Pamphlet entitled Apollo Mathematicus* (Edinburgh, 1696).[31]

Hepburn was summoned to appear before the College to answer for his action in publishing the pamphlet without first obtaining permission. Pitcairne, together with several others, lodged a protest, urging that the College was acting *ultra vires*. As a result he found himself officially suspended from his fellowship on 22 November 1695 on the grounds that his protest was 'a calumnious scandalous false and arrogant paper refuseing ye authority of ye president and colledge and contrair to the promissory engadgement'.[32] Hepburn was suspended a month later.

These events fit into a larger pattern. The College had split into two parties, one the political and religious sympathies of which were Jacobite, the second Williamite. The scientific position of the former appears to have been with the Moderns, that of the latter with the Ancients. Initially the Jacobites had been the stronger. For most of 1694 their leader, Pitcairne's father-in-law Sir Archibald Stevenson, had been President. On 6 December he was succeeded by Dr Robert Trotter (1648–1727) in what seems to have been a difficult election. The election meeting for the next year (1696) was held in Dr Trotter's house on 5 December 1695, a Saturday, and so technically feriate. The election was likely to be closely contested. Pitcairne ignored the sentence of suspension against him and was present. Dr Trotter, however, had made his preparations. Also present were two Baillies (magistrates) of the city, together with their Officers (in effect, policemen):

---

[29] *Tarrugo Unmasked*, 'To the Reader'.
[30] See 30.
[31] David E. Shuttleton, '"A modest examination": John Arbuthnot and the Scottish Newtonians', *British Journal for Eighteenth-Century Studies* 18 (1995), 47–62. Cf. Johnston, *Best of our owne*, 65, letter 52, which shows that in 1711 Pitcairne still thought that Sibbald was the author of *Apollo Mathematicus*.
[32] Craig, *History*, 411, quoting *College Minutes*, 22.xi.1695.

INTRODUCTION

'Dr. Pitcairn was Removed by the Town of Edinburghs Officers, after having protested against the Violence used against him, three other Members also pretended to be Suspended were pointed at, and the Bailie desired to Remove them, but they thought fit to prevent the hard usage their Colleague had mett with, and with the Plurality of the College did withdraw to Dr. Stevinson's house, and there unanimously Elected him President in the usual form and manner, and did also Constitute the other Officers of the College.

This Election being free and Legal, Dr. Stevenson with the Censors and others came to the Ordinary place of Meeting to Intimate the Election, but finding Dr. Trotter there and the other Physicians removed, the Chair emptie and the Books on the Table, Dr. Stevenson having signified to Dr. Trotter that he was Chosen President by the pluralitie of the Colledge, took Possession of the Chair by way of Instrument in the Clerks hands, and Dr. Trotter going about to carry away the Books, he was hindred, but without any Force or Violence, for some he let fall on the Floor, and others he threw down on the Table.'[33]

This account comes from Stevenson. The College Minutes simply record that:

'The qlk day the Colledge chosed Sr. Thomas Burnet Sr Robt Sibbald Drs Trotter Sinclair Cranstoune Mitchell Dicksone to be counsellors for this year and they removeing to another Room choose Dr. Trotter president, Drs Mitchell and dicksone censors, Dr Dundas secretary and Dr ffreir treasurer for the ensewing year.'[34]

Sir Robert Sibbald's name appears only once in the documents quoted, but it is likely that hostility between him and Pitcairne contributed substantially to the dispute, the so-called 'Ryot' in the College. The points at issue were taken to the Court of Session, the supreme court for civil actions in Scotland, which in a series of judgements found for Trotter and Sibbald. The expulsion of Pitcairne (and Stevenson) was thus confirmed. Various attempts at reconciliation were made, but it was not until 30 November 1704 that Pitcairne again figured at a meeting of the College. He was never again elected to office. 'No aspersion on Pitcairne is implied in saying that, in its efforts to consolidate restored stability, the College adopted a wise course.'[35]

The affair does not seem to have affected Pitcairne's position as a physician. His practice in Edinburgh continued to flourish. He assisted in the preparation of the posthumous *Plantarum Historiæ Universalis Oxoniensis Pars Tertia* (Oxford, 1699) by the Robert Morison, already mentioned. To this he also contributed an account

---

[33] Ibid., 413–414, quoting R.C.P.E. (1696) Miscellaneous papers, no. 98.
[34] Ibid., 412, quoting *College Minutes*, 5.xii.1695.
[35] Ibid., 419.

of Morison's life. In 1699 he received the honorary degree of MD from King's College, Aberdeen.

On his homeward journey from the graduation, Pitcairne found himself stormbound at Laurencekirk in the Mearns. The local schoolmaster, Thomas Ruddiman (1674–1757) provided him with company and conversation. Pitcairne was much impressed by the young man and invited him to Edinburgh. There he obtained for him a post in the Library of the Faculty of Advocates, now the National Library of Scotland, paid him generously for tutoring his son, Andrew, and recommended him as tutor to others. Ruddiman eventually became Keeper of the Library; he gained an international reputation as Latinist and editor; in addition, he became a printer and publisher, who, among much else, printed many of Pitcairne's poems as broadsheets and edited the posthumous *Selecta Poemata* (Edinburgh, 1727).[36]

Pitcairne's interest in human anatomy has already been noted. Partly as a consequence, after his expulsion from the College of Physicians, he tended to associate more with surgeons than with physicians. On 16 October 1701 he had the rare distinction, for a physician, of election as a Fellow of the Incorporation (later Royal College) of Surgeons of Edinburgh.

Jacobites and the Scottish colonial enterprise; Pitcairne arrested

The various Navigation Acts (1650, 1651, 1660, 1663, 1696) passed by the English Parliament gave Englishmen and English colonists a legal monopoly of all trade between England and its colonies, and operated against trade by outsiders, including Scots. In reaction to this, The Company of Scotland Trading to Africa and the Indies was established in 1695, with much Scottish popular support and financial investment. The intention was to create a Scottish equivalent of the English and Dutch East India Companies. Predictably, the response of the English government was hostile. Despite this, in 1698 and 1699 the new Company dispatched ships to the Isthmus of Darien (now partly in Colombia, partly in Panama), there to establish a trading colony, Caledonia, with access to both Atlantic and Pacific Oceans. The venture turned out a tragic failure. Climate, disease and Spanish intervention were major factors, as was the hostility of King William and English vested interests. The Scots colonists defeated the invading Spaniards in a minor skirmish at Toubacanti (Tubuganti) on 4 February 1700. The victory however was transitory. Articles of Capitulation were signed on 31 March and on 12 April the colony was abandoned. Only a few colonists ever saw Scotland again.

The news took a long time to arrive. On 10 June Jacobites in Edinburgh expressed their opposition to King William and his policies by openly celebrating in the streets the birthday of the Prince, the Old Pretender, with bonfires and drawn pistols. Pitcairne produced one of his best Latin poems for the occasion,

---

[36] Douglas Duncan, *Thomas Ruddiman* (Edinburgh and London, 1965), especially pp. 2, 15–23.

INTRODUCTION

Fabulæ 2 Lib. 1. Phædri Metaphrasis,[37] the story of King Oak and King Stork. Ten days later, when news of Toubacanti arrived, rioting broke out, which led to the rioters taking control of the city. The Duke of Hamilton and other gentlemen with Jacobite sympathies drank toasts to Toubacanti at Steill's tavern, the Cross Keys.[38] A more committed Jacobite, the Earl Marischal, sent out his servants with wine and toasted Caledonia from his doorway. Hugh Paterson, a surgeon, and Pitcairne's friend, the printer James Watson the younger were forcibly, if temporarily, released from the Tolbooth where they had been imprisoned for writing and publishing Jacobite and pro-Darien pamphlets. The stunning news of the capitulation and final abandonment of the colony, which soon followed, served only to strengthen hostility to William and the English generally. Final dissolution of the Company came only with the signing of the Act of Union in 1707. Some £233,000 was awarded in compensation to shareholders and other sufferers. We have not been able to find whether or not Pitcairne was a shareholder, but the probabilities suggest that he was. The failure of the Company helped to force Scotland to accede to the 1707 Union.

On 16 January 1700 an intercepted letter from Pitcairne to his friend Dr Gray in London caused him to be arrested and briefly imprisoned in the Heart of Midlothian, the Edinburgh Tolbooth. The letter concerned an Address from the people of Scotland to King William and the English parliament, protesting at their behaviour towards the Company of Scotland. William had written ordering the Privy Council to make his displeasure known and to stop the Address. The predictable effect was to make thousands demand the right to sign. To enable them to do so, copies were sent to all the shires and burghs. It 'became a people's protest, a declaration of loyalty to Scotland's Company and Scotland's Parliament'.[39]

The contents of the letter are preserved in Privy Council papers on the case:[40]

'Mr Archbald Pitcairne Doctor of medicine … Did presume on ane or other of the days of December last to write and send a Letter all written and Subscrived with his hand to one Doctor Gray in London wherin he ffalsely Represents That the said Address for the Parliament goes on unanimously Throw the whole nation, and that only a few Courtiers and Presbeterian ministers oppose it, But in vain, and That twice so many have signed since the proclamation anent Petitioning, as signed it before, And Bids him take Notice That there is one sent to Court with a Title Different, To beguile the Elect of the Court, If it were possible, And that all the corporations and all the Gentlemen have signed the address and himself among the rest, And That it is now a National Covenant And by Jove it would produce a Nationall

---

[37] 12.
[38] 19(a), 13–14 and n.
[39] John Prebble, *Darien. The Scottish Dream of Empire* (London, 1968; Edinburgh, 2000), 270.
[40] Johnston, *Best of our owne*, 30–32, letter 11.

and Universall – To which he adds That he is Thinking after a lazie Way, To Reprint his papers, But hopes there shall be news E're they are printed, And That he is calculating the fforce of the Musculi Abdominis in Digesting meat, and is sure he can prove they can doe it, une belle affair.'

The Privy Council professed itself outraged. The final remarks were held to have a particularly sinister significance.

After two days' imprisonment, Pitcairne was released on the grounds of his admission that 'through the Influence of a small Excess He wrot in a privat Letter, now in their Lo[rdshi]ps hands severall groundless news upon unExamined reports with some affectationes of ffancy, which he heartily condemnes, But does seriously protest, It was without the least design Either directly or Indirectly against his Majestys Government.'[41] It would seem that the Councillors were only in part satisfied. His release was under the condition that he should 'live peaceably under and with all submission, to the present Government of his Majesty King William, And that he shall not Act Consult or Contrive any thing in prejudice therof, nor shall not Converse or Correspond with any Rebells And that he shall appear before the saids Lords of Privy Councill whensoever he shall be called or Required therto, under the penalty of Two Hundered pounds sterling, In caice he shall ffaill or transgress in any pairt of the premises.'[42] Obviously he was regarded as a Jacobite sympathiser and potential rebel, as indeed he remained for the rest of his life.

Events in Europe

By 1701 two major European wars had broken out. In 1700 the grandson of Louis XIV, Philip of Anjou (1683–1746), succeeded the Spanish king Charles II (1662–1700) as Philip V of Spain. The link thus created between France and Spain upset the balance of Europe and, in an attempt to restore something like the *status quo*, other powers, including England and Holland, took up arms to promote an alternate king, the boy Charles (1685–1740), second son of the Hapsburg Emperor Leopold I. Thus began the War of the Spanish Succession (1701–1714). Jacobites naturally supported Philip, while Whigs were on the side of Charles, at least until 1711, when on the death of his elder brother Joseph he became Emperor and so once more upset the European balance.

In England Marlborough had returned to favour, in 1702 becoming Captain General of the English forces engaged in the war. He won remarkable victories at Blenheim (1704), Ramillies (1706), Oudenarde (1708) and Malplaquet (1709), the last however only at great cost. The war became unpopular. In 1710 the moderate Tory, Robert Harley (1661–1724), came to power and in 1711 Marlborough was

[41] Ibid., 28.
[42] Ibid., 32.

dismissed. So far as Britain was concerned, the Treaty of Utrecht (1713) brought the war to a close.

Charles XII of Sweden invaded Denmark in 1699, thus beginning the Great Northern War which ended in 1720, two years after Charles himself had been killed at Frederiksten in Norway. The other belligerents were Poland, Saxony and Russia. By 1706 Charles had established himself firmly in Saxony, giving rise to fears in a Vienna already much occupied by the War of the Spanish Succession. The general belief was that Charles had come to an agreement with Louis XIV. If we are to trust Pitcairne, a rumour even arose that marriages had been diplomatically arranged between Charles and Louisa, younger sister of the Pretender, and between the Pretender and Charles's sister Ulrika, marriages which potentially united a restored Stuart monarchy in Great Britain with Sweden, France and Spain in an alliance against the remaining Allies. Charles turned his arms against Russia in 1708 and in 1709 was defeated by Peter the Great at Poltava and forced to take refuge in Turkey, from which he returned only in 1714, well after Pitcairne's death. Even so, the rumour persisted.

It may not have been altogether baseless. In 1716 Count Gyllenborg, the Swedish minister in London, promised the Jacobites that 10,000 Swedish troops would invade Britain. That plot was nipped in the bud.

Pitcairne kept in touch with these events. Probably in 1702 on the occasion of Philip V's marriage to Maria Louisa of Savoy, he wrote verses in the form of an optimistic prophecy.[43] The denunciation of the Hapsburg claimant to the Spanish throne[44] was probably written when Charles became Emperor in 1711. Pitcairne celebrated the fall of Marlborough in '[*Ad Annam R. MDCCXI*]';[45] he saluted Harley's achievement at Utrecht in an epigram,[46] and praised Swift in two Sapphic stanzas[47] for his support of Harley's policies. He wrote [*Ad CAROLUM XII. Suecorum Regem.*][48] in the knowledge that the king had begun a campaign against Russia, but before news of the defeat at Poltava had reached Scotland. The epigram on Louisa[49] was written for her eighteenth birthday in 1710, the day when she came of marriageable age. Louisa died in 1712 and poem **122** takes the form of an address by her spirit in which she commends to Ulrika's wifely and maternal care the Pretender and his British subjects.

[43] 118.
[44] 119.
[45] 91.
[46] 96.
[47] 93.
[48] 120.
[49] 121.

INTRODUCTION

Pitcairne's later life

During his later years Pitcairne remained a controversialist, but became more observer than active participant in external affairs. The information we have about his life and relationships during the period is derived chiefly from his poetry and his letters, occasionally from other writings. He commemorated the death of James VII on 6 September 1701[50] and, more virulently, that of King William on 8 March 1702.[51] The accession of James' daughter, Anne, meant that at least a Stuart was again on the throne. Pitcairne seems to have regarded her as primarily a regent, who would give way to her half-brother, James Francis, when he came of age.[52] Pitcairne retained his faith that the succession would finally revert to the Prince.

In the Parliament of 1703 the Earl of Strathmore proposed an act extending toleration to oppressed Episcopalians. Two counterproposals were put forward, one, by the Duke of Argyle, 'ratifying the late Revolution and all that followed thereupon,' the other, by the Earl of Marchmont, aimed at securing the Presbyterian government. In face of such competition no action was taken on the Strathmore proposal. Pitcairne is the probable author of an anonymous satirical play, *Tollerators and Con-Tollerators; A Comedy Acted in My Lord Advocat's Lodgeing, June 10, 1703*,[53] a play in which there is little action, but which introduces all the main characters in the debate.

Under 30 November 1704 David Gregory has an interesting note:[54] 'This day being St Andrews day was first told me the intrigue betwixt My Lord Roxburgh, Dr Pitcairn, Dr Cheyn, &c. of reforming Colleges &c. in Scotland, & of the Plan printed by Dr Pitcairn at Edenburgh. Mighty things were said of the constant Correspondence betwixt My Ld Roxburgh & Dr Pitcairn, the constant dining of Dr Cheyn with My Lord or My Lord with him, & My Lords pressing Dr Cheyn to return to his Country, &c.'

On 5 January 1705 Gregory has another note:[55] 'Dr. Cheyne braggs that next summer he is to goe to Scotland and together with Dr Pitcairn settle all the Practice of Physick, and publish unalterable Principles therof. He talks to Dr Mead the same but makes York the place of meeting.'

My Lord Roxburgh is John Ker (c. 1680–1741), 5th Earl and 1st Duke of Roxburghe.[56] George Cheyne (1671/2–1743), an Aberdeenshire Episcopalian, moved to Edinburgh, probably about 1690, where he studied medicine with Pitcairne

---

[50] 10.
[51] 81, 82, 83.
[52] See 11 and commentary.
[53] George R. Kinloch (ed.), *Babell; A Satirical Poem on the Proceedings of the General Assembly in the Year M.DC.XCII.*, Maitland Club (Edinburgh, 1830), 70–78.
[54] *David Gregory, Isaac Newton and their circle. Extracts from David Gregory's memoranda, 1677–1708*, ed. W.G. Hiscock (Oxford, 1937), 21.
[55] Hiscock, *Gregory*, 23.
[56] 21.

and mathematics, probably with Thomas Bower.[57] He supported Pitcairne in the dispute with the College of Physicians. In 1701 he published anonymously *A New Theory of Fevers*. He graduated MD of King's College, Aberdeen, and then moved to London, where in 1702 he became a Fellow of the Royal Society. He offended Newton with his *Fluxionum methodus inversa* (1703), thus losing his connection with the Royal Society. He became tutor in mathematics to William Ker, younger brother of the Earl. In 1705 he published his Newtonian *Philosophical Principles of Natural Religion*. His health broke down, forcing him to return to Scotland, where he fell under the influence of the Quietist George Garden (1649–1733), an Episcopalian and Jacobite clergyman, deprived from St Nicholas, Aberdeen, and later regarded as a possible Bishop of Aberdeen.[58] Garden influenced all Cheyne's later work, medical and scientific.

In the second note, Dr. Mead is the Richard Mead, already mentioned as Pitcairne's pupil at Leiden.

As a number of his notes indicate, Gregory disliked Cheyne intensely. It is thus difficult to assess the credibility of his account. Cheyne and Roxburghe are both often mentioned in Pitcairne's correspondence but there is no hint of any scheme resembling the one mentioned. Pitcairne certainly wrote letters to gain men of whom he approved posts in the Scottish universities, but the appeals which have survived[59] are for the most part later than Gregory's notes and directed, not to Roxburghe, but to John Erskine (1675–1732), 22nd Earl of Mar and from 1705 to 1709 'Her Majesties principal Secretary of State For the Kingdom of Scotland'[60] (later he became the ineffective leader of the 1715 Jacobite rising). Roxburghe, it is true, held the Secretaryship for some nine months in 1704–1705. One letter to him, dated 21 October 1704,[61] at least hints at an effort to gain Thomas Bower some kind of post. But it is probably best to accept Pitcairne's own account[62] of the relation: 'Take notice that Dr Gregorie & Dr Cheyne are not indissoluble friends, tho both are mine'. Gregory may simply have been jealous that Cheyne was on intimate terms with Pitcairne, and so gave a maliciously exaggerated account of the matter.

In 1705 Pitcairne's father-in-law, Sir Archibald Stevenson, retired as Physician to Heriot's Hospital – a statutory post in the charitable foundation for the sons of Edinburgh burgesses who had died, leaving their families in straitened circumstances, established in terms of the will of George Heriot (1563–1624), a wealthy but childless Edinburgh goldsmith who in 1603 had accompanied James VI to London and died there. The Hospital was to be modelled on a London institution, Christ's Hospital. The statutes were drawn up by Heriot's nephew, Walter

---

[57] 58.
[58] Goldie, *Episcopal Church*, 41–42, 47.
[59] Johnston, *Best of our owne*, 43–46, 52–53, 54–56, letters 25–28, 37–38, 41–43.
[60] Thus styled in Pitcairne's letters to him.
[61] Johnston, *Best of our owne*, 40, letter 21.
[62] Johnston, *Best of our owne*, 39, letter 18.

INTRODUCTION

Balconquhall (1586–1645), Dean of Rochester and subsequently Durham. An Episcopalian form of worship was prescribed. Stevenson and others, it seems, had been able to preserve that tradition even after the Revolution. In 1702 however John Watson, a well-known Covenanter, was appointed House-Governor and Head-Master and began to institute changes. In 1705, when Stevenson retired at the age of 76, he cancelled a claim for £200 against the Hospital on condition that the Governors appointed as his successor another Fellow of the Royal College of Physicians, the Episcopalian and Jacobite George Mackenzie (1669–1725). This led to open conflict which ended only with the second dismissal of Mackenzie in 1714.

Pitcairne anticipated Mackenzie's appointment in a poem sent by Heriot himself from beyond the grave.[63] Another[64] is more directed against the Governors of the Hospital, among whom the ministers of Edinburgh were included, and may belong to the later stages of the conflict.

On the surface, Pitcairne seems to have been little affected by the prospect of the 1707 Union of Parliaments. In a letter to the earl of Mar, dated 28 May 1706,[65] he says: 'I am perfectlie blythe to hear Your Lordship, and the Countess of Mar is in good health. If the Union can perpetuat that good health, I am for the Union, tho our Colledge should break'. Only the reference in the final clause is obscure. Pitcairne developed a tendency to use the word 'Britons' where formerly he would have said 'Scots', occasionally even revising the text of his earlier poems.[66]

Second thoughts are perhaps implicit in the brief elegy[67] on John Hamilton (1656–1708), 2nd Baron Belhaven, who died in London under custody for suspected involvement in the attempted 1708 French invasion in support of the Jacobite cause. Two phrases, *Quam nimis indigné Scotis avelleris oris!/ Si quis nunc Scotas dicere Fata sinunt* (3–4), and *raptosque Penates* (7), both have Virgilian overtones which carry the implication that for Scots the consequences of the Union have been like those of the fall of Troy for the Trojans.

In the spring of 1708 a French fleet with the Pretender and 6000 troops on board had briefly appeared in the Firth of Forth. No landing was made, but a group of Stirlingshire lairds riotously demonstrated their support. They were tried on a charge of high treason, but acquitted on a verdict of Not Proven. Pitcairne expressed his pleasure at the verdict.[68]

In a letter dated 27 December 1709[69] Pitcairne attacked Gregory's former Edinburgh student, the mathematician and astronomer John Keill (1671–1721). The letter was addressed to Doctor Walkinshaw, a Scottish physician with a London

---

[63] 43.
[64] 111.
[65] Johnston, *Best of our owne*, 44, letter 26.
[66] See for instance 2, 15–16 and notes.
[67] 16.
[68] 87.
[69] Johnston, *Best of our owne*, 56–57, letter 44.

practice, and is about the publication (London [Edinburgh], 1709) of *A letter from Dr James Walkinshaw to Sir Robert Sibbald*, which answers the anonymous *A letter from Sir R- S-, to Dr Archibald Pitcairn*, and may in turn have led to the publication of Sibbald's long-delayed reply to Pitcairne's *Dissertatio de Legibus Naturalis Historiae* (above, p. 7), *Vindiciae Scotiae Illustratae, sive prodromi naturalis historiae Scotiae, contra prodromomastiges, sub larva libelli de legibus historiae naturalis latentes* (Edinburgh, 1710).

Pitcairne's anger at Keill is explained in a MS note on the flyleaf of the NLS copy of the *Letter of Sir R- S-*,[70] a note which must have been written after Keill had obtained the Savilian professorship at Oxford in 1712 (he failed to obtain it on the death of Gregory):

'This letter which pretends to pass under the name of Sir Robert Sibbald M.D. was written, at least owned privately by Will. Cockburn[71] physician at London. But the answerer [i.e., 'Walkinshaw'] supposes it to be wrott by John Keill, Sav prof. of Astronomy at Oxford whom he means p. 3, line 20 of his answer. If Cockburn wrott it, as it is certain he published it, he must surely have had the assistance of Keill or some other mathematician. Keill disowned having any hand to it. The answer was published by Dr Pitcairne in Dr Walkinshaw's name, whose consent he had to do so, tho' he never saw it & happened to die before it was printed. But the real author of it is Dr Thomas Bower prof. of Mathematicks at Aberdeen. It is printed at Edinburgh tho' it bears London. Dr Pitcairne layd the mistakes in calculation at Dr Cheyne's door who undertook to do them & revise his dissertations for the press.'

Bower has already been several times mentioned as a protégé and friend of Pitcairne.

Pitcairne's letter to Walkinshaw begins with a discussion of methods for circulating copies of the pseudonymous *Letter*, but soon turns to Keill, his publications, and these of his brother, the physician James Keill (1673–1719), like Pitcairne himself (and probably influenced by him) an iatromathematician:

'Doctor, This day I have Your most oblidging letter of the 12th. The title is as yow order. I send the remaining sheets, and the errata. On thursday or fryday I send by land 400 copies which will not come to yow till after 20 days. Mean tyme Send me your sure address, and I am to send on saturday The carriers place where yee can call for the Cargo, for it shall be directed to Yow according to Your old address. I shall also send yow the investigation and calcul of the spherrois at length. Keil stole his *principia physices vera*[72] word

---

[70] Shelfmark 1.593(23).
[71] One of Pitcairne's former Leiden students; see above, p. 8.
[72] A reference to Keill's *Introductio ad veram physicam* (Oxford, 1701).

by word from Dr Gregorie's dictates, but what ever is in it is said better by others before him, and not one word of the book is his except the barbarous Latin, and confus'd expression. He abus'd The Great Des-car-tes[73] in print, Who first invented The true Method of Tangents from which and of which, Dr Barrows method, and Sir Isaac Neuton's fluxions, and Leibnitz's calcul are only Corollaries or abridgements, as shall be seen if I live a little longer, but without reflection on these great men. Mr Whiston wrote on the way of the deluge.[74] It was a paper given him by Mr Neuton. Mr Whiston needlesslie spoke of other things too. Keil fell upon him scurrilouslie i.e. upon Mr Neuton reallie (this lost him the profession at Oxford) and wold needs prove by geometrie that the deluge was a miracle i.e. That the rules of Attraction demonstrate by Sir Isaac are false. but the ill natur'd cur, thinking to please a popish humour that sticks to some protestant divines, did not see That if Mr Whiston's i.e. Mr Neuton's thought was wrong, no deluge could have been Let the bees see to That, boy.

His brother the doctor's *Anatomie*[75] is Bourdon's translated word [for word] from French. his book of animal secretion,[76] where it is right, is word for word Bellini's if yee'l put the word Cohesion for Attraction, and even that is needless since Bellini always says *Cohesio cum nisu partium in se mutuo*, which looks like attraction.'

Early in 1710 Pitcairne heard from Dr Gray that Dr Walkinshaw had died. He transferred to him disposal of the 400 copies of the *Letter*, particularly requesting that one copy should be given to Dr Arbuthnot, and that he should not 'let Cockburne &c. see it, till the rest are ready to appear, which are on the road'.[77]

Sibbald had not been directly involved in the exchange, but was clearly affected by it, prefacing his *Vindiciae* (three copies of which he sent to Pitcairne) with an 'Ode *Paraenetica* ('hortatory') *Ad Archibaldum Pitcarnium M.D.*' This concludes with the tribute:

Docte Pitcarni, impavide labora
Patriæ laudes cumulare magnis
Fructibus miri ingenii vigens dum
    Sufficit ætas.

---

[73] In *An examination of Dr Burnet's Theory of the Earth. Together with some remarks on Mr Whiston's new Theory of the Earth* (Oxford, 1698).

[74] Ibid.

[75] James Keill, *Anatomy of the Humane Body, Abridg'd* (London, 1698).

[76] James Keill, *An Account of Animal secretion, the Quantity of Blood in the Humane Body, and Muscular Motion* (London, 1708).

[77] Johnston, *Best of our owne*, 57–58, letter 45.

INTRODUCTION

Cassius quærit, luminisque morbi
Jam diu mente meditata, lucem
Videant tandem, viridesque nectent
   Tum tibi lauros.   (41–48)

He also claimed that Pitcairne had informed him that he was not the author of *De legibus*. Pitcairne commented on all this in a letter to Dr Gray dated 6 January 1711:

> 'Yee know the bearer: he brings yow the rarest piece of lies and nonsense I ever saw. *Scribit et in tergo nec dum fr(e)nabit* – The author gave me 3 copies in a compliment, of which I send one to yow, and one to Dr Arbuthnot as an answer to his modest examination.[78] The author told me that by My telling him I was not author of the *Dissertatio de legibus historiae naturalis* (which he tels indeed and lyes) he meant in alledging this upon me onlie to hinder me from answering him since he in his *Vindiciae* had commended me so much. An excellent reasoning and which made me smile in place of being angrie. He told me he wold let no body else see it till he had got the approbation of all the learned to it.'

Fairly clearly Pitcairne still believed that Sibbald was responsible for *Apollo Mathematicus*. Published works and private letters together illustrate the vindictive deviousness of scientific controversy in the late seventeenth- and early eighteenth-century.

Somewhere between 1706 and 1708 Sir Archibald Stevenson, seems to have suffered an illness so nearly fatal that Pitcairne composed a funeral ode.[79] After his recovery, Pitcairne transformed the poem into a celebration of Stevenson's approaching eightieth birthday. Once again, his action was premature and on Stevenson's death just before the anniversary it became necessary to turn the poem back to something like its original form. Not long afterwards, Stevenson's wife also died.[80]

Pitcairne's verses are full of Virgilian reminiscences, especially of the *Aeneid*. He once refers[81] (20.II, 11–12) to the influential Middle Scots translation of that poem[82] by Gavin Douglas (c. 1474–1522), Bishop of Dunkeld. This forms part of an address, supposedly by Dennistoun, to the earlier Scots Latinist, George Buchanan:

---

[78] See above, n. 24.
[79] 40(a).
[80] 41.
[81] 20.II, 11–12.
[82] David F.C. Caldwell (ed.), *Virgil's Aeneid*, 4 vols., Scottish Text Society (Edinburgh and London, 1957–1964).

INTRODUCTION

Ergo redi: non te redeuntem deserat ille
  Qui cecinit Scotis, Arma virumque, modis

The reference occurs in a poem printed by Watson in 1700; at that date, perhaps, plans were already afoot for Symson and Freebairn's edition of the translation (Edinburgh, 1710), to which Pitcairne became a subscriber. The *Proposals* for subscriptions is undated, but cannot have been later than 1708, because included in the 'List of such of the Subscribers Names and Designations as have come to our Hands' is 'The most Reverend Father in God, John Lord Arch-Bishop of Glasgow', John Paterson, that is to say, who died in that year. Paterson had lost his archiepiscopal authority in 1690; the inclusion at so late a date of his full dignities is enough to show that the edition was a Jacobite and Episcopalian venture. One of the printers, Andrew Symson (c. 1638–1712), had been the Episcopalian curate of Kirkinner in Wigtownshire and Douglas in Lanarkshire, who had taken to the trade after being deprived of his charge. Freebairn was known as 'the Pretender's printer'. Jacobites, it is well known, made use of the *Aeneid* to serve their own political purposes. The best-known example is Dryden's translation (1697).[83]

Pitcairne did more than subscribe; he actively assisted in the enterprise. In the Preface the printers felt themselves 'bound to acknowledge the Obligations we owe to the Right Reverend Father in God, William Lord Bishop of Carlile; to the Learned, Famous and Ingenious Physitians Sir Robert Sibbald, Dr Archibald Pitcairn, and Dr John Drummond; and to the Worthy Mr John Urry of Christ Church. Oxon.' (Note, in passing, the careful distinction of the style, 'Right Reverend', appropriate to a bishop as opposed to 'most Reverend', appropriate to an archbishop.) Pitcairne is in interesting company. The Bishop of Carlisle, William Nicolson (1655–1727) was no Jacobite, but a defender of the rights of the Church of England and an opponent of the 1707 Union because he feared the possible influence of Scottish Presbyterianism. He was an antiquarian and an early student of Scottish antiquities, who threw doubt on the traditional history, earlier defended by Sir George Mackenzie of Rosehaugh. It should perhaps be noted that Sir Robert Sibbald sprang to the defence of the traditional account, which Pitcairne in his later years clearly abandoned.[84]

John Urry (1666–1715), primarily a textual critic, came from an Aberdeenshire family. Because he refused to acknowledge King William, he was deprived of his Studentship at Christ Church, Oxford. He is now best remembered for the edition of Chaucer's works which appeared in 1721, six years after his death. Sibbald is mentioned primarily as a learned man; despite his earlier misadventures, he was no Jacobite, although he may have retained Episcopalian leanings. It was for his

---

[83] See especially Pittock, *Poetry and Politics*, 94–107.
[84] 2,15–16nn.

Scotia Illustrata that Symson had originally prepared the valuable *Larger Description of Galloway*, which however remained unpublished until 1823. Symson published Sibbald's *Answer to the second letter to the right reverend, the Lord Bishop of Carlile* [i.e., William Nicolson] … *Wherein the Scots antient possession in Britain is asserted* (Edinburgh, 1704).

There is no positive evidence that Pitcairne was personally acquainted with Nicolson or Urry. Dr John Drummond however was a colleague and friend, brother of the lawyer David Drummond, already mentioned. He was secretary to the Edinburgh Royal College of Physicians 1706–1708, and President 1722–1727. After Pitcairne's death Drummond wrote the sympathetic obituary notice quoted below.

In 1709 the English High Church clergyman Henry Sacheverell (c. 1674–1724) delivered a virulent sermon against Whigs and Nonconformists, 'The Perils of False Brethren.' For this he was put on trial before the House of Lords in 1710. The verdict was Guilty, but the light sentence imposed was regarded by his party as a triumph. Pitcairne later used the case for Jacobite propaganda.[85]

In 1711 he celebrated the birthday of Anne Stamfield, hostess at the Greping-office, in a poem[86] which shows the lighter side of his talent. A eulogy of the Duchess of Gordon[87] commemorates her gift to the Faculty of Advocates of a medal, on the obverse of which was a head of the Pretender, on the reverse a map of the British Isles with the motto *Reddite*, 'give back'. Acceptance of the medal by the Faculty, on 30 June, subsequently led to a humiliating withdrawal.

In 1712 he wrote an epigram[88] on the death in a duel of the 4th Duke of Hamilton, by this time regarded as chief hope of the Jacobites. In one version he sought to implicate Marlborough in a plot against the Duke.

Most of the verses of his later years are brief Jacobite and religious pieces which often make creative use of the church calendar and the complexities of New and Old Style dating. These among them relating to Harley and the Peace of Utrecht have already been mentioned. One[89] shows an alarmed realisation that the Hanoverian succession is a possibility, the realisation of which fortunately he did not live to see. The last of his books, an expanded version of *Dissertationes medicae* (Edinburgh, 1713) is dedicated to God and the Prince, *Deo suo et Principi opus hoc consecrat Archibaldus Pitcarnius Scotus, 10 Junii, 1713*.

Pitcairne died on 20 October 1713.

---

[85] 113.
[86] 69.
[87] 89.
[88] 94.
[89] 97.

INTRODUCTION

Pitcairne's private life. Books and conviviality

We know a certain amount about his private life. He was a great collector of books. Some he obtained from England. In a note, dated 16 October 1695, addressed to David Gregory,[90] he requests him: 'To send me Wallis's' works, his *Aristarchus & Pappus & Ptolemey* my broth^r paying for them. To give me ane account of Connor's book *de antris lethiferis* To endeavour to get Neuton's papers about the mythologies & Christian religion for me To send me Hooks *philos. collections*.'

The three volumes of Wallis's *Opera Mathematica* were published at Oxford in 1693, 1695 and 1699; Pitcairne refers to the first two volumes. Wallis had earlier produced editions of several Greek mathematicians and astronomers; the *Harmonicorum libri tres* of the Alexandrian, Ptolemy (Oxford, 1682); the *De magnitudinibus et distantiis solis et lunae* of Aristarchus and the surviving fragments of the *Collection* of Pappus, a handbook of Greek mathematical sciences (Oxford, 1688).

Bernard Connor (c. 1666–1698) was an Irishman, born in County Kerry. As a Catholic, he was debarred from university education in the British Isles. He went to France where, like Pitcairne, he obtained the degree of MD at Rheims. He became something of a specialist on spondylitis, an arthritic disease of the spine. Early in 1695 he came to England and lectured in London, Oxford and Cambridge. In the same year he was elected Fellow of the Royal Society and a year later Licentiate of the Royal College of Physicians. In 1695 he published at Oxford the work to which Pitcairne refers *Dissertationes medico-physicæ. De antris lethiferis. De montis Vesuvii incendio. De stupendo ossium coalitu. De immani hypogastria sarcomata.* Clearly he had made a considerable impression on English physicians and scientists; Pitcairne wished to remain in touch with current developments.

Newton is mentioned for his unpublished and unorthodox theological writings, some of which apparently circulated in MS form. Pitcairne also refers to these in a letter to Dr Gray, dated 24 October 1694: 'I have desired Gregorie to procure me a scheme of Mr Neuton's divine thoughts, (I hope yee'l not laugh) that I may write a demonstration for our religion: but this will be a tale of two drinks. I am confident that better things may be said to that purpose than hitherto has been said.'[91]

Robert Hooke (1635–1703), a distinguished scientist, edited the *Philosophical Collections* of the Royal Society in the late 1670s and early 1680s.

Gregory answered this request, as is shown by a passage in a letter to Dr Gray dated 27 February 1701,[92] a passage which also gives a revealing glimpse into Pitcairne's domestic arrangements: 'I shall write to you about Hooks *Collections*. I am ordering my books in a large roome, they are now all lying on the floor, so I cannot say anything about Hook.'

---

[90] Johnston, *Best of our owne*, 21–22, letter 6; cf. Hiscock, *Gregory*, 3–4.
[91] Johnston, *Best of our owne*, 19, letter 4.
[92] Johnston, *Best of our owne*, 36, letter 15.

Pitcairne corresponded with the physician Sir Hans Sloane (1660–1753),[93] who became Secretary to the Royal Society in 1693, and whose collections eventually formed the basis of the British Museum. Sloane obtained books for Pitcairne, while Pitcairne sent him books and any objects which might be of scientific interest.

Not all purchases were made in England. There were also good opportunities in Scotland. Pitcairne, for instance, thanked Sloane for sending him a *Cæsalpinus*,[94] but continues: 'If in the auctions that are shortlie to be made here any thing occurres fit for yow I shall assuredlie procure it. I wish yee could be at the pains to make a list of what books yee desire to have and send it me: for I sometymes find bookes here that I have long sought in vain elsewhere. As last day, after I had receiv'd the books Doctor Gray bought for me at Dr Bernards auction, I found the *Rosa Anglica*[95] in good condition & bought it for 1^s 2^d, which I pairted with to a comarad, having pay'd for it at Bernards ij^s. I had given commission to the D^r to buy at the auction *Cæsar Magatus de rara medicatione vulnerum*.[96] He writes he could not buy it, it went so high. Last day I found it & bought it here at 3^s 4^d in good condition. There is one here that has a vast collection of physic books, but has no printed catalogue.[97] Wee look on his written one, & he being ane owted minister and ignorant generallie of the prices of our books, wee get them for a small matter.'

Despite his loyalties, in the matter of book-buying, Pitcairne showed no hesitation in taking advantage of an ejected Episcopalian priest.

The books mentioned are mainly scientific or medical. The full range of the collection is shown by the catalogue,[98] published after his death, presumably for an auction. The entire library was purchased by the Russian Czar, Peter the Great (1672–1725), for inclusion in the newly-founded (1714) Library of the Russian Academy of Sciences.

Like most professional men and landowners of his time, Pitcairne enjoyed his wine and the taverns which supplied it. His favourite among the Edinburgh taverns was the so-called Greping-office, 'a suite of dark underground apartments in the Parliament Close, opening by a descending stair opposite the oriel of St Giles's, in a mass of buildings called the Pillars ... Here, it seems, according to a custom which lasted even in London till a later day, the clever physician used to receive visits from his patients. On one occasion a woman from the country called to consult him respecting the health of her daughter, when he gave a shrewd hygienic advice in a pithy metaphor not to be mentioned to ears polite. When, in consequence of

---

[93] Johnston, *Best of our owne*, 24–25, letter 10; 37, letter 16.
[94] Andreas Caesalpinus (1519–1603), Italian botanist and physician.
[95] *Rosa anglica medicine*, a medical treatise by the Englishman, John of Gaddesden (d. 1348/9).
[96] Cesar Magatus, *De rara medicatione vulnerum, seu de vulneribus raro tractandis, libri duo* (Venice, 1676). Johnston, *loc.cit.*, mistranscribes *rara* as *eara*.
[97] Almost certainly Andrew Symson.
[98] *Catalogus librorum Archibald Pitcairne* (EUL, La.III.629).

following the prescription, the young woman had recovered her health, the mother came back to the Greping-office to thank Dr Pitcairn and give him a small present. Seeing him in precisely the same place and circumstances, and surrounded by the same companions as on the former occasion, she lingered with an expression of surprise. On interrogation, she said she had only one thing to speer at him (ask after), and she hoped he would not be angry.

"Oh no, my good woman."

"Well, sir, have you been sitting here ever since I saw you last?" '[99]

This is legend rather than history, as is Wodrow's comment: 'he got a vast income, but spent it upon drinking, and was twice drunk every day.' It is true that a fair number of Pitcairne's poems are concerned with taverns, particularly the Greping-office, and with convivial gatherings, usually to celebrate some Jacobite occasion. Pitcairne took pains with these poems, as is demonstrated, for instance, by the complicated textual history of **19**. The style, however, is usually ironic, sometimes even hostile, as in **9**, where he laments the death of Mark Learmonth in a drinking bout and talks of *venena Greppæ* (l. 40).

A letter to Dr Gray, dated 27 February 1701,[100] shows that Pitcairne had a physician's awareness of the likely consequence of heavy drinking: 'I must tell you That I weigh'd My Lord Kinaird's liver (*hepar*) It weighed 8 pound, 2 ounces, at 16 ounce per pound. It was very schirrous ['indurated, covered with hard excrescences', from the same Greek root as 'cirrhosis']. It compress'd his stomach & its blood vessels so that the stomach was entirely & highlie inflamm'd, nothing could pass doune, & he oblidged to vomit every thing; Whereas Sir James Oswald whom I caus'd open that day too had a schirrous liver highlie, but it weigh'd only 3 pound: My Lords stomach was full of liquor; Sir James's had none, who dyed of a jaundice & dropsie.'

It is perhaps unlikely that the author of these remarks would have over-indulged himself in drink, but it must be remembered that seventeenth-century concepts of over-indulgence differed somewhat from our own – and not in the direction of moderation. Pitcairne drank copiously, but probably not quite to the extent suggested by his detractors.

His precise religious beliefs are difficult to determine. His opponents[101] called him an atheist or deist, to some extent, probably, as the result of what another physician called 'the generall scandall of my profession, the natural course of my studies, the indifferency of my behaviour, and discourse in matters of religion.'[102] Rather more accurately, Dr Anita Guerrini calls him 'a devoted, if not devout, Episcopalian'.[103] Several among his later poems (especially **104–116**) commemorate Church festivals which are at once Christian, Jacobite and not celebrated by

---

[99] Chambers, *Traditions*, 159–160.
[100] Johnston, *Best of our owne*, 36, letter 15.
[101] For instance, Eizat, author of *Apollo mathematicus*.
[102] *Religio Medici*, *Sir Thomas Browne: selected writings*, ed. Sir Geoffrey Keynes (London, 1968), 7.
[103] *OxfDNB*, s.v.

Presbyterians. His friend Robert Calder (?1650–1723), a dispossessed Episcopalian clergyman, who wrote a verse-commentary on **109(a)**, Pitcairne's Christmas poem for the year 1712, claimed him for a model Christian in the Episcopalian tradition: 'Pitcairne, this, your Confession of the Christian faith, was a live faith, as your good deeds prove. You were prompt to relieve the destitute with your goods, the sick with your remedy, or to cheer up the sad with your witticisms. This faith was unacquainted with the doctrines of Arius or Socinus, nor had it any smack of the business of the bloody rebel. Led by this faith, you learned to give to each his own, whether to Caesar or Irus, and to despise the world's wealth.'

The final two sentences have decided Jacobite as well as religious, overtones. The references to Arius and Socinus show something of the charges which others brought against him. Arius was the fourth-century Alexandrian heresiarch who denied the doctrine of the Trinity and whose views were most strongly opposed by Athanasius (c. 296–373), Bishop of Alexandria. Socinus belongs to a later period; the reference is to the Italian, Fausto Paolo Sozzini (1539–1604), an early Unitarian, who denied the essential divinity of Christ and rejected the natural immortality of man. There is evidence that Pitcairne's beliefs in fact came close to theirs.

In *Epistola Archimedis ad Regem Gelonem*, as part of a discussion of the authority of faith in the religion of a mathematician, he includes the following passage:

> *Testimonio nititur esse Ducem* Pœnorum *in* Italia Hannibalem; *testimoniis quoque creditur eum* Romanos *ad* Ticinum, *deinde ad* Trebiam, *nuperque ad Lacum* Transumenium *magno prælio superasse. At si quis adfirmarit* Hannibalem *eas tres pugnas eodem tempore pugnasse uno eodemque usum exercitu, fidem apud peritos haud inveniret, (quod ea res testimoniorum vires superet) quamvis etiam extricandi sui caussa persuadere vellet unicum quidem esse* Hannibalem, *sed qui tres Duces diversos unus in se ha[e]ret, nempe* Ticinensem, Trebianum & Trasumenium, *tam diversa sunt in quibus pugnatum est loca. Quippe testimoniis id unum nititur, esse* Hannibalem *in* Italia Pœnorum *Ducem, qui tribus præliis variis temporibus dissitisque locis* Romanos *superarit. At eum unicum in tres partiri postulato nulli respondet, cum etiam in homines quatuor hominem unum* Hannibalem *eodem jure possint partiri, si fors ille de* Romanis *quartam victoriam aliquando reportaverit.*

Hannibal did, in fact, win a fourth victory over the Romans at Cannae in 216 BC, a fact known to Pitcairne, but not yet, apparently, to Archimedes. The assumed date of the *Epistola* is thus after the victory at Lake Trasimene (217 BC), but before Cannae. Archimedes himself died in 212 BC.

The *Epistola Archimedis* is, as has been noted, directed primarily at Presbyterians and Roman Catholics; the relevance of this passage to Trinitarian theology and the doctrine (in whatever form) of the Real Presence in the communion elements would be fairly clear even if Pitcairne had not himself made it explicit in a holograph note (EUL MS, Dc.4.103):

INTRODUCTION

Hoc unum Te moneo Lector ut quæ de Hannibalibus tribus aut Quattuor Commemoro pagina 43,[104] *Ea de ijs accipi debere Qui Christum in Dissitis infinite locis eodem tempore Corpus suum velut Hostiam exhibere comedendum panis facie tradunt, rem impossibilem et forsan ab aliquot plebeijs Papistis, et ab omnibus Lutheranis creditam … Cave tamen, Lector, credas Archimedem vel Archiam*[105] *putare potuisse Tres esse Deos, vel unum esse Tres, hoc est, duo esse Quattuor, Nam si unus faciat Tres, alter Unus, hoc est Duo, facient Quattuor, Rem Archiæ incredibilem et Blasphemam, Quæque testimonijs Omnium hominum Divorumque probari non potest.*

The Trinity and the Real Presence are, it should be noted, as much part of Episcopalian as of Roman Catholic and even Presbyterian belief. For the most part, Pitcairne's Latin verse appears to exhibit an orthodox Episcopalianism. There is one major exception, the once-famous Epicurean poem, 22. In his prose he accepts that Jesus was the offspring (*progenies*, not *filius*)[106] of God, but rejects Trinitarianism as absurd.

Pitcairne's interest in Newton's unpublished theological writings has already been mentioned. He pretends to jest about them, but his own opinions, so far as we can judge, came close to some of these he mocked.

'It did not take Newton long to read himself right out of orthodoxy. He became fascinated with the theological struggle of the fourth century as a result of which trinitarianism was established as Christian orthodoxy. For Athanasius, the principal architect of trinitarianism, he developed more than a mere antipathy – passionate hatred is a better description … Newton enlisted himself among the disciples of Athanasius's opponent, Arius, for whom Christ was not an eternal part of the Godhead but a created intermediary between God and man, a doctrine similar to but not identical to modern unitarianism.'[107]

This brings Pitcairne and Newton close together. He also resembled Newton in that he had 'a vast propensitie to writ the *Relligio mathematici*, or *Euclidis* &c. but it cannot be printed *me vivo*. If I write it, I'l certainlie laugh in my grave if I can but understand then what a work there shall be made to answer it by those who'l not understand it. The paper (if ever I write it) shall be ane immortal confutation of poperie & of every thing that smels of poperie. But yow'l think me made to meddle in such affaires.'[108]

Unlike Newton, he never wrote a *Relligio mathematici*. The Epistola Archimedis is as close as he ever came. Nevertheless in his religious, as in his scientific and medical work, he was a Newtonian.

---

[104] In fact, as noted, 32–34.
[105] i.e., Archibald ('Archie') Pitcairne.
[106] *Progeniem Suam Christum*, EUL MS Dc.4.103.
[107] Richard S. Westfall, 'Sir Isaac Newton', *OxfordDNB*.
[108] Johnston, *Best of our owne*, 18, letter 3, to Dr Gray, 23 September 1694.

Selecta Poemata includes[109] verses by friends in commemoration of his life and achievements. In 1715 Robert Hepburn[110] published in London a brief *Dissertatio de scriptis Pitcarnianis*, devoted, for the most part, to his prose works, but including comments on the poems. The dedication includes the claim: *Ipsum* [Pitcairne] *equidem ego existimo ingenti adeo ingenio & labore non pænitendo, versus fecisse; ut non verear eum anteferre omnibus Lyricis, qui ab Horatii temporibus ad nostrum usque ævum vixere.*

The dedication is to Joseph Addison, a Whig, and, as might be expected, is less than enthusiastic about Pitcairne's Jacobitism:

Latini sermonis mirâ peritiâ omnes hujus seculi scriptores facilè superabat, ob id solùm meritò culpandus, quod sæpissimè in condendis carminibus obscurus fiat.
In causa erat animus in Jacobæorum partes studio nimio, & (ut verum fateor) senili abreptus.

Hepburn directly discusses only two poems, **40(c)**, the ode to Sir Archibald Stevenson on his 80th birthday, and **22**, *Gualteri Dannistoni ad Amicos*.

The most judicial and sympathetic assessment of Pitcairne's career is to be found in a letter written by Dr John Drummond[111] to his Aberdeen colleague, Professor Thomas Bower:[112]

'I told you in my last, that Dr Pitcairne was confined to the house, and I made too sure a prognostic, that he would never come again abroad, for on Friday, the 20th of October, about ten o'clock at night, he died, to the great detriment of learning, and the vast regret, I am sure, of all learned men, both at home and abroad. I was in the country when he died, but I am well informed that all the while he kept the house, he was in the greatest tranquillity and composedness of mind imaginable; and after this manner, without pain or trouble, and with just apprehensions of God and religion, as he constantly lived, left the world; – and we may expect just accounts of him, *quem odio aut gratia meis exemit*. And I am confident his character will be as bright and shining as any of the greatest worthies our nation can boast of, either in the present or past ages.

He was the most learned Physician that this kingdom ever bred. He was professor of Medicine at Edinburgh and Leyden, and he graced and adorned these chairs, with uncommon learning and knowledge. His excellent dissertations are lasting monuments of his noble genius, and of what advantage and light, he has thrown into the darkest parts of Medicine. In them, he proved

---

[109] pp. 88–98.
[110] see **126, 127**.
[111] see **37**, 1n.
[112] Kinloch, *Babell*, iv–viii. The letter is said to be '*penes* Robert Pitcairn, Esq.'. We have not been able to trace the original.

the continuities of the veins and arteries, without which, the circulation of the blood was imperfect. He has demonstrated the necessity of obstructions happening in the arteries, rather than in the nerves, and in the nerves, rather than in the veins, and that from their make and figure. He both explained respiration and the structure of the lungs, and has proved that the air does not penetrate through the coats of the vessels to mix with blood in them, contrary to the opinion of the great Borelli. He has told us how digestion is performed, viz. by the strong muscles of the stomach, and the muscles of the diaphragm and abdomen, and all this in a due mathematical way. He has destroyed ferments in the stomach, and other parts of the body, for correcting of which, so many unnecessary drugs were given by physicians. He has established the circular figure of pores and defeated the contrary opinion, and has given sufficient hints, by which secretion and nutrition may be explained. He has banished materiæ subtiles, occult qualities, and such other gibberish, and has shown that acids and alkalies, as such, cure no diseases. He has demonstrated the evacuations proper in fevers, by exact calculation. He has explained vision, and demonstrated the nature and diseases of the eye, and their causes. To be short, he has joined the Physician and Mathematician so happily together, that he has given us in a manner, an œconomia animalis, at least he has explained and demonstrated the most difficult and most considerable things in œconomia animalis, that his dissertations are so far the only solid institutions of Medicine we now have. Neither were these idle speculations and vain amusements, for he founded on them a rational practice, which he had so universally here for many years, and performed with so great judgment and success, that even these Physicians who had no good will at him were forced to acknowledge his inventions, and follow his method in curing diseases, which is the best now known in any part of the world, being short and proper, and free from the idle pomp and unnecessary farrago of too many drugs.

The calumny of Atheism objected against him by fanatical and enthusiastical spirits, who brand both good and learned men with this odious name, that cannot come up to their ridiculous opinions and notions, is absurd and false; for no man believed more firmly the existence of a God, and demonstrated it more clearly, as may be seen in his dissertation, De circulatione sanguinis in animalibus genitis et non genitis, in which he has proved against Des Cartes and others, that an animal cannot be mechanically produced, but must owe its original to a Supreme Being; whose existence he has demonstrated to the satisfaction and conviction of all mankind.

For his Poetry, which was always in latin, he not only equalled, but excelled the best poets of his age. We find in all his poems, a justness of thought, a vivacity of spirit, excellent turns of wit, a preciseness of style, and a happy imitation of the best antient authors; so that he may be compared to our great Buchanan himself. If we consider in what haste and hurry, the most of his performances were done, by reason of the crowd of business he was engaged in, it is still more surprising; but this is only known to some few in this place, and not to be observed by those who read his works, which are absolutely complete and perfect in their kind.

There is a design of collecting his poems, and printing them altogether. Some of his verses, made of late years, are to be omitted as not having the ordinary life and spirit in them, and not being of a piece with the former ...

[He] was not only a learned man, but a Mæcenas too, and an encourager of learning through the whole course of his life. His great care of the poor ought not to be omitted ... he did not spend all his money on his pleasure and freaks, but erected a most noble Library ...

His love to his country, and loyalty to his Prince, were extraordinary – they seemed always to fill his head and heart – and in all his discourses and verses, we find a mighty penchant and byass that way. Loyalty was still the burden of all his songs. In a word, he was one of the greatest geniuses that this age produced; being an excellent Mathematician and Philosopher, a learned and skilful Physician, a quaint and delicate Poet, a judge and master of all polite learning, a generous and charitable man, and a most loyal and dutiful subject.'

The Poems

Scottish neo-Latin verse is generally seen in terms of the achievement of the great George Buchanan (1506–1582) and of the later, mostly lesser, poets who figure in the two volumes of the *Delitiae Poetarum Scotorum* (Amsterdam, 1637). The best-known are Andrew Melville (1545–1622), Mark Alexander Boyd (1563–1601), Sir Robert Ayton (1570–1638), David Wedderburn (1580–1646) and John Barclay (1582–1621). The *Delitiae* was commissioned by Sir John Scott of Scotstarvet (1585–1670) and edited by Arthur Johnston (1587–1641), himself, after Buchanan, the best-known Scottish neo-Latin poet.[113] At Scott's insistence, Johnston's own *Parerga* and *Epigrammata* were included in the first volume.[114]

These poets were all born in the sixteenth century. With the exception of the long-lived Scotstarvet, all were dead before the execution of King Charles I in 1649 and the subsequent Cromwellian interlude. Pitcairne belongs to an appreciably later period, and his verse bears the mark of these later events, still more of the others which led to the reign (Pitcairne would have said usurpation) of King William. and the Hanoverian succession which he did not live to see. Throughout his adult life he composed Latin verse. The earliest is probably **45**, the shorter of the two poems to Robert Lindsay, written before Lindsay's death in 1675, perhaps during the time both spent at the Tounis College in Edinburgh.

---

[113] See Robert Crawford (ed. and trs.), *Apollos of the North. Selected Poems of George Buchanan & Arthur Johnston* (Edinburgh, 2006).
[114] pp. 439–647.

INTRODUCTION

'A Poem on the King and Queen of Fairy', the earliest version of ΜΟΡΜΟΝΟΣΤΟ-ΛΙΣΜΟS (**123**), is tentatively dated 1670 in the catalogue of the British Library. In the 1691 print the translation is attributed, probably in jest, to Walter Dennistoun, another fellow-student of Pitcairne, who became 'schoolmaster' (headmaster) of the grammar school at Musselburgh, six miles from Edinburgh, and who died in 1700. Pitcairne described him as 'a pitiefull Poetaster', adding 'but at Colledge with me'.[115]

Dennistoun's surviving verse is not distinguished, but Pitcairne's harsh verdict may be partly the result of political, religious and scientific disagreements. Dennistoun was as clearly a Presbyterian Whig as Pitcairne was an Episcopalian Jacobite. There are also indications that Dennistoun was committed to an 'Ancient' rather than Pitcairne's Newtonian, 'Modern', view of the Universe. He died in 1700.

Lindsay and Dennistoun both influenced Pitcairne's own verse, although in different ways. At College, Lindsay had joined with him in the study of Plato as interpreted by Ficino and the later Cambridge Platonists.[116] Both were familiar with the Platonic Underworld depicted in Book 6 of the *Aeneid*. These joint interests led to the pledge 'that whoever died first should give an account of his condition', with the consequent apparition which had so great an effect on Pitcairne. The state of the dead, posthumous existence in the Underworld and the possibility of return became a recurrent theme in his poetry, developed in a variety of ways. Sometimes he seems to identify the return of the dead with the restoration of the male line of the House of Stuart.

Pitcairne addressed Dennistoun in two poems, one, **49**, written during Dennistoun's lifetime, the other, **9**, a somewhat peculiar address to his recently departed spirit. Pitcairne also used the name as a pseudonym, often to express sentiments very different from any held by the real Dennistoun.[117] Many were written after 1700 and presented as communications from the world of the dead.

Whether or not written in his own person, Pitcairne's Latin poems are usually occasional and brief. They tend towards the epigrammatic as exemplified chiefly by Martial. The longest, *Gualteri Dannistoni ad Georgium Buchananum Epistola* (**20**), is in three parts, but, even so, only 219 lines long. Next in length is *Poema Pitcarnii M.D.* (**19(b)**), with 78 lines. Only a few of the others exceed 50 lines. Most of the poems take the form of addresses or dramatic monologues in elegiac couplets; good examples are *Ad Rob. Lindesium. 1689* (**1**), *In Geo Makinnium* (**5**), and *To Mr B. Stote concerning the Edenburgh Taverns* (**19(a)**).

This last, addressed to the Englishman (Sir) Bertram Stott,[118] is a mock-heroic version of the traditional *encomium urbis*, a form with a long history, exemplified, for instance, by Arthur Johnston's *Encomia Urbium*, a series of 24 poems on Scottish

---

[115] Oxford, *Bodleian MS Antiq.d.x.7(4)*, second hand.
[116] **1**, introductory Note.
[117] In eight poems, **20, 21, 22, 50, 60, 68(a), 85, 123**. Five, **21, 22, 60, 68(a), 85**, purport to be posthumous communications from the next world.
[118] See **21, 39, 58(a), 59, 60**.

towns, beginning with Edinburgh.[119] 'Holyrood and the Castle form the extremes: the Parliament House and St Giles' fill up the middle of the picture, and the whole has for centre the crown of St Giles''.[120]

In Pitcairne, the opening lists the traditional interests of the traveller:

Advena, qui nostros cupies cognoscere Divos,
  Et populi mores, ingeniumque loci –

The cathedral of St Giles', once representing *Divos*, is now a desecrated shrine, ruined by the Presbyterian revolution; the real life of Edinburgh – *populi mores, ingeniumque loci* – is to be sought underground, in the taverns, and especially the one known as the Greping-office, which has become a type of the Elysium of the happy dead (primarily the Jacobites) as presented in *Aeneid* 6.

Pitcairne produced personal *encomia* for his family and friends, the series, for instance, on his daughters (23, 25–28), which reflect his Jacobitism as well as his fatherly feelings, the poem on Pythagoras and Newton (47), that on James Dalrymple, Viscount Stair (51), on Andrew Fletcher of Saltoun (67), and, in lighter vein, the birthday poem for Anne Stamfield, landlady of the Greping-office (69). The verses on Viscount Dupplin, his wife, and his father (68), take the form of an exchange of letters between the deceased Dennistoun and Pitcairne, with the printer Robert Freebairn intervening. Another brief posthumous epistle (85) comes from Dennistoun to the Edinburgh Professor of Law, John Cunningham, beseeching him to return to the world of the dead as court of last resort in quelling the disturbances which have followed the arrival there in 1702 of that notorious trouble-maker, William of Orange. The poem to Elizabeth, Duchess of Gordon (89), congratulates her on her loyalty to the Stuarts, contrasting her with the infamous Elizabeth I of England, who in 1587 had ordered the execution of Mary Queen of Scots, whose claim to the English throne was better than her own.

Many of the briefer poems in elegiacs are epitaphs, sometimes serious, sometimes not, sometimes even premature. To the first group belong the epitaphs on Lockhart, Graham and Mackenzie (3, 4, 5), on Margaret Hay, his first wife (24), on Sir Andrew Balfour (29), on James Aitken, Bishop of Galloway (48), and on Charles Wilson (56). A good example of the second kind is the epitaph supposedly written for his wife by George Farquhar of Leith (57). In the third, we have the virulent 'epitaph' for Sir Robert Sibbald (30), still very much alive and destined to be an object of dislike for the remainder of Pitcairne's life.

As indicated above, some of the poems are dramatic monologues, apparently spoken by the person commemorated. In *Balfoureus moriens loquitur* (29), Balfour

---

[119] *Musa Latina Aberdonensis*, 3 vols., Spalding Club: ed., 1 and 2, Sir William Duguid Geddes, 3, William Keith Leisk (Aberdeen, 1892–1910), 2, 255–287; a selection in Crawford, *Apollos of the North*, 86–103, 146.
[120] Ibid., 255.

sets out his scientific idealism, extending beyond death. In *Heriotus Senatui a se constituto sapere* (**43**), George Heriot comes back from the dead to make his wishes clear to the current Governors of his Hospital. George Farquhar of Leith speaks for himself in **57**. The Duke of Lauderdale speaks from the grave in **72**; James VII does the same in **80**, and Louisa Maria Theresa, younger sister of the Old Pretender, in **122**. The monologue sometimes becomes a dialogue, as in the untitled **111**, involving Heriot, Pitcairne and Robert Calder, or **115**, *Presbyteri Scoti Petro*, involving St Peter and the Scottish Presbyterian ministers.

More extended and elaborate versions of the monologue form appear in *Poema Pitcarnii M.D.* (**19(b)**), where the voice is that of a professor in some academy of drinking instructing his favourite student, and in *David and Venus* (**18**), where a Presbyterian minister, David Williamson, dedicates himself to the service of Venus, rather than Christ or Mahomet, and Venus accepts him as her priest, saying that she will abandon Paphos for Scotland, where she will establish her cult, with Williamson as high priest.

Archibaldi Pitcarnii Scoti. Carmen. Anno Aetatis suae LX (**22**) is the final version of a poem which under its earlier titles, *Joannis Sylvij de seipso carmen*, and *Gualterus Dannistonus Ad Amicos*, had been presented as a dramatic monologue. Matthew Prior's well-known English paraphrase preserves the third title.

The calendrical pieces, finally, which make up Section 7, are mostly written in elegiac couplets. Only the introductory *Ad Josephum Scaligerum* (**103**) takes the form of a Horatian ode in sapphics. The Julian calendar (Old Style, O.S.), still used in England, had been replaced elsewhere by the Gregorian (New Style, N.S.). By Pitcairne's time the difference between the two was such that 29 May (O.S.) was 10 June (N.S.). The twenty-five year reign of Charles II, for Pitcairne the golden age of Stuart monarchy, was ushered in by his Restoration on 29 May 1660, which also happened to be his birthday. It was thus a date of much significance for Jacobites, for whom a Restoration in the past became a type of one in the future. The fact that 29 May was the same as 10 June, the Pretender's birthday was regarded as a good omen.

Ad Marcum Lermontium (**7**) is an epistolary invitation in sapphics to the advocate, Mark Learmonth, to enjoy a celebratory dinner with him on a 29th May, when successes for the French forces in the Nine Years War had renewed hopes of a second Restoration. The ode is reminiscent of the dinner invitation sent by Horace to Maecenas in *Odes* 3, 8, *Martiis caelebs quid agam Kalendis?* Similar is *Pitcarnius rogat Tho. Kinkadium ut ad se veniat Decima Junii, quæ sacra est Divæ Margaritæ Scotorum Reginæ* (**37**). St. Margaret, who in 1069 married the Scottish king, Malcolm III (1031–1093), was sister of Edgar the Ætheling, *de jure* heir to the English throne, which in 1066 had been forcibly usurped by William the Conqueror. The family situation bears an obvious resemblance to that of James VII and his son. The reference in l. 10 to Charles II and his nephew probably indicates that June 10 and May 29 are now to be regarded as equivalent.

INTRODUCTION

The epistolary form is clear in *Davidi Dromondio Jurisconsulto Archibaldus Pitcarnius S.* (**64**). Like Pitcairne, David Drummond was born on 25 December, and he is invited to a joint, if muted, celebration of their natal day. Mortality is the theme, remembrance of dead friends and anticipation of oneself leaving behind such friends as Prior, Addison and Gray. There is consolation, however, in the thought of once more seeing his professional predecessors, the great physicians Borelli and Bellini, and his closest friend, the astronomer David Gregory. Meanwhile, he must do his best to help his country and his fellow-citizens – a half-disguised reference to Jacobitism.

Two other odes develop similar themes. *Q. Horatio Flacco Archibaldus Pitcarnius Caledonius* (**31**) is, in effect, a mythical history of medicine to the time of Pitcairne, ending with a tribute to two Moderns, Robert Gray and John Bateman, regarded as the main living exponents of scientific medicine. *Roberto Graio Scoto Londini Medicinam Profitenti Archibaldus Pitcarnius Scotus S.* (**39**), another epistolary ode, is addressed to the same Robert Gray, and expresses the isolation which Pitcairne in Edinburgh is beginning to feel, a feeling much enhanced by the recent death of his friend, David Gregory, whom he imagines in the Elysian Fields, delighting Euclid and Archimedes with news of the discoveries recently made by Newton and Halley, and reunited with his distinguished uncle, James Gregorie. Pitcairne and Gray are both bereft of his support and attention.

In obitum Archibaldi Stevensoni, Medicorum sui seculi facile princeps (**40**) is primarily a commemoration of the life of Pitcairne's father-in-law and close ally, Sir Archibald Stevenson. The textual history is complicated.

Several briefer poems, including one (**93**) addressed to Jonathan Swift, are in sapphics. Another of these, *Thomæ Boero Scoto, Matheseos & Medicinæ Professori, Arch. Pitcarnius Scotus S.* (**58**), is ingeniously built from a single Horatian stanza, *Odes* 1, 12, 17–20.

That same ode, in its entirety, provides the model for the two satiric Imitations entitled *Proceres Scotorum Anno* MDCXC (**76**). Horace's ode maps the divine purpose which had shaped Roman history in its heroic course from Romulus to Augustus. Pitcairne's imitations deal with the dire sequence of Presbyterian heroes who by 1690 had brought Scotland to such a sorry pass.

In alcaics, only two odes have survived, a drinking poem, *Thomæ Kinkadio Chirurgo, Archibaldus Pitcarnius Chirurgus S.D.* (**38**) and one (**59**), extant in two versions, the first entitled *Ad Andream Tenant*, the second *Ad Thomam Kinkadium*. The two latter deal, or fail to deal, with a problem common in early eighteenth-century Scotland, gifted friends who are thinking of moving south to London. In the first, Sir Bertram Stott is at least an Englishman by birth, but in the second Kinkaid's own brother is the object of concern.

In Nuptias Comitis Levinii (**77**) is a satirical Imitation of Horace, *Odes* 3, 28, preserving the metrical form, Asclepiadean Strophe No. 2, Glyconic alternating with Lesser Asclepiad in four-line stanzas. The subject is the rigorously Presbyterian wedding on 3 September 1691 between Lady Anne Wemyss and the Earl of Leven.

INTRODUCTION

Seven poems are in hendecasyllables, a metre favoured by Catullus, but also by such later classical poets as Martial and Statius. *Monopennius J.C.* (**55**), a witty and moving poem on the death of a witty friend, contains some Catullan reminiscences. Three others, *Ad* ✱✱✱ (**6**), *Ad Hugonem Dalrimplium, Supremi Senatus Juridici in Scotia Præsulem* (**53**), and *Ad Comitem Cromarteum* (**87**), are parodies of Catullus, 49, *Disertissime Romuli nepotum*, a mock-humble address to the learned orator, lawyer and statesman, Marcus Tullius Cicero. Pitcairne plays significant variations on the initial adjective. In **6** it becomes *Prudentissime*; in **53** (the least satiric) *Consultissime*, in **87** *Vivacissime*. Each has its point in relation to the man addressed. A more distant version may be found in *Ad Haium Comitem Kinulium* (**68(e)**), linked not so much by its first as by its final line, *Doctis omnibus esse ter patronum*.

The remaining two poems are longer and unrelated to Catullus. *Ad Dannistonum* (**9**) may owe a little to Statius's account of revelry at the Saturnalia, the *Kalendae Decembres* (*Silvae* 1, 6), but essentially it is original. The style is compressed. In 45 lines it combines an account of Priapic revelry in the Greping-office with the narrative of the behaviour of one Hugh Cuninghame, 'ane Ignorant Lawyer, a profest Hypocrite, ane abominable Presbiterian or Holy Drunkard',[121] behaviour which led to the tragic, and needless, death of Pitcairne's friend, the advocate Mark Learmonth, who has already been mentioned. At the same time, the poem celebrates the posthumous apotheosis of Greppa, landlady of the Greping-office, and is a threnody for Walter Dennistoun, who had died just before Greppa. The overtones are Jacobite.

Fabulæ 2. Lib. 1. Phædri Metaphrasis (**12**) has already been mentioned for its connection with the Darien expedition.[122] In a sense, as the title indicates, it too is an Imitation, but there is no verbal or metrical similarity to the fable of Phaedrus on which the piece is based. The structure leads beautifully to the little birthday ode in sapphics with which it ends.

The poems reflect Pitcairne's powerful personality, frequently at odds with his times and circumstances. His nature had two sides, one conservative, the other radical. The first appears in his Jacobitism and Episcopalianism, both of which have their remote origins in Ghibelline ideas formulated during the struggle between supporters of the Papacy (Guelphs) and supporters of the Empire (Ghibellines). Most famously they are given expression in Dante's *De Monarchia*. During the period of the Reformation they developed into the doctrine of the Divine Right of Kings, a doctrine which saw the monarch as a sacred figure, intermediary between God and his subjects and head of Church as well as State. Succession to the monarchy was hereditary and immutable by way of male primogeniture. With the monarch as head, the organization of the Church was necessarily hierarchical, Episcopalian. Adherents of these views set themselves against any form of church absolutism, whether Papal or Presbyterian. 'The two systems, Papal and

---

[121] **9**, introductory note.
[122] Above, pp. 15–16.

Presbyterian, are alike in that they both regard the state as the mere handmaid of an ecclesiastical corporation, and would, in the last resort, place the supreme direction of politics in the hands of the rulers of the church.'[123]

Pitcairne's radical side appears in his position as a scientific Modern, working by the application of mathematical analysis to experimental evidence. This is in conflict with his more conservative beliefs to the extent that it led him into theological difficulties with the doctrine of the Trinity and the Real Presence, but left him otherwise, apparently, unaffected. Although he wrote verses on church subjects, he seldom himself went to church or took part in religious ceremonies. Nevertheless, he remained on very good terms with a number of Episcopal clergymen.

The usurpation by William of Orange challenged Pitcairne on both fronts, and it is no surprise that his best poems were, for the most part, written during that reign. William had broken the immutable succession to the monarchy, just when the birth of the Prince had apparently most clearly established it. In Scotland, something like Calvinist absolutism had been asserted with the General Assemblies of 1690 and 1692. The rift at the College of Physicians had been between Ancients and Moderns, and the Ancients had won at least a temporary victory.

The first twelve of the seventeen poems in *Poemata Selecta*[124] were written during William's reign. They portray a society in dissolution after the loss of its King, its Church, and the greatest figures of its civil and military life. Even so, elements of comfort are present. Events abroad sometimes favour King James. One Stuart, Charles II, lived to see the Restoration of his line; if he should now return, he may bring about another — especially after William's providential death in 1702. The picture is not wholly dark.

A number of poems already discussed fit into this general scheme. *David and Venus* (18), *Proceres Scotorum Anno MDCXC* (76), and *In Nuptias Comitis Levinii* (77), for instance, all show in different ways what the Church has come to, and cast some light on the general state of society. They come close to Pitcairne's vernacular writings of the same period, his comedy, *The Assembly*, and his Hudibrastic epic, *Babell*.

In *Pythagoras Samius et Isaacus Neutonus Anglus* (47) Pitcairne presents himself as a scientific Modern, not only by his subject-matter, but also by the quasi-mathematical way in which he assesses the Greek and the Englishman against each other. Almost the same is true of *Thomæ Boero Scoto, Matheseos & Medicinæ Professori, Arch. Pitcarnius Scotus S.* (58), where Newton is again the main subject. The sapphic ode, *Ad Josephum Scaligerum 29 Maij 1710* (103) is a playful tribute to Joseph Scaliger (1540–1609), the great mathematician of the calendar, and is followed by a series of poems based on calendrical peculiarities.

---

[123] Figgis, *Divine Right*, 193.
[124] Section 1 below.

INTRODUCTION

Pitcairne saw the quarrel between Ancients and Moderns more in terms of medicine and natural history than of mathematics; witness the virulent attacks on Sir Robert Sibbald (30) and Sir David Hay (34). Others he treated more favourably; see, for instance, *Balfoureus moriens loquitur* (29), *Q. Horatio Flacco Archibaldus Pitcarnius Caledonius* (31), and *Ad Robertum Morisonum. M.D. et Botanices Professorem Oxoniensem* (32).

Many of the poems stand outside either category. Some are simple expressions of good-fellowship, as, for instance, the ode (38) to Thomas Kinkaid and his surgeon friends, or that to William Carmichael (54). Fatherly pride dominates the poem to his young daughter, *Ad Annam Pitcarniam* (23), grief, and pride of a different sort, that on the death of his first wife, *In Uxorem suam* (24). He wrote moving epitaphs for his friends. *Monopennius J.C.* (55) has already been mentioned; others, *In obitum Alexandri Monteith Chirurgi* (44), *In Carolum Wilson* (56), might be added. A comic epitaph, worthy of Martial, is *Georg: Ferquhard Lethensis ad uxorem demortuam* (57). And there is the birthday poem to Anne Stamfield (69). Standing apart from all these is the noble tribute to Viscount Stair (51), a man politically opposed to everything for which Pitcairne stood, but a great lawyer.

Pitcairne saw and judged his Scotland in terms of imperial Rome. Where his verse is most relaxed, he writes like a Horace or Virgil under the principate of Augustus, in the darker poems more like a Juvenal remembering Domitian. He assumes that the natural state of Scotland is Augustan, as it had been during the golden reign of Charles II. He calls Edinburgh *Augusta*[125] and makes the phrase *Fergusi nepotum*,[126] the Scots, descendents of the legendary first king of Scotland, Fergus, equivalent to *Romuli nepotum*, used by Catullus of the Romans, descendents of Romulus, their legendary first king. The abused Scottish institutions are seen in terms of their Roman equivalents – *Jura silent, torpent classica, Rostra vacant*.[127]

Pitcairne is not wholly dependent on classical sources. He is acquainted with such neo-Latin authors as Jacopo Sannazaro (1458–1530) and George Buchanan (1506–1582). He was also himself the central figure in a small group of late Scottish neo-Latin poets, the most notable of whom were Sir William Scott of Thirlestane, Thomas Kinkaid, Pitcairne's friend and fellow-surgeon in Edinburgh, and a younger man, John Kerr, professor of Greek in King's College, Aberdeen, 1717–1731. *Selecta Poemata, Archibaldi Pitcarnii Med. Doctoris, Gulielmi Scot a Thirlestane, Equitis, Thomæ Kincadii, Civis Edinburgensis, et Aliorum* (Edinburgh, 1727) gathers together some of their work.

To the editor of this last publication, Robert Freebairn, or perhaps Thomas Ruddiman, the last word may be given. After praising Pitcairne's medical works and claiming that he easily holds the primacy among the poets just mentioned, he continues:

---

[125] 40(c), 15 below.
[126] 6, 1; 53, 1; 87, 1.
[127] 5, 26.

INTRODUCTION

Ad ea autem quod attinet, quæ nunc afferimus magni illius Viri poemata, non est quod pluribus, Lector benevole, tecum agamus. Id nobis summatim suffecerit dixisse, ea quoque in suo genere præstantissima esse: &, cum pleraque omnia Epigrammaticæ indolis sint, quod in ejusmodi carmine decebat, eam in stylo puritatem, in dicendo salem & leporem, in sententiis denique vim & acumen ubique eminere, ut ad normam antiquorum expressa, & ad ipsius Catulli *vel* Martialis *lucernam evigilata videantur.*

The Texts

Selecta Poemata Archibaldi Pitcarnii Med. Doctoris, Gulielmi Scot a Thirlestane, Equitis, Thomæ Kincadii, Civis Edinburgensis, et Aliorum (hereafter SP) was much read in the eighteenth and early nineteenth centuries, but has now become little more than a collector's item. The title proclaims that the contents are only a selection, and in fact many other poems have survived, usually as broadsheets which Pitcairne had privately printed for circulation among friends. A 'Note of School Authors printed & sold by Mr Tho. Ruddiman now in his possession 2 Sept. 1732,' (an account book; Edinburgh, NLS, MS 763) records the printing of several individual poems during the years 1712 and 1713. MS copies also circulated. These ephemera were sometimes later brought together. Two purely broadsheet collections, R[1] and R[2], are in the Edinburgh Room of the Edinburgh Central Library (*Reliquiae Pitcairnianae*, ref. qy R489P68, Accession nos. 13817 and 36553). Another is held in HRHRC (Harry Ransom Humanities Research Center, University of Texas at Austin) for the most part under shelf-mark PR 3619 P54. Fifteen are held in Bodleian, Oxford, under shelf-mark *Antiq.d.x.7 (BA(4a))*. The Beinecke collection in Yale University Library holds a few items (YB). Broadsides are combined with MS items in N (Edinburgh, NLS, H.23.a.16), an extensive collection, which may have been put together by the publisher Archibald Constable (1774–1825), and in BA(4), (Oxford, Bodleian, *Antiq.d.x.7*). BD (Oxford, Bodleian, *Don.c.58*) is entirely MS. Broadsides and MSS alike seem to date from Pitcairne's lifetime.

Pitcairne occasionally claims authorship in the title or the body of a poem. For the most part however the poems are anonymous or attributed to Walter Dennistoun. Confirmation of authorship is sometimes to be found in his correspondence, for example, in a letter of 16 June 1712 addressed to John Ker (c. 1680–1741), 5th Earl and 1st Duke of Roxburghe:[128]

> 'I send your Grace 3 copies about Barberini [80], one for Janet, another for Peggie, and one for Louise, 2 for June [105], one for May, which was the Ascension-day [104], One for this Emperour [119], 4 for Juppiter Hammon [83]. They say that in Raguels roll the Hammilts are famos for joining the Inglis-men against Robert de Bruss and now a loun is added. I wrote this in good humour. I send 3 for Sannazarius [50].'

---

[128] Johnston, *Best of our owne*, 67, letter 53.

INTRODUCTION

The jest is probably aimed at the 4th Duke of Hamilton, in September 1711 created 1st Duke of Brandon in the British peerage, but denied a hereditary seat in the House of Lords. Interestingly, Pitcairne assumes that women, or at least daughters of the nobility, will be able to appreciate some of his Latin verse.[129]

Printer, date and place of printing are sometimes indicated, for example in E, *Gualteri Dannistoni ad Georgium Buchananum* EPISTOLA *et Buchanani* RESPONSUM. MDCC, EDINBURGI, *Typis Jacobi Vatsoni* (**20**). A later print is dated 1706. D (*Die* XXV *Decembri; Anni* MDCCXII [**109(a)**]) is subscribed *A.P.* and annotated *Apud Robertum Freebairn, 1712*. A (*Ad Haium Comitem Kinulium* [**68(e)**]) has EDINBURGI, *Apud Robertum Freebairn Typographum* REGIUM, but no date.

Among these prints, the most important is PS (*Poemata Selecta 9ab5c2d8eg2h14i3l8-m10n5o4p7r6s7t6v*), printed in quarto, probably in Edinburgh. The latter part of the title is in cipher, the almost useless key to which is preserved in EUL, MS Dc.4.103.[130] The text is given in the form of a list enumerating the number of times each letter of the alphabet appears in it. This particular example should convey something like *Selecta Poemata Archibaldi Pitcarnii Anno Ær[æ] Christianæ Millesimo Septingentesimo Nono*, 'Selected Poems of Archibald Pitcairne in the One Thousand Seven Hundred and Ninth Year of the Christian Era',[131] but the number of letters does not precisely correspond with the code. The pamphlet which appears never to have been bound, contains seventeen poems, written at various dates between 1689 and 1708, all Jacobite. It was probably produced in anticipation of the Tory electoral triumph in 1710 and the consequent increased likelihood of a Jacobite restoration. All the poems are included in SP, but in a different order and with some variant readings. After Pitcairne's death, PS was included as an appendix to his collected medical works, *Archibaldi Pitcarnii, Scoto-Britanni, medici celeberrimi, Opera omnia, duobus tomis comprehensa: quorum unus continet elementa medicinæ physico-mathematica: alter dissertationes medicas, cum quibusdam aliis opusculis Archibaldi Pitcarnii* (The Hague, 1722, and subsequent editions).

---

[129] A letter to Dr Gray dated 6 August 1697 (*Best of our owne*, 23, letter 8) includes a text *of In effigiem Rob. Morisoni* (**32**). Another (27 February 1701; *Best of our owne*, 36, letter 15) refers to *Gualteri Dannistoni ad Georgium Buchananum Epistola et Buchanani Responsum* (**20**), apparently to the 1706 edition. Another (to the Earl of Mar, 20 September, 1707; *Best of our owne*, 47–48, letter 31), includes a text of *Ad Bertramum Stotum* (**60**), attributing it to Walter Dennistoun. Letters dated 2 September 1710 and 26 February 1711 (*Best of our owne*, 63, letter 50, 66, letter 53) refer to *Gualterus Dannistonus Ad Amicos* (**22**). Finally, a letter dated 1 September 1712 (*Best of our owne*, 68, letter 56) includes a text of *Harlaio* (**96**).

[130] *Tertiamque Reddidi rursus auctam nomine meo literis involuto Quas cuivis non erat Oedipo facile explicare.Adpellavi tunc eam Archimedis Epistolam ad Regem Gelonem Albae Graecae repertam Anno Aerae Christianae 1688.Literae Involventes hae sunt adhibitae.25 A, 3B, 8C, 6D, 21E, 3F, 8G, 3H, 18I, 9L, 7M, 9N, 16O, 8P, Q, iiR, 10S, 15T, 10V, X, 2Y. Explicatio.Conficta ab Archibaldo Pitcarnio Scoto olim Professore Medico in Academia Lugduni Batavorum Editaque Anno Vulgaris Aerae Supra Mille et Septingentos Sexto Amstelodami. Typis Georgii Gallet Praefecti Typographiae Huguetanorum.*The cipher represents (approximately only; Pitcairne's arithmetic is sometimes faulty) the final paragraph.

[131] See NLS, *H.23.a.16*, fo.1ʳ.

INTRODUCTION

Several copies of PS survive. It forms part of N and of both R¹ and R². Yale University Library has a copy (YB, GR 17 43), as does the Harry Ransom Humanities Research Centre in the University of Texas at Austin (PR3619 P54 A61709).

In some ways more important than any of these is the Bodleian copy (BA[1]), first item in the collection already mentioned. On the obverse of the first leaf after the title page is a letter in Pitcairne's hand, under his Dennistoun pseudonym, addressed to Robert Arbuthnot,[132] Jacobite brother of Pitcairne's friend already mentioned, the physician Dr John Arbuthnot (1667–1735). This reads as follows:

> 'Sir, *Patroa Virgo* is the Sun.
>
> For Gods sake tell me if you have got the *Poemata Selecta* of which this is the key. Write often to me.
>
> Your Walter Danniston
>
> For Mr Robert Arbuthnet.'

The opening sentence refers to an epigram (**121**), addressed on her eighteenth birthday in 1710 to the exiled youngest daughter of James VII, Louisa Maria Theresa (1692–1712), '*Ad Mariam Lodovicam Teresam, ipso suo natali die XVII Junii, MDCCX*':

> *Fratre tuo viso, derisit Apollo Gradivum,*
> *Quo fuerat coelo fortius ante nihil:*
> *Tu simul exorta es, coelo formosior ipso,*
> *Abscondit victum virgo patroa caput.*

Arbuthnot had difficulties with the word '*patroa*' in the final line. Pitcairne was aware that there were difficulties in his poems and responded with an interpretation just as difficult, while at the same time sending a Key, which would assist in the understanding of his recently-printed collection, PS. Even his closest friends sometimes found Pitcairne's poetry difficult – *Multa stylo obscuro Pitcarnus carmina scripsit*, Robert Calder remarked (**109(b)**) – and it seems clear that explications were often in demand.

On the verso of the same leaf, in a more formal hand, but with corrections possibly in Pitcairne's autograph, is the 'Key,' for poems **1, 6, 7, 9** and **10** of the pamphlet. These are included in the relevant notes below. They begin impersonally, with Pitcairne mentioned as AP. In later references the words 'me,' 'our,' 'we' and 'I' are used.

---

[132] H. See and A. Cormack, 'An Aberdeen Trader Two Hundred Years Ago,' *Aberdeen University Review* XV (1927–1928), 32–36; Lenman, *Jacobite Risings*, 104.

The more formal hand bears some resemblance to the one used in the selection of Pitcairne's poems making up the second part of *BA(4)*. This also contains annotations, with the pronoun 'we' used once. The hand may be that of one of the amanuenses sometimes used by Pitcairne.[133]

Other surviving copies of *PS* have on the final leaf the list *Mutenda [sic] & Corrigenda*. This is lacking in the Bodleian exemplar, but in the text the same alterations and corrections (with one exception) are inserted in what appears to be Pitcairne's hand. These, it may be assumed, he subsequently had the printer insert as a list of *errata* in copies yet to be distributed. The Bodleian exemplar, in other words, is particularly valuable for the insights provided into Pitcairne's original intentions and the final form of the poems. We may probably also assume that the barbarous form *Mutenda* is the responsibility of the printer rather than Pitcairne — and, with equal probability, that the printer was not Ruddiman.

In the Texas copy of *PS*, after *Mutenda & Corrigenda*, the same MS explicatory notes appear, including a brief additional note on poem 12. This last was probably once present in the Bodleian exemplar, but lost in cutting or binding. The notes break off with the words, 'Sir *Patroa Virgo* is the Sun.' Fairly clearly, the whole thing is copied from the Bodleian Key.

N contains no annotations, but has a preliminary MS page, perhaps by Archibald Constable. It reads 'Select Poems of Dr Archibald Pitcairn, 1709, with a page of MS annotations very curious and interesting. At the end is a MS copy of verses on Dr Archd. Stevenson's birthday printed in the 12mo volume [i.e., *SP*] p. 36.' The reference is to poem 40c below. On the reverse of the page, the 'MS annotations' form an abbreviated version of the Key, followed by the interpretation of the cipher in the title of *PS* already mentioned.

S, BL MS, *Sloane 3198*, is a miscellaneous collection of prose documents with mainly Scottish connections, all bound together. The sixth item, in Pitcairne's sometimes illegible hand and described in the prefatory list of contents as 'Robert Lindsay's Apparition to AP', is a version of the Key in some ways better than any of these already mentioned. It ends however with notes on a poem not included in *PS*, '[*Ad Kirktonum Chirurgum*]' (35), followed by a text of that poem and a reference forward to another, probably '*Ad Georgium Kirtonum, Proserpinæ a Potione*' (36). A final note suggests that it was addressed to Dr Gray.

In general, the notes are on poems the occasion for which might have been obscure even to a Scot in the early eighteenth century. The occasion for the others is pretty well self-evident. One should note that Pitcairne was prepared to explicate poems other than those in *PS*.

PS is a Jacobite anthology, ranging in tone from early despair to a later guarded optimism. As it is the most extensive collection of Pitcairne's Latin verse un-

---

[133] Cf. *Best of our owne*, 23, letter 8: 'I gave it [32] to a master of arts & minister to doe [i.e., make a fair copy].'

doubtedly produced under his own supervision, it seems natural to put it first in this edition.

The most extensive MS collection is APP (EUL MS, *Archibaldi Pitcarnii M.D. Poemata. Oct^ri An. 1703*), bound in with the printed *Catalogus Librorum Archibald Pitcairne*, shelf-mark La.III.629. There are 58 quarto pages, the last two blank. The first is also blank, save for the words '*this and the Lat:*'. The title appears on p. 2. The MS is in two hands, the first not identified, but perhaps that of an amanuensis, the second, on pp. 13–18 and 32–57, that of David Gregory. A different paper is used for these latter pages. The word '*finis*' is written on p. 33 below the poem entitled '*Monnopennius J.C.*' (**55**). The concluding poem is '*Ad Dominum de Belhaven mortuum Londini Junio MDCCVIII*' (**16**), followed by the date '*July 10. 1708*'. Belhaven died on 21 June 1708; Gregory himself on 10 October 1708. It is clear that between October 1703 and July 1708 Gregory continued to add poems to the collection. The final total is 55. As in SP and BA(4), the first is '*Joannis Sylvij de seipso carmen*' (**22**).

A puzzling feature is the inclusion of '*In Obitum Archibaldi Stevensoni Medicorum sui seculi facile principis*' (**40(a)**). Sir Archibald Stevenson died only in 1710.

BA(4), tentatively dated 1710, and headed 'Poemes by doctor Pitcarne' is written in two main hands. The first is florid, decorative, and rather careless (there are deletions, insertions and blots), and occupies ff.2.r.-14.r. The final words are 'Edinburgh,' followed by an illegible date, indicating where and when the 30 poems included (10 also in PS) were copied. There are parallels with SP and APP. in the order and titles.

The second hand, resembling that in the Key to the Bodleian PS, begins on f.18.r., and ends with a series of notes occupying most of f.22. These form an abbreviated version of the Key. There are texts of six poems, five also included in PS, together with a scabrous prose parody, '*ad Dominum de Courson Te Deum.*'

F, an early eighteenth-century MS (GUL, *Ferguson 108*), contains as the third item *Poema Pitcarnii M.D.* (**19(b)**).

This Edition

The text of the individual poems is followed by an English translation, notes on textual sources and variants, metre, and a literary and historical commentary. We have made no comment on the metre when it is the usual elegiac couplet. PS takes pride of place, followed by a group of longer poems, mainly satiric. As already noted, the longest (**20**) was separately published by Watson in 1700; on the title-page it is attributed to Walter Dennistoun. Often several poems turn on the same or a closely related subject and it has seemed sensible to group them together, rather than attempt an entirely chronological sequence which would obscure any such relationship. The chronology is often tentative. Almost all the poems might have been classified as Jacobite. The extent, however, to which this is so varies considerably. Jacobitism may be combined with other themes, and we have made some effort to separate those which are simply Jacobite from others in which a different theme predominates or at least holds the balance. First come family poems, then those referring to members of Pitcairne's profession. Next come friends and acquaintances. The next section is political, mainly Jacobite. A separate and distinctly Episcopalian group turns on the calendar and the church year. Europe governs the next. The final section contains translations from English and Scots.

Within each section we have, so far as possible, kept a chronological order of composition.

Editorial treatment obviously must vary from poem to poem. In general, we have used the oldest printed version as text and listed substantial variations whenever these are found. We prefer printed to MS sources, but when no printed text is available, we have used the best MS version. Sometimes variations are so great that it has seemed better to print alternative texts in their entirety.

Archibald Pitcairne (1652–1713)
[Photo courtesy of the Royal College of Physicians, Edinburgh]

James Francis Stuart (1688-1756), The Old Pretender
[Photo courtesy of the National Portrait Gallery, London]

James VII and II (1633-1701) [Photo courtesy of the Scottish National Portrait Gallery, Edinburgh]

Louisa Maria Theresa Stuart (1692–1712)
[Photo courtesy of the National Portrait Gallery, London]

Poem. I. Robert Lyndsay, Grandchild or Great=Grandchild to the said Lyndsay of Pitscottie, Son King cot Dumfries: being intimat Comrade with Sir Robt Bertrand and about That whoever Died first should give account of the Condition, if possible. It happen'd that Sir Robt about the end of 1679 while he was at Paris, and the very night of his Death, Sir Robt apear'd that he was at Edinbr where Lyndsay attack'd him thorough the said R: Berlayes Son in Law "No Robin. Ay. But How?— Ou=ie—Any Say in the Graufriars. I am about the grave to
"Sit in a place, whereof the Measures cannot be express'd in Scotch, Greek or Latine. Shall I never
"Rest Seeing small use to Lord Lord to carrie your Mind.—— Robin. No go with you Bob rest
"till I go to Hu [unclear] & Bent of Rhan & take leave of my Parents. Obidie, Sais Robt Alliance
"Lyndsay Farewell. He come for your at another time. And saving a Tangerine, Sacheveral and 1694
"was told by Robin. Hight well forbid for a time, and that it was properly his fate to carrie him
off. But was Discharged to tell with.

Poem. VI with fires ✱✱✱ is britallin.
Poem. VII. Mayer Lermont Edward Rapp'd with me on a 29th of may when our Army
could not go to the fields, when Chanbery was taken &c: and as several places near Made. Vaudemi—
The fr=fil Devide in a Sun.

Poem VIII. Od: Greppam.
Gilt wine in Spain.
This was delightful. But the show that time at 32 yeres the seris yers the indemnity, to Give Leipt 143 Gr=pp= yeres, which was other nonsense.
Know not, but Rape by Ann price. — Vair Did pris 1681, the Pharaohs to reside in Greppam. I never in his
end of the yere— told me we did Ketch grief entirely, its old calvor wine, where—his other Livers were—
It ink'd to give Hebron by Mayerhoffs, for 20 Anno, a poet, to Lome, to Geneva. A little Ann than Greppam had now put in Mr Gilt Bruce, our Ship Manch, who is supposed to be married to Mr Claymore
bottle is another such Br: who is maried to Gartman the Chief of such sort of Saints.

Poem. IX. is explained by what is
How have both the Greyhys who would [unclear] in shown here by the Lord [unclear] from [unclear] the Mr Lock with
Christie's, Wooden Gratitude was in a proveron. [unclear]
Stone about his neck.—This is

X Hugh Cunningham a my as [unclear] Hepburn in Edinburgh. But as son for he went
intended Surveyor of [unclear] Robert your Company — in a [unclear] but for [unclear] made to Rent. If not for hi [unclear]
Wife Did. This first Strand always in Grippell, was yet to [unclear] Tennant has expert of short cabby
Our present Couting is a Abner Handfriend [unclear] to Abner A [unclear] called Haunty to R—

BIBLIOGRAPHY

A. Works by Archibald Pitcairne

i. *Latin Verse*

[*A Poem on the King and Queen of Fairy* (English and Latin) Broadside (n.p., s.n., n.d.; ?London, ?1670)]
[*ΜΟΡΜΟΝΟΣΤΟΛΙΣΜΟΣ, sive Lamiarum Vestitus. A POEM on the King and Queen of FAIRY. Translated into Latine, by Mr Walter Dennestone.* (n.p., s.n., 1691)]
[*Gualteri Dannistoni ad Georgium Buchananum EPISTOLA et Buchanani RESPONSUM* (Edinburgh: James Watson, 1700)]
Archibaldi Pitcarnii M.D. Poemata. Oct^{ri} An. 1703 (MS, bound in with *Catalogus librorum Archibald Pitcairne* below)
Poemata Selecta 9ab5c2d8eg2h14i3l8m10n5o4p7r6s7t6v ([Edinburgh]: 1709)
'Ad Haium Comitem Kinulium' (Broadside) (Edinburgh: Robert Freebairn, n.d.)
'Die XXV Decembri; Anni MDCCXII' (Broadside) (Edinburgh: Robert Freebairn, 1712)
Selecta Poemata Archibaldi Pitcarnii Med. Doctoris, Gulielmi Scot a Thirlestane, Equitis, Thomæ Kincadii, Civis Edinburgensis, et ALIORUM (Edinburgh: [Robert Freebairn], 1727)
GUL, MS Ferguson 108 (*Poema Pitcarnii M.D.*)
HRHRC [University of Texas at Austin] PR 3619 P54 (broadside collection)
NLS, H.23.a.16 (broadside and MS collection)
Oxford, *Bodleian Antiq.d.x.7* (broadside and MS collection)
    Bodleian Don.c.58 (MS collection)
Reliquiae Pitcairnianae, ref. qyR489P68, accession nos. 13817, 36553 (broadside collections, Edinburgh Room, Edinburgh Central Library.)

ii. *Other Works*

Exempla additionis, subtractionis ... ad quorum reflectionem Joannem Young invitat Archibald Pitcairne (Broadside, EUL, Dc.1.61/187) (Edinburgh: March 1, 1683)
Quamvis Johannem Young publice fuerit ab Archibaldo Pitcairne invitatus ut problemata duo solveret ... (Broadside, EUL, Dc.1.61/187) (Edinburgh: March 20, 1683)
Solutio problematis de historicis; seu de inventoribus dissertatio (Edinburgh: John Reid, 1688)
Archibaldi Pitcarnii oratio qua ostenditur medicinam ab omni philosophorum secta esse liberam; et exemplo docetur quantam utilitatem medicis offerre possit mathesis (Leiden, 1692: Edinburgh: John Reid, 1696)
Disputatio de curatione Febrium quae per evacuationes instituitur ([Edinburgh]: George Mosman, 1695)
Dissertatio de Legibus Historiæ Naturalis (Edinburgh: John Reid, 1696)

Archibaldi Pitcarnii Dissertationes medicae (Rotterdam: *typis Regneri Leers*, 1701)

Epistola Archimedis ad Regem Gelonem Albae Graecae reperta 1688 (n.p., n.d., s.n.: ?1706; ?1710)

Archibaldi Pitcarnii Dissertationes Medicae. Quarum multae nunc primum prodeunt. Subjuncta est Thomae Boeri M.D. ad Archibaldum Pitcarnium epistola, qua responditur libello Astrucii Franci (Edinburgh: Robert Freebairn, 1713)

Archibaldi Pitcarnii, Scoto-Britanni, medici celeberrimi, Opera omnia (Hagæ Com: Apud Henricum Scheurleer, 1722)

The Assembly, a comedy, by a Scots Gentleman (London: s.n., 1722)

The Assembly; or Scotch reformation: a comedy. As it was acted by the persons in the drama. Done from the original manuscript written in the year 1692 ([Edinburgh]: s.n., 1752: Edinburgh: s.n., 1766)

[*The Assembly by Archibald Pitcairne* ed. Terence Tobin (Lafayette, Indiana: Purdue University Studies, 1972)]

Babell; or The Assembly, a Poem MDCXCII. *Written originally in the Irish Tongue and Translated into Scottish for the Benefite of the Leidges. By A.P. a Well Wisher to the Cause*, ed. George R. Kinloch (Edinburgh: Maitland Club, 1830)

[*Tollerators and Con-Tollerators; A Comedy Acted in My Lord Advocat's Lodgeing, June 10, 1703*, in *Babell*, above, 70–78]

The best of our owne: letters of Archibald Pitcairne, 1652–1713, Ed. W.T. Johnston (Edinburgh: Saorsa Books, 1979)

Praxis medica Pitcarniana (2 vols.; MS, n.p., n.d., c. 1700; Library of RCPE)

Collegium medicinæ practicum secundum methodum Riverianum ordinatum Edinburgh (MS, n.p., n.d., c. 1700; bound in with *Praxis*, above, vol. 2)

Catalogus librorum Archibald Pitcairn (n.p., n.d.; EUL, La.III.629)

BL, MS *Sloane 3198* (item 6, 'Robert Lindsay's Apparition to AP')

B. Secondary Works before 1800 (alphabetic by author or title)

Addison, Joseph, *Works of the Right Honourable Joseph Addison Esq* (London: Jacob Tonson, 1721)

Almeloveen, Theodoor Jansson van, *Inventa novantiqua. Id est brevis enarratio ortus & progressus artis medicae, ac praecipue de inventis vulgo novis ... in ea repertis* (Amsterdam: *apud Janssonio-Waesbergios*, 1684) Utrecht University Library, MS 995 III 6K12

——, *Apollo Staticus, Or, The Art of Curing Fevers by the staticks: Invented by D^r. Pitcairn and Publish'd by him in Latine: Now Made English by a Well-wisher to the Mathematicks* (Edinburgh: James Watson, 1695)

Aquino, Carolo de, *Sacra exequialia in funere Jacobi II Magnæ Britanniæ regis ab ementiss. Carolo cardinali Barberino in templo sancti Laurentii in Lucina. Oratio in funere Jacobi ii* (Rome: s.n., 1702)

[Arbuthnot, John], *A Modest Examination of a Late Pamphlet entitled Apollo Mathematicus* (Edinburgh: James Watson, 1696)

Barclay, John, *Ioannis Barclaii Argenis* (Paris: Nicolas Buon, 1621)

——, [*John Barclay. Argenis*, ed. and trs. Mark Riley and Dorothy Pritchard Huber (2 vols.; Royal Van Gorcum, Tempe Az., 2004)]

BIBLIOGRAPHY

Boece, Hector, *Scotorum Historiæ a prima gentis origine,: cum aliarum & rerum & gentium illustratione non vulgari* (Paris: Iodocus Badius Ascensius, 1527)

——, *Bond Book of the Royal Company of Archers* (NAS, ref. B52/11/5)

Buchanan, George, *Rerum Scoticarum Historia* (Utrecht: Elzevir, 1668)

——, *Georgii Buchanani Scoti Poemata* (London: R. Griffin, 1686)

Burnet, Gilbert, *History of his own time* (London, 1724–1753)

Calder, Robert, *The Lawfulness and Expediency of Set Forms of Prayer* (Edinburgh: s.n., 1706)

——, *The Lawfulness and Necessitie of observing the Anniversary Fasts and Festivals of the Church maintain'd, particularly of Christmas* (Edinburgh: s.n., 1710)

Campbell, Alexander, *Introduction to the History of Scotch Poetry, from the XII century to this time* (Edinburgh: Andrew Foulis, 1798)

Cheyne, George, *New Theory of continu'd Fevers* (Edinburgh: John Vallange; London: G. Strachan, 1701)

——, *Fluxionum methodus inversa; sive Quantitatum fluentium leges generaliores: Ad celeberrimum virum, Archibaldum Pitcarnium, Medicum Edinburgensem* (London: J. Matthews, 1703)

——, *Philosophic Principles of Natural Religion* (London: George Strahan, 1705)

Choice Collection of Comic and Serious Scots Poems both Ancient and Modern (3 vols.; Edinburgh: James Watson, 1706, 1709, 1711) [ed. Harriet Harvey Wood (2 vols.; Edinburgh: STS, 1977, 1991)]

Connor, Bernard, *Dissertationes medico-physicae. De antris lethiferis. De montis Vesuvii incendio. De stupendo ossium coalitu. De immani hypogastria sarcomata.* (Oxford, 1695)

Cunningham, John, *Joannis Cuningamii j. cti. oratio inauguralis recitata Edinburgi; cum primum jus civile docere cœpit* (Edinburgh: James Watson, 1705)

——, *A discourse by Mr. John Cuninghame advocate, at the beginning of his lessons upon the Scots law* (Edinburgh: James Watson, 1705)

'Curate, Jacob' (pseudonym), *Scotch Presbyterian Eloquence* (London: Randal Taylor, 1692)

Dalrymple, James, 1st Viscount Stair, *Institutions of the Law of Scotland* (revised edn.; Edinburgh: heir of Andrew Anderson, 1693) [ed. David M. Walker (Edinburgh: EUP, 1981)]

[Defoe, Daniel], *The Vision, a poem* (on Lord Belhaven) ([Edinburgh: s.n., 1706])

Delitiæ Poetarum Scotorum hujus ævi Illustrium (2 vols.; Amsterdam: Johannes Blaeu, 1637)

Disticha Catonis, *Dionysii Catonis Disticha de Moribus ad Filium* (Amsterdam: *Officina Schouteniana*, 1754)

Douglas, Gavin, Bishop of Dunkeld, VIRGIL *Æneis, Translated into* SCOTTISH *Verse, by the famous Gawin Douglas Bishop of Dunkeld* (Edinburgh: A. Symson and R. Freebairn, 1710)

——, [*Virgil's Aeneid Translated into Scottish Verse by Gavin Douglas Bishop of Dunkeld*, ed. David F.C. Caldwell (4 vols.; Edinburgh and London: STS, 1957–1964)]

Dryden, John, *Astræa Redux. A Poem on the Happy Restoration and Return of His Sacred Majesty Charles the Second* (London: Henry Herringman, 1660)

——, *Britannia Rediviva, A Poem on the Prince Born on the 10th of June 1688* (London: J. Tonson, 1688)

——, *The Works of Virgil: containing his Pastorals, Georgics and Æneis, Translated into English by Mr Dryden* (London: J. Tonson, 1697)

——, [*Poems of John Dryden*, ed. James Kinsley (4 vols.; Oxford: Clarendon Press, 1958)]

D.S. earl of Buchan (David Steuart Erskine, 11th Earl of Buchan), *Essays on the Lives and*

Writings of Fletcher of Saltoun and the Poet Thomson: Biographical, Critical, and Political (London: s.n., 1792)

[Eizat, Sir Edward], *Apollo Mathematicus, or the Art of Curing Diseases by the Mathematicks, according to the Principles of Dr. Pitcairne. A work both profitable and pleasant, and never published in English before. To which is subjoined a discourse of certainty, according to the principles of the same author* ([London]: s.n., 1695)

Fraser, James, *Memoirs of the life of the very Reverend Mr James Fraser of Brea, Minister of the Gospel at Culross, written by himself* (Edinburgh: Thomas Lumisden and John Robertson, 1738)

Gaddesdon, John of, *Rosa anglica practica medicine a capite ad pedes Ioanis anglici nouiter impressa & perquam diligentissime emendata per mag. Nicolaum Scyllacium* (Papie: l. birreta, 1492)

Garth, Sir Samuel, *The Dispensary. A Poem in Six Cantos* (London: John Nutt, 1699)

Glanvill, Joseph, *The vanity of dogmatizing; or confidence in opinions* (London: s.n., 1661)

——, *Scepsis Scientifica: or Confest ignorance, the way to science* (London: s.n., 1665)

Goldie, Frederick, *Short History of the Episcopal Church in Scotland from the Restoration to the Present Day*, 2nd edn. (Edinburgh: St Andrew Press, 1976)

Gregory, David, *Astronomiæ Physicæ et Geometricæ Elementa* (Oxford, 1702)

——, Εὐκλείδου τὰ σωζόμενα. *Euclidis quæ supersunt omnia*, ed. D. Gregory (Oxford, 1703)

——, *Apollonii Pergæi Conicorum libri octo et Sereni Antissensis de sectione cylindri & coni libri duo*, ed. Edmund Halley (with D. Gregory) (Oxford, 1710)

Hepburn, George, *Tarrugo unmasked: or, An Answer to a late pamphlet intituled, Apollo Mathematicus* (Edinburgh: s.n., 1695)

Hepburn, Robert, *The Tatler. To be published weekly by Donald MacStaff of the North* (Edinburgh: James Watson, January – May 1711)

——, *An idea of the modern eloquence of the Bar. Together with a pleading out of every part of law* (Edinburgh: Robert Freebairn, 1711)

——, *Dissertatio de scriptis Pitcarnianis* (London: Bernard Lintott, 1715)

Hobbes, Thomas, *Leviathan, or the matter, form and power of a commonwealth, ecclesiastical and civil* (London [Amsterdam]: s.n., 1651)

——, [*Thomas Hobbes. Leviathan* (London and New York: Everyman's Library, 1914)]

J.M., Sir and Ja:S (Sir John Mennie or Mennes, and Dr John Smith), *Musarum Deliciæ: Or, The Muses Recreation, Conteining severall select Pieces of sportive Wit* (London: Henry Herringman, 1655)

Johnson, Samuel, *The Vanity of Human Wishes: the tenth satire of Juvenal imitated* (London, 1749)

——, *Dictionary of the English Language* (2 vols.; London, 1755)

Johnston, Arthur, *Epigrammata Arturi Ionstoni Scoti, medici Regii* (Aberdeen: Edward Raban, 1632)

——, *Parerga Arturi Ionstoni, Medici Regis* (Aberdeen: Edward Raban, 1632)

——, ['Parerga et Epigrammata' in *Delitiæ Poetarum Scotorum*, above, i, 439–647; *Musa Latina Aberdonensis*, below, i and ii.]

Keill, James, *Anatomy of the Humane Body, Abridg'd* (London: s.n., 1698)

——, *An Account of Animal Secretion, the Quantity of Blood in the Humane Body, and Muscular Motion* (London: s.n., 1708)

Keill, John, *An examination of Dr Burnet's Theory of the Earth. Together with some remarks on Mr Whiston's new Theory of the Earth* (Oxford, 1698)
——, *Introductio ad veram physicam* (Oxford, 1701)
——, *Letter from Sir R- S- to Dr Archibald Pitcairn* (Edinburgh: s.n., 1709)
Lindsay, Sir David, of the Mount, *Ane Dialog betuix Experience and ane Courteour, off the Miserabyll Estait of the Warld* (St Andrews: J. Scot, 1554)
——, [*The Works of Sir David Lindsay of the Mount 1490–1555*, ed D. Hamer (4 vols.; Edinburgh and London: STS, 1931–1936)]
Mackenzie, George, *Lives and Characters of the most eminent writers of the Scots nation* (3 vols.; Edinburgh: James Watson, 1708, 1711, William Adams Junior, 1722)
Mackenzie, Sir George, of Rosehaugh, *Aretina or the Serious Romance ... Written originally in English. Part first* (Edinburgh: Robert Broun, 1660)
——, *Religio Stoici: with a friendly address to the phanaticks of all sects and sorts* (Edinburgh: R. Broun, 1663)
——, *Idea eloquentiae forensis hodiernae: una cum actione forensi ex unaquaque juris parte* (Edinburgh: heirs of Andrew Anderson, 1681)
——, *Institutions of the Laws of Scotland* (Edinburgh: John Reid, 1684)
——, *Jus Regium or the first and Solid Foundation of Monarchy in General and more particularly of the Monarchy of Scotland; against Buchanan, Naphtali, Dolman, Milton etc* (Edinburgh: heir of Andrew Anderson; London: R. Chiswell, 1684).
——, *A Defence of the Antiquity of the Royal Line of Scotland in answer to William Llloyd, Bishop of St Asaph, with a True Account when the Scots were governed by the Kings in the Isle of Britain* (Edinburgh: heir of Andrew Anderson; London: R.C., 1685)
Magatus, Cesar, *De rara medicatione vulnerum, seu de vulneribus raro tractandis, libri duo* (Venice: s.n., 1676)
More, Henry, *The Immortality of the Soul, so farre forth as it is demonstrable from the Knowledge of Nature and the Light of Reason* (London: s.n., 1659)
Morison, Robert, *Præludia Botanica (Hortus regius Blesensis auctus ... Præludiorum botanicorum pars prior)* (London: Thomas Roycroft, 1669)
——, *Plantarum Historiæ universalis Oxoniensis. Pars secunda* (Oxford, 1680)
——, *Plantarum historiæ universalis pars tertia* (Oxford, 1699)
Newton, Sir Isaac, *Philosophiæ Naturalis Principia Mathematica* (London: Royal Society, Joseph Streat, 1687)
——, [*Sir Isaac Newton's Mathematical Principles*, ed. and trs. Florian Cajori (Berkeley, Los Angeles, London, University of California Press, 1934)]
Nicolson, William, Archbishop of Cashel (Bishop of Carlisle), *The Scottish historical library: containing a short view and character of most of the writers, records, registers, law-books, &c. which may be serviceable to the undertakers of a general history of Scotland, down to the union of the two kingdoms* (London: T. Childe, 1702)
——, *Octupla: hoc est Octo Paraphrases Poeticæ Psalmi CIV Authoribus totidem Scotis* (Edinburgh: heirs and successors of Andrew Anderson, 1696)
——, *Philosophical Collections* (in continuation of *Philosophic transactions of the Royal Society*) Ed. R. Hooke (London: s.n., 1679–1682)
Prior, Matthew, *Poems on Several Occasions* (London: Jacob Tonson and John Barber, 1718)

Scaliger, Joseph Juste, *De emendatio temporum* (*Iosephi Scaligeri Iulii Cæsaris F. Opus Nouum de emendatione temporum in octo libros tributum*) (Paris, 1583)

Scotch Presbyterian Eloquence. See 'Curate, Jacob (pseudonym)'

[Steward, Sir Simeon], *Description of the King and Queene of Fayries, their habit, fare, their abode, pompe, and state, Being very delightful to the sense, and full of mirth* (London: Richard Harper, 1634)

Swift, Jonathan, *Conduct of the Allies* (London: Morphew, 1711)

——, *History of the last Four Years of the Queen* (London: A. Millar, 1758)

Sibbald, Sir Robert, *Nuncius Scoto-Brittanicus* (Edinburgh: David Lindsay and partners, 1683)

——, *Scotia Illustrata sive Prodromus Historiæ Naturalis* (Edinburgh: Kniblo, Solingen and Colmar, 1684)

——, *Answer to the second letter of the right reverend, the Lord Bishop of Carlile ... Wherein the Scots antient possession in Britain is asserted* (Edinburgh: Andrew Symson, 1704)

——, *Vindiciæ Scotiæ Illustratæ, sive prodromi naturalis historiæ Scotiæ, contra prodromomastiges, sub larva libelli de legibus historiæ naturalis latentes* (Edinburgh, Andrew Symson, 1710)

——, [*Autobiography of Sir Robert Sibbald, knt., M.D., to which is prefixed some account of his MSS*, ed. James Maidment (Edinburgh: T. Stevenson, 1833)]

[Sinclair, John], *True Account of the proceedings at Perth;: the debates in the secret council there; with the reasons and causes of the suddain finishing and breaking up of the rebellion/ Written by a rebel* (London: J. Baker and T. Warner, 1716)

Urry, John (ed.), *The works of Geoffrey Chaucer, compared with former eds. and MSS. By J. Urry, together with a glossary* (London: Bernard Lintot, 1721)

Volusenus, Florentius, *De Animi Tranquillitate Dialogus* (Lyons: S. Gryphius, 1543)

[Walkinshaw, Dr James], *Letter from Dr James Walkinshaw to Sir Robert Sibbald* (London [Edinburgh], 1709)

Wallis, John, *Opera Mathematica* (3 vols.; Oxford, 1693, 1695, 1699) (ed.) *Harmonicorum libri tres* (Ptolemy) (Oxford, 1682) (ed.) *Aristarchi Samii de magnitudinibus & distantiis solis et lunæ liber ... Pappi Alexandrini secundi libri mathematicæ collectionis fragmentum, ed., Lat. Fecit, notisque illustr. J. Wallis* (Oxford, 1688)

Webster, Charles, *Account of the Life and Writings of Dr. Pitcairne* (Edinburgh: Gordon & Murray; London: Richardson and Urquhart, 1781)

Willdey, George, 'Great Britain and Ireland ... 1715', BL, Maps c.11.a.2.

Wishart, William, and John Dundas, *Seasonable Warning by the Commission of the General Assembly concerning the danger of popery* (Edinburgh: relict of Andrew Anderson, 1713)

B. SECONDARY WORKS SINCE 1800

(*References to classical Latin and Greek texts are usually to the appropriate volumes in* **Scriptorum Classicorum Bibliotheca Oxoniensis**, *Oxford Classical Texts* [*Oxford: Clarendon Press*], *or in the* **Loeb Classical Library** [*Cambridge, Mass., and London: Harvard University Press*])

Adams, James W.L., 'The Renaissance Poets (2) Latin' in *Scottish Poetry: A Critical Survey*, ed. James Kinsley (London: Cassell, 1955), 68–98

BIBLIOGRAPHY

Aldis, H.G., *List of Books Published in Scotland before 1700* (new edn. with additions; Edinburgh: NLS, 1970)

Allen, M.J.B., *Marsilio Ficino and the Phaedran Charioteer* (Berkeley, Los Angeles, London: University of California Press, 1981)

——, *The Platonism of Marsilio Ficino: A Study of his Phaedrus Commentary, Its Sources and Genesis* (Berkeley, Los Angeles, London: University of California Press, 1984)

Bacon, Francis, *Francis Bacon*, ed. Brian Vickers (Oxford, New York: OUP, 1996)

Barbour, John, *The Bruce*, ed.& trs. A.A.M. Duncan (Edinburgh: Canongate Classics, 1997)

Barrow, G.W.S., *The Kingdom of the Scots* (London: Edward Arnold, 1973)

Biographia Presbyteriana, ed. Patrick Walker and the Rev. Alexr. Shields (2 vols.; Edinburgh: D. Speare and J. Stevenson, 1827)

Black, George F., *Surnames of Scotland. Their Origin, Meaning and History* (New York: New York Public Library, 1946)

Boog Watson, Charles B., *Roll of Edinburgh Burgesses and Guild-Brethren, 1701–1760* (Edinburgh: SRS, 1930)

Book of Scotish Pasquils, 1568–1715, ed. James Maidment (Edinburgh: William Paterson, 1868)

Boswell, James, *Boswell's Journal of a Tour to the Hebrides with Samuel Johnson LL.D. 1773*, Ed. Frederick A. Pottle and Charles H. Bennett (Melbourne, London, Toronto: Heinemann, 1963)

——, *Boswell's Life of Johnson* (2 vols.; London: Everyman's Library, 1949)

Bradner, Leicester, *Musae Anglicanae: A History of Anglo-Latin Poetry 1500–1925* (New York: Modern Language Association of America, 1940)

Browne, Sir Thomas, *Sir Thomas Browne: selected writings*, ed. Sir Geoffrey Keynes (London: Faber and Faber, 1968)

Burns, Robert, *Poems and Songs of Robert Burns*, ed. James Kinsley (3 vols.; Oxford: Clarendon Press, 1968)

Carnall, Geoffrey, 'Hepburn, Robert' in *Oxford Dictionary of National Biography* (q.v., below), s.v.

Catullus, Gaius Valerius, *Catullus*, ed. C.J. Fordyce (Oxford: Clarendon Press, 1961)

——, *Catulli Tibulli Propertii Carmina*, ed. L. Mueller (Leipzig: Teubner, 1892)

Chambers, Robert, *Traditions of Edinburgh* (new edn.; Edinburgh: William and Robert Chambers; London: Wm. S. Orr, 1847)

Complete Baronetage, ed. G.E.C. (i.e., George E. Cokayne), (5 vols.; Exeter: W. Pollard & Co., 1900–1906)

Cook, A.B., *Zeus: a study in ancient religion* (3 vols. [in 5]; Cambridge: CUP, 1914–1940)

Cowan, Ian B., *The Scottish Covenanters 1660–1688* (London: Victor Gollancz, 1976)

Craig, W.S., *History of the Royal College of Physicians of Edinburgh* (Oxford: Blackwell, 1976)

Crawford, Robert, *Apollos of the North: Selected Poems of George Buchanan & Arthur Johnston* (Edinburgh: Polygon, 2006)

Crawford, T., *Love, Labour and Liberty: the eighteenth-century Scottish lyric* (Cheadle Hulme: Carcanet, 1976)

Curtius, E.R., *European Literature and the Latin Middle Ages*, trs. Willard R. Trask (London: Routledge and Kegan Paul, 1953)

Daiches, David, *Scotland and the Union* (London: John Murray, 1977)

David Gregory, Isaac Newton and their circle. Extracts from David Gregory's memoranda, 1677–1708, ed. W.G. Hiscock (Oxford: For the editor, 1937)

Declaration of Arbroath, trs. A.A.M. Duncan in *The Bruce* (q.v., s.v. Barbour, John), 779–782

Dictionary of National Biography, ed. Leslie Stephen and Sidney Lee, Compact Edition, 2 vols. (Oxford, 1975)

Dictionary of Surnames, ed. P. Hanks and F. Hodges (Oxford: OUP, 1988)

Davie, G.E., *The Democratic Intellect* (2nd. edn.; Edinburgh: EUP, 1964)

Devine, T.M., *The Scottish Nation 1700–2000* (Harmondsworth: Allen Lane The Penguin Press, 1999)

Donaldson, Gordon, *Scotland James V to James VII* (Edinburgh and London: Oliver and Boyd, 1965)

——, and Robert S. Morpeth, *Dictionary of Scottish History* (Edinburgh: John Donald, 1977)

Dow, Frances, *Cromwellian Scotland 1651–1660* (Edinburgh: John Donald, 1979; reprinted 1999)

Dunbar, William, *Poems of William Dunbar* ed. Priscilla Bawcutt (2 vols.; Glasgow: ASLS, 1998)

Duncan, A.A.M., *The Kingship of the Scots, 842–1292* (Edinburgh: EUP, 2002)

Duncan, Douglas, *Thomas Ruddiman* (Edinburgh and London: Oliver and Boyd, 1965)

——, 'Scholarship and Politeness in the Early Eighteenth Century' in *History of Scottish Literature* (q.v., below), ii., *1660–1800*, 51–64

Ferguson, William, *Scotland 1689 to the Present* (Edinburgh: Oliver and Boyd, 1968)

Fergusson, Robert, *Poems of Robert Fergusson*, ed. Matthew P. McDiarmid (2 vols.; Edinburgh and London: STS, 1954, 1956)

Figgis, John Neville, *The Divine Right of Kings* (2nd edn.; Cambridge: CUP, 1922)

Fletcher, H.R. and W.H. Brown, *The Royal Botanic Gardens, Edinburgh, 1670–1970* (Edinburgh: HMSO, 1970)

Ford, Philip J., *George Buchanan Prince of Poets* (Aberdeen: AUP, 1982)

Fordyce, C.J., see under 'Catullus, Gaius Valerius'

Foxon, David F., *English Verse, 1701–1750* (2 vols.; London: CUP, 1975)

Fraenkel, E., *Horace* (Oxford: Clarendon Press, 1957)

Gairdner, John, *List of Fellows of the Royal College of Surgeons, Edinburgh* (Edinburgh: s.n., 1874)

Galt, John, *Ringan Gilhaize or The Covenanters* (3 vols.; Edinburgh: Oliver and Boyd, 1823) ed. Patricia J. Wilson (Edinburgh: Scottish Academic Press, 1984)

Grant, F.J., *The Faculty of Advocates in Scotland 1532–1943* (Edinburgh: SRS, 1944)

Green, Roger P.H., *Latin Epics of the New Testament* (Oxford: OUP, 2006)

Guerrini, Anita, 'Pitcairne, Archibald' in *Oxford Dictionary of National Biography* (q.v., below), s.v

Grierson, H.J.C. (ed.), *Metaphysical Lyrics & Poems of the Seventeenth Century* (Oxford: Clarendon Press, 1921)

Handbook of British Chronology, ed. E.B. Fryde, D.E. Greenway, S. Porter and I. Roy (3rd edn.; London: Royal Historical Society, 1986)

Harry the Minstrel (Blind Harry), *Hary's Wallace*, ed. M.P. McDiarmid (2 vols.; Edinburgh and London: STS, 1968, 1969)

Henderson, T.F., 'Pitcairne, Archibald' in *DNB*, Compact Edition, 2 vols. (Oxford, 1975), 1669

Henryson, Robert, *Poems and Fables of Robert Henryson*, ed. H. Harvey Wood (2nd edn.; Edinburgh and London: Oliver and Boyd, 1958)

——, *Poems of Robert Henryson*, ed. Denton Fox (Oxford: Clarendon Press, 1981)

Historia Brittonum: 3. The Vatican Recension, ed. D.N. Dumville (Cambridge: D.S. Brewer, 1985)

History of Scottish Literature, gen. ed. Cairns Craig (4 vols.; Aberdeen: AUP, 1987–1988)

Hoppit, Julian, *A Land of Liberty? England 1689–1727* (Oxford: Clarendon Press, 2000)

Howie, W.B., 'Sir Archibald Stevenson, his Ancestry, and the Riot in the College of Physicians at Edinburgh' in *Medical History* XI (1967), 269–284

Jack, R.D.S., *Scottish Prose 1550–1700* (London: Calder and Boyars, 1971)

Johnson, David, *Music and Society in Lowland Scotland in the Eighteenth Century* (London: OUP, 1972)

Jones, Richard F., *Ancients and Moderns: A Study of the Background of the Battle of the Books* (2nd edn.; St Louis: Washington University Publications, 1961)

Keith, Robert, *An Historical Catalogue of the Scottish Bishops down to the year 1688* (new edn.; Edinburgh: Bell & Bradfute, 1824)

Kennedy, James, 'Aeneas Britannicus' in *Musa Latina Aberdonensis* (q.v. below), iii, 175–185

Kirkton, James, [*The Secret and true*] *history of the Church of Scotland from the Restoration to the year 1678*, ed. C.K. Sharpe (Edinburgh: James Ballantyne and Co., 1817) ed. Ralph Stewart (Lewiston/Queenston/Lampeter: Edwin Mellen Press, 1992)

Knox, John, *John Knox's History of the Reformation in Scotland*, ed. William Croft Dickinson (2 vols.; London and Edinburgh: Nelson, 1949)

Lang, Andrew, *Sir George Mackenzie, King's Advocate, of Rosehaugh: his life and times, 1636?-1691* (London: Longmans, 1909)

Lenman, Bruce, *The Jacobite Risings in Britain 1689–1746* (London: Eyre Methuen, 1980; new edn., Aberdeen: Scottish Cultural Press, 1995)

Lewis, C.T. and C. Short, *A Latin Dictionary* (Oxford: Clarendon Press, 1975 [1879])

Lockhart, George, of Carnwath, *Scotland's Ruine* [*Memoirs Concerning the Affairs of Scotland From Queen Anne's Accession to the Throne To the Commencement of the Union of the two Kingdoms of Scotland and England in May 1707*] ed. D. Szechi (Aberdeen: ASLS, 1995)

mac Mhaighstir Alasdair, Alasdair (Alexander MacDonald), *The Poems of Alexander MacDonald*, ed. and trs. Rev. A. MacDonald and Rev. A. MacDonald (Inverness: Northern Counties Newspaper and Printing and Publishing Company, 1924)

Macrobius, Ambrosius Theodosius, *Saturnalia, In Somnium Scipionis Commentarii*, ed. Iacobus Willis (Leipzig: Teubner, 1970)

Macqueen, James G., 'Scottish Latin Poetry' in *History of Scottish Literature*, (q.v. above), i., 213–225

MacQueen, J., *Progress and Poetry* (Edinburgh: Scottish Academic Press, 1982)

——, 'From Rome to Ruddiman: the Scoto-Latin Tradition' in *Edinburgh History of Scottish Literature*, ed. Ian Brown, Thomas Clancy, Susan Manning and Murray Pittock (2 vols., Edinburgh: EUP, 2006), i., 184–208

McFarlane, I.D. (ed.) *Renaissance Latin Poetry* (Manchester: Manchester University Press, 1980), *Buchanan* (London: Duckworth, 1981)

McIntyre, John, 'St Margaret and the Scots College, Rome' in *Innes Review* XLIV.2 (Autumn 1993), 187

Mann, A.J., *The Scottish Book Trade 1500–1720* (Phantassie, East Linton: Tuckwell Press, 2000)

Milton, John, *John Milton. Complete Poems and Major Prose*, ed. Merritt Y. Hughes (New York: Odyssey Press, 1957)

Molhuysen, P.C., *Bronnen tot de Geschiedenis des leidsche Universiteit* IV ('s-Gravenhage: Rijks geschiedkundige Publicatien, 1920)

Money, D.K., *The English Horace: Anthony Alsop and the Tradition of British Latin Verse* (Oxford: British Academy, OUP, 1998)

Munk, W., *Roll of the Royal College of Physicians of London* (London: Longman, Green, Longman and Roberts, 1861)

Musa Latina Aberdonensis, ed. Sir William Duguid Geddes and William Keith Leisk (3 vols.; Aberdeen: New Spalding Club, 1892–1910)

Oxford Book of Greek Verse, chosen by Gilbert Murray, Cyril Bailey, E.A. Barber, T.F. Higham and C.M. Bowra (with corrections; Oxford: Clarendon Press, 1946)

Oxford Book of Latin Verse, chosen by H.W. Garrod (Oxford: Clarendon Press, 1912)

Oxford Classical Dictionary, ed. N.G.L. Hammond and H.H. Scullard (2nd edn.; Oxford: Clarendon Press, 1970)

Oxford Companion to Law, ed. D.M. Walker (Oxford: Clarendon Press, 1980)

Oxford Dictionary of National Biography, ed. H.C.G. Matthew and Brian Harrison (61 vols.; Oxford: OUP, c. 2004) online edn. (Oxford: OUP: 2004–)

Oxford Dictionary of Saints, ed. David Hugh Farmer (Oxford, New York: OUP, 1987)

Oxford Dictionary of the Christian Church, ed. F.L. Cross (London: OUP, 1957)

Paul, Sir James Balfour, *Scots Peerage. Founded on Wood's edition of Sir Robert Douglas's peerage of Scotland* (9 vols.; Edinburgh: s.n., 1904–1914)

Penguin Book of Greek Verse, ed. Constantine A. Trypanis (Harmondsworth: Penguin Books, 1971)

Perosa, A. and J. Sparrow (eds.), *Renaissance Latin Verse. An Anthology* (London: Duckworth, 1979)

Philp, James, of Almerieclose, *Grameidos Libri Sex*, ed. A.D. Murdoch (Edinburgh: SHS, 1888)

Pinkerton, J.M. (ed.), *Minute Book of the Faculty of Advocates* (2 vols.; Edinburgh: Stair Society, 1976–1980)

Pittock, Murray G.H., *Poetry and Jacobite Politics in Eighteenth-Century Britain and Ireland* (Cambridge: CUP, 1994)

——, *Jacobitism* (Houndmills, Basingstoke, Hampshire and London: Macmillan Press, 1998)

——, 'Philp, or Philip, James, of Almerieclose' in *Oxford Dictionary of National Biography* (q.v. above), s.v.

Ramsay, Allan, *The Gentle Shepherd*, in *The Works of Allan Ramsay*, ed. Burns Martin, John W. Oliver, Alexander M. Kinghorn and Alexander Law (6 vols.; Edinburgh and London: STS, 1951–1974), ii, 205–277.

Riley, P.W.J., *King William and the Scottish Politicians* (Edinburgh: John Donald, 1979)

BIBLIOGRAPHY

Ritchie, Robert Peel, *The Early Days of the Royall Colledge of Phisitians, Edinburgh. The extended oration of the Harveian Society, Edinburgh delivered at the 114th Festival* (Edinburgh, 1899)

Robertson, John, 'Fletcher, Andrew, of Saltoun', in *Oxford Dictionary of National Biography* (q.v. above), s.v.

Satirical Poems of the Time of the Reformation, ed. J. Cranstoun (2 vols.; Edinburgh and London: STS, 1891–1893),

Schlapp, Robin, 'The Contribution of the Scots to Mathematics' in *Mathematical Gazette* LVII (1973), 1–16

Scots Peerage, see 'Paul, Sir James Balfour' above

Scott, Sir Walter, *The Antiquary* (3 vols.: Edinburgh: J. Ballantyne for A. Constable, 1816) ed. David Hewitt (Edinburgh: EUP, 1995)

——, *The Tale of Old Mortality* (3 vols.: Edinburgh: William Blackwood; London, John Murray, 1816) ed. Douglas S. Mack (Edinburgh: EUP, 1993)

——, *The Heart of Midlothian* (4 vols.: Edinburgh: A. Constable, 1818) ed. Andrew Lang (London: Macmillan, 1906) ed. David Hewitt and Alison Lumsden (Edinburgh: EUP, 2004)

——, *Redgauntlet* (3 vols.; Edinburgh: A. Constable; London: Hurst Robinson, 1824) ed. G.A.M. Wood and David Hewitt (Edinburgh: EUP, c. 1997)

See, H. and A. Cormack, 'An Aberdeen Trader Two Hundred Years Ago' in *Aberdeen University Review* xv (1927–1929), 32–36

Shirlaw, Leslie, 'Dr Archibald Pitcairne and Sir Isaac Newton's "Black Years" (1692–1694)' in *Royal College of Physicians, Edinburgh, Chronicle* 5 (Jan. 1975), 23–26

Shuttleton, David E., '"A modest examination": John Arbuthnot and the Scottish Newtonians' in *British Journal for Eighteenth-Century Studies* 18 (1995), 47–62

Simpson, S.M., 'An Anonymous and Undated Edinburgh Tract' in *The Book Collector* (1966), 67

Steven, William, *History of George Heriot's Hospital* (new edn.; Edinburgh: Bell & Bradfute; London: Simpkin, Marshall, 1859)

Symson, Andrew, *Large Description of Galloway, by Andrew Symson, Minister of Kirkinner*, M.DC.LXXX.IV (Edinburgh: W. and C. Tait, 1823)

Thackeray, William Makepeace, *The History of Henry Esmond, Esq., a colonel in the service of Her Majesty Q. Anne, written by himself* (London: Smith, Elder & Co., 1852)

Underwood, E. Ashworth, *Boerhaave's Men at Leyden and After* (Edinburgh: EUP, 1977)

Vulgate, *Biblia Sacra Iuxta Vulgatam Versionem* (Stuttgart: Deutsche Bibelgesellschaft, 1994 [1967])

Waquet, Françoise, *Latin or the Empire of a Sign, from the Sixteenth to the Twentieth Centuries*, trs. John Howe (London, New York: Verso, 2001)

Wendel, François, *Calvin: The Origins and Development of his Religious Thought*, trs. Philip Mairet (London: Collins, 1963)

Westfall, Richard S., 'Sir Isaac Newton' in *Oxford Dictionary of National Biography* (q.v. above), s.v.

Williams, R.D. (ed.), *The Aeneid of Virgil* (2 vols.; London: St Martin's Press, 1972–1973)

Wodrow, Robert, *Analecta: or Materials for a History of remarkable Providences, mostly relating to Scotch Ministers and Christians* (4 vols.; Glasgow: Maitland Club, 1842–1843)

Yates, Frances A., *Astræa: The Imperial Theme in the Sixteenth Century* (London: Routledge and Kegan Paul, 1973)

Young, John R., 'Hamilton, John, second Lord Belhaven and Stenton' in *Oxford Dictionary of National Biography* (q.v. above), s.v.

I

The *Poemata Selecta*

Selected Poems

POEMATA SELECTA

I

(a) *Ad Rob. Lindesium, 1689.*

[(b) *Ad Robertum Lindesium*]

Lindesi, stygias jamdudum vecte per undas,
    Stagnaque Cocyti non adeunda mihi,
Excute paulisper Lethæi vincula somni,
    Ut feriant animum carmina nostra tuum.
5 Te nobis, te redde tuis, promissa daturus
    Gaudia; sed Proavo sis comitante redux.
Namque novos cives mutataque regna videbis,
    Passaque Teutonicas Sceptra Britanna manus,
Legatosque Deûm Populo mandata ferentes;
10   Nam vulgus nunc est maxima cura Deûm.
Illis non Phoebi notæ, non Palladis artes,
    Numina sunt Bardis hæc peregrina novis.
Queis Deus est quicunque furit, quicunque potentem
    Vertit in imbelles immeritosque manum.
15 At licet a Superûm doceant se Rege venire,
    Quoque modo facilem fas sit habere Jovem;
Sola tamen Ditis mysteria nosse videntur,
    Et Ditis solas incoluisse domos.
Hunc crepat, hoc omnis Legio se vindice jactat,
20   Aëris hic fluctus Oceanique regit;
Solus in obscœnas homines transire figuras
    Cogit, & exutum scit revocare genus:
Quæ pater ipse Deûm sibi Naturæque negavit,
    Ille potest, illis si sit habenda fides.
25 Ergo domi natum propera visurus Avernum,
    Et Phlegetonta novum, non prohibente Jove.
Hic scelera agnoscas eadem quibus affluit Orcus,
    Tartareos vultus, Tartareumque pecus.

1 Title: (a) PS, 3; (b) APP, 8, BA(4), f.4ᵛ., SP, 8. Text: PS, 3–4, thus. SP, 8–9, offers occasional typographical differences; with one exception, noted below, the text is otherwise identical. APP, 8–9 and BA(4), f.4ᵛ.-f.5ʳ., include some verbal variants; 4: *animam* for *animum* and *tuam* for *tuum* (APP only). 13: *Nam* for *Queis* (so also SP). (APP only) *tonat* for *furit* and *furentem* for *potentem*. 18: *Atque Erebi* for *Et Ditis*. 19: (APP only) *hunc* for *hoc*. 23: *Quæ rerum natura Iovisque fata negarunt* for *Quæ pater ipse Deum sibi Naturæque negavit*. 24: (APP only) *Hic* for *Ille*. 27: *queis personat Orcus* for *quibus affluit Orcus*. 29: *nec* for *&*.

I

(a) *To Robert Lindsay 1689*

[(b) *To Robert Lindsay*]

'Lindsay, long since borne across the Stygian waves and the swamps of Cocytus, which I am not permitted to approach, shake off the bands of Lethæan slumber for a little while, allowing my verses to touch your spirit. Restore yourself to us, to your own, to give us promised joys, but come back accompanied by your great-grandfather. For you will see a new citizenry and changed kingdoms, the British sceptre suffering the grasp of a German, and the deputies of the Gods transferring their commission to the people. The Gods now care chiefly for the common people. The arts of Phœbus and Pallas are unknown to them: these divinities are foreign to the new-fangled Bards. Whoever rages, whoever turns a potent hand against peaceful people deserving better – to them he is God. But although they teach that they come from the king of the Gods and the way in which it is legitimate to keep Jove well-disposed, it is with the mysteries of Dis only that they seem to be familiar, and only the halls of Dis that seem their natural home. He is the divinity acclaimed by the whole gang; under his protection they bathe in their own conceit; he governs the ebb and flow of wind and wave. He alone has the power to transform men into indecent shapes and knows how to call back a deprived race. If we must believe them, he is able to perform acts, which the very father of the Gods has denied to himself and to Nature. So hurry to see Avernus homegrown and a new Phlegethon which has arisen with Jove's permission. Here you will recognize the same wickedness with which Orcus overflows, diabolical faces and

Hic neque jam Furiæ desunt, & Tartara nondum
30   Te, licet hic fueris, deseruisse putes.
Unus abest scelerum vindex Rhadamanthus; amice,
Dî faciant reditus sit comes ille tui.

2

[(a) *Scotia Martio. 1689*]

[(b) *Deploratio status Regni Scotici*]

Cum despecta Fides scelerato excederet Orbe,
   Desereretque suum patria nostra Patrem;
Tum placuit patriis aeternum abscindere terris
   Scotia Dîs genitos quos alit alta viros.
5 Tum tetigit Fati furiis opressus acerbi,
   Facundo Stygias ore LOCARTUS aquas.
Et magnam posuisti animam, fortissime GRAME,
   Marsque videbatur, te moriente, mori.
Nil superest quod ficta fides, quod subdola lingua
10   Perdere, sacrilegæ vel potuere manus.
Postquam homines deerant, sævitum in Templa, Deosque est,
   Et quotquot doctæ crimina mentis habent.
Omnia vulgus erat, scelerisque licentia vulgo,
   Res tamen Auctores induit acta Deos.
15 Dî, quorum hortatu Scythico de littore Scotus
   Picta Caledoniis intulit arma jugis,
Si vos læsa movet Majestas inclyta juris,
   Si Cœlos Hominum tangere cura potest,
Æquævum vestro Populum servetis Olympo,
20   Reddite Grampigenis Jura Patremque jugis:
Illa dies Superos indigno crimine solvet,
   Tum nobis vulgus desinet esse Deus.

2 Title: PS, 4, BA(4), f.2ᵛ., none; (a) APP, 4; (b) SP, 4.   Text: PS, 4–5, APP, 4–5; SP, 4–5. After 14, BA(4) inserts an additional couplet: *Et jam fata Chaos vicit, fulmenque Tonanti/ Vix servire suo turba profana sinit*, 'And now chaos has conquered the Fates, and the unholy row scarcely permits the thunderbolt to serve his Thunderer'. 20: APP and BA(4) read *viris* for *jugis*.

a diabolical herd. Nor from here are the Furies absent – if you were actually here, you would think that you had never left Tartarus. One figure only is missing, Rhadamanthus, the avenger of crimes. God grant, friend, that when you return it may be in his company.'

2

[(a) *Scotland in March 1689*]

[(b) *Lament for the State of Scotland*]

'When despised Loyalty had withdrawn from the polluted world, and our fatherland had abandoned its father, then it pleased fate to separate for ever from their native land these men, born of the Gods, whom high Scotland had nourished. Then Lockhart, with all his eloquence, was overwhelmed by the furies of a harsh destiny and reached the waters of Styx. And you laid down your great soul, most valiant Claverhouse – with your death Mars himself seemed to die. Nothing remains which feigned loyalty or deceitful tongue or sacrilegious hands could destroy. When no men were left to be victims, the target for destruction became the temples and the Gods, and everyone who lay open to the reproach of possessing an educated mind. The mob became everything, and the licence given to the mob to commit crime. To the Gods however was imputed all responsibility for events.

Ye Gods, who encouraged Scotus to bring his painted arms from the Scythian shore to the Caledonian ridges, if treason against the glorious sovereignty of law moves you, if the trouble of men can touch the heavens, save a people coeval with your Olympus, return to ridges born of the Grampians their laws and their Father! That day will free the Powers above from an unworthy accusation. Then the mob will cease to be our God.'

POEMATA SELECTA

3

(a) *In Geo. Locartum.*

[(b) *In Georgium Lockartum*]

[(c) *In D. Geo. Locartum, Supremi Fori juridici Præsidem*]

[(d) *In Mortem Dom: Georg: Locarti Præsidis etc.*]

    Esse Deum postquam te mors infanda coegit,
        Oblita est Juris Fergusiana tribus.
    Non pudet illicitis metiri moribus æquum;
        Relligio est priscam non violare fidem:
5 Quodque nefas Natura parens animantibus esse
        Monstravit, nomen nunc Pietatis habet.
    Una malis tantis par est medicina, LOCARTO
        Judice si Scoti facta notanda putent.

---

3 Title: *PS*, 5, thus; (b) *APP*, 6; (c) *BA(4)*, f.3ʳ.; (d) *SP*, 3.   **Text**: *PS*, 5, thus; *APP*, 6, *SP*, 3–4, and *BA(4)* have the same text save for details of punctuation and capitalization.

3

(a) *On George Lockhart*
[(b) *On George Lockhart*]
[(c) *On George Lockhart, Lord President of the Court of Session*]
[(d) *On the Death of George Lockhart, Lord President etc.*]

'After unspeakable death compelled you to be a God, Clan Fergus forgot Law. There is no shame now in measuring equity by the misapplication of customary law. Religion means the maintenance of ancient belief. Whatever Mother Nature once revealed to mankind as forbidden now has the reputation of piety. Only one medicine is equal to evils of such magnitude, that Scots should think it worthwhile to note what was done when Lockhart was judge.'

4

(a) *In mortem Vicecomitis Taodunensis.*

[(b) *In Mortem Vicecomitis de Dundee*]

    Ultime Scotorum, potuit quo sospite solo
        Libertas patriæ salva fuisse tuæ;
    Te moriente novos accepit Scotia Cives,
        Accepitque novos te moriente Deos.
5 Illa tibi superesse negat, Tu non potes illi,
        Ergo Caledoniæ nomen inane vale:
    Tuque vale gentis priscæ fortissime ductor,
        Optime Scotorum atque ultime, GRAME, vale.

---

4 Title: (a) PS 5, SP, 4; (b) APP, 6, BA(4), f.3ᵛ. **Text**: SP has a different version of the final line, *Ultime Scotorum, atque ultime Grame, vale*. This has some point; see the note to line 8 below. 5: APP and BA(4), *Illa tibi superesse nequit, nec tu potes illi*.

    A MS of the late 17th or early 18th century, NLS *Adv.MS 32.3.1*, which also contains the *Memoirs touching the Revolution in Scotland* written by Graham's friend, the Jacobite Colin, 3rd Earl of Balcarres (1654–1723), includes a version, for the first four lines identical with that in PS, but differing thereafter:

        Illa nequit superesse tibi, tu non potes illi,
          Ergo Caledonia nomen inane vale,
        Tuque vale nostræ gentis fortissime Ductor,
          Ultime Scotorum atque optime Grame vale.

The final -*a* of *Caledonia* is short, where metrically it should be long. By comparison with *priscæ*, *nostræ* lacks point. It seems likely that this version is a memorial transcript, accurate for the opening lines, less so for what follows.

    CUL MS *Add. 5962*, an anonymous poetic miscellany of the early eighteenth century, contains (fo.13) another version, with minor variations in punctuation and capitalization. Line 5 has the same reading as APP and BA(4). The final line is almost the same as that in NLS *Adv.MS 32.3.1*.

    The Cambridge MS has a note, 'This Englished by Mr Dryden.' See below.

    We are grateful to Dr Money for this last reference. These variant readings suggest that Pitcairne himself may have altered 5 and 9. In 5, *negat* seems better than *nequit* as strengthening the personification of *Scotia*. In 9, he may have made experimental variations in the position and use of *optime* and *ultime*.

4

(a) *On the death of Viscount Dundee*

[(b) *On the Death of the Viscount of Dundee*]

'Last of the Scots, only your survival could have maintained the freedom of your native land: with your death Scotland has received new citizens and with your death she has received new Gods. She proclaims that she cannot survive you, nor can you survive her: therefore, farewell the empty name of Caledonia! And farewell you! mightiest leader of an ancient race, best and last of the Scots, Graham, farewell!'

POEMATA SELECTA

5

(a) *In Geo. Makinnium*

[(b) *Sepulchrum Georgii Mackenzy. In Mortem Locarti, Grahami & Mackenzii*]

[(c) *In Mortem Dom: Georgii M'kensi reg: Adv:*]

[(d) *In D. Geo Makinnium, Advocatum Regium. In Eundem*]

   Non hic Cæsarei surgunt monumenta sepulcri,
      Sedibus his Numen Cæsare majus inest:
   Ille Caledonii Regni Regumque Patronus,
      Quem patria Indigetem credidit esse Deum,
5 Qui sua tot victor Reges in Regna reduxit,
      Qui Cives quæ sint Regia jura docet,
   Occidit, & tumulo gaudet MAKINNIUS isto,
      Ista Hominem moles sola fuisse docet.

   Ergo Caledoniæ luimus perjuria turbæ,
10   Nec prodest toties tamque fuisse pios!
   Scilicet everti voluerunt Grampia Divi
      Regna, nec Heroum tot superesse genus!
   Aspera jam magnum rapuerunt Fata LOCARTUM,
      Ultimus Astræe filius ille fuit.
15 Sed non illa animos, non fortia pectora, clades
      Perculit; Est tanto par medicina malo:
   Est GRAMUS, qui jura armis, qui milite Leges
      Protegat: haud utinam prodigus ipse sui.
   Ah! Nimium Gramæa potens Dîs visa propago:
20   Exitio virtus te tua, Grame, dedit.
   Jam nobis super unus erat MAKINNIUS, unus
      Eloquio patrias qui repararet opes:
   Mors illum tamen atra tulit, jacet artis & æqui
      Oblitus, nostri fama decusque Fori.
25 Quo rapto, post fata Locarti, fataque Grami,
      Jura silent, torpent classica, Rostra vacant.

---

5 **Title**: (a) PS, 5; (b) APP, 6; 7; (c) BA(4), f.3ᵛ.; (d) SP, 6. **Text**: PS, 5–6. In APP, 6–8 and SP, 6–7, ll. 1–8 and 9–26 are printed as separate poems with different titles. 1: PS reads *Cæsarici*, corrected in *Mutenda & Corrigenda* and in the other texts; in B¹(1), the Bodley copy of PS the second *c* has been manually altered to *e*. 3: PS, APP, BA(4) and SP read *Caledoniæ*, altered to *Caledonii* in the B¹(1) and in *Mutenda & Corrigenda*. 6: for *sint* APP and BA(4) read *sunt*; they then insert 25–26. 21: APP *Tum* for *Jam*; BA(4) MAKINNIUS for *Mckenzius*. 23: for *illum tamen* APP and BA(4) *tamen illum*.

5

(a) *On George Mackenzie*

[(b) *The Tomb of George Mackenzie. On the death of Lockhart, Graham and Mackenzie*]

[(c) *On the death of Lord George Mackenzie, King's Advocate*]

[(d) *On Lord George Mackenzie, King's Advocate. On the Same*]

'It is not a Caesar's monumental tomb that rises here; this temple contains a divinity greater than any Caesar. Patron of the Scottish kingdom and kings; after his death deified, as his country believed; he who victoriously restored so many kings to their kingdoms, who teaches his fellow-citizens the foundations of monarchy, is dead, and Mackenzie rejoices in that tomb, that pile, which affords the only proof that he was mortal.

Thus we pay for our treasonous turmoils in Scotland. There is no profit in our former patriotism, however often and extensively proved! Evidently the Gods have willed the overthrow of the Grampian kingdom and the extinction of the race which has produced so many heroes! Already a harsh fate has snatched away great Lockhart, the last son of Astraea. But that disaster failed to deject our spirits, our brave hearts; there is a medicine to remedy even so great an injury. Graham survives to defend right with his weapons, the Law with his army – if only he were less prodigal of himself. Ah! The gods thought the progeny of Graemus overmighty. Your valour, Graham, gave you up to destruction. Now Mackenzie was the only hope left to us, the only one whose eloquence could restore our country's power. Black death however bore him away; the glory and honour of our Courts, he lies forgetful of art and equity. With his death, after the fate of Lockhart, the fate of Graham, Law has fallen silent, the war-trumpets are dumb, the rostrum stands empty.'

POEMATA SELECTA

6

(a) *Ad* ★★★.

[(b) *Ad Vice-Comitem Tarbatium*]

[(c) *Ad Georgium Vicecomitem Tarbatium*]

Prudentissime Fergusî Nepotum
Quot Phœbus videt, aut videbit olim,
Te nunc illa ferox [manus] Brigantum,
Plus justo Superis sibique fisa,
5 Et pulcri nimium tenax & æqui,
Supplex invocat, ac abesse nullum
Te præsente putat genus Deorum.
Benignissime Fergusî Nepotum
Adsis, & Veteri piæque Genti
10 Promptus subvenias, opem petenti
Solos non puduit Deos negare;
Qui Te si videant patrocinantem
Genti Fergusiæ superba passæ,
Fortassis requiem dabunt, miserti
15 Duræ sortis & irriti laboris,
Virtutisque vagæ; Viroque fient
Fessis auspice Dî benigniores.

6 Title: (a) *PS*, 6, thus. The version of the Key in *S* reads: 'Poema VI with 3 asteresc is Bredalbins who made the pacification for the highlanders, but Cromartie it is to him who never did good to any mortal'; a similar note but lacking the reference to Cromartie occurs in the Bodleian Key and the version in *N*; (b) *APP*, 20, *BA(4)*, f.7[v].; (c) *SP*, 7.   **Text**: *PS*, 6–7, *APP*, 20, *SP*, 7–8. The poem once appeared in *BA(4)*, f.6[r]., but 1–8 have been obliterated. 9: *APP*, 9. and *BA(4)*, *promptus* for *Genti*; 10 *Stirpi* for *Promptus*; 12 *Hi* for *Qui*. The complete version in *BA(4)*, f.7[v]. preserves the same readings, and in 6 has *Te supplex vocat* for *Supplex invocat* (as does *APP*, 20).

6

(a) *To* ★★★

[(b) *To Viscount Tarbet*]

[(c) *To George, Viscount Tarbet*]

'More prudent than any other of Clan Fergus, seen or to-be-seen under the sun, that fierce company from Brigantium, putting its confidence more than is right in the Gods and in itself, and holding too much to the beautiful and the just, now beseeches you as a suppliant, thinking that with you in charge no one of the race of Gods will desert us. Kindest of Clan Fergus, bring a quick subvention to an ancient and pious race. The Gods alone felt no shame in rejecting someone who sought their resources, but if they see you granting favours to the race of Fergus, which has endured tyranny, perhaps they will give us rest, pitying our hard fate, our useless labour, and wavering courage. When a real man is our leader, the Gods may become gentler to the weary.'

7

(a) *Ad Marcum Lermontium.*

[(b) *Ad Marcum Leir^{mt}.*]

    Caroli festæ jubeant quid Horæ
    Quoque fas gestu gravidam movere
    Amphoram, non te nimis est necesse,
        Marce, moneri.

5 Hic dies regnis Carolum Britannis
    Primus ostendit, patriæque dixit
    Sospitatorem, meritosque jam nunc
        Servat honores.

    Hic & injusto posuit labori
10 Principis finem, scelerique metas
    Civico, & plebis rabidæ cruentas
        Contudit iras.

    Tum suos regno populos beavit
    Aureo, & tuta requie STUARTUS,
15 Tum Diis visi nimium potentes,
        Marce, Britanni.

    Ergo ter centum cyathis ovantes
    Vina libemus Superûm cohorti,
    Quam recens hospes Jovis, Indigesque
20   Carolus auget.

    Sunt mihi mensæ pateris onustæ,
    Et coronatum stat, amice, vinum,
    Te leves risus, sale cum pudico,
        Opperiuntur.

25 Pone mordaces super orbe curas
    Brittonum, hostiles trepidant catervæ,
    Et nivis ritu, superante Solis
        Igne, liquescunt.

7 Title: (a) PS, 7, APP, 23, SP, 15; (b) BA(4), f.9ʳ. **Text:** PS, 7–8; SP, 15–16, the same with minor typographic variations. APP and BA(4), f.9, have similar variations, and in 14 read *dulci* for *tuta*.

7

(a) *To Mark Learmonth*

[(b) *To Mark Learmonth*]

'Mark, you don't need to be advised about the seasonal ordinances for Charles' festival and the proper ritual for the disturbance of the laden wine-jar.

This day first showed Charles to the British kingdoms and declared him saviour of his country; now it preserves the memory of his well-earned honours.

This day also marked the end of the prince's undeserved toils, put an end to civic crime, and crushed the bloody rage of the rabid commons.

Thereafter Stuart blessed his people with a golden reign and secure repose; thereafter, Mark, the Gods thought the Britons excessively mighty.

Therefore exultingly with thrice a hundred measures let us pour out wine as a libation to the company of Saints, reinforced by Charles, the recent guest of Jove and father of his nation.

My tables, friend, are laden with dishes and the wine stands crowned. Light-hearted laughter with modest wit awaits you.

Lay aside gnawing cares about the world of the Britons; the enemy bands tremble and melt away, like snow overcome by the heat of the Sun.'

8

Ad Greppam

    Diva, que cellis habitas Avernis,
    Et rubro Manes pelago coerces,
    Dic quibus lucis CAROLUS quietum
        Transigat ævum.

5 Ille si sciret Generis sacrati
      SPEM procul regnis profugam paternis,
    Non leves inter latitaret umbras,
        Lentus inersque.

    Sed gravis dudum remeasset ultor
10 Fratris, & magni Pueri, annuente
    Cœlitum cœtu, superis Deorum
        Gratus & imis.

    Ergo tu mœstæ pia vota gentis
    Perfer, & longam Caroli quietem
15 Rumpe, nunc fas, nunc Acheronta tempus,
        Diva, movere.

    Nam tibi lati Dominator Orci,
    Vocibus Bacchi Patris excitatus,
    Æmulos gnatæ Cereris dicavit
20   Nuper honores.

8 Title: *PS*, 8, *APP*, 13, *BA(4)*, f.21ʳ. (second hand), *SP*, 16–17, all thus.   **Text**: *PS*, 8, thus. 1: *SP*, 16–17, *quæ* for *que*. 2: *APP*, 13 *fluvio* for *pelago*; 3: *Quere quo luco* for *Dic quibus lucis*; 6: *regno* for *regnis*. 3: *BA(4)* reads *Ede quo luco* for *Dic quibus lucis*. All differ otherwise only in capitalization and punctuation.

POEM 8

8

To Greppa

'Goddess, who inhabitest the cells of Avernus and confinest the dead with a red sea, say in what sacred groves Charles passes a tranquil eternity.

He, if he knew that the hope of his anointed race is an exile from the kingdoms of his fathers, would not lie hidden, unconcerned and indolent, among the disembodied shadows.

But long since would have returned in triumph, stern avenger of his brother and the mighty Boy, pleasing to Gods above and below, with full consent of the assembled Deities.

Do you therefore fulfil the prayers of a mourning people and break Charles' long repose. Now is the time, Goddess, to move Acheron!

For to you the Master of wide Orcus, stirred up by the voices of the followers of Father Bacchus, has just now proclaimed honours to rival the daughter of Ceres.'

9

(a) *Ad Dannistonum.*

[(b) *Deploratio*]

[(c) *In Mortem Deploratio Denistoni Poetæ et Greppæ Cauponæ &c.*]

[(d) *Ad Gualt. Dannistonum*]

    Dannistone meæ Patrone Musæ,
    Quis te casus, amice, quis Deorum
    Te sub Tartara misit invenusta,
    Tum cum Greppa foret canenda nostro
5   Nubens Ægidio, Proserpinæque
    Ditem linquere gestiens Avernum?
    Qualis nox fuit illa, Dii, Deaeque,
    Qua Greppa Ægidium fovere molli
    Amplexu voluit, senisque Divi,
10 Ligno aut cortice siccioris omni,
    Alto gurgite proluebat inguen,
    Limosoque iterum lacu imbuebat?
    At vos Ægidii senis ministri,
    Cum queis ille dies terebat omnes
15 Fabellis generis novi audiendis,
    laudes Dominæ novæ frementes,
    Rauco carmine personate Templum,
    Templum atque atria Cœlitis superba.
    Dannistone meæ patrone Musæ,
20 Quanto dignius elegantiusque
    Sedes Ægidii, deæque Greppæ,
    Intrasses duce Libero triumphans,
    Vitatis Erebi silentis undis?
    Quæ tum gaudia poculi bibisses?
25 Quae libamina tum Deo Deæque
    Fudisses, duce Libero triumphans?
    Annam dum sitiens vocaret Hugo,

9 Title: (a) PS, 9; (b) APP, 24; (c) BA(4), fo.10.r. (in left margin) (d) SP, 17. **Text**: PS, 9–10, thus; also, with minor typographical variants, SP, 17–19. APP, 24–26, BA(4), fo.10. APP, 24–26 and BA(4) have the following variant readings: 11: *Pleno gurgite proluit pudenda.* 26: *Libero duce* for *duce Libero.* 29: *prius lubentem* for *Diis dicatus.* 34: (Bodleian MS only) in place of *nec alter olim*, the reading *nihil merentem* is indicated, followed by *Te cum ante diem abstulere flentes / Te cum ante patrem abstulere, Marce,* 'when weeping they have taken you away before your time, when they have taken you away, Mark, before your father'. 40: *Deæque* for *venena.* 41: *repullulantem* as variant for *Stygi domandam.* 42–43 are omitted.

POEM 9

9

(a) *To Dennistoun*

[(b) *Threnody*]

[(c) *Threnody on the Death of the Poet Dennistoun and the Landlady Greppa etc.*]

[(d) *To Walter Dennistoun*]

'Dennistoun, Patron of my Muse, what chance, friend, what God banished you beneath horrible Tartarus, when it was incumbent to raise a song for Greppa marrying our Giles and exultantly leaving Avernian Dis to Proserpine? Gods and Goddesses! What a night it was, when Greppa desired to fold Giles in a soft embrace. She used deep water to wash the privy parts of the old God, more dessicated than any wood or cork, and plunged them again in a muddy lake. But you, in whose company he used to wear out all his days with new and gripping tales, as they clamoured to praise their new Lady, you ministers of old Giles, make the temple resound with hoarse song, the temple and the proud halls of the Celestial!

   Dennistoun, patron of my Muse, would not your dignity and elegance have been enhanced if you had entered the seats of Giles and the Goddess Greppa, triumphantly led by Liber after your avoidance of the silent waves of Erebus? Triumphantly led by Liber, what joys would you then have found in your cups, what libations poured to the God and Goddess? While thirsty Hugh would

POEMATA SELECTA

    Atque ad prælia liberaliorum
    Marcum pelliceret, Diis dicatus
30 Lucusque omnis, Jo, sonaret, Anna!
    Sed Marcum Superi, mihi invidentes,
    Longam vivere maluere noctem;
    Quo non flebilior bonis honestisque
    Alter procubuit, nec alter olim
35 Terras candidior reviset hospes:
    Qui vir si proprium suis fuisset
    Donum, si patria seneret urbe,
    Qua nunc alite dicerem disertus,
    Et Marco et Patre Libero jubente,
40 Fraudes Ægidii, venena Greppae,
    Hugonisque sitim Stygi domandam.
    Hæc mî Cynthius, hæc novem Sorores
    Læto carmine prosequi dederunt:
    Sed tu debueras adesse nobis,
45 Dannistone, meæ patrone Musæ

10

[(a) *Ad Jacobum VII*]

[(b) *Ad Jacobum II*]

[(c) *In Mortem Jacobi Regis septimi*]

[(d) *Ad Jacobum* ------- (7 dashes)]

    Ergo magna Tui tellurem liquit Imago,
      Illa Tui qua non sanctior ulla fuit?
    Te mox aspiciet contentus Rege STUARTO,
      Virtuti similis semideusque Cato.

---

10 Title: (a) *PS*, 10; (b) *APP*, 26; (c) *BA(4)*, f.10.v.; (d) *SP*, 19. **Text**: *PS*, 10, *SP*, 19, thus, with minor differences of spelling, punctuation and capitalization. In *APP* and the *BA(4)* the first four lines differ substantially:

    Ergo magna tui sub terras ibit Imago.
      Privatus curis cum satis ante aferes.
    Jam tibi similem vidisti, credo, Catonem,
      Virtuti similem semideumque virum.

'So your great spirit will go beneath the earth, deprived of worries, although previously you brought enough of them on yourself. Now you have seen, I believe, Cato, a demigod resembling you, resembling you in virtue.'

summon Anna and entice Mark to the battles of the over-liberal, the God's chosen victim and the entire sacred grove would resound 'Io, Anna!' But the Gods destined Mark, in my despite, to enter the long night. In the contest he came second, and fell, none more worthy than he of lament by good and honest men, nor will a second whiter [than he] ever again visit the earth. If he had been given back to his friends, if he had grown old in his native city – made fluent by that omen, commanded by Mark and Father Liber, I would speak of the delusions of Giles, Greppa's poisons, and Hugh's thirst, to quench which Styx was demanded. But these things Cynthius and the Nine Sisters have empowered me to present [only] in merry song. But you ought to have been there with us, Dennistoun, patron of my Muse.'

10

(a) *To James* VII

[(b) *To James* II]

[(c) *On the Death of King James* VII]

[(d) *To James* ------- (7 dashes)]

'Has your great spirit, then, left the earth, that spirit of yours more sacred than any other? Soon the demi-god Cato, whose virtue resembled yours, will look upon you, contented with the Stuart king. What better, what more accurately, can the

5   Quid melius de Te, quid dicet rectius, ille
        Manibus impositus dicere jura piis?
    Quam quod Te vita, quam quod te moribus esse
        Dissimilem Genero Dî voluere tuo.

11

(a) *Ad Carolum* II

[(b) *Ad Carolum* II *Martii 8ᵛᵒ, 1702.*]

    Carole, si pratis iterum reddare paternis,
        Quem mox custodem, jusseris esse gregis?
    Cui calamos tradas cum pastoralibus armis,
        Prataque Teutonico nuper adempta Lupo?
5   An Fratri rursus? Vel, quæ præsentior Annæ?
        An PUERO Fratrem quem vocat Anna suum?
    At Frater nimium prisci virtute Catonis
        Gaudet, & ad Superos non revocandus abest.
    ANNA igitur calamos & pastoralia sumet,
10   Quæ reddet Fratri, si sapit Anna, suo.

11 **Title**: (a) *PS*, 11, *SP*, 20; (b) *APP*, 32. *BA(4)*, f.12.r., lacks a title. **Text**: *PS*, 11, *SP*, 20–21, thus, with minor typographical differences. In l. 3, *APP* and *BA(4)* read *trades* for *tradas*, and in l. 4 *Bovi* for *Lupo*; in ll. 7–8 they read: *At frater Batavo permisit ovile Bubulco/ Vexavit glaucis hic tua Regna Lupis*, 'But your brother has surrendered the sheepfold to the Batavian ploughman; *he* has plagued your kingdoms with grey wolves'. The final line in both is *Quæ tradet Fratri, si placet illa suo*. *BA(4)*, however, precedes this line with *Quæ fratri tradet, si sapit illa suo*.

One set to pass judgement on the righteous dead say of you than that in life, as in character, the Gods willed you to be unlike your son-in-law?'

11

(a) *To Charles II*

(b) *To Charles II on 8th March 1702*

'Charles, if you were restored again to your ancestral meadows, whom would you ordain to be the next shepherd of your flock? To whom would you hand over your reed-pipes with the shepherd's weapons and the meadows recently snatched away from the Teutonic wolf? To your brother again? Or to Anne, who is nearer at hand? Or to the Boy whom Anne calls brother? But your brother rejoices too much in the virtue of old Cato and has passed irrevocably to the Saints above. Anne therefore will assume the reeds and pastoral equipment, which, if Anne has any sense, she will presently return to her own brother.'

POEMATA SELECTA

12

(a) *Fabulæ 2. Lib. 1. Phædri Metaphrasis.*

[(b) *Darien*]

[(c) *In Decimum diem Junii*]

[(d) *In decimum Diem Iunii natalem Principis*]

[(e) *Fhædri Fabul:' Liber Primus Fab: 2*]

Ranarum proceres paludis hujus,
Et prati indigenæ palude cincti,
Nonne audistis avos, patresque vestros,
Securos potuisse stagna circum
5 Exultare sua, & venusta prata?
Rex ILIGNUS iis dabat beatam
Vitam, atque otia non periculosa.
Tunc quæ me puerum puella Rana
Castis, Juppiter, osculata labris!
10 Quot dein rettulit osculationes,
Et cura vacuas metuque tristi!
Quot tunc millia vidimus profecta
Ad ripæ ulterioris inquilinos?

---

12 Title: (a) PS, 11, SP, 21. A contemporary hand has added (b) to PS in R^1; (c) APP, 20. (d) BA(4), f.8.r. (first hand); (e) BA(4), f.18.r. (second hand). **Text**: 4–5. APP reads: *Securos potuisse prata cursu/ Insultare sua ac aquas natatu*, 'without a care in the world have been able to hop around their meadows when they travelled and their waters when they swam'. BA(4) has the same reading, but with the impossible *potuisti* for *potuisse*.

In APP and BA(4): 8. *me* is omitted. 19. (Bodleian only) *potest diu* for *diu potest*.

25. missing. 26. *At nunc Rex colitur Ciconiarum* for *Optatur novus inquiesque Rector*. 35. *non satis est* for *nonne sat est*. 37. *ut jam* for *jam ut*. 49. *ne te nimis fatigem* for *si nos vetus arbor audis*. 58. *Stagnicolarum* for *Praticolarum*.

The second Bodleian hand has variants: 4–5. as in first hand. 21–22. *Libertasque gravis, graves penates,/ Et saturnia displicebat Ilex*. 25–26. missing. 27. As in APP and first hand. 35. as in APP and first hand. 51. *aves* for *Ales*.

There are also minor variations of spelling, capitalization, and punctuation.

On f.17.v. of the BA(4) (between the two hands) appears a note, apparently written by Pitcairne:

'Instead of (in Ranarum proceres &c.) *Quousque*
– *Sed ipsa tandem*
Libertas gravis, et graves penates,
Et Saturnia displicebat ilex.

This shows him revising the text, almost attaining the final form found in PS.

The version written in the second hand concludes with an attribution to *Danistone* (Dennistoun), Pitcairne's usual pseudonym. In the copy of PS preserved as R^2, there is a hand-written attribution to *Danesen*.

12

(a) *Paraphrase of Phaedrus, Fable 2, Book 1*

[(b) *Darien*]

[(c) *On the tenth of June*]

[(d) *On the Tenth of June, Birthday of the Prince*]

[(e) *Fables of Phaedrus, First Book, Fable 2*]

'Chiefs of the Frogs of this marsh and of your native meadow girt by the marsh, have you not heard that your fathers and grandfathers were able to live in happiness and security around their pools and attractive meadows? King OAK gave them a happy life and safe enjoyment of their leisure. Then in my youth, which Frog girl kissed me with chaste lips (Jupiter!)? How many more carefree kisses did she then get back with no gloomy fear? How many thousands did we see setting out to be tenants of the further shore? What old and new games did we play there together,

Quos illic veteres novosque lusus
15 Unà lusimus advenæ hospitesque,
A sole èxoriente ad occidentem?
Sed Ranæ fuimus, fuit paludis
Ingens gloria, lausque clara prati.
Ah! Sors nulla diu potest placere
20 Ventoso populo! Sed ipsa tandem
Libertas gravis, & graves Penates,
Ut Saturnia displiceret ILEX,
Quæ prati indigenis palude cincti
Ranis otia fecerat beata.
25 Irato Jove Cœlitumque cœtu
Optatur novus inquiesque Rector,
Rectorque eligitur Ciconiarum,
Quarum exercitus Ales hæc pererrat;
Hæc impune pererrat atque vexat,
30 Ranarum patria ac avita stagna;
Nec nos visere nunc licet cohortes
Ranarum per amœniora fusas
Pratorum æquora, & invidenda regna.
Obscœnæ volucres, malæque pestes
35 Stagni, nonne sat est vorasse gentem
Nobis sanguine moribusque junctam,
Nullæ ut jam superest in Insula illa
Ranæ legibus atque Rege junctæ?
At vos, O proceres ducesque nostri,
40 Clari militiæ domique clari,
Si stirpem Veterem, incolamque prati
Servatam cupitis palude cincti,
Hæc gratis animis, labrisque castis,
Mecum ter memorate verba læti;
45 Et nulla audeat hic natare Rana
Quæ non hæc memoret ter ipsa verba.

ILICIS sacræ Geniale Numen,
Quippe te priscæ coluere Ranæ,
Juniis, si nos vetus arbor audis,
50   Annue votis.

Quæ tuas Ales peregrina Ranas
Certat infesto violare rostro,
Sedibus nostris abigatur omnis
    Trans mare magnum.

strangers and hosts, from sunrise to sunset? But we are Frogs no longer; the great glory of the marsh and the fair fame of the meadow has departed. Ah! No kind of fortune can keep a fickle people happy for long. Liberty herself at last becomes onerous and household divinities burdensome, with the result that the Saturnian OAK, which had provided blissful leisure for the Frogs indigenous to the meadow girt by the marsh, proved no longer to their taste. To the annoyance of Jove and the company of Heaven, a new and restive governor is desired and a governor chosen from among the Storks, who make up this winged army that wanders around. It wanders around unchecked and troubles the Frogs' ancestral pools. Nor are we permitted to visit the tribes of Frogs scattered across the friendlier levels of their meadows, their enviable kingdoms. Obscene birds! Evil plagues of the pool! Is it not enough that you have devoured a people linked to us by blood and way of life, so that now no Frogs who remain faithful to their laws and their King survive in that island?

But you, our chiefs and dukes, famous in the field and famous at home, if you want to preserve the ancient stock and the people of the meadow girt by the marsh, gladly recall these words time and again with thankful minds and chaste lips. Let only these Frogs who have become word-perfect dare to swim here!

"Genial Spirit of the sacred OAK, insomuch as the first Frogs worshipped you, if you hear us, ancient Tree, nod assent to our Junian vows.

The winged foreigner who tries to upset your Frogs with pestilent beak, let every one of them be driven from our homes across the great sea.

55 Nos tua nobis ope restitutæ
　　Ilicis circum saliemus aram,
　Principis laudes celebrare gratæ
　　Praticolarum.

13

(a) *In 30. Januarii 1708*

[(b) *30 Januarii*]

Ergo nefasta dies, & secli dedecus acti,
　　Quam solam decuit non rediisse, redit.
Quæ scelus armavit divino nomine Juris,
　　Et Juris numen sustulit una, redit.
5 Quam bene pro Jano venisset Junius ultor?
　　Mensibus atque annis JUNIUS omne decus.
Ille modum longis posuisset ritè querelis,
　　Et lacrymis finem, Scotia mœsta, tuis.
Sed veniet Lux grata, venit tot conscia votis
10 　Junia, mortales ore favete viri.
Res agitur magnis jamdudum credita Divis,
　　Non opis humanæ, Jupiter, illa fuit.

14

(a) *In 30. Januarii 1709.*

[(b) *30 January 1709*]

Hæc est illa dies quæ sacræ conscia cœdis
　　Tot genuit pestes, stulte Britanne, tibi.
An potuit Divi non ultor Jupiter esse?
　　An poterit Nati non memor esse Deo?

---

13 Title: (a) PS, 13, SP, 24; (b) BA(4), f.21, r, (second hand).　Text: there are no significant variations.
14 Title: (a) PS, 13, SP, 24; (b) BA(4), f.22.r. (second hand).　Text: PS, 13–14; SP, 24; BA(4), f.22ʳ. There are no significant variations.

When we are restored to ourselves by your help, we shall jump thankfully around the altar of the Oak to sing the praises of the prince of the dwellers in the meadow."'

13

(a) *On 30 January 1708*

[(b) *30 January*]

'Thus the accursed day, blackest of the last century, the only day which should not have returned, returns. It returns, although it reinforced crime with the divine name of Law, and by itself did away with Law's divine spirit. How appropriately would Junius have come as avenger of Janus, Junius who gives a perfect embellishment to every month and year! He would have set the proper limit to your long complaints and put a stop to your tears, grieving Scotland! But the Day of grace will come, the June day comes in full awareness of your many vows – mortal men keep a religious silence! Something long entrusted to the great Gods is taking place, something, by Jupiter! beyond all human means.'

14

(a) *On 30 January 1709*

[(b) *30 January 1709*]

'This is the notorious day, accessory to the horrible crime which produced so many plagues for you, foolish Briton. Could Jupiter leave the Divinity unavenged? Can he possibly forget the Offspring of the God?'

POEMATA SELECTA

15

Ad Janum. 1709

Jane, jam Menses abiere sacri, &
Grampio dudum populo nefasti,
Verba dicamus bona nunc & apta,
    Auspice Maio.

5 Junius venit, viridi juventa
Gratus, & Solem nimis imminentem
Noctibus, dulcique hominum quieti,
    Sistere princeps.

Nunc nec amissum puero parentem
10 Flere, nec nati meminisse matrem
Fas: Ceres tandem steriles revisit
    Impigra terras

Et comes Baccho Venus, hæc columbas
Læta, mansuetas Pater ipse tigres
15 Frænat: Hæc nobis dedit illa formo-
    sissima Junî

Lux, & eversum reparavit annum,
Primaque insanas hyemes amœnis
Veris antiqui spatiis coegit
20   Nuper abesse.

Gaudio rursus nitet omnis ætas,
Ipse Saturnus redit, exul olim
Rege Dictæo, superos Deûm qui
    Miscuit imis,

25 Atque Ranarum malè bellicosis
Auream rupit populis quietem, &
Pace florentem Furiis replevit
    Impius Orbem.

---

15 Title and Text: *PS*, 14–15; *SP*, 25–27. The MS alterations in *B¹(1)*, the Bodleian copy of *PS* (2, 43–44), elsewhere indicated in *Mutenda & Corrigenda*, which limit the application of the poem to Scotland rather than Britain as a whole, are ignored in *SP*.

15

To Janus 1709

'Janus, now that the detestable months, long hated by the Grampian people, have gone away, let us proclaim the good news appropriately forecast by May.

June in his green youth has come pleasantly, first to bring to a standstill the Sun, which was bearing down too hard on the nights and the sweet quiet of men.

Now it is improper for the boy to lament his lost father, or the mother to remember her son; unwearied Ceres has at last revisited the barren fields.

So too has Venus, companion to Bacchus; joyfully she bridles her doves, the Father the tigers which he has tamed. These gifts that most beautiful day in June has given us

And has repaired the topsy-turvy year, and recently was first to compel the insane winters to abandon the pleasant spaces formerly occupied by spring.

Each generation shines joyously again. Saturn himself returns, long exiled by the Dictaean king who mingled the Gods above with those below,

And who destroyed golden quiet for the unwarlike Frog people and impiously filled the world, then flourishing in peace, with Furies.

Junio rursus tamen annuente,
30 Scota lustrabunt & avita prata
   Gramus, ingentisque Locartus oris,
      Makiniusque;

Ad salutandam Cererem remissi ab
Dite placatam venerante socrum,
35 Et Patri Baccho, comitique Bacchi,
      Dona ferentes.

Nosque adhuc lenti dubitamus almi
JUNII augusto Genio litare?
Quem colunt Reges super atque subter
40   Astra potentes.

Ille sit felix propriusque nobis,
Vota nos illi faciamus uni,
Mensibus semper pius præsit
   Scotobrigantum.

However, with June once again nodding assent, Graham, Lockhart with his great eloquence, and Mackenzie will purify their hereditary Scottish meadows,

Sent back by Dis, out of respect for his appeased mother-in-law, to greet Ceres, bearing gifts also for Father Bacchus and the companion to Bacchus.

And shall we have any lingering doubts about sacrifice to the august Genius of fostering June, worshipped by Kings whose powers extend above and below the stars?

May he be benign and favourable to us! Let us make our vows to him alone! May he ever piously preside over the months of the Brigantine Scots!'

POEMATA SELECTA

16

(a) *In Johannem Belhavenium*

[(b) *Ad Dominum de Belhaven mortuum Londini Junio* MDCCVIII]

[(c) *on My Lord Belhaven*]

[(d) *In Joannem D. Belhavenium*]

Dum Cives servare studes, dum Grampia regna,
    Dignus Hamiltonia dum cupis esse domo,
Quam nimis indignè Scotis avelleris oris!
    Si quas nunc Scotas dicere Fata sinunt.
5 At quoniam Fato tollet se gloria vatum
    Altior, atque Tui fama perennis erit,
Non Te jam Divum, sed nos raptosque Penates
    Flebimus, O vates non habiture parem!

17

(a) *In Geo. Makinnium Georgii filium.*

[(b) *In Georgium Mackenzy a Valle Rosarum mortuum Kal. Octob. Anni* MDCCVII]

Quamvis dura tulit me mors, oriente juventa,
    Divinoque parem noluit esse Patri:
Non tamen aut Divos, incusavi-ve Sorores,
    Quæ me, me sociis abripuere meis:
5 At Matris dolor ille meæ, mihi durior ipsa
    Morte, minus gratum reddidit Elyzium.

---

16 Title: (a) *PS*, 15; (b) *APP*, 56; (c) *BA(4)*, f.16ʳ, inset; (d) *SP*, 36. **Text**: *PS*, 15; *APP*, 56; *BA(4)*, f.16ʳ, inserted in a later hand; *SP*, 36–37. In l. 2, *SP*, and *BA(4)* have *Hamiltona* for *Hamiltonia*. In the final line *BA(4)* has the impossible *habituera* for *habiture*. There are also minor differences of capitalization and punctuation.

17 Title: (a) *PS*, 16, *SP*, 37; (b) *APP*, 52. **Text**: *PS*, 16, *APP*, 52, *SP*, 37, thus, with minor typographical differences.

16

(a) *On John Belhaven*

[(b) *To Lord Belhaven who died in London in June 1708*]

[(c) *on My Lord Belhaven*]

[(d) *On John, Lord Belhaven*]

'Despite your engagement in the service of your countrymen and the Grampian kingdom, despite your desire to be worthy of the house of Hamilton, how less than worthily have you been dragged from the shores of Scotland – if indeed the Fates now permit any shore to be called Scottish! But since the glory of seers raises itself higher than Fate and your fame will be everlasting, it is not you, now a God, whom we lament, but ourselves and our stolen household divinities, you seer who will never have an equal!'

17

(a) *On George Mackenzie, son of George.*

[(b) *On George Mackenzie of Rosehaugh who died on the Kalends of October 1707*]

'Although harsh death has taken me in the flower of my youth, and forbidden me to rival my divine father, yet I have not berated the Gods or the fatal Sisters who have snatched me unhappy from my companions. But that grief of my mother, harsher to me than death itself, has made Elysium a less pleasing place.'

2

Satiric and Philosophical Poems in Elegiac Couplets

SATIRIC AND PHILOSOPHICAL POEMS IN ELEGIAC COUPLETS

18

DAVID AND VENUS

(a)

David Veneri / Venus Davidi

DAVID VENERI,

MILITIS infesti me vis urgebat inermem,
  Nec superum quisquam ferre parabat opem,
Ad tua Castra, VENUS, fugi, Tibi, Diva, litavi,
  Et sprevi miles militis arma tuus.
5 Dum lito me densa circumdas optima nube,
  Aeneae qualis profuit ante pio.
Ipse Deae numen grata in caligine sensi,
  Et VENUS in media nube secunda fuit.
Illa feros hostes nubes mihi depulit illa
10   Cultorem jussit Numinis esse Tui.
Sancta VENUS quantos solvam tibi tutus honores!
  Quam Te non ficta Relligione colam!
Te Dea, Te Supplex cunctis venerabor in oris,
  Tu mihi pro Superis omnibus una cluis.
15 Nil tuus *Aeneas* sine Te, nil maxima pollet
  Tot quamvis alijs Roma superba Deis.
Sola facis mites ad signa venire puellas,
  Et jam templa Deum sunt tua Castra VENUS.
Mirentur *Mahometem Arabes,* mirentur & *Indi,*
20   Alteriusque alios Numinis urat Amor.
Ast ego furtivae VENERIS proeconia dicam,
  Illi sacra lubens Tempus in omne feram.

VENUS DAVIDI,

DELICIAE generis nostri, mihi rebus in arctis
  Cognite, militiae gloria magna meae,
25 Qui VENERI Phoebum socias & pectora versas
  SCOTICA DAVIDICAE relligione Lyrae,

18 Title: (a) *N(8)*, a single sheet, folio, printed on one side; *T*, D32 1710; (b) APP, 9, with *Williamson* inserted above, between *David* and *ad Venerem*; BA(4), f.5ʳ; SP, 9, 10, with reverse order of poems; (c) *R²*, item 11. **Text**: (a) as above; (b) APP, 9–11, BA(4), ff.5ʳ–6ʳ; SP, 9–11. 10. (a) *Tui*, (b) *sui*. 17–18. SP omits. 20. (a) SP, *Alteriusque alios,* BA(4), *Europam alterius.* 22. (a) *lubens*, (b) *libens*. in (b), after 22, seven couplets not in (a). (a) 33, SP, 47, *sperata*, (b) 47, *promissa*. (a) 35–36, (b) 49–50, omitted in SP. (a) 36, *Arcadicus*, (b) 50, *Arabicus*. There are also typographical variations.

102

18

(a) *David to Venus / Venus to David*

DAVID TO VENUS

'The violence of a hostile soldiery pressed me hard; I was defenceless, nor was any of the Gods prepared to come to my aid. To your stronghold, Venus, I fled; to you Goddess, I made an acceptable sacrifice, and, as your soldier, rejected a soldier's weapons. While I made my sacrifice, best of ladies, you surrounded me with thick cloud such as long ago helped the pious Aeneas. In welcome dense gloom I felt in myself the power of the goddess and Venus was favourable in the midst of the cloud. That cloud drove fierce enemies away from me and compelled me to become a worshipper of your divinity. Holy Venus, no sacrifice is enough to repay you for my salvation; there is nothing feigned in the worship I give you. You, Goddess, you will I venerate as your suppliant in every clime; you alone, in preference to all the Gods, will I honour. Without you, your Aeneas was nothing, nor could greatest Rome accomplish anything, no matter how many other Gods she was proud to possess. Let the Arabs and Indians worship Mahomet, and let the love of another divinity burn up other people; I shall sing the praises of a furtive Venus, and gladly make sacrifices to her for ever.'

VENUS TO DAVID

'Darling among my offspring, acknowledged by me as master in northern affairs, great glory of my army, you who unite Phoebus and Venus and turn Scottish hearts snatched away by the worship of David's lyre – you will be my David, you have

SATIRIC AND PHILOSOPHICAL POEMS IN ELEGIAC COUPLETS

Tu mihi DAVID eris, Tu me deducere Coelo
  Non sola placidi Carminis arte vales.
Jam pudet *Anchisen* gremio fovisse, pudetque
30 Oscula loripedi mille dedisse seni,
Quamvis ille Deis haud paucis fortior esset,
  Hic Deus aeterno vinctus amore mihi.
Ergo CALEDONIIS veniam sperata Puellis,
  Posthabitaque colam Grampia rura *Papho*.
35 Illic multa mihi fumant Altaria, noster
  Illic Arcadicus creditur esse Puer.

(b)

David ad venerem
[*David ad venerem / Venus ad Davidem*]

Militis infesti me vis urgebat inermem,
  Nec superum quisquam ferre parabat opem;
Ad tua Castra Venus fugi, tibi Diva litavi
  Et sprevi miles militis arma tuus.
5 Dum Lito me densâ circumdas optima nube,
  Æneæ qualis profuit ante pio.
Ipse Deæ numen grata in caligine sensi
  Et Venus in media nube secunda fuit
Illa feros hostes, nubes mihi depulit illa
10 Cultorem jussit numinis esse Sui
Sancta Venus quantos solvam tibi tutus honores
  Quam te non fictâ Relligione colam,
Te Dea te supplex cunctis venerabor in oris,
  Tu mihi pro superis omnibus una cluis,
15 Nil tuus Æneas sine te nil maxima pollet
  Tot quamvis alijs Roma superba Deis
Sola facis mites ad signa venire puellas
  Et jam templa deûm sunt tua Castra Venus.
Mirentur Mahometem Arabes, mirentur et Indi,
20 Europam alterius Numinis urat Amor
Ast ego furtivæ Veneris præconia dicam,
  Illi sacra libens tempus in omne feram.
Illa dedit sanctum populo plaudente videri
  Nullaque non voluit credere virgo Deæ.
25 Illa dedit stolido mysteria pandere vulgo;
  Et dolus in nulla pæne fefellit anû.
Illa mihi Gentem spondet cui millia cedent

the power to draw me down from heaven, not only by the art of your gentle song. I'm ashamed now that I've cherished Anchises in my bosom, and I'm ashamed that I've given a thousand kisses to an old man with bandy legs. However much the latter may have excelled the potency of most of the other Gods, this God is bound to me by eternal love. Therefore I shall come, long desired by Caledonian girls, and cherish the Grampian fields, scorning Paphos. There many altars smoke to me, there it is believed that my Boy is a mountaineer.'

(b)

David to venus
[*David to venus / Venus to David*]

'The violence of a hostile soldiery pressed me hard; I was defenceless, nor was any of the Gods prepared to come to my aid. To your stronghold, Venus, I fled; to you, Goddess, I made an acceptable sacrifice, and, as your soldier, rejected a soldier's weapons. While I made my sacrifice, best of ladies, you surrounded me with thick cloud such as long ago helped the pious Aeneas. In dense gloom I felt in myself the benevolent power of the Goddess and Venus was favourable in the midst of the cloud. That cloud drove fierce enemies away from me and compelled me to become a worshipper of her divinity. Holy Venus, no sacrifice is enough to repay you for my salvation; there is nothing feigned in the worship I give you. You, Goddess, you will I venerate as your suppliant in every clime; you alone, in preference to all the Gods, will I honour. Without you, your Aeneas was nothing, nor could greatest Rome accomplish anything, no matter how many other Gods she was proud to possess. You alone make gentle girls rally to the colours; even now the temples of the Gods, Venus, have become your strongholds. Let the Arabs and Indians wonder at Mahomet, let love of another Divinity consume Europe; I shall sing the praises of a furtive Venus and gladly make sacrifices to her for ever. To popular applause, she gave me the appearance of a saint; there isn't a girl but puts her trust in the Goddess. She grants the revelation of her mysteries to the stolid multitude, and her trickery has remained undetected in virtually every old woman. She promises me a posterity to whom shall bow all the thousands whom

SATIRIC AND PHILOSOPHICAL POEMS IN ELEGIAC COUPLETS

   Omnia Romulei quæ genuere patres.
  Illa regit terras et sunt jam sydera terræ,
30   Illa sacerdotes protegit usque suos.
  Grampia quod veteres mutarunt Regna Penates
   Et perculsa suum deserûere patrem,
  Debent fata tibi; duce te Bacchata Caledon
   Et juga fœmineo Grampia pressa choro.
35 Tu mihi Diva doces Cœlis sit quanta voluptas
   Tu Cupido cœlos sola patere facis.

   Venus ad Davidem

  Deliciæ generis nostri, mihi rebus in arctis
   Cognite, militiæ gloria magna meæ
  Qui Veneri Phœbum socias et Pectora versas
40   Scotica Davidicæ rapta furore Lyræ
  Tu mihi David eris, tu me deducere cœlis
   Non sola placidi Carminis arte vales.
  Jam pudet Anchisen gremio fovisse, pudetque
   Oscula Loripedi mille dedisse Seni.
45 Quamvis ille Deis haud paucis fortior esset,
   Hic Deus æterno vinctus amore mihi.
  Ergo Caledonijs veniam promissa puellis,
   Posthabitaque colam Grampia rura Papho
  Illic multa mihi fumant Altaria, noster
50   Illic Arabicus creditur esse puer

the Roman fathers begat. She rules the earth, and earth has now become heaven; she protects her priests to the limit. The fates owe it to you that the Grampian kingdom has now changed its old household gods and has been so beaten down that it has deserted its own father; under your captaincy Scotland has turned bacchanal and the Grampian ridges have been oppressed by a troop of Maenads. You teach me, Goddess, how much pleasure there is in heaven; you alone open heaven to a lustful man.'

Venus to David

'Darling among my offspring, acknowledged by me as master of northern affairs, great glory of my army, you who unite Phoebus with Venus and turn Scottish hearts snatched away by the fury of David's lyre – you will be my David, you have the power to draw me down from the heavens, not only by the art of your gentle song. I'm ashamed now that I've cherished Anchises in my bosom, and I'm ashamed that I've given a thousand kisses to an old man with bandy legs. However much the latter might have excelled the potency of most of the other Gods, this God is bound to me by eternal love. Therefore I shall come, as promised to the Caledonian girls, and cherish the Grampian fields, scorning Paphos. There many altars smoke to me, there it is believed that my boy is Arabian.'

19

Edinburgh Taverns

(i)

(a) *To M^r. B. Stote concerning the Edenburgh Taverns*.

[(b), (c) No title.]

[(d) *Ad Advenas*.]

Advena, qui nostros cupies cognoscere Divos,
 Et populi mores, ingeniumque Loci,

19 Title: (a) APP, 54; (b) APP, 29; (c) BA(4), f.13.r.; (d) SP, 27. **Text**: APP, 54–56. After l. 4 all other versions insert:

> Olim bruta Cohors sed formidata Gigantum
> Ausa fuit magnis bella ciere deis:
> Montibus impositos calcabant Agmina Montes
> Astraque tum cives extimuere novos.
> Ille pater Divum, Rex ipsorumque Gigantum,
> Juppiter hæc fati maximus Auctor ait:
> Non his freta dolis, non bellatoribus istis
> Speret ad ætherias surgere terra Plagas
> Sed Juga vesanam promittunt Scotica stirpem
> Quae cœlum terris misceat atque Stygi.
> Surget Edinburgum vel Olympo celsius ipso
> Et dis invisum tollet in astra Genus
> Juppiter hæc: urbem nostram delubraque divûm
> Sic visum fatis tristis Erinnys habet.

'Once upon a time a stupid but formidable band of Giants dared to make war on the great Gods. Their army trod under foot mountains piled on mountains, and the stars then grew afraid of their new fellow-citizens. The Father of the Gods and King of the very Giants, mightiest source of destiny, Jupiter, spoke thus: "Let not earth hope to rise to the celestial regions, relying on these tricks, on these warriors. The Scottish ridges, mingling heaven with earth and hell, foretell an insane race. Edinburgh will rise, more lofty even than Olympus itself, and carry to the stars a race inimical to the Gods." Thus Jupiter. As fate willed, our city and the shrines of our Gods fell under a heavy curse.'

8: for *furiis eripiesq[ue], nobis*, other versions: *cui Jani in mense quotannis/ Mactatur patriis, dite jubente, Deus./ Sic te Bacchus amet, sic te conservet Apollo/ Advena sic furiis eripiare novis*, 'for whom, as Dis instructs, the God of their forefathers is sacrificed in January every year. May Bacchus be favourable to you, may Apollo keep you; may you be snatched away, stranger, from such new Furies!' (reference to Presbyterian celebrations of the anniversary of the execution of Charles I, 30 January 1649, an Episcopalian fast-day). After 48: BA(4): '**Finis/ Finis/** *At the end of the poem about the taverns was the following verses made by the same Authour which I think will trouble you a little to understand smartly*'. Lines 49–54 then follow. 55–56: BA(4), *Nam vicinus adest, ipso vigilantior Argo/ Qui tibi pro verbis vulnera forte dabit*, 'For a neighbour is there, more vigilant than Argo himself, who will perhaps give your words a painful reply.'

APP, 29–32, 3: for *cœlum feriantia, cœlo imitantia* with *cœlum ferientia* as an alternative; 12: *strenuus* for *impiger*; 14: *peperit* for *genuit*; 19: *Te quoque* for *Sæpeque*; 22: *alma* for *assa*; 39: *fluenta bibentes* for *gurgite nantes*; 40: *Adspicies* for *Agnoscas*; 41: *superis quid agatur in oris* for *rerum terræque relictæ*; 42: *mortali non memoranda* for *purpureo nectaris ore*; 49: *Sed* for *At*; 52: *gaudia clausa* for *promere vina*.

19

(i)

(a) *To M^r. B. Stote concerning the Edenburgh Taverns*

(b) (c) No Title

[(d) *Ad Advenas.*]

'Stranger, if you want to know our Gods, the ways of the people, and the genius of the place, investigate the Edinburgh city tenements which support the sky, and

Urbis Edinburgi cœlum feriantia tecta
  Antraque Cocyto pæne propinqua pete.
5 Protinus Ægidii triplicem te confer in ædem,
  Tres ubi Cyclopes fanda nefanda boant,
Verbaque dant populo, sed te, si Stotus es, ipse
  Servabis, furiis eripiesque; nobis
Bacchi sacra colas, et Phœbi numen adores,
10 Incolumis libes pocula multa Jovi.
Auspice nunc Luna, nunc auspice Sole bibendum,
  Potabis noctes impiger atque dies.
Nunc te Clavigeri delectent pocula Styli,
  Quem genuit Baccho pulchra Garumna patri.
15 Deinde alii heroes, navis quos accipit Argo,
  Monstrabunt veterum pocula magna Ducum.
Et nunc suaviloquam Buchanani exquirito Kettam,
  O, quoties placuit frons mihi læta viri!
Sæpeque Barcina decorati tempora vite
20 Commoda Tennenti visere tecta decet,
Ipse dabit vinum vultu suadente bibendum,
  Ostreaque in testis inferet assa coquus.
At si crescit amor pisces condire Lyæo,
  Et socios lepores piscibus esse cupis,
25 Instructus canibus, variisque Cuthelius hamis,
  Optatas mensæ suppeditabit opes.
Fors etiam volucres adjungere piscibus audes,
  Et vetitis epulis accubuisse placet?
Has tibi Redæo quæ nunc viret arbor in horto,
30 De Paradisiaco littore rapta dabit.
Sed nos Haia vocat non ditior altera vini
  Fœmina, nec tota blandior urbe cluet.
Denique speluncam penetrare juvabit Avernam,
  Antraque quæ nunquam Phœbus Appollo videt.
35 Sed placare memento canem quæ limina servat;
  Adferet indigenam protinus Anna merum.
Interiora petas, sedesque invise beatas,
  Hae norunt solem, cum præit Anna, suum.
Quas illic animas Lethæa gurgite nantes
40 Agnoscas, quales patre jubente jocos!
Scilicet immemores rerum terræque relictæ
  Gaudia purpureo nectaris ore bibunt
Sed superas iterum vos eructare sub auras
  Hoc opus, hic ingens est aliquando labos.

their cellars, which almost border the banks of Cocytus. Take yourself directly to the triple temple of Giles, where three Cyclops bellow unspeakable sermons, cheat their congregations. But if you are Stott, you will save yourself by your own efforts. Cultivate the rites of Bacchus with us, and revere the power of Phoebus, safely pour many libations to Jupiter. Under the auspices, now of the Moon, now of the Sun, you must drink, you will quaff diligently by night and by day. Now let the cups of key-bearing Steill delight you, whom the beautiful Garonne bore to father Bacchus. Afterwards other heroes, the crew of the ship Argo, will show you deep cups of ancient princes. And now look for the smooth-talking Katy who serves Buchanan. O how often the happy appearance of the man has pleased me! You must also visit the commodious premises of Tennant, whose temples Catalan vine adorns. With persuasive countenance he'll give you wine to drink; his cook will serve you roasted oysters in their shells. But if a desire grows in you to season fish with wine, and you want hare to accompany fish, Cuthel, who can handle dogs and a variety of hooks, will abundantly supply the resources you desire for your table. Perhaps you're bold enough to combine fowl with fish and you want to take your place at forbidden feasts? These the tree which now grows green in Reid's garden, snatched from the shore of Paradise, will provide for you.

 But Hay calls us; in the whole city no other woman is held to be richer in wine, nor more charming. Then you will be delighted to penetrate the cave of Avernus and the grotto which Phoebus Apollo never sees. Don't forget to placate the bitch guarding the threshold. Anna will at once bring you the wine of the country, neat. Go inside, visit the seats of the blessed, who will have acknowledged Anna, when she goes before them, as their own Sun. What souls will you see there, swimming in the water of Lethe, what wit, if Father [Bacchus] orders! Forgetful for sure of business and the world they have left, they drink the joys of nectar with empurpled lips. But to belch yourself forth again under the breezes of heaven, this is sometimes a task, a mighty labour. So, when you make the descent, take to

45 Ergo tibi fidum cape descensurus Achatem;
   Dic Annæ 'Comiti vina negato meo.'
Artibus his olim Castor et Pollux ab antro
   Ditis ad æthereas emicuere domos.
Sed simul ac iterum sub cœli veneris axem,
50   Et veteres nostra videris urbe faces,
Proderit astriferos Rossi cognoscere vultus,
   Grajaque Vasconicis gaudia clausa cadis,
Hic sapiens fies, et fortis, Gallica sed tu
   Hospitia et reges commemorare cave
55 Nam vicinus agit, quem impune lacessere, censor,
   Crede mihi, nulli bis potuere. Vale.

(ii)

Poema Pitcarnii M.D.

Qui mihi combibulus puer es cupis atque jocari
   Huc ades et manibus pocula sume tuis.
Mane tibi primo generosos accipe potus,
   Hispano miscens pinguia jura mero.
5 Attamen in primo facies ut rubra meroque
   Sint madidæ vestes prompta cervisia.
Desidiam fugiens cum te schola nostra vocavit,
   Adsis, nec totum sit bibere ulla mora.
Me præceptorem cernis cum vina bibentem
10   Pota combibulis ordine quisque tuis.
Tu quoque fac sedeas, quando tibi stare negatu[m]
   Amplius, ac, nisi sis solus, abire cave.
At magis ut quisque est potandi munere clarus,
   Hoc magis is clara sede locandus erit.
15 Nicotiana, tubi, calices et gallica vina
   Sint semper nugis anteferenda tuis.
Non tua rimosis fas est concredere testis
   Vina, sed humanis illa reconde cadis.
Sæpe propinato vinumque revolve palato
20   Cum sitias; nunc ex his bibe; nunc ex aliis.
Qui sitit et qui sæpe bibi[t] mea sceptra tenebit;
   Dum raro sitiens ejiciendus erit.

19 Text and Title. *F*(3). 11: we have substituted *negatum* for *negatus*; 21: *bibit* for *bibi*. 53–78 correspond to 11–48 of (i), with minor differences.

yourself a faithful Achates; say to Anna "No drinks for my friend!" By such arts Castor and Pollux once escaped from the cave of Dis to their homes in the sky.

But as soon as you reappear under the axle-tree of heaven and see in our city the ancient torches, it will be useful for you to recognise the starry features of Ross and Greek joys enclosed in Gascon flasks. Here you'll practise the sterner virtues; don't make a toast to French hospitality and kings. A censor plies his business in the neighbourhood, whom none, believe me, can provoke twice with impunity. Farewell!

(ii)

Poem by Dr Pitcairne

'You who are my pupil in social drinking and who also wish to play the fool, come here and take the cups in your hand. First thing in the morning, receive liberal draughts, mingling rich brose with Spanish wine. But still make it your first concern that your clothes have been visibly dampened with red beer and wine. Laying sloth aside, when my school-bell has summoned you, answer the roll-call and settle down at once to serious drinking. When you see me, your teacher, drinking wines, drink, each of you, in turn to your fellow-drinkers. Take care to find a seat when you're no longer able to stand and don't dare go away unless you're the only one left. The better the marks obtained in the drinking exercise, the better the place to be gained in class. Let tobacco, pipes, cups and French wines always be put before your trifles. Don't entrust your wines to cracked pots; lay them up in human vessels. When you thirst, always roll your wine on a pledged palate; drink now from these, now from those others. The thirsty man who drinks often will wield my canes, while the man who is seldom thirsty will be expelled.

Nil tam difficile quod non temulentia vincat;
    Bachare, et parta est gloria perpetua.
25 Nam veluti flores tellus nec semina profert,
    Ni illam humectat impluvialis aqua,
Sic calices manibus nocturnis atque diurnis
    Versandi vester ne sterilescat ager.
Estque inter socios Lex certa tenenda bibendi,
30   Ne nos offendat nescia garrulitas;
Incumbens cyathis submissa voce loqueris;
    Cum fueris potus, voce canorus eris.
Et quoscunque bibas calices vertantur ad unguem;
    Tum famulis hausto pocula redde mero.
35 Sed cave ne tangat bibituri brachia quisquam,
    Quod vino damnum non mediocre parit.
Si potum dedero, sic tu potare studebis,
    Principis ut palmas et mereare decus.
Et quoties potas, græcari rite memento
40   Et veluti scopulos pocula parva fuge.
Porro combibulis quoties te cunque rogabunt,
    Præbibe; qui sitiunt ad mea vota trahe.
Qui, licet haud sitiens, sitienti potat amico,
    Inde magis reliquis ipse sitire queat.
45 Nunquam tu tetricos imitabere Mohamedanos,
    Humani generis dedecus atque probrum,
Quorum tam rigidus nemo aut tam barbarus ullus
    Quem non potantem Francia tota probet.
Recte potandi si vis a me cognoscere leges,
50   Sumere si cupias fusius ore merum,
Perspice qui madidi dederunt exempla Catonis,
    Et quos Authores turba faceta colit.
Auspice nunc Luna, nunc auspice Sole bibendum;
    Potabis noctes strenuus atque dies.
55 Nunc te clavigeri delectent pocula Steeli,
    Quem peperit Bacho pulchra Garumna patri.
Deinde alii heroes, navis quos recepit Argo,
    Monstrabunt veterum pocula magna Ducum.
Et nunc graviloquam Buchanani exquirite Kittem;
60   O quoties placuit frons mihi læta viri!
Hinc te digressum Dallasius accipit, Heros
    Et major proavis Briggnis ille suis.
Dumque speluncam penetrare juvabit Avernam,
    Antraque quæ nunquam Phœbus Apollo vidit.

POEM 19

Nothing so difficult but drunkenness will beat it. Play the Bacchanal and everlasting glory comes to birth. For as earth causes neither flowers nor seeds to grow unless it is moistened by rainwater, so, to maintain the fertility of your field, your cups must be plied in your hands by day and by night. There is one certain rule for drinking with boon-companions, not to permit ignorant chatter to offend us. Speak with a hushed voice when devoting yourself to your goblets; when you have finished drinking, you will be in full musical voice. And whatever you drink, turn your glasses fully up, then return them to the barmen with the wine fully drained. But take care not to jostle someone's arms when he's in the act of drinking; nothing damages wine so much. If I stand you a drink, take care to drink it in a way which will put you in line for the glory of the dux medal. And whenever you drink, keep in mind to play the Greek properly; steer clear of little cups as if they were reefs. Rather, drink to your fellow-drinkers as often as they ask you; drag the thirsty ones to my devotions. Anyone who is not thirsty but who drinks to a thirsty friend, as a result is himself able to thirst more than the rest. Never imitate the gloomy Mohammedans, the shame and disgrace of humanity. Not one of them is so inflexible or so barbarous that the whole of France might not approve of him if he drank. If you want me to teach you the laws of drinking properly, if your desire is to savour wine more copiously in your mouth, observe those who have quoted the distichs of drunken Cato and the *auctores* frequented by the merry band. You must drink under the auspices, now of the Moon, now of the Sun; you will quaff energetically night and day. Now let the cups of key-bearing Steel delight you, whom the beautiful Garonne bore to father Bacchus. Afterwards other heroes, the crew of the ship Argo, will show you deep cups of ancient princes. And now look for the grave-talking Kitty who serves Buchanan. O how often the happy appearance of the man has pleased me! When you leave, the Dallasian hero, greater than his Briggnian ancestors, receives you. Finally you will be delighted to penetrate the cave of Avernus and the grotto which Phoebus

65 At pacare memento canem qui limina servat.
    Tum cyathos puri nectaris Anna dabit.
Interiora petas; sedes invise beatas;
    Hæ norunt solem, cum præit Anna, suum.
Quas illic animas lethæa fluenta bibentes
70   Aspicies, quales patre volente jocos.
Scilicet immemores superis quid agatur in oris
    Gaudia mortali non memoranda bibunt.
Sed revocare gradus superasque evadere in auras,
    Hoc opus, hoc ingens est aliquando labor.
75 Ergo tibi fidum cape descensurus Achatem;
    Dic Annæ, famulo vina negare meo.
Artibus his olim Pollux et Castor ab Antro
    Ditis in æthereas emicuere Domos.

Finis

POEM 19

Apollo has never seen. Don't forget to placate the bitch guarding the threshold. Then Anna will give you cups of pure nectar. Go inside; visit the seats of the blessed, who acknowledge Anna, when she goes before them, as their own Sun. What souls will you see there, drinking the waters of Lethe! what wit, if Father [Bacchus] permits! Forgetful for sure of events in the world above, they drink joys which human memory cannot retain. But to recall your steps and escape to the airs of heaven, this is the task, this is sometimes the mighty labour. So, when you make the descent, take to yourself a faithful Achates, say to Anna, 'No wine for my man!' By such arts Pollux and Castor once escaped from the cave of Dis to their homes in the sky.'

End

20

Gualteri Dannistoni ad Georgium Buchananum Epistola et Buchanani Responsum

Gualterus Dannistonus Lectori S.D.

Cum essem Georgio Buchanano scripturus, non dubitavi, quod eum talibus delectari nossem, ad ipsum mittere Psalmi Davidici a me in Latinos modos versi Exemplar: quo viso magnus ille Vates non poterit non sibi plaudere, mihique ipsum æmulari nequicquam conanti gratias agere.

I

Dexteram invictam canimus Jovemque,
Qui triumphatis hominum & Deorum
Præsidet regnis, animatque magnam
  Numine molem.

5 Quam tuæ virtus tremefecit orbem
Juppiter dextræ! sacra tu sereni
Pandis, immensum veluti volumen,
  Atria Cœli.

Orbis ac uni tibi nota summa
10 Orbium, & nantes per inane vastum
Vi tua Terræ, Jovis esse clamant
  Omnia plena.

---

20 Title: 1700 print thus; so 1706 print; SP, 56 (save for place and name of publisher). APP, 35, is headed *Ad Georgium Buchananum 1705*. APP, 42, is headed *Paraphrasis sequens* (i.e., the translation), *una cum subnexo Carmine ad G. Buchananum, edita est Anno* MDCCVI. On p. 47 appears *Ad Georgium Buchananum*, on p. 49 *Georgius Buchananus Gualtero Dannistono Sapere*. Titles and texts in APP are in Gregory's hand. **Text**: 1700 print, pp. 1–15, with unnumbered page of *Corrigenda* and *Mutanda*; APP, 35–36 (an abbreviated version of II only, lacking *Corrigenda* and *Mutanda*); APP, 42–49, preceded on pp. 37–41 by a transcription of Dennistoun's translation in *Octupla*; SP, 56–66; *Corrigenda* and *Mutanda* are inserted above the line as alternative readings.

Under *Corrigenda* there are two entries, ten under *Mutanda*. In the text, we have incorporated *Corrigenda*, simple corrections of printing errors. The *Mutanda* are improvements suggested by Pitcairne, and as all occur in verses by Dennistoun (see below), we have included them under **Notes** rather than in the text. For the most part they are incorporated in SP.

The printer was the Jacobite, James Watson (1664–1722), best known for his *Choice Collection* (Edinburgh, 1706–1711); see too below, **35**, 3n, Harriet Harvey Wood (ed.), *James Watson's Choice Collection of Comic and Serious Scots Poems*, II, STS (Aberdeen, 1991), ix–xvi. In APP, the titles suggest that later editions of the present collection were printed in 1705 and 1706. As noted under **Title**, an edition, probably also printed by Watson, appeared in 1706, *Gualteri Dannistoni ad Georgium Buchananum epistola, conscripta anno aerae Christianae* M.DCC.VI.; this appears to be the one to which Gregory refers. He seems not to have known the 1700 edition.

20

The Letter of Walter Dennistoun to George Buchanan and Buchanan's Reply 1700. At the Press of James Watson in Edinburgh

Dear Reader,

When I started to write to George Buchanan, I had no hesitation in sending him a copy of a Psalm of David which I had paraphrased in Latin verse, because I knew that he was charmed by such translations. When he has seen my version, that great poet cannot but congratulate himself and thank me for my vain attempt to rival him.

Walter Dennistoun.

I

'We sing the invincible right hand of Jove who holds sway over the conquered kingdoms of men and Gods, and whose spirit animates the mighty mass.

How has the power of your right hand, Jupiter, made the world tremble! You open the sacred halls of peaceful heaven like a huge book

The world and the totality of worlds known only to you, the earths by your power swimming through the vast inane – all proclaim that they are full of Jove.

Tu domos priscæ penetras Abyssi,
Tu rotis nubes vehis inquietis,
15 Et manus ventis tua Dædaleas
    Assuit alas.

Jura tu brutis facilesque leges
Rebus imponis, quibus antra parent
Æoli, parent rapidæ fluenta
20   Fervida flammæ.

Illa quam nobis patriam dedisti
Nobilem, Tellus, hominum stativis,
Fert tuas laudes per aprica nostri
    Littora Solis.

25 Tu jubes illam placita revolvi
Orbita, gyros sibi constitutos
Audeat ne quo violare quondam
    Avia saltu.

Tu Salo victis dominante ripis
30 Merseras Terras Hominesque, & omnis
Montis illusit juga vis aquarum,
    Iraque Ponti.

Voce sed magna monitæ Tonantis
In suas Undæ recidere sedes,
35 Et minas Ponti domat infrementis
    Reddita Tellus.

Illa disjectis moderanter undis
Vox, salutari penitus ruina,
Montium nasci juga, valliumque
40   Æquora jussit.

Arduum sævis Marium procellis
Littus opponis, tumidumque arenæ
Aggerem, quem non superabit æstu
    Unda rebelli.

45 Attamen dulces latices in omnem
Depluis vallem, tibi quos ab alveo
Phœbus excivit Maris, atque nubes
    Traxit ad altas;

You penetrate the homes of primeval Chaos, you bear the clouds on restless wheels, and your hand has stitched Daedalean wings to the winds.

You impose duties and easy laws on brute matter, which the caves of Æolus obey, which the glowing streams of swift fire obey.

That Earth, which you gave to us as noble home, to serve as dwelling place of man, bears your praises throughout the warm shores of our Sun.

You command her to return by the track which pleases you, lest she should ever in any way dare to go out of the path and leap to violate the course set for her.

You had drowned lands and men when the ocean tyrannized over its conquered margins, and the entire force of the water, the wrath of the sea, made sport with the mountain-ridges.

But the waves returned to their natural place, admonished by the great voice of the Thunderer, and the restored Earth tamed the threats of the roaring Sea.

When the waves had been brought under control, that Voice ordered the mountain-ridges and the valley-plains to be born in a beneficial internal convulsion.

Against the savage tempests of the seas you set the steep shore and the swelling bulwark of sand, which the wave will not conquer with insurgent tide.

For all that, you rain down on every valley sweet showers which Phœbus at your behest has called from the sea-bed and has dragged to the high clouds;

Quos bibunt densæ pecorum catervæ,
50 Quos feræ potant, aviumque turmæ,
Queis sitim pellunt Onagri colentes
    Invia tesqua.

Tu doces lætas volucrum cohortes
Ramulos parvis onerare tectis,
55 Et levi, propter latices, morari
    Otia cantu.

Proluit siccam pluvialis Æther
Barbam, & arentes humeros Atlantis,
Gratum opus glebæ sitientis agris
60   Agricolisque.

Ebria epotis alacrisque Tellus
Nubibus gramen pecori dicatum,
Divitem, humani pretium laboris,
    Sufficit herbam.

65 Vita frumentis alitur, Falerno
Redditur vivax, Oleo nitescit
Frons, & ærumnas animis abesse
    Indicat atras.

Syderum invadit patriam propago
70 Arborum potis animosa rivis,
Et caput Cedrus Libani voluptas
    Nubibus infert.

Cedrus incertis Avium catervis
Dat lares dulces, Abies Pelargum
75 Accipit civem piceo salubris
    Grataque succo.

Cuncta Divini regit ordo fati,
Montium Damis juga destinantur,
Inter & rupes latebras Echinus
80   Invenit aptas.

Tu stato Lunam reditu fatigas,
Solis alternas radiis corusci
Objicis Terras, retrahisque furvæ
    Noctis in umbram.

Which the close-packed herds of cattle imbibe, which the wild beasts and the flocks of birds drink, by which the wild asses that inhabit the trackless deserts quench their thirst.

You teach the joyful companies of birds to load the branches with their little dwellings, and because of the showers to delight their leisure with cheerful song.

The rain of the atmosphere washes out the dry beard and the withered shoulders of Atlas, a task most acceptable to the fields of the thirsty land and to farmers.

The eager Earth, drunk from the clouds it has swallowed, furnishes rich grain dedicated to the herd, rich grass, the reward of human labour.

Life is sustained by the corn; it is invigorated by Falernian wine; the forehead begins to glitter with olive-oil, and shows that black troubles have gone away from our minds.

The progeny of the trees, animated by the rivulets it has drunk, invades the country of the stars, and the cedar, the delight of Lebanon, lifts its head to the clouds.

The cedar gives sweet homes to the uncertain troops of birds, the silver fir, pleasingly wholesome with sap black as pitch, accepts the stork as an inhabitant.

The order fixed by divine fate rules all things; the mountain ridges are destined for fallow deer, and the hedgehog has found a suitable hiding-place among the crags.

You weary the moon by returning it to its [former] state. You expose lands in succession to the rays of the brilliant sun and drag them back to the shadow of dusky night.

85 Eripis Soli, tenebrisque Terras
    Tradis ereptas, Fera tum relictis,
    Ut famis suasit rabies, cavernis
        Territat Orbem.

    Ille prædonum Leo sævientum
90 Rex, & ipsarum Domitor Ferarum,
    Inverecundo licet ore, supplex
        Te rogat escam.

    Sol, ut aversæ rediere Terræ,
    Cogit occultis stabulis Leones,
95 Tum levant turmæ Pecorum diurno
        Corpora somno.

    Tum quoque ipsorum Domitor Leonum
    Excutit somnos Homo, tum labores
    Impiger poscit, reficitque sero
100   Membra sopore.

    Quanta solertis Monumenta Dextræ
    Eminent! Dextræ, freta quæ facesque
    Syderum, & terras moderatur omni
        Sole calentes.

105 Quæ per immensas Pelagi paludes
    Piscium mutos populos, pecusque
    Sole vix utens agit, & profundo
        Gurgite versat.

    Hic volant Puppes, choreasque Cete
110 Improbas campo celebrant in udo,
    Humidum vulgus stupet, & per imas
        Diffugit undas.

    Quæ fovet Tellus, fluidumque Regnum
    Tethyos, turmas miserans egenas,
115 Tu foves solus, recreasque dulci
        Munere vitæ.

    Dividis seclis alimenta, Dextram
    Laudat altricem Tribus omnis, & Te
    Exigit vitæ variam statutæ
120   Auspice sortem.

You take lands away from the sun and hand them, thus deprived, over to darkness. The wild beast then leaves his dens, as the frenzy of hunger urges, and puts the world in terror.

The very lion, king of savage predators and lord of the beasts themselves, begs food from you as a suppliant, although with shameless mouth.

As the lands which had been turned away return, the sun forces the lions back to their secret dens. Then the herds of cattle raise their bodies from daily sleep.

Then too Man, lord of the very lions, shakes off sloth; then he is diligent in demanding work and renews his limbs with slumber in the evening.

How pre-eminent are the works of your skilful right hand, your right hand which controls the straits and the torches of the stars and the lands warmed by every sun!

Which conducts the mute fish population, and the herd which scarcely experiences the light of the sun, through the immense oozes of the main and occupies it in the ocean depths.

Here ships run before the wind, and the whales perform their monstrous dances in the wet open sea; the watery folk are amazed and scatter through the depths of the waves.

Pitying the needy multitudes, you alone foster and refresh with the sweet gift of life that which the Earth and the liquid kingdom of Tethys fosters.

You distribute nourishment through the ages; every tribe praises your fostering right hand and completes the varied lot of life determined under your auspices.

Tu relegatas animas in Orcum
Trudis, & vitæ rubicunda rumpis
Stamina, occlusis adytis viisque
    Sanguinis almi.

125 Ast ubi fibris residem ciere
In suos flexus placuit cruorem,
Tum ferax natis subito renidet
    Terra Colonis.

Omnis Hunc Tellus colet, omnis Ætas
130 Dicet æterno celebrem triumpho,
Ipse lustrabit placido beatas
    Lumine Terras.

Illius nutu trepidare magnus
Orbis, excelsi trepidare Montes,
135 Et metum mista tremulo favilla
    Prodere fumo.

Juppiter carmen mihi semper, illum
Nostra clarabit Lyra, dum nec anni
Denegant vires, neque sanguis arti
140   Tardior obstat.

Juppiter solus mihi Rex, & auctor,
Illi ego inducam choreas ovantes
Victor, Eois numeris peritus
    Pangere Carmen.

145 Ipse des, Terra Pietas ut omni
Regnet, & Virtus rediviva Cœlo
Æquet Humanum Genus, illud a Te
    Juppiter ortum.

II

Ad Georgium Buchananum

Regia deseritur Ditis, Proserpina Matrem
    Quærit, & ad superos prima capessit iter.
Æacus & Minos vacuo spatiantur in Orco:
    Nec, quos castiget, Rex Rhadamanthus habet,

You thrust souls which have had their day into Orcus, and break the ruddy thread of life, when the sanctuaries and routes of the nourishing blood have been shut up.

But when it has pleased you to urge into its windings the blood that remains in the fibres, then suddenly the fruit-bearing Earth shines again at the birth of husbandmen.

The whole earth will worship him, every age will call him renowned in everlasting triumph. He will himself make the blessed lands bright with mild light.

At his nod the great globe shakes, the exalted mountains shake and betray their fear by ashes mingled with wavering smoke.

Jupiter is my song for ever; him my lyre will celebrate so long as the years keep my powers undiminished and more sluggish blood does not hinder my art.

Jupiter alone is my king and creator; for him I shall bring forward choral celebrations of my victory, skilled to compose a song in Eastern measures.

For your part, grant that Piety may reign over all the earth, and that renovated Virtue may equate with heaven the human race, itself sprung from you, Jupiter.'

II

To George Buchanan

'The palace of Dis is deserted; Proserpina seeks her mother and is first to make the journey back to those who live on Earth. Aeacus and Minos stroll about in an empty Orcus; King Rhadamanthus has no one to punish. And are you still

5 Et tu lentus adhuc dubitas, Buchanane, redire?
     Nec Patriam curas visere rursus Humum?
  Quæ nunc assidue tua Regni Jura reposcit,
     Et dolet oblitam se nimis esse tui,
  Oblitam nimis esse sui, quam sævior hoste
10   Impius exagitat Relligionis amor.
  Ergo redi; non te redeuntem deserat ille
     Qui cecinit Scotis, Arma virumque, modis,
  Non cui dicta volat divini Gloria Vallæ,
     Non cui Brussiades Nobile Carmen erat.
15 Primus ad Æthereas remeabit Gramius auras
     Adsuetus Vallum scandere, Roma, tuum.
  Duglasiûmque sequetur ovans Exercitus omnis,
     Hajaque Nobilitas, Indomitusque Kethus.
  Non tamen his cedent, fortissima pectora, Keri,
20   Non Homii virtus nescia stare loco,
  Non Leslæa virum Dîs formidata propago,
     Quam colit & semper Regia Fifa colet.
  Non Moravûm Proceres, Vallæque Dromondius ultor,
     Non animis ingens Setoniana manus.
25 Non aberunt Clarii genus insuperabile, non qui
     In Pelagus Vemia celsus ab arce tonat.
  Non alii Heroes, quos Scoticus extulit Orbis,
     Queisque dedit paucos Anglia Terra pares.
  Hi, Duce te, Cœli rursus convexa subibunt
30   Grampia; Quos plausus tum Buchanane feres!
  Unus eris, quem nos semper venerabimur, Unus
     Æacus & Minos & Rhadamanthus eris.
  Ergo redi; Musamque refer, quâ sæva domabas
     Monstra, Sacerdotum Pontificumque genus.
35 Nunquam major erat Musam tibi Caussa ciendi,
     Non aliud tali tempus egebat ope.
  Quippe tui Cives, mutato nomine tuti
     Rursus Hamiltoni Præsulis ora vident.
  Ille redit, secumque trahit quot Erinnyas Orcus,
40   Quotque Sacerdotes Pontificesque fovet.
  Ficta Fides comes est, perjuria mille sequuntur,
     Fictaque Paupertas, Impietasque furens.
  Hic tamen huc rediit, Buchanane, scelestior illo
     Cui tua Tartareas Musa dicavit aquas;
45 Credibile hunc illum est Nomen mutasse genusque,
     Et Circen nostris antetulisse Diis.

lazily hesitating to return, Buchanan? Have you no wish to revisit your native soil, which once more eagerly demands your *De Jure Regni* and laments that it has been overforgetful of your work, overforgetful of itself, agitated as it is by an impious love of superstition, more savage than any foe. So come back! As you return, may he not desert you who sang *Arma virumque* in Scottish measures, nor he whose poem on the glory of the divine Wallace spreads its wings, nor he who wrote that noble epic, the *Bruce*. Grim will be first to return to the breezes of the upper air, Grim accustomed to storming the Wall which was yours, o Rome! The entire triumphant army of the Douglases will follow, the nobility of Hay and Keith the indomitable. The Kerrs, bravest hearts, will not yield place to them, nor will the restless courage of Hume, nor the men of the House of Leslie, feared by the gods, a house which the kingdom of Fife honours, and always will honour. Nor will the Earls of Moray be absent, Drummond avenger of Wallace, the great-souled Seton family, the unconquerable kindred of Sinclair, and the noble race which thunders to the sea from Wemyss castle. Nor will the other heroes whom the realm of Scotland extols, whose equals have seldom been found in England. Under your leadership, all these will ascend once more to the Grampian vault of the sky. What applause will then be yours, Buchanan! You will be the one whom we shall always hold in reverence, you will be our Aeacus and Minos and Rhadamanthus. So come back, and bring with you the Muse, by whose influence you tamed savage monsters, the race of priests and bishops. Never was their greater need for you to set your Muse to work, no other period demanded such a task. Once more your countrymen see the face of an Archbishop Hamilton, disguised by a change of name. He returns, and with him drags all the Furies, all the priests and bishops taken by Orcus to its bosom. Feigned Loyalty is his companion; a thousand Perjuries follow, feigned Poverty and mad Impiety. But yet he returns, Buchanan, a man more wicked than he for whom your Muse decreed the waters of Tartarus. Possibly the two are one, with a change of name and family, and a preference for Circe over our native gods. Both are known to you, for who could

Notus uterque tibi, Quis enim te fallere speret?
  Quo nemo speret plenior esse Deo.
Incute Vim calamis, & diâ Carminis Arte,
50 Ista sub Infernas Monstra retrude Domos.

III

Georgius Buchananus Gualtero Dannistono
SAPERE.

Dannistone, meæ quid turbas otia vitæ,
  Quam juvat Elysias ducere propter aquas?
Nonne fuit satius tentare poemata nostri
  Davidis, & Lamias sollicitare leves;
5 Quam Cereri natam rursus promittere? non est
  Materies isthæc viribus æqua tuis.
Illa quidem priscis licuit cantare poetis,
  Cum caruit tutâ fabula nulla fide.
Sed manes meliora vident, quos detinet Orphei
10 Barbiton, & terris castior Orcus habet.
Hic secura quies, nulla hinc exire cupido,
  Hic placet, hic solum sors sua cuique placet.
At tua jampridem se lævi moribus Orci
  Induit, & vitiis Tartara vincit humus.
15 Nec Rhadamanthus adest, populusque impune scelestus
  Criminibus certat turpior esse novis.
Ergo omnis Terras Orco periere relicto
  Illa Sacerdotum perniciosa cohors,
Et quicunque dabant Rhadamantho vindice pœnas,
20 Quam bene Virgilio cognita turba meo!
Et tu vane pios revoces ad secula manes
  Impia, & Elysias depopulere domos?
Tu potius terras perituraque regna relinque,
  Pitcarnumque viæ, si volet, adde tuæ.

hope to escape your notice, you, than whom no one could aspire to be more fully in touch with God. Put vigour in your pen, and use the divine art of poetry to thrust these monsters back to their infernal abodes.'

III

George Buchanan to Walter Dennistoun
BE SENSIBLE!

'Dennistoun, why do you disturb my leisurely life which I am happy to lead by the waters of Elysium? Surely it was more than enough to make an attempt at the Psalms of our David and conjure up bug-a-boos? Which daughter do you propose to return to Ceres? That theme is beneath your powers. Such a subject was indeed permitted to early poets, when every story received unqualified assent. Better visions are reserved for the blessed dead, whom the lute of Orpheus detains and a purer Orcus holds in his realms. Here there is lasting repose; there is no wish to leave. This is the place to be, the only place where everyone is contented with his lot. But your land has long since clothed itself with the customs of an ill-omened Orcus and has outdone Tartarus in its vices. There is no Rhadamanthus there, and the wicked population strives unchecked to invent new, more vicious slanders. Thus that whole pernicious cohort of priests and all who were paying the penalty with Rhadamanthus as avenger – a mob very familiar to my Virgil! – have abandoned Orcus and spilled over every land. Are you vainly trying to call holy souls back to an unholy age and lay waste our Elysian homes? Rather, give up the world and its transient kingdoms, and, if he is willing, bring Pitcairne on the same road as yourself.'

SATIRIC AND PHILOSOPHICAL POEMS IN ELEGIAC COUPLETS

21

(a) *Joanni Duci Roxburgi, Archibaldus Pitcarnius S.D.*
[(b) *Gualterus Dannistonus Georgio Buchanano S.*]

Cum me nuper participem fecerit Mercurius carminis, quo Dannistonus noster, Georgium Buchananum, nemoris Elysii tum novus hospes, compellavit; rem auribus tuis haud indignam facturus mihi videor, si carmen ipsum ad te transmittam, & animum ordinandæ Reipub. natum, ejusque summa negotia librantem, paulisper alliciam ad hæc levia, & inimicas corpori curas aspernantia, consulamque civis illius saluti, cujus beneficio multi mortales vitam in otio transigunt nullis periculis adfini. Vale.

   Tandem regna mei pereuntia liquit imago,
    Alloquerer Manes ut, Buchanane, tuos.
   At comes esse viæ Pitcarnius abnuit; illum
    Detinet Albini nobilis ordo soli,
5 Ante omnes Kerus; quis enim non dicere Kero
    Carmen amet? solus carmina Kerus amat.
   Solus digna facit divino carmine, solus
    Defendit patriæ Tartara vestra suæ.
   Ille suis arcet Lethæa fluenta poëtis,
10   Et negat effœtæ credere carmen aquæ.
   Ille epulis Divûm vates accumbere jussit
    Primus, & ætherei nectaris esse potes.
   Jamque bibit nectar pleno Pitcarnius ore,
    Jam Kerum læti Stotus & ille canunt.
15 Anne putes illos, si Kerum linquere vellent,
    Nectare florentes linquere posse cados.

21 **Title and Text**: *SP*, 39–40; *APP*, 50 (with **Title**, (b), but without prose introduction). In *APP* the text directly follows 20.

21

Archibald Pitcairne writes to John, Duke of Roxburghe.

'*Since Mercury recently delivered me a copy of the poem in which our Dennistoun, then a new guest in the Elysian grove, addressed Buchanan, it seemed to me that I would be doing something not unworthy of your ears if I were to send the actual poem off to you, and attract a soul, born for the common weal and pondering its supreme affairs, to these light-weight matters which despise Care, foe to the body, and that I should look after the welfare of that citizen, by whose benevolence many mortals pass life at leisure far from any hazard. Farewell.*'

'At last my ghost has left the realms that perish, in order that I may speak to your spirit, Buchanan. But Pitcairne has refused to accompany me on my way — the noble families of the Albine soil detain him, Ker more than any other, for who would not like to compose a poem to Ker? Ker alone loves poetry. Alone he does deeds worthy of divine song, alone he keeps your Tartarus at a distance from his native land. He keeps the streams of Lethe away from his poets and refuses to entrust a poem to degenerate water. He is foremost to invite bards to recline at the banquet of the Gods and to be [drinkers?] of celestial nectar. Now Pitcairne drinks his fill of nectar. Now Stot and he sing joyously of Ker. Even if they were willing to desert Ker, do you really think that they could abandon their jugs frothing with nectar?'

SATIRIC AND PHILOSOPHICAL POEMS IN ELEGIAC COUPLETS

22

(a) *Archibaldi Pitcarnii*
Scoti. Carmen.
Anno Aetatis suae LX.

[(b) **Joannis Sylvij** *de seipso carmen.*]

[(c) **Gualterus Dannistonus**
Ad Amicos]

Dum moriens laetor redeuntis munere vitæ
　Adfectoque viam sedibus ire Deum,
Brittanna Druidum Sophia, Gallisque superbus
　SCOTUS avis, animas morte carere cano.
5 Has ego corporibus profugas ad sidera mitto,
　Sideraque ingressis otia blanda dico.

22 Title. (a) *N(7)*; (b) APP, 3 (not in Gregory's hand), BA(4), f.2, SP, 1; (c) *N(98), (99)*; BA(4), 2, 3; BA(4a), 1; BD(b). **Text**. In versions (a), (b), and (c), as above, the first four lines differ according to title. The text printed is that under (a), from its title to be dated late in 1712 or early in 1713, perhaps during Pitcairne's last illness.

Under (b), dating from 1703 or earlier, the reading is:

Dum brevis adnitor momentum fallere vitæ,
Et somni æterni non nimis esse memor:
Demonstro; quæ sit sophiæ Natura: quis hospes
Pectoris, atq[ue] animas posse perire nego.

'As long as I exert myself to ignore the moment of brief life and to forget, so far as I can, the everlasting sleep, I demonstrate what is the nature of wisdom, and who dwells in the heart, and I deny that it is possible for souls to perish.'

(c), in library catalogues usually dated 1710, reads:

Dum Studeo fungi fallentis munere vitæ,
Adfectoque viam sedibus Elysiis,
Arctoâ florens Sophiâ, Samiisque superbus
Discipulis, Animas morte carere cano.

'While I am busy carrying out the duty of deceitful life and strive to find a way to the Elysian Fields, singing that souls are immortal, I abound in Northern wisdom and am made arrogant by the disciples of Samos.'

In (a) the text is so arranged that ll. 1–10 stand visually as well as thematically separate from the remainder of the poem.

Prior's paraphrase (see *Commentary*) is based on (c) and usually printed with it. In *N(7)*, however, it is printed with (a) and includes a translation of the appended Pauline quotation.

9: for *Cœlicolis*, (b) and (c) read *Cœlitibus*. 11: for *Divi*, (b) and (c) read *cœli*. 15: for *& vitæ*, (b) reads *ac vitæ*; for *mittere*, (b) reads *fallere*. 19–20: not present in (b) and (c). 24: for *atque*, (b) reads *ac*.

In (b) and (c) there is no footnoted quotation from *1st Corinthians*. There are also minor typographical differences between the three versions.

22

(a) *Walter Dennistoun To his Friends*

(b) *Poem about himself by Johannes Sylvius*

(c) *Poem by Archibald Pitcairne, Scot, when he was sixty years old*

'While I am busy carrying out the duty of deceitful life and strive to find a way to the Elysian Fields, singing that souls are immortal, I abound in Northern wisdom and am made arrogant by the disciples of Samos. Souls I despatch to the heavens, refugees from the body, and when they have entered the heavens, I proclaim for

Qualia conveniunt Divis, Queis fata volebant
  Vitai faciles molliter ire vias.
Vinaque Cœlicolis media inter gaudia libo,
10 Et me quid majus suspicor esse viro.
Sed fuerint nulli, forsan, quos spondeo, Divi,
  Nullaque sint *Ditis* Numina, nulla *Jovis*;
Fabula sit terris agitur quae vita relictis,
  Quique superstes, Homo, qui nihil, esto Deus:
15 Attamen esse hilares & inanes mittere curas
  Proderit, ac vitae commoditate frui,
Et festos agitasse dies aevique fugacis
  Tempora perpetuis detinuisse jocis.
Omnibus interea mortalibus esse benignos,
20 Atque, etiam *nullis*, solvere vota Diis.
His me parentem praeceptis occupet Orcus;
  Et mors seu Divum, seu nihil esse velit:
Nam Sophia ars illa est quae fallere suaviter horas
  Admonet, atque Orci non timuisse minas.

PAULUS *ad Corinthios Epistolae Primae, Sectione 15mo, Paragrapho 19ma.*

Si huius duntaxat vitae gratia in Christo spem habemus, omnium sumus mortalium miserrimi.

them soothing repose, such as befits Gods for whom the Fates willed that they should travel smoothly on the effortless paths of life. I pour wine in libation to the Celestials in the midst of their joys and fancy that I am something more than man. But even if the heavens, to which I pledge myself, had no existence, even if there were no powers of Dis, none of Jove – if it were a fable that life carries on after the world has been abandoned and that whoever has survived as a human being, though he is nothing, let him be God – even so, it would profit us to be merry and abandon all futile cares, enjoying the benefits of life, celebrating days of festival, and lengthening our fleeting span with perpetual rejoicing. May Orcus take me as a follower of these rules, and Death, whether it intends me to be one of the Gods or nothing. Wisdom is the science which advises me to beguile the hours pleasantly and to have had no fear of the threats of Orcus.

PAUL, in the 19th verse of the 15th chapter of the First Epistle to the Corinthians:

"If we have hope in Christ for the sake of this life only, we are of all Men most miserable."'

3
Wives and Daughters

23

Ad Annam Pitcarniam

Anna mihi genuit te Margaris Haia, nulli
    Inferior forma vel pietate Deae.
Non Matri cedis, si quam decet esse perennam,
    ANNAE divinae Erroliaeque places.

24

(a) *In Uxorem suam*

[(b) *In Mortem Uxoris* Pitcarnii]

[(c) *In Margaretam Haiam conjugem suam*]

Quam cito te nobis, Longe Gratissima Conjunx,
    Eripuit fati deproperata dies.
Scilicet haec ipsos Contemnunt fata Poetas,
    Parsq[ue] mei potuit, Me superante, mori.
5 Haud ita perpetuam spondent tibi Carmina vitam
    Nostra, nec extingui me superante potes.
Si potuit virtus et honestae gratia mentis,
    Ante diem Stygio praeda fuisse Duci:
At non Haia tamen Pitcarni, regna silentum
10   Adspiciet, versu facta perenna meo.

23 **Title and Text**: two identical prints, *N(83)*.
24 **Title**: (a) APP, 19; (b) BA(4), f.7ʳ; (c) SP, 13. **Text**: APP, 19, thus; BA(4), f.7; SP, 13–14.

23

To Anne Pitcairne

'Anne, you were borne to me by Marjorie Hay, inferior to no goddess in form and piety. You don't yield place to your mother, if it is fitting for any woman to be Perenna, you please the divine Anna and her of the race of Errol.'

24

(a) *On his Wife*

[(b) *On the Death of Pitcairne's Wife*]

[(c) *On his wife, Margaret Hay*]

'How quickly the day hastened on by fate has snatched you from me, most deeply beloved wife! These Fates certainly consider even poets of no importance, and a part of me could have died, even when I was still alive. Not so! – my poems promise you eternal life; while I am still alive in them, your light cannot be put out. Even if virtue and the beauty of an honourable mind could, before its time, have become the prize of the lord of Styx, even so, Hay, wife of Pitcairne, will get no glimpse of the kingdom of the silent, transformed by my verse into Anna Perenna.'

25

(a) AD
Elisam Pitcarniam
10 *Junii*, 1710.

[(b) *Ad* **Elisam Pitcarniam** x.
die **Junii** *natam*]

Te quoque Sol vidit nascentem, Filia, luce,
   Qua Dominum nasci viderat ante Tuum.
Ille Deum nulli cedit pietate nec armis,
   Et tua nullius forma secunda Deæ.

26

AD
JOANETAM PITCARNIAM
Decimo **Junii** *Natam.*

Te placidus vidit Sol nasci, Filia, luce,
   Qua **Dido** nasci viderat ante meam.
Tu similis **Didus** maternis moribus esto,
   Pitcarna Regem relligione colens:
5 Relligione colens Pitcarni, cujus avita
   Est pro **Jacobo** laus voluisse mori.

27

AD
MARGARITAM PITCARNIAM

OCTAVUS Martis Te jussit, Filia, nasci,
   Et te, **Nassovi**, nemine flente mori.
Felix ille mihi fulsit Populisque **Britannis**,
   Proveniant tales terque quaterque Dies.

---

25 Title: (a) N(22); BA(4a),6; R¹, 22; HRHRC, PR 3619 P54 A82 1710; (b) SP, 67. **Text**: as above; SP, 67, 3, reads *fulget virtute secundus* for *cedit pietate nec armis*. Note that in SP there is no indication of year of composition.
26 Title and Text: N(50).
27 Title and Text: N(25); HRHRC, PR 3619 P54 A86 1712; SP, 68. In l. 2, SP has N....vi for Nassovi.

25

To Eliza Pitcairne, 10 June 1710

[*To Eliza Pitcairne, born on the 10ᵗʰ day of June*]

'The Sun saw your birth, daughter, on the day on which he had previously seen the birth of your Lord. He yields to none of the gods in piety or arms, and your beauty comes second to that of no goddess.'

26

To Janet Pitcairne, Born on the Tenth of June

'A mild sun saw your birth, daughter, on the day which had previously seen the birth of my Dido. Keep to the customs of Dido your mother, maintaining the Pitcairne faith by reverencing the King, maintaining the faith of Pitcairne, whose ancestral renown is to have been willing to die for James.'

27

To Margaret Pitcairne

'The eighth of March ordained your birth, daughter, and your unlamented death, Nassau. Happy was the dawn of that day for me and for the British people! May such days befall us time and again!'

28

AD JANUM

    Jane, Tui sexto mihi Filia prodiit *Agnes*,
        Agnes ter fausto digna venire die.
    Ter decimum *Jani Agnes* indignata videre,
        Quem nemo lacrymis orba videre potest,
5 Incidit in luctus, et morti paene propinqua,
        Octavo *Martis* denique salva fuit.
    Et Decimo *Juni* maternis risit in ulnis,
        Illo saepe die rideat Illa Patri.

28 Title and Text: *N(24)*; HRHRC, PR 3619 P54 A76 1712; *SP*, 68. In *SP*, l. 3 reads *Agnes ter decimum Jani indignata videre*; otherwise the texts differ only typographically.

28

To Janus

'Janus, on the sixth of your month my daughter Agnes was born, Agnes thrice worthy to arrive on a festal day. Vexed to see the thirtieth of January, which no one can see without tears, she became grievously ill and almost close to death, then at last on the eighth of March recovered. On the tenth of June she smiled in her mother's arms. May she often smile at her father on that day!'

4
Physicians and Surgeons

PHYSICIANS AND SURGEONS

29

(a) BALFOUREUS *moriens loquitur*

[(b) *In D.* AND. BALFOUREUM, *M.*
D. Equitem auratum]

    Quis magis aut sapere, aut vitæ plus optat habere:
        Vixi dum licuit vivere et esse probum:
    Vixi dum terræ prius haud mihi visa ferebant
        Regnaque Neptuni dum nova monstra dabant.
5 Omnia nam vidi quæ tellus educat omnis
        Omnia quæ Thetidos divitis unda vehit
    Jamque nimis notæ terræque undæque valete
        Nunc juvat ignoti scire quid astra premant.

30

(a) *In Robertum Sibaldum. M.D.*

[(b) *In Robt: Sib:*]

[(c) *In* D. ROBERTUM SIBBALDUM *de Cyphiis*, MD. *Equitem auratum*]

    Te quoque Grampicolæ viderunt cedere fatis,
        Et patrio condi vir Cyphiane solo
    Fata tamen cedent famæ cinerique Superstes
        Diceris Bodiis par similisque Tuis.
5 Dum procul a Geneva se Summovet Inclyta Roma,
        Quod quam sit Longum, scit Cyphianus iter:
    Dum Coi præcepta senis, Senecæque legentur,
        Tot quibus annorum futile turget opus
    Dumque tot Inculti queis horret Scotia, montes
10   Exiles fundent squalidulasq[ue] rosas:

---

29 Title: (a) *APP*, 24, *BA(4)*, fo.9ᵛ, first hand; (b) *SP*, 14. **Text:** *APP*, 24; *BA(4)*, fo.9ᵛ, first hand; *SP*, 14. The texts differ only in punctuation.

30 Title: (a) *APP*, 12 (b) *BA(4)*, f.6ᵛ; (c) *SP*, 12. **Text:** *APP*, 12; *BA(4)*, ff.6ᵛ–7ʳ, where, in l. 3, *famæ* has been inserted for deleted *fata*; in l. 6, the *u* in *longum* for deleted *a*. Save for the alterations, the text in *SP*, 12–13, is essentially identical.

29

(a) *Balfour speaks as he dies*

[(b) *On Sir Andrew Balfour, M.D.*]

'Whoever wishes to extend his knowledge or to enjoy a longer span, *I* lived as long as it was permitted me to live and keep my integrity. I lived as long as the land brought me things I had not seen before, as long as Neptune's realm produced new monsters for me. For I have now seen everything which the entire earth brings forth, everything which the wave of rich Thetis bears. Farewell, land and water now over-familiar! My intended pleasure is to know the secrets concealed in the stars.'

30

(a) *On Robert Sibbald* MD

[(b) *On Rob*ᵗ. *Sib.*]

[(c) *On Sir Robert Sibbald of Kipps,* MD, *Knight*]

'The Grampian people have seen you too, Kipps, yield to the Fates and be interred in your native soil. The Fates however will yield to Fame and you will outlive your ashes and be named as precisely resembling your Boyds. As long as famous Rome stays far from Geneva (Kipps knows well how long the road between them is), as long as the precepts of the old man of Cos and of Seneca are read (with references to whom swells your futile work of so many years), and so long as the multitude of uncultivated peaks, with which Scotland bristles, produces meagre and miserable little roses, the ungrateful oblivion of ages to come will not oppress

Non te ingrata prement venturi oblivia sæcli,
　Nec deerunt Cyphijs carmina digna tuis
Verum digna Deis atque immortalia furta
　Quid majus facient te, Cyphiane, viro.

31

Q. Horatio Flacco
Archibaldus Pitcarnius Caledonius

Dive, dic vatem medicumve Phœbo
Editum, quem nunc referam, moneque
Qua via possim quoque gratiosus
　　Dicier illi;

5 Quo potest terris nihil exoriri
Inscio, invitove repullulare;
Qui pater vatum viget, et medentum
　　Ultimus auctor:

Et bonum vestris, Epidaure, misit
10 Anguibus virus, docuitque, Chiron,
Te suas artes, voluitque nato
　　Esse magistrum, et

Scire quo luco legeretis herbas
Utiles ægris, pater ipse queis se
15 Præbeat pulcro deditis et æquo
　　Sæpe colendum.

Ille te duxit pater, Æsculapi, in
Aonas montes, equitemque nondum
Orphei ritu satis assuetum
20　　Carmine morbos

Pellere, et mores animi rebellis
Corpori infestos cithara domare, et
Mollibus lenire modis nocentem
　　Pectoris æstum.

31 **Title and Text**: *N(16)*; HRHRC, PR 3619 P54 Q2 1708; *SP*, 48–50. The texts differ only typographically.

you, nor will songs worthy of your Kipps be lacking. Your immortal thefts, worthy of the Gods, will turn you, Kipps, into something truly greater than a man.'

31

Archibald Pitcairne, Caledonian, to Quintus Horatius Flaccus

'Departed spirit, sing the poet or physician begotten by Phoebus, whom I shall now invoke. Explain the way or method by which I may come to his favour.

Nothing can rise from the earth without his knowledge, or burgeon once more against his will, he who flourishes as father of poets and final authority for physicians.

And he gave your serpents, Epidaurus, a beneficial poison, and he taught you, Chiron, his arts, and chose you as teacher for his son, and

To know the grove in which you might collect herbs helpful to the sick, himself the father who offers himself for worship to those dedicated to the beautiful and the equitable.

As your father, he led you, Aesculapius, into the Aonian mountains, and to a horseman not yet fully accustomed to the expulsion of illnesses by song in the Orphic manner,

And to use the lyre to tame the habits of a rebel mind inimical to the body, and to calm with gentle harmonies the hurtful surge of the heart.

25   Hæc sed incrementa fuere Phœbi,
     Ante Trojani furias duelli,
     Quo ferox Pelei suboles parabat
        Carmen Homero.

     Ad meum veni, Venusine, seclum,
30   Quo novus Pollux, novus atque Castor
     Brittonum cœlo micuere grato
        Munere Phœbi.

     Castor es Grai, Batemanne, Pollux,
     Sonticos ambo superare morbos
35   Inclyti, ac iram superum periti a–
        vertere terris.

     Castor et Pollux mihi nunc vocandi,
     Brittonum semper populis adeste,
     Et viæ ignaris medicis favete
40   Sidere fausto.

32

[(a) *Ad Robertum Morisonum. M.D.*
et Botanices Professorem Oxoniensem]

[(b) *In Effigiem* ROB. MORISONI, *Botanices*
in Academia **Oxoniensi** *Professoris.*]

Quæ, Morisone, viro potuit contingere major
    Gloria, Pæonium quàm superasse genus?
Ipse Tibi palmam Phœbus concedit Apollo,
    Laureaque est capiti, quælibet herba Tuo.

Aliud

5 Dum genera herbarum divinâ digeris arte,
    Evolvisque alto semina mersa chao,
  Quid possint hominum vires, verique labores,
    Quamque Deo similis sis, Morisone, doces.

---

32 Title: (a) APP, 34; *(b)* SP, 82. **Text**: S, f.22 (in letter of Pitcairne to the Dr Robert Gray, dated 6 August 1697 [Johnston, *Best of our owne*, 23, letter 8 – part quotation], written as liminary verses for R. Morison and J. Bobart, *Plantarum Historiæ Universalis Oxoniensis Pars Tertia* [1699]); APP, 34; SP, 82. The second epigram is found only in APP.

But these were the actions of Phoebus before the mad passions of the Trojan War, in which Peleus' fierce issue provided an epic for Homer.

I have arrived at my own time, Venusian, in which a new Pollux, and also a new Castor, have glittered in the British heaven by Apollo's gracious gift.

Gray, you are Castor, Bateman Pollux, both famously skilled in conquering serious diseases and turning away from Earth the wrath of God.

I now call on Castor and Pollux to help the British peoples at all times and to extend the happy influence of their sign on physicians unacquainted with the way.'

32

(a) [*To Robert Morison, Doctor of Medicine and Professor of Botany at Oxford*]

(b) [*On the portrait of Robert Morison, Professor of Botany in Oxford University*]

'What greater glory can come to a man, Morison, than to have outdone the Paeonian race? Phoebus Apollo himself grants you the palm. Every plant is a laurel for your head.'

Another

'While you classify plant species with divine skill and unfold their origins sunk in deep chaos, you demonstrate the capabilities of human powers in the search for truth, and your own resemblance to divinity, Morison.'

33

AD PHOEBUM APOLLINEM

Dic mihi qui Medicae mortalibus Auctor es artis,
    Qui mores hominum nocte dieque vides,
Dic mihi si dignus potuit Te Phoebe videri,
    Si fuerit Clarii Numine dignus avi,
5 Qui natos negat esse Patrum quos orbis adorat,
    Quique negat Divos ante fuisse viros.
Hunc Tu si nescis, *Pitcarnius* Ille docebit
    Qui *Phaeton* alter debuit esse Tibi.

34

(a) *In Davidem Haium Medicum*

[(b) *In Mortem Dav: Hay M.D.*]

[(c) *In D.* DAVIDEM HAIUM, *M.D. Equitem auratum.*]

Haie cui primos pepererunt flagra triumphos,
    Et medici titulos Abredonensis Anus,
Quemque opibus Conjunx alienis fecit opimum,
    Quemque Legi indignus nobilitavit Arabs.
5 Te tandem tuus Orcus habet, te Civibus Orci
    Gratius haud unquam misit Apollo Caput.
Quippe tuo jussu terras Liquere, putentque
    Tartara se jussu Linquere posse tuo.

---

33 Title and Text: *N(23)*; *BA(4a)*,12; *SP*, 67. In l. 8, *SP* reads *Phaethon* for *Phaeton*. Other typographical differences are minor.

34 Title: (a) *APP*, 11, not in Gregory's hand; (b) *BA(4)*, fo.6ᵛ; (c) *SP*, 12. **Text**: *APP* thus; so *BA(4)*, but with abbreviations, indicated by a colon; *SP*, 12. In l. 1 *SP* has *Hai* for *Haie*, but otherwise differs only typographically.

33

To Phoebus Apollo

'Tell me, you who established the medical art for mortals, who see night and day the ways of humanity, tell me if he has seemed worthy of you, Phoebus, and if he will have seemed worthy of the spirit of his Sinclair ancestor, he who denies that children are the offspring of fathers whom the world adores, and who denies that the Gods previously were men. If you don't know this fellow, that Pitcairne of yours will show you who ought to have been a second Phaethon to you.'

34

(a) *On Dr David Hay*
[(b) *On the Death of David Hay, M.D.*]
[(c) *On Sir David Hay, M.D., Knight*]

'Hay, for whom whips produced your first triumphs and medical qualifications from the old wife of Aberdeen, and whose lady enriched you with another's money, and whom an Arab not worth reading ennobled, your Orcus has you at last – Apollo never sent a head more gratifying than yours to the citizens of Orcus. They abandoned Earth, in fact, on your prescription; let them think that by the same prescription they can now get out of Tartarus.'

35

[(a) *Ad Kirktonum Chirurgum*]

[(b) *Ad* GEO. KIRKTONUM Chirurgum.]

Dum nimis indulges sævo Kirtone dolori,
    et frustra sospitum vis revocare patrem,
eriperis nobis Quid nos Quid Grajus et Qui
    plus Oculis placuit Clarkius Ille tibi?
5 Nempe quod extinctis fecisses Optime nobis
    Manibus offerimus pocula sæpe Tuis.

36

(a) A D

Georgium Kirtonum,
PROSERPINÆ a Potione

Nuper *Hamiltonus* vacuæ pertœsus *Edinæ*,
    Fugit ad Elysium flebilis umbra nemus.
Vir bonus, & quo non recti servantior alter,
    Et quem qui nosset *Saxo* vel hostis amet,
5 *Potterius* comes est, ambo Junonis alumni,
    Quæ lucem humano commodat alma gregi,
Hos ad Reginæ Thalamum, perducito vestræ
    Infernum *Diti* parturit Illa Jovem.
Fata novum spondere Jovem cecinere poetæ,
10   Qui Superum posset non minor esse Deo;
Quique patrem regno spoliaret ut alter opimo,
    Ter gratum Bardis temporis hujus opus.
Et jam tota sacro vexantur Tartara bello,
    Diffugiunt manes quâ data porta pii.
15 Dis redit ad *Gallos*, & *Pictos Scoto-Brigantas*,
    Et nemus Elysium deserit ipse Cato.
Macte novo Domino, mihi fas sit, Dive Georgi,
    Libare antiquo pocula sæpe Jovi.

---

35 Title: (a) APP, 27; (b) SP, 31. **Text**: S thus; APP, 27, Oxford, BA(4), fo.12ᵛ, SP, 31 differ as follows: 2: *ereptum* for *sospitum*. 3: *Uatsonus* for *Grajus*. 4: BA(4) reads *tui* for *tibi*. Otherwise the texts differ only in details of abbreviation, punctuation and capitalization.
36 Title and Text: (a), N(66); (b), SP, 31–32.

35

[(a) *To Kirkton, Surgeon*]

[(b) *To George Kirkton, Surgeon*]

'Kirkton, while you abandon yourself to devouring grief and wish in vain to call back your late father, you are being snatched from us. How do I react? How does Gray and that Clark of yours who pleased you more than your eyes? Why, Sir, as you would have done, had we been the ones to die – we offer frequent libations to your shade.'

36

(a) *To George Kirkton, from the Draught given to Proserpine*

'Recently Hamilton, disgusted by an empty Edinburgh, fled, lamented shade, to the Elysian grove, a good man and unrivalled observer of right, whom anyone who had known him, Englishman or enemy, would love. Potter is his comrade, both fosterlings of Juno, who graciously bestows light on the human race. Guide them to the bedroom of your Queen. She is in travail with Infernal Jupiter to Dis. Poets have sung that the Fates promise a new Jupiter, who would not be less than any other of the gods above, and who, like the other, would despoil his father of a rich kingdom, a procedure thrice gratifying to bards of this age. And now Tartarus entire is troubled by a holy war. The pious shades disperse by any exit available. Dis returns to the French and the painted Scoto-Brigantes, and even Cato himself deserts Elysium. Good luck to the new Master! but may it be lawful for me, sainted George, to pour frequent libations to the old Jove!'

(b) *Ad Eundem*

Clarkius, & quæ te quondam lætata sodali
    Floruit, ah! nimium nunc lacrymosa cohors,
Te salvere jubent; Manesque decentia castos
    Gaudia non fictâ relligione vovent.
5 Noster Hamiltonus nuper, nunc vester, Edinæ
    Prætulit amplexus deliciasque tuas.
Vir bonus, & quo non recti servantior alter,
    Et quem qui nôsset Saxo vel Anglus amet:
Poterus comes est, ambo Junonis alumni,
10   Quæ lucem humano commodat alma gregi,
Hos ad Reginæ thalamum perducito vestræ,
    Infernum Diti parturit illa Jovem.
Fata novum debere Jovem cecinere poëtæ,
    Qui supero posset se perhibere parem.
15 Hæc etiam nostris placuit sententia Bardis,
    Queis nulli plures percoluêre Deos.
Macte novo Domino, liceat mihi, care sodalis,
    Libare antiquo pocula sæpe Jovi.

37

PITCARNIUS *rogat* THO. KINKADIUM *ut ad se veniat Decima* Junii, *quæ sacra est Divæ* MARGARITÆ *Scotorum Reginæ.*

Kinkadi, jucunde comes Dromondi,
Sis Die mecum, Dea Margarita
Quâ Deos olim voluit sodales
    Visere rursus.

5 Alvous tecum, Buchananus ille,
Atque Fribarnus veniant amici,
Queis Deûm nullus magè te colentes
    Mittere speret.

Namque græcandum est, decimàque Juni
10 Vina libandum Carolo & Nepoti,
Quem suis misit decus adfuturum
    Diva Britannis.

37 Title and Text: SP, 41–42.

POEM 37

(b) *To the Same*

'Clark, and the fellowship which flourished in your company – once joyful, now, alas! overfull of grief – wish you well, and in a spirit of true religion vow the celebrations appropriate to your chaste spirit. Recently Hamilton, once ours, now yours – a good man who was more observant of right than anyone else, and who would be loved by anyone who knew him, Angle or Saxon – preferred your embraces and delights to Edinburgh. Potter is his companion, both fosterlings of Juno, who graciously bestows light on the human race. Guide them to the bedroom of your Queen. She is in travail with Infernal Jupiter to Dis. Poets have sung that the Fates owe us a new Jupiter, who would be able to declare himself equal to the Capitoline, and this prophecy pleased the bards of our own time, who have honoured more gods than anyone else. Good luck to the new Master! but may it be permitted to me, dear comrade, to pour frequent libations to the old Jupiter!'

37

Pitcairne invites Thomas Kinkaid to visit him on the Tenth of June which is a feast-day of St Margaret Queen of Scotland

'Kinkaid, Drummond's light-hearted companion, be with me on the day on which St Margaret once wished to see her saintly cronies again.

Let your friends Alves, the famous Buchanan, and Freebairn come with you. None of the saints would hope to send anyone more favourably disposed to yourself than these.

For on the Tenth of June we must feast like Greeks, and pour out libations to Charles and his Nephew, whom the saint has sent to be the future glory of her Britons.'

38

THOMÆ KINKADIO *Chirurgo*, ARCHIBALDUS
PITCARNIUS *Chirurgus*, S.D.

    O salutaris militiæ decus,
    Spes Æsculapi, spes Podalirii,
        Fessi laborum te vocamus,
           Et vocat, ipse vocat, Lyæus

5 Te fratre gaudens; Phœbus ubi cadit
    Linquitque cassos luce Machaonas,
        Nostros revisurus labores,
           Kinkadiumque sibi secundum.

    Princeps coronet vina Dromondius,
10 Haurire cogat pocula Barclius,
        Ridere Clercus, cum jocosis
           Nos salibus volet esse lætos.

    Manè ad labores ritè redibimus,
    Te salutaris militiæ Duce,
15   Nos tum Æsculapi, rursus ægris
           Adspicietis opem ferentes.

39

Roberto Graio
Scoto
Londini Medicinam Profitenti
Archibaldus Pitcarnius
Scotus
S.

    Ille qui terris latitat Britannis,
    Solus, aut nullo sapiens amico,
    Ille quam debet miser inquefelix
        Vivere, Grai?

---

38 Title and Text: SP, 42–43.
39 Title and Text: N(15); HRHRC, PR 3619 P54 R62 1708; SP, 46–47. In the title SP has 'Arch.' for 'Archibaldus'; otherwise the texts differ only typographically.

38

Archibald Pitcairne, Surgeon, greets Thomas Kinkaid, Surgeon

'Pride of the company of healers, hope of Aesculapius, hope of Podalirius, wearied by our labours, we summon you: Lyaeus too summons you, gives you a personal summons,

Rejoicing in you as a brother, when Phoebus sets and leaves the Machaons bereft of light, but will soon see our work beginning again, and Kinkaid second only to himself.

Let Drummond be preses and crown the wine, Barclay compel us to drain our cups, Clerk make us smile, since he wants us to be merry with his jolly witticisms.

In the morning we shall duly return to work, with you as leader of the company of healers. You will then see us once more bringing to the sick the help of Aesculapius.'

39

Archibald Pitcairne, Scotsman, writes to Robert
Gray, Scotsman professing medicine in London.

'He who lurks in Britain, alone or as a friendless savant, what obligation has he, Gray, to live in wretched unhappiness?

PHYSICIANS AND SURGEONS

5 Audiit nunquam meditante Stoto
 Carmina Eoas domitura tigres,
 Proximum aut Phœbo Priorum canentes
  Dulce Camœnas.

 Ille quid credat redeuntia astra
10 Solis ac lunæ sibi dedicari,
 Se nisi ut solum miserumque posset
  Sæpe videre?

 Quid putes mi nunc animi esse soli,
 Postque tot raptos inopi sodales,
15 Te fere solo superante, Te, ca-
  rissime Grai?

 Namque nos liquit decus illud ævi
 Scotici, sic Di voluere, liquit
 Regiæ stirpis decus atque fama
20 Gregorianæ.

 Ille Neutonum incolumem lubenti
 Narrat Euclidi Siculoque Divo,
 Miraque augusti docet almus Angli
  Cœpta stupentes

25 Deinde Pergæum reducem novumque
 Acris Halleii studiis; sed ipse
 Quam graves nuper tulerit labores
  Dicere parcit.

 Ista necquicquam memoramus: Ille
30 Immemor nostri, patruoque gaudens,
 Nos ope & cura sapientis orbos
  Liquit amici.

He has never heard Stott meditating songs able to tame Eastern tigers, or the Muses sweetly singing Prior, closest to Apollo.

Why should he believe that the returning months and years deserve his attention when he is able to see himself as often lonely and miserable?

What do you think my state of mind is, now that I'm lonely and poor, now that so many of my companions have been taken, with you almost the lone survivor, you, most beloved Gray?

As the Gods have willed, that ornament of the era in Scotland, that ornament and renown of the royal race of Gregor, has left us.

He is now giving news of Newton, still with us, to a delighted Euclid and the divine Sicilian: he graciously instructs his astonished audience in the wonderful work undertaken by the great Englishman

Then [he tells how] the Pergean has been recovered with new material produced by the labours of acute Halley: but he modestly refrains from talking about the important tasks recently undertaken by himself.

We bring them to memory in vain. Forgetful of us, and happy to see his uncle again, he leaves us bereft of the support and attention of our philosopher friend.'

40

(a) *In obitum* Archibaldi Stevensoni,
   Medicorum sui seculi facile principis

[(b) *In obitum* Archibaldi Stevensoni, *Medici Regii*.]

    Linquis invitas, venerande, Terras,
    Octies denos hilaris per annos,
    Qui salutato toties dedisti
        Gaudia Phœbo.

5   Quam putas illum rediise lætum
    Mane, tot vestrâ sibi restitutos
    Arte cernentem, reducesque dias
        Lucis in auras?

    Mille vixisse bene sanus æra,
10 Causa ni mortis gravis ingruisset
    Mors Homj, longè tibi carioris
        Lumine Phœbi;

    Mors Homî, cui non simile aut secundum,
    Ire sub terras potuit, nec alter
15 Acrior Rogis, Patriæ vindex
        Æthere vesci.

    Hunc sequi curas, et es assecutus;
    Jungitis dextras, lacrymasque gaudî
    Funditis plenas, melioris orsi
20   Stamina vitæ.

    Ergo concordes animæ valete,
    Usque dicendæ mihi, dum nec orcus
    Poscet effœtum, neque denegabit
        Carmen Apollo.

---

40 Title: (a), APP, 53 (in Gregory's hand); (b) SP, 34–35; (c) *N(10)*; HRHRC, PR 3619 P54 A94 1709; (d) R^1, 25. **Texts**: as above (a), (c), (d). The text of (b) resembles (a), but in 9 and 13–15 readings are as in (c).

40

(a) *On the Death of Archibald Stevenson,*
easily prince of the physicians of his time

(b) *On the Death of Archibald Stevenson, Royal Physician*

'You leave the reluctant earth, venerated one, blithe through your eighth decade, you who have so often renewed your joys after greeting the Sun.

How joyful do you think that he has returned, seeing so many restored to him by your art, and brought back to the breezes of the light of day?

You would have led your life in full vigour through three generations, had not a heavy cause of death fallen violently upon you, the death of Home, far dearer to you than the light of the Sun.

The death of Home, to whom nothing equal or second could pass to the world below, nor could another partake of the upper air, more grievous to pyres, avenger of his country.

You are striving to follow him, and now you have caught up. You shake hands and shed tears full of inward joy, beginning to weave the warp of a better life.

Therefore farewell, twin souls! to be ever commemorated by me, until Death demand my worn-out body and while Apollo does not reject my song.'

(c) Archibaldo Stevensono

Equiti, Scotorum Archiatrorum Comiti, Octogenario,
Socero suo,
Archibaldus Pitcarnius
S.

    Pallidi vivis bene spretor Orci,
    Octies denos alacer per annos,
    Qui salutato toties novasti
        Gaudia Phoebo.

5 Quam putas illum rediise lætum
    Mane, tot vestra sibi restitutos
    Arte cernentem, reducesque dias
        Lucis in auras?

    Duceres vitam viridis triseclem,
10 Caussa ni luctus gravis incubaret
    Mors Homi longe tibi carioris
        Lumine Phœbi:

    Mors Homi, quo non alium licebat
    Ire sub terras venerantiorem
15 Stirpis Augustæ, neque digniorem
        Æthere vesci.

    Attamen curas lacrumasque inanes
    Pone, spes gentis superat vetustæ,
    Qui tibi reddet placitum paterni
20   Oris honorem.

    Nos cito heroem adsequemur,
    Hoc quod est vitæ simile exuentes;
    Tumque sinceræ, Socer, ordiemur
        Stamina vitæ.

(d,1) *In undecimum* Martii, *quo ante*
annos octoginta natus est Archibaldus

Stevensonus *Medicorum apud* Scotos *facile Princeps*

    Lux optata nitet, quæ soles noctibus æquat,
      Quæque STEVENSONO stamina prima dedit
    Mortalis vitæ, quam multis ille tropæis
      Auxit, & in longam distulit arte viam;

POEM 40

(c) Archibald Pitcairne greets Archibald Stevenson,
Knight, Fellow of the Scottish College of Leading
Physicians, Octogenarian, his Father-in-law.

'You live well, despising pale Death, active through eighty years, you who have so often renewed your joys after greeting the Sun.

How joyful do you think that he has returned, seeing so many restored to him by your art, and brought back to the breezes of the light of day?

You would have led your life in full vigour through three generations, had not a heavy cause of sorrow worn you down, the death of Home, far dearer to you than the light of the Sun,

The death of Home, by comparison with whom no other of Edinburgh stock was permitted to pass below more greatly honoured, more worthy to enjoy the upper air.

For all that, lay aside sorrow and useless tears. The hope of the ancient race survives, who will restore to you the pleasing honour of his father's face.

We shall catch up with the hero quickly enough, laying aside this thing which resembles life. And then, father-in-law, we shall begin to weave the warp of a life uncorrupted.'

(d,1) On the eleventh of March, the day which,
eighty years before, saw the birth of Archibald
Stevenson, easily Prince of Physicians among the Scots.

'Now dawns the wished-for light which makes daytime and night equal, and which gave Stevenson the first threads of mortal life, augmented by him with many victories, and protracted a long way by his art. Fearing that mortals would

5 Quam ne mortales artem perdiscere possent,
 Ad superos ILLUM Juppiter arte tulit.

(d, 2) *On The Chief Physitian* SIR ARCHIBALD STEVENSON

Fancy the great *Hippocrates's* Art,
A faithfull Subject from a loyal Heart,
Kind Husband, tender Father, steady Friend,
Quick Wit, and solid Wisdom of the Mind:
5 Great STEV'NSON, who in all these did abound,
With Laurels never fading shall be crown'd.
His Soul was fixt to Monarchy and Church,
And ne're abandon'd either in the Lurch.
He all his Life with diverse Changes try'd,
10 Kept firm his first Uprightness till he dy'd.
STEV'NSON, who so cou'd die, and so cou'd live,
In spite of Death it self must still survive.

41

AD
ELISAM RAMISAEAM
ARCHIBALDI STEVENSONI
Medicorum Principis Conjugem,
ARCHIBALDUS PITCARNIUS

Magnanimis *Scotisque* Atavis dignissima vixti,
 Et *Stephani* Conjux digna fuisse, socrus
Pitcarni, Qui se Divina jactet *Elisa*,
 Et Medici Regis gaudeat esse gener.
5 Tu vigeas Qualis *Stephano* florente vigebas,
 Elysij Tales non habuere duos.

41 Title and Text: *N(62)*.

completely master the art, Jupiter exercised his own and took Stevenson to the heavens.'

41

Archibald Pitcairne on Eliza Ramsey, wife of the Prince of physicians.

'You have lived your life as most befitted your great-souled Scottish ancestors, and as worthy to have been Stevenson's lady, mother-in-law to Pitcairne, who is proud of the divine Eliza and glad to be son-in-law of the Royal Physician. May you continue to flourish as you did during Stevenson's lifetime! The Elysian Fields have never seen a couple to match you.'

42

[AD GULIELMUM KETHUM
Magnum Scotiæ *Mariscallum,*
Anno MDCCXII.]

    Jam te, Dive, tenent *Homius*, sapiensque *Stevinus*,
        Qui tecum verè vivere semper ament.
    Vivetis placidè, ac, velut hic vixistis, amicè,
        O' utinam memores, Dià caterva, mei.
5 His me narrabis lentum me credere Coelo,
        Dum SCOTUS Morino lentus ab orbe redit.
    JACOBO dices, ut Fratres *Issachar* omnes,
        Sub plusquam Pharium jusserit ire jugum.
    Singula dum memoras, Divos hortaberis altos,
10   Ut Domui vestrae semper adesse velint,
    Ut Patre Dite fatis faveant concordibus armis,
        Et Vallam jubeant rursus adesse suis.
    Te praeter nemo poterit Dis Gratior esse,
        Teque magis nemo Patrius esse Deus.
15 Contigit haud alii Majestas tanta leporis,
        Haud alij tantus contigit oris honos.

43

HERIOTUS
Senatui a se constituto sapere.

    Cnoxiaci nostram faedastis Fraudibus Aedem
        Doctrinae dociles impedijsse vias.
    At mihi *Makinius* si concedatur amicus
        Et Medicus, nostris mox erit alma Salus;
5 Et cum *Makinio* Leiturgia grata redibit,
        Quam *Martyr* voluit *Carolus* esse Meam.

42 Title: only in SP. Text: *N(37)*; HRHRC, PR 3619 P54 J3 1712; SP, 78–79. The texts differ only in minor points of typography.
43 Title and Text: *R¹*, 28.

42

[To William Keith, Grand Marischal of Scotland, in the year 1712]

'Now they hold you fast, blessed spirit, Home and wise Stevenson, whose wish would always be to live truly in your company. You will live, all three, in peace and friendship, just as you lived here. Remember me, divine brotherhood! You will tell them that while Scotus is slow to come back from France, I too am slow to entrust myself to heaven. You will tell Jacob how Issachar ordered all his brethren to submit to a yoke more than Pharaonic. While you are still giving individual bits of news, you will beseech the high gods that they may always champion your house, that they may unite with Father Dis and the Fates to favour our arms, and that they bid Wallace return to champion his people. No one will be dearer to the gods than you, no one more god of your family. Such dignity combined with charm, such high praise from men's lips, has never befallen another.'

43

Heriot, to the Board of Governors appointed by him, Be sensible

'By the deceits of the Knoxian you have defiled our temple and made difficult the docile path of learning. But if Mackenzie is confirmed as my friend and physician, deliverance and restoration will soon come to our children, and with Mackenzie will return the blessed Liturgy which Charles the Martyr decreed should be my own.'

44

In obitum ALEXANDRI MONTEITH *Chirurgi.*

Te quoque Kirktono comitem, Montethe, dederunt
  Parcæ, fatalem quàm nimis ante diem!
Nil tibi profuerant docti bona pectoris, et nil
  Arte Machaoniâ vix habuisse parem.
5 Dum patriæ servire studes, solarier ægros,
  Atque salutares tendis ubique manus,
Mors vetat everso quenquam succurrere sæclo,
  Et tibi Kirktonum suadet adire meum.

44 Title and Text: SP, 34.

44

On the Death of Alexander Monteith, Surgeon

'You too, Monteith, the fates have made a companion to Kirkton by how excessively untimely a death! The blessings of a learned heart had availed you nothing, nor did the fact that you scarcely had an equal in Machaon's profession. While you are doing your best to serve your country, to comfort the sick, and are extending everywhere your healing hands, Death forbids anyone to come to the aid of a world turned upside down, and persuades you to join my friend Kirkton.'

5
Friends and Opponents

45

AD
Robertum Lindesium,

Vidimus hæc pueri, Juvenes hæc vidimus arva,
    Hæc nos arva senes exanimesque vident.
At nova nos olim feret hæc super arva Juventus,
    Arva senectutis Libera facta minis.
5 Inque vices Telluris erunt Hominumque perennes
    Nunquam Lassandis gaudia vecta rotis.

46

(a) *In Joannem Patersonum*

[(b) *Inscriptio Domus Johan: Patersoni*]

[(c) *In Ædes* JOAN. PATERSONI.]

Cum victor Ludo, Scotis qui proprius, esset,
    Ter tres victores post redimitus avos,
Patersonus, humo tunc educebat in altum
    Hanc quæ victores tot tulit una, Domum.

---

45 Title and Text: *N(65)*.
46 Title and Text: (a) APP, 19 (not in Gregory's hand); (b) BA(4), f.7ᵛ; (c) SP, 33.

45

To Robert Lindsay

'These fields – we have seen them in boyhood, we have seen them in youth; in old age and death these fields see us. But one day renewed Youth will carry us over these fields, fields made free of the threat of old age. In the eternal vicissitudes of Earth and human beings, there will be joys borne on wheels that never weary.'

46

(a) *On John Paterson*

[(b) *Inscription on John Paterson's House*]

[(c) *On John Patersone's Tenement*]

'Since he became champion in the game which belongs to the Scots and was crowned as had been thrice three of his champion ancestors before, Paterson then raised from the ground to its present height this house which on its own had produced so many champions.'

47

(a) PYTHAGORAS SAMIUS
ET
ISAACUS NEUTONUS *Anglus.*

[(b) *De Neutono*]

[(c) ISAACO NEUTONO *Anglo*,
Mathematicorum omnis aevi Principi,
ARCHIBALDUS PITCARNIUS *Scotus*,
Plusquam *Nestoreos* Annos, hoc est, plusquam *Samios* optat.]

[(d) *In D. Isaacum Neutonum*]

Pythagora jactet *Samius* se fundus alumno
   Neutono Tellus gaudeat *Angla* suo
Magna utriusque quidem victuraque gloria glebæ
   Dum vaga *Phoeboeis* terra vehetur equis.
5 Sed *Samius* Magno toties superatur ab *Anglo*,
   Est major quoties *Anglia* Terra *Samo*.

Scribebat *Archibaldus Pitcarnius Scotus*.

---

47 Title: (a) N(9); (b) APP, 12, BA(4), f.7ʳ. (first hand); (c) HRHRC PR 3619 P54 T4 1710; (d) SP, 13. **Text**: N, thus. APP and BA(4): 1: *Jactet Pythagora* for *Pythagora jactet*. APP inserts *Aristarcho* as an alternative above *Pythagora*. 2: *gestit terra Britanna* for *Tellus gaudeat Angla*. 3: *Par* for *Magna*. 5: *Nam* for *Sed*; *tanto*[?] *magno* for *Magno toties*. 6: *Est quanto major terra Britanna* for *Est major quoties Anglia Terra*.
  HRHRC: 2: *gestiat* for *gaudeat*. 3 *cluet, mansuraque* for *quidem victuraque*. Title and Text follow 58.
  SP, 1: *jactat* for *jactet*. 2: *gaudet terra Britanna* for *Tellus gaudeat Angla*. 3: *mansuraque* for *victuraq*;. 5: *At* for *Sed*; *magno tantum* for *Magno toties*. 6: as in APP and BA(4).

47

(a) *Pythagoras the Samian and Isaac Newton the Englishman*

[(b) *On Newton*]

[(c) *For Isaac Newton, Englishman, Prince of Mathematicians of all times, Archibald Pitcairne, Scot, wishes more years than those of Nestor, that is, more than Samian*]

[(d) *On Sir Isaac Newton*]

'Let the Samian glebe pride itself on Pythagoras, its foster-child. Let the land of Britain exult in its own Newton. Great is the glory of either piece of ground, to live as long as the planetary Earth is carried by the horses of Phoebus. But the Samian is as many times surpassed by the great Englishman as England is bigger than Samos.'

FRIENDS AND OPPONENTS

48

(a) *D. Atkins Episcopus Orcadensis*
[(b) *In Mortem Episcopi Gallovidiensis*]
[(c) *In Jacobum Atkinsium Episcopus Candidae Casae*]

    Maximus Atkinsi pietate et maximus annis
        Ante diem Invitâ relligione cadis
    Ni caderes nostris Inferret forsitan oris
        Haud Impune suos Roma superba Deos.

49

Ad Walterum Dennistonum Ludi Magistrum Mussilburgensem

    Dennistone Deo nunquam non plene quis ausit
        Versibus armato displicuisse tibi?
    Massius ipse tuæ metuit jam fulmina Musæ
        Qui toties homines spreverat atque Deos
5 Et tandem bonus esse Cupit, si credere fronti
        Fas foret, aut posset Massius esse bonus.

48 Title and Text: (a) APP, 4; (b) BA(4), f.2ʳ; (c). SP, 3.
49 Title and Text: APP, 3. The poem has been crammed into the foot of the page by a hand different from either of the two principal hands in the MS.

48

(a) *Atkins, Orcadian Lord Bishop*
[(b) *On the Death of the Bishop of Galloway*]
[(c) *On James Atkins, Bishop of Candida Casa*]

'Greatly distinguished for piety and for length of years, you are nevertheless dead before your time, Aitken, and against the interests of true religion. If you were still alive, you might have ensured that proud Rome failed to import her Gods to our shores.'

49

To Walter Dennistoun Schoolmaster of Musselburgh

'Dennistoun, you who are perpetually filled by the God, who has dared displease you in your armour of verse? Massie himself, who so often had despised men and gods, has just now learned to fear the thunderbolts of your Muse and at long length wishes to become respectable – if only one could trust appearances or Massie were capable of respectability.'

50

(a) **Gualterus Danistonus**
SCOTUS
Sannazario Veneto
Propriam quietem
Gratulatur

[(b) *In* BELGAS]

Tellurem fecere Dii, sua littora *Belgæ*,
    Immensæque fuit molis uterque labos.
Di vacuo sparsas glomerarunt æthere terras,
    Nil ubi quod posset fallere cœpta fuit.
5 At *Belgis* operæ Divûm, naturaque rerum
    Obstiterat; tamen Hi verba dedere Diis.

MS insertion: *Obstitit; Hi tandem* –

ALITER

Tellurem fecere Dii, sua littora *Belgæ*,
    Immensæque fuit molis uterque labos.
Dî vacuo sparsas glomerarunt æthere terras,
10 Nil, ubi quod cœptis officiebat, erat.
At Belgis maria & cœli naturaque rerum
    Obstitit; obstantes Hi domuere Deos.

---

50 Title: (a) N*(100)*; HRHRC, PR 3619 P54 G8 1700Z; (b) APP, 5, BA*(4)*, f.3ʳ; SP, 3. **Text**: as under Title. In APP, BA*(4)* and SP the text is identical with the second version printed above, apart from 10, where the reading is *Nil ubi quod cœptis possit obesse fuit*, and 11, which has *Ast* for *At*.

50

(a) *Walter Dennistoun, a Scot, congratulates Sannazaro Venetian, on the repose he has deserved*

[(b) *On the Dutch*]

'The Gods made the Earth, the Dutch their own shores; both tasks were enormously difficult. The Gods fashioned the scattered lands into a globe in empty space, where there was nothing that could disappoint their plans. But the works of the Gods and natural law had obstructed the Dutch; however, these people cheated the Gods.'

Otherwise

'The Gods made the Earth, the Dutch their own shores; both tasks were enormously difficult. The Gods fashioned the scattered lands into a globe in empty space, where there was nothing that obstructed their plans. But sea and sky and natural law stood in the way of the Dutch; these people subdued the Gods who stood in their way.'

FRIENDS AND OPPONENTS

The Dalrymples

51

(a) *Vice-Comes de Stairs*

[(b) *Ad* JACOBUM *Vicecomitem de* **Stairs**.]

    Si potuit virtus, si numina juris et æqui
        Victurum toto nomen in orbe dare,
    Fama tibi crescet nullo delebilis ævo,
        Atque tuas laudes Phœbus uterque leget.
5 Sed quamvis meritis non essent numina testes,
        Nec legeret laudes Phœbus uterque tuas,
    Quatuor illa fori, proles tua, fulmina nostri,
        Fulmina mox nostro plura datura foro,
    Illa tuas celebrent laudes animasque quaternas,
10   Quas uni voluit Juppiter esse tibi:
    Munera, namque togæ feliciter omnia functas,
        Quæ nunc sunt nati quatuor, unus eras.

52

Ad D. DAVIDEM DALRYMPLIUM *Equitem &c.*

    Cum mihi difficili caussa licèt sis semper patronus,
        Et præstes linguæ juripotentis opem,
    Solvere conantem postico fallis amicum,
        Verbaque das Medico judicibusque simul.
5 Quid mihi nunc superest, quo te, patrone, rependam?
        Scilicet ut morbis dem quoque verba tuis.

---

51 Title. (a) APP, 34 (b) SP, 51. Text: APP, 34, thus. SP, 4: *canet* for *leget*; 6: *caneret* for *legeret*.
52 Title and Text: APP., 34; SP, 50–51.

POEM 52

The Dalrymples

51

(a) *Viscount Stair*

[(b) *To James, Viscount Stair*]

'If virtue, if the spirits of law and equity, have been able to grant you a name which will live all over the world, your reputation will grow untouched by the passage of time, and either Apollo will recite your praises. But even if the spirit should not bear witness to your merits, nor either Apollo recite your praises, let those four luminaries of the Scottish bar, your sons, soon going to give even greater brilliance to our bar, celebrate your deserts and the fourfold soul which Jupiter destined you as a single person to have: for you carried out with distinction all your services to the robe, and in your sole capacity were what your four sons now are.'

52

To Sir David Dalrymple, Baronet, etc.

'Since you are always my advocate in a difficult case and demonstrate your wealth of legally persuasive language, you practise witchcraft to win a backside release of your would-be friend, and deceive physician and judges alike. What's left for me now with which to repay you, my advocate? Of course, that I too should talk away your illnesses.'

FRIENDS AND OPPONENTS

53

Ad HUGONEM DALRIMPLIUM, *Supremi Senatus Juridici in* **Scotia** *Præsulem.*

Consultissime juris, atque rite
Fori juridici supreme Præses,
Gratias tibi maximas Mathesis
Agit, nobilis artium Patrona,
5 Tanto nobilior Patrona, quanto
Es tu gratior æquiorque Musis.

54

Ad Gulielmum Carmichael

Si Gulielme diem placido vis fallere risu,
  Frangere vis noctem si Gulielme mero;
Mitte fori rixas, et nos invise bibentes
  Ecce tuos clamans O Epicure deos.

55

(a) *Monopennius J.C.*

[(b) *In Mortem Gulliel*[mi] *Monneyp*[ennii] *Advocati.*]

[(c) *In* GUL MONNEIPENNIUM, *I.C.*]

Risus atque Joci Deorum Alumni
Læto pectore, libero ore nati,
Vos dehinc Iubeo miser valere
Nam qui vos coluit nimis, nimisque
5 Monneipennius ille, vester ille
Monneipennius omnium sodalis

---

53 Title and Text: HRHRC, PR 3619 P54 A72 1712; SP, 71.
54 Title and Text: APP, 33.
55 Title: (a), APP, 33 (in Gregory's hand); (b) BA(4), f.12ᵛ.; (c) SP, 32. Text: as (a), with contractions expanded within square brackets. The texts otherwise differ only in capitalisation and punctuation.
  In APP the text is followed by the word *Finis*.

186

53

*To Hugh Dalrymple, Director of the
Supreme Court of Law in Scotland*

'Most learned of lawyers and most properly Lord President of the Court of Session, heartfelt thanks are extended to you by Mathematics, noble patroness of the Arts, the nobler a Patroness, the more pleasing and friendlier you are to the Muses.'

54

To William Carmichael

'William, if you want to beguile the day with a gentle laugh, if you want to shorten the night, William, with unmixed wine, forget your legal wranglings and visit us as we drink, exclaiming, "Epicurus, behold your gods!"'

55

(a) *Moneypenny J.C.*

[(b) *On the Death of William Moneypenny, Advocate*]

[(c) *On William Moneypenny, I.C.*]

'Nurslings of the gods of laughter and mirth, born with light heart and free mouth, from this day forth I bid you farewell, for he who enjoyed your company (too much! too much!) that Moneypenny, that friend of yours, Moneypenny, boon companion to everybody, who conquered our mortal race with his sallies, has

FRIENDS AND OPPONENTS

Qui mortale genus jocando vicit
Vos secum rapuit, suo sepulchro
Vos condi voluit, facetiasque
10 Omnes in Stygii ablui fluento
Quare in perpetuum valete – manes
Conditi sale plurimo, valete.

56

(a) In Carolum Wilson

[(b) *Ad* ----------- VOLUSENUM.]

Vixisti Volusene tuis pergratus Amicis
   Te quoque non Musis gratior alter erat,
Sed frustra Musis frustra tot amatus Amicis
   Filia cum Cereris non sat Amica foret,
5 Illa quidem mœstos nimis aspernata sodales
   Te nobis proprium noluit esse Decus
Non totus moriere tamen Volusene sed Orci
   Effugies avidas, me revocante, manus
Quodque negant Medico concedent Fata Poetæ
10   Hic Superis reddet quem dedit ille neci.

57

(a) *Georg: Ferquhard ad uxorem demortuam.*

[(b) *Georgius Ferchard ad uxorem demortuam.*]

Qua mihi non vixit vexatior altera Conjux,
   Nec potuit nostro dignior esse jugo
Me sine securam per sæcla silentia vitam
   Esse solet qualis manibus Uxor age:

---

56 **Title**: (a) APP, 27 (b) SP, 30. **Text**: APP, 27; BA(4), f.11ʳ.; SP, 30.
   SP, 2: *Tu, quo* for *Tu quoque*; 10: *His* for *Hic*.
57 **Title**: (a) APP, 28, with *Lethensis* inserted above the line; (b) BA(4), f.14ʳ. **Text**: APP, 28; BA(4), f.14ʳ; SP, 33. APP and SP lack place and date.
   In BA(4) the epigram is the final poem to be copied by the first hand. Place and date apply to the entire first section of the MS. Unfortunately no year is indicated.

snatched you with him, wishes you to be entombed with him, and all his jokes to be washed in the waters of Styx. Therefore, Farewell for ever! Spirits well-seasoned with Attic salt, Farewell!'

56

(a) *On Charles Wilson*

[(b) *To ------------ Wilson*]

'Your life, Wilson, was very pleasing to your friends and the Muses loved no other more than you. But the love of the Muses and so many friends did not help you, when the daughter of Ceres was not sufficiently your friend. Indeed she too much despised your grieving companions, not wishing you to continue as our own special ornament. However, Wilson, you will not wholly die, but escape the greedy hands of Orcus, called back by me. Whatever the Fates deny to the Physician, they will concede to the Poet. The Physician passed sentence of death on you. The Poet will restore you to the upper air.'

57

(a) *George Ferchard to his Deceased Wife*

[(b) *George Ferchard to his Deceased Wife*]

'Spouse, than whom no other lived more vexatious to me, nor could be more deserving of my yoke, without me, wife, lead in security through the ages of

5 Impositumque tuo saxum prægrande sepulchro
    Non Leve præteriti pignus Amoris habe.

[Edinburgh
Feb'y 1]

58

THOMÆ BOERO Scoto, **Matheseos et Medicinæ** Professori,
ARCHIBALDUS PITCARNIUS Scotus, S.D.

1 Salutatum properè virorum
  Maximum, cui te placuisse lætor,
  Cuique nil vidit simile aut secundum
    Dia Mathesis.

5 Illa se salvam meritò fatetur
  Esse, Neutono revocata ab Anglo,
  Proximus illi tamen occupabit
    Scotus honores.

59

(a) *Ad Andream Tenant*

Andrea, facetis grate sodalibus,
Cum quo diurnis addimus horulis
  Noctes morantes, et jocosum
    Pectore concipimus Lyæum

5 Stotusne ditem cogitat Angliam,
  Urbemque Romæ nobilis æmulam,
    Spreto Lyæo, Disque nuper
      Plus Tyberi Tamesin placentem.

---

58 Title and Text: HRHRC, PR 3619 P54 T4 1713; SP, 48. In HRHRC, it is printed together with **47**.
59 Title and Text: (a) APP, 51, in David Gregory's hand, added after 1703, (b) APP, 28–29 (not in Gregory's hand); BA(4), fo.11ᵛ; SP, 38–39. BA(4) 10: Instructa Cœlo subripiet suo; 15–16: Quam Scota clarebit Thalia,/ Pallade jam nimia superbam. SP, 16: Pallade jam nimia superbam.

silence such life as the shades usually pass. And as no light pledge of our past love, I have set on your grave a very large stone.'

[Edinburgh
Feb'y 1]'

58

Archibald Pitcairne, Scot, greets Thomas Bower, Scot, Professor of Mathematics and Medicine

'Go! to give appropriate veneration to the greatest of men, whom I am delighted that you have pleased, and to whom Divine Mathematics has seen nothing similar or second.

    She confesses, quite properly, that she has been redeemed, recalled by the Englishman Newton. Next to him however a Scot will claim the honours.'

59

(a) *To Andrew Tenant*

'Andrew, delight of your witty cronies, in whose company we lengthen the little hours of day, delaying the nights, and receive a jovial Bacchus in our hearts,

    Is Stott, in contempt of Bacchus and the Gods, considering rich England and the city which aims to rival noble Rome, and the Thames which has recently become more pleasing than the Tiber?

    Ille invidendis pectora dotibus
10 Armata nostro subripiet Jovi,
       Musasque ab Arctis invocantes
        Audiet haud facilis redire.

    Quæ tum querelæ, quæ lacrymæ tibi
    Cum Stotus illam migrat in Angliam,
15   Quam cælos augebit supellex
       Pallade jam nimiâ tumentem.

    Et nos oportet vivere languidos,
    Rapto eruditæ militiæ duce,
      Quin nos recedentem Sodales
20   Ad Tamesin comitamur omnes.

  (b) *Ad Thomam Kinkadium.*

    Thoma facetæ Militiæ decus
    Cum quo diurnis addimus horulis
      Noctes morantes, et jocosum
        Pectore concipimus Lyæum.

5 Fraterne rursus cogitat Angliam,
    Urbemque Romæ nobilis æmulam,
      Nobis relictis, jamque Divis
        Plus Tiberi Tamesin placentem.

    Ille invidendis pectora dotibus
10 Instructa nostro subripiet solo
      Musasque Civesque Invocantes
        Audiet haud patrio sub axe.

    Quæ tum querelæ quæ Lachrymæ tibi
    Cum Frater illam migrat in Angliam
15   Quam Scota ditabit Suppellex
       Jam nimia tumidam Minervâ.

    Et nos oportet vivere Languidos
    Rapto facetæ militiæ duce;
      Quin mox recedentem Sodales
20   Ad Tamesin comitamur omnes.

He will snatch away from our clime a nature enviably endowed, and will scarcely hear the Muses of the North imploring him to return.

How you will complain and weep when Stott emigrates to that England, already swollen with an excess of talent, which his gifts will augment [to the skies].

And when the leader of our learned company has been snatched away, we must live forlorn, unless we all follow him in comradeship as he leaves for the Thames.'

(b) *To Thomas Kinkaid*

'Thomas, pride of the company of wits, in whose company we lengthen the little hours of day, delaying the nights, and receive a jovial Bacchus in our heart,

Does your brother have England once more in mind, and the city which rivals noble Rome, and the Thames more pleasing than the Tiber, abandoning us and our gods?

He will snatch away from our soil/ from his own clime/ a nature enviably endowed, and will no longer hear in his native clime the pleas of the Muses and his fellow-countrymen.

How you will complain and weep when your brother emigrates to an England/ already arrogant in an excess of talent, which Scottish gifts will further enrich/ which, although already swelling with an excess of talent, a Scottish Thalia will render illustrious/

And when we have lost the leader of the company of wits, we must live forlorn, unless we all follow him in comradeship, soon to leave for the Thames.'

60

(a) AD
BERTRAMUM STOTUM *Equitem Anglum*,

[(b) *In* BERTRAMUM STOTUM *Armigerum* **Anglum**.]

[(c) '*poor Stote's epitaph made by Wattie Danniston*']

Stote Tuae moerens astat *Pitcarnius* urnae,
    Qui sibi tam plausit se placuisse Tibi.
Ille Tuos animi mores veneratus, & artes
    Reddere, Quae Superis Te valuere parem,
5 Te jubet invitus, jubet invitusque valere
    Dimidiumque animae Deliciasque suae.

Scribebat *Archibaldus Pitcarnius Scotus*.

61

Ad JOVEM.

Optime, quàm gratos mihi fundis ab æthere nimbos!
    Sit tibi perpetuus, Juppiter, iste labos.
Sic decuit terras, sic æquora claudere Phœbo,
    Quem dio clausum pectore STOTUS habet.

---

60 Title: (a), *N(12)*; (b), SP, 38; (c), SRO, MK, GD.124, 15/512/5–6. **Text**: *N(12)* thus; SRO, MK, GD.124, 15/512/5–6 (Johnston, *Best of our owne*, 48, letter 33); SP, 38. SRO, 4: after *Reddere, Te superis quæ potuere parem*; 6: *Deliciasque animae, dimidiumque suae*. The final note, *Scribebat … Scotus*, is found only in (a).
61 Title and Text: SP, 37.

60

(a) *To Bertram Stott, Knight, Englishman*

(b) *On Bertram Stott Esquire, Englishman*

(c) as above.

'Stott, Pitcairne, who so applauded himself because he had pleased you, mourns as he stands at your tomb. He who venerated your character and arts unwillingly bids you give back the qualities, which had the power of putting you on a par with the gods. Unwillingly he bids you farewell, the darling half of his soul.'

Archibald Pitcairne, Scot, wrote this.

61

To Jove

'Highest, how gratifying it is to me that you are pouring clouds of rain from the sky! May that task be yours, Jupiter, for ever! It was appropriate that lands and seas should thus shut themselves off from Phoebus, whom Stott holds shut off in his divine heart.'

62

IN
BARBARAM & MARGARITAM
CAROLI STUARTI Comitis *Traquarij*
Filias Gemellas.

Tertia *Septembris* vos orbi misit ovanti,
 Et Te *Cromvelli* Sacre tyranne Stygi.
Quam gratum errorem Matrique Patrique creatis?
 Quam cupidos dabitis, quam timidosque procos?

63

In DAVIDEM DRUMMONDUM *in*
certamine Sagittariorum **Edinburgensi**
Victorem, Anno ------

Phœbe, genus dic atque virum cui nuper honores
 Felici peperit missa sagitta manu.
Ille suam credit, cui cessit palma, sagittam;
 Nos illam scimus, Phœbe, fuisse tuam.

64

Davidi Dromondio
Jurisconsulto
Archibaldus Pitcarnius
S.

Me brevis mimum peragente vitæ
Verbaque ægrotis medicata dante,
Te rei nobis reliquæ studentem,
 Fide Dromondi,

---

62 **Title and Text**: *N(36)*, *R¹*, 24, thus; *SP*, 78. *SP*, 2: for *Sacre, dire.*
63 **Title and Text**: *SP*, 76.
64 **Title and Text**: *N(13)*; HRHRC, PR 3619 P54 D34 1708; *SP*, 43–45. In *SP* the final abbreviation, *St. vet.*, is missing.

62

*On Barbara and Margaret, Twin Daughters
of Charles Stuart, Earl of Traquair*

'The third of September sent you to a rejoicing world, and you, Cromwell, accursed tyrant, to the Styx. How pleasing is the uncertainty you create for your mother and father! What passions will you provide for your suitors, what nervousness too!'

63

*On David Drummond, Victor in the Archery
Contest held in Edinburgh in the year ------*

'Phoebus, declare the lineage of the man whose happy hand released the arrow which won him honours. He believes that the arrow which won the prize was his own, but we know, Phoebus, that it was yours.'

64

Archibald Pitcairne writes to David Drummond, Advocate

'I pass through the farce of brief life, giving doctored advice to the sick; you busy yourself with the affair left behind to us, faithful Drummond.

5 Di diu servent vegetum, piumque;
   Qualis exactis steteras ab annis,
   Qualis aut velles etiam Catoni
       Ipse videri.

   Hoc die ad cœnam venias, paratus,
10 Namque natalis tuus est meusque,
   Poculis doctis recreare fesso
       Pectus amico.

   Tum Scoti grate memores Beveli
   Flebimus, læti socium beatum,
15 Quo nihil terris melius, nec Orco
       Sanctior umbra.

   Ille præcessit, sequar ipse, sero
   Te secuturum fugiens, & illum
   Graium linquens mihi plus ocellis
20   Semper amatum:

   Linquam & æternæ Priorum potitum
   Laudis, ac vatum decus Addisonum,
   Mercuri, qui te aerias favente
       Carmine vicit

25 Alpium rupes. Ego te Borelli,
   Teque, Bellini, videam superbus;
   Sed prius caste veneratus astrum
       Gregorianum.

   Nunc vices lætas iterare vitæ
30 Dum licet, puri superis litemus,
   Et patri Baccho, Cererique matri
       Sacra feramus.

   Et quod in nobis opis auxiliique est,
   Civibus demus patriæque caræ;
35 Hæc Deum sedes pietas recludit
       Una, Dromondi.

   25 *Decemb.* 1708,
   St. vet.

May the Gods long keep you active and dutiful, just as you stood firm in past years, or as you yourself might wish to appear even to Cato.

Come to dinner today – it's your birthday and mine – prepared to give new heart by learned cups to your worn-out friend.

Then we shall gratefully remember the Scot Bevelus and weep, though glad our friend is now among the blessed. He was the world's best, and Orcus holds no holier shade.

He has gone before, I shall follow him myself, leaving you to follow later, abandoning that Gray too whom I have always loved better than my eyes.

I shall leave Prior also, winner of eternal praise, and Addison, glory of poets, who, with your favour, Mercury, conquered in song the lofty Alpine crags.

Proudly shall I see you, Borelli, and you, Bellini, but only after chastely worshipping the star of Gregory.

Now, while we may repeat the joyous vicissitudes of life, undefiled let us make an acceptable offering to the gods, and carry the sacred vessels to Father Bacchus and Mother Ceres.

And let us give whatever resources and help we can to our fellow-citizens and beloved country. This, Drummond, is the only piety by which the abodes of the Gods are opened to us.'

25 December 1708, Old Style.

65

AD
Gulielmum **Benedictum Equitem Auratum**
Grubetii **Agri Dominum**
Archibaldus Pitcarnus.

    Hunc, *Benedicte*, tuo cineri *Pitcarnus* honorem
        Dat meritum gratus saepe placensque Tibi.
    Verba dabas Medicis multo ditata lepore,
        At nobis laetus pocula docta dabas.
5 Et nunc Te nobis iterum, Divine, dedisti,
        Intersis Scotis Indiges Alme diu.

66

Ad GUL. BENEDICTUM *de*
Grubbet, *Equitem* ----- A.P.

    Hunc, Benedicte, tuo meritum Pitcarnus honorem
        Dat cineri, priscâ te pietate colens.

    Tu colis Elysios gratissimus advena cœlis,
        Dum terras absens Tartara mœsta facis.

5 Sed tuus, ille tuus, Dîs quo non dignior & te,
        Filius, hic patriâ liberiore frui

    Nos faciet, cœloque dabit Scotosque beatos;
        Intersit nobis Indiges ille diu.

---

65 **Title and Text**: *N(17)*; HRHRC, PR 3619 P54 A66 1713.
66 **Title and Text**: SP, 52.

65

*Archibald Pitcairne to William Bennet,
Knight, Laird of Grubbet Field.*

'As one who was often grateful and dear to you, Pitcairne gives this merited honour to your ashes, Bennet. You practised deceit on physicians in the most charming way, but also regaled us with learned cups. And now, departed spirit, you have given us yourself again. May your presence as kindly patron of Scots long be with us!'

66

To William Bennet of Grubbet, Knight ----- A.P.

'This deserved honour, Bennet, Pitcairne gives to your ash, devoting himself to you with an antique sense of duty.

    As a most welcome arrival to the heavens, you stay in the Elysian Fields, while your absence makes Earth as desolate as Tartarus.

    But your son, that son of yours, than whom none is more deserving in the eyes of the gods and yourself, may he make us delight in a freer country

    And he will bring fortunate Scots to heaven. May he long be with us as Patron!'

67

Andraeae Flechero
Regulo Saltonio.
Archibaldus Pitcarnius
S.D.

QUOD repetita sequi nollet *Proserpina* Matrem,
   Si caussam quaerit, FLECHERUS, Illa fuit.
Nondum natus erat Mundo SALTONIUS Ille
   Qui solus *Cereris* debuit esse gener.

68

VISCOUNT DUPPLIN, his WIFE and his FATHER

(a) *Dannistonus*
PITCARNIO
S.D.

Pitcarni quereris quod nullo carmine laudem
   Duplinium Patriae Spem Columenque suae.
Sed Flaccus nuper docuit, monuitque decere
   Me Maecenati non nimis esse gravem:
5 Et brevibus verbis adfari rite Patronum,
   Cujus non debent Tempora ferre moram.
Illi Fribarnum non Commendaris inepte,
   Leslaeique velis non minus esse memor.
Et potes ipse, Tuus si sit modo dexter Apollo,
10   Duplinii Meritis Carmina digna dare.

---

67 Title and Text: *N(34)*, HRHRC, PR 3619 P54 A9 1712, thus. SP, 77, differs only typographically and in a single abbreviation, ARCH. for *Archibaldus*, in the title.
68 Title and Text: (a)–(c), *R²*, Broadside H; SP, 54–56: (a) HRHRC, PR 3619 P54 D3 1710; (d), *N(33)*; SP, 75: (e), *N(31)*; HRHRC, PR 3619 P54 A68 1712; SP, 75–76.

67

Archibald Pitcairne greets Andrew Fletcher, Kinglet of Saltoun

'Ceres asks why Proserpine shouldn't want to go with her mother after her rescue; Fletcher was the reason. In the upper world, that famous Laird of Saltoun, the only appropriate son-in-law for Ceres, had yet to be born.'

68

VISCOUNT DUPPLIN, his WIFE and his FATHER

(a) *Dennistoun writes to Pitcairne*

'Pitcairne, you complain that I don't sing the praises of Dupplin, the hope and pillar of his country. But Flaccus recently taught and advised me that it was not proper to be overburdensome to Maecenas, and that the correct thing was to use few words in addressing my Patron, whose circumstances forbid any long-windedness. You are right to commend Freebairn to him, and you wish him also to keep Leslie equally in remembrance. And if only your Apollo is propitious, you can yourself compose poems befitting the merits of Dupplin.'

(b) *Pitcarnius*
DANNISTONO
S.D.

Dannistone jubes me digno dicere versu
    Duplinium Patriae Spem Columenque suae.
Haec Te sed ridens jussit mihi scribere Flaccus
    Romanae Fidicen primaque Fama Lyrae.
5 At Maro me monuit, nil majus viribus aude,
    Duplinius nostro debuit ore cani.

(c) *Maecenati Duplinio*
ROBERTUS FRIBARNUS
S.D.

MAEcenas volui grates tibi solvere, musa
    Sed mea par animo noluit esse mea,
Nec potuit, quamvis et Dannistonius illi,
    Et mihi Pitcarnus ferre parabat opem.
5 Ille tuos solus celebrare valebat honores,
    Qui cecinit, Scotis, ARMA VIRUMQUE, modis.
Ille tuos caneret, sinerent modo fata, Labores
    Quos te pro Patria sustinuisse Juvat.

(d) ARCHIBALDO PITCARNIO
GUALTERUS DANNISTONUS
Εὐχαίρειν.

Me vis Duplinii divinas dicere laudes;
    Sed res est longi temporis atque moræ:
Serus enim in coelum Mæcenas ille redibit,
    Quem patrem doctis Juppiter esse jubet.
5 Leslæo interea lætetur, sæpe Boëro,
    Fribarnoque: egeat nil opis ille tuæ:
Sed cum Britannâ jucundus Pallade vivat,
    Atque senex ritu Nestoris astra petat.

Dabam ex Horatii villa Tiburte Elysia.

POEM 68

(b) *Pitcairne replies to Dennistoun*

'Dennistoun, you urge me to celebrate in appropriate verse Dupplin, the hope and pillar of his country. Horace, the poet and chief glory of the Roman lyre, told you to write these things to me, but he was joking. Virgil advised me, "Don't tackle something beyond your powers – it is *my* voice that should celebrate Dupplin."'

(c) *Robert Freebairn writes to Dupplin as Maecenas*

'I wished to thank you, Maecenas, but my muse lacked the will to be the equal of my spirit, nor had it the power, although Dennistoun proposed the undertaking to Pitcairne, and he to me. The ability to celebrate your honours was held by one alone, him who sang *Arma virumque* in Scottish measures. Had the Fates permitted, he would have celebrated the labours which it has pleased you to undertake on behalf of your country.'

(d) *Walter Dennistoun wishes all the best to Archibald Pitcairne*

'You want me to sing the praises of Dupplin as a divinity, but that would take a great deal of time and involve long delay, for that Maecenas, whom Jupiter ordains to be a father to the learned, will be late in his return to heaven. Meanwhile, may he often rejoice in Leslie, in Bower, and in Freebairn; may he lack nothing of *your* help. But long may he live happily with the British Minerva, and may he reach the old age of Nestor before he seeks the stars.

I write from Horace's Tiburtine villa in Elysium.'

(e) *Ad* HAIUM *Comitem* Kinulium.

  Felix Dupplinio, nuruque felix,
  Quæ, si Juppiter alteram annuisset
  Mundo Pallada, Pallas altera esset,
  Alternisque Jovis subiret ædes.
5 Te Pitcarnius ille vester, & qui
  Se totum tibi dedicat tuisque,
  Te salvere jubet, jubet valere,
  Et florere diu Boëro amicum,
  Te quem patria ter lubens fatetur
10 Doctis omnibus esse ter patronum.

69

Ad ANNAM *Sexto* **Februarij**, *Anni* **1711**.

ANNA, *Sibyllino* Quam nos veneramur in Antro,
 Quæ nos responsis *Nocte Dieque* beas;
Hæc Te prima tulit placidis vagitibus hora
 Mulcentem Tygres indomitasque feras.
5 Ast homines postquam miserata es nuper agrestes
 Queis puteus potus, victus avena fuit,
Non homines tantum sibi naturæque reducis,
 Nectare Dîs homines efficis, Alma, pares.
Accipe nos hodie facilis, lætosque remitte;
10 Sic Tu nos *Homines*, Te faciesque *Deam*.

---

69 Title and Text: *R¹*, Broadside 20; SP, 71–72. In the title SP has VI for *Sexto*, MDCCXI for **1711**.

(e) *To Hay, Earl of Kinnoull*

'Happy in Dupplin and happy in your daughter-in-law! Had Jupiter ordained a second Minerva for the world, she would be that second Minerva, and would take turns with her counterpart to enter Jove's palace. Your old friend Pitcairne, who dedicates himself totally to you and yours, wishes you health, wishes you strength, and to live long as Bower's friend, you whom your country thrice joyfully declares thrice patron of all scholars.'

69

To Anna, 6 February 1711

'Anna, to whom we pray in the Sibylline cave, and who bless us night and day with your responses, this is the day of your birth, when you soothed tigers and wild untamed beasts with your peaceful squalling. But afterwards it was on men that you took pity, men recently mere savages, to whom a well was drink, oats were victuals. You do more than restore men to their natural selves – with your nectar, bountiful one, you make men equal to gods. Receive us graciously today, and send us away happy. Thus you will make us men, and yourself a goddess.'

70

ROBERTO FRIBARNIO, *Typographo Regio, Et in certamine Sagittariorum Regiorum Victori, Archibaldus Pitcarnius sagittarius s.d.*

Prisca pharetratis quae fulsit gloria Scotis,
   Per te ter faustum nunc rediviva cluet.
Illa diu decoret **Drommondum, Kinkadiumque**,
   Et te, tres animas deliciasque meas.

71

A D
ARCHIBALDUM REIDIUM
Joannis Reidij Typographi Optimi Filium.

Vive diu felix, et laetos redde Parentes
   Pitcarnique Senex ede vigentis opus.

23 Junij, 1713.

---

70 **Title and Text**: BA(4a), 13; HRHRC, PR 3619 P54 R6 1713; SP, 52. In the title SP has '**A.P.** *S.D.*' for '*Archibaldus Pitcarnius sagittarius s.d.*'; for *quae fulsit, & propria*.

70

*A.P. greets Robert Freebairn, Typographer Royal, Victor
in the Competition of the Royal Company of Archers.*

'The ancient glory which shone for the quiver-bearing Scots is now famous, revived by thrice-fortunate you. May that glory long adorn Drummond and Kinkaid and you, three souls whom I love.'

71

To Archibald Reid, Son of John Reid Best of Printers

'Live long and happy, and give joy to your parents, and in old age print the work of a Pitcairne still in his prime.'

23 June, 1713

6

Political, mainly Jacobite

POLITICAL, MAINLY JACOBITE

72

(a) *Lauderdaliæ Dux*

[(b) *In Obitum Ducis Lauderiæ &c.*]

[(c) *In Joannem Ducem Lauderiae*]

Ille ego Lauderiæ Dux, hoc inclusa sepulchro
    Et Jussi, et Volui membra jacere mea.
Si mihi contingat vitæ par vita peractæ,
    Aut Jovis aut Ditis summus Amicus ero.
5 Ni Jovis aut Ditis regnavero Summus Amicus,
    Et tenebras Linquam Ditis et astra Jovis.

73

JACOBO Septimo
Ejus Nominis,
SCOTIAE REGI,
Die *Octobris* **Decimo quarto,**

HIC est Ille Tuus natalis, *Septime*, qui Te
    Germanum *Carolo* jusserat esse pio.
Octobri quantas persolves *Scotia* grates?
    Qui *Juni* Decimum fecit adesse Tibi.

74

AD PHOEBUM

PHOEBE Pater, Manes non hic vexare sepultos
    Fert Animus, superi nunc mihi carmen erunt:

Sed breve carmen erunt, nam non ego, luctibus impar,
    Sustineo longis esse Poeta malis.

---

72 Title and Text: (a) APP, 4; (b) BA(4), f.2ᵛ.; (c) SP, 2. Text as in (a).
73 Title and Text: R¹, 29; BA(4a), 4.
74 Title and Text: N(30); HRHRC, PR 3619 P54 A88 1710; SP, 73. SP, 6: *Quæ* for *Quot*. 7: *cœlestis & ipse* for *Parnassius, ista*. 8: *Ipse tuus nollet fors meminisse pater* for *Ille tuus nollet facta fuisse pater*.12: *Sancta* for *Lecta*.13: *alter* for *Ios*.18: *ridebis* for *damnabis*. Other variants are typographic only.

72

(a) Duke of Lauderdale

[(b) On the Death of the Duke of Lauderdale etc.]

[(c) On John, Duke of Lauderdale]

'As famous Duke of Lauderdale, I ordained and desired my limbs to lie enclosed in this tomb. If my future life follows the pattern of my past life, I'll be a great friend either of Jove or of Dis. If I shan't reign as great friend of either, I'll abandon both the shades of Dis and the stars of Jupiter.'

73

To James, seventh King of Scotland of that Name, on the Fourteenth of October

'This is the famous day of your birth, Septimus, which had ordained you to be brother of Charles of blessed memory. What thanks, Scotland, will you pay to October, who made the Tenth of June come to your aid?'

74

To Phoebus

'Father Phoebus, my spirit does not urge me to vex departed spirits here: the living will now be the subject of my song.

But they will be the subject of a lay that is brief, for I am not up to these griefs, nor can I bear to be a poet for long misfortunes.

 5 Nec te, *Phœbe*, juvat lacrymoso dicere vati,
  Quot Bardi nuper damna tulere tui.

Ista animus meminisse, horret Parnassius, ista
 Ille tuus nollet facta fuisse pater.

Denique quis sanus narranti talia credat,
10 Qualia nec *Cretes* commemorare solent?

Vendiderit Fratres, & jusserit *Issachar* amens
 Lecta Cananæum colla subire jugum.

Prodiderit patriam sociis servilibus *Ios*,
 Merserit & *Batavo* prata *Britanna* salo.

15 Hæc ego si memorem, si scribere tristia tentem,
 Et plusquam Iliacum condere nitar opus,

Ipse sacros vultus avertes, *Phœbe*, canenti,
 Et tu damnabis carmina nostra, *Prior*.

75

(a) **Ad G. B.**

Juppiter est hominis facie te fallere passus,
 Impiaque in patrios fundere verba Deos.

O rem non dignam Divumque hominumque parente,
 Et cujus pudeat poeniteatque Jovem!

5 At cito si feriet te fulmine Juppiter, idem
 Juppiter ex illo tempore noster erit.

(b) **Ad** GILB. BURNET. *Scotum,*
A.P. *Scotus.*

Vejovis est hominis facie te fallere passus,
 Impiaque in patrios fundere verba Deos.

O rem vix ipso, vix ipso Vejove dignam!
 Et cujus pudeat poeniteatque *Stygem*.

---

75 Title and Text: (a) *N(47)*; HRHRC, PR 3619 P54 A64 1710; (b) *N(48)*; another copy in *R²*, Broadside D. (b) is a more virulent version of (a).

Nor are you happy, Phoebus, to tell a tearful prophet, how many of your bards have recently suffered harm.

The Parnassian mind shudders to recollect such things, your distinguished father would wish that they had never taken place.

Then too what sane mind would credit someone telling stories such as not even Cretans are in the habit of relating?

How in his madness, Issachar would have sold his brothers and ordered them to submit their chosen necks to the Canaanite yoke.

How Ios would have betrayed his country to his servile associates, and sunk the meadows of Britain in the Batavian sea.

If I were to relate these things, if I were to try to write my own *Tristia*, and if I were to strive to compose a work greater than the *Iliad*,

You will yourself, Phoebus, turn your sacred countenance away from the singer, and you, Prior, will condemn our lays.'

75

(a) *To G.B.*

'Jupiter has allowed you to deceive with a human face and pour out blasphemies on your ancestral gods.

An action unworthy of the father of gods and men. May it shame Jupiter and cause him to repent!

But if Jupiter will quickly strike you with a thunderbolt, from that time onwards the same Jupiter will be on our side.'

(b) *A.P., Scot, to Gilbert Burnet, Scot*

'Vejovis has allowed you to deceive with a human face and pour out blasphemies on your ancestral gods.

An action scarcely worthy, scarcely worthy even of Vejovis himself. May it shame Styx and cause it to repent!

5 At cito si feriet te fulmine Vejovis, Ille
  Mox Jovis ex Illo tempore noster erit.

76

(a) **Proceres Scotorum Anno** MDCXC

Quam pudet Clio memorare gentem?
Quos senum mores, iuvenumve formas?
Quem vivum? Cujus recinet jocosa
   Nomen imago

5 Aut in obscuro Vemiensis antro
  Aut Monimella, Strutherave sylva?
  Unde vocalem temere insecuta
     Rothea prius.

  Quid prius dicam solitis Parentis
10 Laudibus, qui res hominum et deorum
   Turbat, et longi novitate monti[s]
      Terruit Urbem?

   Vnde nil majus generatur ipso,
   Nec viget quicquam simile aut secundum,
15 Proximus illi tamen occupabit
      Janrus honores.

   Prœliis audax neque te Levine
   Non canam, sævis metuende flagris,
   Quem colunt nautæ per amena Fifæ
20   Littora sparsi.

   Davidem post hos primus, an quieta
   Regna Rulæi memorem, an superbos
   Labii fasces, dubito, an Georgii
      Pauperis aurum.

25 Crescit occulto velut arbor ævo
   Fama Crafordii: micat inter omnes
   Kennedis sydus, velut inter ignes
      Luna minores.

76 Title and **Text**: *APP*, 15–18 (in David Gregory's hand).

But if Vejovis quickly strikes you with a thunderbolt, from that time onwards he will be Jovis, on our side.'

76

Scots Worthies in the Year 1690

'What race, Clio, is it shameful to mention? What morals of the old or natures of the young? Whom among the living? Whose droll image resounds a name
   either in the obscure cave of Wemyss, or in Monimail, or in Anstruther wood, whence it had first rashly followed melodious Rothes?
   How shall I begin but with the customary praises of the Father who disturbs the affairs of men and gods and has terrorised the City with the novelty of the long mount?
   Whence nothing greater than himself is born nor does anything flourish his equal or second. Closest to him however Janrus will seize the honours.
   Nor shall I fail to sing thee, Leven, audacious in battle, fearsome with your savage whips, whom the sailors scattered across the pleasant shores of Fife cultivate.
   I don't know whether I should call David first to mind after these, or the quiet kingdom of Rule or the proud rods of Law or the gold of poor George?
   The reputation of Crawford grows like a tree from a hidden age. Among them all, the star of Kennedy sparkles, like the Moon surrounded by lesser fires

POLITICAL, MAINLY JACOBITE

    Gentis Albanæ, pater atque custos
30 Orte Nassavo, Tibi cura Magni
    Kennedis fatis data, Tu secundo
        Kennede regnes.

    Ille seu scortis juvenes amicos
    Egerit justo domitos triumpho,
35 Sive subjectos populos avari
        Præsulis ira,

    Te minor nostrum reget unus orbem:
    Tu gravi curru quaties Olympum
    Tu parum castis inimica mittes
40   Fulmina Lucis.

(b) Aliter

    Quem virum aut Heroa lyra vel acri
    Tibia sumis celebrare Clio?
    Quos senum mores, juvenumve formas
        Attinet Echo

5 Aut latebrosis Vemiarum in antris.
    Aut super Largo, Strutherisve in udis?
    Unde vocalem temere insecutæ
        Rothea silvae

    Quid prius dicam solitis parentis
10 Laudibus? Qui res hominum ac deorum
    Miscet, et longi novitate monti[s]
        Terruit urbem?

    Vnde nil majus generatur ipso,
    Nec viget quicquam simile aut secundum:
15 Proximus illi tamen occupabit
        Janrus honores:

    Prœliis audax neque te Levine
    Non canam, certis metuende flagris,
    Quem colunt nautæ per amœna Fifæ
20   Littora sparsi.

    Et parem Alcidæ Superisque dicam
    Davidem, grato superare furto
    Nobilem; cujus simul alba Nymphis
        Stella refulsit,

POEM 76

Father and Guardian of the Scottish race, risen from the Nassovian, the care of great Kennedy has been granted to you by the Fates. May you hold sway with Kennedy for deputy!

He – whether he will have led in a well-deserved triumph conquered youths friendly to harlots or peoples laid low by the anger of a greedy Moderator –

though less than you, he will be sole ruler of our world. You will shake Olympus with a weighty chariot; you will send unfriendly thunderbolts on polluted groves.'

Otherwise

'What man or hero, Clio, are you setting out to celebrate on lyre or shrill flute? What morals of the old or natures of the young does Echo touch

either in the secret caves of Wemyss, or over Largo, or in the damp Struthers from which the woods have rashly followed the singing of Rothes?

How shall I begin but with the customary praises of the Father who throws into confusion the affairs of men and gods and has terrorised the City with the novelty of the long mount

whence nothing greater than himself is born, nor does anything flourish his equal or second. Closest to him however Janrus will seize the honours.

Nor shall I fail to sing thee, Leven, audacious in battle, fearsome in the certainty of your whips, whom the sailors scattered across the pleasant shores of Fife cultivate.

And I shall call David the equal of Hercules and the Gods for the seduction of a noblewoman by a pleasant trick. Simultaneously, the glistening of his star has promised favours to Nymphs.

25 Defluit membris agitatus humor;
   Concidunt iræ, fugiuntque flatus,
   Et ferox (sic Di voluere) lecto
       Virgo recumbit.

   Kirtonum post hos prius an quietum
30 Reguli regnum memorem, an superbos
   Labii fasces, dubito, an Georgii
       Pauperis aurum.

   Dem Vieræum, Clelanumque dulcis
   Prodigum vitæ, superante Scoto,
35 Lætus insigni referam Camœna
       Reimoriumque

   Hunc et incomptis Orocum capillis
   Vtilem rixis tulit, et Breæum
   Sæva paupertas, et avitus arcto
40   Cum Lare fundus.

   Crescit occulto velut arbor ævo
   Fama Crafurdii: micat inter omnes
   Kennedis sydus, velut inter ignes
       Luna minores.

45 Gentis Albanæ pater atque custos
   Orte Nassavo, tibi cura magni
   Kennedis fatis data: Tu secundo
       Kennede regnes.

   Ille seu mistas pueris puellas
50 Egerit justo domitas triumpho,
   Sive subjectos populos avari
       Præsulis iræ,

   Te minor nostrum reget unus orbem,
   Tu solum curru quaties Britannum,
55 Tu parum gratis inimica mittes
       Fulmina templis.

The fluid roused pours down from his members, their passions fall together, their breaths flee, and the spirited girl (so the Gods willed) lies back on the bed.

I don't know whether I should call Kirkton first to mind after these, or the peaceful kingdom of Rule, or the proud rods of Law, or the gold of poor George.

Let me give you Weir, and, rejoicing in my distinguished Muse, may I call Cleland to mind, careless of sweet life, since the Scot was victor, and Rymore.

Harsh poverty and a hereditary farm with northern Lar bore him and Orrock with unkempt hair, a handy man in brawls, and Brae.

The fame of Crawford grows like a tree from a hidden age; the star of Kennedy sparkles, like the Moon among lesser fires.

Father and Guardian of the Scottish race, risen from the Nassovian, the care of great Kennedy has been granted to you by the Fates. May you hold sway, with Kennedy for deputy!

He – whether he will have led girls, conquered in a just triumph, together with boys, or people subjected to the wrath of a greedy Moderator –

Though less than you, he will be sole ruler of our world. You alone will strike the Briton with your chariot. You will dispatch hostile thunderbolts on churches that displease you.'

77

In Nuptias Comitis Levinii
Horat. Lib.3. Ode 28

    Festo quid potius die
Cromuelli satagam? Promere amabilem
      Festina puer Hastulam
Et Claustris adhibe vim cupientibus.

5   En queis hora volat votis!
Tu, dum testiculis et genibus vales
      Duffeum dubitas agrum
Primus davidico findere vomere?

    Nos cantabimus invicem
10 Cromuellum et madidos sanguine regis
      Patres: Tu vesanos Lyra
Mortonam et tumida facta [filisthiæ]

    Summo Carmine, Cui patre
Ventosi placuit Brittonis insula
15   Pulso, nocte litabitur
O Cromuelle tibi sanguine virginis.

78

Ad --------- MALAVILLAM.

Post tot demersos Lethæo gurgite cives
    Arte malâ, Circe te sociante sibi,
Aggrederis tandem Vemias submergere terras,
    Quæ vitas hominum Sole hiemante fovent.
5 Si nihil hæc Superi se sunt curare professi,
    Si brutis mittunt ludicra tela jugis,
At scelera ulcisci decuit Malavillia cives,
    Et Vemius dudum debuit esse tonans.

---

77 Title and Text: APP, 14 (in David Gregory's hand).
78 Title and Text: SP, 81–82.

77

On the Wedding of the Earl of Leven

Horace, Book 3, Ode 28

'What better occupation could I have on Cromwell's birthday? Hurry, boy, to bring out the little spear of love and apply your force to the bulwarks of desire.

Lo! with what vows the hour flies! While you remain robust in testicles and knees, have you any doubt of being the first to cleave Macduff's field with David's plough?

In turn we shall celebrate Cromwell and the Commission soaked in the blood of a king. Your part is to celebrate on your lyre madmen, the woman Morton and the arrogant deeds of Filisthia

With your final song. To you, Cromwell, whom the island of fickle Britto has pleased by expelling its father, by night the blood of a virgin will be sacrificed.'

78

To --------- Melville

'After so many citizens had been drowned in the Lethaean stream by sorcery, with Circe bringing you in as her accomplice, finally you set about submerging the lands of Wemyss which nourish the lives of men during the winter. If the gods have declared that they don't care about this, if they send ridiculous weapons to a brutish team of yoked beasts, yet his countrymen ought to have punished the crimes of Melville, and Wemyss has long deserved to be the Thunderer.'

79

Hectoris exuvias indutum cernite *Mosen*,
Huic homines, Agni praeda fuistis ei.

Lo! Moses wrapt in Hector's *Skin*,
This worried Lambs, the other Men.

80

(a) [*In* JACOBUM II. **Britanniæ** *Regem*.]

(b) [**In** IACOBUM **Secundum Britanniae Regem**]

Barbarus exclusit tumulo me *Nassus* avito,
Perfidia fretus, *Marleboroe*, Tua.
Urbs caret exuvijs, at *Barberinus* inultos
JACOBI Manes fecit in Urbe coli.

Quod non fecere Barbari, fecere Barberini.

81

(a) *In mortem Gulielmi Aurasionensis*

[(b) *In diem 4 Nov: 1702.*]

[(c) *In Octavum Martii.*]

Prisca redit virtus, Pietasque refulget avita,
Promite Tyrrhenis vina reposta cadis
Missaque de cœlo Terras Astræa revisit,
Promite Lætifici Liquida dona patris:

---

79 Text: APP, 33 (in Gregory's hand, immediately after *finis*); N(72); HRHRC, PR 3619 P54 H4 1712.
80 Title and Text: HRHRC, PR 3619 P54 152 1712, R¹, 19, untitled. In R¹, title (a) together with an attribution to Archibald Pitcairne, has been added in pencil, in a much later hand. SP, 41, has title (a); 1: *te Nasus* for *me Nassus*; 2: *fidens* for *fretus*, Marl-----oe for *Marleboroe*. BA(4a) has title (b), reads *fidens* for *fretus*, and lacks final prose line.
81 Title: (a) APP, 28 (not in Gregory's hand); (b) BA(4), fo.11ʳ; (c) SP, 20. BA(4a), 11, has no title.
Text: as under **Title**; In l. 4, BA(4a) reads *Fundite* for *Promite*; in ll. 7–8, for *cui tellus … equum*, it reads *cui Scotia fuderat olim/ Littoris ex utero Bellerophontis Equum*. For *extulit*, SP reads *fuderat*, and for *Ex utero glebæ, Littoris ex utero*. For *extulit*, BA(4) reads *educat*.

79

'Behold Moses clad in the spoils of Hector! As men, you were prey to one, as lambs to the other.'

80

[*On James II, King of Britain*]

'The barbarian, Nassau, excluded me from my ancestral tomb, relying, Marlborough, on your treachery. The city lacks my remains, but Barberinus made sure that the unavenged spirit of the departed James should be honoured in the city.'

What the Barbarians failed to do, the Barberini accomplished.

81

(a) *On the Death of William of Orange*

[(b) *On 4 November 1702*]

[(c) *On 8 March*]

'Ancient virtue returns and ancestral piety shines out once more – bring out the wine laid up in Tyrrhenian jars! Sent from heaven, Astraea visits Earth again – bring out the liquid gifts of the father who produces joy! The Hydra that laid

   5 Occidit Imperii Populatrix hydra Britanni
      Omnibus incolumes Solvite vota Diis
    Primaque Neptuno, cui tellus extulit olim
      Ex utero glebæ parturientis equum.

82

HORATIUS ad *LUCIFERUM*.

Lucifer, nam Te Docilis Magistro
Nassovus movit Sacra mentiendo
Hostium nuper nimis impeditos
    Fraudibus *Anglos*.

 5 Ille nunc narrat Facies quot ausus
Est tuo jussu scelerum patrare,
Sed novis Heros Equus *Armistrangi*
    Obstitit ausis.

Tertius nunc est *Usinulca* vestri
10 Ordinis, quam nos petimus *Britanni*
Ut fiet Tecum Sacer omnis Ille,
    Lucifer, Ordo!

83

Hac *Jovis Hammonis* cineres conduntur in urna,
    Qui se *Saturno* praedicat esse fatum.
Saepe vafer voluit *Saturni* regna potiri,
    Sed frustra, hunc Tumulum *Cretica* Terra dedit.
5 At *Saturne* Tui vivis regnator Olympi,
    Haeredem indignans *Creticum* habere nothum.

82 Title and Text: *N(49)*.
83 Text: *N(73)*.

waste the British Empire has fallen – now that you are saved, fulfil your vows to all gods, and first to Neptune, for whom the Earth once brought forth a steed from the womb of a field in labour.'

82

Horace to Lucifer

'Satan, your apt pupil Nassau, by falsifying holy things has troubled the English, overmuch hindered recently by the deceits of enemies.

He now tells how many faces of crime he has ventured to commit at your bidding. But a hero, Armstrong's Horse, has stood in the way of his new ventures.

Usinulca is now third in your Brotherhood. How we Britons ask that all members of that accursed Brotherhood may join you, Satan!'

83

'In this urn are buried the ashes of Jupiter Ammon, who predicted that he would be Saturn's Nemesis. He often craftily plotted to gain possession of Saturn's kingdom, but in vain – the land of Crete provided him with this tumulus. Saturn, you live as ruler of your Olympus, thinking it unworthy to have a Cretan bastard as heir.'

POLITICAL, MAINLY JACOBITE

84

In Marchionem Montis Rosarum

Dis Genite et Geniture deos, tibi surget avita
    Gloria, materni pullulat oris honos.

85

GUALTERI DANNISTONI *Epistola ad* JOANNEM CUNINGAMIUM *Juris Antecessorem, ut maturet reditum ad Inferos.*

   Sancte Cuningami, quæ nunc tibi causa morandi?
      An patriæ magnæ non memor esse potes?
   An Ditis, qui te lucis præfecit Avernis,
      Ante Hecates raptum, perplacitamque fugam?
5 Ah! dum tu nimium nimiumque oblite tuorum,
      Arma quibus decuit reddere, jura dabas,
   Tartara læva locos subitò invasere beatos,
      Et Manes lacerant impia turba pios!
   Jam Cato nos liquit, majorque Catone Locartus,
10   Unica spes Ditis deliciæque, redi.
   Non opus est armis, nec possunt arma juvare:
      Solus opus nobis, ipse Lycurge, veni.
   Redde patrem nobis, alio non Rege beatis,
      Qui tibi, Galle, pater, qui tibi, Scote, fuit.

86

Ad CYCLOPAS ALPINOS
Virgilius Aeneidos Libro Octavo

Tollite cuncta ---- caeptosque auferte labores
Alpini Cyclopes, et huc advertite mentem.
Arma viris facienda ----- nunc viribus usus,
Nunc manibus rapidis, omni nunc Arte Magistra.
Praecipitate moras.

---

84 Title and Text: *APP*, 19 (written in or before October 1703; not in David Gregory's hand); *BA(4)*, f.7ᵛ (with no title). *BA(4)*,1: *resurgit* for *tibi surget*.
85 Title and Text: *SP*, 74.
86 Title and Text: *N(51)*.

84

On the Marquess of Montrose

'In you, child of gods and destined progenitor of gods, the glory of your ancestors will rise again, the honour of the shores that bore you flourishes.'

85

Walter Dennistoun's Letter to John Cunningham, Professor of Law, to hasten his Return to the World of the Dead.

'Sainted Cunningham, what cause have you now for delay? Have you no memory of your great fatherland, none of Dis, who put you in charge of the groves of Avernus before the rape of Hecate and her happy escape? Ah! while you were establishing a system of law, overforgetful of your own, whose weapons it was your duty to restore, ill-omened Tartarus suddenly invaded the realms of the blessed, and an unholy mob is now mangling the pious dead. Now Cato has left us, and Lockhart, greater than Cato. Sole hope and darling of Dis, return! There's no need for weapons, nor can weapons help. Our only need is that you should come, Lycurgus in person. Restore our father to us, blessed only in that king who was your father, Frenchman, and yours too, Scot.'

86

To the Alpine Cyclopes (Virgil, Aeneid 8)

'Take away everything! ---- stop the tasks you have begun, Alpine Cyclopes, and direct your minds hither! Arms are to be made for heroes ----- Now there is occasion for your strength, now for your swift hands, now, instructed by your whole art, fling away delays!'

POLITICAL, MAINLY JACOBITE

87

Ad Comitem Cromarteum.

Vivacissime Fergusi nepotum
Quoi virtus nova pullulat per annos,
Gratias tibi maxime merenti
Agunt quinqueviri, immerensque turma
5 Vexatissima nuper illa, tanto
Vexatissima pro fidem Deorum
Quanto tu optimus, optimusque Iudex.

88

A D

JACOBUM GALLOVIDIUM,
Equitem Caledonium.

Quis fuero, cum Tu *Jacobe* redibis in Urbem,
   Quaeritis, is qui Te Rus abeunte fui.
Atque Equites nostri sunt quales ante fuere,
   Et memores vestri *Gallica* vina bibunt.
5 Presbyteri *Cnoxi* pejora Parentibus audent.
   Et *Gallovidium* Rure redire vetant.

89

Elisae Havartae **Principi** *Gordoniae*
A.P. *Scotus* S, D.

Quantus erat *Mariae* vindex *Havartus, Elisae*
   Essexae tanto Carnificina fuit
Foedior, et tanto truculentior improbiorque
   Iratos nobis quae jubet esse Deos.

---

87 Title and Text: BA*(4)*, f.21ᵛ (second hand).
88 Title and Text: N*(59)*, *(60)*. The text printed is that of *(59)*. *(60)*: 5. *Discipuli* for *Presbyteri*; *majora* for *pejora*; 6: *Hæc melius poteris scire*, PATRONE, *Redux* for *Et Gallovidium Rure redire vetant*. These readings may represent a later recension.
89 Title and Text: N*(35)*, HRHRC, PR 3619 P54 E4 1712, thus; SP, 77, differs only typographically.

230

87

To the Earl of Cromarty

'Liveliest of clan Fergus, in whom new vigour sprouts as the years go by, five men offer you the thanks you have more than deserved, as does that squadron recently and undeservedly most persecuted, most persecuted in face of their loyalty to the gods proportionately as you are the finest of men and the finest of judges.'

88

To James Gallovidian, Caledonian Chevalier

'James, you ask what kind of existence I shall have when you return to the city. I shall be the same as I was during your absence in the country. And our chevaliers continue to be just as they have been in the past, and drink French wine remembering you! Knox's priests continue to dare evils worse than their parents and are still forbidding the Gallovidian to come back from the country.'

89

A.P., Scot, greets Elizabeth Howard, Duchess of Gordon

'Howard was the great protector of Mary; much fouler, much more ferocious and dishonourable was the hangman's role played by Elizabeth, betrothed to Essex, which roused the gods against us. You arise as a second, but better, Elizabeth, you

5 Altera sed melior nobis exsurgis *Elisa*,
   Quae *Maria* natis Numina fausta voves.
Sis felix faveasque tuis *Havarta Britannis*
   Havartaeque domus *Gordoniaeque* decus.

90

Ad Homerum
Catulli carmen ex Græco Sapphûs versum,
& Albæ Græcæ repertum, Anno
vulgaris Æræ 1711.

Te poetarum coluere Regem
Junij natum decimo Camenæ;
Non tui deerit venerationi
   Lesbia Sappho,

5 Te salutantes animans puellas,
Quæ modos nondum tibi forte noti
Carminis ludunt hodie repertos
   Virginis arte.

Te pater gaudens oriente Phœbus
10 Hesperum illusit, voluitque curru
Impiger totam volitare noctem, &
   Regis Homeri

Omne per cœlum celebrare dotes;
Atque vicinam populis Britannis
15 Ultimam Thulen, voluitque vatem
   Palladis artes

Scire, queis Reges reditum pararent,
Et procos gazis Ithaci imminentes
Tollerent, pœnas sibi civibusque
20   Lege daturos

Regiâ, plaudente Deûm ★ ★ ★
         ★ ★ ★
         ★ ★ ★
            ★ ★

---

90 Title and Text: HRHRC, PR 3619 P54 A7 1711. Opposite **Homerum** in **Title** is a MS insertion: *i.e. Jacobu[m] 8*u[m] *Reg: M. Britt.*, 'that is, James 8th King of Great Britain'.

who have made your offering for fate to favour Mary's descendants. May you be happy and favour your Britons, Lady Howard, glory of the house of Howard and Gordon!'

90

To Homer

A Poem of Catullus translated from the Greek of Sappho and discovered at Alba Graeca in the Year of the common Era 1711.

'The Muses have worshipped you, born on the tenth of June, as King of Poets. The Lesbian Sappho will not be wanting in reverence for you, encouraging the girls who are acclaiming you, who today perform a measured song, as yet perhaps unknown to you, devised by the art of a virgin.

At your rising Father Phoebus mocked the Evening Star and wished to fly the entire night in his chariot and to celebrate the endowments of King Homer throughout the firmament and Ultima Thule, neighbour to the British peoples. He wished the bard to know the arts of Athena, by which Kings might provide for the return of the Ithacan and make away with the Suitors threatening his treasures and intending to crush him and his fellow-islanders by royal *fiat*, to the applause of the Gods --------------------- King, help your girls today,

POLITICAL, MAINLY JACOBITE

  Rex Tuis adsis hodie puellis,
   Pontifex adsis facilis bonusque
  Casta sic solvat Tibi vota Thules
25   Incola vati.

91

[Ad Annam R. Anno MDCCXI]

 Credidimus terras *Hydram* liquisse *Britannas*
  Tempore quo mensis nomina *Martis* habet;
 Credidimus stulte, nam sævior *Hydra* revertit,
  Multiplicis capitis mista venena ferens.
5 Quas strages, qualemque luem dedit illa *Britannis*,
  Pauperiem quantam fecit, & *Hydra* famem!
 Pæne vetus poteras in *Lernæ* nomen abire,
  Orba tuis populis, *Albion*, atque Diis;
 Non erat *Alcides*, nec *Vallas* fortior illo,
10 Qui posset tantis obvius ire malis:
 Una fuit Superum tanto par ANNA labori,
  Quae merito nobis ANNA *Perenna* cluet;
 Non oblita sui, non immemor ANNA suorum,
  Perculit *Hydrarum* fulminis igne genus.
15 Illa Deum vitam, sed *Avum* prius ulta *Patremque*,
  Accipiet, Superis omnibus Vna placens.

92

 Goddolphine Stygem potas et Averna fluenta,
  Qua laevas Orco Dis jubet ire vias.
 Noluit ad dextram Te Dis allabier oram,
  Ne sibi patrares *Sidnie* tale scelus,
5 Quale paravisti Regi, Quem mergier undis
  Jussisti, vetuit sed Soror Illa sui.

91 **Title and Text**: *N(29)*; BA(4a), 8; HRHRC, PR 3619 P54 C7 1710; SP, 72. The title appears only in SP.
92 **Text**: BA(4a), 14.

help them as high-priest mild and good. Her chaste vows let the woman of Thule thus pay to you, the bard.'

91

[*To Queen Anne in the year 1711*]

'We believed that the Hydra had left British lands at the time in which the month has the names of Mars. We were stupid to believe it, for the Hydra has returned even fiercer, bearing the mixed venoms of its multiple head. What carnage and what pestilence that Hydra inflicted on the Britons, what poverty and hunger it made! Bereft of your people and Gods, Albion, you were almost forced to become the [modern] equivalent of the ancient Lernaean marshes. There was no Hercules, no Wallace, stronger even than Hercules, to go to meet such evils. Anna, whom we rightly call Anna Perenna, was the only Divinity equal to such a labour. Not forgetful of her self nor of her own, Anna struck the race of Hydras with the fire of lightning. When she has avenged her grandfather and her father, may she be granted the life of the gods, since she alone pleases all the Immortals.'

92

'Godolphin, you are drinking Styx and the waters of the infernal regions, where Dis orders that you follow the left-hand path in Orcus. Dis did not want you to land on the right-hand bank for fear, Sidney, that you would commit on him such a crime as you intended for the King, whom you ordered to be submerged by the waves, but that Sister of his forbade it.'

93

A D

JONATHANEM ----------
— **Novembris Anni** MDCCXII

Davidis fautor *Jonathan* fuisti,
Qui dedit Regem populo *Israelis*
Sive *Jacobi, Solomone* tandem hae-
rede beandi.

5 Jamque favisti *Jonathan Roberto*
Terque Ter Soter, facias ut Is se
Davidem praestet generi *Israelis*
Semper amicum.

94

IN
JACOBUM
PRINCIPEM HAMILTONIUM
Virum Fortissimum,
Parricidio foedissimo trucidatum, Londini
Die quindecimo Novembris Anni MDCCXII

(a)

Dum Patriae servire studes Patriaeque Parenti,
Dignus *Hamiltona Regificaque* Domo,
Es Parricidio sublatus, Qualis et *Ios*
Hibernusque negent *Vejovis* esse rei.

(b)

Dum Patriae servire studes Patriaeque Parenti,
Dignus *Hamiltona regificaque* Domo,
Es Parricidio raptus, Fortissime, Quale
Barbariem *Hibernam* nunc pudet esse suum.

---

93 Title and Text: *N(77)*.
94 Title and Text: (a) *N(38)*; (b) *R²*, Broadside E; HRHRC, PR 3619 P54 I5 1712; SP, 79.

93

To Jonathan ----------, ---- November 1712

'Jonathan, you were the supporter of David, who gave a King to the people of Israel or Jacob, blessed at last in Solomon, his heir.

Now that you, Jonathan, thrice three times saviour, have extended your favour to Robert, may you ensure that he will maintain himself as David, ever friend to the people of Israel.'

94

On James, Duke of Hamilton, a very brave man, cut down by the foulest parricide in London on 15 November 1712

'While you strive to be the servant of your fatherland and of your fatherland's Father, in a way worthy of the royal and king-making House of Hamilton, you have suffered by parricide. Let the like of Ios and the Irish Vejovis deny their guilt.'

'While you strive to be the servant of your fatherland and of your fatherland's Father, in a way worthy of the royal and king-making House of Hamilton, you have been snatched away, bravest one, by a parricide which Irish barbarity is now ashamed to acknowledge as its own.'

95

Delphinis quanto Balaena *Britannica* fertur,
 Et quanto Catulis fortior esse *Leo*,
Tu tanto superas Homines pietate Deosque,
 Quam sibi *Pitcarnus* Te volet esse Domi.

96

HARLAIO

ARBITER *Europae*, mandatu Brittonis ANNAE,
 Qui nunc pace SCOTOS *Angligenasque* beas.
Quid debet quantumque Tibi *Britannia*, quid quae
 Ultima non meruit nominis esse Sui?

97

ARBITER *Europae*, mandato *Brittonis* ANNAE,
 Qui pacem *Scotis Angligenisque* facis.
Quid Regina tibi debet, Quantumque STUARTA?
 Ultima quae non vult nominis esse Sui.

98

AD
ANNAM BRITANNAM

ANNA *Stuartorum* Decus et Spes altera Regum,
 Quos Sibi, quos reddi prisca *Caledon* avet,
Este bonae, Faustaeque Tuis Rex *Anna Stuartis*,
 Et nos *Teutonico* non onerate jugo.

---

95 Text: *N(78)*.
96 Title and Text: Broadsheet attached to NLS, MS *583*, f.904b, reproduced in Johnston, *Best of our owne*, 68, letter 56.
97 Text: *N(84)*.
98 Title and Text: *N(86)*.

95

'As the British Whale is said to be more powerful than Dolphins, and the Lion than Whelps, by the same measure you surpass men and gods in your sense of duty. How Pitcairne wishes he had you at home!'

96

To Harley

'Arbiter of Europe, you who under commission of the Britoness, Anna, are now gladdening Scots and English with peace, what debt, what huge debt does Britain owe you, what does [the Queen] who has not deserved to be the last of her name?'

97

'Arbiter of Europe, who are making peace for Scots and English under commission from the Briton, Anna, what does the Queen owe you, how much does the Stuart, who does not wish to be the last of her line?'

98

To the Briton Anna

'Anna, ornament and second hope of the Stuart Kings, for whose restoration ancient Caledonia longs, may you, Anna, and the King together be good and favourable to your Stuarts. Do not burden us with a Teutonic yoke!'

99

Saxonas ac Anglos olim Germania fudit.
    Nunc fundit solos, Angle Britanne, tuos.

100

Annae Reginae
Archibaldus Pitcarnius **Scotus**
[S.D.]

Anna Caledoniae quae nunc felicior orae,
    Missa per innumeros Sceptra tueris avos,
Illa diu vigeant, quae, cum vos fata jubebunt
    Linquere, GERMANO, Linquite, Diva, Tuo.

101

Multa tulere sacrae, Te, Rex, absente columbae
    Atque IMPUNE Tuo saevijt orbe furor:
Tu dabis his finem, Divi genus, et Deus, AC TU
    VEXABIS CORVOS, accipitresque truces.
5 Te cito, Te Patrem videat rediviva *Caledon*,
    Cumque pio veniat *Caesare* casta *Venus*.
Quae Tua rursus erunt *Europe*, gaudia salvae!
    Quo[t] surgent Tauro Templa superba *Jovi*.

---

99 Text: HRHRC, PR 3619, P54 S2 1712.
100 Title and Text: HRHRC, PR 3619 P54 A92 1712; BA(4a), 15. S.D. erased in HRHRC, present in Bodleian. In l. 4, Bodleian reads *grata* for *Diva* and *suo* for *Tuo*.
101 Text: N(54), (55), (56); BA(4a), 2;R¹, 26. The text printed is that of N(55), with one alteration in 8, *Quot* for *Quod*, as in (54) and (56). (54) differs further: 3: *huic* for *his*; 4: *Tu Decus omne Tuis* for *accipitresque truces*. 7: *sylvae* for *salvae*.
    In (56) we have; 2: *Impius et vestro* for *Atque* IMPUNE *Tuo*; 3: *aureus* for *et Deus*. 4: *feros* for *truces*. In R¹, *truces* is retained, but the text otherwise corresponds to (56).

99

'Germany once poured forth Saxons and Angles. Now, Anglo-Briton, it casts down only your own people.'

100

Archibald Pitcairne, Scot, greets Queen Anne

'Anna, whose better fortune it now is to guard the sceptre of the Scottish shore, passed down through innumerable generations, may it long retain authority, and when fate ordains that you must leave it, leave it, Goddess, to your Brother.'

101

'Your sacred doves have borne much during your absence, o King, and madness has raged unchecked in your world. You will put an end to this, son of a god and a divinity yourself, AND YOU WILL HARASS THE CROWS and the grim hawks. May a revived Caledonia quickly see you, her Father, and with the pious Caesar may there come a chaste Venus. How will the joy of the redeemed be yours again, Europa! How many proud temples will rise to Jove, the Bull!'

102

AD
Jacobum Dromondum,
Dominum Stobhallum,
Archibaldus Pitcarnius Scotus.

Salve, dignus Avis, exoptatusque *Dromondis*,
 Dignus *Havartaea Gordoniaque* Domo,
Qui semper Patriam propugnavere Patremque,
 Jacobumque suum visere rursus avent.
5 Illum quam videant, videant cito rure reverti?
 Quam nobis aderis tunc Anabella favens?

Natus est JACOBUS STOBHALLUS *Undecimo Maii, Anni* M.DCCC.XIII.

102 Title and Text: *N(14)*; HRHRC, PR 3619 P54 A72 1712; SP, 45.

102

Archibald Pitcairne, Scot, to James Drummond, Lord Stobhall

'Greetings, child worthy of your grandparents, greatly desired by the Drummonds, worthy of the house of Howard and Gordon, who have always rallied to the defence of their fatherland and its Father, who long to see their own James again. How they wish to see him, see him again, returning soon from the country! Then how much more favourable will you be to us, Annabella!'

James Stobhall was born 11 May 1713

7
Calendar and Church Year

103

AD
JOSEPHUM SCALIGERUM
29 Maij 1710.

    Scaliger, quo nil voluere Musæ
    Doctius Gallo volitare cœlo,
    Quemque jamdudum veneratur orbis
        Scoto-Brigantum;

5 Dic quibus terris, stimulante Phœbo,
    Culta tot quondam neque non colenda
    Gentibus, Maji properata lux vi-
        gesima nona

    Ibit in Junii decimam: Quot hujus
10 Tum dies ludi, quot & hinc honores
    Vestient annos etiam sub Orci
        Axe fluentes!

    Quam tibi gratus novus hic redibit,
    Carle, natalis, potior priore,
15 Qui sibi reddet populum potenti
        Dite creatum.

104

(a) **In Maij vigesimam nonam,**
Anno MDCCXII

    Hac CHRISTUS voluit patrio se reddere cœlo,
        Hac CAROLUM regno rursus adesse suo:
    Hac jus cuique suum tribui de monte jubebat,
        Esseque Christicolam qui data monte colit.
5 Vina SCOTI Regum Regi, stirpique STUARTAE
        Fundite, quae vobis nomina prisca dabit.

---

103 **Title and Text**: *N(22)*; BA*(4a)*, 6; R[1], 22; HRHRC, PR 3619 P54 A82 1710.
104 **Title and Text**: (a) *N(18)*; SP, 53: (b) *N(19)*: (c) *N(20)*.

103

To Joseph Scaliger, 29 May 1710

'Scaliger, whose work is more learned than any other which the Muses willed to soar in the Gallic heaven, and whom the world of the Scoto-Brigantes has long revered,

Say in what lands, spurred on by Phoebus, the twenty-ninth day of May, until now observed as a feast, and still to be observed in the future by so many nations, has been hurried on

And will transform itself into the tenth of June. How many days of this festival, how many consequent offerings, will then adorn the years, these even that are gliding under the axis of Orcus!

How gratifying to you, Charles, will be the return of your new natal day, better than the old, which will restore to itself a people created by the power of Dis.'

104

(a) *On 29 May 1712*

'On this day Christ willed his Ascension to his Father's heaven, and the Restoration of Charles to his kingdom. On this day from the Mount he ordered that each should be paid what was due to him, and that anyone who observes the commandments given on the Mount is a Christian. Pour out libations, you Scots, to the King of Kings, and to the House of Stuart which will give you back your ancient renown.'

CALENDAR AND CHURCH YEAR

(b) IN MAII XXIX,
Sive JUNI X,
Anni MDCCXII.

Hac CHRISTUS *voluit patrio se reddere coelo,*
  Hac **Carolum** *Regno rursus adesse suo.*

Hac jus cuique suum reddi de monte jubebat,
  Esseque *Christicolam* Qui data monte colit.
5 **Grampia** gaudebis cum *Maio Junius* haeres
  Numina prisca Tibi, tempora grata dabit.

(c) **In Maij vigesimam nonam**,
Anno MDCCXII.

Hac CHRISTUS voluit patrio se reddere coelo,
  Et *CAROLUM* regno rursus adesse suo:
Hac justos voluit gaudere, hac flere scelestos:
  Quae nobis potuit gratior esse dies?
5 Vina SCOTI Regum Regi, stirpique STUARTAE,
  Fundite, quae vobis nomina prisca dabit.

105

(a) **Ad Junium**

Juni, Te Regem jam mensibus esse fatetur
  Julius, Augusto non renuente prior.
Nunc Valeant Menses Septembres atque Novembres,
  Et nobis annus Junius unus eat.

(b) *Ad Junium Anni* MDCCXII

Juni, te regem nunc annis esse jubemus,
  Atque tui decimum mensibus esse decus.
Nunc abeant, abeant Septembres atque Novembres,
  Et nobis annus Junius unus eat.

105 Title and Text: (a) N(21); HRHRC, PR 3619 P54 A84 1712; (b) SP, 54.

(b) *On 29 May or 10 June 1712*

'On this day Christ willed his Ascension to his Father's heaven, and the Restoration of Charles to his kingdom. On this day from the Mount he ordered that each should be paid what was due to him, and that anyone who observes the commandment given on the Mount is a Christian. Land of the Grampians, you will rejoice when June, heir to May, restores you your ancient divinities and happy times.'

(c) *On 29 May in the Year 1712.*

'On this day Christ willed his Ascension to his Father's heaven, and the Restoration of Charles to his kingdom. On this day he willed that the just should rejoice and on this day that the wicked should weep. What day could be more gratifying to us? Pour out libations, you Scots, to the King of Kings, and to the House of Stuart which will give you back your ancient renown.'

105

(a) *To June*

'June, the former July declares that you are now King over the months, and August does not disagree. Now, farewell to the months of September and November, and may the year pass for us as a single June.'

(b) *To June 1712*

'June, we ordain you now to be king over the years, and your tenth to be the glory of the months. Now let Septembers and Novembers disappear, and may the year pass for us as a single June.'

106

(a) IV. Nov. M.DCC.XII.
Ad Calvini Discipulos

(b) *Ad* JOHANNEM CALVINUM

(c) *Ad* JANUM CALVINUM

Quod non quinta dies potuit patrare Novembris,
    Aut fors non voluit quinta patrare dies,
Vos voluit, vos quarta dies scelerata Novembris
    Ter decuma Jani proditione prior.

107

AD

JACOBUM MAGNUM

Quarta dies abiit Te Salvo, MAGNE, *Novembris*,
    Et nunquam voluit quinta nocere Tibi:
Sexta ter optatum patriae Te debuit aurae,
    Sed *Juno, Juno* non satis aequa fuit.
5 Septima ter tandem Te vidit laeta tremensque;
    Illa debueras, MAGNE, redire die:
Et redis, atque Jubes *Phoebo* fulgere *Novembrem*,
    Illo, cui placuit *Junius* ille tuus.

On *George Main*'s Son *James*, Born on the 7th of November 1711.

---

106 Title and Text: (a) HRHRC, PR 3619 P54 A62 1712; (b) HRHRC, PR 3619 P54 A8 1712; (c) SP, 54. In ll. 3–4, (b) and (c) read: *Discipulos, Calvine, tuos trigesima Jani/ Plusquam sacrilega vidit obire manu.*
107 Title: BA(4a), 9, 10. **Text**: BA(4a), 10. BA(4a), 9 lacks the final couplet and Gloss.

106

(a) *November 4 1712*

To Calvin's Disciples

(b) *To Janus Calvin*

'The accursed fourth day of November, surpassing the treachery of the thirtieth of January, decreed that you, you, should achieve what the fifth day of November could not achieve, or what destiny forbade the fifth day to achieve.'

107

To James the Great

'The Fourth of November passed without harming you, Great One, and the Fifth had no wish to do you any injury. The Sixth owed you, thrice desired, to your native breezes, but Juno, Juno, was not now sufficiently favourable. The Seventh, trembling with a triple joy, at last beheld you; your duty, Great One, had been to return on that day. And you do return and command November to shine with the same Sun in which that June of yours once took pleasure.'

On George Main's Son James, Born on the 7th of November 1711.

108

Die xxx *Novembris, Anni* MDCCXII.
Ad Andream CHRISTI **Apostolum**.
Qui SCOTIS *dedit esse Christianis*.
A. P.

Andraea, vixti *Jacobo* semper Amicus,
    Atque *Caledoniis* semper Amicus eras,
Rursus nos visas *Scotis* ter Sancte Patrone,
    Visas *Jacobo* sed redeunte redux.
5 Ille fidem officiis, non relligione malorum,
    Officiis nostris & pietate probet.

109

(a) *Die* xxv. *Decembris, Anni* MDCCXII.

Hac Christus jussit se nostram sumere formam,
    Ipse hominum Rector, Filius ipse Dei.
Hac homines jussit mortales esse beatos,
    Qui Patris vellent, qui sua jussa sequi,
5 Jussa sequi, queis ille Pater, queis Filius ille,
    Vos homines fecit semideosque viros,
Atque alii voluit faciendum quod tibi velles;
    Atque homines jussit *reddere cuique suum*:

---

108 Title and Text: *N(85)*.

109 Title and Text: (a) *N(26)*; *R¹*, 23; YB, BrSides By6 1712; all copies of a single print; SP, 69.

After the colophon, *N(26)* has a MS note in Pitcairne's hand: 'For Grubet from the Goodman and AP [monogram] in Prats's.' For the Bennets of Grubbet and Wideopen, see above, **65, 66**. 'Prats's' we have not identified.

In SP, 3: *Hic* for *hac*; 6: *Vos fecêre pios* for *Vos homines fecit*; 7: *Jusseruntque alii* for *Atque alii voluit*; 8: *Jusseruntque homines* for *Atque homines jussit*. 9–10 only in SP.

(b) SP, 96–98, apparently consisting of four short poems, the first and the last two by Robert Calder, on whom see below, **106**, introductory note. The second is a variant of (a). The poems appear in the part of SP devoted to memorial celebrations of Pitcairne, and in fact together form a single elegy, the main purpose of which is to defend Pitcairne against the charge of atheism or other form of unorthodox belief. The Christmas poem is central to the defence. The text has been modified, perhaps by Calder himself. Calder's own Latin verse is somewhat stilted.

7: *sibi* for *tibi*; 8: *numisma tui Cæsaris esse* for *homines jussit reddere*. This may show the influence of (a), 9–10, found only in SP, 69.

108

On 30 November 1712

A.P. to Andrew, Apostle of Christ, who granted the Scots Christianity

'Andrew, during your life you were always James's friend, and you were always a friend to the Caledonians. Visit us again, thrice-holy Patron of the Scots, visit us, but return with the restoration of James. May he approve our loyalty, accompanied, not with the superstition of malignants, but with the ceremonial forms that are ours, and with our piety.'

109

(a) On 25 December 1712

'On this day Christ, himself Ruler of men, himself Son of God, ordained that he should assume our form. On this day he ordained that mortals should be blessed who decided to follow the commandments given by the Father and Himself – to follow the commandments by which he, the Father, made you men, by which he, the Son, made you demigods. And he willed that you treat another as you might wish to be treated yourself, and he ordered human beings to render to each

      [Reddere cuique suum, primo si Cæsare major,
10   Sive sit is Cæsar, Cæsare sive minor.]
      Hac te, Christe, die natus Pitcarnius olim
        Auspice, te coluit, te colit, atque colet.

A.P.

Apud ROBERTUM FREEBAIRN, 1712.

(b) DAVIDI DRUMMONDO, Edinburgi, xxv Decembris MDCCXIII.

    Natalis Christi lux felicissima mundo,
      Te cum Pitcarno protulit illa dies,
    Nexus amicitiæ vestræ, Drummonde, juvabit
      Pitcarni Manes hâc memorare die.
5 Multa stylo obscuro Pitcarnus carmina scripsit,
      Perspicuo calamo ast asserit ille fidem.

Posuit R. CALDER.

Confessio Fidei ARCHIBALDI PITCARNII,
Die xxv. *Decembris, Anno* MDCCXII.

    Hac Christus jussit se nostram sumere formam,
      Ipse hominum rector, Filius ipse Dei.
    Hac homines jussit mortales esse beatos,
10   Qui patris vellent, qui sua jussa sequi;
    Jussa sequi, queis ille Pater, queis Filius ille
      Vos homines fecit, semideosque viros.
    Atque alii voluit faciendum quod sibi vellet,
      Atque numisma tui Cæsaris esse suum.
15 Hac te, Christe, die natus Pitcarnius olim
      Auspice, Te coluit, Te colit atque colet.

A.P.

Illatio ex Confessione PITCARNII.

    Hæc tua, Pitcarni, fidei Confessio Christi,
      Viva fides fuerat, quod benefacta probant.
    Fortunis inopes, ægrosque levare medelâ
20   Promptus eras, tristes aut hilarare jocis.

his own. [To render to each his own, whether he is greater than the first Caesar, whether he is that Caesar, whether he is less than Caesar.] Pitcairne, born this day under your protection, Christ, has worshipped you, does worship you, and will worship you.'

A.P.

Printed by Robert Freebairn, 1712

> (b) *To David Drummond at Edinburgh, 25 December 1713*

'The day of Christ's birth, light most auspicious to the world, that day brought you into the world, together with Pitcairne. On this day the close bond of your friendship, Drummond, will take pleasure in calling to mind the shades of Pitcairne. Pitcairne wrote many poems in a difficult style, but he affirmed his Creed with a lucid pen.'

R. Calder *composed this.*

> **Archibald Pitcairne's** *Confession of Faith, 25 December 1712*

'On this day Christ, himself ruler of men, himself Son of God, ordained that he should assume our form. On this day he ordained that mortals should be blessed who decided to follow the commandments given by the Father and himself – to follow the commandments by which he, the Father, made you men, by which he, the Son, made you demigods. And he willed that you do to another what he might wish for himself, and that the coin of your Caesar should be his own. Pitcairne, born this day under your protection, Christ, has worshipped you, does worship you, and will worship you.'

A.P.

> *Logical Inference from Pitcairne's Confession*

'Pitcairne, this, your Confession of the Christian faith, was a live faith, as your good deeds prove. You were prompt to relieve the destitute with your goods, the sick with your remedy, or to cheer up the sad with your witticisms. This faith

Non sapit hæcce fides Arii, nec dogma Socini,
  Sanguinei praxin neve rebellis olet.
Hâcce fide ductus didicisti Cæsari, & Iro,
  Et dare cuique suum, temnere & orbis opes.

Epitaphium.

25 Ecce Mathematicum, Vatem, Medicumque Sophumque,
    Pitcarnum magnum hæc urnula parva tenet.

R. CALDER.

110

AD
JESUM CHRISTUM
Dei Filium
ARCHIBALDUS PITCARNIUS *Scotus.*

Natali vestro, lacrymis jejunia pascunt
  Discipuli Cnoxi, quos *Usinulca dedit. *Calvinus

Quippe *Pharisaei* mutata voce fuere,
  Adventumque Tuum, maxime *Christe*, timent.

5 Ne monstraretis, parendum Regibus esse,
   Atque juberetis reddere cuique suum.

Nunc postquam terras placuit tibi linquere, gaudent
  Esse sibi festum fas agitare diem.

Et ridere Deum, qui nobis talia suasit,
10 Qualia *Cnoxiacis* esse nefasta placet.

Andream nobis Tu *Jacobum*que remitte,
  Qui Te, *Cnoxiacis*, auspice, verba dabunt.

110 Title and Text: *N(67)*; HRHRC, PR 3619 P54 A78 1713.

was unacquainted with the doctrines of Arius or Socinus, nor had it any smack of the business of the bloody rebel. Led by this faith, you learned to give to each his own, whether to Caesar or Irus, and to despise the world's wealth.'

Epitaph

'See, this tiny little urn holds the great Pitcairne, Mathematician, Poet, Physician and Sage both.'

R. Calder

110

Archibald Pitcairne, Scot, to Jesus Christ, Son of God

'On your birthday, the disciples of Knox, whom Usinulca produced, feed their fast-day with tears.

Because they were Pharisees under a different name, and they fear your Advent, greatest Christ,

Lest you should show that kings should be obeyed, and should order them to return to each his own,

Now after it has been your pleasure to leave Earth, they rejoice that they are permitted to insult a festal day,

And to deride God, who persuaded us to accept the very things it pleases the Knoxians to call forbidden.

Do You send back Andrew and James to us, who under Your guidance will confound the Knoxians.'

111

Cur Tibi Natalem felix *Heriote* quotannis
    Knoxiadae, at CHRISTO non celebrare solent?

Respondet HERIOTUS.

Hoc Aenigma Tibi solvet *Pitcarnius*, ergo
    Noli Tu Manes sollicitare meos.

PITCARNIUS.

5 *Presbyteris Scotis* nummos *Heriote* dedisti,
    At CHRISTUS nullos, spernitur ergo DEUS.

ROBERTUS CALDERUS.

Presbyteris Scotis CHRISTUM liquisse negabas
    Pitcarni nummos, quantus at error erat?
Nonne graves Illos nummorum pondere cernis,

PITCARNIUS Respondet.

10 Nam pretium *Caroli Martyris* omnes gerunt.

112

Ad JANUARIUM *Anni* MDCCXIII,
ARCHIBALDUS PITCARNIUS
Anno Aetatis suae LXI.

Jane, Senex optat *Pitcarnius* esse velitis
    Junius, & *Juveni* gratior atque Seni.
Quam vellet *Juvenem* se grato mense videre,
    Et caedes nunquam, *Jane*, videre *Tuas*.

---

111 **Text**: *N(63)*.
112 **Title and Text**: *N(71)*.

111

'Why is it an annual custom for the Sons of Knox to celebrate your birthday, blessed Heriot, when they don't celebrate Christ's?'

Heriot replies

'Pitcairne will solve this riddle for you, so give up vexing my ghost.'

Pitcairne

'You gave money to Scots ministers, Heriot, but Christ gave none, and so God is despised.'

Robert Calder

'You said, Pitcairne, that Christ left no money to the Scots ministers, but aren't you making a big mistake? Don't you see them loaded with money?'

Pitcairne replies

'Yes, they have their reward for Charles's martyrdom.'

112

Archibald Pitcairne, in his sixty-first year, to the January of 1713

'Janus, old Pitcairne desires that you should wish to be June, a more pleasing month to young and old alike. How he would wish to see himself young in a pleasing month, and never to see your murders, Janus.'

113

Dum Tibi laudatur *Maii* Vigesima Nona,
    Sis Decimae *Juni Sacheverele* memor,
Qui memorem *Maii* faciet Te, nosque beabit,
    Et reddet Populis aurea Secla suis.

Festo Ascensionis, et CHRISTI *in Regnum suum reditus, Anno* 1713 *scribebat Archibaldus Pitcarnius, Scotus.*

114

MARGARITA
REGINA et *DIVA*
SCOTORUM,
Ad *Maij* Vigesimam Nonam Anni MDCCXIII.

Sacra Dies olim Marti *Caroloque* fuisti,
    Arbitraque *Europae, Brittonibusque* Salus.
Saturnus genuit Te rursus Secla daturam
    Aurea, quae reddet *Junius* Ille meus.
5 Ille meus Sacer est Qui *Marti Mercurioque,*
    Arbiter, *Europe,* Qui Tibi Magnus erit.

115

Presbyteri Scoti PETRO.

Esse Tibi notum *Christum* ter *Petre* negasti,
    Quam vis Ille Tuus Rex foret atque *Deus.*

Respondet Sanctus *Petrus.*
29 *Junij,* 1713.

Mox me poenituit, sed vos non poenitet esse
    Perjurosque *Deo,* Regibus atque Tribus.

---

113 **Text**: *N(76).*
114 **Title and Text**: *N(57), (58)* – two copies of the same print.
115 **Title and Text**: *N(75).*

113

'While you regard the Twenty-Ninth of May as a festival, you should remember the Tenth of June, Sacheverell, who will make you remember May, and make us happy, and restore the Golden Age to his peoples.'

Archibald Pitcairne, Scot, wrote this on the Feast of the Ascension and return of Christ to his own Kingdom, 1713.

114

Margaret, Scottish Queen and Saint, on 29 May 1713

'You have long been a day sacred to Mars and to Charles, you have been Arbiter of Europe and Salvation to Britons. Saturn begat you to give back the Golden Ages, which that June of mine will restore. That June of mine is sacred who, as arbitrator between Mars and Mercury, will be great for you, Europa.'

115

The Scots Presbyters to Peter

'Peter, you thrice denied that you knew Christ, although He was your King and God.'

St Peter Replies, 29 June 1713

'I soon repented, but you don't repent that you have abjured God and three Kings.'

116

XXV *JULII* MDCCXIII

Quam Te prisca cupit gens *Grampia*, Sancte, redire!
    Et nullam *Romae* prorsus habere fidem!
Et *Genevae* nullam fictrici Relligionis,
    Quae peperit populis impia facta tuis.

117

CALDERUS

Visharto, qui se Moderatorem, hoc est, vel Deum aut Regem vocat: sacerdos spurius ex infima *Fanaticaque* Plebe.

    Proclamas omnes *Papistas* esse *Fugandos*,
        Normannumque simul Relligione colis,
    Qui *Lutheri* semper, Qui nunc Solennia *Papae*
        Sacra facit, si quid credis Amice mihi.

    Vishartus **Moderator**.

5 Omni sacra facit *Papae*, nunc Gratus haberi
    Vult *Knoxi* Papis, Quos *Usinulca* dedit.

---

116 Title and Text: *N(61)*.
117 Title and Text: *N(53)*.

8
European

118

(a) *Vaticinium*.

Austriacas acies & fultos Saxone Belgas,
    Fulmine disjicies, magne Philippe, tuo.
Sed dare te dignum, dignumque Ammone puellum,
    Qui regat Eoas occiduasque plagas,
5 Orbis opes, solis naturæ munus Iberis,
    Hic manet, hic unus teque Jovemque labos.

(b) *Vaticinium in Sepulcro Caroli Quinti repertum 1710*.

Teutonicas Acies, postremaque Cæsaris Arma
    Fulmine disjicies, Quinte Philippe, meo.
At dare Te Dignum, Dignumque Ammone Puellum,
    Qui Regna occiduis jungat Eoa plagis,
5 Orbis opes, solis naturæ munus Iberis,
    Hic manet, hic unus Teque Jovemque labos.

119

Carole, si similis Fratris, similisve Parentis,
    Et proavum indignus nullius esse cupis:
Finge Dei Matrem, si qua est, tibi semper amicam,
    Et cœptis adhibe Numina cæca tuis.
5 Relligione tumens, contemptor juris & æqui
    Sis pius, et visas sæpe sepulcra Deum,
Nil bello valeas, sis cultor pacis iniquus,
    Et scelerum sociis furcifer auctor eas,
Ganeo quæ turpis vel haruspex suaserit, aude;
10   Tu sic *Austriacus*, CAROLE, *Cæsar* eris.

---

118 Title and Text: (a) *R¹*, 27; SP, 70: (b) HRHRC, PR 3619 P54 V3 1710; BA(4a), 5, where -e- in *Teutonicas* is omitted but inserted by hand above the line.
119 Text: *N(80), (81)*; *R²*, Broadside B; HRHRC, PR 3619 P54 C32 1712. *N(80)* and *N(81)* differ typographically; *(81)*, 6: *visis* for *(80) visas*; 8: *Et socium sceleris Furcifer agmen agas* for *Et scelerum sociis furcifer auctor eas. Rel.* The text in *R²* resembles that in *N(80)*, but was printed separately in different types. In particular it lacks the ornate initial capital.

118

(a) *A Prophecy*

'Great Philip, you will scatter with your lightning the Austrian ranks and the Dutch supported by the Saxon. But this labour, this one labour, is waiting for you and for Jove, to grant you a boy worthy of you and worthy of Ammon, to rule Eastern and Western lands, the riches of the world, the gift of Nature to the Spaniards alone.'

(b) *Prophecy found in the Tomb of Charles v, 1710*

'Philip the Fifth, you will scatter with my lightning the German ranks and the ranks of the Emperor in the rear. But this one labour awaits you, awaits Jove, to give you a son worthy of you and worthy of Ammon, who can join the Eastern kingdoms to the Western territories, the riches of the world, the gift of Nature to the Spaniards alone.'

119

'Charles, if you want to be like your brother, like your parent, and unworthy of none of your ancestors, make sure that the Mother of God, if she exists, is always your friend, and summon blind powers to your enterprises. Swollen with superstition, you should piously despise law and equity, and often visit the tombs of the Saints. You should have no aptitude for war, but rather be a villainous peace-maker; you should go your way as a gallowsbird traitor to your allies. Dare to do whatever the vile debauchee or fortune-teller suggests. Thus, Charles, you will be Austrian Emperor.'

120

(a)

[*Ad* CAROLUM XII. **Suecorum** *Regem*.]

Carole *Gothorum* longe Fortissime Ductor,
    Gallia cui solum detinet ora parem,
Perjuros hostes, & barbara numina temne
    Sauromatûm, & dextro confice cæpta pede.
5 Dî Te victorem mox in Tua regna reducent,
    Et Patriam nulli non pietate parem.
Sis felix faveasque Tuis *Suecissime Cæsar*,
    Sic faveat *Lodoix Gallobritanna* Tibi.

(b)

CAROLE *Gothorum* Ductor fortissime, solus
    Cui par JACOBUS, non *Alaricus* erit.
Perjuros hostes, & barbara numina temne
    Sauromatum, & dextro confice caepta pede.
5 Di Te victorem mox in Tua Regna reducent,
    Et Patriam nulli non pietate parem.
Sis felix faveasque bonis, *Suecissime Caesar*,
    Di Tibi sic faveant, & Soror Illa Tui.

---

120 Title: SP, 70, only. **Text**: (a) N(27); HRHRC, PR 3619 P54 C3 1711; SP, 70. SP, 4: *cœpta* for *cæpta*; 7: *bonis*, the reading in (b), for *Tuis*; otherwise the texts differ only typographically. (b) N(28); R², Broadside C. The texts are identical.

120

(a) [*To Charles XII, King of Swedes*]

'Charles, by far the bravest leader of the Goths, whose only equal is detained on the Gallic shore, despise your perjured enemies, and the barbarous spirits of the Slavs, and complete the task which you began under favourable auspices. The gods will soon return you victoriously to your kingdom, your fatherland unequalled for its sense of duty. May you be fortunate and favour your own, most Swedish Caesar! So may Gallobritannic Louisa favour you!'

(b)

'Charles, bravest ruler of the Goths, whose only equal will be James, not Alaric, despise your perjured enemies and the barbarous spirits of the Slavs, and complete the task which you began under favourable auspices. The gods will soon return you victoriously to your kingdom, your fatherland unequalled in its sense of duty! May you be fortunate and favour the good, most Swedish Caesar! May the gods and that sister of yours thus favour you!'

121

i

(a) LODOIX MARIA STUARTA.

[(b) *Ad* MARIAM LODOVICAM TERESAM,
ipso suo natali die XVII. **Junii,** MDCCX.]

Fratre Tuo viso derisit Apollo Gradivum,
  Quo fuerat coelo fortius ante nihil.
Tu simul exorta es coelo formosior ipso,
  Abscondit nitidum Virgo patroa caput.

ii

(c) Ad Lodoicam Stuartam, *Ipso suo natali, die Decimo septimo Junii 1710.*

Risit *Apollo* tuo felici sidere fratri,
  Quo nihil in toto fortius orbe viget,
At simul exorta es, se longe pulcrior ipso,
  Abscondit nitidum victus *Apollo* caput.

122

(a)

MARIA LODOIX BRITANNA
AD
ALARICAM SUECAM

Juppiter arripuit Sibi Me, *Fratrem*que jubebit
  Esse suis Reducem cum volet ANNA soror;
Tunc Ego Te *Matrem Britannis* esse jubebo,
  Nam Magni *Conjux* sola micare potes.
5 Tu fias *Mater* qualis *Soror* ante fuisti,
  Et Magni Populos tres, ALARICA, bees.

---

121 Title: (a) N(74); R², Broadside A; (b) SP, 53; (c) BA(4a), 7. **Text**: For i, N and R² have the text printed. SP, 4, has *victum* for *nitidum* and differs slightly in capitals and punctuation. For ii, BA(4a), 7.
122 Title and Text: N(68) and (69).

121

i

(a) *Louisa Maria Stuart*

[(b) *To Maria Louisa Theresa on her birthday, 17 June 1710*]

'When your brother appeared, Apollo mocked Mars, who up to that point had been the bravest ever seen in heaven. As soon as you appeared, fairer than the very heaven, the Patroan Virgin hid her shining head.'

ii

(c) *To Louisa Stuart, on her birthday, the seventeenth day of June 1710.*

'Under a fortunate star, Apollo smiled on your brother. Nothing in the whole world enjoyed so vigorous a life as he. But as soon as you were born, more beautiful by far than himself, Apollo was conquered and hid his shining head.'

122

(a) *Maria Louisa, the Briton, to Ulrika, the Swede*

'Jupiter has snatched me to himself, and will ordain my brother's restoration when sister Anne decides. I will order you then to be a Mother to the Britons. As wife of a great one, you alone can shine. May you become such a Mother as formerly you were a Sister, and be a blessing to your great one's three peoples, Ulrika.'

(b)

Maria Lodoix Stuarta,
AD
Alaricam Suecam.

Juppiter arripuit sibi me, JUNONE relicta,
    Quod REGI fuerit non satis aequa meo.
Nunc volo REGINAM Te ALARICA vigere Britannum,
    Cumque meo REGE et FRATRE valere diu.

POEM 122

(b) *Maria Louisa Stuart to Ulrika, the Swede*

'Jupiter has taken me to himself, leaving Juno, because her rank was not equal to that of my king. Now I wish you, Ulrika, to lead your life as Queen of the Britons and enjoy long life with my Brother, the King.'

9
Translations

TRANSLATIONS

123

(a) **ΜΟΡΜΟΝΟΣΤΟΛΙΣΜΟΣ**
sive
Lamiarum Vestitus

A POEM
on the
KING and QUEEN
of
FAIRY

Translated into Latine by Mr. *Walter Dennestone*
Printed in the Year, MDCXCI

[(b) A POEM on the **King** and Queen of *Fairy*]

TO THE
VIRTUOSI

Ye *Virtuosi* hav't to you assign'd
The Natural causes of all things to find.
We cloath the *Fairies* in their proper dress;
And leav't to you, What force they have? to guess.

AD
PHILOSOPHOS

Naturæ, & rerum veras expendere caussas
Sorte datum vobis, Ingeniosa cohors.

123 Title and Text: (a), NLS, *1943.12.(2[1])* (?Edinburgh, 1691); (b), BL, *C.121.g9.(29)* (?London, 1670). Although it is later, we have chosen (a) for our textual basis. It has the longer, and for the most part the better text, and contains, in the attribution to Walter Dennestoun, the most probable indication of Pitcairne's authorship. The subtitle *In Oreadum Regem*, is lacking in (b). In stanza 2 (English), (b) has *Spider* for *Spiders*; in 5.5 *When* for *New*. In 6.3–4 (Latin), (b) has *ut sine fine moveret/ Aera si Cynips uel prætereundo feriret* for (a), *ut trepidaret ad auram/ Quam musca aut cynips prætervolitando feriret*. (b) 8.4 (English) has *unctious* for *unctuous*; 8.4 (Latin) *Instita* for the meaningless *Iustita* of (a). In *On the* QUEEN, 1.1 (English), (b) has *attyr'd* for *atryr'd*; in 2.1 (Latin), the less evocative *lumine* for *lampade*; in 3.2 (Latin), *variis* for *varius*; in 4.3 (English), *But* for *Bnt*; in 6.1 (Latin), the nonsensical *orba* for *alba*; in 6.3 (Latin), the meaningless *nagagate* for *gagate*. In 7.3 (English), (b) has *to Trade*, (a) *to tread*.

For the most part, the readings in (a) are corrections or improvements. A few corruptions have also been introduced.

A further text is to be found in *A Choice Collection of Comic and Serious Scots Poems both Ancient and Modern* (3 vols., Edinburgh: James Watson, 1706, 1709, 1711), i, 135–141, most easily consulted in Harriet Harvey Wood (ed.), *Watson's Choice Collection* 1, 136–141. Watson's text is directly based on (b).

123

To the Natural Philosophers

'The task allotted to you, scientists, is to decide the true laws of nature and reality. For our part, we veil the bodies of the Shades with a tenuous cloak. It is for you to define the power, the force, inherent in them.'

Corpora nos Lemurum tenui velamus amictu:
Dicite vos, Quæ vis? quis vigor insit eis?

On the KING of FAIRY.

Upon a time the Fairy Elves,
Having first array'd themselves,
Thought it meet to cloath their King,
In Robes most fit for Revelling.

In Oreadum Regem.

Monticolæ quondam Lamiæ circumdata amictu
Corpora prætenui choreis & lusibus apto;
Talibus inde suum Regem quoq; vestibus ornant
Quæ deceant numerosq; leves festasque chorêas.

(2)

He had a Cobweb-Shirt more thin,
Than ever Spiders since could spin;
Bleach'd in the whiteness of the Snow,
When the Northern Winds do blow.

Ejus araneoli scutulata subucula filo
Rarior, eximiæ quod texuit artis Arachne:
Intactæque nivis fuit insolata nitore,
Quam rigidus gelidâ Boreas diffundit ab Arcto.

(3)

In that Waste and open Air
No Shirt half so Fine or Fair:
A rich Waste-Coat they did bring
Made of the Trout-flies Golden Wing.

Nec sub Hyperboreo tam pura camisia tractu
Usque adeò tenuis tamque alba apparuit usquam:
Proxima cura fuit tunicellam imponere Regi
Hepiali textam mirè ex aurantibus alis.

POEM 123

On the King of the Oreads

(1)

'Once upon a time the mountain-Witches wrapped their bodies in filmy cloaks suited to dances and revels; afterwards they adorned their king too with such garments as befit light music and festive dances.'

(2)

'His check-shirt was finer than the little spider's thread woven by the choice art of Arachne. It was bleached with the brightness of untrodden snow which harsh Boreas has spread from the frozen North.'

(3)

'Nowhere in the Hyperborean region did so clean and fine and white a shirt appear. Their next business was to dress their King in a waistcoat miraculously woven from the moth's golden-glistening wings.'

(4)

Dy'd Crimson in a Maidens blush,
And lin'd with Humming-Bees soft Plush.
At which his Elf-ship 'gan to fret
And sware 'twould cast him in a sweat.

Virginis eximiæ roseo quæ tincta rubore,
Atque apis Hyblææ duplicata est vellere molli:
Tum fremere & jurare Heros gestamine tanto
Pressus, & exili manare à corpore sudor.

(5)

He for his Coolness needs would wear
A Waste coat made of Downy Hair,
New taken from an Eunuchs Chin,
It pleas'd him well; 'twas wondrous thin.

Post, refrigerii caussâ, subtile theristrum
Curari fecit consutum more decoro,
Nuper ab Eunuchi malâ & lanugine sumptum:
Hoc placuit, quia erat tenui subtemine textum.

(6)

His Hat was all of Ladies love,
So passing light that it would move
If any Gnat or Humming Fly
But beat the Air in passing by.

Ejus erat (capitis tegumentum insigne) galerus,
Ut referunt, è femineo conflatus amore;
Qui levis usque adeo fuit ut trepidaret ad auram,
Quam musca aut cynips prætervolitando feriret.

POEM 123

(4)

'Which was dyed with the rosy blush of a handsome maiden, and lined with the soft fleece of the bee of Hybla. Then the Hero began to fret and swear because he was oppressed by so great a weight, and sweat was trickling from his slender body.'

(5)

'Next, to keep him cool, he had them prepare a thin summer-garment, becomingly stitched together, and taken from the down on a Eunuch's chin. This pleased him because it was woven with a subtle woof.'

(6)

'His bonnet, the distinguished covering for his head, as they say, was fused from woman's love, and was so light that it trembled at the breeze caused by a gnat or gall-fly fluttering past.'

(7)

About it went a wreath of Pearle
Dropt from the Eyes of some poor Girle,
Pincht because she had forgot
To leave clean Water in the Pot.

Ambijt hunc circum speciosa & gemmea spira
Ex oculis teneræ tremulis modò lapsa puellæ;
Quam malè multarunt Lemures quòd linquere in ollâ
Oblita est puras, nocturno tempore, lymphas.

(8)

His Breeches and his Cassock were
Made of the Tinsel Garsummer:
Down it's seam there went a lace
Drawn by an unctuous Snails slow pace.

Denique fiebant saga cum femoralibus ejus
Lineolâ é tenui per summa cacumina campi
Extensâ, quorum suturam rara tegebat
I[n]stita ducta pigri limacis tramite pingui.

On the QUEEN

No sooner was their King atryr'd
  as never Prince had been,
But as in duty was requir'd
  they next array their Queen.

In REGINAM

Postquam Rex tali fuit insignitus amictu
  Membra cui Regum nulla tulere parem.
Mox etiam, veluti ratio poscebat & æquum,
  Reginæ parili corpora veste tegunt.

(7)

'Round this went a beautiful coil of precious stones just fallen from the trembling eyes of a delicate girl, whom the Shades cruelly punished because she forgot to leave fresh water overnight in the pot.'

(8)

'Then his cloak and his breeches were made from the delicate little thread which extends from tip to tip of the shoots in the meadow. A flounce fashioned by the spruce course of an indolent snail concealed the seam.'

On the QUEEN

'After the King was arrayed in clothing finer than any Kings' limbs had previously borne, soon, as reason and equity demanded, the body of the Queen too they clothed in equally splendid garments.'

(2)

Of shining threed shut from the Sun
  And twisted into Line,
On the light Wheel of Fortune Spun
  was made her Smock so fine.

Illius ex auro clarâ de lampade solis
  Emisso, scitè facta erat interula.
Stamina cujus erant solerti pollice ducta,
  Sortis in ambiguæ torta levique rotâ.

(3)

Her Gown was very colourd fair
  The Rain-bow gave the dip;
Perfumed by an amber Air,
  Breath'd from a Virgins lip.

Palla fuit, qualem spectabilis induit Iris,
  Quam varius radiis pingit Apollo suis.
Talis odor, qualis fragranti spirat ab ambrâ,
  Halitus aut qualis Virginis esse solet.

(4)

The Stuff was of a Morning dawn
  When Phebus did but peep,
B[u]t by a Poets Pencil drawn
  In Chloris lap asleep.

Materies fuit Auroræ de lumine primo
  Phœbus ubi Eois surgit honorus aquis.
Peniculo vatis qui pingebatur amatæ
  Chloridis in gremio membra quiete levans.

(2)

'Her smock had been skilfully made of gold sent out from the bright torch of the sun, the warp of which a clever hand had woven on the crooked and fickle wheel of doubtful Fortune.'

(3)

'Her robe was like that donned by Iris when she appears, painted by variegated Apollo with his beams. The scent was like the air which breathes from fragrant amber, or like that which a maiden usually has.'

(4)

'The material was provided by the first light of Aurora, when Phœbus confers glory arising from the Eastern waters, whom the brush of a poet portrayed quietly raising his limbs from the lap of his loved Chloris.'

(5)

Her Vail was white and pale-fac'd by,
  Invented by a Maid,
When she (poor Soul) by some bad spy
  Had newly been betray'd

Candidulumque habuit velamen, pallidulumque,
  Dextra puellaris texuit illud opus,
Qui color idem erat ac pellucet in ore puellæ
  Prodita ab infausto quæ modo forte viro.

(6)

Her Necklace was of subtile tye
  Of glorious Atoms, set
In the pure Black of Beauties eye,
  As they had been in Jet.

Illius alba decens ornabat colla monile
  Formosum pulchris conspicuisque atomis:
Quæ velut in puro nigroque gagate fuissent
  Impositæ, miris emicuere modis.

(7)

Her Shoes were all of Maiden-Heads
  So passing thin and light
That all her care was how to tread;
  A thought had burst them quite.

Calceolique sui perquam tenuesque levesque
  Facti de claustris virginitatis erant.
His igitur verita est incedere, namque pusillus
  Sensus amoris eos rumperet absque morâ.

(5)

'She had a tiny little veil, both white and pale-faced. A girl's right hand wove that work. It had the colour visible in the face of the girl who somehow or other finds herself betrayed by an unhappy man.'

(6)

'Her white neck was adorned by a becoming necklace, finely formed from beautiful and striking atoms. As if they had been set in pure black jet, they shone amazingly.'

(7)

'Her sandals were fashioned from maidenheads so dainty and light that she feared to walk in them, for the least trace of love would burst them immediately.'

(8)

The revells ended, she put off
  Because her Grace was warm:
She fann'd her with a Ladies scoff,
  And so she took no Harm.

Ludis exactis, quoniam sudore madebat
  Confestim vestes exuit ipsa suas.
Et se femineo vannavit scommate demum
  Nec quidquam damni pertulit inde sibi.

FINIS

124

An Inscription on JOHN BELL
JOHN BELL *liv'd in* Annandale, *on the Scots Side, and has a Stone* (200 *Years old*) *on him, with this Inscription.*

I Jocky Bell o' Braiken-brow lyes under this Stane;
  Five of my own Sons laid it on my Wame:
I liv'd aw my Days but Sturt or Strife,
  Was Man of my Meat, and Master o' my Wife.
5 If you done better in your Time than I did in mine,
  Take the Stane aff my Wame and lay it on o' thine.

Imitated by ARCHIBALD PITCAIRN, **M.D.** Scotsman.

(a)

Hoc saxum mihi filii induerunt
Quinque, Mercurio Beloque digni,
Privatos tenui lares tumultu,
Uxoris Dominus, famis Magister,
5 Si rem me melius gerendo vixti,
Hoc saxum licet induas, amice.

124 Title and Text: HRHRC, PR 3619 P54 153 1712; SP, 80–81.

(8)

'Immediately the revels were ended, she doffed her clothes by herself, because she was dripping with sweat, and finally she fanned herself with a lady's taunt, nor did it bring her any harm.'

The End

124

An Inscription on JOHN BELL

(a)

'This stone my five sons, worthy to belong to Mercury and Bell, put on me. I kept my household free from trouble, was Lord of my wife and Master of my hunger. If your life has been better managed than mine, you, my friend, may don this stone.'

(b)

Hic Belus abscondor, caput objectare periclis
    Impiger, & prædam sæpe referre novam:
Scota domum conjux castam servabat, & illi
    Prima fuit semper cura placere mihi.
5 Si qua tuo, Lector, favit fortuna labori,
    Aut mage virtuti dextra Laverna tuæ,
Tolle tibi hoc saxum quod nobis incubat, isti
    Inscribas laudes quot libet ipse tuas.

John Bell's *Monument is in* Reid *Kirk-Yard, now in the parish of* Graitney, *belonging to the Right Honourable the Viscount of* STORMONT.

POEM 124

(b)

'Here, a Bell, I'm hidden away, unwearied in putting my head into dangers, and often bringing back fresh booty. My Scott wife kept my house chaste, and her first care was always to please me. If fortune has in any way favoured your work, reader, or a more favourable Laverna promoted your virtue, take up for yourself this stone which lies on me, and on it inscribe as much self-praise as you like.'

10

Dubia. Poems by Walter Dennistoun and Robert Hepburn

125

In
Annum Millesimum Septingentesimum

Post mille exactos à partu virginis annos,
    Et tria bis porro sæcula, lapsa priùs.
Centuriam claudit *septenam* hic omine fausto,
    Tempora lætitiæ totus & annus habet.
5 Nunc emittendi captivi ex carcere cœco,
    Et miseris largâ munera danda manu.
Hactenus attriti fuimus bellisque fameque,
    Interiitque gravi frigore turba frequens.
Sed nunc bella silent, torpent lituique canori;
10   Et Cereris premium est vilius atque fuit.
Ipsa soli & cœli facies blanditur amicè,
    Cessat & iste hyemum qui fuit ante rigor.
Eque *Caledoniâ* manarunt nuncia grata,
    Unde brevi ingentes, spero, vehentur opes.
15 Auspiciis igitur tantis cum cuncta gerantur,
    Scotia mox lætum tollet ad astra caput.
Cuique suum dabitur: terras *Astræa* reviset,
    Incolet & nostros copia paxque Lares.

Interea afflicti, lector, memor esto Poetæ,
20   *Qui premitur podagrâ, pauperieque simul.*

W.D.

126

Ricardio Stilio Anglo,
Viro hujus Sæculi Maximo,
Robertus Hepburnius Scotus.
S.D.

Dicite Heroem Sociumve, Musæ,
Libero Patri, Venerique gratum,
Cujus immensas merito laborem
    Pangere laudes.

125 Title and Text: HRHRC, CE 97 W2 1700.
126 Title and Text: EUL, Df.2.47; HRHRC, PR 3619 P54 R5 1713.

125

On the Year 1700

'After a thousand years have passed since the Virgin Birth and in addition twice three centuries before that have gone by, this year as a whole closes the seventeenth century under good omen and possesses a time of joy. Now captives are to be released from dark imprisonment and gifts are to be given to the wretched with generous hand. Thus far we have been worn down with wars and famine. Multitudes have often perished in the severe cold. But now wars are silent, the sonorous war-trumpets are inactive and the cost of corn is cheaper than it was. The very face of earth and heaven entices in a friendly fashion and that wintry rigour of the past is wanting. So too from Caledonia pleasing news has spread abroad, from which, I hope, great riches will soon be brought along. Therefore, since everything is developing under such good auspices, Scotland will soon raise her joyful head to the stars. To each his own will be given. Astraea will revisit Earth. Plenty and Peace will live in our homes too.

Meanwhile, Reader, remember the afflicted Poet, who is oppressed simultaneously by gout and poverty.

W.D.'

126

The Scot, Robert Hepburn, greets English Richard Steele, Greatest Man of this Age

'Sing, Muses, of the Hero or Comrade, friend of Father Liber and Venus, for whom I earn the task of composing a boundless panegyric.

    5 Ingeni magni melior quis Auctor,
        Sæpius mecum tacitus revolvo,
        Quidve Mortales Superis adæquos
           Reddere possit.

        Sive sit certus Deus; anne Venter
 10 Ingeni largitor: aberrat autem,
        Si quis his causis putet obvenire
           Nobile pectus.

        Rectius dices nihil absque Vino
        Posse præclarum fieri, atque nasci
 15 Pulchrius, possit quod & hunc in annum, &
           Vivere plures.

        Laudibus Vini meritis putatur
        Esse Vinosus, Pater ille Vatum,
        Qui graves Trojæ cecinit labores,
 20   Magnus Homerus.

        Ennius nunquam, nisi Potus, arma
        Ausus est forti resonare plectro:
        Nam Duces sævos melius canebat
           Plenus Jaccho.

 25 Ipsa narratur veteris Catonis
        Sæpius Vino caluisse Virtus:
        Romuli fæci tamen est luendæ
           Censor in annum.

        Teque, Ricardi, minuisse curas,
 30 Te ferunt Vino: emeritos labores,
        Dive, quis Cælo & Superis redonet
           Carmine digno.

POEM 126

Often I turn over silently in my own mind what source of great ability could be better, or what [else] could make mortals the equals of the gods,

Or whether the source is certainly a God. Surely the Belly doesn't bestow genius? But if anyone were to think it is for these reasons that noble inspiration comes as his lot, he makes a bad mistake.

You would more correctly say that without wine nothing that could live both for this year and more could become distinguished and have a beautiful birth.

Great Homer, that Father of Bards, who sang the heavy labours of Troy, is regarded as a drunkard because he gave to wine the praises it earned.

Save when drunk, Ennius never dared resound war on his mighty lyre, because he used to sing fierce leaders better when he was filled with Iacchus.

The very virtue of old Cato is said to have become heated by wine more often than not, yet he was appointed Censor for a year to purge the Roman dregs.

They say that you, Richard, have lessened your cares with wine. Who may restore your well-earned labours, Saint, to heaven and the gods by a song worthy of you?'

127

Ad
GEORGIUM MAKENZIUM,
Regium, olim, apud *Scotos*,
ADVOCATUM
Roberti Hepburnij, Scoti,
CARMEN SAPPHICUM.

Te sequor læta calidus Juventa:
Fidus interpres tua scripta cultu
Patrio donavi, abiens in oras,
    Advena, *Belgum*.

5 Ore facundo, *Theopompum*, et atras
Regias cædes, simulata obumbras
Fabula; ac magnos, Juvenis, labores
    Præripis *Orco*.

Me quater denas *Satiras* dedisse
10 Civibus gratum juvat, et decoro
More lusisse haud pudet insecantem, in
    Tempore, Ludum.

Pœnitet lingua tamen *Anglicana*
Esse descriptas. Brevioris Ævi
15 Patrius sermo est; aliisque terris
    Non bene notus.

127 Title and Text: EUL, Df.2.47.

127

*To George Mackenzie, umquhile King's Advocate for
Scotland, a Sapphic Ode by Robert Hepburn, Scot.*

'I follow you in the warmth of light-hearted Youth. A faithful translator, I have rendered your writings in native style while as a stranger I was visiting the shores of the Dutch.

With eloquent lips you disguise Theopompus and the black slaughter of a king in a counterfeit tale, and, while still a young man, you snatch from Orcus your mighty labours.

I'm pleased to have published forty *Satires* which have given pleasure to the public, and I'm not ashamed to have pursued my game decently at the appropriate time.

I'm sorry, however, that the *Satires* were written in English. Our native tongue has relatively recent origins and it is not well known in other countries.

COMMENTARY

1

Notes. Robert Lindsay was the eldest son of James Lindsay of the Mount, Fife, and his wife, Anna, daughter of Sir Patrick Hay of Pitfour, Perthshire. Robert died in 1675/6, before his father. The family were collateral descendents of the poet, Sir David Lindsay of the Mount (c. 1490–1555), whose satirical verse remained popular well into the eighteenth century. During Pitcairne's lifetime at least seven editions of the *Works* were published (D. Hamer [ed.], *The Works of Sir David Lindsay of the Mount*, 4 vols., STS [Edinburgh and London, 1931–1936], iv, 284 [genealogical table], 86–95 [bibliography]).

The Key, particularly the version in S, gives details of the close relationship between Lindsay and Pitcairne:

'Robert Lindsay, grandchild [sic] to Sir David Lindsay of the Mount Lyon King at Armes etc. and whose sister was married to David Lyndsay Melforts Davie was most intimat condisciple with AP. These two reading in the summer 1671 when both graduated by Sir Wm. Paterson, Plato and some bits of Dr Henrie More, Ficinus, made a bargain that whoever died first should give an account of his condition. Robert Lyndsay succeeded his father as a Clerk to the exchequer, Mount or Month (a mile north-west from Coupar in Fife) being on his 800 merks a year, still in his possession but really belonging to his father's creditors. He dy'd of an Iliac passion in the winter 1675 and 1676 when AP was at Paris. That very night, in which Lyndsay died, as AP's letter and Boghall's letter given at Paris agreed, AP dream't (as a man at Eise) That Lindsay cme to him thus, Archie perhaps you heard I'm dead. No Robin. Ay but they have buried my body in the Gray-Friars, I am tho alive and in a place the pleasures of which cannot be exprest in Scots Greek or Latin. I have come with a well sayling small ship to Leith Road to carry you thither. Robin Jll go with You but wait till I go to Fife and take leave of my father and mother ([who d]welle at Pitcairne Gren) and next to East Lothian to take leave of my aunt Rothlan. Archie I have but the allowance of one tide and you shall not make your visits in so short a tyme. Forsooth Archie, J'll come for you at another tyme.

AP never sleeps a night Since that tyme without dreaming that Robin Lindsay told him that [he] was alive, and in the year 94 when AP had a sickness that every body thought insuperable, as he could not walk without being supported, had never any fear of himself, Robin told him he was delay'd for a time but he was order'd and was properlie put to his task to carry off AP at a tyme nor was discharged to tell [when].'

Sir William Paterson is probably Sir William Paterson of Granton (d. 1709), third son of John Paterson, bishop of Ross (1604–1679) and younger brother of John Paterson (1632–1708), later archbishop of Glasgow (below, 20(II), 37–38n.). Sir William became an advocate and was later clerk to the Privy Council; at this time he may have been the regent responsible for Pitcairne and Lindsay's progress through college. Plato is mentioned primarily in terms of the *Phaedrus* myth of the soul as charioteer, and the vision of Er with which the *Republic* closes, both demonstrating the immortality of the human soul. The Florentine Neoplatonist Marsilio Ficino (1433–1499) wrote a famous commentary on the *Phaedrus*, in which he gave much attention to the myth (M.J.B. Allen, *Marsilio Ficino and the Phaedran Charioteer* [London, 1981]; *The Platonism of Marsilio Ficino; A Study of His Phaedrus Commentary, Its Sources and Genesis* [London, 1984]). The Cambridge Platonist, Henry More (1614–1687) is probably mentioned for his *The Immortality of the Soul, so farre forth as it is demonstrable from the Knowledge of Nature and the Light of Reason* (London, 1659).

A somewhat garbled version of the story appears in *Analecta; or Materials for a History of remarkable Providences, mostly relating to Scotch Ministers and Christians* (4 vols., Maitland Club [Glasgow, 1842–1843], iii, 520–521) by Robert Wodrow. According to this, Pitcairne was the close friend of David Lindsay, Clerk to the Council at Edinburgh, with whom he had been at school and college. Lindsay died when Pitcairne was in Paris. Before the news reached there, he had a dream in which he found himself in Edinburgh and was told of the death, but afterwards met his friend in the Lawnmarket. David assured him that in fact he was dead, but desired that he might go with him. They went down the street together, but were unable to enter several houses where they used to drink. They went by way of Leith Wynd to the Calton Hill, where Lindsay entered a slap ('pass or shallow valley between hills') and disappeared from sight. The dream was repeated ten or twelve times before news of the death arrived from Edinburgh. Lindsay continued to appear nightly for the rest of Pitcairne's life.

Wodrow (1679–1734), who had been Librarian of Glasgow University, but for most of his life was minister of the rural parish of Eastwood in Renfrewshire, only gradually pieced his version together. He claims that the story was widely known in Edinburgh, but the name of the revenant, he thought at first (*op. cit.*, ii, 47–48) was Stevenson, a name associated with Pitcairne, whose second wife was the daughter of the physician Sir Archibald Stevenson (1630–1710; see **40**); only later did he discover that it was Lindsay. The Christian name he gives is David, not Robert, and he describes him as Clerk to the Council in Edinburgh, when in fact he was a Clerk to the Exchequer. He probably confused two Lindsays. He regards the episode as taking place shortly before Pitcairne's own death in 1713. Pitcairne however did not visit Paris in his later years, but stayed there in 1671 or 1672, and again from 1675 to 1680. The second visit fits with the death of Robert Lindsay.

The short poem, *Ad Robertum Lindesium* (45), is probably related.

The story is undeniably interesting, but seems to have only a limited relevance to the poem that it is intended to introduce. The world of the dead from which Lindsay is invited to return differs considerably from the 'place whereof the pleasues cannot be exprest,' nor is there any hint that Lindsay has already made at least one return trip with an invitation for Pitcairne to join him in Elysium. Instead, he has passed the time since his death in Lethaean sleep. The concept of the revenant is the only feature common to poem and story. Primarily the poem is a powerful satiric portrait of Scotland transformed by recent events into an adjunct of the classical Hades. Pitcairne may however intend that the present state of Scotland has at last made him ready to be summoned by Lindsay.

Title *1689*: the year of the accession of William of Orange and Mary as joint monarchs, thus completing the Revolution which Pitcairne did not regard as Glorious.

1–3 *stygias undas … Stagnaque Cocyti … Lethæi vincula somni*: references, probably derived from *Aeneid* 6, 295–316, 125–136, 703–715, to the streams of the classical underworld. Lindsay on his return, is to shake off the forgetfulness caused by the waters of the river of forgetfulness, Lethe.

5–6 *promissa daturus/ Gaudia*: the pact to provide details of the hereafter, 'if possible.'

6 *Proavo*: the satirist and reformer, Sir David Lindsay of the Mount. The most relevant among his works are probably the play, *Ane Satyre of the Thrie Estaitis*, the first recorded performance of which was in 1552 at Cupar in Fife, and *The Monarche (Ane Dialog betuix Experience and ane Courteour, off the Miserabyll Estait of the Warld)*, written c. 1548–1553, with the first printed edition appearing at St Andrews or Edinburgh in 1554. After the death of James V in 1542, his daughter, the young Queen Mary, was sent to France in 1548. For later Jacobite eyes, the situation resembled that which followed the flight of James VII and the infant Prince of Wales to France in 1689. Like the Jacobites, Lindsay had some hope of amendment:

> *Thoucht God with mony terrabyll affrayis*
> *Hes done this cuntrie scurge by divers wayis,*
> *Be Iuste Iugement, for our greuous offence,*
> *Declare to thame thay sall haue mery dayis*
> *Efter this trubyll, as the Propheit sayis:*
> *Quhen God sall se our humyll Repentence,*
> *Tyll strange pepyll thoucht he hes geuin lycence*
> *To be our scurge Induryng his desyre,*
> *Wyll, quhen he lyste, that Scurge cast in the fyre.* (*Monarche*, 82–90)

It was easy to equate 'strange pepyll' with William of Orange and his followers.

7 *novos cives*: adherents of William of Orange, including members of the formerly outlawed Presbyterian conventicles; cf. **4**, 3.
mutataque regna: Scotland, England, and Ireland, changed by the success of King William.

8 *Teutonicas*: perhaps simply 'Dutch,' but possibly a derogatory reference to Nassau, the district north of Wiesbaden in Hesse, which formed a significant part of the patrimony of the House of Orange-Nassau, 'King Willie, that Bullie of Twenty or Thirty *German* Lairds' (Tobin, *Assembly*, I, i, p. 41). Compare the use of *Nassovus* or *Nassus* for William, **27**, 2; **83**, 2.
sceptra: poetic plural for singular, or perhaps a reference to the individual sceptres of the three kingdoms.

9 *Legatosque Deûm*: members of the government.

11 *non Phœbi ... artes*: Pitcairne regarded many of the Presbyterians as uneducated. The arts of Phœbus are poetry and medicine, of Pallas (Minerva) philosophy.

12 *Bardis ... novis*: Presbyterian ministers and teachers.

13–14 *Queis Deus ... manum*: a discreet reference to King William is probably included. The author of a mock-epitaph (*Christ Church, Oxford*, Wake MSS 18.514; Money, *English Horace*, 206) is more direct, describing him as *trium patris Regnorum fur improbus ... pseudorexque ... Britanniarum*, 'the wicked thief of his father's [i.e., father-in-law's] three kingdoms ... and pseudo-king of the British Isles.'

14 *imbelles immeritosque*: Episcopalians generally; cf. the words of Mr Covenant Plain Dealer: 'they call themselves Ministers of the Episcopal Perswasion, but we'll give no Favor to any such people, we'll root out the Canaanites, and not leave one of them alive i' the land' (Tobin, *Assembly*, II, iii, p. 55).

20 *Aëris ... regit*: an ironic echo of the disciples' words after Christ had calmed the storm: 'What manner of man is this that even the winds and the sea obey him!' (Matthew, 8, 27).

21–22 *in obscœnos ... cogit*: i.e., dresses them in the costume of a Presbyterian minister. 'Go get a double necked Cloke, an high-crown'd Hat: and all the other Appertinencies of a *Presbyterian* Minister' (Tobin, *Assembly*, III, i, p. 61).
obscœnos also carries implications of sexual impropriety, like that of Mr James Wordy, the Old Lady's Presbyterian chaplain, who seduces Mrs Rachel, her daughter, or that attempted by Mr Solomon Cherry Trees, a Preacher, against Mrs Laura (Tobin, *Assembly*, I, ii, pp. 43–45; III, ii, pp. 63–65). The exploits of David Williamson, minister of the West Kirk in Edinburgh, the hero of '*David ad Venerem*' (below, **18**), are caricatured in those of Mr Solomon Cherry Trees.
obscœnos: cf. **12**, 34n.

22 *exutum ... genus*: Presbyterians, who had been refugees in Holland during the reigns of Charles II and James VII, but who returned with King William.

23–24 *Quæ ... potest*: another discreet reference to William, whom Jacobites (and others) credited with homosexual tendencies. The anonymous author of the mock-epitaph already quoted calls him *Mas-stuprator, Sodomita, Misogynos*, three words with the same meaning. Cf. too 'An Ode inscribed to King William' by the noted Jacobite Alexander Robertson of Struan (c. 1670–1749), most readily consulted in T. Crawford (ed.), *Love, Labour and Liberty: the eighteenth-century Scottish lyric* (Carcanet, 1976), 92–93. We are grateful to Dr Money for this reference.

There may also be a reference to the disruption, in the person of William, of the divinely ordered royal succession.

25–31 *Avernum … Rhadamanthus*: the places and figures mentioned all appear in *Aeneid* 6; see especially 125–136, 273–281, 295–316, 703–715.

28–29 *Tartareos … Tartareumque … Tartara*: note the effective rhetorical repetition with variations.

31 *Rhadamanthus*: judge of the dead.

2

Notes. For Lockhart and Graham, see the next two poems. William and Mary were accepted as joint monarchs of Scotland by the Convention of the Estates in April 1689. On 7 June 1690 they finally approved an act establishing Presbyterian government of the church. By the Act Concerning Patronages of 19 July 1690 the right to present ministers to vacant charges devolved upon the heritors and elders of the parish under the oversight of the presbytery. The unrepresentative General Assembly of November 1690, composed of some 180 ministers and elders, none from the Episcopalian heartland, the area north of the Tay, pressed ahead with plans to purge the church and universities of unyielding Episcopalians, a task performed with much zeal and little discretion. In 1692 the meeting of an equally unrepresentative Assembly was eventually dissolved by the royal commissioner, but to little effect. The proceedings of this last are caricatured in Pitcairne's *The Assembly* and in his *Babell; A Satirical Poem on the Proceedings of the General Assembly in the Year* M.DC.XCII (ed. G. Kinloch, [Edinburgh, 1830]). The present poem is probably earlier. It belongs to the period between the 1690 Assembly and the death of Sir George Mackenzie of Rosehaugh on 8 May 1691; see 5.

1 *Fides … Orbe*: Pitcairne follows Claudian (*In Rufinum*, 1, 53; M. Platnauer [ed.], *Claudian*, 2 vols., Loeb Classical Library [Cambridge, Mass. and London, 1922], i, 30–31) in associating Fides (Loyalty) with Astræa, the virgin goddess of Justice, who lived on earth during the Golden Age, but afterwards abandoned it to take up residence in Virgo, one of the twelve zodiacal constellations, now named for her. The 1660 restoration signified her return, and the beginning of a new Golden Age; cf. Dryden's *Astræa Redux* (1660). With the Glorious Revolution of 1689 Astræa once more abandoned earth. For this and later developments,

see M.G.H. Pittock, *Jacobitism* (London, 1998), 71–72. For earlier use of the figure see Frances A. Yates, *Astræa: The Imperial Theme in the Sixteenth Century* (London, 1973).

2 *patria nostra*: in BA(1) manually altered to *terra Britanna*, a reading which elsewhere appears only in *Mutenda & Corrigenda*. The change is probably an attempt to make the poem more British after the 1707 Union. The balance of *patria* with *Patrem* is lost.
Patrem: James VII, possibly also God.

3 *exscindere*: so MS correction in BA(1) and in *Mutenda & Corrigenda*; elsewhere, *abscindere*, 'extirpate.'

5 *opressus*: so in PS; *oppressus* in SP and BA(4).

11 *in Templa*: the purgation of the churches.

12 *quotquot ... habent*: the purging of the universities. Probably foremost in Pitcairne's mind was the expulsion of Alexander Monro (d.?1715), Principal of Edinburgh University 1685–1690, in favour of Pitcairne's *bête noire*, Gilbert Rule (1629–1701). A brief account of the affair will be found in the preface to *The Assembly* (Tobin, *Assembly*, 27–28). In the play itself Rule is caricatured as Mr Salathiel Little-sense.

15–20 ... *Di* ... *Si* ... *Si* ... *servetis* ... *Reddite*: the classical Latin verse prayer formula; cf., e.g., Catullus, 76, 17–26, *Aeneid* 1, 603–605; 2, 689–691; 5, 687–689. 'The *si*-clause, which is regular in such appeals, far from implying any doubt in the petitioner's mind, expresses his confidence in the power he invokes' (C.J. Fordyce [ed.], *Catullus* [Oxford, 1961], 368).

15–16 *Scythico ... Scotus ... Picta*: MS correction in BA(1), afterwards incorporated in *Mutenda & Corrigenda*; elsewhere *Morino ... Gallus ... Scota*. The words deleted refer to the Scottish origin legend. In *Picta* there may be a reference to that other people of early Scotland, the Picts. But cf. also *Aeneid* 9, 581–582, *stabat in egregiis Arcentis filius armis/ pictus acu chlamydem*, or rather perhaps to a line from *Aeneas Britannicus* (1663), an adaptation by James Kennedy of the *Aeneid* to the exploits of Charles II (Aeneas) from the battle of Worcester (1651) to the Restoration, and his subsequent marriage to Catherine of Braganza (Lavinia): *In medio chlamyde et pictis conspectus in armis* (MLA, iii, 181, 73).
For Jacobite use of Aeneas and the *Aeneid*, see Pittock, *Poetry and Politics*, 27–28, 38–40.
The Morini were a Belgic people, whose territory lay on what is now the French side of the Straits of Dover. *Gallus* is literally 'Gaul,' but Pitcairne probably intends a reference to Gaidhil Glas, in the origin legend eponym of the *Gaelic*-speaking Scots and Irish.
Pitcairne began by accepting the full origin legend, but in a letter dated 8 May 1710 to the mathematician, the Revd. Colin Campbell of Ardchattan, he remarks: 'it is plain wee highlanders (and I am one of those from father to sone who beat the Picts) came from Gallia by the shortest cut, Calais and Dover, in small boats very long; for wee must have come from the neightest continent

and a continent in which our language was spoke, as ours is at this day in basse Bretagne, i.e. Aremorici &c.' (Johnston, *Best of our owne*, 60, letter 49). The Morini are mentioned in an enclosure to the same letter. By 1710 Pitcairne, it is clear, had revised his adherence to the older tradition. He retained belief however in the figure of Gaidhil Glas.

17 *læsa … Majestas*: a play on *crimen læsæ maiestatis*, 'the crime of injured majesty or treason' (OCL, 709), with an obvious allusion to James VII.

19 *Æquævum vestro Populum … Olympo*: cf. the similar use of *æquævus* in Claudian: *æquævumque videt consenuisse nemus* ('De sene Veronensi,' 16); closer *urbs æquæva polo* (*De Bello Gothico*, 54; Platnauer, *Claudian*, ii, 194–195; 130–131).

20 *Grampigenis*: 'born upon the Grampians,' 'Scottish.' Earlier poets also use the adjective; Arthur Johnston, for instance, has *Anglia Grampigenas extructis molibus hostes/ Arcuit* ('Ad Iacobum Ionstonem, Baronem de Ionston,' 9–10; MLA, ii, 46). The word is frequent in *Aeneas Britannicus*. Claudian may have provided the model: *Apenninigenis cultas pastoribus aras* (*De Sexto Consulatu Honorii Augusti*, 505; Platnauer, *ut cit.*, ii, 110–111). Pitcairne's conjunction with *jugis*, 'ridges,' is unexpected and striking – apparently on Pitcairne's part the result of a happy second thought; see **Text**.

Patremque: James VII.

3

Notes. The Scottish Estates met on 14 March 1689 to consider the question of the monarchy. On 25 March they recognized William. On 31 March the Lord President (head of the Scottish judiciary), Sir George Lockhart (c. 1630–1689) of Carnwath, Lanarkshire, was shot in the High Street of Edinburgh by John Chiesley of Dalry in revenge for a judgement requiring him to pay an aliment or income of £93 out of his estate to his presumably estranged wife and their children (Chambers, *Traditions of Edinburgh*, 75). There is no direct evidence that Lockhart's strongest sympathies were with King James, or that these had anything to do with his murder, but Pitcairne choses to regard him as the first Jacobite martyr. His son, also George Lockhart of Carnwath (1681–1732), author of *Memoirs Concerning the Affairs of Scotland From Queen Anne's Accession to the Throne To the Commencement of the Union of the two Kingdoms of Scotland and England, In May, 1707* (D. Szechi [ed.], *Scotland's Ruine*, ASLS [Aberdeen, 1995]), together with his younger brother Philip, executed for his part in the 1715 rising, were active, and indeed notorious, Jacobites.

The elder Lockhart was second son of Sir James Lockhart, Lord Lee (d. 1674). He passed advocate in 1656. Under the Commonwealth, he was elected MP for Lanark and adjacent burghs (1656), and for Lanarkshire (1658). In 1658, he became 'sole attorney' (the equivalent of Lord Advocate). After the Restoration he was pardoned as a reward for his father's loyalty. In 1663 he was knighted. In 1674 he

COMMENTARY

took part in the unsuccessful impeachment of the Secretary of State for Scotland, the Duke of Lauderdale (1616–1682), who subsequently took action against him, debarring him from pleading during 1674 and 1675. He defended a number of Covenanters, including the Earl of Argyll (1681). In 1685 he became Lord President. In 1686 he became a Privy Councillor and a Commissioner of the Exchequer. With two others he was summoned to London to discuss King James's proposals for the removal of Catholic disabilities, which, after initial opposition, he eventually accepted on his return to Edinburgh.

Lockhart was the most successful and eloquent pleader of his times, his only rival being Sir George Mackenzie (see 5).

The poem was probably written immediately after the murder. Pitcairne plays variations on the topos The World Upside Down (Curtius, *Latin Middle Ages*, 94–98). For him the murder marked a significant stage in the transformation of Scotland to the Hades of poem 1.

1 *Esse Deum*: echo of the ironic last words of the Roman emperor Vespasian (9–79): *Væ, puto deus fio*, 'Alas! I think I'm becoming a god' (Suetonius, *Vespasian*, 23). Pitcairne's intentions are also ironic.
2 *Fergusiana tribus*: the Scots, the clan of Fergus I, who in terms of the Scottish origin legend became first king of the Scots in Scotland (as opposed to Ireland) in 330 BC. James VII was regarded as descended from Fergus I.
3 *illicitis ... æquum*: the immediate reference may be to John Chiesley's argument that in terms of the customary *jus mariti* he was not liable to provide aliment for his wife. 'By the custom of Scotland the wife is in the power of the husband' (Stair, *Institutes*, 1, 4, 13). Lockhart's decision had a more equitable basis, and his subsequent murder was in effect a return to the ancient custom of blood-feud.
moribus; in APP, *viribus* is inserted as an alternative reading above *moribus*.
4 *priscam ... fidem*: Cf. Aeneid 6, 878–879: *heu pietas, heu prisca fides invictaque bello/dextera!*, 'Alas for duty, alas for pristine faith and hands unconquered in war!' Cf. *gentis priscæ*, 4, 7, and contrast *ficta fides*, 2, 9.
7 *medicina*: note the metaphor based on Pitcairne's profession. Cf. 5, 16, *Est tanto par medicina malo*.

4

Notes. On 18 March 1689, John Graham of Claverhouse (1648–1689), recently created Viscount Dundee and Lord Graham of Claverhouse and appointed commander of King James's forces in Scotland, withdrew from the Convention of Estates and left Edinburgh, accompanied by fifty of his own troops, to raise an army in the Highlands for King James. In a battle (27 July) at the head of the pass of Killiecrankie, north of Pitlochry, Perthshire, he defeated the Williamite army led by General Mackay, but was himself killed. Graham's second-in-command, Colonel Cannon, attempted to follow up the victory, but was repulsed at Dunkeld (21 August). The poem was probably written shortly afterwards.

Graham was seen by Pitcairne as tragic hero and lost national saviour; cf. *Grameidos Libri Sex* by James Philp, or Philip, of Almerieclose (1654/5–1714/25), an epic modelled on the *Aeneid* and on the *Bellum Civile* of the Roman poet Lucan (ed. A.D. Murdoch, SHS, series I, vol. 3 [Edinburgh, 1888]; Money, *English Horace*, 26; Murray Pittock in *Oxford DNB, s.v.*). His military service began on the Continent, ironically under William of Orange, whose life he is said to have saved at Seneff in 1674. He left the Dutch service in 1677 and was afterwards commissioned in the Duke of Montrose's horseguards to curb covenanting activities in Scotland. He became sheriff-depute of the county of Dumfries and stewartry of Annandale. On 1 June 1679 he was defeated by an armed covenanting conventicle at Drumclog in Ayrshire, but afterwards defended Glasgow and was on the winning side at Bothwell Brig (29 June). After the Sanquhar Declaration (22 June, 1680), in which Richard Cameron and his associates renounced allegiance and declared war on King Charles and his followers, and the subsequent defeat (22 July) of the Cameronians by a detachment of Graham's troops at Airds Moss in Ayrshire, he was appointed hereditary sheriff of Wigtown and steward-depute of Kirkcudbright, with authority to prosecute recalcitrants throughout the south-west. The severity of 'bluidy Clavers' has become legendary. Nevertheless he used his powers sparingly. The number of lives taken by him did not exceed ten (Donaldson, *James V – James VII*, 372, n. 44; cf. Cowan, *Scottish Covenanters*, 111–112). In October 1688 he was second-in-command of the Scottish forces sent southward to resist William's invasion, but after the flight of James he returned, with some difficulty, to Scotland.

The poet Dryden (1631–1700), whose sympathies were Jacobite, made an English version of the poem:

Oh Last and best of Scots! Who did'st maintain
Thy Country's Freedom from a Foreign reign;
New people fill the Land, now thou art gone,
New Gods the Temples, and new Kings the Throne.
Scotland and Thee did each in other live,
Nor would'st thou her, nor cou'd she thee survive.
Farewel! Who living did'st support the State,
And coud'st not fall but with thy Country's Fate.

This catches Pitcairne's classical qualities and the sense in which he used the word *Libertas* (l. 2), but misses the overtones of Scottish history and legend, less familiar to Dryden.

For vivid but substantially opposed imaginative portraits of Graham, see Scott's *Old Mortality* (1816) and Galt's *Ringan Gilhaize* (1823).

COMMENTARY

1   *Ultime Scotorum*: Graham was the last true Scot because he was the last to uphold the line of Fergus I; see **3**, 2.
2   *Libertas*: i.e., national liberty, the right of the Scots to live free of foreign domination under their own kings. The concept is central to Scottish history and historical propaganda, at least from the fourteenth century; cf., e.g., the Declaration of Arbroath (1320): *Cui* [i.e., Robert Bruce], *tamquam illi per quem salus in populo facta est, pro nostra libertate tuenda, tam jure quam meritis, tenemur, et volumus in omnibus adherere ... Non enim propter gloriam, divicias aut honores pugnamus, sed propter libertatem solummodo, quam nemo bonus, nisi simul cum vita, amittit.* Pitcairne, in effect, adds Graham to the list of heroic defenders of Scottish freedom.
3   *novos ... cives*: adherents of William of Orange, including members of the formerly outlawed conventicles.
4   *novos ... Deos*: Presbyterian in place of Episcopal order.
6–8   *vale ... vale ... vale*: the triple 'Farewell' customary in Roman funeral rites; cf. Ovid, *Fasti*, 3, 563–564 (Anna over the ashes of her sister Dido): *terque, 'vale,' dixit, cineres ter ad ora relatos / pressit, et est illis visa subesse soror.*
7–8   *Tuque ... vale*: Pitcairne may have had in mind lines from the conclusion of Statius' 'Consolatio ad Claudium Etruscum' (*Silvae*, III, 3, 208–210), in which the word *sospite* (cf. l. 1) also occurs: *Salve supremum, senior mitissime patrum, / supremumque vale, qui numquam sospite nato / triste chaos mæstique situs patiere sepulchri.*
7   *gentis priscæ*: a reference to the antiquity of the Scots in terms of the origin legend. For *priscæ* cf. **3**, 4.
8   *ultime, Grame*: the variant reading in SP, which lacks the comma, has some point. The Graham lineage included the royalist James Graham (1612–1650), 5th Earl and 1st Marquess of Montrose, who conducted a brilliant campaign against the Covenanters in 1644–1645, together with the more legendary Græmus, father-in-law of Fergus II, 40th or 45th king of Scots. Græmus restored power to the Scots by overthrowing the Roman Antonine Wall, known as Graham's or Grim's Dyke. With the death of Claverhouse and the subsequent acceptance of King William such actions became impossible for any future heroic Graham. See too **85**.
The two readings complement each other. They may indicate a deliberate ambiguity on Pitcairne's part.
The name Graham is in fact a by-form of the English place-name Grantham (Lincs.), introduced to Scotland at the beginning of the 12th century by William de Graham, holder of the manor (P. Hanks and F. Hodges [eds.], *Dictionary of Surnames* [Oxford, 1988], 222; G.W.S. Barrow, *The Kingdom of the Scots* [London, 1973], 118).

5

Notes. Sir George Mackenzie (1636–1691) of Rosehaugh in the Black Isle (Ross and Cromarty) passed advocate in 1659 under the Commonwealth, and was readmitted to the Faculty in 1661 after the Restoration. Before 1668 he had been knighted. In 1669 he entered the Scottish parliament as member for Ross, where he persistently opposed the policies of Lauderdale (**72**). Lockhart was his chief rival as an advocate, and relations between them eventually grew bitter. Mackenzie became Lord Advocate (chief public prosecutor) in 1677, and his subsequent harshness towards the Covenanters gained him the nickname 'Bluidy Mackenzie.' In 1682, as Dean of the Faculty of Advocates, he was responsible for the foundation of the Advocates' Library, now the National Library of Scotland. In 1686 his opposition to James VII's policy of religious tolerance brought about his dismissal as Lord Advocate, but in 1688 he was restored. He opposed the deposition of King James and, as a consequence of the bitter hostility which he subsequently encountered in Edinburgh, he retired to Oxford. He died at Westminster on 6 May 1691 and was buried in Greyfriars Churchyard, Edinburgh, where an impressive tomb was erected over his remains. The poem was probably composed on the completion of the monument.

Mackenzie was twice married. By his second wife, Margaret Haliburton, he had a son, George, 'a Gentleman Commoner of University College, Oxford, who died without issue in 1707,' (A. Lang, *Sir George Mackenzie, King's Advocate, of Rosehaugh: his life and times, 1636?-1691* [London, 1909], 310) and who is commemorated in **17** below.

Mackenzie was called by Dryden 'that noble wit of Scotland' ('Discourse concerning Satire,' *Poems of John Dryden*, ed. J. Kinsley, 4 vols. [Oxford, 1958], ii, 666). He was devoted to literature. Particularly relevant to the present poem are his historico-legal writings. His belief in the legendary sequence of Scottish kings from Fergus I to the present was so great that if its attempted refutation had been perpetrated in Scotland, it would have been his duty as Lord Advocate, he declared, to prosecute the offender. In pursuit of his ideal he wrote *Jus Regium or the first and Solid Foundation of Monarchy in General and more particularly of the Monarchy of Scotland; against Buchanan, Naphtali, Dolman, Milton etc.* (London, 1684 and 1685) and *A Defence of the Antiquity of the Royal Line of Scotland in answer to William Lloyd, Bishop of St Asaph, with a True Account when the Scots were governed by the Kings in the Isle of Britain* (London, 1685). Better known at the present day is his *Institutions of the Laws of Scotland* (Edinburgh, 1684). His opus also includes a novel, *Aretina or the Serious Romance* (London, 1661), a work modelled on Greek romance by way of such Renaissance intermediaries as Sir Philip Sidney's *Arcadia* (1590), John Barclay's Latin *Argenis* (1621), and Madame de Scudery's *le grand Cyrus* (1649–1653). The work has political overtones, with the third of its four books containing 'a lightly disguised allegory of the Civil War, overthrow of Charles I, rise of Cromwell and return of Charles II' (Jack, [ed.], *Scottish Prose 1550–1700*

COMMENTARY

[London, 1971], 34; extracts from text, 156–165). Also worth mentioning is *Religio Stoici* (Edinburgh, 1663).

Title *Makinnium*: the spelling is a Latinization of the original pronunciation of the name Mackenzie, Gaelic *MacCoinnich*, 'son of Kenneth.' The *z* in the modern written form originally represented the letter yogh, sometimes represented by *y*. The form in BA(4) suggests that the false modern spelling pronunciation already existed in the early eighteenth century.

1 *Cæsarei*: i.e., of a Roman emperor, a Cæsar, after his death regarded as deified.
monumenta sepulchri: the classically styled monument in Greyfriars Kirkyard.
2 *Sedibus ... inest*: hyperbole. As expositor of the theory of kingship and restorer to historic credibility of so many beleagured kings (Fergus I and his descendents), Mackenzie was greater than any individual emperor or king.
3 *Caledonii ... patronus*: by way of his *Jus Regium* and more particularly his *Defence of the Antiquity of the Royal Line of Scotland*.
4 *Indigitem*: The Indigetes were 'heroes elevated to the rank of gods after their death and regarded as the patron deities of their country' (*Lewis and Short*).
5 *Qui ... reduxit*; in *Defence ... of the Royal Line*.
6 *Qui ... docet*: in *Jus Regium*.
9 *Caledoniæ ... turbæ*: cf. *Georgics* I, 502: *Laomedontiae luimus periuria Troiae*.
perjuria turbæ: the events of the Glorious Revolution.
10 *toties ... pios*: by way of former Scottish patriotic heroes such as Graemus, Wallace and Bruce.
13 *Locartum*: see 3.
14 *Astræae*: cf. 2, 1.
16 *medicina*: cf. 3, 7.
17 *Gramus*: see 4.
18 *prodigus ... sui*: cf. Horace, *Odes*, I, 12, 37–38, *animaeque magnae/ prodigum Paulum*.
19 *Nimium ... propago*: modelled on Virgil's account of the meeting in the underworld between Aeneas and his distant descendant Marcellus (42–23 BC), the brilliant but ill-fated nephew of the Emperor Augustus: *nimium vobis Romana propago/ visa potens, superi, propria hæc si dona fuissent* (*Aeneid* 6, 870–871). In Jacobite symbolism Claverhouse corresponded to Marcellus; cf. **7**, 15–16, where the corresponding figure, rather less convincingly, is Charles II.
21 *Mackinnius*: for the triad of Lockhart, Claverhouse and Mackenzie, cf. **15**, 31–32.
21–22 *unus ... opes*: a possible reminiscence of Virgil's adaptation of Ennius (Book XII, fragment 1): *tu Maximus ille es,/ unus qui nobis cunctando restituis rem* (*Aeneid* 6, 845–846). Ennius' and Virgil's reference is to the dictator Quintus Fabius Maximus Cunctator who employed delaying tactics against Hannibal after the Roman defeat at Trasimene (217 BC). Pitcairne may have seen a

correspondence between these tactics and Mackenzie's use of his eloquence to delay full implementation of Williamite policies.

Notice how much of the language in this poem is based on *Aeneid* 6, the account of a journey to the underworld. Cf. 1.

24 *artis*: i.e., his mastery of legal procedure.
26 *Jura … vacant*: an ironic variation on a theme found in Claudian's 'De sene Veronensi': *non freta mercator tremuit, non classica miles,/ non rauci lites pertulit ille fori* (Platnauer, *Claudian*, ii, 7–8, pp. 194–195). The trouble-free existence of the old man is the opposite of the desolate peace which descended on Scottish institutions with the deaths of Lockhart, the judge (*Jura*), Claverhouse, the soldier (*classica*), and Mackenzie, the advocate (*Rostra*).

Claudian's verse is itself a variation on Horace, *Epodes*, 2, 5–8: *neque excitatur classico miles truci,/ neque horret iratum mare,/ forumque vitat et superba civium/ potentiorum limina*. Pitcairne seems closer to Claudian than to Horace.

Rostra: the platform for speakers in the Roman forum, hence the place in court for the advocate to make his case.

After 24, APP and BA(4) substitute (punctuation ours):

> *Ille jacet, simul alta jacet miseranda Caledon;*
>   *Jura silent, torpent classica, Rostra vacant.*
> *Diis aliis alii placeant; sit Pallas Ulyssi*
>   *Æque sit Aonii fautor Apollo chori;*
> *Illi omnes uni tribuerunt omnia divi,*
>   *Heu quanta est Stygio præda parata diti.*

'With *his* ruin, great Caledon lies pitifully ruined; law has fallen silent, the war-trumpets are dumb, the rostra stand empty. Some may have a close relationship with a single god. Pallas may look favourably on Ulysses, Apollo equally on the Aonian choir, yet all those gods surrender everything to a single divinity. Alas! What a huge prize has been provided for Stygian Dis.'

The final couplet is powerful and effective. Pitcairne may however have felt that the first had the makings of a good ending and that the second was somewhat inadequate.

6

Metre. Hendecasyllabic.
Notes. The Keys and SP are in apparent conflict, the first indicating that the person primarily addressed is John Campbell of Glenorchy (1635–1717), created 1st Earl of Breadalbane in 1681, the second that he is Sir George Mackenzie

of Tarbat (1630–1714), created Viscount Tarbat in 1685, and in 1703 Earl of Cromarty. *S* is ambiguous. The difference however may not be so very great. In 1689 and afterwards the Government badly needed some kind of pacification of the rebellious Highlands. Most of the clans were Jacobite and Episcopalian or Catholic, and had supported Claverhouse at Killiecrankie. The Scottish Treasury had few resources available to finance action by the small military force available. 'Therefore, the other policy, of trying to buy off the rebels, had its attractions, even if it were only to secure temporary gains' (W. Ferguson, *Scotland 1689 to the Present* [Edinburgh, 1968], 17). The task was assigned, first in 1689 to Tarbat, with £5000 at his disposal, and afterwards in 1691 to Breadalbane. In June 1691 a meeting with the chiefs at Achallader in Argyll led to an arrangement, the deadline for which was 1 January 1692. By then all the chiefs with the exception of Glengarry, Clanranald, MacLean of Duart and MacIan of Glencoe, had submitted. After strenuous attempts to be on time, the last had in fact done so on 6 January, but as his clan was small and their position vulnerable, they were chosen for punishment – the Massacre of Glencoe on 13 February 1692.

The poem is a satiric comment on Breadalbane's mission. Conceivably it was written after the massacre. If so, there is no direct reference and Pitcairne is not usually so restrained in his comments. The poem was more probably composed during the early months of 1691. Events at Glencoe must however have coloured most later reactions.

The poem parodies Catullus 49, a mock-humble address to the Roman statesman and orator Marcus Tullius Cicero (106–43 BC):

Disertissime Romuli nepotum,
Quot sunt, quotque fuere, Marce Tulli,
Quotque post aliis erunt in annis,
Gratias tibi maximas Catullus
Agit pessimus omnium poeta,
Quanto tu optimus omnium patronus.

Other meanings of *patronus* are subliminally present, exploited by Pitcairne in the word *patrocinantem* in 12. The occasion for Catullus' poem is not known, but his underlying intention was almost certainly satiric, as of course was Pitcairne's. Both poems are fine specimens of rhetorical *allegoria*, which *aliud verbis, aliud sensu ostendit* (Quintilian, *Inst.*, 8.6, 44)

Cf. 53, 1; 88, 1.

1–2 *Prudentissime ... olim*: direct parody of *Catullus* 49, 1–3.
1 *Prudentissime*: a double-edged epithet, which might imply that Breadalbane exercised the cardinal virtue of Prudence, or alternatively that he was quick to adapt himself to prevailing financial circumstances. It was widely (and probably

POEM 6

falsely) believed that much of the money set aside for the pacification ended up in Breadalbane's pocket. Incidents of his earlier career had certainly been unsavoury.

Fergusi nepotum: cf. 3, 2n.

3 [*manus*]: inserted by hand in BA(1); in other copies in *Mutenda & Corrigenda*. Present in BA(4), f.7ᵛ.

Brigantum: not the Brigantes, the British tribe which in Roman times occupied the modern Yorkshire and neighbouring territories, but the Scots, and particularly the Highlanders, as descendants, according to legend, of the people of Brigantium in N.W. Spain, perhaps the modern La Coruña.

4–5 *Plus ... æqui*: Pitcairne differs from most Lowlanders of his time in emphasizing the virtues of the Highlanders, even when he is apparently dismissing them. They are faithful, holding to the beautiful and the just, in terms of fidelity to the just and beautiful cause of James VII and Episcopalianism.

9 *Veteri piæque Genti*: the Highlanders, as descendants of Gaidhil Glas, are an ancient race, as maintaining Episcopal order and ceremony they are pious; cf. Pittock, *Poetry and Politics*, 41 ff.

10 *subvenias, opem*: both words have pecuniary suggestions. Despite the widespread Lowland opinion, the suggestion that the Highlanders are beggars is probably intended as ironic.

In BA(1) a comma has been manually inserted after *subvenias*, and a full stop after *petenti* has been partially erased. In *Mutenda & Corrigenda* elsewhere: 'L.10 post subvenias adde (,) & del (.) post petenti.'

12 *patrocinantem*: see above, introductory paragraphs.

14 *miserti*: a shortened form, introduced *metri causa*, for *miseriti*, past participle of the deponent *misereor*, 'I feel pity.' Lewis and Short give two examples, both with possible relevance to this passage: *cui Venus postea miserta est* (Hyginus, *Fabulae*, 58), and (impersonal construction) *quo me reipublicae maxime misertum est* (Macrobius, *Saturnalia*, 2.10, attributed to Scipio Africanus). Unfortunately, the reference given for the latter quotation seems not to correspond to anything, at least in Willis' edition of Macrobius (Teubner, 1970). For the use of the verb in a similar context, cf. *Aeneid* 2, 143–144 (the plea to the Trojans of the treacherous Sinon): *miserere laborum/ tantorum, miserere animi non digna ferentis*.

16–17 *Viroque ... benigniores*: Dr Money suggests an echo of Horace, *Odes*, 1, 7, 25–32, the speech to his comrades made by Teucer on being exiled from his father's kingdom of Salamis:

> *quo nos cumque feret melior fortuna parente,*
> > *ibimus, o socii comitesque.*
> *nil desperandum Teucro duce et auspice: Teucri*
> > *certus enim promisit Apollo*
> *ambiguam tellure nova Salamina futuram.*
> > *o fortes peioraque passi*

315

mecum saepe viri, nunc vino pellite curas;
   cras ingens iterabimus aequor.

Notice particularly the use of *auspice* in ablative absolute construction, and the parallel between *Viroque* and *viri*. The near hopeless situation resembles that of Scottish Jacobites in 1691. At the same time, they looked for a happier outcome.

7

Metre. Sapphic stanza.
Notes. the entry in the Bodleian Key reads: '**Poem** VII Marc Lermont avocat supp'd with me on a 29th of May when our Forces could not go to the Fields, When Charleroy was taken &c: and the secret peace was made. You know the Fr. Kn.s devise is a Sun.' *S* is similar, but omits the date.

The Key in *N* differs slightly: 'Carm. 7 Marc Lermot an advocat who suped that 29th of May at the author that Charleroy was taken & the secret peace made. The last line refers to the King of France's Devise which is the Sun.'

29 May is the anniversary both of Charles II's birth and of the Restoration, the day in 1660 on which his return was recognised by the two houses of the English Parliament at Whitehall, where, more than eleven years before (30 January 1649), his father, Charles I, had been executed. Pitcairne likes to refer to this date. Indications for the year of composition are less certain. The dinner took place during the war (1689–1697) between France, under Louis XIV, and the allied powers, Spain, the Empire, Britain, Holland and Savoy. On the allied side, the leading spirit was William of Orange. Subsumed to this Nine Years War was the struggle, mainly carried out in Ireland, between James VII, under the patronage of Louis XIV, and William.

The Key alludes to three incidents during the war. Early in 1692 the Earl (later Duke) of Marlborough was dismissed as Commander-in-Chief of the English forces; probably as a consequence the English army was unable to take the field. A subsequent series of brilliant French successes in 1692–1693 culminated in the capture of Charleroi, in modern Belgium, in October 1693. In June 1696 the Duke of Savoy submitted to Louis in a secret treaty, not made public until August of that year. The poem is earlier than the Peace of Ryswick (30 October 1697), which more or less restored the *status quo ante bellum*. Pitcairne favoured the French cause; hence his quiet satisfaction at the way things appeared to be going when he wrote the poem.

Mark Learmonth, eldest son of Thomas Learmonth, advocate, was himself admitted to the Faculty of Advocates on 17 December 1679. Thereafter, until 1692, he was in some trouble for non-payment of entry-money (to be used, incidentally, to stock the new Advocates' Library). On 5 June 1683 he married

Jean, daughter of Thomas Hay of Alderston. He died in 1701 (F.J. Grant, *The Faculty of Advocates in Scotland 1532–1943*, Scottish Record Society [Edinburgh, 1944], 122; J.M. Pinkerton, *The Minute Book of the Faculty of Advocates*, vol. 1, Stair Society [Edinburgh, 1976], 38, 54, 70, 111). His death resulted from the drinking contest described in **9**. See also Money, *English Horace*, 145.

The poem is not quite an imitation, but, as Money notes, contains verbal echoes (ll. 1, 3, 5, 7, 17, 25) of Horace, *Odes* 3, 8, *Martiis caelebs quid agam Kalendis*, an invitation to Maecenas to join him at dinner on the anniversary of his narrow escape from a falling tree. Horace thinks that Maecenas may be puzzled to receive an invitation from a bachelor to celebrate what should be a festival of married women, the Matronalia on 1 March. Learmonth needs no such explanation for the invitation.

The poem exemplifies the calendrical interests also found in many other of Pitcairne's poems.

5   *Hic dies*: cf. *Martiis caelebs*, 9: *hic dies anno redeunte festus*.
6   *primus ostendit*: i.e., at his birth.
6–7 *patriaeque ... sospitatorem*: i.e., at the Restoration.
9–10 *labori principis*: the hardships suffered by Charles II during the Civil War and protectorate.
10–11 *scelerique ... Civico*: the Civil War, 1642–1652; cf. Horace, *Odes*, 2, 1, 1, *Motum ex Metello consule civicum*, referring to the Roman Civil Wars, regarded by Pollio (76 BC–AD 4) in his *Historiae* (now lost) as beginning in the consulship of Quintus Caecilius Metellus Celer (60 BC).
14 *Aureo*: i.e., the reign was a Golden Age.
15–16 *Deis ... Britanni*: a reminiscence of *Aeneid* 6, 870–871, *nimium vobis Romana propago/ visa potens, superi*. Cf. **5**. 19. The reference is to Marcellus, nephew, son-in-law and designated heir to the Emperor Augustus, who died in 23 BC at the age of 19. The lines draw an effective emotional parallel between Marcellus and James, the future Old Pretender, son of James VII, nephew of Charles II, and half-brother of Queen Anne. The vocative *Marce* is perhaps deliberately intended to recall Marcellus.
25–26 *mordaces ... Brittonum*: cf. *Martiis caelebs*, 17, *mitte civilis super urbe curas*. Learmonth is to dismiss cares about the exiled British monarch, cares which French successes made seem less oppressive than had previously been the case.
26–28 *hostiles ... liquescunt*: the armies of Louis XIV, the Sun King, had made the opposing forces of the Allies melt like snow.

8

Metre. Sapphic stanza.
Notes. The Key in S reads: 'P.8. Greppa. Mistris Henderson, who by a nickname and by malice was called Greppa, Kept the best wyne in towne. When our wyne was at 32 pence the Scots pint, She suddenlie sold her's at 20 pence the pint. This was oblidging. but she Knew the new french wine wol'd be suddenlye home, which the other vintners knew not, but kept up their prices. Wee did our selves the pleasure to drink in Greppa's ill wjne (in the end of the year) at the old Scots price, and she sold all her wjne, when the other vintners were forc'd to give theirs, (hogheads) for 20 Shillings a piece to be turn'd to Aqua Vitæ. A little tyme thereafter Greppa died, was put in S:t Giles's church (our high church) and so is suppos'd to be married to Sanctus Ægidius [St Giles], which is an honor next to her who is matched to the chief of such sort of saints.

This will serve to explain the po.ix, for Walter Danniston dy'd a few days before the Greppa and so could not be at Greppa's marriage with AEgidius Nota that Aegidius's wooden statue was in a procession by [the Rable drown'd in the] Nor-loch with a stone about his neck this is limosoque iterum.'

An almost identical passage is found in the Bodleian Key. A note in BA(4), f.22:r., reads: 'Denniston (a pitiefull Poetaster but at Colledge with me) dyed in 1700. M:rs Hendersone who sold wine in ane house underground dyed a little after him. She brewed her wine with half boyled brandie. Her woman Anne hath the house now. M:rs Hendersone was calld Greppa from ane obscene suspicione. Ad Greppam was written after her death, when wee suposed she was married to S:t Giles in whose church she was buried to the compleat defilment of that Church.' The obscene suspicion is that the Greping-office was a brothel as well as a drinking-den.

On f.22:v there is a continuation: 'Nota that Greppa had before her death brought her wine from 40 [d.] to 20 [d.] the Scots pint, which we think to be so meritorious as to procure her marriage with that Church (excised) St. Giles.'

Mrs Henderson's house was known as the Greping-office, 'a suite of dark underground apartments in the Parliament Close, opening by a descending stair opposite the oriel of St Giles, in a mass of buildings called the Pillar. By the wits who frequented it, it was called the *Greping-office*, because one could only make way through its dark passage by groping' (Chambers, *Traditions of Edinburgh*, 159). Pitcairne suggests a different explanation of the name.

The Key in N reads: 'Carm 8. Greppa, a nickname to Mrs Henderson – who kept a tavern, & dying, was laid in S:t Giles's and so is supposed to be Marryed to that Saint.'

Pitcairne's intentions are difficult to assess. By virtue of her posthumous mock-marriage to St. Giles (also commemorated in the following poem) and consequent deification, Greppa receives credit for supernatural power and authority, which she is asked to use in rousing Charles II from death to reinstate his brother

James VII, and establish the future Old Pretender as heir-apparent. In the afterlife Charles is described as *Lentus inersque*, which to a degree corresponds to his character in life. At best, he seems an unlikely avenging revenant. The satiric point may be that Jacobitism is now confined to the tavern, to return only in the unlikely event that a revenant Charles II will preside over a second Restoration. Cf. the account of Edinburgh in *The Assembly*, I, i (Tobin, *Assembly*, 39): 'A Man who had walked betwixt the *Strait Bow* and the *Cross*, would imagine he had marched out of King *William's* Territories to King *James'*: They have both their Kingdoms in this Town; I' Faith, Only with this Difference, King *James'* domineers in the Taverns, and *King William's* at the Council-Table'.

The revenant nevertheless is generally for Pitcairne a figure for the return of the Stuarts and the *ancien régime*. For other versions, see 1, 11, 15.

The poem was written after the death of Greppa, but before that of James VII on 6 September 1701.

1–2 *Diva ... coerces*: the dead Greppa is a power in the halls of the underworld (Avernus), as during her life she had been a power in the Greping-office. The term *Diva* indicates that after her death, like classical heroes and Roman emperors, she had been deified.

2 *rubro ... pelago*: the Red Sea in which the Egyptians were overwhelmed as they pursued the Israelites (Exodus 14: 23–28), allegorically corresponding to the Styx, the boundary between living and dead. Also the sea of claret by means of which the subjects of Greppa in this world convince themselves that William of Orange and his forces will be destroyed.

3 *Carolus*: Charles II.

5–6 *generis sacrati Spem*: James, the future Old Pretender, son of James VII. The word *sacrati* presupposes the doctrine of the Divine Right of Kings.

9 *remeasset*: the return of the saviour in triumph. Cf. *Aeneid* 2, 95: *si patrios umquam remeassem victor ad Argos*.

10 *fratris*: James VII.
magni Pueri: the future Pretender.

15–16 *Acheronta ...movere*: an echo of Juno's threat (*Aeneid* 7, 312) to rouse civil war in Italy: *flectere si nequeo superos, Acheronta movebo*. Pitcairne realized that civil conflict would inevitably result from any attempt at the restoration of James VII.

17 *dominator Orci*: Pluto, lord of the Underworld, who raped Proserpine and made her his Queen.

18 *Vocibus Bacchi Patris*: i.e., drunken revelry in the Greping-office during the marriage of St. Giles to Greppa, mentioned in the introductory paragraphs and narrated in 9.

19 *gnatae Cereris*: Proserpine, daughter of Ceres.

19–20 *Æmulos ... honores*: i.e., as a result of her marriage to St. Giles, the posthumous status of Greppa is second only to that of Proserpine. The honours of Proserpine are listed by Claudian, *De Raptu Proserpinae* (Platnauer, *Claudian*, ii, 277–306).

9

Metre. Hendecasyllabic.
Notes. see the introductory paragraphs to **8** above. The Key for **10** also applies to this poem; we give the version in *S*: 'Hugh Cunningham, a profest hypocrite & true presbyterian, but who eternallie intruded himself into honest men's Company, and in faith I could not be free of him, for he spoke as wee did. This Hugh drank always in Greppa's, and ruin'd Marc Lermont my easie friend. Our pre-sent Greppa is Anne Stamphield a worthie woman, and whose wyne you drank latelie, when servant to old Greppa. Hugh call'd always for her.'

A continuation of the note on fo. 22.r. of *BA(4)*, quoted in the Introduction to **8** above, reads 'Mark Learmont was a very honest man, but facilis was murdered by one Hugh Cuninghame ane Ignorant Lawyer, a profest Hypocrite, ane abominable Presbiterian or Holy Drunkard'. On fo.22.v. is found: 'Nota. St Giles statue was throne into the north Loch by the rable in Queen Marys tyme'; cf. **8**, introductory note, §2.

The Key in *N* reads: 'Carm 9 Denniston dyed before Mrs Henderson & so could not be at her marriage.

Nota. Ægidius's wooden statue was in a procession by the rabble drown'd in the North Loch with a stone about his neck, this is Limosoque iterum &c.'

The alternative title given in *BA(4)* offers a rather better idea of the development of the poem, which on the surface combines lamentation for Dennistoun with celebration of the mock-exequies for Greppa. But it still misses a good deal. With the death of Learmonth during the drinking-contest the tone alters, implying malice (on the part of Hugh Cuninghame) leading to the subsequent tragedy. The repetition of the opening line marks the beginning of the change. The final return brings the poem to a close with the suggestion (implicit throughout) that Dennistoun would have approved the method used to bring about the death of Learmont.

Although the total effect is very different, Pitcairne may have modelled this poem on one by Statius, *Kalendae Decembres* (*Silvae*, 1.6), which is in hendacasyllables and gives an account of reverly at the Saturnalia:

quis spectacula, quis iocos licentes,
quis convivia, quis dapes inemptas,
largi flumina quis canat Lyaei?
iam, iam deficio tuoque Baccho
in serum trahor ebrius soporem. (93–97)

1 *Dannistone ... Musae*: Walter Dennistoun was schoolmaster at Musselburgh, six miles from Edinburgh, and a minor writer of Latin verse. He took his MA at Edinburgh, where Pitcairne was a fellow-student, and wrote a Latin verse paraphrase of Psalm 104, dedicated to the Faculty of Advocates in 1691 (*Minute Book*, I, 94). As noted already, he died in 1700, a few days before Greppa. Pitcairne often used Dennistoun as a stalking-horse for his own verse; thus, as early as 1691, we have *ΜΟΡΜΟΝΟΣΤΟΛΙΣΜΟS ... Translated into Latin by Mr. Walter Dennestone*, but in fact probably by Pitcairne (**123**). It is for this reason that he is described as 'Patron' of Pitcairne's Muse. Attributions to Dennistoun are more than once mentioned in Pitcairne's correspondence (Johnston, *Best of our owne*, letter 31, p. 48, dated 20 September 1707; letter 50, p. 63, 2 September 1710; letter 53, p. 66, letter 26 February 1711: see too General Introduction above). These letters are all later than Dennistoun's death.

3 *sub Tartara*: i.e., in the lowest abyss of Hell.

invenusta: literally 'without Venus.' In Tartarus there are no marriage celebrations of the kind described in the poem. A precise and unexpected use of the adjective – cf. the use of the word in Catullus 10, 3–4: *scortillum ... non sane illepidum neque invenustum*.

5–6 *Nubens Ægidio ... Avernum*: Ægidius is St Giles, to whom the main Edinburgh church, elevated to a cathedral by Charles I, is dedicated. The Greping-office was close by, and Greppa was buried in the church. A wooden image of the saint was taken from the church and destroyed by Protestant rioters, probably in 1557. Pitcairne may have had John Knox's words in mind: 'in Edinburgh was that great idol called Saint Giles, first drowned in the North Loch, [and] after burnt, which raised no small trouble in the town' (Dickinson, *Reformation in Scotland*, i, 125). Knox, like other Protestants, equated such images with pagan idols and demons. The marriage of Giles and Greppa is an unholy affair, with Greppa in consequence becoming a demon, second only to the actual Queen of the Underworld, Proserpine wife of Dis. Cf. **8**, introductory note, 19–20n.

Some part of the image may have survived to be used in the celebration almost a century and a half later. 'Saint Giles's day [1 September 1558] approaching, they [the Scottish bishops] gave charge to the Provost, Bailies, and Council of Edinburgh, either to get again the old Saint Giles, or else upon their expenses to make a new image' (Dickinson, *ut cit.*, i, 127).

The wooden image is treated as Priapic, corresponding to the *ruber hortorum custos, membrosior aequo,/ Qui tectum nullis vestibus inguen habet* (*Priapea*, ed. Mueller [Leipzig, 1892], I, 5–6); cf. *Quom sim ligneus, ut vides, Priapus/ Et falx lignea, ligneusque penis* (VI, 1–2); also, *Quod partem madidam mei videtis,/ Per quam significor Priapus esse:/ Non ros est, mihi crede, nec pruina,/ Sed quod sponte sua solet remitti,/ Cum mens est pathicae memor puellae* (XXXXVIII).

For a more distant parallel, cf. Horace, *Satires*, I, 8, 5 (the speaker is Priapus): *obscenoque ruber porrectus ab inguine palus*

The North Loch 'filled the low ground, where the railway now runs, between the Old Town and the New Town [of Edinburgh]' (Dickinson, *ibid.*).

10 *Ligno ... siccioris*: the wood of the image had dried out and therefore impotent.

11–12 *Alto ... imbuebat*: possibly the image was taken back to the North Loch and once more washed in the muddy water. The alternative reading in BA(4) suggests a different interpretation.

13 *Ægidii senis ministri*: i.e., the revellers. There is a hint that (Presbyterian) ministers of St Giles' church, or at least members of the congregations, took part in the ceremony. The reference may however be only to Hugh Cunninghame.

16 *Dominæ novæ*: 'Our New Lady,' i.e., Greppa, now married to St Giles. Cf. too the phrase used by Virgil of Theseus and Pirithous: *hi dominam Ditis thalamo deducere adorti* (*Aeneid* 6, 397).

17–18 *Templum ... superba*: i.e., the Greping-office, with a side-reference to St Giles' church.

21 *Sedes ... Greppæ*: the Greping-office.

22 *Libero*: Liber, a Roman equivalent of Bacchus.

23 *Erebi ... undis*: i.e., the Styx, the river separating the world of the living from that of the dead. Erebus is the Underworld, the silence of which is contrasted with the din of the Greping-office.

The motif of the revenant is at least subliminally present in this and the immediately surrounding lines.

25 *Deo Deæque*: St Giles and Greppa.

27 *Annam*: Anne Stamfield, successor to Greppa as landlady: cf. 69.
Hugo: Hugh Cuninghame.
prælia: for a drinking-contest with a happier ending see Money, *English Horace*, 190–193, 318–319.

28 *liberaliorum*: i.e., over-indulgers in drink. There is a side-reference to Liber, perhaps also to the Liberalia, the festival of Liber, held on 17 March.

29 *Marcum*: Mark Learmonth. See 7 and the introductory note to this poem.
pelliceret: the word implies treacherous or criminal intentions; cf. *invidia ... pellacis Ulixi* (*Aeneid*, 2, 90).
Diis dicatus: Mark as a dedicated sacrificial offering.

30 *Lucus*: a grove sacred to a deity or group of deities, where rites and sacrifices were performed – in this case the Greping-office with tutelary deities St Giles, Greppa and Anna. The priest is Hugh Cunninghame, the revellers are worshippers, and Mark the sacrificial victim.
Jo: 'Io,' a ritual cry in classical religious ceremonies. Cf. Horace, *Odes*, 4, 2, 49–51:

> *terque, dum procedis, io Triumphe,*
> *non semel dicemus, io Triumphe,*
> *civitas omnis.*

POEM 9

Cf. *duce Libero triumphans*, 23 above.

31 *Sed Marcum*: at this point the poem begins to modulate considerably in tone.
mihi invidentes: perhaps indicating that Pitcairne as physician warned Mark to give up.

32 *Longam vivere ... noctem*: a striking phrase, meaning 'to die.' Cf. Catullus, 5, 6: *nox est perpetua una dormienda*.

33–35 *Quo ... hospes*: cf. Horace, *Odes*, 1, 24, written on the death of Quintilius Varus, a friend not only of Horace and Virgil, but possibly also of Catullus (see *Catullus*, 10):

> *multis ille bonis flebilis occidit,*
> *nulli flebilior quam tibi, Vergili.* (9–10)

34 *alter ... alter*: the balance of the two words involves a contrast. The first refers to Learmonth and indicates that he came second in the contest (i.e., lost). The reference in the other is more general, *any* future visitant.

34–35 The alternative reading in BA(4), 34, has a possible mark of excision; the following two verses are overlined, presumably to indicate excision; in both the scansion is defective.

35 *candidior*: Cf. Horace, *Satires* 1, 5, 41–42: *Animae qualis neque candidiores/ terra tulit*; also a covert reference by way of colour symbolism to Mark's Jacobitism.

38 *alite*: *ales* is literally 'a bird,' but as birds were regarded as instruments of augury, the word in poetry sometimes came to signify 'omen,' especially an omen at a wedding ceremony. Cf. Catullus, 61, 19–20, the marriage song of Manlius Torquatus and Junia Aurunculeia: *bona cum bona/ nubet alite uirgo*. The omens at the wedding of Giles with Greppa were less promising.
disertus: Pitcairne may have had in mind the vulgate text of Catullus, 12, 8–9: *est enim leporum/ disertus puer ac facetiarum*, with *leporum* and *facetiarum* taken as limiting genitives after *disertus*. 'The basic implication of *disertus* is clarity and articulateness of speech' (Fordyce, *Catullus*, 131).

40–41 *Fraudes ... domandam*: the illusions of the first thirty lines are finally shattered.

41 *Stygi domandam*: *repullulantem*, 'sprouting forth again,' the alternative reading in BA(4), is an extremely rare and technical word, in classical Latin found only in Pliny the Elder and Isidore. It is appropriately ugly, but may lack more sinister implications. Pitcairne uses the uncompounded verb *pullulare* elsewhere, **85**, 2 and **88**, 2, in probably pejorative contexts.

42 *Cynthius*: Apollo, god of poetry, born on Mount Cynthus in the Greek island of Delos.
novem Sorores: the nine Muses, attendants of Apollo.

COMMENTARY

10

Notes. James VII died at St Germain, near Paris, on 6 September 1701. See also **81**.

1 *Imago*: cf. Dido's words as she prepares for her own death: *et nunc magna mei sub terras ibit imago* (*Aeneid* 4, 654). The variant version in APP and BA(4) is closer to this than the text in PS.
2 *sanctior*: James had been consecrated by the anointment at his coronation.
3–4 *aspiciet ... Cato*: see Money, *English Horace*, 147. Cato Uticensis (95–46 BC), constitutionalist and Stoic philosopher, committed suicide at Utica after Julius Caesar's defeat of the Pompeians at Thapsus. He figures prominently in Lucan's epic, *Bellum Civile*, which formed the model for the Jacobite *Grameid* by Pitcairne's contemporary, James Philp of Almerieclose (1654/5–1714/25). James, who devoted much of his last years to religious observance, resembled Cato in virtue and in steadfast adherence to a lost cause, adherence which made Dante (in the *Convito* and *De Monarchia*) accord Cato almost divine status. Pitcairne may have recalled the scene in *Purgatorio* (1, 31–108), where Cato waits at the foot of Mount Purgatory to welcome the redeemed as they disembark from the ship of souls.
5 *ille*: i.e., Minos, judge of the righteous dead.
7 *Quam ... esse*: the heavy spondaic beat of this hexameter stands in deliberate contrast to the metrically lighter final pentameter with its unexpectedly subversive and witty point.
8 *Genero*: William of Orange, who in 1677 had married James's eldest daughter Mary.

11

Notes. the poem was written after the death of King William following a riding accident on 8 March 1702; cf. **82–84**. The motif of the revenant is again present.

1–4 *pratis ... prataque*: cf. the similar use of the word in **12**, 2, 5, 18, 23, 41, **15**, 30.
3 *calamos ... armis*: Pitcairne treats Charles II's reign as a pastoral Golden Age, which a subsequent legitimate monarch might be able to restore. Anne, as a Stuart, is included, but only if on her succession she hands over the crown to her half-brother.
'The literary culture of Jacobitism in England often expressed itself in terms of the English countryside depicted in idealized ruralism' (Pittock, *Jacobitism*, 19). The present text shows that the topos was not restricted to England; cf. too for example, Allan Ramsay's *The Gentle Shepherd* (Burns Martin and John

W. Oliver, *The Works of Allan Ramsay*, II [STS, Edinburgh and London, 1953], 205–277).
4 *Teutonico … Lupo*: King William; see 1, 8, note. Money (*English Horace*, 146–147) suggests a reference to the Hanoverian succession. The date proposed for the poem reduces the possibility. In subsequent correspondence, Dr Money has suggested to us that at a later date it might be re-read with altered significance – a possibility, although the word *adempta* might seem to argue against it. Dr Money however suggests that the translation might be regarded as 'taken away by the Teutonic wolf [from the rightful owners].'
5 *Fratri*: James VII, lately deceased. In this version, the word *nimium* (7) suggests a certain lack of enthusiasm for James, made much more explicit in *BA(4)*, probably, as in 10, an earlier, less diplomatic, draft.
Annæ: Anne, second daughter of James VII by his first wife, Anne Hyde; reigned 1702–1714.
6 PUERO: James (1688–1766), son of James VII by his second wife, Mary of Modena; after his father's death recognized by Louis XIV and Jacobites generally as James VIII (and III), to others the (Old) Pretender.
7 *Catonis*: see 10, 3–4, note.
9–10 ANNA … *suo*: i.e., Anne will act as Regent until her half-brother comes of age.
10 *reddet*: For Anne's attitude to her half-brother, see Lenman, *Jacobite Risings*, 111–112, Hoppit, *Land of Liberty?*, 306–307. She had no wish for his succession.

12

Metre. hendecasyllabic, 1–46; sapphic stanza, 47–58.
Notes. the fable is loosely based on the poem by Phaedrus (c. 15 BC – c. AD 50), '*Ranae Regem Petierunt*'; see the edition by J.P. Postgate (OCT, Oxford, 1919). In 1–9, it should be noted, Phaedrus puts the fable into the context of the seizure by the tyrant Pisistratus of political power in Athens (561 BC), a seizure in which some at least of the Athenian citizenry collaborated. This forms a classical parallel to the usurpation by William of Orange. Pitcairne modifies the first episode in Phaedrus, where the immediate response of Jupiter to the frogs' request for a king is the gift of a log, a gift which they almost instantly reject. His King Oak, by contrast, is long established and actively benevolent, but the Frogs turn against him. The fable was widely used in Jacobite literature and propaganda (Pittock, *Poetry and Politics*, 47).

A note in *BA(4)*, f.22.r. (second hand) reads: '*Ranarum proceres &c.* was wrote when the proclamations of Darien came out.

Ilex is the Royal Oak. *Ales peregrina* is the Dutch Stork.

At vorasse gentem &c. are meant the forfaulters in Ireland in the P of O's tymes all is in imitation of Phaedrus 2 fable bk j.'

The Key in *N* reads: 'Carm 12 Darien.'

COMMENTARY

An obscurely worded note in *S* reads: 'Poem xij. This is Darien. Lately was heard of old Seaforth (General Dyce etc.) appearing in the north cf. Vol page – we can raise the dead as easilie as an invasion was brought 2 years ago. [I] begin to suspect all stories [of] resurrection.' The apparent reference is to Kenneth Mackenzie, 4th Earl of Seaforth (1661–1701), a member of James VII's Privy Council. He followed James to exile in France and accompanied him to Ireland, from which James wrote in 1689 to say that he was sending Seaforth to give support to Colonel Cannon, Dundee's replacement after Killiecrankie. Preparations began, but the defeat at Cromdale in May 1690 prevented further developments.

In 1697, after various misfortunes and imprisonments at home, Seaforth returned to France. At the height of the Darien crisis, it would appear, rumours of a second attempt on his part to provoke a rising began to circulate, rumours fanned by the belief or hope that a restored James would set right the wrongs done to Scotland by King William. In the fable, the final sapphic stanzas turn on the belief that such a rising could be successful.

As noted in the Introduction (pp. 15–16), the poem was written, in the context of the Darien expeditions, as part of the Edinburgh celebrations for the birthday of the exiled Prince of Wales on 10 June 1700. Darien was an attempt to alleviate the desperate economic and political plight of Scotland in the last years of the seventeenth century. Pitcairne puts the entire blame for the situation on William and his Dutch followers. Everything will be put right, he suggests, when William is expelled and the Stuart male line restored.

1   *proceres*: the nobility and gentry.
    paludis: i.e., the sea, effectively denied to Scottish merchant shipping. Significantly the word, or the variant *stagna*, is repeated throughout the poem.
2   *prati*: Great Britain, but probably Scotland especially.
3–5 *avos ... prata*: i.e., before 1688.
6   *Rex ILIGNUS*: the Stuart line, including James VII, but with a particular reference to Charles II, whose reign Pitcairne always treats as a Golden Age. 'The oak tree, originally the clan badge of the Stuarts ... In the aftermath of 1688, however, it remained explicitly Jacobite' (Pittock, *Jacobitism*, 72). Probably also intended is a reference to the Royal Oak at Boscobel, Shropshire, in which Charles found a miraculous refuge after his defeat with the Scottish army at Worcester (1651). Charles' indomitable hatred of taking trouble, and his consequent habit of leaving his Scottish subjects to their own devices (which incidentally included the persecution of the Covenanters) well suited him for the role of King Log.
7   *otia non periculosa*: i.e., leisure activities without fear of intervention by informers. This may refer primarily to Pitcairne's brief imprisonment for writing an indiscreet and obscurely seditious private letter in December 1699 to his friend Dr Gray in London, a letter the contents of which, he believed, were revealed to the authorities by an informer (Introduction, pp. 16–17; cf. **19**(a), 53–56). The tone of the letter is unmistakeably Jacobite.

POEM 12

8–11   *Tunc ... tristi*: a reminiscence of Catullus, 1, 7–9. *Juppiter* (9) corresponds to the same word, in the same metrical position, in Catullus, 1, 7.

8–9   *Tunc ... labris*: in a communication, Dr Money has suggested a humorous allusion to the story of the Frog Prince.

8   *me puerum*: Pitcairne as narrator makes himself part of the action, probably referring to his French visits during the 1670s. An element of allegory is present. Pitcairne went abroad to study – something no longer possible when the poem was written. The lips which gave him kisses were chaste (*castis ... labris*, 9), primarily because they were those of Learning. There may be a *double entendre*.

11   *cura ... tristi*: the kisses were free from care, because Pitcairne had no political (Jacobite) worries, free from fear because he was not yet subject to William's oppressive interference.

13   *ripae ulterioris*: Pitcairne had France in mind, now barred to Scots. But he also intended other territories, Nova Scotia, for instance, and Darien, with which King William had forbidden Scots to deal. The phrase echoes *Aeneid* 6, 314, *tendebantque manus ripae ulterioris amore*, and implies a desire for the restoration not only of King James and the Auld Alliance, but also of the freedom of the seas.

inquilinos: an uncommon word, in verse especially so, here probably echoing Martial 1, 86, 11–13 (also in hendecasyllabics): *Migrandum est mihi longius vel illi/ vicinus Novio vel inquilinus/ sit, si quis Novium videre non volt*. Novius was Martial's close neighbour, whom he never saw.

The visitors were tenants because they were students or merchants temporarily resident abroad.

14   *lusus*: the processes of education or trade.

16   *Sole ... occidentem*: probably a reference to Louis XIV, whose sun was rising in the 1670s, but beginning to set by the time of the Peace of Rijswijk in 1697.

17–18   *Ranæ ... prati*: cf. *Aeneid* 2, 325–326, *fuimus Troes, fuit Ilium et ingens/ gloria Teucrorum*. Despite the fall of his city, the mission of Aeneas was to found a new Troy in Italy. *Fuimus Troes* thus became 'the repeated mantra of Jacobite disappointment' (Pittock, *Jacobitism*, 72).

20   *Ventoso populo*: cf. Pliny, *Panegyric*, 31, 2: *uentosa et insolens natio* (of the Egyptians in relation to the Romans).

21   *graves Penates*: the guardian gods of the household; here the Episcopal form of worship.

22   *Saturnia*: i.e., belonging to the Golden Age; cf. Virgil, *Eclogues* 4, 6, *Aeneid* 8, 319–327; cf. **84**. Dr Money, in a communication to us, has made the excellent point that during the Golden Age Saturn, like James VII, was an exile, living in Italy as James lived in France; cf. *Aeneid*, 8, 319–320: *Saturnus ... arma Iovis fugiens et regnis exsul ademptis*. Saturn was the father of Jupiter, who drove him into exile: James was father-in-law to William of Orange.

COMMENTARY

26 *novus ... Rector*: William. In Phaedrus the new ruler is not a stork but a water-serpent (*hydrus*). William's notorious long nose may go some way to explain the alteration.

27–30 *Ciconiarum ... stagna*: the genitive plural indicates that William arrived with followers, his army together with the returned ministers and elders of the Presbyterian church, now established, who under Charles II and James had been exiles in Calvinist Holland. Together these form the *exercitus* of 28.

31–33 *cohortes ... regna*: people overseas with whom Scots could no longer associate, and whose lands were happier because not under William's control.

34 *obscœnæ volucres*: cf. *Aeneid* 3, 241 (of the Harpies): *obscenas pelagi ferro foedare volucres*. In his edition (*Aeneid I–VI*, 288) R.D. Williams comments that *obscenas* is 'a very strong word.' Pitcairne probably intended a reference to the sexual behaviour of some among the returned clergy; see **18** and *The Assembly*, passim. Cf. too **1**, 21–22n.

35–36 *gentem ... junctam*: the Irish. Irish supporters of James VII were defeated at the Boyne (1690) and Aughrim (1691). By the terms of the subsequent Treaty of Limerick (1691), 12000–15000 Irish soldiers, the 'Wild Geese,' left for France, 'so that now no Frogs who remain faithful to their laws and their King survive in that island.' Pitcairne notably recognizes the kinship of Irish and Scots.

39 *ducesque*: reference to the Earl of Seaforth? The word may however refer to the Dukes of Argyll, Hamilton, and Queensberry, all prominent figures in Scottish politics around the turn of the century. Alternatively, it may simply mean 'leaders.'

47–58 *ILICIS ... Praticolarum*: a birthday votive ode for James, only son of James VII, born June 10, 1688, a date observed as a Jacobite festival; note *Juniis ... votis* (49–50). It is addressed to the protecting Genius of the Stuart line. See **Title**, (c), above.

58 *Praticolarum*: a good ending, with a single-word adonic.

13

Notes. This is the first of three poems commemorating two anniversaries, 30 January 1649, when Charles I was executed, and 10 June 1688, the birthday of the Old Pretender. From 1662 to 1859 a special service for 30 January was annexed to the Book of Common Prayer. The anniversary was kept as a day of national fasting and humiliation. Charles, that is to say, was treated as a saint, 'Charles, King and Martyr'. In terms of the second anniversary, the poem is a genethliacon or birthday celebration, a form popular both in classical and in Neo-Latin verse; cf. the closing sapphics of **12**. Pitcairne refers to four classical examples of the form, all celebrating the dead poet and advocate of the old order, Lucan (39–65 AD), one (*Silvae* 2, 7) by Statius and three much shorter examples by Martial (7, 21; 22;

23). He also echoes the speech of Aeneas to the Trojans on the first anniversary of his father Anchises' death (*Aeneid* 5, 45–71). The general effect depends largely on rhetorical repetition and variation (*polyptoton*), balancing different parts of the verb *redire* and *venire*, *nomine* and *numen*, *Janus*, *Junius* and *Junia*, giving the poem an almost ritual tone.

1–2 *Ergo … redit*: cf. *Aeneid*, 5, 49–50: *iamque dies, nisi fallor adest, quem semper acerbum, / semper honoratum (sic di voluistis) habebo.*

3–4 *nomine … numen*: note the paronomasia.

4 *numen*: cf. *Aeneid* 5, 56: *haud equidem … sine numine divum*.

5 *Jano*: Janus, Roman god of beginnings, whence January.

Junius: i.e. *Junius mensis*, 'month of Juno,' 'June,' but also the Roman gentile name, *Junius*, 'member of the clan devoted to Juno,' with primary reference to L. *Junius* Brutus who overthrew the Tarquins and established the Roman republic and/or to M. *Junius* Brutus who took part in the murder of Julius Caesar but failed to re-establish the republic. Both attempted to overthrow regimes regarded as tyrannical and usurping. Cf. below *Junia*, feminine in agreement with *Lux*, (9–10).

8 *Scotia mœsta*: cf. *Aeneid*, 5, 48, *maestasque sacravimus aras*.

9 *Lux*: literally 'light'; for the meaning 'day,' and particularly 'birthday,' cf. the opening of the second genethliacon for Lucan by Martial (7, 22, 1–2): *Vatis Apollinei magno memorabilis ortu / lux redit*. In the third (7, 23, 3) we have: *Quid tanta pro luce precer?* Cf. too Juvenal, *Satire* 12, 1: *natali die mihi dulcior haec lux*. Cf. also 40(d), 1: *Lux optata nitet* (of Stevenson's birthday).

conscia votis: cf. the opening of Martial's first genethliacon for Lucan (7, 21, 1–2): *Haec est illa dies, magni quae conscia partus / Lucanum populis et tibi, Polla, dedit*. Polla was Lucan's widow. Cf. also 13, 1.

votis: cf. *Aeneid* 5, 53, *annua vota*.

10 *Junia*: i.e., 10 June.

ore favete: cf. *Aeneid*, 5, 71 (marking the transition to the religious ceremony at the tomb): *ore favete omnes et cingite tempora ramis*; Statius, *Silvae* 7, 19–20: *Lucanum canimus, favete linguis, / vestra est ista dies, favete, Musae*.

11 *Res agitur*: probably the greater commitment of Louis XIV to the Jacobite cause which led to the attempted invasion of Scotland (March 1708) by a French fleet with the Pretender on board. 'The catalyst for the abortive invasion was the union of 1707, which had a transforming effect on the Stuart cause … now the Jacobites could pose as the champions of Scottish nationalism and the defenders of Scottish liberty' (Devine, *Scottish Nation*, 36–37).

14

Notes. See introductory note to the previous poem.

1 *HÆc ... cœdis*: a variation on Martial, 7, 21, 1: *Haec est illa dies, magni quae conscia partus*; see **13**, 1, n.
2 *pestes*: i.e., the Commonwealth period and government by Oliver Cromwell; probably also the Glorious Revolution and government by King William.
3 *Divi*: i.e., Charles I, after his death regarded by many as a saint. Pitcairne often translates Christian into pagan terms; cf. **3**, 1.
4 *Nati ... Deo*: i.e., the Old Pretender, grandson of Charles I. Compare the phrase *nate dea*, 'child of the goddess (Venus),' in Virgil often used to address Aeneas (e.g., *Aeneid* 2, 289).

15

Metre. Sapphic stanza.
Notes. The poem celebrates the attainment on 10 June 1709 by the Pretender of his full legal majority, unrealistically regarded as combined with the assumption of full royal power and the consequent return of the Golden Age. The vision was inspired partly by the marked increase of Jacobitism and separatism in Scotland after the 1707 Union, partly by the fortunes of the Whig administration under Godolphin and Marlborough, which began to wane during 1709, eventually leading to the triumph of Harley and the Tories in the general election of 1710. In the first stanza Janus symbolizes not so much the execution of Charles I as the wintry (from a Jacobite point of view) period from the Glorious Revolution to the Pretender's coming of age.

Ceres, Bacchus and Venus, mentioned in the poem, are all fertility powers who return with the true king to restore the fertility of the land. Similar associations are to be found elsewhere in Jacobite poetry. Compare, for instance, lines from 'Oran mu Bhliadhna Thearlaich', 'A Song for the Year of Charles' (i.e., Prince Charles Edward Stuart), by the Gaelic poet Alasdair mac Mhaighstir Alasdair (c. 1700–1770):

Thig soinnion leis an righ,
Teichidh sneachd is eire bhuainn;
Fògrar dòruinn shion,
Thig sòlas, falbhaidh pian;
Gach seòrsa de gach fion
Thig bho'n Fhraing 'n a thunnaichean,
'S gu'n caisg sinn uil' ar n'ìot ...
O, sheannchaidhnean 's an am,

POEM 15

Glacaibh dubh is peann,
So a' bhliadhna chòrr,
An tilg a' ghrian le maoth-bhlàs biadhchor
Gathan ciatach òirnn;
Bidh driùchd air bàrr an fheòir,
Bainne 's mil gun luach, gun mhargadh,
Airgiod agus òr.

Sunshine will come with the king, snow and frost will flee from us; vexation of weather will be banished, joy will come, distress will go; every kind of wine will come from France by the barrel, so that we shall all put an end to our thirst ... Chroniclers of our time, take ink and pen to record this remarkable year in which the sun will shed the tender, fruitful warmth of his goodly ray upon us. There will be dew on the tips of the grass, milk and honey, silver and gold, will be had for the asking.

The year may be the year of the Young Pretender, but the King is still the Old Pretender, 'gentle James', *Sheumàis chaoimh*; see A. and A. MacDonald (eds.), *Poems of Alexander MacDonald* (Inverness, 1924), 118–125.

Unusually, the poem is often reminiscent of other poems in the collection, especially **2**, **3**, **4**, **5** and **12**.

1. *Jane ... Menses*: i.e., the months of winter, but symbolically the period from King William's usurpation to the present of the poem.
   sacri: i.e., 'laid under a curse', 'devoted to the powers of the Underworld'.
2. *Grampio dudum populo*: so altered by Pitcairne (see **Text**) from *Brittonum semper populis*.
3. *auspice Maio*: the beginning of summer in May preludes the abundance of June. There is probably also a reference to the birth of Charles II on 29 May 1630 and his Restoration on 29 May 1660; see **7**; probably also to the fact that 29 May Old Style corresponds to 10 June New Style; see **103**.
4. 6–8 *Solem ... princeps*: a reference to the Summer Solstice, which under the Old Style calendar fell on the Pretender's birthday. A similar reference is to be found in 'Oran a' Gheamhraidh', 'Song to Winter', of mac Mhaighstir Alasdair (MacDonald and MacDonald, *ut cit.*, 28–35; J. MacQueen, *Progress and Poetry* [Edinburgh, 1982], 77–82).
5. 9 *puero*: the Pretender.
   parentem: the deceased James VII.
6. 10 *nati*: again the Pretender.
   meminisse: i.e., to remember that her son has lost his inheritance.
   matrem: Mary of Modena (1658–1718), second wife of James VII and mother of the Pretender.
7. 11 *Ceres*: goddess of harvest and abundance. After the rape of her daughter Pros-

COMMENTARY

erpine, Ceres abandoned her office. The resulting wintry dearth was ended by the temporary return of Proserpine, leading to a new Spring.

13 *comes Baccho Venus*: i.e., wine and love.

13–15 *columbas ... Frænat*: doves draw the chariot of Venus, Indian tigers that of Bacchus.

17 *Lux*: cf. 13, 9n.

eversum ... annum: the return of the Pretender will restore the proper order of the seasons, the *insanas hyemes* (18), brought about by the rule of an usurper; cf. Virgil, *Georgics* 1, 498–501: *di patrii ... hunc saltem everso iuvenem succurrere saeclo/ ne prohibete*. The reference here is to the peace established (30 BC) in the Roman world by the young Augustus after the tumultuous events of the previous half-century. The Pretender and Augustus are in effect equated.

22 *Saturnus*: king of the gods until overthrown by his son Jupiter and exiled to Italy, where he presided over a Golden Age; cf. **12**, 22n., **84**.

23 *Rege Dictæo*: Jupiter, born in the Dictaean cave in Crete, here equated with William of Orange. Saturn was Jupiter's father; James VII was William's father-in-law.

23–24 *superos ... imis*: reference unclear.

25 *Ranarum*: a continuation of the figure introduced in **12**.

27–28 *Furiis ... orbem*: William dragged Britain into the Nine Years War (1688–1697); his policies continued during the War of the Spanish Succession (1702–1713).

30 *avita prata*: cf. **11**, 1, 4; **12**, 2, 5, 18, 23, 41.

31–32 *Gramus ... Locartus ... Makiniusque*: cf. **2**, **3**, **4**, **5**. Note once more the motif of the revenant.

34 *socrum*: i.e., Ceres.

35 *comitique Bacchi*: i.e., Venus; cf. 13.

37–38 *almi ... Genio*: i.e., the Stuart royal line.

39–40 *Quem ... potentes*: i.e., the Stuart line is protected both by dead (deified) monarchs, in particular Charles I and II and James VII, and by Louis XIV of France and the Pretender, both still alive.

43–44 *Mensibus ... Scotobrigantum*: MS alteration in the Bodleian and Yale exemplars from the printed *Ille Saturno pius imperante/ Jura det annis*, 'May he dutifully make law for the years under the sway of Saturn', an alteration also indicated in *Mutenda & Corrigenda*. Saturn is the exiled Pretender; cf. **12**, 22; **84**.

44 *Scotobrigantum*: cf. **6**, 3n.; **36** (a), 15. The improved ending with a single-word adonic recalls that in **12**.

16

Notes. John Hamilton, second Baron Belhaven (1656–1708), was not originally a Jacobite; he was in fact one of the Scottish noblemen who in January 1689 invited William to assume the government of Scotland and summon a convention of the Three Estates. William's failure to support the Darien scheme changed his attitude; in particular he became a passionate opponent of the 1707 Union, which he denounced on 2 November 1706 in a remarkable speech to the Estates, a speech subsequently published in Edinburgh and London. David Daiches remarks (*Scotland and the Union* [London, 1977], 147): 'Belhaven's speech consisted largely of a series of pictures of what Scotland would become as the consequence of an incorporating union.' The climax was:

> 'But above all, My Lord, I think I see our Ancient Mother CALEDONIA, like Caesar sitting in the midst of our Senate, Rufully looking round about her, Covering her self with her Royal Garment, attending the Fatal Blow, and breathing out her last with a *Et tu quoque mi fili.*'

Lord Marchmont replied that a short answer to this long and terrible speech would suffice: 'Behold, he dreamed, but lo! When he awoke, behold it was a dream.' Hence the title, 'The Vision' (Edinburgh, 1706), given to a contemporary verse attack (by Defoe) on Belhaven. Pitcairne accepts the title, but regards Belhaven not as a dreamer but as an inspired seer (*vates*).

As a consequence of his opposition to the Union, Belhaven was imprisoned in Edinburgh and in April 1708 brought in custody to London on suspicion of favouring the abortive Jacobite invasion of that year. He died there on 21 June 1708. Pitcairne's verses must have been composed shortly afterwards.

See the article on Belhaven by J.R. Young in *OxfDNB*.

1–2 Almost the same couplet is used in Pitcairne's epitaph (**95**) for James Douglas, fourth Duke of Hamilton (1658–1712), leader of the Country (or Patriotic) Party in the Scottish parliament, killed on 15 November 1712 in a duel with Lord Mohun. The second line repeats, but to opposite effect, line 10 of George Buchanan's hostile epigram on Archbishop John Hamilton of St Andrews (1512–1571): *Dignus Hamiltonæ dum cupis esse domo* (*Epigrammatum* 2, 30).
1 *Dum ... regna*: i.e., by activities in the Scottish parliament.
2 *Dignus*: note the effective balance with *nimis indignè* in the following line.
   Hamiltonia ... domo: probably, in the first place, a reference to the leader of Belhaven's party, the Duke of Hamilton, not in fact a blood-relation.
3 *indignè ... avelleris*: i.e., when he was taken to London and died there.
4 *Si ... sinunt*: i.e., after the 1707 Union. A distant echo of the Virgilian *fuimus Troes.*
5 *vatum*: cf. 8, *vates*, and see introductory note above.

7 *raptosque Penates*: i.e., after the Union, Scottish domestic affairs are to be settled in London rather than Edinburgh. The phrase stems from the Virgilian *victosque Penates* (*Aeneid* 1, 68). Belhaven, it is suggested, was a possible Aeneas, unsuccessful however in the re-establishment of his household gods.

17

Notes. The poem commemorates the death on 1 October 1707 of George, the only surviving son of Sir George Mackenzie of Rosehaugh (5, introductory note) by his second wife, Margaret Haliburton. At the time of his death, the younger Mackenzie was a Gentleman Commoner of University College, Oxford. The poem is as much directed to the mother as to the son.

1 *Dura ... mors*: balanced against *oriente juventa* and, later, *durior ipsa/ Morte* (5–6).
2 *Patri*: Sir George Mackenzie.
3 *Sorores*: the Fates.
4 *me, me*: in BA(1), the comma is a later insertion by hand. It appears elsewhere in *Mutenda & Corrigenda*, and is sometimes inserted. The repetition is emphatic. Compare in *Aeneid* 9, 427, the exclamatory and absolute *me, me, adsum qui feci, in me convertite ferrum, / o Rutuli!*
5 *Matris*: Margaret Haliburton.
6 *Elyzium*: Elysium, the abode of the virtuous dead.

18

Notes. The poem is a satire in Ovidian mock-heroic style: *Militat omnis amans et habet sua castra Cupido* (*Amores* 1, ix, 1 – the entire poem is an elaboration of the conceit). The hero, David, is David Williamson, latterly Presbyterian minister of the West Kirk, Edinburgh, known to his contemporaries as Daintie Davie. In his earlier years, before the battle of Bothwell Brig (1679), he had preached at conventicles in Teviotdale. For this he was much later imprisoned on the evidence of papers found on the person of the Cameronian James Renwick (1662–1688), captured in January 1688 and executed a month later. Williamson was released after the flight to France of James VII (*Biographia Presbyteriana* [Edinburgh, 1837], 149–167). He is best known however for the exploit recorded in *Scotch Presbyterian Eloquence* (1692), written under the episcopalian pseudonym 'Jacob Curate' (in fact, probably Robert Calder; see 111, introductory note) and ironically dedicated to William Lindsay (1644–1698), eighteenth earl of Crawford – Lord Whigridden, that is to say, 'a *Presbyterian* Peer, a rigid Fool' in Pitcairne's *The Assembly*.

POEM 18

'Nay, generally, they are of Opinion, that a Man is never a true Saint, till he have a sound Fall, such as that of *David*'s with *Bathsheba*. The following Narration of a well-known Truth shall serve for instance.

A Party of King *Charles* the Second's Guards being sent to apprehend Mr. *David Williamson* (one of the most eminent of their Ministers now in *Edinburg*) for the frequent Rebellion and Treason he preached then at Sield [*sic*]-Meetings; and the Party having surrounded the House where he was, a zealous Lady, Mistress of the House, being very sollicitous to conceal him, rose in all Haste from her Bed, where she left her Daughter of about 18 Years of Age; and having dressed up the Holy Man's Head with some of her own Night-Cloaths, she wittily advised him to take her Place in the warm bed, with her Girl; to which he modestly and readily consented; and knowing well how to employ his Time, especially upon such an extrordinary [*sic*] Call, to propagate the Image of the Party, while the Mother, to divert the Troopers Enquiry, was treating them with strong Drink in the Parlour, he, to express his Gratitude, applies himself with extraordinary Kindness to the Daughter; who finding him like to prove a very useful Man in his Generation, told her Mother she would have him for her Husband: To which the Mother, though otherwise unwilling, yet, for concealing the Scandal, out of Love to the Cause, consented, when the Mystery of the Iniquity was wholly disclosed to her. This whole Story is as well known in Scotland, as that the Covenant was begun, and carried out by Rebellion and Oppression.'

(1738 edn. [Rotterdam and London], 5–6)

Williamson figures by name in *Babell*, and as Mr Solomon Cherry-Trees in *The Assembly*. Compare in the Preface to the latter: 'Mr David Williamson is called Mr Solomon Cherry-trees, for that famous action of his, in getting with child the Lady Cherry-Trees daughter, in that instant when the soldiers were searching the house to carry him away to suffer the just punishment of a rebel and a traitor' (Tobin, *Assembly*, 30).

The exemplars are later but the poems were probably written during the early 1690s, at much the same time as *Babell*, *The Assembly*, and *Scotch Presbyterian Eloquence*. In the first the mock-heroic element is provided by the story of Dido and Aeneas, an element still liminally present in the second, although there the story of David and Bathsheba has a stronger presence. It is curious to note that Aeneas, and even his appearance from a cloud at Carthage, became part of Jacobite typology (Pittock, *Poetry and Politics*, 27–28, 38–40; *Jacobitism*, 72), and that Dryden in *Absalom and Achitophel* figuratively applied King David's marital peccadilloes to events in the reign of Charles II.

For many years Williamson's exploit retained some notoriety; throughout this period the poem retained some personal interest. The satire also has a general application, to the hypocrisy which Pitcairne saw at the heart of Presbyterian orthodoxy, present in both versions but given additional, more obvious, emphasis in the second and longer. Compare Burns's 'Holy Willie's Prayer', in which a particular individual, William Fisher, elder in Mauchline parish, Ayrshire, also emerges as a universal, comic and despicable figure.

An English paraphrase appears in R^2 as Broadside 11:

The Priest's Address to Venus/ Venus Answer to the Priest

For much curious information relative to Mr David Williamson the reader is referred to Kirkton's Church History, p. 349. This and the Answer are translations from Dr Pitcairn.

The Priest's Address to Venus

When, in late times of sin, an angry crew
Of armed souldiers harmless me persue,
I cry'd to Heav'n for aid, but all in vaine;
The gods were deaf, and careless of my paine.
5   *At length to Venus' camp I do repaire,*
And offerings for the goddess fitt prepare
When fortified with Love's inchanting armes,
I rest secure from all these feirce alarms.
Whilst at thy altar I devotlie bow,
10   *The sacrifice was streight consum'd by you,*
Blest deitie, still unto thy servants true.
Thy powerful succors in the cloud I felt,
And in Love's liquid rapture fainting melt.
By thee, my foes subdued, and I set free,
15   *Shall of thy godhead still adorer be.*
Dear Venus, safe, I'll of thy praises sing,
And to thy altars, willing gifts shall bring;
Thy name thro' all the world I will make known –
Thou, more than other gods, thy love hath shown.
20   *Without thy aid, Æneas, thy own son,*
No famous act, no valiant deed had done.
Proud Rome, with all her saints, thou dost outdo –
As many votaries hast, and martyrs too.
By thy sweet charms allured, and for thy sake,
25   *The Scots their ancient laws and rites forsake.*
By thee made drunk, their chains asunder brake,
And tamelie to a female yield their neck.
Love's mysteries, thou goddess makes me know,
And heavenly pleasures how to use below.
30   *Yea, with one breath love's gate does open blow.*

Thou maiden blushes quickly can subdue,
Their fiercenes tame, and make the proudest low.
Temples, where divine service ought to be,
Are now made waste, and dedicat to thee.
35 *Let Eastern nations Mahomet adore,*
And holy Europe their own God implore.
And I thy praise, dear Venus, shall proclaime,
My chief devotion shall run in thy name.
Yea, blest by thee, I holy shall appear,
40 *And every wench shall Venus love and fear.*
By her, in secret mysteries skill'd, I grew,
With which we cheat the poor unthinking crew,
And each old hag the pious fraud persue.
She promis'd me a nation, which should be,
45 *Throw all the world renown'd for bigotrie,*
Which with true zeal purg'd from the dross of Rome,
That to be fooles and knaves took for their doome.
In fyne, she rules the Earth, and will protect
Those priests that ne'er her service shall reject.

Venus Answer to the Priest

50 *Darling of all, our love, my chiefest joy,*
Your vowes we heard, nothing shall you annoy.
In adverse times thou was well known to me,
And of my heroes chiftain thou shalt be.
Thou undeceivest the world, and let's them see
55 *Religion and lust do weell agree.*
Scotsmen, rejoice, and celebrate the day
That Davie's harp you heard soe sweetly play.
Thou art my David, and can quickly cure
All the distempers love-sick maids endure.
60 *Thy weell-tun'd instrument makes me forsake*
The Gods, and dwell on Earth for thy dear sake.
When I thy sweet embraces call to minde,
I blush to think that ever I was kind
To old Anchise, or that I could touch
65 *Distorted Vulcan, whom I loath'd so much;*
Though he amongst the Gods had got a name,
And was not meanly skill'd in Cupid's game.
But thou my god and faithful lover art,
Ty'd with the strictest bonds we'll never part.
70 *I'll come then, as I promis'd, to thy land,*

COMMENTARY

And leaving Paphos (empty), will command
That many smoking altars burn for me,
And thou, dear saint, my faithful priest shall be.

The reference under the title is not directly to *A History of the Church of Scotland* by James Kirkton (1628–1699), which contains nothing immediately relevant to the poem, but to the edition printed in 1817 by C.K. Sharpe under the somewhat misleading title *The Secret and true history of the Church of Scotland from the Restoration to the year 1678*. Sharpe's notes include the story of Daintie Davie. The print in R^2 must be later than 1817; it appears to be of early- to mid-nineteenth century date. The translation itself is certainly older; spellings and the occasional rhyme show that the linguistic basis is Scots. One couplet, not directly paralleled in the Latin, 'By thee made drunk, their chains asunder brake,/ And tamelie to a female yield their neck' (26–27), suggests a date of composition during the reign of Anne (1702–1714). There is at least a possibility that Pitcairne was the author.

(a), (b), 1–22

1–4 *Militis … tuus*: these lines set out the basic situation, the pursuit of the preacher by government troops and his finding refuge in Venus's stronghold (*Castra*), the bedroom of the house which gave him refuge and, by implication only, the young woman whom he found there.
3 *litavi*: i.e., he performed the act sacred to Venus.
4 *sprevi … tuus*: i.e., he used the weapons of Venus rather than those of a soldier.
miles: for the figure of love as military service under the command of Venus, cf. introductory note above; also, e.g., Horace, *Odes* 3, 26, 1–2: *Vixi puellis nuper idoneus/ et militavi non sine gloria*. The figure retained importance for many centuries.
5–6 *me densa … pio*: the darkness of the bedroom, likened to that in *Aeneid* 1, 411–414, where Venus conceals in cloud her son Aeneas and his comrade Achates as they approach Carthage, ruled by Dido, whom the goddess plans that Aeneas shall seduce. Note the ironic suggestion that *pius*, the essential epithet of Aeneas, also applies to Williamson.
11 *Sancta Venus*: in effect, 'Saint Venus.' In classical usage the participial adjective *sanctus* (from *sancio*) does not often qualify the personal name of a divinity, and when it does, the usage is not simply adjectival and the flavour is archaic. Thus, to illustrate the Virgilian phrase *sancte deorum* (*Aeneid* 4, 576), addressed to Mercury, Servius quotes from Ennius the phrase *Juno Saturnia sancta dearum*. In both poets, the dependent genitive shows that the function of *sanctus* remains substantially participial ('regarded as holy among the gods'). In Pitcairne *Sancta* is purely adjectival, and the phrase is used ironically as if Venus were a Christian saint to whom petitions might properly be addressed.
12 *non ficta Relligione*: i.e., the Calvinism which he outwardly professes is a mere show.

POEM 18

14 *cluis*: for this (mock-) heroic idiom, see *Lewis and Short*. Cf. Milton, *Paradise Lost* 3, 7: 'Or hear'st thou rather pure Ethereal stream?'

16 *Roma*: the city was founded by Romulus and Remus, descendents of Aeneas, and so of Venus. 'As Venus Genetrix (= the mother of the *gens Iulia*) she was prominent in imperial cult' (*OCD*, s.v.). Pitcairne perhaps has most in mind the proem to Lucretius' *De Rerum Natura*, which celebrates the universal power of Venus, *Aeneadum genetrix*.

18 *templa Deum*: i.e., Presbyterian churches.

19–20 *Mirentur ... Amor*: Williamson rejects the two major religions known to him, Islam and Christianity.

20 (a) *Alteriusque alios*, (b) *Europam alterius*: in both versions *alterius* most probably refers to Christ. (b) is the more explicit.
(a) *alios*: Christians generally.
urat amor: cf. Virgil, *Eclogues* 2, 168: *me tamen urit amor*.

21 *Ast ego ... dicam*: cf. Money, *English Horace*, 128. The phrase however is primarily dramatic. Pitcairne is speaking as Williamson rather than personally.
furtivae Veneris: cf. Ovid, *Amores* 2, 8, 7–8: *num verbo lapsus in ullo/ furtiuae Veneris conscia signa dedi?*; *Ars Amatoria* 1, 33–34: *nos Venerem tutam concessaque furta canemus*; ibid., 275: *utque uiro furtiva Venus, sic grata puellae*.

(b) 23–36

23 *sanctum*: cf. above 11n. 'Saint' here means Presbyterian minister.

25–30 *Illa ... Illa ... Illa ... Illa ... Illa ...*: perhaps a reminiscence of the rhetorical repetition of *te*, addressed to Venus, in Lucretius 1, 6–24, the invocation of Venus.

26 *Et dolus ... anu*: i.e., every old woman has, in her time, endured (or enjoyed) the trickery of Venus.

27 *Gentem*: i.e., the child mentioned in the introductory note above; perhaps also others fathered by Williamson.

28 *Romulei ... patres*: apparently the ancient Romans, but in fact a reference to the pre-Reformation Roman clergy, whose promiscuity was much emphasised by Protestants; *patres* thus has the double significance of 'priest' ('Father') and 'progenitor.'

31 *veteres ... penates*: i.e., traditional Episcopalian forms of worship; cf. 12, 21n.

32 *patrem*: the exiled James VII; cf. 2, 2.

33–34 *Bacchato ... choro*: cf. Virgil, *Georgics* 2, 487–488: *virginibus bacchata Lacaenis/ Taygeta*; *Aeneid* 3, 125: *bacchatamque iugis Naxum*. Like Sparta and Naxos, Scotland is now given over to orgiastic worship

35–36 *Cœlis ... cœlos*: in classical Latinity the masculine plural form of *caelum* is rare and poetic (Lucretius 2, 1097: *caelos omnis conuertere*), but in ecclesiastical Latin it is frequent: *Caeli enarrant gloriam Dei* (Vulgate *Psalm* 18:1). Here the ecclesiastical overtone is probably deliberate.

COMMENTARY

(a) 23–36. (b) 37–50

23–24, 37–38 *Deliciae ... meae*: the language of love modulates into that of military service. Venus begins with a term of endearment, *deliciae* (cf., e.g., Catullus 2, 1; Virgil, *Eclogue* 2, 2), but goes on to speak as supreme commander, awarding commendation.

23, 37 *rebus in arctis*: i.e., in Scottish affairs; cf. below, 22,3 and n.

24, 38 *gloria*: Venus is granting David the amatory equivalent of a Roman military triumph; cf. Ovid, *Amores* 2, 12 (a poem beginning *Ite triumphales circum mea tempora laurus*), 11–12: *at mea seposita est et ab omni milite dissors/ gloria*: also Horace, *Odes* 3, 26, 1–2, cited above 4n.

25, 39 *Qui ... socias*: Apollo is god of poetry, in mythology not usually linked to Venus.

25–26, 39–40 *pectora ... Lyrae*: the phrase *Lyra Davidica* usually refers to the Psalms of the biblical King David, celebrated among much else for his seduction of Bathsheba, wife of Uriah, and the unsavoury events leading to their subsequent marriage (*II Samuel*, 11). The king and David Williamson are linked by their exploit, and by the fact that both were poets, or at least that Williamson was much given to biblical poetic language, especially from the *Song of Songs* (attributed to Solomon, King David's son by Bathsheba) as an aid to seduction. Pitcairne describes him as 'so famous for love-intrigues, who preaches so oft out of the Canticles, and talks so much, in his sermons, of beds of roses and dams of love' (Tobin, *Assembly*, 30). For the lyre as phallic symbol and weapon of love, cf. Horace, *Odes* 3, 26 (already quoted), 3–4: *defunctumque bello barbiton*.

28, 42 *Non sola ... vales*: by implication, his second attraction is his potency as a lover.

29, 43 *Anchisen*: Anchises, the mortal father of Aeneas by a union with Venus. In the *Aeneid* he is an old man, but of course by then Aeneas had reached full maturity and himself fathered a child.

30, 44 *loripedi ... seni*: the lame god Vulcan, married to Venus.

31, 45 *ille*: Vulcan.

32, 46 *Hic Deus*: Williamson, ironically given divine status.

33, 47 *sperata/ promissa Puellis*: with the reading *sperata* the girls are agents, with *promissa* recipients. The word *puella*, as often in Catullus, Horace and Ovid, is used in the sense 'sweetheart, mistress.'

34, 48 *Posthabitaque ... Papho*: cf. *Aeneid* 1, 15–16 (of Carthage): *quem Iuno fertur terris magis omnibus unam/ posthabita coluisse Samo*. Samos was Juno's major cult-centre as Paphos was for Venus.

36, 50 *Arcadicus/ Arabicus*: *Arcadicus* is the better reading. Scotland, like Arcadia, is mountainous and remote. *Arabicus* is a corruption, perhaps influenced by *Arabes* (19).

Puer: Cupid.

19

Notes. The two poems in this section bear an obvious relationship to each other. Both are dramatic monologues, one directed towards an inquisitive visitor to Edinburgh, the other in the character of the master at a drinking academy delivering instructions to a willing pupil. The climax of each is an almost identical catalogue of Edinburgh taverns. There are also considerable differences. The lines preceding the catalogue bear no resemblance to each other. The overtones in 19(a) are strongly Jacobite and Episcopalian; nothing of this is present in 19(b). In 19(a), 39–46, imply that Greppa is still alive, with Anne Stamfield as her servant in the Greping-office. In 19(b), 66–68, only Anne is mentioned, presumably as sole proprietrix. Greppa, it will be remembered, died in 1700 and was succeeded by Anne. 19(a) is thus probably the earlier, written during the hated reign of King William and before the death of Greppa. 19(b) probably belongs to the more hopeful (from a Jacobite point of view) reign of Queen Anne.

As has already been noted in the General Introduction, 19(a) parodies the conventional *encomium urbis*, as practised, for instance, by Arthur Johnston (*MLA* 2, 255–287) and earlier by such poets as Julius Caesar Scaliger (1484–1558) and the late-classical Ausonius (d. c.395). Like Johnston, Pitcairne stresses the height of Edinburgh's situation and buildings. Johnston however, unlike Pitcairn, ignored the depths. Pitcairne's general tone is mock-heroic, with references to the *Gigantomachia*, the episode of the Cyclopes in *Odyssey* 9, the quest of the Golden Fleece, and the descent to the underworld in *Aeneid* 6. The underground Edinburgh taverns make this last the predominant image.

'In the long inserted passage quoted in the textual notes, the primary reference is to the *Gigantomachia*. In attacking the Gods, the Giants attempted to pile mountains on mountains – Pelion on Ossa and Ossa on Olympus; cf. *Aeneid* 6, 582-584, *Georgics* 1, 278-282. There are overtones of the building of the Tower of Babel (Genesis 11:4); compare Pitcairne's vernacular satire on the Kirk, *Babell*, written 1691/2. Pitcairne sees as Giants/builders the French theologian Calvin (1509–1564) and his followers, the ministers of the Presbyterian Church of Scotland, the latter firmly established in the early 1690s at the expense of the Episcopalians. Their triumph corresponds to the early success of the Giants/builders. Pitcairne expected that the power of Jupiter, and the consequent return of the Stuart monarchy, would ensure the reversal of the situation.

invisum ... Genus are the Presbyterian clergy.

Erinnys was a Fury who punished notable sinners.

Jani in mense: 30 January was the anniversary of the execution in 1649 of Charles King and Martyr, observed by Episcopalians as a fast-day, by Presbyterians as a festival.

dite is Dis, i.e. Satan.'

Chambers paraphrased parts of this version (*Traditions of Edinburgh*, 158–159).

19(b) is a satirical lecture on the art of drinking, supposedly given by a schoolmaster to a willing pupil, the *puer* of 1. For the most part, the poem is written in proverb-like closed couplets which parody the style of the *Disticha Catonis*, much used as a school-text in the Middle Ages and later. Practical advice on 'reading' is given in the final lines (53–78).

The poem bears some resemblance to a macaronic *jeu d'esprit*, very doubtfully attributed to Pitcairne, beginning with a 'Formula Lauream Candidatis dandi in Collegio Buterensi' to be found in *A Choice Collection of Comic and Serious Scots Poems both Ancient and Modern*, 3 vols. (Edinburgh: James Watson, 1706, 1709, 1711), iii, 56–69, most readily consulted in the first volume of Harriet Harvey Wood (ed.), *James Watson's Choice Collection of Comic and Serious Scots Poems*, 2 vols., STS (Edinburgh, 1977, 1991). No copies seem now to be extant of an earlier edition, *The Institution and Progress of the Buttery College at Slains in the Parish of Cruden, Aberdeenshire, with a Catalogue of the Books and Manuscripts in the Library of that University* (Aberdeen: John Forbes, 1702). Pitcairne may have seen a copy of this work, then written his own version, transferring the college to Edinburgh.

(a)

3–4   *Urbis ... propinqua*: Edinburgh was celebrated for the height of its tenements and for the cellars beneath, entered from below the street and often used as shops or taverns.

5   *Aegidii triplicem ... aedem*: St Giles' Cathedral in Edinburgh, originally a collegiate church, raised by Charles I to the status of a cathedral, seat of the newly-created bishopric of Edinburgh. Bishop Rose and his congregation abandoned the building in 1690. It was subdivided into three (later four) Presbyterian churches.

6   *Cyclopes*: gigantic loud-voiced shepherds with a single eye in the middle of the forehead. They also formed the workforce of Vulcan's noisy stithy; cf. **82** below. Here, the ministers of the three St Giles' congregations.

9   *Bacchi ... Phoebi*: gods respectively of wine and of music and poetry. Phoebus is also called Apollo (1.34). The only refuge from the dominant church is to be found in the life of the taverns.

11   *Luna ... sole*: taverns the signs of which were the Moon and the Sun.
bibendum: cf. Horace, *Odes* 1, 26,1, on the death of Cleopatra.

13   *Clavigeri*: the tavern-sign was probably the Cross Keys.
Styli: John Steill, a man of some culture, subscriber to the 1721 and 1728 volumes of Allan Ramsay's *Poems*. He was a teacher of music and a performer; concerts by him are on record in 1700, 1707 and 1711. His tavern was well-known for musical performances. Here the Edinburgh Musical Society held their meetings in the 1720s (Johnson, *Music and Society*, 32–34). He seems to have retired from business or died in 1729. Ramsay claims that his tavern was

POEM 19

equal to the best in London ('Epistle to Robert Yarde of Devonshire Esquire', 19–24; Martin and Oliver, *Allan Ramsay*, ii, 57–58).

14 *Garumna*: the Garonne, the river which flows through the claret-producing area around Bordeaux.

15 *Argo*: the crew of the ship Argo made the long voyage to Colchis to recover the Golden Fleece. Chambers suggests that the tavern was called 'The Ship'.

17 *Kettam*: Chambers renders 'Katy' (*Traditions*, 158).

19 *Barcinia*: adjective from *Barcino*, the ancient name of Barcelona, capital of Catalonia. Tennant presumably specialized in Spanish wine. French wine was more highly regarded.
decorati tempora vite: cf. *Aeneid* 6, 665.

22 *Ostreaque*: oysters were a favourite Edinburgh delicacy; cf. Robert Fergusson's 'Caller Oysters' (McDiarmid, *Poems of Robert Fergusson*, ii, 66–68).

31 *Haia*: the proprietrix of the Greping-office; see **8**, 'Ad Greppam,' where Pitcairne calls her Mrs Henderson. Perhaps 'Hay' was her maiden name.

33–34 *Denique ... videt*: cf. Virgil's description of the cave of Avernus, entry to the underworld (*Aeneid* 6, 237–242).

35 *Sed placare ... servat*: the bitch corresponds to Cerberus, guardian-dog of the underworld. With *servat*, cf. *Aeneid* 6, 298, 417–423.

36 *indigenam ... merum*: i.e., whisky.
Anna: Anne Stamfield, servant in, and eventually landlady of the Greping-office; see above **9**.27 and n.; **69**.

37 *sedesque ... beatas*: the interior of the tavern corresponds to the Elysian Fields (*Aeneid* 6, 639).

38 *norunt solem ... suum*: cf. *Aeneid* 6, 641.

39–42 *quas ... bibunt*: cf. *Aeneid* 6, 713–715, 748–751.

43–44 *superas ... labos*: a clever variation on *Aeneid* 6, 128–129.

45 *fidum ... Achatem*: cf. *Aeneid* 6, 158 etc. Achates was a close comrade of Aeneas, but did not in fact accompany him to the underworld.

47–48 *Artibus ... domos*: cf. *Aeneid* 6, 121–122. Castor and Pollux were twin sons of Jupiter and Leda, the first mortal, the second immortal. When Castor died, Pollux rescued him from the underworld. They were placed in the sky as the constellation Gemini, the Twins.

49–56 *Sed ... Vale*: Pitcairne seems to have added these lines after the completion of the poem.

50 *veteres ... faces*: the stars, but also the lanterns carried at night by the caddies, the errand-boys of the Edinburgh streets.

51 *Rossi*: not identified.

52 *Grajaque*: 'Greek', i.e, 'treacherous'; *timeo Danaos et dona ferentis* (*Aeneid* 2, 49).

54 *reges*: the 'Kings over the Water', James VII, and Louis XIV of France.

55–56 *Nam ... Vale*: the variant text in SP may represent a further revision by Pitcairne. Both versions refer to Williamite informers on the look-out for Jacobites.

(b)

1 *jocari*: i.e., by playing the part of a schoolboy.
5–6 *Attamen ... cervisia*: in effect, make sure that your clothes correspond with school regulations, put on school-uniform.
rubra: ablative, although scansion dictates *rubră*.
8 *adsis*: 'Adsum' is the proper response at a school morning roll-call.
10 *ordine*: the pupils are arranged in order of abilities.
14 *clara sede locandus*: i.e., he will be made top of his class.
15 *Nicotiana*: tobacco, introduced to Europe by J. Nicot (1530–1600).
tubi: i.e., tobacco pipes; cf. Alsopp, *Odes* 2, 15, 1–2: *Dum tubum, ut mos est meus, ore versans/ Februis penso quid agam Calendis* (Money, *English Horace*, 308).
21 *sceptra*: the rods or ferrules formerly used by masters on recalcitrant pupils.
38 *palmas*: the award, usually a medal inscribed with palms, given to the academically most accomplished pupil, the dux.
39 *græcari*: cf. Horace, *Satires* 2, 2, 10–11: *vel si Romana fatigat/ militia adsuetum græcari*; cf. also 37, 9.
45 *Mohamedanos*: i.e., probably, the Turks. Alcohol is forbidden to Mohammedans.
48 *Quem ... probet*: a possible reference to a Franco-Turk alliance.
51 *Catonis*: the author of *Disticha Catonis*, as distinguished from Cato the Censor or Cato Uticensis. Pitcairne refers primarily to his own couplets above.
52 *Authores*: i.e., *auctores*, the curriculum authors used in schools; here the tavern-keepers and taverns catalogued below. The *turba faceta* is the crowd of customers who frequent these places.
53–78 As in 18(a), the style of the catalogue is mock-heroic, but the effect is greater because in this version the style corresponds to the status of the tavern-keepers as *auctores*. The catalogue culminates in a visit to the Virgilian Underworld and Elysian Fields. Cf. the notes to 18(a), 26–56.
61–62 *Dallasius ... Heros ... Briggnis*: not identified; not mentioned in 18(a). His name may have been Brigg or Briggs and he may have come to Edinburgh from Dallas in Moray. Alternatively he may have been a Dallas whose people lived near a bridge, perhaps the one at the east end of the Nor' Loch in Edinburgh.

20

Metre. Sapphic stanza (I) and elegiac couplet (II and III).
Notes. A book entitled *Octupla: Hoc est Octo Paraphrases Poeticæ Psalmi CIV Authoribus totidem Scotis* was published in Edinburgh in 1696 (Pitcairne had a copy in his library). The first of the eight paraphrases included was by the great George Buchanan (1506–1582), whose version of the Psalms in classical metres was his best-known, and in some ways most brilliant, work. The eighth was by Pitcairne's former fellow-student, Walter Dennistoun, a version introduced by a fulsome dedication to the Senators of the College of Justice, the Faculty of Advocates, and

the Society of Writers to the Signet – the entire Scottish legal profession, that is to say, judges, counsels and solicitors. The text is taken from a print, probably of 1690 or early 1691. Under 19 February 1691 the *Minute Book of the Faculty of Advocates* (vol. 1, ed. J.M. Pinkerton [Edinburgh, Stair Society, 1976], 94) has the following entry: 'And haveing lykwayes taken into their consideratione Mr. Walter Dennistoune his paraphrase on the hundred and fourthe psalme which he dedicated into the Facultie they appoynted him three pound sterling out of the stock purse. And ordained Mr. John Richardsone ther thesaurer to pay the same'.

The association thus provided of Dennistoun with Buchanan gave rise to Pitcairne's poem. The psalm version is Dennistoun's, with alterations and additions by Pitcairne, who made it at once more pagan and classical, more scientific, and at the same time improved the Latin. In the first line, for instance, Dennistoun has *Dexteram invictam canimus Jovamque*, in which the last word is intended as a contracted form of *Jehovamque*. Pitcairne emended to *Jovemque*, accusative of *Juppiter*, name of the supreme Roman god. In ll. 3–4, Dennistoun has *animatque vasto / Numine mundum*, which Pitcairne alters to *animatque magnam / Numine molem*, thus introducing a Virgilian reminiscence. In ll. 5–6, Dennistoun has *Quam tuæ magnus stupefecit orbem / Gloriæ Splendor!* The phrase *magnus stupefecit* is relatively weak; the substitutions made by Pitcairne and his exploitation of the earlier *Jovem* and *Dexteram* make a considerable improvement: *Quam tuæ virtus tremefecit orbem / Juppiter dextræ!* Pitcairne inserted further references to Juppiter in the three final stanzas of the paraphrase (ll. 137, 141, 148).

In Dennistoun there is no equivalent of stanzas 3 and 6 (9–12, 21–24). These are by Pitcairne and the underlying cosmology is not biblical but rather Newtonian. It also presupposes the plurality of worlds. Presumably to Dennistoun the entire concept would have been anathema. Pitcairne makes his version, and indeed the entire pamphlet, a document in the battle of the late-17th early-18th century between Ancients and Moderns. His reverence for the Ancients, his classicism, is combined with a scientific modernism.

On one occasion (45–48) Pitcairne has replaced a stanza by one of his own composition, which is at once more scientifically accurate than Dennistoun's original and contrives to introduce the name of another classical divinity, Phœbus. In general Pitcairne's concern is to remove obviously prosaic or imprecise diction and to avoid such stylistic solecisms as, for instance, the immediate juxtaposition of an adjective or participle with the noun which it qualifies.

Farther differences, other than typographical, between Dennistoun's version and Pitcairne's are recorded in the notes to the appropriate line.

The second item, the 'Epistle to Buchanan', may also be based on a poem by Dennistoun, but if such a thing once existed, it does not appear to have survived. The 'Epistle' centres on the return from exile of John Paterson (1632–1708), appointed Episcopalian archbishop of Glasgow in 1687. Before 1695 he had been banished to England, where he was restrained in London, finally obtaining permission to return in, or shortly after, 1696. His return worried some at least of

COMMENTARY

the Presbyterians. Dennistoun is made to compare him to John Hamilton (1512–1571), Roman Catholic archbishop of St Andrews 1549–1571, a supporter of Queen Mary and the object of intense Presbyterian hostility, given full expression by George Buchanan and John Knox. By his denunciation of Paterson, and by his paraphrase of Psalm 104, Dennistoun aims to become the later equivalent of Buchanan. It is a neat stroke on Pitcairne's part to have Buchanan himself quash these ambitions in his 'Reply'.

I

Although stanzas 1–5 loosely correspond to Psalm 104, vv. 1–4, they come closer to Cleanthes *Hymn to Zeus*, 1–8, reinterpreted in terms of Newtonian science.

Stanzas 6–20, dealing with the Flood and the subsequent restoration of the Earth, correspond to vv. 5–18, again reinterpreted in Newtonian terms.

Stanzas 21–25 correspond to vv. 19–23.

Stanzas 26–29 deal primarily with the sea, and correspond to vv. 24–27.

Stanzas 30–32 celebrate the omnipotence of God, and correspond to vv. 28–30.

Stanzas 33–36, praise of God, correspond to vv. 31–34.

There is little correspondence between stanza 37 and v. 35.

1–6   *Dexteram ... dextrae*: see introductory note.
1   *Dexteram*: the right hand of God, as symbolising his power, is often mentioned in the Psalms, for instance in 98:1. Psalm 104 contains no direct reference.
3–4   *animatque ... molem*: cf. Virgil, *Aeneid* 6, 727: *mens agitat molem*.
9–12   *Orbis ... plena*: see introductory note.
11–12   *Jovis ... plena*: cf. Aratus, *Phaenomena*, 2–4, whence Virgil, *Eclogue* 3, 60: *Iovis omnia plena*.
15–16   *Dædaleas ... alas*: the reference is to the story of Daedalus' construction of waxen wings to enable his son and himself to escape from the Cretan Labyrynth (Ovid, *Metamorphoses* 8, 183–235).
17   *facilesque*: Dennistoun *rigidasque*.
21–24   *Illa ... Solis*: see introductory note.
25   *illam placita*: Dennistoun *terram solitam*.
26–28   *gyros ... saltu*: in *Mutanda* Pitcairne proposes for these lines: *Rerum placita Parenti/ Nulla qua terræ potuit colonis/ Gratior esse*. SP, 57, preserves the original reading.
29   *Tu*: Dennistoun *Hanc*.
29–32   *Tu ... Ponti*: the reference is to the Flood.
30   *Merseras ... omnis*: Dennistoun *condidit mersam Deus, & superba*.
31   *Montis*: Dennistoun *montium*.
33   *monitæ*: Dennistoun *moniti*.
34   *In ... recidere*: Dennistoun *Pristinas fluctus petiêre*.
35   *infrementis*: Dennistoun *aestuantis*.

346

37 *moderanter*: Dennistoun *violenter*.

45–48 *Attamen ... altas*: Dennistoun *Et tamen valles salientis undæ/ Rivulos potant, tua quos cavernis/ Montium excivit, rapuitque in imos / Dextera campos*. See introductory note.

58 *Barbam ... Atlantis*: cf. Aeneid 4, 250–251 (of Atlas): *nix umeros infusa tegit, tum flumina mento/ praecipitant senis, et glacie riget horrida barba.*

59–60 *Gratum ... agricolisque*: Dr Money points out that this echoes a phrase from the discarded opening lines of the *Aeneid* (1,1ᵈ): *gratum opus agricolis*. In *Mutanda* Pitcairne proposes an alternative reading: *Thuriis prægnans opibus Sabæas/ Ornat arenas*. His diction is more elevated than the rather prosaic original, and maintains the exoticism with which the stanza opens. The emendation is accepted, *SP*, 59. Pitcairne may have had in mind Buchanan's rendering of Psalm 72, ll. 38–40 (v. 8): *regesque Arabum beati,/ Thuris & dites venient Sabæi,/ Dona ferentes*. The resemblance between *Thuriis* and *Thuris* is of course coincidental.

66 *vivax*: Dennistoun *fœlix*.

67–68 *& ærumnas ... atras*: in *Mutanda* Pitcairne substitutes: *& ultrices jubet exulare/ Pectore curas*. With *ultrices ... curas* cf. Aeneid 6, 274: *ultrices ... curas*.
Pitcairne is probably rejecting the mainly pre-classical *ærumnas*, and improving the prosaic *indicat*.

70 *rivis*: Dennistoun *lymphis*.

75 *salubris*: Dennistoun *salubri*.

75–76 *piceo ... succo*: perhaps a reference to the preparation of medicinal turpentine from the sap of coniferous trees.

79 *Echinus*: in Vulgate Psalm 103:18, *erinaciis*, 'hedgehogs'; in AV, Psalm 104:18, 'conies.'

83 *furvæ*: Dennistoun *densam*.

89–90 *Ille ... Ferarum*: the Aesopic concept of the lion as king of beasts.

91 *Inverecundo ... ore*: an oblique reference to the demanding intensity of the lion's roar: 'the young lions roar after their prey, and seek their meat from God,' AV, Psalm 124:21. Dennistoun has transformed the original paradox into conceit.

95 *Tum*: Dennistoun *tunc*.

97 *ipsorum ... Leonum*: Man as Lord of Creation.

99 *reficitque*: Dennistoun *recreatque*.

103–104 *moderatur ... calentes*: Dennistoun *agitat sub omni/ sole jacentes*.

106–107 *mutos ... utens*: Dennistoun *ignotos populos, marique/ Barbaras gentes*.

107 *agit*: Pitcairne proposes the more vivid *regit*, adopted in *SP*, 61.

109–110 *choreasque ... udo*: an elaboration on 'there is that leviathan whom thou hast made to play therein,' AV, Psalm 124:26; cf. Aeneid 5, 822–823: *tum variae comitum facies, immania cete,/ et senior Glauci chorus*; cf. Iliad 13, 27–28.

111 *imas*: Dennistoun *omnes*.

117 *seclis*: Dennistoun *cunctis*.

119 *variam*: Dennistoun *placidum*.

120 *sortem*: Dennistoun *tempus*.

123–124 *occlusis ... almi*: a reference to the circulation of the blood as established by William Harvey (1578–1657).
130 *Dicet*: Dennistoun *Cernet*.
133–136 *Illius ... fumo*: 'he looketh on the earth and it trembleth: he toucheth the hills and they smoke,' (AV, Psalm 104:32).
133 *nutu trepidare*: cf. *Aeneid* 9, 106 (of Jupiter): *adnuit, et totum nutu tremefecit Olympum*.
137 *Juppiter carmen mihi*: Dennistoun *Ille dicetur mihi;*. See introductory note.
138 *Lyra*: particularly appropriate for a poem in sapphic stanzas; cf. Ovid, *Amores* 2, xviii, 26: *Aoniae* (? leg. *Aeoliae*) *Lesbis amata lyrae*. *Lesbis*, 'Lesbian woman', is Sappho.
141 *Juppiter ... auctor*: Dennistoun *Sola nam nobis Deus est voluptas*.
142 *Illi*: Dennistoun *Huic*.
143 *Eois numeris*: i.e., the sapphic stanza, originating in the eastern Mediterranean island of Lesbos.
144 *Pangere*: Dennistoun *Condere*.
145–148 *Ipse ... ortum*: very different from the final verse of the psalm: 'Let the sinners be consumed out of the earth, and let the wicked be no more. Bless thou the Lord, O my soul. Praise ye the Lord.' Pitcairne's's conclusion is Stoic or Socinian rather than Calvinistic.
145 *Ipse des*: Dennistoun *Det Deus*.
146–148 *Virtus ... ortum*: Dennistoun *æterna pietate Regum/ Mens colat Regem, preferatque casto/ Pectore Laudes*. This differs significantly from Pitcairne's version, but also from the psalm.
147–148 *illud ... ortum*: cf. Aratus, *Phaenomena*, 5, Acts, 17:28.

II

1–2 *Proserpina ... iter*: Proserpina spent the months of growth and harvest with her parent, Demeter, the Earth-mother, the remainder of the year as Queen in Hades. The figure introduces a spring poem, perhaps because Paterson returned to Edinburgh at that time of year.
In the absence of Proserpina the other rulers of Hell enjoy a vacation.
7 *Regni Jura*: Buchanan's treatise *De Regni Jure apud Scottos*.
10 *Impius ... Relligionis amor*: i.e. Episcopalian rites and beliefs.
11–12 *ille ... modis*: Gavin Douglas (1474–1522), Bishop of Dunkeld, translator of the *Aeneid*, which opens with the words *Arma virumque*.
13 *cui ... Vallæ*: Harry the Minstrel (fl.1470–1492), also known as Blind Harry, author of *The Acts and Deeds of Sir William Wallace*.
14 *cui Brussiades ... erat*: John Barbour (?1320–1395), Archdeacon of Aberdeen, author of *The Brus*, chronicling the achievements of Robert I (1306–1328).
15 *Gramius*: Græmus or Grim; see 4, 8n.
17–26 *Duglasiûmque ... tonat*: a catalogue of historically important noble families,

POEM 20

for the most part associated with Robert I and the War of Independence. Many were Jacobites and Episcopalians. Note too that both John Barbour and Gavin Douglas held high office in the pre-Reformation church.

17 *Duglasiumque*: Sir James Douglas (c. 1286–1330) was a close associate of Robert I. and in effect founded the fortunes of the Douglas family.

In the 1690s the most prominent members of the family were James Douglas (1662–1711), 2nd Duke of Queensberry and Duke of Dover, 'The Union Duke,' on the whole a supporter of the new order, and James Douglas (1658–1712), 4th Duke of Hamilton and 1st of Brandon, colonel of the Oxford regiment under James VII. A Jacobite and Episcopalian, he was imprisoned after the Revolution. He became parliamentary leader of the Cavalier (Jacobite) party, opposed to the Union. He was planning an arrangement by which the Old Pretender should succeed Queen Anne, when he was killed under suspicious circumstances in a duel with Lord Mohun. Cf. **42**, 7n; **74**, 11n; **94**.

18 *Hajaque*: in or about 1309 Robert I made his supporter, Sir Gilbert Hay of Errol (d. 1330), hereditary Constable of Scotland. The earldom of Errol was created for the family in 1452. The earldom of Kinnoull and earldom (later marquessate) of Tweeddale belonged to collateral branches. The family was strongly Episcopalian and Jacobite. John Hay (1626–1697), 2nd Earl and 1st Marquis of Tweeddale, became Chancellor in 1692 and in 1695 became Commissioner to the parliament which met that year. His support for the Darien scheme put King William in an awkward position. In 1696 he was dismissed as Chancellor.

Pitcairne's first wife, Margaret, was a Hay, daughter of Colonel James Hay of Pitfour; see **23**, **24**. Cf. too **68**.

Kethus: probably Sir Robert Keith (d. 1346), who commanded the Scottish horse for Robert I at Bannockburn, created hereditary Marischal of Scotland. The family became Earls Marischal in 1458. Later they were notably Episcopalian and Jacobite. The earldom was forfeited in 1716. Cf. **42**.

19 *Keri*: the Kerrs of Cessford, Roxburghshire, Wardens of the Eastern Marches (with England), Earls, and finally (1707), Dukes of Roxburghe. The last date speaks for itself. Cf. **21**.

20 *Homii*: the Earls of Home. Charles (d. 1706), 5th Earl of Home, belonged to the Cavalier party. Cf. **40**(a), 11 and n: **42**, 1.

21 *Leslæi*: the Leslie family (from Leslie, a village in Fife), Earls (1680–1681, Duke) of Rothes. John Hamilton or Leslie (1679–1722), 9th Earl of Rothes, was a member of the Country party, generally in opposition to the Williamite government; a handful of the members were Jacobite. Writing of him, Lockhart observes (*Scotland's Ruine*, 64): 'No man was more forward in the Country party, nor did any profess greater regard to the Royal family [James VII and his son] than his lordship, and that with repeated oaths and asseverations, but, alass, he had neither enough of sense nor honesty to resist the first temptation.' Cf. **76**(a), 8.

23 *Moravûm Proceres*: The Earls of Moray. The 1st Earl, Thomas Randolph (c. 1280–1332), was one of Robert I's closest adherents. The 20th Earl, Alexander Stewart (1634–1701), was Secretary of State for Scotland, 1680–1688, and a supporter of James VII's policies. On the accession of William and Mary, he was deprived of office, but remained in Scotland till his death.
Dromondius: the Drummond family of Stobhall, Perthshire, from 1605 Earls of Perth. James Drummond (1648–1716), 4th Earl and 1st titular Duke of Perth, Chancellor 1684–1688, became a close adherent of James VII and also a Catholic convert. After the revolution he was imprisoned until 1693. On release, he went first to Rome, then to the court at St. Germain, where he remained until his death. His brother John (1649–1714), 1st Earl and titular Duke of Melfort, Secretary of State 1684–1688, also became a convert, and in 1688 fled to France, where he spent the rest of his life; cf. **112**, introductory note.
We do not understand *Vallæque … ultor*

24 *Setoniana manus*: the Seton family, of Seton in E. Lothian. In 1314 Sir Alexander Seton deserted Edward II for Robert I on the eve of Bannockburn. In 1690 Alexander Seton (d. 1694), 4th Earl of Dunfermline, who belonged to a collateral branch of the family, was forfeited for Jacobitism.

25 *Clarii genus*: the Sinclair (St Clair) family, originally of Roslin, Midlothian, Earls of Orkney 1379–1470, Earls of Caithness 1455–. Henry Sinclair of Roslin (d. 1330) fought at Bannockburn and was a signatory to the Declaration of Arbroath (1320). Robert I regarded his brother, the fighting William Sinclair, Bishop of Dunkeld 1309–1337, as 'my Bishop'. Henry's son, Sir William Sinclair of Roslin (d. 1330), accompanied Sir James Douglas on his proposed journey to the Holy Land with Robert I's heart. With Douglas he was killed in Spain. In a collateral branch of the family, Henry Sinclair (1660–1723), 10th Lord Sinclair, was the only peer who publicly protested against the accession of William of Orange to the throne of Scotland. His son, John (1683–1750) took a prominent part in the 1715 rising and wrote *Memoirs of the Rebellion*. See also **33**.

25–26 *non qui … tonat*: the earldom of Wemyss, Fife, was created in 1633 for John, Lord Wemyss of Elcho (c. 1604–1649) whose ancestor, Sir David, had been a signatory to the Declaration of Arbroath. Cf. also **76, 77, 78**.
The lands of Wemyss were believed to have belonged originally to the Macduffs, Earls of Fife c. 1124–1389. In *Mutanda* Pitcairne proposes *Duffides*, 'descendents of Macduff', for *In Pelagus* (26). The amended form appears in SP, 64.

28 *pares*: in *Mutanda* Pitcairne here inserts a couplet (included, SP, 64), *Inter quos, Annande, micas, pietate refulges, / Vel proavis major, Balmerinoe, tuis.*
Annande: William Johnstone (c. 1660–1721), 3rd Earl of Annandale and Hartfell, 1st Marquis of Annandale (1701), a member of 'the Club,' a group which opposed the Williamite settlement and which met in Penston's tavern in the High Street of Edinburgh. The leader was Sir James Montgomerie of Skel-

morlie (d. 1694, in Paris), with whom Annandale joined in a plot to restore James VII. When the plot was discovered, Annandale, like others, confessed. He was briefly imprisoned in the Tower of London, but was soon able to recover his position. In 1693 he was created a Lord of Session extraordinary, and he was president of the parliament which in 1695 received the report on the Glencoe massacre. His career thereafter was moderately distinguished, but both sides always regarded him with suspicion. 'Even those of the Revolution party only employed him as the Indians worship the Devil, out of fear' (*Scotland's Ruine*, 110). He opposed the terms of the 1707 Union.

Balmerino: John Elphinstone (1652–1736), 4th Baron Balmerino (from Balmerino in Fife), was a Jacobite, 'testifying, on all occasions, an unshaken loyalty to his prince' (*Scotland's Ruine*, 111). His second wife was Anne, daughter of Arthur Rose, last Episcopalian Archbishop of St Andrews 1684–1704. Their son, Arthur Elphinstone (1688–1746), 6th Baron Balmerino, was executed on Tower Hill for his part in the '45 rising.

33–34 *Musamque ... genus*: see Buchanan, *Epigrammatum Liber II*, 30, 'Joanni Hamiltono fani Andreæ Archiepiscopo,' and especially 31, 'Eidem.'

37–38 *Quippe ... vident*: the return of Archbishop Paterson; see above, introductory note.

John Paterson (1632–1708), son of John Paterson, Bishop of Ross 1662–1679, belonged to an Aberdeenshire family of some distinction. A graduate of St Andrews, he became Bishop of Galloway in 1674. In 1686 he supported, with some reservations, King James' policy of religious tolerance and in 1687 was appointed Archbishop of Glasgow. For some time after the Revolution he lived in Edinburgh. In 1692 he was accused of corresponding with the exiled court and was imprisoned in Edinburgh Castle. By 1695 he had been banished to England and restrained in London, but in 1696 or 1697 he was allowed to return, regaining his complete liberty in 1702 on the accession of Queen Anne. During his last years he attempted to raise funds for the support of the extruded Episcopalian clergy. He was buried in the Chapel Royal of Holyrood.

Lockhart (*Scotland's Ruine*, 54–56) paints a generally unfavourable portrait, calling the Archbishop a renegade, apparently because he accepted the legitimacy of Queen Anne's succession. Paterson was much hated by Presbyterians, but had one or two defenders; see old DNB.

38 *Hamiltoni Præsulis*: John Hamilton (1512–1571), natural son of James Hamilton (c. 1475–1529), 2nd Earl of Arran, became Archbishop of St Andrews in 1549 and made some attempt at church reform. In 1558 he may have been responsible for the burning of the aged Walter Myln as a Protestant heretic. In 1563, after the Protestant Reformation, he was briefly imprisoned for saying Mass. He was favoured by Queen Mary, and in 1566 officiated at the baptism of her son, the future James VI. He was accused of complicity in the murders of Darnley (1567) and the Regent Moray (1570). He continued his active support for the

queen after her defeat in 1568 and subsequent flight to England. In 1571 he was captured after the fall of Dumbarton Castle and hanged at Stirling. He was denounced by Buchanan (in his *History* as well as his *Epigrammata*), and by John Knox, who called him 'that cruel murderer of our brethren, falsely called Archbishop of St Andrews' (*Reformation*, ii, 197). See too 'The Bischoppis lyfe and testament,' (*Satirical Poems of the Time of the Reformation*, ed. J. Cranstoun, 2 vols. [STS, Edinburgh and London, 1891–1893], i, 193–200, ii, 129–140). In the Paisley Missal however his death as a martyr is entered by hand under 7 April.

45 *Nomen mutasse genusque*: i.e., from John Hamilton, Archbishop of St Andrews, he has become John Paterson, Archbishop of Glasgow.

46 *Circen*: an enchantress and temptress, representing the Roman Catholic church. Presbyterians tended to describe Episcopalians as a 'Popish, Prelatical, and Malignant Faction' (*Scotch Presbyterian Eloquence*, 49).

47 *Notus uterque tibi*: i.e., Buchanan knew the Hamiltons' true nature and was notoriously hostile to the Roman Catholic Church.

III

4 *Lamias*: the classical Lamia was a witch, said to suck children's blood.

4–6 *Lamias … tuis*: Pitcairne is in effect criticizing 'Dennistoun' for exaggeration, or worse, and as a consequence failing to observe the Horatian precept: *ficta voluptatis causa sint proxima veris, / ne quodcumque velit poscat sibi fabula credi, / neu pransae Lamiae vivum puerum extrahat alvo* (*Ars Poetica*, 338–340).

5–6 *non est … tuis*: cf. Horace, *Ars Poetica*, 38–39: *sumite materiam vestris, qui scribitis, aequam / viribus.*

7–8 *Illa … fide*: i.e., 'Dennistoun's' poem is primitive and barbarous.

9–10 *Sed manes … habet*: by implication at least Pitcairne's own poetry is more up-to-date and civilized – Augustan rather than primitive.

13–16 *At tua … novis*: cf. above, 1, 25–32. *tua … humus* is Scotland.

18 *Sacerdotum perniciosa cohors*: Presbyterian clergy rather than, as in Dennistoun, Episcopalian.

20 *Virgilio cognita turba*: see *Aeneid* 6, 566–569.

24 *Pitcarnumque*: as noted above, the name is in effect a signature, claiming authorship.

21

Notes. This poem of light-hearted, self-interested compliment to John Ker (c. 1680–1741), 5th earl and 1st duke of Roxburghe, is a sequel to 20. When that was written, Dennistoun was still alive; the exchanges concluded with an invitation from Buchanan for Dennistoun and Pitcairne both to join him in Elysium. Dennistoun died in 1700, the year in which 20 was published, and so moved directly into the orbit of the dead Buchanan. The present poem is his posthumous epistle to Buchanan, explaining how Pitcairne failed to accompany him because he could not give up the terrestrial hospitality extended by Ker. Mercury, messenger of the gods, brought Pitcairne a copy.

In 1696, while still very young, John Ker was served heir to his deceased brother in the earldom. Not long afterwards he began his political career by associating himself with the Country party, which inclined towards Jacobitism and opposed union with England. In 1704 he became a leader in the breakaway New Party, later known as the *Squadrone Volante*. In 1704–1705 he was one of the Secretaries of State for Scotland. 'By November 1705 Roxburghe was convinced that the Court was determined to push an act of union through the parliaments. He concluded that it might well succeed in the Scottish parliament: "The motives will be, Trade with most, Hanover with some, ease and security with others." If this were so, and the New Party could claim no credit for helping to carry the union, then its future would be bleak indeed. Gradually Roxburghe cleverly steered the majority of the *Squadrone* to his way of thinking' (Ferguson, *Scotland 1689 to the Present*, 51–52). The Treaty of Union was ratified by the Scottish parliament on 16 January 1707, and 25 April saw the creation of Roxburghe's dukedom.

Lockhart says of him: 'John, Earl, afterwards Duke, of Roxburgh, made his first appearance in the world to the general satisfaction of all men. He was a man of good sense, improven by so much reading and learning that, perhaps, he was the best accomplished young man of quality in Europe, and had so charming a way of expressing his thoughts that he pleased even those against whom he spoke. And it was a thousand pities a man so capable to do good should have proven the very bane and cut-throat of his country, by being extreamly false and disingenuous, and so indifferent to the ties of honour, friendship, vows and justice, that he sacrificed them all, and the interest of his country, to his designs, viz. revenge and ambition' (*Scotland's ruine*, 64).

Ker's later views were opposed to Pitcairne's. It therefore seems probable that preface and poem were written before the New Party had been founded, or at least before the *volte-face* of late 1705. To begin with, at least, Pitcairne was overcome by Roxburghe's charm and hospitality. The two men also had overlapping scientific interests; Roxburghe was a fellow of the Royal Society and, much later, a pall-bearer at Newton's funeral (1727) in Westminster Abbey.

In the title Roxburghe is styled 'Duke.' If we are right about date of composition, this must be an alteration made after 1707 – perhaps as late as 1727, when SP was published.

Preface, 2 *nemoris ... hospes*: i.e., after Dennistoun's death.
3–4 *animum ... librantem*: i.e., Ker was a member of parliament, and so concerned with state affairs.

COMMENTARY

Poem, 1 *regna ... liquit*: cf. **20**, III, 23: *perituraque regna relinque*.
3 *comes ... Pitcarnius abnuit*: cf. **20**, III, 24: *Pitcarnumque viæ, si volet, adde tuæ*.
4 *Albini*: perhaps the usurer whose educational methods are satirized in Horace, *Ars Poetica*, 325–332. This is combined with a pun on *Alba*, 'Scotland' in the adjectival form *Albanus*. A dig at the grasping nature of the Scottish nobility?
5–6 *quis enim ... amat*: cf. Virgil, *Eclogue* 10, 3: *neget quis carmina Gallo*?
8 *Defendit ... suæ*: i.e., as a member of the Country party, he is opposed to the devilish forces of the Presbyterians and Williamites.
9–10 *Ille suis ... aquæ*: a clever variant on the doctrine put forward by Horace, *Epistles* 1, 19, 2–3: *nulla placere diu nec vivere carmina possunt/ quæ scribuntur aquæ potoribus*: cf. **126**, 14–15.
11 *epulis Divûm*: cf. Horace, *Satires* 2, 6, 65: *o noctes cenaeque deum*.
12 *nectaris*: the drink of the gods.
   potes: form not recognised.
14 *Stotus*: the Englishman Sir Bertram Stott, author of a Latin verse-epistle to Pitcairne (*SP*, 84–87). Pitcairne commemorated his death in two poems (**58**, **59**). Cf. too above, 19(i).

22.

Notes. In his *Journal of a Tour to the Hebrides* (ed. Potter and Bennett [London, 1963], 38) Boswell records a comment by Johnson: 'He did not allow the Latin poetry of Pitcairne so much merit as has been usually attributed to it, though he owned that one of his pieces, which he mentioned but which I am sorry is not specified in my notes, was "very well." It is not improbable that it was the poem which Prior has so elegantly translated.'

In his own time Pitcairne was termed atheist, perhaps simply because, like his older contemporary, Sir Thomas Browne (1605–1682), he was a physician: 'For my Religion, though there be severall circumstances that might perswade the world I have none at all, as the generall scandall of my profession, the naturall course of my studies, the indifferency of my behaviour and discourse in matters of Religion ...' (*Religio Medici*, 1). More than anything else, however, this famous poem was the cause of his reputation. In terms of late seventeenth- and early eighteenth-century Edinburgh and Scotland, the content is nothing short of outrageous. In all three texts the primary reference is to the author, in (a) as himself; in (c) under his *persona* as Dennistoun. In (b) the title is puzzling, but may be enlightening; the most probable reference is to Franciscus Sylvius (1614–1672), Franz or François de la Boë or Du Bois, physician, physiologist, anatomist and chemist, who, like Pitcairne, had been a professor at Leiden (1658–1672). Sylvius held that all the phenomena of life and disease were based on chemical action. 'His studies helped shift medical emphasis from mystical speculation to a rational application of universal laws of physics and chemistry' (*Encyclopædia Britannica*

CD2000). With G.A. Borelli (1608–1679) and Lorenzo Bellini (1643–1704), he was one of the founders of the more scientific school of medicine to which Pitcairne belonged. (Sylvius, incidentally, was also the first to distil gin as an inexpensive medicine. This too may have interested Pitcairne.) Joannes Sylvius may simply mean a follower of the materialistic doctrines of the great physician. It is also likely that the name was chosen with some reference to the Late Latin philosophic use of *silva*, 'wood,' as the equivalent of Greek ὕλη, in the sense '(brute) matter.'

While admitting the possibility of a purely material world, the poem is not simply atheistic. There is a balance of Pythagorean/Druidic beliefs against the Epicureanism of the latter part of the poem. Even the first part however has an Epicurean flavour. If the gods exist, they live at ease, unconcerned with human affairs, though it may be possible for individual souls to join their company. The whole tenor of the poem nevertheless suggests that the possibility is illusory and that the present life is the only one. The poem is also Epicurean in the suggestion that, despite the imminence of death, the proper purpose of existence is the enjoyment of the pleasures which life has to offer. There are occasional Lucretian (i.e., Epicurean) overtones in the diction.

The 17th-century rise of 'mechanical philosophy,' one side of which is to be seen in the work of Sylvius, Borelli and Bellini, is related to a revival of Epicureanism, best illustrated by the writings of Pierre Gassendi (1592–1655), the French scientist, mathematician and philosopher. His Epicureanism was combined – in terms of the present poem perhaps significantly – with a reasoned belief in a rational and immortal soul.

Pitcairne refers to this poem in a letter to the Rev. Colin Campbell dated 2 September 1710: 'Sir, I have nothing of Mathematical news to send you. I send, in place of them, Wattie Danniston's creed.' In another, dated 26 February 1711, addressed to Mr John McKenzie of Delvin, he remarks: 'In 2 days I'l send in print to you Mr Prior's Imitation of my Gualterus Dannistonus ad amicos, in English, which he bids me print with the Latin' (Johnston, *Best of our owne*, 63, 66).

Matthew Prior (1664–1721), English diplomatist and man of letters, began as a Whig and Williamite, but later became a Tory and crypto-Jacobite, negotiator of the Peace of Utrecht in 1713. After Queen Anne's death he was imprisoned for two years. His *Poems on Several Occasions* was first published in 1707. See **40**, 7; **62**, 21; **73**, 18. The 'Imitation', much celebrated in its day, reads as follows:

Walter Danniston, **Ad Amicos.**

Imitated by Mr. *Prior*.

Studious the busy Moments to deceive,
That Fleet between the Cradle and the Grave,
I credit what the *Grӕcian* Dictates say,
And *Samian* sounds o'er *Scotia*'s Hills convey.
5 When mortal Man resigns his transient breath,

The Body only I give o'er to Death:
The Parts dissolv'd and broken Frame I mourn;
What came from Earth, I see to Earth return:
The Immaterial Part th' Ætherial Soul,
10 Nor can Change vanquish, nor can Death control:
Glad I release it from its Partner's Cares,
And bid good Angels waft it to the Stars.
Then in the flowing Bowl I drown those sighs,
Which Spite of Wisdom from our Weakness rise;
15 The Draught to the Dead's Memory I commend,
And offer to the now immortal Friend.
But if oppos'd to what my Thoughts approve,
Nor *Pluto*'s rage there be, nor Pow'r of *Jove*,
On its dark side, if thou the Prospect take,
20 Grant all forgot beyond black *Lethe*'s Lake:
In total Death suppose the Mortal ly,
No new Hereafter, nor a future Sky;
Yet bear thy Lot content, yet cease to grieve;
Why, ere Death comes, do'st thou forbear to live?
25 The little Time, thou hast 'twixt Instant now
And Death's Approach, is all the Gods allow:
And of this little hast thou ought to spare
To sad Reflection, and corroding Care?
The Moment past, if thou art wise, retrieve,
30 With pleasant Mem'ry of the Bliss they gave.
The present Hours, in present Mirth imploy,
And bribe the Future with the Hopes of Joy.
The Future (few or more, how e'er they be)
Were destin'd e'rst, nor can by Fate's Decree
Be now cut off, betwixt the Grave and Thee.

1 (version (c)) *fungi ... munere*: cf. *Aeneid* 6, 885–886, *fungar inani/ munere*.

3–4 (version (c)) *Arctoâ ... discipulis*: the Samian disciples are the followers of Pythagoras, born on Samos, who taught the immortality and transmigration of souls. Prior is probably right to assume that *Arctoâ* refers to Scotland. The two phrases form a kind of hendiadys: 'I am proud, arrogant, to proclaim in Scotland the doctrine which I acquired from Pythagoras and his followers.' Note that Pitcairne's admiration for Pythagoras was less than whole-hearted; see **47**. Like Pythagoras, incidentally, Epicurus was born in Samos.

The reading in (b) is less specific, while that in (c) changes the emphasis to the doctrines of the Druids as reported by Caesar (*Bellum Gallicum* 6, 14) and others. Pitcairne's presentation of himself as a descendent of British and Gaulish druids implies the modification of the Scottish origin-legend found in **2**, 15.

POEM 23

4 (version (c)) *Animas ... carere*: cf. the words given to Pythagoras by Ovid (*Metamorphoses* 15, 158–159): *morte carent animae semperque priore relicta/ sede novis domibus vivunt habitantque receptae.*

6–8 *otia ... vias*: the Epicurean position on the gods is set out in Lucretius 2, 646–651.

8 *Vitai*: this archaic disyllabic form of the genitive singular is characteristic of Lucretius; cf., e.g., 2, 79: *et quasi cursores vitai lampada tradunt.* In Virgil it occurs no more than four times (*vitai* in none), in Ovid not at all.

12 *Ditis ... Jovis*: cf. *Aeneid* 3, 543: *tum numina sancta precamur/ Palladis*, Horace, *Epodes*, 17, 3: *per et Dianae non movenda numina*; cf. also Lucretius 3, 18: *divum numen.*

17 *ævique fugacis*: perhaps a reminiscence of Horace, *Odes* 2, 14, 1–2: *Eheu fugaces, Postume, Postume,/ labuntur anni.*

23 *Sophia Ars*: i.e., (Epicurean) philosophy.

23–24 *Sophia ... minas*: cf. Bacon's contrast of Stoic and Epicurean attitudes towards death: 'Ought they [the Stoics] not to have taught men to die as if they lived and not to live as though they continually died?' ('Of Tribute,' Vickers, *Francis Bacon* [Oxford, 1966], 26).

23

Notes. Pitcairne's first marriage was brief. In or about 1685 he married Margaret Hay, daughter of Colonel James Hay of Pitfour, Perthshire, who belonged to a cadet branch of the Hays, Earls of Errol. The couple had a son, name unknown, who died in infancy, and a daughter, Anne, who was still alive in 1694, but whose subsequent fate is uncertain. The poem was written shortly after Anne's birth, probably in 1687 or 1688.

1 *Margaris*: not the usual form for 'Margaret'; here perhaps the pet-form 'Marjorie.'

3–4 *perennam ... Annae*: a partly disguised reference to Anna Perenna, Italian goddess of the returning year, whose festival was held on the Ides (15th) of March, probably Anne's own birthday. Pitcairne, like Ovid, also plays on the adjective *perennis*: *amne perenne latens Anna perenna vocor* (*Fasti* 3, 654). A wish, probably unfulfilled, that the baby might be long-lived is implied.

4 *Erroliaeque*: i.e., Margaret Hay, who herself is called [Anna] Perenna in the final line of 24, next below. The adjective is also applied to Queen Anne, 91, 12. Obviously the name had a particular resonance for Pitcairne.

24

Notes. see introductory paragraph to preceding poem. The date of the poem is probably late April, 1690.

2–3 *fati ... fata*: the impersonal singular (*fatum*, the immutable law of nature) is transformed to the personified plural (*fata*, the Fates), with overtones of hostility, even malignity, towards mere human beings.
4 *parsque mei*: cf. Horace, *Odes* 3, 30, 6–7: *multaque pars mei/ vitabit Libitinam*. Horace refers to his poetry, Pitcairne to his wife.
  Me superante: i.e., during his lifetime, as opposed to the same phrase in 6, which refers to the eternal life of great verse.
5–6 *perpetuam ... nostra*: for the topos see Curtius, *Latin Middle Ages*, 476–477, 485. A Renaissance commonplace, less frequent in the later seventeenth-century; cf. 56, 7–10.
8 *Stygio ... duci*: Pluto or Dis, lord of the dead beyond the Styx.
9 *silentum*: the dead.
10 *Perenna*: see preceding poem, 3–4n.

25

Notes. Pitcairne married Elizabeth Stevenson on 8 August 1693 (below, 40, introductory note). The couple had one son and four daughters. Elizabeth, the eldest daughter, was born 10 June, ?1695, and died 18 March, 1718. The poem was thus probably written for her fifteenth birthday.

2 *Dominum ... Tuum*: the Old Pretender.
3 *cedit ... armis*: the alternative reading in SP has a better verbal balance with the following line and is perhaps to be preferred.
3–4 *Ille ... Deæ*: for the topos of outdoing, see Curtius, *Latin Middle Ages*, 162–165.

26

Notes. Pitcairne's second daughter by Elizabeth Stevenson, Janet or Jane, was born, like her mother and sister, on 10 June, the birthday of the Pretender. She became the wife of Alexander Erskine (died 1756), 5th Earl of Kellie, and mother of the composer Thomas Alexander Erskine (1732–1781), 6th Earl of Kellie, and the poet Andrew Erskine (1740–1793). She died in 1776.

POEM 29

2   *Dido*: i.e., Elizabeth Stevenson. She is called Dido because the Phoenician name of the Queen of Carthage was Elissa (*Aeneid* 4, 335: *nec me meminisse pigebit Elissae*), which resembles the name Eliza or Elizabeth.
3   *Didus*: rare genitive of *Dido*, not found in the *Aeneid*.
4–5 *relligione ... relligione*: Episcopalianism, with belief in the Divine Right of Kings, is implied.
6   *Jacobo*: probably James VII, indicating that Janet was born and the poem written before the king's death on 6 September 1701.

27

Notes. Margaret, born on 8 March 1702, was third daughter of Pitcairne's second marriage. She died in 1777.

2   *Et te ... mori*: King William died on 8 March 1702; see below **82**.
    Nassovi: William was Prince of Orange-*Nassau*. Pitcairne refuses any recognition of him as King of Great Britain.

28

Notes. Agnes, fourth daughter of Pitcairne's second marriage, became the wife of Colin Arthur, surgeon-apothecary in Fife (Ritchie, *Early Days*, 201).

1   *Jane*: here, as usual, 'January'; cf. **13**, 5n; **15**, 1.
    sexto: Epiphany, Twelfth Night. Church feasts were not observed by Presbyterians. By the combination of the date with the phrase *fausto ... die* (2), Pitcairne indicates that he and his family belonged to a different tradition.
3   *Ter decimum*: Charles I was executed on 30 January. Episcopalians observed the day as a fast; cf. **13**.
6   *Octavo Martis*: **27**, 2n.
7   *Decimo Juni*: the Pretender's birthday.

29

Notes. Andrew Balfour was born in 1630. He graduated in Arts at St Andrews, before going to London, then spent some years in France, for the most part in Paris, where he studied medicine, anatomy and botany. In 1661 he became MD of Caen. After some more time in London he was appointed tutor to the youthful John Wilmot (1647–1680), second Earl of Rochester, with whom he spent some three years (1661–1664) in France and Italy. In all, he 'spent some fifteen years abroad, continually observing not only the natural history of the European countries he visited, but also their antiquities, laws and customs' (H.R. Fletcher, W.H. Brown, *The Royal Botanic Gardens, Edinburgh 1670–1970* [Edinburgh, HMSO, 1970], 4). Soon after his return to Scotland he settled in Edinburgh, where, with the assistance of Robert Sibbald (30), he established a small botanic garden. Most of the credit for the establishment (1670) of the larger Physic Garden, which eventually developed into the Royal Botanic Garden, belongs to Sibbald. Balfour also played a substantial part in the establishment (1681) of the Royal College of Physicians, of which he became third President in 1685, in succession to Sir Archibald Stevenson (1681–1684; 40) and Sibbald (1684–1685), the term of the latter being cut short by his conversion to Catholicism. In 1682, together with Sibbald and Stevenson, he was knighted by the Duke of York, the future James VII, at Holyrood. On 9 January 1694 he died suddenly while walking in the High Street of Edinburgh.

Pitcairne was a bidder at the sale of Balfour's books, which began on 4 February 1695 (Johnston, *Best of our owne*, 21, letter 5). He probably wrote the poem immediately after Balfour's death. It is a fine expression of late-17th-century scientific idealism.

1 *Quis ... habere*: Pitcairne comments ironically on the final couplet of Claudian's 'De sene Veronensi', which contrasts the traveller with the old man who has never left his village: *plus habet hic vitae, plus habet ille viae* (Platnauer, *Claudian*, ii, 196). Balfour travelled extensively and had an exceptionally wide experience of life.
6 *Thetidos*: Thetis was a Nereid, daughter of the Old Man of the Sea.

30

Notes. The poem is a mock-epitaph for the physician, botanist, and geographer, Sir Robert Sibbald (1641–1722), who inherited the lands of Kipps near Torphichen, West Lothian from his mother Margaret, daughter of Robert Boyd of Kipps, Advocate. Sibbald, with Sir Andrew Balfour, was co-founder of the Edinburgh Physic Garden (1670), and was largely instrumental in the foundation of the Royal College of Physicians of Edinburgh (1681), of which he became President in 1684, in succession to the first President, Sir Archibald Stevenson. In 1685 he became first Professor of Medicine in Edinburgh University. His medical writings are largely based on the treatises attributed to the Greek Hippocrates (fl. 425 BC), and the writings of his classical and Arabic followers, involving the balance of the bodily humours and the extensive use of herbal remedies. To Pitcairne this was old-fashioned and obscurantist. The ultimate occasion for the poem was the publication in 1684 at Edinburgh of Sibbald's *Scotia Illustrata sive Prodromus Historiae Naturalis in quo Regionis natura, Incolarum Ingenia & Mores, Morbi iisque medendi methodus, & Medicina Indigena accurate explicantur*, which is described on the title-page as *Opus viginti Annorum*. Pitcairne severely attacked this publication in *Dissertatio de Legibus Historiæ Naturalis* (1696), to which Sibbald replied in 1710 with *Vindiciæ Scotiæ Illustratæ, sive Prodromi Naturalis Historiae Scotiae, contra Prodromomastiges, sub larva libelli de legibus historiae naturalis, latentes* (D. Duncan, 'Scholarship and Politeness in the Early Eighteenth Century', *The History of Scottish Literature 2, 1660–1800*, ed. A. Hook [Aberdeen, 1987], 55–57). Sibbald wished however to remain on reasonable terms with Pitcairne, as the latter later rather sourly noted (Johnston, *Best of our owne*, 65–66).

There are some difficulties in dating the epitaph. The 'roundel' quoted below may suggest that the poem was written about 1686, not long after the publication of *Scotia Illustrata*. The roundel however is almost entirely concerned with Sibbald's shifting adherence, now to Presbyterianism, now to Catholicism, both, so far as Pitcairne was concerned, thoroughly objectionable forms of worship, but playing a relatively minor part in the present poem.

During the later 1680s and early 1690s relations between the two seem to have been relatively cordial. By 1694 things were changing. Two College parties were forming, one led by Sibbald and Thomas Burnet, Physician to the King in Scotland, the other by Pitcairne and Stevenson. In November and December 1695 Pitcairne and Stevenson, together with George Hepburn and several others, were suspended. It was late 1704 before either again attended a meeting (*Introduction*, pp. 13–14; R.P. Ritchie, *The Early Days of the Royall Colledge of Phisitians, Edinburgh* [Edinburgh, 1899]; W.B. Howie, 'Sir Archibald Stevenson, his Ancestry, and the Riot in the College of Physicians at Edinburgh,' *Medical History* XI [1967], 269–284; W.S. Craig, *History of the Royal College of Physicians of Edinburgh* [Oxford, 1976], 408–419; A. Guerrini in *Oxford DNB*.). Pitcairne felt that Sibbald was responsible for the entire turn of events.

The *Dissertatio de Legibus Historiæ Naturalis* is a document in the warfare between the two groups. In three points – the reference to Mark Alexander Boyd, to *Rosa Ciphiana*, and to Sibbald's sapphic ode – the poem echoes points made in the *Dissertatio*; see below, 4n, 9–10n, 12n. Most probably the two belong to the same period.

Title *Cyphiis*: i.e. Kipps.
2 *patrio condi ... solo*: i.e., by the publication of *Scotia Illustrata*, and by the number of references to Kipps found therein.
vir Cyphiane: the Scots custom was to address a landowner by the name of his property. In Walter Scott's *The Antiquary*, for instance, the Antiquary himself, Jonathan Oldbuck of Monkbarns, is usually addressed as 'Monkbarns'. So here. Cf. *Cyphianus* (6), *Cyphiane* (14).
4 *Bodiis*: the Boyd family, to whom in 1574 the lands of Kipps had been assigned in feu-ferm (*RMS, 1546–1580*, no. 2186). Pitcairne probably also refers to the emphasis placed by Sibbald on the poet Mark Alexander Boyd (1563–1601), whom he regarded as a kinsman, one of whose poems he prefixed to *Nuncius*

Scoto-Brittanicus (Edinburgh, 1683), a kind of flier for *Scotia Illustrata*, and to whose life as an eminent Scot he paid disproportionate attention (II.iii.2, pp. 2–4).

5 *Geneva*: headquarters of Calvinism; here the Presbyterian (Calvinist) Scottish church.
inclyta Roma: i.e., the Catholic Church; for the phrase, cf. Ennius, *Incertae Sedis Fragmenta*, no. 75: *Augusto augurio postquam incluta condita Roma*: *Aeneid* 6, 781: *illa incluta Roma*. The phrase also occurs in Joachim du Bellay, 'Romae descriptio', 138 (A. Perosa and J. Sparrow, *Renaissance Latin Verse* [London, 1979], 397).

6 *scit Cyphianus iter*: a reference to Sibbald's brief conversion to Catholicism (1685–1686); compare the 'Roundel on Sir Robert Sibbald, 1686' (R^2, 12), which begins:

> There is lost, there is lost
> On the Catholic coast,
> A quack of the college's quorum,
> Tho' his name be not shown,
> Yet the man may be known
> By his *opus viginti annorum*.

7 *Coi ... Senecaeque*: The writings of Hippocrates of Cos and the younger Seneca, 'the Philosopher' (c. 4 BC – 65 AD). Seneca was the author of *Naturales Quaestiones*, a work of no real scientific value, used in the Middle Ages and later as a text-book of natural science. Sibbald constantly refers to both as sources and thus excites Pitcairne's ridicule.

8 *sutile*: In *Nuncius Scoto-Brittanicus* Sibbald included a questionnaire, appealing for information on various aspects of Scottish life and society. Some at least of the information he received – not always of the best quality – was subsequently incorporated, stitched into, *Scotia Illustrata*.

9–10 *inculti ... rosas*: these lines contain verbal reminiscences (for the most part pejorative) of entries in the plant catalogue in part II of Sibbald's *Scotia Illustrata* (pp. 46, 61): **Rosa Ciphiana, seu Rosa pimpinellae foliis minor nostras ... Quod in Praedio meo Ciphiano sponte nascatur Ciphianum appellavi ... Nascitur in colle quodam Praedii nostri Ciphiani Austro obverso, declivi admodum, cautibus squalido, nec alibi, quod sciam, conspicitur**. Sibbald subjoined (61–62) a sapphic Ode, addressed to his colleague Sir Andrew Balfour, including the lines *Rosa, digna* **faustis/ Montibus** (as opposed to Pitcairne's *inculti ... montes*), and *Caulis* **exilis**. Sibbald obviously thought he had discovered a previously unknown plant. In fact, as Pitcairne recognised, it is relatively common except in SE Britain. In modern terminology it is the Burnet Rose, *Rosa pimpinellifolia* – Hugh MacDiarmid's 'little white rose of Scotland/ that smells sharp and sweet – and breaks the heart.'

12 *Cyphiis ... tuis*: i.e., poems like the sapphic ode just quoted.

13 *furta*: As mentioned above, Sibbald's book is partly based on answers to his questionnaire in *Nuncius Scoto-Brittanicus*. Pitcairne disapproved, apparently regarding this collecting-method as theft.

31

Notes. The conflict between Ancients and Moderns figured prominently in late-seventeenth-century literary and scientific controversy; see R.F. Jones, *Ancients and Moderns*, 2nd edn. (St Louis, 1961). Pitcairne sided with the moderns and saw the dispute in the Edinburgh Royal College of Physicians as part of the struggle. The ode refers to the dispute. It begins from the reliance of ancient medicine, represented by such figures as Chiron and Aesculapius, on herbs and incantations, a reliance continued, by implication, in the work of Sibbald and his associates, with whom Pitcairne contrasts his London-based fellow-moderns, Gray and Bateman. Why the ode should be addressed to Horace is unclear to us.

1   *Dive*: i.e., Horace, deified after death.
    vatem medicumve: Aesculapius (Asklepios), mythical patron of physicians and surgeons, son of Phoebus Apollo and the nymph Coronis. Apollo was god of medicine and also of inspiration and poetry. Aesculapius combined both in his medical work.
6   *repullulare*: cf. **9**, 41n.
9–10 *bonum ... virus*: the most celebrated temple of Aesculapius was at Epidaurus in the Greek Argolis. The sick passed the night there and, while sleeping, were cured by serpents licking their faces.
10 *Chiron*: the wise Centaur, who taught Aesculapius.
18 *Aonas montes*: the mountains of Boeotia. Mt. Pelion, where Chiron lived, is in fact in Thessaly.
    equitemque: the upper part of Chiron's body was human, the lower that of a horse.
19 *Orphei ritu*: the music of Orpheus had remarkable powers, almost enabling him to restore Eurydice to life.
26 *Ante ... duelli*: the figures so far mentioned belonged to the mythical period before the Trojan War, in which Podalirius and Machaon, sons of Aesculapius, played a part: see **38**, 2. Cf. also Horace, Odes 4, 9, 25: *vixere fortes ante Agamemnona*.
    By the Trojan War Pitcairne may intend the English and Scottish civil wars of the middle-seventeenth century. Earlier medical theory and practice he regarded as primitive. Modern scientific medicine he probably regarded as beginning with William Harvey (1578–1657), whose major works span the main period of conflict.

duelli: *duellum* is an archaic form of *bellum*, appropriate in a reference to the Trojan War.

27–28 *Pelei suboles ... Homero*: Achilles son of Peleus is the hero of Homer's *Iliad*.

30–31 *Pollux ... micuere*: the Tyndaridae, Castor and Pollux, saved seamen from shipwreck. After their death they were translated to become the two brightest stars in the constellation Gemini; cf. Horace, *Odes* 4, 8, 32–33: *clarum Tyndaridae sidus ab infimis/ quassas eripiunt aequoribus ratis*.

33 *Castor ... Grai, Batemanne, Pollux*: Robert Gray MD was a London-based Scot, a close friend of Pitcairne; see especially **39**. Nine of Pitcairne's letters to him, and the abstract of a tenth, have survived (Johnston, *Best of our owne*, letters 3, 4, 5, 8, 11, 13, 15, 45, 46, 52). The earliest was written on 23 September 1694, the latest on 6 January 1711. For the most part they deal with medical and anatomical matters, but one at least (11) led to serious trouble.

Gray is the Robert Gray MD elected an Honorary Fellow of the Royal College of Physicians, London, in 1664, and subsequently 'constituted a Fellow of the College by the charter of King James II, and ... admitted as such by the Comitia Majora Extraordinaria of 12th April, 1687. The College having been required by the House of Lords to give in a list of such of their members as were "Papists, reputed Papists, or criminals," we find in the return dated 1st July, 1689, Dr Gray's name under the head of "criminals or reputed criminals"' (W. Munk, *The Roll of the Royal College of Physicians of London*, 2 vols., [London, 1861], i, 454). This last indicates that Gray was a Jacobite, but not a Roman Catholic. Munk suggests that he moved to Newcastle-upon-Tyne, where a doctor of the same name became the town's physician and died before 31 March 1701. That is impossible if he is the same as Pitcairne's Dr Gray, domiciled in London throughout their correspondence. Rob. Gray, as a Senior Fellow, is a signatory of the 'Instrument ... of the College of Physicians,' dated 22 December 1696, quoted in the prefatory material to Sir Samuel Garth's poem, *The Dispensary* (1699). He must have been reasonably prosperous; the signatories agreed that each should contribute £10 towards the cost of drugs for use in the new dispensary.

On 4 October 1705, Gray, together with Sir Hans Sloane, was elected an Honorary Fellow of the Royal College of Physicians, Edinburgh (Craig, *History*, 1072). Gray seems to have been a friend, perhaps a relative, of the physician and botanist Robert Morison, on whom see **32**.

John Bateman MD was educated at Merton College, Oxford, where he proceeded MD in 1682. In 1685 he became a Fellow of the Royal College of Physicians, London, in which he subsequently held a number of offices. He was President 1716–1718. He died 11 September 1728 (Munk, *Roll*, i, 435). Like Gray and Sloane he was a signatory of the Instrument quoted above. He is said to be portrayed as Celsus in the final Canto VI of *The Dispensary*: the name is taken from the first-century writer on medicine, Aulus Cornelius Celsus. He is the delegate summoned by Hygeia, goddess of health, to accompany her

POEM 32

to the Elysian Fields, where Harvey's spirit will give advice on how to bring the internal quarrels of the College to a peaceful conclusion:

> With just Resentments and Contempt you see
> The foul Dissentions of the *Faculty*,
> How your sad sick'ning Art now hangs her Head,
> And once a Science, is become a Trade.
> Her Sons ne'er rifle her Mysterious Store,
> But study Nature less, and Lucre more.

The link of Bateman with the great Harvey is perhaps an indication of why Pitcairne admired this contemporary.

The two are called Castor and Pollux presumably because their influence protected younger members of the new school of medical practice from professional shipwreck at the hands of their unenlightened elders. Jointly they may have played some part in composing the troubles at the Edinburgh College.

39 *viæ ignaris medicis*: physicians who clung to the old style of medicine.
40 *Sidere fausto*: the benevolent constellation Gemini.

32

Notes. Robert Morison (1620–1683) was born in Aberdeen, where he graduated MA in 1638. In the civil wars he was a Royalist, eventually fleeing to Paris, where he studied botany and anatomy. In 1648 he graduated MD of Angers. In 1650 he became physician to the Duke of Orleans and a keeper of the ducal gardens at Blois. Here he attracted the attention of the exiled Charles II, with whom he returned to England at the Restoration to become royal physician and botanist, and keeper of the king's gardens. In 1669 he was elected Professor of Botany at Oxford. His main publications were *Præludia Botanica* (1669), *Plantarum Historiæ Universalis Oxoniensis Pars Secunda* (1680) and the posthumous *Pars Tertia* mentioned above, completed by his former student Jacob Bobart (1641–1719). Pitcairne contributed *Roberti Morisoni Vita* to this last, a work also preserved as item 7 in *S. Pars Prima* was never published.

Morison appears to have been a friend, perhaps a relative, of Dr Robert Gray, who wrote of him: 'He was communicative of his knowledge, a true friend, an honest countryman, true to his religion, whom neither the fair promises of the papists, nor the threatenings of others would prevail upon to alter' (BL, *Sloane MS 3198*).

2 *Pæonium ... genus*: Paean was a title of Apollo as god of medicine. The Paeonian race is made up of physicians as a profession.

33

Notes. The poem is an attack on Matthew St. Clair or Sinclair (?1654–1728), an original Fellow of the Royal College of Physicians, first on record in 1674 as a medical student in Leiden. He was President of the College in 1698 and 1708, and was the longest surviving of the original 21 Fellows. His MS lectures are preserved in the Library of the College (Craig, *History*, 65, 944). His presidency in 1698 shows that he supported Sibbald in the dispute which split the College in the 1690s. The dispute, and his election, may be the original occasion for the poem.

Title *Phoebum Apollinem*: Apollo was patron of the medical arts; cf. **31**, introductory note. His image appears in the College coat of arms immediately beneath the motto *Non sinit esse feros*. The supporters are two wild men pacified by the god.

4 *Clarii*: the Sinclair family, barons of Roslin and Ravenscraig, earls of Orkney and Caithness; see **20** (II), **25**.

5 *natos ... Patrum*: a reference to the disputes about the Pretender's birth. St. Clair, it is to be assumed, was a Whig, who accepted that fraud had been committed, that the Pretender was not, in fact, James VII's son.

6 *Quique ... viros*: i.e., who deny that the martyrdom of Charles I had made him a saint.

8 *Phaeton*: Phaethon, son of Apollo and the heroine Clymene, who almost destroyed the world when he attempted to drive his father's chariot of the sun. Jupiter struck him down with a thunderbolt.

34

Notes. Sir David Hay, MD of Aberdeen, was one of four physicians called in 1680 to give their advice on a legal dispute between the Edinburgh Apothecaries and the Faculty of Surgeons. His name comes first in the list of Fellows in the original patent (1681) of the Royal College of Physicians of Edinburgh. In 1684 he became a Physician-in-Ordinary to the King in Scotland. He died in 1699 (Craig, *History*, 60, 61, 65, 683).

It seems likely that Hay was an opponent of Pitcairne's Iatrophysical theories and sided with Sibbald in the dispute which split the College in the 1690s; see **30** and Introduction, pp. 13–14. The poem may or may not have been written after Hay's death; the epitaph on Sibbald was written when Sibbald was still very much alive.

1 *flagra*: corporal punishment was still practised in 17th-century universities; cf. Aubrey's remark on Milton's time at Christ's College, Cambridge: 'His 1st tutor there, from whom receiving some unkindness [whipped him], he was

POEM 35

    afterwards (though it seemed opposed to the rules of the college), transferred to the tuition of one Mr Tovell' (*Collections for the Life of Milton*, By John Aubrey, F.R.S., in M.Y. Hughes [ed.], *John Milton Complete Poems and Major Prose* [New York, 1957], 1023).
2 *Abredonensis Anus*: Aberdeen University, probably specifically King's College, the older foundation. *Anus* is deliberately ambiguous; it may be the fourth-declension feminine *anus*, 'old woman' or the second-declension masculine *anus*, 'arse, posterior.' Neither word is meant to be complimentary.
3 *Conjunx*: not identified. Pitcairne implies that she had been a wealthy widow, but we have found no corroborative evidence.
4 *quemque ... Arabs*: i.e., Hay gained his reputation and his knighthood by work based on the writings of medieval Arabic physicians such as the *Kitab al-Qanun fi al-tibb* or *Canon of Medicine* of Avicenna (980–1037) and the *Liber Canonis* of Averroes (1126–1198). These were standard university text-books until the mid-seventeenth century, but regarded as outmoded by a later generation of physicians.
5 *tuus Orcus*: Hell is called *tuus* because Hay's medicines sent so many of his patients there.
6 *Apollo*: presiding deity of medicine; cf. **31, 32, 33**.
7–8 *Quippe ... tuo*: Hay's prescriptions efficiently despatched his patients to the next world, where the hope now is that there they will be equally efficient in returning them to this world. Note the clever verbal balance between *Liquere* (7) and *Linquere* (8).

35

Notes. Although not found in any extant version of PS, the poem is included in the version of the Key found in S between the first and second part of an entry:

'George Kirton surgeon, my good comrad, a merry fellow, no presbyterian, son to the famous Mr James Kirton, and brother to Capt. Kirton in your Fleet. He was married to Gray of Wariston's Sister and dyed too soon after his father's death. Robin Clark was his most intimat.'

   [*Text*]
'After Kirton's death dy'd James Hamilton M.D. a Perseus Scotus my kind
   friend, most excellent. Look to page fifth.
     For Dr Gray
     For the care of Mr John Pitcairne merchand
       London.'

The words 'page fifth' seem to refer to **36**. Neither poem is included in PS.

COMMENTARY

George Kirkton was a surgeon, elected Fellow of the Incorporation in 1696. His father was the Rev. James Kirkton (1620?-1699), a Covenanter and conventicler who in 1691 became minister of the Tolbooth Kirk and a commissioner for the 'purging' of Edinburgh University. He was author of *A History of the Church of Scotland 1660–1679*, which circulated in manuscript and was first printed in 1817; see the edn. by R. Stewart (Lewiston/Queenstown/ Lampeter, 1992; cf. **18**, note on text). He was much disliked by Episcopalians. Pitcairne in *The Assembly* gives a satiric portrait of him as Mr Covenant Plain Dealer.

Pitcairne's description of George Kirkton as 'a merry fellow, no presbyterian' shows that the latter had diverged from the ways of his father. The poem was written after James Kirkton's death, not long before that of George. The suggestion that excessive grief for his father led to the melancholy illness (and eventually the death) of George may or may not be serious. The tone of the poem is certainly light, but compare the treatment of Mark Learmonth's death, for Pitcairne certainly a serious matter, in **9**. The Key illuminates certain details, but leaves others in darkness.

3 *Grajus*: Dr John Gray; see **31**, **33**n. He was the recipient of the S. The *Uatsonus* of the variant reading is most probably James Watson (1664?-1722), the Episcopalian (or Catholic) printer; see Introduction, p. x; **20**, **Text**.
   Grajus is to be scanned as a dactylic trisyllable, *Gra-j-us*.

4 *Clarkius*: Robert Clark, the Robin Clark of the Key, was born in 1664, the fifth and youngest son of Sir John Clerk, first baronet of Penicuik, and uncle of the third baronet, the celebrated Sir John Clerk of Pericuik (1676–1755). He was elected Fellow of the Incorporation of Surgeons, Edinburgh in 1689, and in 1701 Deacon. He declined the latter office and was suspended, but his privileges were restored when James Hamilton (see introductory note, **36**) was appointed to the post. Robert's surgical skill saved his nephew from the loss of a leg, but attendance, with Hamilton, at the birth of his nephew's eldest son, resulted in the death of the mother. He died in 1720; see **36**(b), 1, **38**, 11.

36

Notes. (a) and (b) are palpably variant versions of the same curious elegiac poem, directed to the George Kirkton of **35**, now deceased for some time, and celebrating the skills of two other surgeons, more recently deceased, James Hamilton and Walter Potter. Johnston (*Best of our owne*, 71, Index of Persons) gives Hamilton's dates as 1671–1710. He became a Fellow of the Incorporation of Surgeons in 1695 and was the first Librarian, 1700–1702. From 1702–1704 he was Deacon. While he was in office, the first public anatomical dissections were held, performed chiefly by himself and Pitcairne. He was 'much emploied in midwifery,' and as noted above **35**, 4n., joined Robert Clerk at the birth of the eldest son of Sir John Clerk of Penicuik.

POEM 36

In S (above 35, introductory note), he is called James Hamilton M.D., but there is no other evidence that he had medical as well as surgical qualifications. The term 'Perseus Scotus,' there applied to him, is obscure, but was probably intended as complimentary.

Potter was elected to the Fellowship in 1702. The 'Poterius's pouder' mentioned by Pitcairne in a letter of 6 February 1712 (Johnston, *Best of our owne*, 66, letter 54) may have been a compound manufactured by him.

Hamilton in particular had close associations with Pitcairne, who in his correspondence mentions him several times, always favourably (Johnston, *Best of our owne*, letters 31, 32, 36, 38, 42). Most notable is letter 38 (p. 53), dated 10 February 1708, to the Scottish Secretary of State, John Erskine, 23rd Earl of Mar, where he writes: 'But, My Lord, there is a thing in Your Lordship's power, independentlie of Council or presbyterie, for our friend James Hamilton. It is a post no man in the nation (I mean now the Island) can behave so well in as he can. I beg Y^r Lordship may be forward in it, least some insignificant Southerne put in for it. Our Surgeons are abler far than our neighbours. And it is just wee should be serv'd by the best of our owne.'

We have not been able to discover the post to which Pitcairne refers or the success of his recommendation.

The poem is complex and somewhat puzzling. In (a) it takes the form of an appeal to Kirkton to lead his newly-arrived colleagues to the bedroom where Proserpine, Queen of the Dead, is undergoing a difficult labour. Their particular surgical skills will allow them to be of use. In (b) the appeal is made in the name of Robert Clerk (35, 4n) and other colleagues in the Incorporation who remember Kirkton, Hamilton and Potter with affection and respect. The child of Proserpine and Dis will be Infernal Jupiter. In (a) he will follow the earlier example of the celestial Jupiter by usurping the position of his father Dis, King of the Dead. As Saturn fled before his son to Italy, so Dis will take flight to France and Scotland. In (b) the child will become the equal of Jupiter. In both, sycophantic contemporary poets will applaud the achievement. Let others do what they like, but Pitcairne will stick to the old Jupiter.

Both versions probably belong to 1710. There are obvious underlying references to King William and King James, perhaps also to the possibility of a Hanoverian succession, set out in the 1701 English Act of Settlement, but not accepted by the Scottish Parliament, now defunct. The details however remain obscure. In particular, why should Pitcairne, of all people, wish his friends to assist at the birth of an apparent monster?

(a)

Title *Proserpinæ a Potione*: the meaning of the phrase is uncertain. We have assumed that *Potione* refers to a medical draught administered to Proserpine to assist her in a difficult labour; cf. the methods used by Arthur Johnston at an earlier difficult confinement: *Arte Machaonia letum conabar et herbis/ Pellere quas medicæ præbuit auctor opis* (*'Apologia pro Thaumantia obstetrice' Delitiæ*, 1, 502). The herbs mentioned had presumably been distilled to form a potion.

1 *vacuæ ... Edinæ*: i.e., empty after the final dissolution of the Scottish parliament.

3 *servantior*: the comparative or superlative degree is unusual with participles, but cf. *Aeneid* 2, 426–427: *Rhipeus, iustissimus unus/ qui fuit in Teucris et servantissimus aequi*.

4 *Saxo vel hostis*: cf. (b), **8**: *Saxo vel Anglus*. In both, the assumption is that the English, although united under a single government with the Scots, are naturally hostile to them, but were unable nevertheless to resist Hamilton's virtue and rectitude.

5 *Junonis alumni*: cf. (b), **9**. Juno Lucina was patron of women in childbirth and in this sense bestows light on the human race. Hamilton and Potter were fostered by her as surgeon-obstetricians.

8 *Infernum ... Jovem*: cf. (b), **12**. The phrase would normally be taken to mean 'Pluto' or 'Dis' himself; cf. *Aeneid* 4, 638: *Sacra Jovi Stygio*. Here however the context makes it clear that a son is intended.

9 *poëtæ*: cf. (b), **12**. Probably the Greek and Roman classical poets; see, e.g., Aeschylus, *Prometheus Bound*, 761–768, 908–927. Cf. too the reference to the tomb of Zeus (Jupiter) in Crete, below **84**, 4, and introductory note.

11 *ut alter*: i.e., King William.

12 *Bardis*: cf. (b) **15**. As opposed to *poëtæ*, **9**, poets of the degenerate modern age.

13–16 *Et jam ... Cato*: the Glorious Revolution in Hell and consequent exile of the old order; cf. below, **86**, 7–9. In (b) there is no direct mention of this Revolution.

15 *Dis ... Scoto-Brigantas*: as Saturn went into exile in Italy and James VII in France, so the overthrown Dis goes to Scotland and France, the only countries, Pitcairne optimistically thinks, to keep faith with the Stuarts.

Pictos Scoto-Brigantas: cf. **6**, 3n, **15**, 44. *Pictos*, 'painted,' refers both to the custom among the ancient Britons of tattooing the body, and to the Picts, the race which held the northern parts of Britain conjointly with the Scots.

For the acc. pl. *Brigantas*, cf. Tacitus, *Annals*, 12, 32.

16 *Cato*: cf. **10**, 3–4n, **86**, 9n.

17 *Dive Georgi*: i.e., the deceased George Kirkton; cf. (b), **17–18**. In (a), apart from the title, this is the only indication that the poem is addressed to Kirkton.

17–18 *mihi ... Jovi*: cf. (b), **17–18**. Pitcairne (or in (b) Clerk) reserves the right to drink the health of the ancient Jupiter, i.e., James VII or his son.

(b)

1–4 *Clarkius ... vovent*: Pitcairne addresses Kirkton, not in his own name, but in that of Robert Clerk (**35**, 4n) and his friends, the *nunc lacrymosa cohors*, in the Incorporation of Surgeons.

POEM 37

3 *Te*: Kirkton.
  Manesque: the spirit of the dead Kirkton.
11 *[H]os*: SP reads *Nos. Hos*, the corresponding reading in (a), seems better.

37

Metre. Sapphic stanza.
Notes. There is a brief discussion of the poem in Money, *English Horace*, 145–146. As is there indicated, the invitation is not really to a Catholic commemoration of the translation of the relics of St Margaret, Queen of Scotland (1046–1093), but to a Jacobite celebration of the Pretender's birthday. The joke partly depends on a mistake made by the eminent church historian, Cardinal Cesare Baronius (1538–1607), who was probably confused between the Old and the New Style calendar (cf., below, **103**), when he assigned the festival to 10 rather than 19 June. On the petition of two members of the Leslie family and/or Paul Menzies of Pitfodel, Margaret was named Patron of Scotland in 1673, becoming 'the only Scottish saint to enjoy a universal cult in the Roman calendar' (*ODS*, s.v.). Her feast was fixed on 10 June. In 1678 it was transferred to 8 July where it continued until 1693, when it was transferred back to 10 June 'on the plea of the exiled James VII and II, whose heir had been born on 10 June 1688 and who wished to invoke the protection of St Margaret on the troubled realm which had rejected him' (John McIntyre, 'St Margaret and the Scots College Rome,' *Innes Review* XLIV.2 [Autumn 1993], 187). The king's action was certain to attract Pitcairne's attention.

The position of Margaret as a member of the legitimate English royal family driven into exile by a usurper, William the Conqueror, bears obvious points of resemblance to that of the Stuarts.

The poem was probably composed in 1693 or 1694. For an ode in similar style, compare **7**, a similar invitation, this time to Mark Learmonth.

1 *Kinkadi*: Thomas Kinkaid (or Kincaid) was born in 1661, and outlived Pitcairne, whose library and dissertations he celebrated in two Latin poems (SP, 92–94). He is described as *Civis Edinburgenus, vir supra sortem doctus, & literis humanioribus bene instructus* (SP, 'Præfatio,' vi). He kept a diary for the years 1687–1688 (NLS, Adv. MS 32.7.7), when he was a medical student, containing much interesting material on how golf was played in the late-seventeenth century. He was one of Pitcairne's intimates, mentioned by him in a letter dated 23 September 1694 (Johnston, *Best of our owne*, 18, letter 3). In other poems he is primarily addressed as a fellow-surgeon, but he was rather late in obtaining his Fellowship at the College; 'from respect to his father [a more distinguished surgeon] and for good deeds done by him to the Incorporation' he was elected 'without examination or payment of fee' on 16 September 1710 (MS note in John Gairdner's *List of*

COMMENTARY

Fellows, 23). He must have been in practice well before this date, but there is nothing in the poem to indicate his profession.

Dromondi: probably John Drummond, secretary of the Edinburgh College of Physicians 1706–1708, President 1722–1727 (Craig, *Royal College of Physicians*, 1078, 1076), brother of David Drummond (**63**, **64**). Pitcairne mentions him in a letter dated 20 February 1701 (Johnston, *Best of our owne*, 35, letter 14).

2–4 *Die ... rursus*: At the translation, the body of the saint was disinterred and moved amid acclamations to a new and more splendid tomb. It is in this sense that St Margaret 'sees her saintly cronies again' – the Scottish churchmen and people. Pitcairne has no great respect for the ceremony. But he too wishes to see his cronies again.

5 *Alvous*: not certainly identified; perhaps William Alves, Writer to the Signet.
Buchananus: Probably the innkeeper of **19** (i), 17–18.

6 *Fribarnus*: Robert Freebairn (c. 1685–c. 1740), printer and publisher, Pitcairne's close friend.

9 *græcandum*: cf. Money, *English Horace*, 146: '*Graecandum* makes a striking gerundive, and is an unusual word; *pergraecor* (to play the Greek, i.e. revel) appears in Plautine comedy. A love of frivolous parties may not be the only Greek quality they need: Greeks were also renowned for cleverness and deceit, essential ingredients for Jacobite success.' Cf. the pejorative use of the adjective *Graia*, 'Greek', in **19**(i), 52 and the famous phrase in *Aeneid* 2, 49: *timeo Danaos et dona ferentis*.

Pitcairne also emphasizes that this will be a Greek (Protestant) rather than a Roman (Catholic) celebration.

10 *Carolo & Nepoti*: Charles II and his nephew, the Pretender. There may well be a subliminal reference to the identity of 10 June NS and 29 May OS; see **103**, introductory note.

11–12 *suis ... Britannis*: Margaret was an English princess and Queen of Scotland. She thus has responsibilities towards both peoples – Britons collectively rather than separately for Scots or English

38

Metre. Alcaic stanza.

Notes. Pitcairne describes himself as 'Surgeon,' so the ode probably postdates his expulsion from the College of Physicians in 1695, is no earlier than 1701, when he was elected a Fellow of the College of Surgeons, and antedates his readmission to the College of Physicians in 1703. For Kinkaid see previous poem.

1 *O ... decus*: cf. the opening of the following poem.
salutaris militiæ: i.e., the College of Surgeons.

2 *Æsculapi ... Podalirii*: the legendary physician Aesculapius had two sons Podalirius and Machaon (6) who also followed his profession, serving with the Greek forces during the Trojan War. Maliciously Pitcairne insinuates that the College of Surgeons, unlike the College of Physicians, maintains their tradition.
4 *Lyæus*: Λυαῖος 'the relaxer, unbender,' an appellation of Bacchus.
5 *Phœbus*: here, the Sun, but also supreme patron of medicine, whence the hyperbolic description (8) of Kinkaid as second [only] to himself.
9 *coronet vina*: cf. *Aeneid* 1, 724.
Dromondius: see previous poem, 1n.
10 *Barclius*: not identified.
11 *Clercus*: see **35**, 4n.

39

Metre. sapphic stanza.
Notes. For the Robert Gray of the title see **31**, 33n. The ode is an elegy for another of Pitcairne's closest friends, the mathematician, astronomer and physician, David Gregory, born 24 June 1661, Kinnairdie, Banffshire, died 10 October 1708, Maidenhead, Berkshire. Gregory was educated at Marischal College, Aberdeen, and Edinburgh University, where his brilliance as a student led to his appointment to the chair of mathematics a month before he graduated MA in November 1683. In March of that year Pitcairne had proposed the solution of a mathematical problem as a public test for Gregory's predecessor in the chair, John Young, whose failure was made the occasion for his dismissal and the appointment of Gregory: see Introduction, p. 6. From February 1687 Gregory and Pitcairne shared lodgings, together with books and information on medicine and mathematics. Their joint work on the method of infinite series was afterwards published in the collected works of the English mathematician John Wallis (1616–1703). Pitcairne was present when Gregory received a copy of a book which was to influence both profoundly, Newton's *Principia* (London, 1687).

Gregory was an Episcopalian whose loyalties at least tended towards the House of Stuart. In 1690 he found himself under investigation in the Williamite and Presbyterian purge of the Scottish universities. In 1691 he went to England, where he was appointed Savilian Professor of Astronomy at Oxford. Newton supported him with a letter of recommendation. In 1692 he became MA and MD of Oxford, where, in addition to his academic work, he seems to have practised as a physician; several of Pitcairne's letters to him give advice on the treatment of patients. In 1695 Anthony Alsop (died 1726) celebrated Gregory's marriage to Elizabeth Oliphant with a Jacobite ode in alcaics (Money, *English Horace*, 284–286; cf. 135–142). In 1705 Gregory was made an Honorary Fellow of the Edinburgh Royal College of Physicians. In 1708 he fell victim to tuberculosis and on his homeward journey from Bath, where he had been sent to take the waters, he died and was buried at Maidenhead, Berkshire.

His most important published work was *Astronomiae Physicae et Geometricae Elementa* (Oxford, 1702), some part of which was contributed by Newton. His knowledge of Greek was limited, despite which he produced an edition of Euclid's works (Oxford, 1703). He collaborated with Edmund Halley (1656–1742) on the *editio princeps* of the *Conics* of Apollonius of Perge (2nd half of 3rd century BC), published in 1710, after Gregory's death.

Six letters from Pitcairne to Gregory survive, written between 16 October 1695 and 24 June 1708 (Johnston, *Best of our owne*, 21, 33, 35, 41–42, 42–43, 53–54). He is mentioned in others, including several to Dr Gray.

The poem was written shortly after Gregory's death. For a brief discussion see Money, *English Horace*, 143–144.

3 *inquefelix*: i.e., *infelixque*. We have found no exact parallel to this usage; cf. however Virgil, *Eclogue* 7, 13: *eque sacra resonant examina quercu*.
5 *meditante*: cf. Virgil, *Eclogue* 1, 2: *musam meditaris*.
  Stoto: see 21, 14n.
6 *Carmina ... tigres*: cf. Horace, *Ars Poetica*, 392–393: *Orpheus, / dictus ob hoc lenire tigris*.
7 *Priorum*: Matthew Prior (1664–1721); cf. 22, introductory note.
9–10 *redeuntia ... lunæ*: cf. Ovid, *Metamorphoses* 10, 479: *redeuntis cornua lunae*; 14, 423–424: *redeuntia solis lumina*.
14 *tot raptos ... sodales*: e.g., Lindsay, Dennistoun, Learmonth, Kirkton ...
19–20 *Regiæ ... Gregorianæ*: the surname 'Gregory' in fact represents 'MacGregor', having been altered as a result of the proscription of the latter after the battle of Glenfruin in 1603. The MacGregors claimed to be descendants of the early Scottish king Giric or Gregorius (878–889); see Black, *Surnames of Scotland*, s.v.; for Giric see A.A.M. Duncan, *The Kingship of the Scots, 842–1292* (Edinburgh, 2002), 11–14.
21–24 *Ille Neutonum ... stupentes*: Gregory, a great modern Scottish mathematician, introduces the achievements of the greatest ever mathematician, the Englishman Newton, to the astonished great mathematicians of antiquity.
22 *Euclidi*: Euclid (fl. 300 BC), Greek mathematician, whose works Gregory edited.
  Siculoque: Archimedes (c. 287–212 BC), Sicilian Greek mathematician and inventor.
25 *Pergæum*: the Greek mathematician Apollonius of Perge in southern Asia Minor; see introductory note.
26 *Halleii studiis*: see introductory note.
27 *graves ... labores*: Gregory's own work on Euclid and Apollonius.
30 *patruoque*: Gregory's uncle, James Gregorie (1638–1675), professor of mathematics, University of St Andrews 1668–1674, first professor of mathematics, Edinburgh University 1674–1675, 'the most original and versatile mathemati-

cian Scotland has produced' (R. Schlapp, 'The Contribution of the Scots to Mathematics,' *Mathematical Gazette* LVII [1973], 1–160).

40

Metre. (a), (b), (c) sapphic stanza. (d) elegiac couplet.
Notes. Archibald Stevenson was the fifth son of the Rev. Andro Stevenson, (1588–1664), Regent in Philosophy and Humanity, Edinburgh University, and subsequently, from 1639, parish minister of Dunbar, East Lothian. Archibald Stevenson was born on 11 March, probably in 1630. In 1659, at rather a late age, he became a medical student at Leiden, graduating MD in 1661. In 1662 he married Elizabeth Ramsay (see 41), by whom he had four sons and four daughters. In 1666 he was appointed physician to Heriot's Hospital, an office which he retained until 1705, when he resigned in favour of Dr George Mackenzie (see 43). In 1681 he became Principal Mediciner to the King in Scotland (*Medicus Regius*) and later in the same year a founding Fellow and first President of the Royal College of Physicians, Edinburgh, of which he again became President in 1693 and 1694. In 1682, together with Robert Sibbald and Andrew Balfour he was knighted at Holyrood by the Duke of York, the future James VII, acting for his brother, Charles II. In 1692 there is a dispensation in his favour of Dolphinton House and Baronies in Lanarkshire. On 8 August 1693 his eldest daughter Elizabeth (25, introductory note) was married to the widowed Pitcairne. Stevenson and Pitcairne were already professionally intimate, and they held together during the College disputes in the 1690s, as a consequence of which both, together with several of their colleagues, were expelled in 1695. The schism continued until 1704 (30, introductory note). In 1700 Stevenson acted as cautioner for Pitcairne during his examination before the Privy Council (Johnston, *Best of our owne*, 32, letter 11). Stevenson died on 16 February 1710 and is buried in Greyfriars Kirkyard (R.P. Ritchie, *The Early Days of the Royall Colledge of Phisitians, Edinburgh* [Edinburgh, 1899]; W.B. Howie, 'Sir Archibald Stevenson, his Ancestry, and the Riot in the College of Physicians at Edinburgh,' *Medical History* XI (1967), 269–284; MS material in Library of the Royal College of Physicians, Edinburgh).

Both Sir Archibald's parents were ardent Calvinists and Covenanters. He held them in high esteem, but seems to have turned against their beliefs. Almost certainly he was both Jacobite and Episcopalian. If, as seems likely, Pitcairne wrote the English poem in (d) above, the line 'His Soul was fix't to Monarchy and Church' certainly refers to the House of Stuart and the Episcopalian church.

Stevenson died in 1710. Pitcairne, however, had completed (a), the first version of the poem on Stevenson's death, before 10 July 1708, the date at which Gregory finished work on APP. The references to 'Home' may help to explain the apparent paradox. 'Home' is most probably Charles Home, 6th Earl of Home, who led the Cavaliers, the party which supported James VII, in the Scottish Parliament, and who died in 1706. His death clearly had a severe affect on Stevenson's health, and it may be that (a) was composed when recovery seemed unlikely. The poem was subsequently adapted in anticipation of Stevenson's eightieth birthday on 11 March 1710, but, when he died in the preceding February, was readapted to the new circumstances.

(a)

Title *Medicorum ... principis*: an echo of the phrase applied to George Buchanan by the younger Henri Estienne (1531–1598): *poeta sui saeculi facile princeps*.

1 *invitas ... terras*: i.e., the world was sorry to see him go.

7 *arte*: i.e., the art of medicine.

11 *Homi*: in an elegy (**42**) for the Jacobite William Keith (c. 1665–1712), 8th Earl Marischal, Home and Stevenson are named as the Earl Marischal's particular friends. All three, it seems likely, were Jacobites. These political sympathies probably rule out any identification of *Homius* with the lawyer and judge Sir David Hume or Home (1643–1707), a kenspeckle figure in the Edinburgh of his day, but a convinced Williamite and Presbyterian. Likeliest candidate is Charles Home (d. 1706), 6th Earl of Home, the leader of the Cavaliers in the Scottish parliament. Lockhart (*Scotland's Ruine*, 133–134) comments on his death: 'One cannot imagine how great a loss the royal family [the exiled Stuarts] and country party sustained by it. ... He ... had a particular talent of procuring intelligence of his adversaries most secret designs ... This proceeded from his being esteemed by people of all parties, on account of his eminently unbyassable honesty and integrity in both private and public matters. He was so faithful to the royal family that he suffered much upon that account and was more relyed upon than any other.' In parliament at least he and Keith sometimes worked together.

Mr John Dallas, Rare Books Librarian to the Royal College of Physicians, Edinburgh, has suggested to us as a third possibility Alexander Home, Clerk to the College of Physicians 1693–1695 and associated with Stevenson during the divisions in the College. We have not discovered whether or not he died before Stevenson and whether he had a son who survived him.

No certainty is possible, but the phraseology of the poem tends to suggest that *Homius* should be identified as the 6th Earl of Home. Whatever his identity, his death drove Stevenson into a decline.

13 *simile aut secundum*: cf. Horace, *Odes* 1, 12, 18: *nec viget quicquam simile aut secundum*, also adapted, **76**(a), (b), 14.

14 *ire sub terras*: cf. *Aeneid* 2, 654: *et nunc magna mei sub terras ibit imago*; 660: *ire sub umbras*; **10**, 1, variant reading.

15 *Acrior Rogis*: i.e., his death was premature.

Patriæ vindex: i.e., he was a Jacobite, working towards the re-establishment of the male Stuart line.

20 *stamina vitæ*: cf., e.g., Tibullus 1, 7: *Hunc cecinere diem Parcae fatalia nentes/ Stamina.*

(c)

1 *spretor Orci*: i.e., despising death by his recovery from the illness caused by the demise of Home.
9 *triseclem*: a century, three generations, as opposed to the mere eighty years which Stevenson was approaching. Variants of the term are usually applied to the wise old warrior Nestor; cf. the term *trisaeclisenex* applied to him by the early Latin poet Laevius.
15 *Augustæ*: *Augusta* was the name of Roman London in the fourth century: *ad Lundinium, vetus oppidum quod Augustam posteritas appellavit* (Ammianus Marcellinus 27, 8, 7). The name was modelled on that of several continental cities, the most notable of which was *Augusta Treverorum*, now Trier, then an Imperial capital. Much later Dryden revived it, but with comic and satiric intent: 'Close to the Walls which fair *Augusta* bind,/ (the fair *Augusta* much to fears inclined)/ An ancient fabrick raised t' inform the sight,/ There stood of yore, and *Barbican* it hight' (*MacFlecknoe*, 64–67). With a rather different purpose, perhaps in an attempt to maintain Scottish dignity after the 1707 Union, Pitcairne used the name to mean Edinburgh.
17–20 *Attamen ... honorem*: Pitcairne urges Stevenson to lay aside his melancholy on the ground that Home has left a son, Alexander Home, 7th Earl (died 1720), who resembles the father whom he has succeeded.
18 *gentis ... vetustæ*: the line of the Earls of Home.
21 *heroem*: i.e., probably Home. The word indicates a member of the aristocracy.

(d,1)

1 *Lux ... æquat*: the birthday fell on the vernal equinox, 11 March, os. For *lux* see 13, 9n.
3 *tropæis*: patients whom Stevenson brought back to health.
5–6 *Quam ... tulit*: Pitcairne implicitly compares Stevenson to Asclepius (Aesculapius), killed by Zeus for daring to bring Hippolytus back to life, but then deified.

(d, 2)

1 *Hippocrates*: Greek physician (5th century BC), supposed author of the medical Hippocratic Oath.
7 *His Soul ... Church*: see above, introductory note.
9 *diverse Changes*: i.e., the Civil Wars, the execution of Charles I, the Cromwellian Commonwealth, the Restoration, the expulsion of James VII and succession of

William and Mary, the division in the College of Physicians, the Union of the Scottish with the English parliament. All fell within Stevenson's lifetime.

41

Notes. Memorial verses for Elizabeth Ramsay, widow of Sir Archibald Stevenson (see **40**, introductory note). She was the daughter of John Ramsay of Idington (?Uddington, Lanarkshire) and his wife Egidia Kellie, and became the mother of eight children, four boys and four girls. She outlived her husband, but died before Pitcairne.

1 *vixti*: shortened form of *vixisti*, 'you have lived (but do so no longer)', 'you are dead.' Cf. Cicero after the execution of the Catilinarian conspirators: *vixerunt*; (cf. also **56**, 1) For a similar usage cf. *Aeneid* 2, 325–326: *fuimus Troes, fuit Ilium et ingens / gloria Teucrorum*.
4 *Medic[i]*: the broadside reads *Medicum*.
 Medici Regis: Stevenson was a Royal Physician; see **40**, introductory note.
6 *Elysij ... duos*: Stevenson and his wife are reunited in the realm of the blessed dead.

42

Notes. William Keith, 8th Earl Marischal, was born c. 1665. He succeeded his father in 1694 and died 27 May 1712. He was probably a close friend of the Earl of Home, with whom he was sometimes politically associated; the poem is evidence of his friendship with Sir Archibald Stevenson. Lockhart says of him: 'The Earl Marischal of Scotland was master of a quick and lively spirit, a great vivacity of wit, an undaunted courage, and, in short, of a soul capable of doing great things. But his misfortune was, he could not seriously, at least for any tract of time, apply himself to business, being loose and irregular in his measures and too bent upon his pleasures. However, being a man of honour and capacity, he was always faithful to his prince and country, did them both great service and merited much from them' (Lockhart, *Scotland's Ruine*, 111).

1–3 *Jam te ... amicè*: cf. **40**(a), 11.
5 *lentum ... Coelo*: Pitcairne does not want to die before the restoration of the male Stuart line.
6 *SCOTUS ... redit*: Scotus is the Pretender, exiled in France. For the phraseology cf. **2**, 15 notes. The eventual return of the Pretender is likened to the original establishment of Scotland by the arrival there from the continent of the eponymous Scotus.

POEM 43

7   *JACOBO*: the Old Testament patriarch; here the deceased James VII.
    Issachar: ninth son of the patriarch Jacob, described thus by his father: 'Issachar is a strong ass couching down between two burdens: And he saw that rest was good, and the land that it was pleasant; and bowed his shoulder to bear, and became a servant unto tribute' (*Genesis* 49:14–15). Cf. the earlier *Ad Phœbum*, 11–12 (**74**). In both James Douglas, 4th Duke of Hamilton may be intended. He was distantly related to the House of Stuart and was widely regarded as a Jacobite, but on 1 September 1705 he successfully proposed a motion in parliament that the choice of Scottish commissioners to negotiate the union with England should be left with Queen Anne, a move which led directly to the 1707 Union. 'From this day may we date the commencement of Scotland's ruine' (Lockhart, *Scotland's Ruine*, 106). Eventually, in September 1711, he received his reward when he became a peer of Great Britain under the titles Baron of Dutton and Duke of Brandon. By his second marriage he had already obtained extensive English estates. Poem **74** probably refers to an earlier lapse. Contrast however **95** below.
10 *Domui vestrae*: i.e., primarily his son and heir George Keith, who took part in the 1715 rising and was consequently forfeited on 30 June 1716. He died unmarried in 1778 and his title died with him.
11 *concordibus armis*: i.e., in any future rising.
12 *Vallum*: the Scottish patriot hero William Wallace (c. 1270–1305).

43

Notes. Early in the eighteenth century Heriot's Hospital in Edinburgh witnessed a skirmish in the long war between Presbyterians and Episcopalians. George Heriot (1563–1624), an Edinburgh burgess, had been goldsmith to James VI and his Queen. In 1603 he followed James to London, where he stayed for the rest of his life. He left no legitimate offspring, and most of his very considerable fortune he bequeathed to the foundation of a Hospital in Edinburgh 'In Imitatione of the publict pios and religious work foundat within the Citie of London callit Chrystis Hospital … for educatione nursing and upbringing of Youth being puir Orphans and fatherles childrene of decayit Burgesses and freemen of the said burgh [Edinburgh] destitut and left without meanes.' This Hospital eventually became the modern George Heriot's School.

    The Hospital at least began as an Episcopalian establishment. Heriot himself worshipped, and was buried, in St Martin's in the Fields, London. The foundation Statutes of the Hospital were drawn up in 1627 by Heriot's nephew, Walter Balconquall (1586–1645), son of an Edinburgh minister, himself eventually episcopalian Dean of Rochester and subsequently Durham. The Governors were to be the Provost, Baillies, Town Councillors and Ministers of Edinburgh, but, in case of dispute, matters were to be submitted to 'those fyve mentioned in the

COMMENTARY

Founderis Will viz. The Lord Chancellour the tuo Archibischopis [of St Andrews and Glasgow] the Lord President of the Colledge of Justice and the Lord Advocat to his Majestie of this realme of Scotland.' The Archbishop of Canterbury, William Laud (1573–1645), played a part in getting the enterprise under way.

At the Hospital something of the Episcopalian tradition survived the 1689 Revolution. For the most part, the staff remained as before. Notably Sir Archibald Stevenson, Pitcairne's father-in-law (40), was Physician from 1666 until he retired in 1705 at the age of 76. He agreed to cancel a claim for £200 against the Hospital on condition that the Governors appointed as his successor another Fellow of the Royal College of Physicians, the Episcopalian and Jacobite Dr George Mackenzie (1669–1725). One probable reason for his action was the appointment in 1702 of John Watson as House-Governor and Head-Master. Watson, Mackenzie later remarked, had been 'taken in open rebellion against King Charles II, and to this hour still prays for the establishment of their wicked covenant.' Mackenzie also expressed serious doubts about Watson's scholarly capabilities.

Watson failed to observe the requirement in the Statutes that set forms of prayer and confession – in effect, those in the *Scottish Prayer Book* of 1637, often erroneously called Laud's Liturgy – should be in daily use. In an anonymous pamphlet, the authorship of which he freely admitted, Mackenzie criticized this practice, and the behaviour of the Governors. For this, he was dismissed in 1711, reinstated in 1713, but finally dismissed in 1714. After the dismissals he was succeeded by Dr Gilbert Rule, a Presbyterian, the son of Gilbert Rule (1629–1701), who had from 1691 to his death been, in Pitcairne's eyes, the usurping and unworthy Principal of Edinburgh University. For an account of the affair (with some natural Whig and Presbyterian bias) see William Steven, *History of George Heriot's Hospital* (new edn., Edinburgh and London, 1859), 90–93.

The affair obviously created some stir. Pitcairne probably wrote the poem in 1705.

In 1714 Mackenzie was made a Physician-in-Ordinary to Queen Anne, an appointment not renewed by George I. He was also a historian and biographer, whose best-known work is *Lives and Characters of the most Eminent Writers of the Scots Nation* (3 vols., Edinburgh, 1708, 1711, 1722).

1 *Cnoxiaci*: coinage, deliberately barbarous in appearance, based on the surname Knox. John Knox (?1512–1572), Protestant reformer and opponent of Mary Queen of Scots, returned in 1559 from the Geneva of John Calvin to Scotland, where he became minister of Edinburgh and a principal agent in the establishment of the Presbyterian church. The immediate reference is probably to John Watson.
3 *concedatur*: the word implies that the Governors must, or at least should, yield to Mackenzie.
4 *nostris*: the boys of the Hospital.

5   *Leiturgia*: the Communion Office from the *Scottish Prayer Book*.
    redibit: the return of Mackenzie implies the return of the Liturgy.
6   *Martyr ... Carolus*: Charles 1. The Scottish Prayer Book owed most of its characteristics to him, together with two Scottish bishops, John Maxwell (c. 1590–1647), of Ross, and James Wedderburn (1585–1635), of Dunblane.

44

Notes. Sir Alexander Monteith, Bt., son of James Monteith of Auldcathie, owned the estate of Todshaugh, now Foxhall, W. Lothian. He served his apprenticeship as a surgeon to William Borthwick (Fellow of the College of Surgeons, 1665; died 1689), then spent some years abroad. In 1691 he was elected Fellow of the College of Surgeons, to which he presented books in 1696. Pitcairne urged him 'to petition the Town Council for the provision of bodies for dissection ... In October 1694 he was granted for dissection the bodies of those who died in the Correction House, as well as infant foundlings, in exchange for free medical care for the poor' (Guerrini in *OxfDNB*; see also Introduction). During 1695–1696 he was President of the College, and again in 1699, but was deposed, probably because he was a Jacobite. In 1700 he petitioned the Scottish Parliament 'that his discovery of drawing Spirits from Malt equal to true French Brandy might be declared a Manufactory.' In 1701 he became acting President of the College because Robert Clerk (**35**, 4n) had refused to accept the post. Pitcairne mentions Monteith in a letter (Johnston, *Best of our owne*, 66, letter 54), dated 6 February 1712, addressed rather unexpectedly to the Whig Patrick Hume of Polwarth (1641–1724), Earl of Marchmont, who had acted for the prosecution in Pitcairne's trial before the Privy Council in 1700: 'My Lord, I have spoken with Mr Monteith, and wee both think That besides bathing the back place with materials which Mr Monteith will send the receipt of, Your Lordship should take 20 grains of Poterius's pouder in your milk.' Gairdner (p. 19) gives the date of Monteith's death as 23 December 1713, but as this is later than Pitcairne's own death on 23 October 1713, Monteith must have died somewhat earlier.

1   *Kirktono*: see **35**, introductory note.
4   *Arte Machaoniâ*; see **31**, 26n, **38**, 2 and n.
5   *Dum ... studes*: cf. **16**, 1n.
    solarier: archaic form of the present infinitive of the deponent verb *solor*.
5–6 *solarier ... manus*: a reference to free medical care for the poor.
6   *ubique*: the reference may also be to the provision of free medical care.
7   *everso ... seclo*: the loss of the Scottish Parliament and the threat of a Hanoverian succession, now imminent with the debility of Queen Anne and the death of the Duke of Hamilton (**95**), have turned the world upside-down.

45

Notes. See above, 1, introductory note. The poem appears to have been written during Lindsay's lifetime – before 1675, that is probably to say.

1   *arva*: Pitcairne and Lindsay's early concern with Platonic ideas (1, introductory note) suggests that the fields are those of the 'plain' or 'meadow of Truth,' τὸ ἀληθείας πεδίον or λειμών, described as lying beyond the heavens in Plato's *Phaedrus*, 248, b-c, part of the myth of the soul as charioteer attempting to control two winged steeds: 'The reason wherefore the souls are fain and eager to behold the plain of Truth, and discover it, lies herein – to wit, that the pasturage which is proper to their noblest part comes from that meadow, and the plumage by which they are borne aloft is nourished thereby' (trs. R. Hackforth, *Collected Dialogues of Plato*, ed. E. Hamilton and H. Cairns [Princeton, 1961], 495). Human souls originate there and eventually return. Also present is the idea, familiar to seventeenth-century Platonists and later revived by Wordsworth, that children and young people retain some memory of their pre-existence on the plain of Truth. Pitcairne, of course, may also have had in mind particular fields known to Lindsay and himself in their childhood.
3   *nova ... Juventus*: the renewed vigour of the soul, liberated after death.
6   *rotis*: the wheels of the chariot of the soul.

46

Notes. This epigram, together with an anagram of the name John Patersone, 'I hate no person,' was inscribed above the door of the tenement in the Edinburgh Canongate, the dimensions of which had been much enlarged by John Patersone, shoe-maker and golfer, on the proceeds of his victory in a foursome in which he partnered the Duke of York, later James VII, to victory. The Duke enjoyed golf on Leith Links during his time in Edinburgh as King's Commissioner, 1681–1685. In a conversation with two visiting English noblemen, he claimed that golf was a uniquely Scottish game. They disagreed, and to settle the matter a match was arranged between the Englishmen and the Duke with a Scottish partner. The Duke chose Patersone, and together they easily won the match. Patersone was duly rewarded. The story is told in Chambers, *Traditions*, 320–322. The match must have been played before the death of Charles II on 6 February 1685.

1   *ludo ... proprius*: golf and the claim which occasioned the foursome. APP has a footnote to the word *Ludo*, 'Gouff'.
4   *victores tot tulit*: the phrase suggests that for generations the Patersone family had lived on the site, perhaps in a single-storeyed house, enlarged and extended after the match. The tenement illustrated in Chambers, p. 320, is six storeys high.

POEM 47

Chambers' translation of ll. 3–4, *humo ... domum*, 'built this mansion, which one conquest raised him above all his predecessors,' is a misunderstanding of the Latin.

47

Notes. Newton's *Philosophiae Naturalis Principia Mathematica* was published in 1687. Pitcairne was present when, soon afterwards in Edinburgh, David Gregory (1659–1708) received a copy. He shared his friend's excitement at Newton's achievement. The poem was probably composed about this time. It is a developed example of the topos *taceat superata vetustas* (Claudian, *In Rufinum*, 1.283; see Curtius, *Latin Middle Ages*, 162–165).

The poem may have been influenced by Martial, *Epigrammaton* I, vii: *Stellae delicium mei Columba, / Verona licet audiente dicam, / vicit, Maxime, passerem Catulli. / tanto stella meus tuo Catullo / quanto passere maior est Columba.*

1 *Pythagora*: The system of Copernicus, perfected by Newton, according to which Earth was a planet, moving like the others in an orbit round the Sun, was often called 'Pythagorean' by such early humanist opponents as George Buchanan. Pythagoras of Samos (6th Century BC) held that Fire occupied the central place, the hearth, of the universe, and that everything else circled around it. This central Fire later Pythagoreans tended to identify with the Sun. Aristotle and common-sense, it was generally held, had combined to refute the doctrine (MacQueen, *Progress and Poetry*, 9–17). Newton himself regarded it as a partial anticipation of his own philosophy (*Sir Isaac Newton's Mathematical Principles*, ed. and trs. by Florian Cajori [Berkeley, Los Angeles, London, 1934], 549–550).

Aristarchus of Samos (3rd Century BC) proposed that the fixed stars and the sun remain unmoved, and that the earth revolves about the sun on the circumference of a circle, the sun lying in the middle of the orbit. He combined with this the rotation of the earth about its own axis (*OCD*, *s.v.* 'Aristarchus').

Here, as in a pamphlet published in 1688, *Solutio problematis de historicis; seu de inventoribus dissertatio*, in which he challenged the view that Hippocrates rather than Harvey had discovered the circulation of the blood, Pitcairne is concerned to uphold the originality and greater scientific validity of modern as compared to ancient science. In the Battle of the Books he was a modernist; cf. *Introduction*, pp. 40–41; Money, *The English Horace*, 143.

Samius ... fundus: literally 'the Samian farm' as opposed to the much larger *terra Britanna* (2) – a contrast exploited in the final couplet.

4 *vaga ... equis*: a metaphor for the control, precisely formulated by Newton, exercised over Earth's orbit by the gravitational pull of the Sun. The phrase *vaga ... terra* implies that Earth too is a planet, a 'wandering' heavenly body; *Phoeboeis ... vehitur equis* indicates that the wanderings are controlled by the Sun.

48

Text. As above. The texts differ only in minor details.

Notes. James Aitken (1613–1687), an Orkneyman (hence *Orcadensis* in (a)), was Bishop of Moray (1677–1680) and subsequently Bishop of Whithorn (Galloway) until his death on 15 November 1687 (*Handbook of British Chronology*, 311) during the reign of the Roman Catholic James VII. His second diocese (Wigtownshire and Kirkcudbright west of Urr) had long been a centre of Covenanting activities. For this reason Aitken was granted a dispensation to live in Edinburgh, and although he once made a visitation, his administration of the diocese was mainly a matter of letters to the synod, presbyteries and individual ministers. 'He was very zealous in opposing the taking off the penal laws' – in their application to Roman Catholics as well as Covenanters. Aitken was buried in Greyfriars Churchyard, Edinburgh, and this epitaph is said to have been fastened upon his coffin (Robert Keith, *An Historical Catalogue of the Scottish Bishops down to the year 1688*, new edition [Edinburgh, 1824], 153).

The epigram, like the one following, is unusual in that Pitcairne seems to put himself in opposition to James VII and his policies.

49

Notes. The poem is a mock-tribute to Dennistoun's verse. It is also uncomplimentary to *Massius*, whoever he may have been. Pitcairne himself may have been the one who on this occasion had displeased Dennistoun. The poem is earlier than Dennistoun's death in 1700, and, as it contains no hint of Jacobitism, may belong to the period before 1688. If *Massius* is in fact the John Massey mentioned below, the poem must have been written in the period 1686–1688.

Title *Walterum Dennistonum*: see 9, 1n.
1 *Deo ... plene*: 'inspired', but possibly rather 'intoxicated'. *Fulmina* (3) indicates that the God is most probably Jupiter, although Apollo, god of poetry and music, may be intended. Bacchus however remains a possibility, particularly in view of the indications in 9 that a night of drunken revelry would have been to Dennistoun's taste.
2 *Versibus armato*: cf. Horace, *Ars Poetica*, 79: *Archilochum proprio rabies armavit iambo*.
3 *Massius*: not certainly identified; possibly Andrew Massie, Regent in the Tounis College who presided over the publication of the graduating *theses philosophicae* in 1683, 1687 and 1695 (Pinkerton, *Minute Book*, 1, 268, n. 1; H.G. Aldis, *A List of Books Published in Scotland before 1700* [with additions, NLS, 1970], 2435, 2725, 3511). More plausibly perhaps he is John Massey (1650/51–1715), a Roman Catholic convert, who in 1686 was appointed Dean of Christ Church,

Oxford, by James VII and II. In 1688 he fled to France, eventually in 1699 becoming confessor to a house of nuns, where he died in 1715 (*OxfDNB*, s.v.).

tuæ ... Musæ: i.e., Dennistoun has published verses hostile to Massius.

fulmina: cf. Cicero, *Familiares*, 9,21,1: *verborum meorum ... fulmina*, an allusion to the thunderbolts of Jupiter, in Pitcairne transferred to the Muse. Pitcairne ironically suggests that Dennistoun's verses have terrified Massius.

4 *Qui ... Deos*: perhaps by his conversion and appointment as Dean of Christ Church – if Massius is indeed John Massey.

5 *bonus*: the *vir bonus* of Roman tradition, a man morally good (usually someone whose opinions and principles accorded with your own – in Pitcairne's terms, a respectable Episcopalian). Massey seems never to have considered a return to Anglicanism.

50

Notes. From spring 1692 until summer 1693 Pitcairne was resident in Leiden as Professor of the Practice of Medicine. The epigram expresses astonishment at Dutch success in reclaiming land from the sea.

The reference in (a) is to Jacopo Sannazaro (1458–1530), a noted humanist of the Italian and French Renaissance, and in particular to his epigram, *De mirabile urbe Venetiis*: *Viderat Hadriacis Venetam Neptunus in undis/ stare urbem et toto ponere iura mari./ 'nunc mihi Tarpeias quantumvis Iuppiter arces/ obiice, et illa tui moenia Martis', ait;/ 'Si pelago Tybrim praefers, urbem aspice utramque,/ illam homines dices, hanc posuisse deos.'* (McFarlane, *Renaissance Latin Poetry*, 26). Men built Rome, the Gods Venice, but the Dutch outdid even the Gods by reclaiming the Netherlands from the sea. Under this title, the epigram is another example of the topos *taceat superata vetustas*; cf. **47**, introductory note.

Title (b) *Belgas*: in classical times the Belgae occupied lands to the north of the Seine and Marne. Pitcairne's emphasis on land-reclamation makes it clear that the Dutch are here intended.

2/8 *Immensæque ... molis*: for construction and sentiment cf. *Aeneid* 1, 33: *tantae molis erat Romanam condere gentem*.

3–4/9–10 *Di ... fuit/ erat*: Pitcairne assumes elements of Newtonian cosmology: 'Bodies projected in our air suffer no resistance but from the air. Withdraw the air, as is done in Mr Boyle's vacuum, and the resistance ceases; for in this void a bit of fine down and a piece of solid gold descend with equal velocity. And the same arguments must apply to the celestial spaces above the earth's atmosphere' (Cajori, *Newton's Principia*, 543). Pitcairne assumes that the same conditions existed at the Creation.

6 *Hi ... Diis*: See following note.

12 *obstantes ... Deos*: the hyperbole may be ironic. Pitcairne hated the Dutch King William's seizure of the British throne from his father-in-law, King James. Cheating or outmanoeuvring the gods was generally regarded as *hubris*, which, Pitcairne may be suggesting, is characteristic of the Dutch.

51

Notes. James Dalrymple (1619–1695), 1st Viscount Stair, Lord Glenluce and Stranraer, was born on the paternal estate in Ayrshire. He studied at Glasgow University, where later (1641–1647) he became regent in philosophy. He was called to the Scottish Bar in 1648, and was one of the commissioners for the administration of justice in Scotland under the Protectorate. After the Restoration, he continued in office. In 1671 he became Lord President of the Court of Session, but in 1681 retired and in 1682 fled to Holland, from which in 1688 he returned with King William. He was reappointed Lord President, remaining in office until his death. In 1690 he was made a Viscount.

In 1681 he published the *Institutions of the Laws of Scotland*, an enlarged edition of which appeared in 1693. 'Stair's *Institutions* has always been regarded as the supreme text on the law of Scotland, in which rules are derived from their underlying principles and their sources in Roman, canon, and feudal law. It remains of the highest authority and in default of contrary later authority is deemed to settle the law' (Walker, *Companion to Law, s.v.*; see too D.M. Walker [ed.], *The Institutions of the Law of Scotland* [Edinburgh and Glasgow, 1981]).

Stair had five sons, four of whom became distinguished lawyers. The eldest, John (1648–1707), was Lord Advocate (1686–1688; 1690–1691), Lord Justice Clerk (1688–1689), and joint Secretary of State for Scotland (1690–1695). His part in the Glencoe Massacre led ultimately to his dismissal. He became 1st Earl of Stair in 1703.

The second son, James, was one of the principal clerks of the Court of Session, but is better remembered as an antiquary. In 1698 he was created a baronet of Nova Scotia.

For the third, Hew (1653–1737), see **53**, introductory note.

A fourth son, Thomas, became physician to Queen Anne. Pitcairne ignores him.

For the fifth and youngest son, David, see **52**, introductory note.

The poem reads as if written immediately after Stair's death. As noted in the Introduction and in **75**, introductory note, Viscount Stair, together with Gilbert Burnet, nominated Pitcairne to the Leiden chair. Even more than Burnet, Stair belonged to the political and ecclesiastical camp opposed to Pitcairne; Lockhart, for instance (*Scotland's Ruine*, 58–59), calls John 'the Judas of his country,' adding 'And what has been said of him may serve for a character of his two brothers, Sir Hugh and Sir David Dalrymple, yea the whole name, only with this difference:

that though they were all equally willing, yet not equally capable of doing so much evil as his lordship.' It is interesting that the present poem and the two following are so unlike that addressed to Burnet.

4 *Phœbus uterque*: Apollo under two aspects, as god of light and reason, and as god of poetry and music. Compare Martial, *Liber Spectaculorum*, 13, 5: *numen utriusque Dianae*, Diana as goddess of childbirth and of the chase; more distantly Catullus, 31, 3: *uterque Neptunus*, Neptune as god of fresh and of salt waters.
7 *Quatuor ... fulmina nostri*: cf. Aeneid 6, 842–843: *geminos, duo fulmina belli,/ Scipiadae*.
9 *animasque quaternas*: Pitcairne outdoes the Platonic concept of the triple soul (*Republic* 4, 434d–441c).
11 *togæ*: the robe of the lawyer or judge; by metonymy, the legal profession.

52

Notes. Sir David Dalrymple of Hailes (c. 1665–1721) was James Dalrymple's fifth son (**51**, introductory note). He was admitted to the Faculty of Advocates in 1688. He acted successfully for the defence when Pitcairne appeared before the Privy Council in January 1700. Later in the same year he was made a baronet. He represented Culross in the Union Parliament (1703–1707), where he became Solicitor-General. In 1706 he became one of the Commissioners for Union, and was subsequently elected to the first Parliament of Great Britain, serving as member for Haddington burghs from 1708 to his death. In August/September 1707 he fell into 'an universal rheumatism', for which he was successfully treated by Pitcairne (Johnston, *Best of our owne*, 48, 51, letters 32, 35). In 1709 he purchased Broughton House, afterwards known as Newhailes. In Parliament he served as Lord Advocate, 1709–1711, 1714–1720, and as Auditor-General of the Exchequer in Scotland, 1720–1721. In 1714 he produced a pirated edition of Lockhart's *Memoirs of the Union*, to which he wrote a hostile preface (*Scotland's Ruine*, 262–272). The publication effectively drove Lockhart from the political scene.

The impressive library wing at Newhailes was begun during the last three years of Dalrymple's life. Like Pitcairne he was a bibliophile, although politically almost completely his opposite.

The poem was probably written after Dalrymple's successful defence of Pitcairne in 1700.

1 *Patronus*: 'Advocate.' for this use cf., e.g., Cicero, *Pro Roscio Amerino*, 2, 5: *his de causis ego huic causae patronus exstiti*.
3 *Solvere conantem postico*: meaning obscure to us. The word *posticum* has several meanings, 'backdoor', 'back part of a building', 'privy', 'backside, arse'. Pitcairne may be exploiting all the possibilities.

4 *Medico*: Pitcairne, the defendant.
Judicibusque: the Lords of the Privy Council.

53

Metre. Hendecasyllabics.
Notes. Sir Hew Dalrymple (1652–1737), Lord North Berwick, was the third son of the 1st Viscount Stair; see **51**, introductory note. In 1698 he succeeded his father as Lord President of the Court of Session, a position which he held until his death. In 1712 he gave judgement in the case between Principal Middleton of King's College, Aberdeen, and Professors Bower and Gordon (**58**, introductory note). The poem, an imitation of Catullus 49 (cf. **6**), commemorates the professors' victory. The poem, like that of Catullus, may be sarcastic.

54

Notes. The Hon. William Carmichael of Skirling was younger son of John, 2nd Lord Carmichael, 1st Earl of Hyndford (1638–1710). He was admitted to the Faculty of Advocates in 1695.

2 *Frangere ... mero*: cf. Horace, *Odes*, 2,7, 6–8: *cum quo morantem saepe diem mero/ fregi.*
4 *tuos ... Epicure deos*: according to the philosophy of Epicurus (341–270 BC), the Gods lead a blissful life, unaffected by worldly cares or concerns: cf. Lucretius, 3, 18–24:

> *apparet divum numen sedesque quietae*
> *quas neque concutiunt venti nec nubila nimbis*
> *aspergunt neque nix acri concreta pruina*
> *cana cadens violat semperque innubilus aether*
> *integit, et large diffuso lumine ridet.*
> *Omnia suppeditat porro natura neque ulla*
> *Res animi pacem delibat tempore in ullo.*

55

Metre. Hendecasyllabics.
Notes. This Catullan threnody is for William Moneypenny, son of Sir John Moneypenny of Pitmilly, admitted to the Faculty of Advocates in 1669, readmitted

in 1676. In 1698 he married Margaret, sister of the 11th Lord Ross. He died 31 March 1700 (Grant, *Faculty of Advocates*, 155). He was presumably one of Pitcairne's cronies. The poem was probably written shortly after his death.

Title (a), (c). *J.C.*, *I.C.*: i.e. *Juris-consultum*, 'advocate'.
5 *Monneipennius ... ille*: cf. Catullus 58, 1–2: *Caeli, Lesbia nostra, Lesbia illa, / illa Lesbia*.
11 *in perpetu[um] valete*: cf. Catullus 101, 10: *in perpetuum, frater, aue atque uale*.

56

Notes. We have not identified the Charles Wilson commemorated. The conceit in the final couplet makes it clear that he was a patient who died despite treatment from Pitcairne. *Volusenus* is a humanistic latinization of the name 'Wilson,' most familiar for its application to himself by the Scottish scholar Florence Wilson (c. 1504–post-1551), 'Florentius Volusenus', author of *De Animi Tranquillitate Dialogus* (Lyons, 1543). An edition of this latter was published by Freebairn in 1707 and may have suggested the use of the form to Pitcairne.

1 *Vixisti*: the perfect tense carries the implication, 'You have lived (but are now dead)'.
1–4 *pergratus ... Amica*: note the effective rhetorical interlacing of *pergratus, gratior, Amicis, amatus Amicis, Amica*.
2 *non Musis gratior alter*: i.e., Wilson was himself a poet. The phrase is a distant reminiscence of the opening of Buchanan's epitaph on Florentius Volusenus (*Epigrammata* 2, 12): *Hic Musis Volusene iaces carissime*.
4 *Filia ... Cereris*: i.e., Proserpine, queen of the dead.
7–8 *non totus ... manus*: cf. the same claim in **24**, 5–6, 9–10. Cf. Horace, *Odes* 3, 30, 7: *non omnis moriar*.
10 *Superis*: the living, as opposed to the dead below; also the Gods.

57

Notes. George Ferchard (Farquhar) may be the George Farquhar, indweller of Leith, whose admission as a burgess of Edinburgh is recorded for 17 January 1672 (Boag Watson, *Roll of Burgesses*, 178).

2 *nec ... jugo*: i.e., the wife was as bad as the husband.
5 *Impositumq[ue]*: a mock-heroic reminiscence of *Aeneid* 6, 308: *impositique rogis juvenes*.
6 *pignus Amoris*: ironic; in normal usage a child rather than a gravestone.

COMMENTARY

58

Notes. Despite its title, the poem is as much concerned with Newton as with Thomas Bower MD, who resembled Pitcairne in that he combined medicine with mathematics. Bower is mentioned in several of Pitcairne's letters between 1703 and 1708. In the first (Johnston, *Best of our owne*, 38, letter 18, 1 October 1703) he is described as 'Cheyn's master,' former teacher, that is, of George Cheyne (1671–1743), in later life a well-known London physician. It would appear that Bower taught Cheyne mathematics rather than medicine; for the latter, Cheyne was Pitcairne's own pupil. In 1706 Pitcairne successfully recommended Bower for the chair of mathematics in King's College, Aberdeen, and by 1708 he was established there (*Best of our owne*, 43–45, letters 25, 26, 28; 52, letter 37). At the 1707 Union, Bower with William Paterson and David Gregory was employed to compute the Equivalent, the compensation granted to the Scots for such part of their revenue as went towards paying the English National Debt. The third item in S is a commission from the Earl Marischal (**42**) to Dr Thomas Bower, dated 1710, making the latter Principal of Marischal College, Aberdeen. In 1712 legal action forced Principal Middleton of King's to abandon the claim that the 1690 Act of Visitation did not give two professors, Bower and George Gordon, both holding chairs of comparatively recent foundation, equal rights with professors of the ancient foundation (Lenman, *Jacobite Risings*, 71). Pitcairne's *Dissertationes Medicae* (Edinburgh, 1713) includes a long epistle from Bower to Pitcairne criticizing the theories of the French physician, Astrucius Francus. Bower died in 1717.

The occasion for the poem was probably a visit made to England by Bower which included a meeting with Newton. In a letter dated 25 February 1706 Pitcairne mentions one such visit which involved a call on David Gregory in Oxford. This may have been connected with the calculation of the Equivalent. There is no reference however to Bower also having seen Newton (Johnston, *Best of our owne*, 42, letter 24). Newton, as Master of the Mint, may well have had some hand in the business. The poem may, however, refer to another occasion.

Note how scrupulous Pitcairne is, even in complimentary verses addressed to a Scots mathematician, to maintain the supremacy of Newton; cf. **39**, 21–24; **47**. Bower, he implies, is fortunate to have this opportunity.

This short ode is based on the fifth stanza from one of Horace's most notable 'Roman' odes, *Quem virum aut heroa* (*Odes* 1, 12, 17–20):

Unde nil maius generatur ipso,
Nec viget quicquam simile aut secundum:
Proximos illi tamen occupavit
   Pallas honores.

By implication, Newton is equated with Jupiter, Bower with Pallas Athene.

1 *1*: addressed to Bower.
   Salutatum: supine, of purpose. Combined with a verb of motion, this supine indicates, sometimes half-humorously, a visit to the shrine of some divinity; cf. Plautus, *Bacchides*, 2.3.113: *deos atque amicos iit salutatum ad forum*; Terence, *Phormio*, 311–312: *ego deos penatis hinc salutatum domum/ devortar*.
1–2 *virorum/ Maximum*: Newton.
3 *Cuique ... secundum*: cf. Horace, *Odes* I, 12, 18.
7–8 *Proximus ... honores*: cf. Horace, *Odes* I, 12, 19–20.
8 *Scotus*: Bower.

59

Metre. Alcaic stanza.
Notes. One of these poems is an adaptation of the other, but we have not been able to establish priorities, partly because we have found no information on either Andrew Tenant or Thomas Kinkaid's brother. For Thomas Kinkaid himself, see **37, 38**. For Sir Bertram Stott, see **19**(1), **21, 39**, 5–6, **60, 61**. Stott died, probably in 1707; (a) at least must therefore be no later. The conclusion might be regarded as a wry and ironic anticipation of Dr Johnson's remark (Boswell, *Life of Johnson*, A.D. 1763, Ætat. 54): 'The noblest prospect which a Scotchman ever sees, is the high road that leads him to England.'

(a)

2–3 *diurnis ... morantes*: cf. 'The very best way to lengthen the day is to steal a few hours from the night, my love'.
4 *Lyæum*: Bacchus; see **38**, 4n.
5 *ditem ... Angliam*: rich, by comparison with the poverty of Scotland, especially after the failure of the Darien scheme.
6 *Romæ ... æmulam*: i.e., the present time of the poem is the English Augustan period.
7 *nuper*: the adverb modifies both *spreto* and *placentem*.
11 *Musasque*: i.e., poems, like the present one, begging him to return to Scotland.
15 *cælos*: the syntax here is something of a puzzle.
   supellex: literally 'household utensils', 'furniture'; here perhaps the word is used in the sense 'qualification'; we have ventured to translate 'gifts'.
16 *Pallade ... tumentem*: the reference is to the poets and prose-writers of the English Augustan period.
   Pallade: the goddess Minerva or Pallas Athene, patron of learning and the arts.

(b)

1 *Thoma ... decus*: cf. opening line of **38**. The first stanza is in effect a summary of that poem, set in deliberate contrast to the remainder of the ode.

60

Notes. For Stott; see **19** (i), **21**, 14 and n: **39**, 5–6: **61**. SRO, MK, GD.*124* is taken from a letter to the Earl of Mar, dated 20 September 1707 and is introduced by the words: 'I send Your Lordship poor Stote's epitaph made by Wattie Danniston' (Johnston, *Best of our owne*, 48, letter 31). It thus seems likely that Stott died in the late summer of that year. Dennistoun is, of course, well-known as a joking pseudonym for Pitcairne.

The junction of the word *Anglum* to Stott's name in the title and *Scotus* to Pitcairne's in the final note of authorship is probably deliberate.

4 *Superis ... parem*: cf. Horace, *Odes* 1, 6, 16: *superis parem*.
4–5 *valuere ... valere*: note the effective verbal balance of the words.
5 *valere*: the usual formula in farewells to the dead; cf., e.g., *Aeneid* 11, 98: *aeternumque vale*.
6 *Deliciasque ... suae*: cf. Horace, *Odes* 1, 3, 8: *animae dimidium meae*. For *delicias* cf. particularly the words used by Suetonius ('Titus', 1) to introduce his account of that emperor: *amor et deliciae generis humani*.

61

Notes. The epigram plays on attributes of the supreme god, Jupiter. As Optimus [Maximus] he is all-just and all-powerful. As god of the sky he is Jupiter Pluvius, who controls the rain. The rain has shut away the sun, Phoebus, from the world, just as death has shut away the sun of Stott's presence from Pitcairne. *Il pleure dans mon coeur/ Comme il pleut sur la ville.*

62

Notes. The Ladies Barbara and Margaret Stewart were twin daughters of Charles, Jacobite 4th Earl of Traquair (d. 1741); they were born 3 September 1708. Margaret died in 1791, Barbara in 1794. Neither married. See 'The Ladies of Traquair,' Chambers, *Traditions*, 286–287.

2   *Cromvelli*: Oliver Cromwell died 3 September 1658. For supporters of the Stuarts the anniversary was a festival. The birth of the twins made it even more festal. Cf. too **77**.

3–4   *Quam … procos*: the twins are identical; distinguishing one from the other is problematical now and will be more so in the future.

63

Notes. The Royal Company of Archers was founded in 1676 and received a charter from Queen Anne in 1707. After the Revolution, the membership was largely Jacobite. The prize for the annual competition held in August was (and is) the Silver Arrow of Musselburgh, won by David Drummond in 1687 and 1707 (*Bond Book of the Royal Company of Archers*, National Archives of Scotland, ref. B52/11/5). The epigram refers to the 1707 competition.

David Drummond (1656–1741) was son of David Drummond, minister of Moneydie, Strathearn, and brother of Dr John Drummond (**37**, 1 and n.). Like Pitcairne, he was born on Christmas Day (cf. **64**, 10). He was admitted to the Faculty of Advocates in 1683, and until 5 June 1688 is more than once mentioned in Faculty minutes, usually in connection with the Advocates' Library. Thereafter, and probably significantly, his name disappears. In 1700 he became treasurer of the Bank of Scotland (founded 1695), a post which he held to his death. He 'was notoriously a Jacobite and treasurer of the funds raised to assist the defence of the Jacobite prisoners' (Lenman, *Jacobite Risings*, 227).

On 20 February 1701 Pitcairne mentions the Drummond brothers in a letter to David Gregory (Johnston, *Best of our owne*, 35, letter 14): 'I have not got what yee wrote 10 days befor this about Mr James Hay. pray write it, if yee can, & put it under a cover to Dr Drummond to be found at the bank-office, where he stays with his brother Mr David treasurer to the bank.'

3   *Phœbe*: the god Phœbus Apollo was archer as well as poet and musician. The full point of the line, however, remains obscure. Pitcairne may be hinting that Drummond, aged 51, required something beyond his own powers to win the prize. The line may also have Jacobite significance. Phœbus with his bow was a slayer of monsters, monsters such as the possibility of a Hanoverian succession. Pitcairne may mean no more than that Drummond shot as if he were himself Phoebus.

COMMENTARY

64

Metre. Sapphic stanza.
Notes. For David Drummond, see **63**. The ode was written after the failure of the 1708 Jacobite attempt and the death of David Gregory and 'Bevelus' later in the same year. Both events probably contributed to the despondent tone, resembling that of **39**, written at much the same time. Both contain an episode set in the next world, but here Pitcairne himself, rather than Gregory, is the new arrival.

1 *mimum*: cf. Seneca, *Epistulae* 80, 7: *hic humanae vitae mimus, qui nobis partes, quas male agamus, adsignat*. The idea became a medieval and Renaiissance commonplace – 'All the world's a stage.'
3 *rei nobis reliquæ*: probably the Jacobite cause.
7 *Catoni*: i.e., the deceased James VII; cf. **10**, 4.
10 *natalis … meusque*: Pitcairne was born 25 December 1652.
13 *Beveli*: not identified.
19 *Graium*: see **31**, 33n., **39**.
21 *Priorum*: see **22**, introductory note.
22 *Addisonum*: Joseph Addison (1672–1719). Probably refers to his Latin verse and his *Letter from Italy*; his best known works, the papers for the *Spectator* and his tragedy *Cato*, are later than this poem. While it is not impossible, there is no actual evidence that Pitcairne and Addison were acquainted. Their political views were very different.
25 *Borelli*: Giovanni Alfonso Borelli (1608–1679), Italian physiologist and physicist, founder of the iatrophysical school of medicine.
26 *Bellini*: Lorenzo Bellini (1643–1704), Italian physician and anatomist who described the collecting, or excretory, tubules of the kidney, known as Bellini's ducts.
Pitcairne regarded Borelli and Bellini as his own immediate medical predecessors.
27–28 *astrum/ Gregorianum*: the spirit of David Gregory and perhaps that of his uncle, James Gregorie (1658–1675).
33–34 *Et quod … caræ*: i.e., continue our support for the Pretender.
36 *Una, Dromondi*: the final Adonic echoes the first, bringing the poem to a rounded and effective conclusion.

65

Notes. Sir William Bennet of Grubbet and Wideopen, Roxburghshire, is a somewhat shadowy figure. In 1647 he succeeded his father, William Bennet, who combined the offices of laird and parish minister. He was made a baronet in 1670. He died c. 1710 (*Complete Baronetage*, 4, 279–280).

POEM 67

Lack of biographical detail makes exposition of the poem difficult. It would appear that Pitcairne was Bennet's physician as well as his friend, perhaps that Bennet had been charmingly successful in concealing his medical condition from Pitcairne, at the same time entertaining him lavishly. The final couplet refers to Sir William's son and heir, also William Bennet, on whom see next poem.

66

Notes. The poem is a variant of the preceding, whether subsequent or prior is not clear.

6 *Filius*: Sir William Bennet, 2nd baronet, who had been a captain in the army and had attended King William from Holland in 1688. He was member for Roxburghshire in the Scottish parliament 1693–1707, and in the Westminster parliament 1707–1708 (*Complete Baronetage*, 4, 279–280). He is addressed in a series of Latin poems by Sir William Scott of Thirlestane (*SP*, 111–113, 119, 119–120 [in fact, 122], 130–132) and another by John Kerr (*SP*, 144–145).

67

Notes. Andrew Fletcher of Saltoun, East Lothian (1653–1716), statesman and political philosopher, now best known for his reasoned opposition to the 1707 Union, was not a Jacobite, but was imprisoned after the abortive 1708 rising. On his release he retired to his Saltoun estate, devoting himself to farming and agricultural improvement. As part of this he encouraged James Meikle to study Dutch agricultural methods. On his return to Scotland in 1710, Meikle constructed a winnowing machine and barley mill at Saltoun, both notable early contributions to the Agricultural Revolution (*OxfDNB*; D. Daiches [ed.], *Andrew Fletcher of Saltoun Selected Writings and Speeches* [ASLS, Edinburgh, 1979], xli). This is the aspect of Fletcher's work extravagantly, perhaps satirically, praised by Pitcairne.

Fletcher and Pitcairne were acquainted, as the following anecdote shows: 'Being in company with the witty Dr. Pitcairn, the conversation turned on a person of learning whose history was not distinctly known. "I knew the man well," said Fletcher, "he was hereditary professor of divinity at Hamburgh." " *Hereditary* professor!" said Pitcairn with a laugh of astonishment and derision. "Yes, Doctor," replied Fletcher, "hereditary professor of divinity. What think you of a hereditary king?"' (*Essays on the Lives and Writings of Fletcher of Saltoun and the Poet Thomson: Biographical, Critical, and Political*, by D.S. [David Steuart] Earl of Buchan [London, 1792], quoted in Daiches, *ut cit.*, xix).

Title *Regulo*, 'kinglet,' may be intended ironically; see immediately above.

COMMENTARY

1   *repetita ... Proserpina*: Pitcairne invented the unwillingness of Proserpine to return.
Matrem: Ceres.
3   *Nondum ... Saltonius*: i.e., the future Laird of Saltoun was still in the underworld awaiting incarnation, like the future heroes of Rome in *Aeneid* 6, 756–892. Proserpine refused to leave because Fletcher was still in her subterranean realm.

68

Metre. (a)–(d), elegiac couplet; (e), hendecasyllabic.
Notes. In (a)–(d) the subject of the verse-correspondence is George Henry Hay (1689–1758), who in 1709, on the succession of his father, Thomas Hay (c. 1660–1719) as 7th Earl of Kinnoull, became titular Viscount Dupplin. Later in 1709 Dupplin married Abigail, second daughter of the now Tory and Jacobite politician Robert Harley (1661–1724), who in 1711 became 1st Earl of Oxford and Mortimer. Abigail is the Pallas (Minerva) of (d) and (e). In the 1710 election to the House of Commons Dupplin became Member for Fawley in Cornwall. Later, in December 1711, he became Baron Hay of Pedwardine, Herefordshire, one of the twelve peers created by Harley and St John to ensure a majority in the House of Lords for the Treaty of Utrecht (1713). In 1715–1716 he was briefly imprisoned in the Tower on suspicion of Jacobitism. In 1719 he succeeded his father as 8th Earl of Kinnoull.

Dupplin is flatteringly styled Maecenas after the Roman statesman (d. 8 BC) who was friend and patron of Virgil, Horace and Propertius. Virgilian and Horatian reminiscences strengthen the association. The nomenclature has a certain point. Dupplin and his father, for instance, are both included in the subscription list for the great edition (1710) of the translation of the *Aeneid* by Gavin Douglas (1474–1522), an edition printed by Andrew Symson and Robert Freebairn, to the preparation of which Pitcairne (together with Sibbald and Dr John Drummond) gave particular assistance, acknowledged in the Preface. The *Aeneid*, of course, was a kind of Jacobite Bible, and Jacobitism, as already indicated, played a part in the production of the edition, obliquely referred to in (c), 5–8.

In 1711 Freebairn and his partners were granted a patent as Royal Printer, *Typographus Regius* (A.J. Mann, *The Scottish Book Trade 1500–1720*, 120–122). It seems likely that Dupplin played some part in obtaining the grant.

We have not been able to identify the Leslie whose name is linked with Freebairn's in (a) and (d).

The precise relationship of (d) to the first three poems is unclear. The general ambience is pretty obviously the same. Like (a), (d) presupposes a request sent by Pitcairne to Dennistoun. In (a) the reference to Horace as immediate adviser, in (d) that to Abigail Harley as Dupplin's wife, shows that at the time of writing Dennistoun was already a well established figure in the Elysian Fields. The reference to Thomas Bower may go some way to keep the two separate. It most probably acknowledges support given to Bower in his dispute with Principal Middleton of King's College, Aberdeen (58, introductory note), a dispute also referred to in (e). This may indicate that (a), (b) and (c) were written in 1711, (d) and (e) somewhat later, in 1712.

(e), as addressed to Thomas Hay rather than his son, stands somewhat apart from the rest, but obviously fits much the same set of circumstances. Only the help given to Bower is specified. Presumably the Earl had no share in the grant of the patent to Freebairn and whatever service was performed for Leslie. Both (d) and (e) strongly suggest that the influence of Abigail Harley affected the actions of her husband and father-in-law.

The poems are no more than ingenious flattery, flattery however at least not intended to bring Pitcairne any personal advantage. The exchange of letters and the fiction of Dennistoun's participation lends a certain charm.

(a)

2   *Columenque*: cf. Horace, *Odes* 2, 17, 4: *columenque rerum* (addressed to Maecenas).
3   *Flaccus*: Horace – Quintus Horatius Flaccus, with whom, Dennistoun's words suggest, he has recently been in conversation.
7   *Fribarnum*: see above, introductory note.
8   *Leslaeique*: not identified.
9   *dexter*: cf. *Aeneid* 8, 302: *dexter adi*.

(b)

4   *Romanae Fidicen Lyrae*: cf. Horace, *Odes* 4, 3, 23: *Romanae fidicen lyrae*.
5   *majus ... aude*: cf. *Aeneid* 10, 811: *majoraque viribus audes*.
6   *nostro ... ore*: i.e., Virgil alone is capable of singing Dupplin's praises; cf. below, (c), 5–6.

(c)

5   *Ille*: i.e., Gavin Douglas. Cf. 20, II, 11–12.
6   ARMA VIRUMQUE: the opening words of the *Aeneid*.

(d)

Title   Εὐχαίρειν: more properly Εὖ χαίρειν. In classical Greek idiom, letters began with χαίρειν (λέγει understood). The εὖ, 'well,' is redundant. The formula corresponds to the Latin *S.D.*, *Salutem dat* or *dicit*.
3   *serus ... redibit*: cf. Horace, *Odes* 1, 2, 45: *serus in caelum redeas* (of Augustus).

COMMENTARY

5 *Boëro*: Thomas Bower (58, introductory note).
6 *egeat ... tuæ*: cf. the phrase of Ennius, quoted in Cicero, *Tusculan Disputations* 3, 19, 44: *opis egens tuae*.
7 *Britannâ ... Pallada*: i.e., Abigail Harley; see introductory note. The Greek Pallas Athena was equated with the Roman Minerva, goddess of wisdom in all its forms, also of spinning and weaving.
8 *ritu ... Nestoris*: the longevity of the Homeric Nestor was proverbial; cf. Statius, *Silvae* 1, 3, 110: *finem Nestoriae precor egrediare senectae*; cf. also 40(a), 9n.

Conclusion *Dabam ... Elysia*: Horace often refers to his villa at Tibur, the Sabine farm; see, e.g., *Epistles* 1, 16, 1–16. Dennistoun writes from the posthumous equivalent in the Elysian Fields.

(e)

1 *nuruque*: i.e., Abigail Harley.
2 *annuisset*: literally 'had nodded (assent to).' Pallas Athena sprang fully-armed from the head of her father Zeus (Jupiter). The verb is thus appropriate.
4 *Jovis ... ædes*: i.e., his dwelling on Mount Olympus. There may be some covert reference.
10 *Doctis ... ter patronum*: a distant reminiscence of Catullus 49, 6: *quanto tu optimus omnium patronum.*

69

Notes. The poem is a graceful mock-heroic celebration of Anne Stamfield on her birthday. She had been servant to Greppa at Pitcairne's favourite Greping-office and on the death of the latter succeeded to her lease; see 9, 27n, 19(i), 36 and n, 38, 46.

1 *Sibyllino ... in Antro*: i.e., the Greping-office; for the reference cf. *Aeneid* 6, 10–11: *horrendaeque procul secreta Sibyllae, / antrum immane*. Anne too lives in the depths and thus corresponds to the prophetic Sibyl. Cf. too 19(a), 33–34.
2 *responsis ... beas*: she responds to her customers' requests for drink as the Sibyl did to requests for oracles. Unlike the Sibyl's, her responses are always favourable.
4 *Mulcentem Tygres*: cf. *Georgics* 4, 509 (of the song of Orpheus): *mulcentem tigres*; for the figure cf. also 39, 6.
5 *avena*: a Scottish touch; cf. Johnson's *Dictionary* (1755): '*Oats*. a grain which in England is generally given to horses, but in Scotland supports the people.'

70

Notes. For the Royal Company of Archers see **63**, introductory note. Robert Freebairn (c. 1685–c. 1740) won the Silver Arrow in 1712 (*Bond Book*). Freebairn was a printer and publisher, granted a royal patent in 1711; see **68**, introductory note. He printed SP and other works by Pitcairne.

2 *rediviva*: Freebairn belonged to the Jacobite party, whose hopes were high in 1712. The word *rediviva* may indicate such hopes.
3 *Drommondum*: David Drummond; see **63**, introductory note.
Kinkadiumque: Thomas Kinkaid; see **37**, 1n. He belonged to the Royal Company of Archers, witnessing the record of the winner of the Silver Arrow in 1687 and 1708 (*Bond Book*).

71

Notes. The elder John Reid operated a printing-house in Edinburgh between 1680 and 1716. His son, the younger John Reid, was active between c. 1699 and 1719 (Aldis, *Books Printed in Scotland*, 119). In Edinburgh several other Reids were active as printers between 1720 and 1750, but we have found no trace of an Archibald. He was probably son of the younger John Reid. The epigram may mark the completion of his apprenticeship to the trade of his father and grandfather.

The epigram exhibits remarkable, perhaps ironic, hopefulness, written, as it was, a few months before Pitcairne's death.

72

Notes. John Maitland, 2nd Earl, 1st (and only) Duke of Lauderdale, was Charles II's corrupt and devious Secretary of State for Scotland 1661–1680. The post was London-based, but from 1669 he combined it with the office of Lord High Commissioner, the king's personal representative, based in Edinburgh during sessions of the Scottish parliament. In England he was a member of the notorious Cabal (1667–1674), the standing committee for foreign affairs which became responsible for much of the process of government. Although personally inclined to Presbyterianism, he attempted to destroy Scottish opposition to Episcopalianism by alternate measures of conciliation and repression, thus gaining the hatred of the Covenanters. Notably he was responsible in 1678 for the quartering of the "Highland Host" on ecclesiastical dissidents in the south-west. He survived a number of attempts to remove him from office, including the affair of the Act of Billeting (1662), planned by Sir George Mackenzie of Tarbat (Donaldson, *Scotland. James V- James VII*, 376; see also **6**, **88**). Another opponent was Sir

George Mackenzie of Rosehaugh (see above, 5), from 1669 member of parliament for Ross in succession to Tarbat. The English parliament made unsuccessful attempts to impeach him in 1674, 1675, 1677 and 1679. Lauderdale was finally forced from office by the Bothwell Brig rising in 1679 and his own ill-health. The poem deliberately ignores his political activities, restricting its satire to the close personal relationship between Lauderdale and the king. Lauderdale died at Tunbridge Wells, Kent, on 20 or 24 August 1682, and on 5 April 1683 was buried at Haddington, East Lothian, near the ancestral Maitland property of Lethington (now Lennoxlove). The poem was presumably written about this time.

1   *Ille ego*: according to Donatus and Servius, these were the words with which Virgil originally opened the *Aeneid*: *Ille ego, qui quondam gracili modulatus avena*. They are parodied in the introduction to Book 2 of Ovid's *Amores*: *Hoc quoque composui Paelignis natus aequosis/ ille ego nequitiae Naso poeta meae*. Lauderdale assumes for himself a mock-poetic and mock-heroic importance.
3   The deliberate syllabic consonance of *vitæ par vita peractæ* is striking, but cannot easily be rendered into English.
4   *Ditis*: Dis or Pluto, ruler of the underworld.

73

Notes. The poem is a celebration of the 55th birthday of James VII on 14 October 1688 and the birth on 10 June of the same year of his son, James Francis, Prince of Wales, later the Old Pretender. The birthday became a Jacobite festival. Cf., e.g., **12, 37, 103**. Cf. too Dryden's almost contemporary *Britannia Rediviva, A Poem on the Prince Born on the 10th of June, 1688* (London, 1688), in which at much greater length he makes the same point as Pitcairne.

The unintended final effect is ironic. On 5 November 1688 William of Orange landed with his forces at Brixham in Devon. James with his wife and son left Whitehall on 11 December and after some misadventures arrived in France on Christmas Day.

1   *Septime*: 'seventh,' i.e., James VII.
2   *Carolo*: Charles II, elder brother of James VII.
4   *adesse*: 'come to your aid,' by apparently ensuring the succession and the future prosperity of the country under a legitimate king.

74

Notes. On 13 February 1689 the English parliament offered the throne to William and his wife, James VII's eldest daughter, Mary. On 4 April the Scottish parliament, with five dissentients, voted that James had forfeited the crown, and on 11 April received the Claim of Right. On 11 May William and Mary accepted the crown of Scotland. The poem is a lament over this sequence of events and the agents who caused it, addressed to Phoebus, god of light and poetry. It was probably written shortly after the event.

1 *Manes ... sepultos*: primarily perhaps Lockhart and Claverhouse; see **3**, **4**; possibly also Mackenzie of Rosehaugh, **5**. But the reference may be more extended, including such figures as Charles I and II.
2 *superi*: for this usage, cf. *Aeneid* 6, 481–482: *Hic multum fleti ad superos, belloque caduci/ Dardanidae*. The *superi* are Issachar and Ios, below, **11**, **13**. Pitcairne may also intend a reference to the god Phoebus, to whom the poem is addressed.
6 *Quot Bardi*: Dryden was deprived of his laureateship in 1689. Pitcairne may have this in mind. Equally probable is a reference to the many deprivations in the Scottish church and universities.
8 *pater*: Jupiter.
10 *Cretes*: Cretans were proverbially regarded as liars; see Titus 1:12.
11 *Issachar*: see **42**, 7 and n. 'To the consternation of all' (Ferguson, *Scotland 1689 to the Present*, 2), the supposedly Jacobite Duke of Hamilton was chosen by William to represent him in the Convention of Estates (Parliament) which opened on 14 March 1689.
12 *Cananæum*: the Canaanites were the pre-Israelitish inhabitants of Palestine, opposed to the incomers. Here in effect the situation has been reversed.
13 *Ios*: cf. **93** (a), 3. Ios is probably John (*Ioannes*) Churchill (1650–1722), from 9 April 1689 5th Earl, later 1st Duke, of Marlborough. Churchill, like Hamilton, had been an associate and friend of James VII and II, but transferred his allegiance almost immediately on William's invasion.
14 *Batavo ... salo*: the Batavians are the Dutch who flooded (rather than drained) the British meadows.
prata Britanna: cf. **11**, 1–3n, 3n.
15 *tristia*: verses like Ovid's *Tristia*, written in and about exile.
16 *plusquam ... opus*: cf. Propertius, 2, 66: *nescio quid maius nascitur Iliade*, referring to Virgil's still uncompleted *Aeneid*. For Jacobites Aeneas in his wanderings, and the prophesied greatness of his descendents, became a type of the exiled Stuarts and their eventual hypothetical glorious restoration.
18 *Prior*: for Pitcairne's relationship with Matthew Prior, see **22**, **Text**. He is mentioned only once in Pitcairne's extant correspondence (Johnston, *Best of our owne*, 66, letter 53), but is called Pitcairne's 'old comrade' in a letter written shortly after Pitcairne's death by Dr John Drummond to Thomas Bower. In

the 1690s and early 1700s his verses were strongly Williamite; see especially his '*Carmen Seculare* for the year 1700'; later he became a Tory. Pitcairne may be deferring to Prior's ability as a Latin poet (though this seems extremely unlikely), or he may be emphasizing (in a playful way?) how far Prior's political views differed from his own.

75

Notes. As is shown by the title in (b), **G.B.** in (a) is Gilbert Burnet (1643–1715), Bishop of Salisbury, today best known for the posthumous *History of His Own Times* (4 vols., London, 1724–1753). Burnet was born in Edinburgh and in 1657 graduated MA of Marischal College, Aberdeen. In 1661 he was licensed to preach and in 1665 became minister of Saltoun, East Lothian. From 1669 to 1674 he was also professor of divinity at Glasgow University. Most of his time thereafter was spent in England. The accession of King James in 1685 forced him to leave the country and he was eventually invited to Holland by William and Mary. In 1688 he returned as one of William's adherents. On 23 December of that year he preached a sermon at St James's on the text 'This is the Lord's doing and it is marvellous in our eyes' (*Psalm* 118:23). On 31 March 1689 he was consecrated Bishop of Salisbury. The non-juring Archbishop of Canterbury, William Sancroft (1617–1693), refused to consecrate him, but was 'prevailed upon' to grant a commission for the purpose to the bishops of the province. Sancroft was himself deprived in February 1690.

In politics Burnet was a Whig, in theology a latitudinarian – both positions anathema to Pitcairne. His episcopate, according to ODCC, was 'a model of zeal and activity.'

In 1691, curiously enough, Pitcairne obtained his Leiden chair on a joint nomination by Burnet and another notable Whig and former Dutch exile, James Dalrymple, 1st Viscount Stair (**51**). Perhaps Burnet's latitudinarianism allowed him to support Pitcairne's candidature.

The poem is obviously directed against Burnet, but he is not the sole target; also involved in (a) is Jupiter, a reference probably to Sancroft, and his failure, as archbishop, to prevent Burnet's consecration. Pitcairne however recognizes Sancroft's underlying sympathy towards the Jacobite cause; if he changes his mind and deprives Burnet – if, as Jove, he strikes him with a thunderbolt – the community will once more recognize his supreme authority.

In (b) Jupiter has been replaced by Vejovis, 'anti-Jupiter,' an obscure Roman deity in whose name the privative and pejorative particle *ve-* has been prefixed to the oblique stem of *Ju*[*piter*], gen. *Jovis*. Ovid (*Fasti* 3, 429–448) records under 7 March the consecration of his temple on the Capitoline; for Pitcairne the date may be significant in terms of Sancroft's behaviour. In Ovid, Vejovis is the young Jupiter – *Iuppiter est iuvenis*, 437 – who as yet had no thunderbolts –

fulmina nulla tenet, 438. This weapon he learned to use only when he had to repel the assault of the Giants on Olympus. Burnet corresponds to the Giants on whom Sancroft, as he matures to become the adult Jupiter, should let loose his weapon.

Vejovis is also regarded as an underworld power. Macrobius (*Saturnalia* 3, 9, 9–14) records a formal curse to devote a hostile city or territory to destruction, a curse which begins with an invocation of the chthonian powers, *Dis pater*, *Vejovis* and the *Manes*. In this context note particularly ll. 5–6, where Vejovis and Styx, the river of the underworld, appear together. If Sancroft exerts his authority, he will become an Olympian as opposed to a chthonian divinity.

Pitcairne combines elements both from Ovid and from Macrobius.

Both (a) and (b) were probably written in the spring of 1689. As more convoluted, (b) is perhaps the later.

5(b). *fulmine*: see introductory material above.
6(b). *Jovis*: not gen. sg. of *Jupiter* but nom. of *Vejovis* with *ve-* removed. The effect, however, is that Vejovis becomes Jupiter.

76

Metre. Sapphic stanza.
Notes. The two poems are parodies, 'Imitations', of Horace, *Odes*, 1, 12, *Quem virum aut heroa*, in which the poet celebrates the divine patrons of Rome, in particular Jupiter Optimus Maximus and the heroic figures who have defended and fostered the state, a sequence culminating in Jupiter's deputy on earth, the first emperor, Augustus. Pitcairne finds a comic and satiric parallel in the Presbyterian establishment, finally established by the packed November 1690 General Assembly of the Scottish church. The part of Jupiter is taken by William Lindsay (1644–1698), 18th earl of Crawford and 2nd earl of Lindsay, who became president of the Scottish parliament in 1689 and in 1690 one of the commissioners for settling the government of the church. He was a single-minded adherent of 'the old resolutioner policies' (Ferguson, *Scotland 1689 to the Present*, 1), and became 'the personification of official integrity whilst in fact creating a screen behind which zealous Presbyterians, with his connivance and even active cooperation, purged the Scottish Church' (P.W.J. Riley, *King William and the Scottish Politicians* [Edinburgh, 1979], 36). Pitcairne saw him as a farcical figure: in *The Assembly* he is Lord Whigridden, 'a *Presbyterian* Peer, a rigid Fool' ('Drammatis [sic] Personae', Tobin, *Assembly*, 34); for his appearance in *Babell* see **80**, **Notes**.

The Moderator (Chairman) of the 1690 Assembly, Hugh Kennedy, corresponds to Augustus. He was MA, Glasgow 1641, minister of West Calder, West Lothian, 1643; deposed, 1660. He returned in 1687 as a consequence of the proclamation of toleration by James VII. In the same year he was translated to Trinity College

Church, Edinburgh. Other individuals, not always now readily recognisable, are set against the demi-gods and heroes of Roman tradition.

Horace's poem has 15 stanzas, 60 lines. Pitcairne's first version, 10 stanzas, 40 lines, is substantially shorter. The second version, 14 stanzas, 56 lines, comes closer to Horace. In it he portrays more of his contemporaries in satirical contrast to figures of the Roman past and present.

The poem was composed in late 1690 or early in the following year.

(a)

1   *Quam pudet Clio memorare gentem?*: contrast in Horace, 1–2: *Quem virum ... sumis celebrare, Clio?*
    Clio: the Muse of history.
2–3 *senum ... vivum*: i.e., young and old, living and dead.
3   *jocosa*: in Horace, 3, 'playful'; less complimentary here.
4   *nomen*: Lindsay or, more probably, Crawford; see below, 26.
5   *Vemiensis antro*: the name 'Wemyss' means 'caves' (Gaelic *uaimh* with English plural -*s*).
5–6 *Vemiensis ... Monimella ... Strutherave*: Wemyss, Monimail and Anstruther are places in the eastern part of Fife associated with the Earl of Crawford or others who shared his beliefs. Lady Anne Wemyss, daughter of Margaret, countess of Wemyss in her own right, was renowned for her Presbyterian rigidity. Her marriage to David Melville or Leslie (1660–1754), 5th Earl of Leven and 2nd Earl of Melville, was much celebrated; see below, 17 and **77**. The couple shared their religious views. The lands and castle of Monimail were purchased by Robert Melville (1528–1621), 1st Lord Melville. George Melville (1636–1707), 4th lord and 1st earl of Melville (below, 23–24) was granted the right to hold two annual fairs in the parish of Monimail. His son, David Melville or Leslie, already mentioned, was born at Monimail.

    In Horace, 5–6, the corresponding locations are Helicon, Pindus and Haemus, places associated with Apollo, the Muses and Orpheus.
7   *insecuta*: the subject is *jocosa ... imago* (3–4).
8   *Rothea*: probably John Hamilton or Leslie (1679–1722), 9th earl of Rothes, by way of his mother, Margaret Hamilton, neé Leslie (d. 1700), countess of Rothes in her own right. He supported the Revolution settlement and was regarded by Jacobites as a turncoat. His grandfather, John Leslie (1630–1681), 7th earl and 1st (and only) duke of Rothes, had been a supporter of Charles II and a notorious persecutor of Covenanters – 'the dissolute Rothes' of 'Wandering Willie's Tale' in Scott's Jacobite tale, *Redgauntlet*. We have found no evidence that Crawford was particularly influenced by Rothes.

    In Horace, 8, the corresponding figure is Orpheus.
8–9 *prius ... prius*: an awkward repetition, not paralleled in Horace.
9   *Parentis*: Crawford. In Horace, 13, Jupiter.

POEM 76

10 *res ... deorum*: i.e., matters of church and state.

11 *turbat*: by his adherence to extreme Presbyterian doctrines and encouragement of action against Episcopalian clergy.

longi ... montis: we have emended *monti* of the MS to *monti*[s]. The reference is obscure, but may be to the lands of the Mount, north-west of Cupar, Fife, in the possession of the branch of the Lindsay family to which Robert Lindsay, the friend of Pitcairne's youth, had belonged; see above, 1. He was no Presbyterian, but it is possible that his younger brother James, who succeeded to the lands, differed in his beliefs.

novitate: Calvinistic doctrine and practice, heresy.

12 *Terruit*: Horace, 16, *temperat*, with reference to the power of Jupiter.

Urbem: Edinburgh, and, by extension, Scotland.

14–15 *Vnde ... secundum*: Horace, 17–18, 'a mighty sentence' (E. Fraenkel, *Horace* [Oxford, 1957], 293); cf. **58**, 3. Crawford is the target.

15–16 *Proximus ... honores*: cf. **58**, 7–8.

16 *Janrus*: not certainly identified. In Horace, 20, the corresponding figure is Pallas (Minerva). Here a possible identification is with James Russell in Kettle (Fife), one of the murderers of Archbishop Sharp on Magus Moor (3 May, 1679). In June 1682, at Talla Linn (Peeblesshire), he founded the exclusive sect known as Russellites which survived into the eighteenth century.

17 *Levine*: David Melville or Leslie(1660–1728), 5th Earl of Leven (Fife) and 2nd Earl of Melville, was born at Monimail (above, 6 and note). He became a soldier of some distinction, entering the service of the elector of Brandenburg through the patronage of Sophia, electress of Hanover. On the continent he raised a regiment of Scots Presbyterian exiles which he brought to England with King William. Soon afterwards they were posted to Scotland. Leven became William's envoy to the Scottish convention of March 1689. At Killiecrankie his regiment, unlike others, did not break and covered the subsequent retreat. He became keeper of Edinburgh Castle and, among other things, commissioner for the plantation of kirks. On 3 September 1691 he married his cousin Anne Wemyss (1675–1702; see above, 5–6 note; **77**). Eventually (1706) he became commander-in-chief Scotland, a post from which he was dismissed in 1712. He looked for favour on the accession of George I, son of his old patron Sophia, electress of Hanover, but suffered disappointment.

Lockhart (*Scotland's Ruine*, 60) says of him: 'David, Earl of Leven, in the beginning of his life was so vain and conceity that he became the jest of all sober men. But as he grew older he overcame that folly in part, and from the proudest became the civilest man alive. He was a man of good parts and sound judgment, but master of no kind of learning. And though he had once the command of a regiment, and was at last created Lieutenant-General and Commander-in-Chief of the forces in this kingdom, yet his courage was much called in question upon sundry accounts not necessary to be mentioned here. He was born and bred an enemy to the royal family, and therefore chearfully embraced, and significantly promoted, everything against its interest. However he was no ways severe, but rather very civil to all the Cavaliers, especially such as were prisoners in the castle of Edinburgh when he was governour. From whence he gained more of their favour than any man in the government.'

For Pitcairne he was a violently comical figure, figuring as Lord Huffy in *The Assembly*, 'A Mere Mad-Cap, *Presbyterian* Peer' (Tobin, *ut cit.* above; Leven is not there recognised as the model), brandishing the whip with which he had 'switched the Lady Mortonhall ... when she reproved him for hunting in her park' (*Babell*, 91; Tobin, *ut cit.*, 49), and using it to disperse his creditors, 'Boatmen, Hirers and Fidlers' (*Ibid.*).

In Horace, 21–24, the corresponding figures are Liber (Bacchus), god of drink, Diana, goddess of the hunt, and Apollo with his vengeful arrows.

18–20 *sævis ... sparsi*: references to Leven's treatment of Lady Mortonhall and the Fife boatmen, as mentioned in the previous note.

21 *Davidem*: David Williamson; see 18. In Horace, 33, the somewhat inappropriate corresponding figure is Romulus, legendary founder and first king of Rome.

22 *Rulæi*: Gilbert Rule (1629?-1701), Presbyterian minister, often in trouble between 1660 and 1688; also a physician (MD Leiden, 1666). In December 1688 he was called to the charge of Old Greyfriars, Edinburgh. In 1690 he became a commissioner for the purging of the University of Edinburgh, of which he became Principal in September of that year, replacing the Episcopalian Alexander Monro (d. 1698).

Rule appears in *The Assembly* as Mr Salathiel Little-sense. Pitcairne disapproved of him and more particularly of his Latin: 'We do not confine ourselves closely to his discourses in the General Assembly, but we take in some of his speeches said in the college this winter. That famous saying of his in a public lecture, *Si aliquis virus colebit falsum Deum, seu verum Deum, ut non præscriptum est, iste virus est guiltus idolatriæ*, is so known through the town, that he is nicknamed Doctor Guiltus from that very thing'.

The *quieta/ regna* (21–22) of Rule are presumably Old Greyfriars church and the University. In Horace, 33–34, the corresponding figure is Numa Pompilius, legendary second king of Rome, who is said to have instituted many state religious practices and institutions.

23 *Labii*: not identified. 'Law' is merely a guess. In Horace, 34–35, the corresponding figure is one of the Tarquinii, legendary Etruscan kings of Rome.

23–24 *Georgii/ Pauperis aurum*: reference uncertain, perhaps to George Melville (1636–1707), 4th Lord Melville and 1st earl of Melville. He joined the Duke of Monmouth the day before the defeat of the Covenanters at Bothwell Brig (1679). He was suspected of involvement in the Rye House Plot (1683) to obtain the succession of Monmouth, illegitimate but Protestant son of Charles II. He escaped to the Netherlands and took no part in the risings of Argyll and Monmouth (1685), but was declared a rebel. His estates were forfeited. James VII later modified the sentence, allowing Melville's son to succeed to the estates, while in return his father paid compensation – £36000 Scots and a yearly rent of £2400 Scots. Melville returned with William and in May 1689 was appointed sole Secretary for Scotland. On 8 April 1690 he was made earl of Melville, viscount Kirkcaldy and Lord Raith, Monimail and Balwearie (all in Fife). In July he recovered his lands and estates. Later in the year he became Commissioner to the General Assembly and presided over the legislation re-establishing Presbyterianism.

The stanza ends with an oxymoron in the concluding Adonic. The adjective *Pauperis* may imply the forfeiture of Melville's estates or the crippling compensations subsequently paid by him, *aurum* his subsequent restoration and the political powers which he exercised. There is also a suggestion that he has made use of bribery.

In Horace, 35–36, the corresponding figure is Marcus Porcius Cato Uticensis (95–46 BC) who, after defeat at Thapsus, committed suicide rather than yield to Julius Caesar.

26 *Crescit … Crafordii*: the earl of Crawford is here mentioned by name for the first time. As a Presbyterian with strong Covenanting sympathies he was virtually confined to his estates during the reigns of Charles II and James VII – whence the phrase *occulto … ævo*.

In Horace, 46, the corresponding figure is Marcellus, probably Marcus Claudius Marcellus (d. 208 BC), five times consul, who fought successfully against the Gauls and the invading Carthaginian general Hannibal. There is also a reference to a later Marcus Claudius Marcellus (42–23 BC), nephew and intended heir to Augustus, who died young; cf. 5,19n. In the following stanzas however the parallel is with Jupiter.

27 *Kennedis sydus*: the star of Hugh Kennedy, the Moderator. In Horace, 47, the parallel phrase is *Iulium sidus*, 'star of the *gens Iulia*', to which Augustus and his great-uncle and adopted father, Julius Caesar, belonged.

29 *Gentis … custos*: i.e., Crawford, now identified with Jupiter.

30 *Orte Nassavo*: Crawford came to prominence only on the arrival of King William, prince of Orange-*Nassau*. There is also a reference to William's most prominent feature, his aquiline nose (*nasus*; cf. 81,1n.).

In Horace, 50, the corresponding phrase is *orte Saturno*, i.e., Jupiter, the usurper who seized the place of his father Saturn. Pitcairne may have intended an inverse ironic correspondence with William, who usurped the place of his father-in-law, James VII; cf. 10, 84.

30–31 *Tibi … data*: the words insinuate an improper collusion between Crawford and Kennedy.

32 *regnes*: in Horace, 52, the word is used appropriately of Jupiter. The suggestion here is that Crawford usurps royal power.

33–36 *Ille … ira*: Horace (53–56) celebrates the future triumphs of Augustus in the East, Pitcairne the more dubious triumphs of Kennedy at home.

COMMENTARY

36 *Præsulis*: in medieval and later Latin *praesul* generally means 'bishop', a term abhorrent to 17th-century Presbyterians. Here used ironically or insultingly of Hugh Kennedy; it is a briefer and more pointed version of Milton's 'New Presbyter is but old Priest writ large' ('On the new Forcers of Conscience under the Long Parliament', 20).

37 *reget unus orbem*: another suggestion of usurping tyranny; in Horace, 57, *reget aequus orbem*.

38 *Olympum*: So in Horace, 58, but here meaning Scotland or Britain as a whole, with associations which suggest spiritual as well as physical domination.

39–40 *parum castis ... Lucis*: so in Horace, 59–60; here ironic, referring to Episcopalian churches and forms of worship.

(b)

1–2 *Quem ... Clio?*: The opening couplet corresponds exactly to that in Horace.

5 *latebrosis*: the adjective has pejorative overtones; cf., e.g., Virgil, *Aeneid* 8, 711–713: *Nilum/ pandentemque sinu et tota veste vocantem/ caeruleum in gremium latebrosaque flumina victos*. After the naval defeat at Actium (31 BC), the Nile provides a lurking place for Cleopatra and her followers, now in effect outlaws. Horace (5) has *in umbrosis Heliconis oris*.

6 *super Largo*: Largo is a burgh on the Fife coast of the Firth of Forth. A hill, Largo Law (952 feet), dominates the local landscape, whence *super* as opposed to *Vemiarum* in *antris* and *Strutherensve* in *udis*.

11 *miscet*: the corresponding verb in (*a*),11, is *turbat*.

21–28 *Et parem ... recumbit*: two stanzas are devoted to David Williamson, who in (*a*) receives only part of line 21. The corresponding lines in Horace (25–32) refer to the demi-gods Hercules (Alcides) and, at greater length, Castor and Pollux, the Dioscuri, protectors of seamen.

21 *Superisque dicam*: Horace, 25, *puerosque Ledae*, the Dioscuri, borne by Leda to Jupiter.

23–24 *cujus ... refulsit*: Horace, 27–28, *quorum simul alba nautis/ stella refulsit*, with a reference to the zodiacal sign Gemini, 'the Twins', of which the two brightest stars are Castor and Pollux. The constellation was believed to possess a calming influence on storms at sea. Williamson's zodiacal sign exercises a calming and seductive influence on women (*Nymphis*).

25–28 *Defluit ... recumbit*: the corresponding lines in Horace (29–32) describe the calming of a storm by the Dioscuri. The grammatical subject of *recumbit* is *unda* rather than *Virgo*.

29 *Kirtonum*: i.e., James Kirkton (1620?-1699), MA, Edinburgh, 1647, minister of Lanark (second charge), 1655, of Mertoun, Berwickshire, 1657; expelled 1662; lived in England and Holland 1676–1687; minister of Edinburgh Tolbooth 1691–1699; commissioner for the 'purging' of Edinburgh University and the church in the south of Scotland. He wrote *A History of the Church of Scotland*

1660–1679, which during the 18th century circulated in MS and was first printed in Edinburgh in 1817 (ed. C.K. Sharpe). More recently it has been edited by R. Stewart (Edwyn Mellen Press, Lewiston, Queenston and Lampeter, 1992). His death is mentioned in a poem (35) addressed to Kirkton's son George, a surgeon and close friend of Pitcairne.

In *Scotch Presbyterian Eloquence* (*ut cit.*, 21) he is called 'Mr James Kirton (the everlasting Comedian of their Party)'. In *The Assembly* he is Mr Covenant Plain Dealer: 'He justly bears the name of plain-dealer; for he opposed the whole Assembly often, and stumbled into many sad truths ... When he takes a freak in his head, he's for moderation; not out of any kindness he has for the Episcopal clergy, but out of an humour of singularity, a spirit of contradiction, and often for want of thinking; for he who speaks without thinking cannot be very consequential to himself, but fall into a great many absurdities' (Tobin, *Assembly*, 'Preface', 29). The 'Preface' and *Scotch Presbyterian Eloquence* correspond in quotations from Kirkton's sermons ('Preface', 28–29; *Scotch Presbyterian Eloquence*, *ut cit.*, 123, 132, 137); the latter contains many other specimens.

33 *Vieræum*: probably the diabolist, Major Weir, 'one of the ten thousand men sent by the Scottish Covenanting Estates in 1641 to assist in suppressing the Irish Papists ... After a life characterised externally by all the graces of devotion, but polluted in secret by crimes of the most revolting nature, and which little needed the addition of wizardry to excite the horror of living men, Major Weir fell into a severe sickness, which affected his mind so much that he made open and voluntary confession of all his wickedness ... He was tried April 9, 1670, and being found guilty, was sentenced to be strangled and burnt between Edinburgh and Leith ... The execution of the profligate major took place, April 14' (Chambers, *Traditions*, 31–33).

In Horace, 37, the corresponding figure is Marcus Atilius Regulus (d.? 249). Each voluntarily gave himself up to death, *atqui sciebat quae sibi barbarus/ tortor pararet* (Horace, *Odes* 3, 5, 49–50). The circumstances however were notably different.

Clelanumque: William Cleland (c. 1661–1689), a student at St Andrews, who joined the militant Covenanters. In June 1679 he commanded at Drumclog and fought at Bothwell Brig, after which he fled to Holland. He took part in Argyll's attempt at a rebellion in 1685, then returned to Holland. On King William's arrival in Britain he was given command of the Cameronian regiment which held Dunkeld against the Jacobite army after Killiecrankie, an action during which he was killed. He was also a poet.

In Horace, 37–38, the corresponding figure is Lucius Aemilius Paullus, the Roman consul who fell at the disastrous battle of Cannae (216 BC), *superante Poeno* (i.e., Hannibal, the Carthaginian general). Pitcairne probably regarded the action at Dunkeld as equally disastrous for the Jacobites. Note the inverse correspondence between the death of the victorious, but Williamite, Cleland, and

COMMENTARY

that of the defeated, but Roman, Aemilius Paullus. Final victory however went to the Romans; Pitcairne insinuates that the same will be true for the Jacobites.

34 *superante Scotto*: the victorious Scot is Cleland; at Dunkeld the Jacobite army was commanded by the Irish successor of Claverhouse, Colonel Alexander Cannon.

36 *Reimoriumque*: probably Henry Rymore, MA, St Andrews, 1633. He became minister of Carnbee, Fife, in 1644. He belonged to 'the moderate and royalist party of resolutioners, who claimed the support of about 750 out of some 900 ministers' (Gordon Donaldson, *Scotland James V to James VII* [Edinburgh and London, 1965], 353). He was deprived in 1664 and restored in 1690, becoming one of the commissioners for the purging of the Universities. He died in 1694. His first wife was a Pitcairne.
Scotch Presbyterian Eloquence concludes (*ut cit.*, 151–152) with two quotations from 'Mr Rymer', who may be the same as the Rymore mentioned here.
In Horace, 40, the corresponding figure is Gaius Fabricius Luscinus, consul in 282 and 278 BC, celebrated for his poverty, austerity and incorruptibility.

37 *Orocum*: probably Alexander Orrock, MA, St Andrews, 1668. In 1687 he was in trouble for his opinions on bishops and the king. He was seized by the archbishop, Arthur Rose (1634–1704) for attempting to preach in St Andrews. He became minister of Hawick, Roxburghshire, in 1690 and died in 1711.
A Mr Orack, 'A Person who was well educated and justly esteemed at St *Andrew's* University', is favourably mentioned in *Scotch Presbyterian Eloquence*, *ut cit.*, 28.
Nothing is known of his hair-style. In Horace, 41, the corresponding figure is the plebeian hero, Manius Curius Dentatus, consul in 290, 284, 275 and 274 BC, like Fabricius celebrated for his humble birth, incorruptibility, and frugality.

38 *Breæum*: James Fraser (1639–1699), of *Brae* in the Black Isle, Ross and Cromarty. His father, Sir James Fraser of Brae, died in 1649. The estate was mismanaged during Fraser's minority, and after his graduation (MA, Marischal College, Aberdeen) in 1658, he found himself crippled by debts and litigation. A protracted spiritual crisis in 1665–1666 eventually led him to accept ordination in 1672 at the hands of ministers deprived as a result of the 1660 Restoration. He was outlawed in 1675; in 1677–1679 he was a prisoner on the Bass Rock, East Lothian, where he studied Hebrew, Greek and oriental languages; in 1681–1682 he was imprisoned, under harsher circumstances, in Blackness Castle, West Lothian. On his release he went to England, but in 1685 found himself in Newgate prison. He returned to Scotland in 1687 and in 1689 became minister of Culross, Fife. He attended the 1690 and 1692 General Assemblies. He died in Edinburgh on 13 September 1699, having witnessed an eclipse of the sun that morning.
His writings were all published posthumously. Best known is *Memoirs of the life of the very Reverend Mr James Fraser of Brea, Minister of the Gospel at Culross, written by himself* (Edinburgh, 1730).

In *The Assembly* Fraser is presented as Mr Timothy Turbulent, thus described in the Preface (Tobin, *ut cit.*, 29): 'Mr Fraser of Brae deserveth the name of Turbulent very well; for he's as huffing, insolent, crossgrain'd a fellow as ever lived. His whole trade, when he was young, was to debauch ladies' waiting-women; but now, when he's graver, he talks obscenely and shews a thing not to be named to the maid, as he did to a great many women lately at the cross of Dunfermling. Now, for women he takes wine, and drinks as great a quantity of hard sack, as curates do of ale. His party calls the fumes of the liquor the operations of the Spirit of God, and his fury and madness they term true zeal.'

In *Babell*, 225–270, he speaks against the use of the Lord's Prayer in worship. In Horace, 42, the corresponding figure is Marcus Furius Camillus, appointed dictator when he was an exile and Rome had been captured by the Gauls (387/6 BC). He returned, defeated the invaders, and recovered the gold used to buy them off. The parallel is at best distant. Pitcairne may have been influenced by the *nomen*, Furius.

39–40 *Sæva ... fundus*: A pretty clear reference to Fraser's ancestral estate of Brae and the poverty associated with it. In Horace, 43–44, the corresponding lines are *saeva paupertas et avitus apto/ cum lare fundus*, where the reference is to the virtuous poverty of Fabricius and Curius. The reference to a farm recalls another early Roman hero, Lucius Quinctius Cincinnatus, in 458 BC summoned from his farm – *quattuor iugerum colebat agrum* (Livy, *Ab Urbe Condita* 3, 26, 8) – to become dictator and saviour of Rome.

45 *Albanæ*: in Horace, 49, *humanae*.

54 *Britannum*: in Horace, 58, *Olympum*; so in (a).

77

Metre. Asclepiadean Strophe No. 2; Glyconic alternating with Lesser Asclepiad in four-line stanzas.

Notes. The earl of Leven (76(a),17n) married Lady Anne Wemyss on 3 September 1691, the anniversary of Cromwell's death (1658) and of his defeats of the Scots at Dunbar (1650) and Worcester (1651). The marriage was apparently performed by David Williamson.

As the title shows, the poem is an 'Imitation' of the delicately erotic Horace, *Odes* 3, 28: *Festo quid potius die/ Neptuni faciam?*. Horace proposes to celebrate the festival of Neptune (23 July) by having the slave-girl, Lyde, bring out wine of an ancient vintage. As they drink together, they will cast philosophy aside and sing, he of Neptune and the Nereids, she of Latona and the arrows of the huntress Diana, and finally of Venus and her sanctuaries. Night will bring the songs to an appropriate conclusion.

Pitcairne's is a nuptial poem in which the marriage takes place on Cromwell's day of ill-omen. The structure more or less follows that of Horace's *Ode*. It also exemplifies Pitcairne's calendrical interests; cf., e.g., **7**; **103–115**.

The marriage roused much contemporary interest and comment. It is mentioned in *Babell*:

> She likewise had a zeallous car'age,
> In a late bussines of mar'age,
> When she a person did neglect,
> Who had both riches and respect,
> And chose one whose 'state was meaner,
> Because his conscience was cleaner,
> And for the good cause ay was ready
> To fight, as he proved on a lady. (1087–1094)

In his notes to the passage (pp. 91–92) Kinloch quotes an anonymous, but obviously Episcopalian, pasquil from the Arniston MS:

Lynes on my Lord Leavine's Mariage with the Countess of Weeme's Daughter.

> In fertile Weems, that soul refreshing place,
> Wnder the droppings of the dew of grace,
> Dorinda liues, the honour of her race!
> Dorinda, chiefe of Covenanted maides!
> Pryde of our Kirk, and glory of our aige!
> Her all, and every pairt wes fram'd so weill,
> No prelat member did the rest excell,
> Bot parity in every limb did dwell.
> So perfect all did justly her account,
> A transumpt of the paterne of the mount.
> Dorinda, only fitt for Ajax love!–
> Ajax, who thunders from his rock lyke Jove;
> Ajax, who does with birchen scepter raigne,
> O'er all the frighted ladyes of the plaine!
> No superstitious rite, nor idle jest,
> But godly psalmes did grace the nuptiall feast.
> In stead of garter loos'd, or stocking flung,
> Sex double verse to Martyrs' tune were sung.
> The bryde wes bedded by the word of God,
> Ane patern of reformed Kirks abroad.
> In the nixt place, a possat made of sacke,
> Which gravely as the sacrament they take.
> After some disputs, curious and nice,
> About postures in the tyme of exercise,

POEM 77

> Sex loud presenters our last good-night did sing,
> The sacred croud did dance it in a ring,
> Untill good sweet mes David did begin,
> Inspyr'd with sack, to sing this nuptiall hymne.

There is obviously more to come, but we have not yet located the MS quoted.

2–3 *Promere amabilem ... hastulam*: Horace, 2–3: *prome reconditum ... Caecubum*.
3 *puer*: the earl of Leven, aged 31 at the time of his wedding. In Horace, 3, the corresponding figure is the girl, Lyde.
4 *et ... cupientibus*: in Horace, 4, *munitaeque adhibe vim sapientiae*. Pitcairne deliberately opposes *cupientibus* and *sapientiae*.
5 *En ... votis*: Horace also stresses the swift passage of time: *inclinare meridiem/ sentis ac, veluti stet volucris dies,/ parcis deripere horreo/ cessantem Bibuli consulis amphoram* (5–8). Obviously the circumstances implied differ.
7 *Duffeum ... agrum*: it was believed that Wemyss Castle had once been a stronghold of Macduff, Thane of Fife in Shakespeare's *Macbeth*. 'Macduff's field' is Lady Anne Wemyss.
8 *davidico*: a reference to David Williamson (**18**, **76** (a), 21, (b), 21–28) as well as to the biblical King David. As noted above, Williamson officiated at the wedding.
vomere: the metaphor is biblical and classical: cf. Vulgate, Judges 14:18: *si non arassetis in vitula mea non invenissetis propositionem meam*; Lucretius, *De Rerum Natura* 4, 1272–1273: [*mulier*] *eicit enim sulcum recta regione viaque/ vomeris atque locis avertit seminis ictum*.
9–11 *Nos ... Patres*: Horace, 9–10: *nos cantabimus invicem/ Neptunum et viridis Nereidum comas*.
11 *Patres*: the members of the English Rump parliament and/or the 159 Commissioners whom they appointed (6 January 1649) to try Charles I.
12 *Mortonam ... [filisthiæ]*: we cannot elucidate this line and are uncertain of the transcription of the final word. The words *Mortonam* and *filisthiæ* are grammatically feminine, corresponding to *Latonam* and *Cynthiae* in Horace, 12. Presumably they refer to women.
13 *Summo ... patre*: Horace, 13: *summo carmine, quae Cnidon*.
13–15 *patre ... pulso*: i.e., the expulsion of James VII.
14 *Brittonis*: Britto, supposed eponymous ancestor of the British race. The form is first found, as a textual variant on the more usual *Brutus*, in the ninth-century *Historia Brittonum* of Nennius (D.N. Dumville, *The Historia Brittonum: 3. The Vatican Recension* [Cambridge, 1985], 66, n. 24).
15 *nocte*: corresponds to *Nox* in Horace, 16.
15–16 *nocte ... virginis*: i.e., the consummation of the marriage is a sacrifice to the divinity of Cromwell (and therefore to be condemned).

78

Notes. The poem is obscure to us, but may well refer to the subject of the previous poem, the wedding of Lady Anne Wemyss and David Melville, or some aftermath of that event. The unusual form *Malavilla* is feminine and so refers to a woman; the usual Latin is the masculine *Melvinus*, as in *Andreas Melvinus*, the Presbyterian church and university administrator, Andrew Melville (1545–1622). Here no doubt the intention is to give prominence to the element *mala*, 'evil, wicked,' an effect strengthened by the reference to the witch Circe in 2.

79

Notes. The first line echoes *Aeneid* 2, 274–275: *quantum mutatus ab illo/ Hectore, qui redit exuvias indutus Achilli*. The reference to Hector may depend on his general reputation as champion of Troy, or perhaps on the epithet, ἀνδροφόνος, 'man-slaying,' sometimes applied to him in the *Iliad*, most notably in 24, 723–724: τῇσιν δ' Ἀνδρομάχη λευκώλενος ἦρχε γόοιο/ Ἕκτορος ἀνδροφόνοιο. Perhaps there is also some trace of the late-seventeenth-century usage of 'Hector' to mean 'a blustering bully'. Moses instituted the sacrifice of the paschal lamb (*Exodus* 12:6), a rite with strong Christian associations.

The satire is directed at William Lindsay (1644–1698), 18th earl of Crawford and 2nd earl of Lindsay (**76**(a), 26n), one of the commissioners for settling the government of the church, and thus a power in the General Assemblies of 1690 and 1692. He figures in *The Assembly* and *Babell*, both referring to the 1692 Assembly; *Babell* includes the following description (the 'mighty deeds' are Lindsay's exploits during the 1690 Assembly):

> At last vprose a noble lord,
> Whose mighty deeds are on record,
> Whom Presbyterians justly call
> Ther Hector, or ther Hanniball;
> And all men in ther wits will grant,
> He's Hector of the Covenant.
> A blockhead, and a mighty droll,
> Whom, in broad Scots, we call a foole.   (890–897)

The epigram was probably written 1690–1692.

80

Metre. Elegiac couplet, with prose gloss appended.
Notes. After the death of James VII (**10**), his body was 'provisionally' transported to the English Benedictine church of St Edmund the Martyr in the Faubourg St. Jacques in Paris, to await the transfer to Westminster Abbey which never took place. His heart and his bowels were presented to other French churches and his brain to the Scots College in Paris. The body was eventually disinterred during the French Revolution and thrown into a ditch. A portion of the bowels survived in the parish church of St Germains and in 1824 at the instructions of George IV were solemnly reinterred.

The poem must antedate William's death in March 1702.

1 *Nassus*: William of Orange-*Nassau*, whose most prominent feature was an aquiline nose (*nasus*, the reading in sp); see Money, *English Horace*, 148.
2 *Marleboroe*: the great general and shady politician, John Churchill (1654–1722), in 1689 created Earl, in 1702 Duke of Marlborough, regarded by Jacobites in particular as double-dealer and traitor. See **74**, 13n.
3 *Barberinus*: from Barberini, a Roman family, the best-known member of which was Maffeo Barberino, Pope Urban VIII (1623–1644).
3–4 *Urbs ... Urbe*: London, Rome.
Gloss: 'Urban VIII's conversion of the brass tubes supporting the roof of the Pantheon,' the church of S. Maria ad Martyres in Rome, 'into the canopy for the high altar at St Peter's and cannons for the Castel S. Angelo, gave rise to the *mot*' (ODCC, s.v. *Barberini*). Here the *Barbari* are William, Marlborough and their followers; the *Barberini* are represented by Cardinal Charles Barberino, named in the title of a volume from Pitcairne's library, *Sacra exequialia in funere Jacobi II exhibita à Carolo Barberino S.R.E. Cardinali, descripta à Carolo de Aquino* (Rome, 1702; *Catalogus Librorum Archibald Pitcairne, Libri in folio*, 302).

81

Notes. The poem celebrates King William's death on 8 March 1702. The date in the Bodleian title is that of William's birth, 4 November 1650.

1–5 For the return from heaven of Astraea, goddess of Justice, accompanied by Virtus, see **2**, 1n. According to Claudian, *In Rufinum*, 1, 52, her return during the reign of the good emperor Theodosius (379–395) was threatened by Rufinus, praetorian prefect in the East, whose activities are compared to those of legendary monsters, in particular the Lernaean Hydra, a seven-headed water-serpent killed by Hercules as his second Labour. Pitcairne equates the Hydra with King William; cf. **91**. He may have inverted the usual connotation. A decorative inset to George Willdey's map of the British Isles in 1715, dedicated to George I (*British Library, Maps, c.11.a.2*) shows Hercules (George) in combat with the Hydra (the Jacobites). In the background Victory or Britannia sounds a blast on her trumpet.

2, 4, 6: *Promite ... Promite ... solvite*: these lines form a kind of refrain, echoing Horace, *Odes*, 1, 37, 1–6, celebrating the death of Rome's principal foreign enemy, the Egyptian Cleopatra. In APP, 4, *Fundite* is inserted in the margin as an alternative to *Promite* in the text.

2 *Tyrrhenis*: in APP, *Vasconicis*, 'Gascon', is inserted as a marginal alternative.

7–8 *Neptuno ... equum*: Neptune is the god of the sea, whose gift to the Athenians was a horse which appeared when he struck a rock with his trident. The reference here is to the horse which on 23 February 1702 William was riding in Richmond Park. It stumbled on a molehill and he was thrown, dying as a consequence of his injuries. The molehill rather than the horse appeared from the earth.

82

Notes. William's death is again the theme. During his lifetime he was Satan's prime agent. His death gives him the equivalent place in Hell, surpassing even that of Calvin. May all Williamites and Calvinists join them!

2 *Nassovus*: William of Orange-*Nassau*; for this and later references, cf., **77**.
Sacra mentiendo: i.e., by breaking the divinely-ordained order of succession to the throne.

3–4 *Hostium ... fraudibus*: perhaps a reference to Marlborough's devious activities.

5 *Facies*: perhaps a covert reference to William's most prominent feature, his nose.

7 *Equus Armistrangi*: the horse which stumbled and threw William; cf. **82**, 7–8. The reference to Armstrong is obscure. In pp. 31–32 of *The memoirs of Sir Robert Sibbald, 1641–1722* (ed. F.P. Hett [London, 1932]), Sibbald refers to a Mr Armstrong who kept a stable in Edinburgh's West Bow, but there is no obvious connection between this and King William's death.
The quantity of the syllables in *Armistrangi* does not fit the metre; -*istr* is long where it should be short.

9–10 *Tertius ... Usinulca ... Ordinis*: *Usinulca* is an anagram of *Caluinus*, borrowed by Pitcairne from John Barclay's *Argenis*, 2, 5 (Mark Riley and Dorothy Pritchard Huber [eds.], 2 vols. [Royal Van Gorcum, 2004], 1, 266–275). Pitcairne's library included the two volume Elzevir edition of 1630 (*Catalogus librorum Archibald Pitcairne, Libri in Octavo & Infra*, 247, 248). Until William's death Calvin had been second in Satan's infernal Brotherhood, but is now demoted.

83

Notes. The poem uses classical mythology to celebrate King William's death. Jupiter/Zeus, son of Saturn/Kronos, usurped his father's throne. Jupiter was born on Crete, where in Cretan mythology he also died; his tomb became a visitor attraction (Cook, *Zeus*, 3 vols. [Cambridge, 1914–1940], I, 157, n. 4). Saturn fled to Italy, where he established a Golden Age. William is equated with Jupiter; his father-in-law, James VII, with Saturn. Crete represents England, Olympus the after-life, where all wrongs are righted, and also Britain as it will be when the male Stuart succession is restored. William's behaviour towards his father(-in-law), like that of Edmund in *King Lear*, proves him a bastard.

1 *Jovis Hammonis*: The Egyptian god Ammon was early equated with Jupiter/Zeus. The compound name emphasizes that William was a foreigner.

84

Notes. The couplet may celebrate the early stages of the career of James Graham (1682–1742), 4th Marquess and 1st Duke of Montrose. Later he became an active promoter of the 1707 Union, as a reward for which he was raised to become Duke of Montrose on 24 April 1707 (a month after the Scottish Parliament passed the Act). Pitcairne's intention may thus be ironic. Lockhart (*Scotland's Ruine*, 92–93) says of him: 'When he first appeared in the world he had enough to recommend him to the love and affection of the nation by being the representative of that noble, loyal and worthy family. And his interest increased to so great a degree by his good behaviour after he came from his travels and in the first session [6 May–16 September 1703] of this Parliament, that, had he continued in these measures, he had the fairest game to play of any young man that ever was in Scotland, since undoubtedly he would have been acknowledged and followed as the head and leader of the Cavaliers [the Tories]. But being of an easy, mean-spirited temper, governed by his mother [Christian Leslie, daughter of John Leslie, 7th Earl and 1st Duke of Rothes] and her relations (the family of Rothes) and extremely covetous, he could not resist the first temptation the Court [the Whigs] threw in his way, and from the time he first engaged with them he adhered closely to their interest, and with the greatest vehemency prosecuted their measures notwithstanding all the friends of his father's family remonstrated to him against it, and that he lost the esteem of them and the Cavaliers.'

1 *Dis*: i.e., earlier, heroic members of the family, in particular his great-grandfather, the Royalist James Graham (1612–1650), 5th Earl and 1st Marquess of Montrose, executed after his spectacular but brutal campaigns on behalf of Charles I and his son, and the legendary ancestral hero, Græmus. Pitcairne

probably also intended a reference to Montrose's kinsman, John Graham of Claverhouse, Viscount Dundee; see **4**, 8n.

Geniture deos: i.e., Graham as himself a potential ancestor of heroes.

2   *pullulat*: cf. **9**, 41n; **31**, 6; **88**, 2.

85

Notes. John Cunningham (1671–1710), MA, younger son of Sir John Cunningham, Bt., of Caprington, Ayrshire, was admitted to the Faculty of Advocates on 23 January 1692, and on 3 January 1693 was appointed as one of the 'privat examinators' for the subsequent year. In 1704 or 1705 he became the third advocate to be appointed Lecturer in Civil (Scots) Law, the post mentioned in the title to the present poem. In 1705 his Latin inaugural lecture, and the first lecture of his actual course (in English), were printed by James Watson, to be sold by Robert Freebairn (*Joannis Cuningamii j. cti. oratio inauguralis recitata Edinburgi; cum primum jus civile docere coepit*; *A discourse by Mr. John Cuninghame advocate, at the beginning of his lessons upon the Scots law*). As already mentioned, both printer and bookseller were Jacobite friends of Pitcairne. The same was true, in all probability, of Cunningham, whose lectures provided the occasion for the present poem (Grant, *Faculty of Advocates*, s.v.; Pinkerton, *Advocates Minute Book* I, 110, 120).

Cunningham's choice of textbook for his course, the *Institutions of the Laws of Scotland* by Sir George Mackenzie (*Discourse*, 5; see **5**, introductory n.) is entirely suited to the task of restoring conservative order to an Underworld undergoing Williamite disturbances.

Dennistoun writes as a distressed inhabitant of the Elysian Fields. The unrest in Tartarus which he reports we may assume to have been fired by the arrival there in 1702 of King William, who characteristically had immediately mounted a rising with the intention of usurping dominion in the Elysian Fields and expelling King James, already established there. Cunningham's task, when he returns, is to use his great legal ability to restore order. He is an avatar, as it were, of Minos or, more probably, Rhadamanthus, whose immemorial task it was to administer justice among the dead (see **1**, 31). His teaching in Edinburgh is a mere dereliction of duty.

The epistle is complimentary to Cunningham, albeit in a somewhat back-handed way. More covertly, it is a call for action by Jacobites in Britain.

1   *Sancte*: Cunningham is addressed as if his place were already among the blessed.

3–5   *An patriæ ... fugam*: Pitcairne suggests a Platonic doctrine of pre-existence like that found in *Aeneid* 6, 703 ff.; cf. **67**, 3n. Cunningham, it is to be supposed, drank the waters of Lethe before undergoing his earthly incarnation.

4   *Hecates*: Proserpine under her infernal aspect.

6 *jura dabas*: cf. *Aeneid* 1, 507, of Dido; also the reference to Minos, 10, 5–6. The reference here is to Cunningham as teacher of law.
7 *subitò*: i.e., immediately after William's death.
9 *Cato*: probably Cato the Censor (234–149 BC), who combined 'legal ability with stern traditional morality' (*OCD*, s.v.); cf. 10, 4 and n. For his pre-existence in the Elysian Fields, see *Aeneid* 6, 841.
  Locartus: Sir George Lockhart (c. 1630–1689); see 3.
12 *Lycurge*: Lycurgus, the legendary Spartan law-giver.
13 *patrem*: James VII. The imperative *Redde* indicates that the insurrection has driven him from Elysium. The verb was also used as a Jacobite slogan; cf. 90, introductory n.
14 *Galle*: James's long residence in France, and the recognition he obtained from Louis XIV, make him father of Frenchmen as well as Scots.

86

Metre. Dactylic hexameter (more or less).
Notes. The parallel drawn by Jacobites between Aeneas and the Pretender has already been mentioned. Pitcairne here adapts a passage from *Aeneid* 8, the instructions given by Vulcan to his Cyclopes to prepare arms and armour for Aeneas (439–443), to fit the circumstances immediately following William's death. It is an appeal to the continental powers, the French in particular, to take military action.

The piece is almost a direct transcript. In 1, to the detriment of the metre, Pitcairne omits the word *inquit* between *cuncta* and *caeptosque*. In 2 *Alpini* has been substituted for *Aetnaei*; in 3 *Arma viris facienda* for *arma acri facienda viro* – again to the detriment of the metre. This last however strengthens the echo of the opening words of the *Aeneid*, *Arma virumque cano*, with its later Jacobite overtones.

87

Metre. Hendecasyllabic.
Notes. Like 6 and 53, the poem is an imitation of *Catullus* 49. It is addressed to the Justice General (chief judge in criminal trials), Sir George Mackenzie of Tarbat (1630–1714), created Viscount Tarbat in 1685 and Earl of Cromarty in 1703; appointed Justice General (for the second time) in 1705.

In 1700 Mackenzie's second marriage, at the age of seventy, to the rich and relatively youthful Margaret Wemyss (1659–1705), Countess of Wemyss in her own right, caused a great stir, as did the fact that the old husband outlived his much younger wife. The marriage is obliquely referred to in ll. 1–2 of the poem, the unusual vigour of the old man emphasized by the verb *pullulat*.

A note in the MS reads 'Ad Cromarteum was sent by the five Stirling Shire

Gentlemen who were tried for their Lives on –'. The five men were five Stirlingshire lairds, James Stirling of Keir, Archibald Seton of Touch, Archibald Stirling of Carden, Charles Stirling of Kippendavie, and Patrick Edmonstone of Newton. In 1708 they openly and riotously demonstrated support for the Pretender, whom a squadron of French ships brought to the Forth estuary, although he was prevented from landing. In November of that year they were brought to trial in Edinburgh on a charge of high treason. Witnesses were unwilling to testify, and the charge was eventually dismissed on the Scottish verdict of Not Proven (Lenman, *Jacobite Risings*, 89–90).

In Lockhart the picture is different: 'Never was a people so much disappointed as the Scots [at the failure of the French fleet to come to port], for all were ready to have shown themselves loyal subjects and good countrymen. Particularly Stirling of Keir, Seaton of Touch, Stirling of Carden and many others, having, as they thought, received certain intelligence that the king was landed, mounted their horses and advanced in a good body towards Edinburgh from the shire of Stirling, but being quickly informed of the bad news, returned home again. However, they were imprisoned and brought to tryal as guilty of treason by being in arms for the Pretender (the title now given to the king), but the probation against them being defective, they were acquitted' (*Scotland's Ruine*, 231).

As Justice General, Cromarty presided at the trial. Pitcairne, of course, was very much on the side of the lairds.

1   *Fergusi nepotum*: cf. **6**, 1n.
2   *pullulat*: cf. **9**, 41n, **31**, 6, **85**, 2.
6   *pro fidem Deorum*: i.e., for their loyalty to the Stuart cause. The preposition *pro* with the accusative is found only very occasionally in late classical Latin with the sense 'before, in front of.' Such a usage is not characteristic of Pitcairne, but is necessary here *metri gratia*.

88

Notes. The poem is one of depression at future prospects, politically speaking. Verbally it is unusually complex. The language is coded to Jacobite sensibilities. *Jacobus*, of course, is the Pretender. In the title, *Gallovidium*, properly 'of, belonging to Galloway (in S.W. Scotland),' is a punning reference to Gaul, France, place of the Pretender's exile, a reference reinforced by the word *Gallica* (4), and the recurring *Gallovidium* (6). The contrast of Galloway, a southern region, and *Caledonium*, a northern, mirrors the Pretender's own situation. His natural place is the north, Scotland, but he is detained in the south, France. Again, Galloway is a remote rural region, *rus*, 'country,' as opposed to *Urbs*, 'city,' most probably representing Edinburgh, seat of the Stuarts' former glory. Less probably London is intended; Pitcairne seems to be thinking in terms only of Scotland.

The title *Equitem*, 'knight,' literally 'horseman, chevalier,' alludes to the Pretender's by-name, the Chevalier de St. George; cf. the later term 'Young Chevalier' for his son, Charles Edward Stuart.

There is also play on the differing significances of the perfect, present and future tenses of the verb 'to be' – *fuero, fui, sunt, fuere* – and the moods and tenses of compound forms of the verb 'to go' – *redibis, abeunte, redire vetant* – reflecting the fluidity of the political situation, the past expulsion, the present exile, and the possible, but perhaps unlikely, future return of the Pretender.

1 *redibis*: the hypothetical future Restoration.
2 *fui*: 'I have been (but no longer am)'; cf. **12**, 17–18n.
3 *Equites nostri*: the Scots gentry.
4 *Gallica vina bibunt*: i.e., they drink toasts to the King over the Water (in France) in French claret, possibly with the implication that they do precious little else. Cf. **8**, 2n, 18n.
5 *Presbyteri*: the meaning 'priests' and the suggestion of 'Presbyterian' makes this a more effective reading than the variant *Discipuli*. Cf. the satirical final line in Milton, 'On the New Forcers of Conscience under the Long Parliament,' 20: '*New Presbyter* is but *Old Priest* writ Large.' Cf. **76**(a), 36n.
   Cnoxi: the Calvinist Reformer John Knox (?1512–1572).
   Parentibus: the predecessors of the present generation of Presbyterian ministers, who had made possible the execution of Charles I and supported the deposition of James VII.
6 *Et ... vetant*: the gloomy final line leaves the poet in the half-dead state of the opening. The variant reading is more optimistic, ending as it does with the coded word *Redux*.

89

Notes. In 1676 Lady Elizabeth Howard, eldest surviving daughter of Henry Howard, 6th (Howard) Earl of Norfolk, became the wife of George Gordon (c. 1649–1716), 4th Marquis of Huntly, later 1st Duke of Gordon. Both were Catholics. There were two children, but the marriage was not particularly happy; before 1697 the Duchess had retired to a convent in Flanders, and in 1707 she succeeded in obtaining a decree of separation from the Duke. She returned to Scotland. On 30 June 1711 she presented to the Faculty of Advocates a silver medal for their collection. On the obverse was the head of the Pretender, on the reverse a map of the British Isles with the motto *Reddite*, 'give back.' This gift the Faculty accepted by a majority vote of sixty-three to twelve. The decision was abjectly rescinded at subsequent extraordinary meetings on 17 and 18 July. Although the reign of Anne still had three years to run, the Minutes record a declaration of allegiance to the House of Hanover 'as by law established' (*Scots Peerage*, IV, 550–551; *Advocates'*

COMMENTARY

Minute Book, 1, 293–295; Scott, *Heart of Midlothian*, ed. Andrew Lang [London, 1906], 182, 815).
   The Duchess of Gordon died in 1732.
   The presentation occasioned Pitcairne's epigram.

1–4 *Quantus ... Deos*: these rather convoluted lines turn on the authorization by Elizabeth of the execution of Queen Mary at Fotheringay in 1587.
1 *Mariae ... Havartus*: Shortly after Mary's flight to England in 1568, secret negotiations began for her liberation and return to Scotland by way of marriage to her fellow-Catholic, the English nobleman, Thomas Howard (1538–1572), 4th (Howard) Duke of Norfolk The northern rising headed by the Earls of Westmorland and Northumberland (1569) and Leonard Dacre (1570), together with the exposure of Rudolfi's plot (1572), put an end to any such hope. Norfolk was executed on Tower Hill 2 June 1572.
1–2 *Quantus ... fuit*: the faithfulness shown by Norfolk stands in contrast to the lack of any such quality in Elizabeth, primarily in terms of Mary's execution, but also by implication in terms of her behaviour towards her favourite, by many regarded as her betrothed, Robert Devereux (1566–1601), 2nd (Devereux) Earl of Essex, whose execution she eventually authorized.
2 *Carnificina*: 'office of executioner.' The primary reference is to Mary, but the executions of Norfolk and Essex give the word added force and relevance.
4 *Iratos ... Deos*: i.e., in the wars and constitutional upheavals of seventeenth- and early eighteenth-century Britain.
   nobis: the people of Britain.
5 *melior*: in her behaviour towards the House of Stewart.
6 *Maria natis*: the House of Stewart and, in particular, the Old Pretender, Mary's great-great-grandson.
7 *Britannis*: for a time after the 1707 Union Pitcairne tends to speak of Britons rather than Scots; cf. 2, 2n.

90

Notes. The medal presented by the Duchess of Gordon to the Faculty of Advocates is again the subject. Here, both Homer and Odysseus (Ulysses), hero of the *Odyssey*, stand for the Pretender, Sappho for the Duchess, and Catullus Pitcairne. Pitcairne had a parallel in mind, *Catullus* 51, *Ille mi par esse deo videtur*, a translation of a lyric by Sappho (frag. 31).

Title *Albæ ... 1711*: cf. *Archimedis Epistola ad Regem Gelonem Albæ Græcæ reperta Anno Æræ Christianæ 1688*, the title of a pamphlet by Pitcairne which also purports to be a translation from the Greek.

POEM 90

Albæ Græcæ: no such place exists, as the adjective *Græcæ* probably implies. Cf. the phrase, the 'Greek Calends', *Kalendae Graecae*, a circumlocution used by the Emperor Augustus to signify 'never'. The Greek calendar contained no *Kalendae*. Pitcairne also probably intended *Alba* to indicate that the poem had its origin in Scotland.

1 *Poetarum ... Regem*: King because the *Odyssey* deals with the return of Odysseus to his island-kingdom of Ithaca, and his defeat there of the usurping band of Suitors, an effective figure for the return of the Pretender to his island-kingdom of Britain and the defeat there of his Whig opponents.

2 *Junij ... decimo*: the Pretender's birthday.

4 *Lesbia*: Sappho belonged to the island of Lesbos in the Aegean. The troubled married history of the Duchess might also suggest that the adjective hints at lesbianism. The use of the word in that sense seems, however, to date only from the nineteenth century.

5 *puellas*: Sappho was 'the leader and chief personality in an institution which trained young girls ... It was, as she herself calls it, a μοισοπόλων δόμος, a house of those who cultivated the Muses ... It was primarily concerned with the cult of Aphrodite, and its members formed a θίασος ['company, troop', assembled for religious observances] ... The Muses were honoured with Aphrodite. It was felt that her ceremonies demanded songs' (C.M. Bowra, *Greek Lyric Poetry* [Oxford, 1936], 187–189). The reference here is presumably to the women attendants of the Duchess. There is also a suggestion that women alone now have the courage to support the Pretender, that males, particularly members of the Faculty of Advocates, are afraid to do so.

6–7 *modos ... ludunt*: the idiom is not classical; for a distant parallel to the sense cf. Catullus 50, 4–5, *scribens versiculos uterque nostrum/ ludebat numero modo hoc modo illoc*.

6–8 *Quæ ... arte*: i.e., the presentation of the medal, metaphorically treated as the performance of a song.

8 *virginis*: the Duchess.

9–10 *Phœbus ... illusit*: i.e., by continuing to shine throughout the night and so preventing the appearance of the Evening Star. The verb *ludere*, this time in compound form (*illusit*, perfect of *illudere*), makes a second appearance. The idea of play, making ridiculous, is prominent in the poem.

15–21 *voluitque ... Regiâ*: The *Odyssey*, rather than the *Aeneid*, becomes the type of Stuart restoration.

15 *Ultimam Thulen*: the extreme northern limit of the ancient world. Here probably Strathbogie, home-territory of the Gordons.

16 *Palladis*: Pallas Athena was the goddess who contrived the eventual homecoming of Odysseus.

17 *Reges*: Alcinous, king of the Phaeacians, dispatched Odysseus on the ship which finally brought him home to Ithaca. Here Louis XIV is intended. The plural is poetic.

COMMENTARY

18 *procos*: Odysseus's final task was to rid himself of the Suitors, who had been besieging his wife Penelope and devouring his substance during his twenty-year absence. Here Whigs, Presbyterians and the turncoat Faculty of Advocates.
Ithaci: Odysseus.

19–21 *pœnas ... Regiâ*: a specific reference to the activities of the Faculty of Advocates.

23 *Pontifex*: the King as head of Church as well as State. A hint that the Pretender should give up Catholicism?

24–25 *Thules / Incola*: the Duchess.

91

Notes. The poem was written early in 1712 (i.e., late 1711, Old Style), to celebrate the dismissal of Marlborough on 31 December 1711. The *sævior Hydra*, the many-headed monster of 3, in broad terms represents Whigs and Presbyterians, but primarily 'the hated triumvirate of Marlborough, Godolphin and Queensberry' (Ferguson, *Scotland 1689 to the Present*, 54). On 7 August 1710 Anne deprived Sidney, 1st Earl of Godolphin (1645–1712), of his office as First Lord of the Treasury, in effect Prime Minister. The election which followed was a triumph for the Tories. On 17 January 1711 Marlborough was forced to return to the queen his duchess's golden key of office. On 31 December the queen made an order dismissing Marlborough himself from all his employments.

1–2 *Credidimus ... habet*: see 82, 5.

5–6 *Quas ... strages*: Pitcairne probably had in mind the disastrous failure of the Darien scheme (1698–1700), together with the general economic and other hardships during the 1690s and the War of the Spanish Succession (1701–1713), for the latter not least the high casualties suffered in Marlborough's near-Pyrrhic victory at Malplaquet (1709).

7 *Lernæ*: Lerna, a forest and marsh near Argos, haunt of the Lernaean Hydra.

8 *Orba ... Diis*: governments after the accession of William II and III, were held responsible for a loss of population to Scotland (by way of famine, war casualties and the Darien scheme), and the sufferings of the Episcopalians.

9 *Alcides*: Hercules, grandson of Alceus.
Vallas: William Wallace (1270–1305), Scottish patriot-hero, celebrated for his physical strength.

12 *Anna Perenna*: Italian year-goddess, bestower of the returning year; cf. **23**, 3; **24**, 10. Despite the Old Style calendar which he cites, Pitcairne regarded 1 January as New Year.
cluet: an archaic word, used by Plautus and Lucretius: *coronam, / per gentis Italas hominum quae clara clueret* (*De Rerum Natura* 1, 118–119). Often, as here, it has mock-heroic overtones.

13 *suorum*: i.e., her half-brother, the Pretender, and his sister, Louisa Maria Theresa (1692–1712).
15–16 *Illa ... placens*: this couplet does not appear in SP – probably a deliberate editorial omission.
15 *Avum*: Charles I.
ulta: i.e., by ensuring that her successor is her half-brother, the Pretender.
Patremque: James VII.

92

Notes. The poem was written after the death on 15 September 1712 of Sidney Godolphin, 1st Earl Godolphin. He had been Lord High Treasurer, head of the Whig administration, from 8 May 1702 until his dismissal on 8 August 1710. Throughout the period he had worked closely with Marlborough. Godolphin was succeeded in office, first, briefly, by the Tory, John Poulett, 1st Earl Poulett (c. 1668–1743), then on 29 March 1711 by Robert Harley (**97**).

1 *Goddolphine*: the spelling *-dd-* is *metri causa*.
2 *laevas*: i.e., 'unlucky, misfortunate'.
5 *Regi*: James Francis, the Old Pretender.
mergier undis: i.e., submerge in the waters of Styx and Avernus; cf. Ovid, *Metamorphoses* 10, 697: *an Stygia sontes dubitavit mergeret unda*. For the phrase in the same line-position, cf. Juvencus, *Evangeliorum Libri Quattuor*, 1, 349: *Tunc meis manibus dignaris mergier undis?*. The speaker here is John, appalled at being asked to baptize Christ in Jordan (Matthew, 3, 14). Is it possible that Pitcairne intended an ironic intertextuality?
We owe this last reference to Roger P.H. Green, *Latin Epics of the New Testament* (Oxford, 2006), 37.
There is no evidence that Godolphin plotted the murder of the Pretender.
6 *Soror Illa*: Queen Anne.

93

Metre. Sapphic stanza.
Notes. Between 1710 and 1712 Jonathan Swift (1667–1745) was closely associated with Robert Harley (**97**), leader of the Tory parliamentary majority which was to bring the unpopular War of the Spanish Succession to an end, and also, Jacobites hoped, obtain recognition for the claims of the Old Pretender. Swift supported Harley by his writings in the *Examiner* (2 November 1710–14 June 1711), and by his pamphlet, *The Conduct of the Allies* (1711). He also worked on the partisan *History of the Last Four years of Queen Anne*, posthumously published in 1758. In

1711 Swift became a founder member of the Brothers' Club, which included as fellow members Pitcairne's friends Prior, Freind and Arbuthnot.

The biblical Jonathan, son of Saul, was the friend and protector of David, even when the latter had been anointed king in place of Saul, and was pursued as an outlaw. After the death of Saul and Jonathan, David became king *de facto* as well as *de jure*. He was Solomon's father (*1 Samuel* 16 – *2 Samuel* 1). The position of Solomon as successor was ensured by another Jonathan, son of Abiathar the priest (*1 Kings* 1:42–53).

The poem draws a rather forced parallel between the relationship of Jonathan Swift and Robert Harley and that of the biblical Jonathan and David. The Solomon of the poem is not Harley's son, but the Old Pretender. Pitcairne, it may be, has conflated the two biblical Jonathans.

2–3 *Israelis/ Sive Jacobi*: the name of the patriarch Jacob was changed to Israel after he wrestled with the angel (*Genesis* 32:28). *Jacobus* is, of course, the Latin form of James, the name of the Old Pretender.

3–4 *hae-/-rede*: Pitcairne emphasizes a word of significant meaning in terms of the Pretender by dividing it between lines.

6 *Terque Ter Soter*: the final word is a borrowing into Latin of Gk. σωτήρ, 'saviour, deliverer,' used as a divine title, especially for Zeus as protector of voyagers and travellers, for human rulers, and for Christ. As applied to Swift, it is unexpectedly strong.

Terque Ter is perhaps a deliberate reminiscence of Virgil's *o terque quaterque beati* (*Aeneid* 1, 94). Macrobius' comment (*In Somnium Scipionis* 1, 6, 43–44) has a possible ironic relevance: *ergo ex his duobus numeris* (i.e., 3 and 4) *constat* διὰ τεσσάρων *et* διὰ πέντε, *ex quibus* διὰ πασῶν *symphonia generatur, unde Vergilius nullius disciplinae expers plene et per omnia beatos exprimere volens ait ... o terque quaterque beati*. Pitcairne's repetition of *ter* produces 9, the square of 3, numerologically even more powerful than 4.

7 *generi Israelis*: the British people.

94

Notes. For the earlier career of James Douglas, 4th Duke of Hamilton, see **42**, 7n; **74**, 11. In 1712 he 'was planning an arrangement whereby the Old Pretender should be recognised as Queen Anne's successor' (Donaldson and Morpeth, *Dictionary of Scottish History*, 93), when he was killed under suspicious circumstances in a duel with Charles, 4th Baron Mohun (1675?-1712). One of Mohun's two seconds, the Irishman Colonel George Macartney (1660?-1730), was accused of treacherously giving the duke his death-blow. Jacobites regarded the affair as a Whig plot to prevent the recognition and eventual succession of the Pretender. The most familiar account is probably that given by Thackeray in *Henry Esmond*, book III, chapter 6:

POEM 95

'The Queen's ambassador to Paris died, the loyal and devoted servant of the House of Stuart, and a Royal Prince of Scotland himself, and carrying the confidence, the repentance of Queen Anne along with his own open devotion and the goodwill of millions in the country more, to the Queen's exiled brother and sovereign'.

1–2 *Dum ... domo*: cf. 16, 1–2 and n. Both poems commemorate members of the Hamilton family.
2 *Regificaque*: the usual sense of this rare word is 'royal, regal, magnificent'; cf. *Aeneid* 6, 605: *regifico luxu*. Pitcairne also makes use of the etymological sense, 'king-making,' appropriate in terms of the mission the duke was about to undertake.
3 (a). *Ios*: i.e., Marlborough; cf. 74, 13n. Tories and Jacobites tended to blame Marlborough for anything working against their interests. Cf. *Henry Esmond*, ut cit.: 'He [Mohun], and Meredith and Macartney were the Duke of Marlborough's men ... I say not that he [Marlborough] was privy to Duke Hamilton's death, I say that his party profited by it; and that three desperate and bloody instruments were found to effect that murder.'
4 (a). *Hibernusque*; (b) *Hibernam*: the reference, direct in (a), in (b) more oblique, is to Colonel Macartney. In (b) *Hiberniam*, the usual form, would not scan; Pitcairne would perhaps have justified *Hibernam* in terms of the less common *Iverna* or *Ierna*.
Pitcairne's scansion indicates that the first -i- in *Hibernus*, *Hibernam*, is long, whereas in classical Latin it is short.
(a). *Vejovis*: see 75(b).
(b). *Barbariem*: this attitude to Ireland differs from that found in 12, 35–38.

95

Notes. An epigram, probably written in 1712, on the supposed heroic qualities of the Pretender. Cf. 119(a), (b), 2; 120, 2.

1 *Delphinis ... Britannica*: cf. Juvenal, *Satire* 10, 14: *quanto delphinis ballaena Britannica maior*. In Juvenal the line has a very different context, the danger of overconfidence in wealth, but it provided Pitcairne with the inspiration for the epigram.
There is a probably dismissive reference to Louis de France (1661–1711), the *Grand Dauphin*, and his eldest son, Louis duc de Bourgogne (1682–1712), who succeeded him as Dauphin only to die ten months later.
2 *Catulis ... Leo*: perhaps a semi-disguised heraldic joke. The lion rampant is the Scottish emblem, the English three leopards passant. The leopard was regarded as begotten in spouse-breach between the lion and the pard, i.e., he was the lion's whelp. Cf. Henryson, *Fables*, 873–879.

3 *pietate*: cf. the heroic *pius Aeneas*, and his Jacobite significance.
4 *Domi*: i.e., returned from exile, restored.

96

Notes. Robert Harley (1661–1724), 1st Earl of Oxford and Mortimer, began as a Whig and Presbyterian, but eventually became the moderate leader of the Tory and Church of England party in Parliament. On 29 March 1711 he became First Lord of the Treasury, in effect Prime Minister. His main political objectives were to conclude the War of the Spanish Succession with a reasonable peace (thus becoming 'Arbiter of Europe'), to put public finances upon a more secure footing, and to avoid Tory extremism. To maintain the support of Tory Jacobites, he covertly offered limited support to the Pretender (Hoppit, *Land of Liberty?*, 303). On the death of the Scottish Secretary, Queensberry, on 6 July 1711, Harley also took upon himself the administration of Scotland.

The subject of the poem is not only peace, but also the unity of Great Britain. By 1713 that unity was in some disarray, particularly so far as Scots were concerned. The abolition of the Scottish Privy Council in 1708 had been unpopular. The case of James Greenshields, an Episcopalian minister who had defied the presbytery of Edinburgh and been imprisoned, only to be cleared on appeal to the House of Lords, led to the Toleration and Patronage Acts of 1712. To Pitcairne and Episcopalians generally, these were cause for rejoicing, but they soured majority Presbyterian opinion. Generally unpopular too was the defeat on 20 December 1711 of the case brought by the Duke of Hamilton and Brandon that he had a rightful claim to a hereditary seat in the House of Lords. In 1713 the English Malt Tax was imposed on Scotland, contrary to the Act of Union, and the cost in money and resources of the War of the Spanish Succession had long been increasing. Harley's Peace of Utrecht, given final form a few months before Pitcairne's death in October 1713, thus had a considerable softening effect on Scottish opinion.

The poem turns on the contrast, between, on the one hand, Harley as *Arbiter Europae*, Queen Anne as *Britto*, and *Britannia*, Great Britain, as the major European power, and, on the other, *Scoti* and *Angligenae*, two wrangling groups of individuals, whose quarrels threaten the Union and the reduction of its influence to a mere cypher. Pitcairne approved of the Union, at least when headed by a Stuart.

The letter accompanying the epigram, addressed to 'Robert Ramsay, Provost of Salvator's Colledge and Rector of the Universitie of St Andrews,' is dated 1 September 1712. The poem was probably written at or about this date.

4 *Ultima ... Sui*: Harley's success made it seem more likely that the successor to Queen Anne would be her half-brother, the Pretender, and that the Stuart dynasty would not be replaced by the Hanoverian.

97

Notes. The epigram is a variation on the preceding, with greater emphasis on peace, less on internal disunity. Queen Anne too is given greater emphasis, as a Stuart, the last monarch of her line, if her half-brother were not to succeed. In this form the epigram may date from 1713, when the queen's health was failing, negotiations for the Treaty of Utrecht were well under way or complete, and the likelihood of the Hanoverian Succession was becoming more obvious.

The poem may be addressed to Harley, but it is at least possible that the intended recipient was Matthew Prior. The negotiations which ended the War of the Spanish Succession depended so much on his diplomatic skills that the subsequent treaty became popularly known as 'Matt's Peace.'

98

Notes. The emphasis on 'Stuart' continues.

1   *Regum*: the Stuart kings.
2   *reddi*: i.e., by the restoration of the Stuart male line.
    Caledon: Scotland.
3   *Rex*: the Pretender, since the death of his father, titular King James VIII. He and Queen Anne are jointly indicated by the pl. imperative *Este*. The pl. adjectives *bonae* and *Faustae* however are feminine, indicating that Anne, as *de facto* monarch, holds the dominant position.
4   *Teutonico ... jugo*: the Hanoverian succession. Contrast 1, 8 where the phrase *Teutonicas ... manus* refers to King William.

99

Notes. A somewhat obscure epigram. We have assumed that Pitcairne used the verb *fundere* in two different senses, in 1, 'pour forth', but in 2, 'cast down'. The subject is the Hanoverian succession, established for England by the 1701 Act of Settlement.

1   *Saxonas ... fudit*: a reference to the Anglo-Saxon invasion of the fifth century, which overthrew the native Britons and established England.
2   *Angle Britanne*: *Angle* parallels *Anglos* in the previous line. *Britanne* is a reminder of the fact that since the Union of 1707 English and Scots alike have become Britons, that, in a way, the conquered Britons have achieved a final success.
    tuos: the Stuart royal line, whose succession in England was precluded by the Act of Settlement.

COMMENTARY

100

Notes. The poem bears an obvious relationship to **97**. It contrasts Queen Anne's good fortune with the misfortunes of the Pretender, misfortunes which the queen can herself rectify.

2 *per innumeros ... avos*: Pitcairne accepts the legendary history of the Scottish monarchy.
4 GERMANO: the Pretender.

101

The epigram turns on the figure of the persecution of the sacred temple doves (Episcopalians and Jacobites) by birds of prey, crows (Presbyterian clergymen) and hawks (perhaps lawyers). This will come to an end with the return to his temple (Scotland) of the god (the Pretender).

The date of the poem is uncertain, but the reference to a possible marriage suggests that it is late; cf. **119, 121**.

1 *Te ... absente*: during the Pretender's exile.
2 *Impune*: an implied allusion to the Scottish national heraldic motto: *Nemo me impune lacessit.*
3 *Divi ... Deus*: i.e., the Pretender is son of a king and himself a king *de jure*.
5 *rediviva*: Scotland will be brought back to life with the Restoration.
6 *Cumque ... Venus*: the king will return accompanied by his queen. Probably Ulrika, sister of Charles XII of Sweden is intended; see **119**(a), 8 and n; **121**.
7–8 *Quae ... Jovi*: Jupiter, in the form of a bull, swam with Europa on his back from Tyre in Asia to Crete in Europe (whence the name), where she bore him several remarkable children. There is a fairly obvious parallel between the legend and the hypothetical good consequences for Europe as a whole of the return of the Pretender, suitably married.

102

Notes. James Drummond (1713–1746), 6th Earl and 3rd titular (i.e., Jacobite) Duke of Perth, came of a notably Jacobite lineage and was himself to die a Jacobite martyr. His grandfather, a convert to Catholicism, had been James VII's Chancellor and shared his exile. His father had been imprisoned in the Tower for raising 200 men in anticipation of the abortive 1708 Rising. On the birth of his son, he made his estates over to him. Subsequently he played an important part in the 1715 Rising, after which he accompanied the Pretender to the continent, where he

430

died (1720) in Paris. His mother was daughter of the 1st Duke of Gordon and Elizabeth, nèe Howard (**89, 90**); hence the reference in 2.

In the '45 James Drummond was one of Charles Edward's senior officers. At Culloden (1746) he commanded the left wing of the Prince's army. Stress and exhaustion killed him as he escaped to France and he was buried at sea.

Stobhall, on the river Tay in Perthshire, is the ancestral home of the Drummonds, from which they took their original title.

3   *Patremque*: the Pretender.
4   *Jacobumque*: again primarily the Pretender, although its position makes the word deliberately ambiguous, with the possibility that it might refer to the young James Drummond.
5   *rure*: i.e., from his exile on the continent.
6   *Anabella*: Queen Anne.
    favens: i.e., by declaring the Pretender her successor.

103

Notes. Renaissance work on chronology and calendars reached its height in the *De emendatione temporum* (1583) of Joseph Justus Scaliger (1540–1609). This established the Julian period, based on a cycle of 7980 years together with a consecutive numbering of days from January 1, 4713 BC, plus the decimal fraction of the day elapsed since the previous noon. Thus the year 2002 began at Julian date 2452275.5; 2003 at 2452640.5. The numbering by days made the system independent of the variable lengths of months and years. It is still used by astronomers for accurate computing work, but was fairly obviously impractical for ordinary day-to-day use.

At the time, calendars were the subject of much discussion. Scaliger's was more accurate than the reformed calendar which had been introduced by Pope Gregory XIII in 1582, and which Scaliger (a Protestant) denounced. In Catholic countries nevertheless it was the Gregorian calendar which replaced the earlier one (Julian calendar), established by Julius Caesar, which by this time had fallen eleven days behind the date indicated by the Sun. Protestant countries were slower to adapt – Britain, for instance, adopted the Gregorian calendar as late as 1752. In 1710 the difference between the two was such that 29 May in the old style (OS) was 10 June by the new (NS). Pitcairne seems to confuse Scaliger's calendar with the Gregorian.

As already often noted (**7**, etc.), both dates were Jacobite festivals; 29 May that of the birth (1630) and Restoration (1660) of Charles II, 10 June the birthday of the Old Pretender. Pitcairne enjoyed the coincidence and in the first poem urges Scaliger, in effect, to appreciate that the use of the Gregorian calendar had had at least one fortunate result. He also seems to anticipate that Britain eventually would

COMMENTARY

adopt the Gregorian calendar, perhaps with the return of the Old Pretender. He is probably also hinting that the pretender is, in effect, a reincarnation of Charles II.
Version (b) of the poem immediately following employs the same conceit.

1–2 *quo ... cœlo*: a reference to *De emendatione temporum*.
2 *Gallo*: although Scaliger's father was Italian, he himself was born and spent most of his life in France.
4 *Scoto-Brigantum*: i.e., Scots; see **6**, 3n, **15**, 44 and n. Scaliger visited Scotland in 1566; his general reputation there was always high.
5 *quibus terris*: i.e., in France and Scotland.
stimulante Phœbo: the fact that the Sun apparently moved faster through the Zodiac than the old calendar had allowed, led to the adoption of the new.
6–7 *quondam ... gentibus*: i.e., in England, once the male Stuart line has been restored. For *quondam* with future reference cf. *Aeneid* 6, 876–877 (of the young Marcellus): *nec Romula quondam/ ulla se tantum tellus iactabit alumno*.
7–8 *vi/gesima nona*: the split in *vigesima* between the final syllable of the third Lesser Sapphic and the Adonic helps emphasize the syntactic continuity of this stanza with the beginning of the next, as also the movement from one calendar to another.
11–12 *etiam ... fluentes*: i.e., in the realm of the dead.
14 *Carle, natalis*: see above, introductory note.
15–16 *potenti ... creatum*: we do not fully understand the significance of this phrase, but cf. **15**, 29–34. The idea here is probably that Dis has sent Charles, in the person of the Pretender, back from the world of the dead to restore Britain to its former glories.

104

Notes. In 1712 the anniversary of the Restoration and the ecclesiastical Feast of the Ascension (celebrated on the 5th Thursday, the 40th day, after Easter) both occurred on Thursday, 29 May (OS). In all versions, although no more than implicit in (a) and (c), there is the additional point that 29 May (OS) is 10 June (NS); see **103**.

3 (a), (b). *jus ... tribui*: cf. *Romans* 13:7: 'Render therefore to all their dues: tribute to whom tribute is due'; *Matthew* 22:21, *Mark* 12:17, *Luke* 20:25: 'Render therefore unto Caesar the things which are Caesar's'. Cf, also Hobbes, *Leviathan* I, 15, 72: 'Justice is the constant Will of giving to every man his own.' Such texts were often used by Jacobites as applying to the exiled James VII and later to his son; cf. **89**, introductory note.
monte: probably the Mount of Olives, traditional site of the Ascension. Christ's words there, as recorded in *Mark* 16:15–18, *Acts* 1:4–8, contain nothing resem-

bling the words attributed to him in this line. Nor does the Sermon on the Mount.

(c). *justos ... scelestos*: cf. *Mark* 16:16, the words of Christ immediately before the Ascension: 'He that believeth and is baptized shall be saved: but he that believeth not shall be damned.' For Pitcairne, the latter clause refers to the Whigs and Presbyterians as non-believers.

4 (b), (c). *Esseque ... colit*: cf. the first clause of *Mark* 16:16, quoted above.
5 (b). *Maio ... haeres*: 10 June is the birthday of the heir of Charles, who was himself born on 29 May.
6 (a), (c). *nomina*: read *numina*, as in (b)?
   dabit: future tense, referring to the hoped-for Restoration of the Pretender.

105

Notes. The two texts appear to be variant versions of an epigram composed in 1712 in the immediate expectation that the Pretender would be named as Queen Anne's successor. June, the month of his birth, is used as a figure for the supposed future king.

1 *Regem*: a half-concealed reference to the Pretender as King, James VIII and III.
2 (a). *Julius, Augusto*: July and August are singled out as months commemorating former rulers, Julius Caesar and his great-nephew, the emperor Augustus. They now give way to the month of the Pretender.
   (b) *decimum*: 10 June, the Pretender's birthday.
3 *Septembres atque Novembres*: months which mark the decline of the year to winter. Correspondingly, Charles II was defeated at Worcester, 3 September 1651; William of Orange landed at Torbay 5 November 1688.

106

Notes. In 1622 Calvinism became the state religion of the Netherlands. In England it was the dominant force behind the Independents (Congregationalists), as in Scotland for the Presbyterians. The Independents, represented by Cromwell and his army, were responsible for the execution of Charles I on 30 January 1649, the Presbyterians for handing him over to the Parliamentary army, and for the later observation of the anniversary of his execution as a festival. The Calvinist William of Orange, born 4 November 1650, os, drove out the legitimate king, James VII and II by an invasion on 5 November 1688, os. Pitcairne sets these dates and events in contrast with another, 5 November 1605, when Guy Fawkes and his fellow-conspirators failed to kill Charles' father, James VI and I, in the Gunpowder Plot.

The epigram was written for the sixty-second anniversary of William's birth, one day before the twenty-fourth anniversary of his invasion. The version found in HRHRC and SF may have been intended for a different occasion. The translation of ll. 3–4 is: 'the thirtieth of January saw your disciples, Calvin, accomplish with worse than sacrilegious hands.'

> **Title** (c): Janus is the Roman god who gave his name to January. *Janus* for *Joannes* Calvin thus indicates the theologian's ultimate responsibilty for events which had given the month a bad name. *Janus* for *Joannes* is common in neo-Latin verse.
>
> 3   *Vos ... vos*: Calvinists, Dutch, Scots and English.
>   *quarta ... Novembris*: the birthday of King William.

107

Notes. The birth of George Main's son James is used as the occasion for a celebration of the return of the Pretender. We have not been able to identify George Main or his son. Presumably Pitcairne was in professional attendance on the child's mother during her pregnancy.

The poem is a conceit, based on the calendar, the name James, *Jacobus*, shared by the child and the Pretender, and the name Main, rendered as *Magnus*. The date 7 November obviously has a special significance which we have not been able to determine with certainty. If it fell on a Saturday, Pitcairne probably associated it with the messianic lines in Virgil:

> *magnus ab integro saeclorum nascitur ordo.*
> *iam redit et virgo, redeunt Saturnia regna,*
> *iam nova progenies caelo demittitur alto.*

The lines, it should be noted, occur in *Eclogue* 4, lines 5, 6, and 7. The numbering thus corresponds closely to that of the dates mentioned in the epigram. Note too how Virgil employs the words *magnus* and *redit*. The fourth *Eclogue* was part of 'the language of Stuart archetypes inherited at the Revolution' (Pittock, *Poetry and Jacobite Politics*, 12).

1   *Quarta ... Novembris*: William of Orange was born 4 November 1650. The ill-omened anniversary passed without harming the unborn child.
2   *quinta*: On 5 November 1688 William of Orange with his forces landed at Torbay in Devon. Another day of ill-omen.
3   *Sexta ter*: The associations of 6 as a birth number are good, primarily because God completed the work of Creation in 6 days. 6 is also the first perfect number, the factors of which, when added together, make up the number itself

(1 + 2 + 3 = 6). Perfect numbers are exceedingly rare and therefore significant. 3 is also fortunate. The child may also be thrice desired because his birth had been expected on 3 successive days.
4 *Juno*: i.e., Juno Lucina, goddess of childbirth. As Lucina, she is mentioned in *Eclogue* 4, 10.
5 *ter*: note the repetition from 3.
6 *redire*: cf. *redis*, 7, and see introductory Note. The juxtaposition with the vocative *Magne* makes the reference obvious.
7–8 and **Gloss**: The lack of these features in BA *(4a)*, 9, may indicate that it represents an early version, felt to be over obscure. The additions would then be intended to dissipate some of the obscurity.
8 *Junius*: a reference to the Pretender's birthday, 10 June 1688.

108

Notes. 30 November is the feast of St Andrew, patron saint of Scotland. The point of the epigram is that the apostle James and the Old Pretender share their name and that St Andrew is friendly to both.

1 *Andraea ... Amicus*: for the friendship of the apostles Andrew and James, see *Mark* 1:16–20, 29, 13:3.
2 *Caledoniis*: The Caledonians inhabited Scotland in Roman times and are generally now regarded as proto-Picts. St Regulus brought the relics of St Andrew to a king of the Picts, Unuist, who won an apparently hopeless battle against the English by the intervention of the saint. 'Caledonia' and 'Caledonians' later became synonymous with 'Scotland' and 'Scots'.
4 *Jacobo*: James, the Old Pretender.
  redux: cf. *Astræa Redux*, Dryden's poem (1660) on the Restoration of Charles II; cf. 2, 1n. In classical Latin the adjective in an active sense is employed as an epithet of Jupiter or Fortuna, in a passive sense of the phoenix after its cremation. Here Andrew is to play the part usually ascribed to Jupiter or Fortune; the Pretender by his return (*redeunte*) that of the phoenix, or Astraea, bringing back the Golden Age. As usual, a parallel is suggested between the return of the Pretender and the 1660 Restoration.
5 *fidem*: i.e., the loyalty shown by Jacobites.
5–6 *officiis, officiis nostris & pietate*: the Episcopalian form of ritual and belief held by Pitcairne and his friends. The repetition gives particular force to *officiis*.
5 *relligione malorum*: Presbyterianism, in which saint's days were not observed.

COMMENTARY

109

Notes. The title in (a) shows that the poem was written for Christmas 1712. The poem is an expression of Episcopalian High Church orthodoxy, which necessarily entailed the restoration to the throne of the male Stuart line in the person of the Pretender. The language is sometimes coded. In (b) the additional material provided by Calder exploits this aspect to the full.

(a)

1   *Hac*: *die* understood from the title.
4   *Patris ... sua jussa*: i.e., the Ten Commandments (*Exodus* 20:3–17) summarised in the Two Commandments of Charity (*Matthew* 22:37–39).
6   *homines fecit*: Genesis 1, 27 (*Vulgate*): et creavit Deus hominem ... masculum et feminam creavit eos.
semideosque viros: demigods were the children of a divinity and a mortal. Pitcairne may have had in mind *John* 1:12–13: 'But as many as received him, to them gave he power to become the sons of God, even to them that believe on his name.'
The word *homines* refers to humankind, male and female alike; the strictly masculine *viros* reflects the masculine 'sons' in the passage from *John*.
7   *alii ... velles*: *Luke* 6:31: 'And as you would that men should do to you, do ye also to them likewise.' The passage has Jacobite undertones.
8–10   *reddere ... minor*: cf. *Matthew* 22:21: 'Render therefore unto Caesar the things which are Caesar's; and unto God the things that are God's.' The passage is given strong Jacobite overtones. Cf. **89**, **104**.
11   *Hac ... die natus*: Pitcairne was born on Christmas day 1651.

(b)

2   *Te cum Pitcarno*: Drummond was born on Christmas Day, 1656; cf. **64**, 10 and n. He too was a Jacobite.
21   *Arii*: Arius (c. 250–c. 336), heresiarch, who denied the divinity of Christ.
Socini: Socinus is the Latinized form of the name of two Italian religious teachers, uncle and nephew, Lelio Francesco Maria Sozini (1525–1562) and Fausto Paolo Sozzini (1539–1604). They were unitarians, denying the divinity of Christ.
During the seventeenth- and early eighteenth-centuries the terms Arian and Socinian 'were often used loosely and indiscriminately against anyone who employed scepticism and reason to question the fundamental tenets of the Established Church' (Hoppit, *Land of Liberty?*, 228). See too Introduction, pp. 30–31.

22 *Sanguinei ... olet*: i.e., he had no sympathy with Cameronians, Covenanters or opponents of Charles I and James VII.
23 *Cæsari, & Iro*: i.e., the highest and lowest ranks of society. Irus is the obstreperous beggar of *Odyssey* 18, but the name is often used simply for an extremely poor man; *Croeso divitior licet fuissem, / Iro pauperior forem* (Martial 5, 39, 8–9).
24 *dare cuique suum*: cf. (a), 8–10n.
   temnere ... opes: cf. Matthew 16:26: 'For what is a man profited, if he shall gain the whole world, and lose his own soul?'

110

Notes. The poem combines elements found in two others. Like **108**, it is a Christmas poem. Like **107**, it includes an appeal to the apostles Andrew and James. Like both, it is Episcopalian in tone, but more directly critical than either of Presbyterian church government, primarily in terms of the observance of Christmas as a fast, but also of their doctrine of kingship. Like both it is strongly Jacobite.

1 *jejunia*: Presbyterians regarded Christmas as a fast rather than a feast.
2 *Usinulca*: as indicated by the gloss, an anagram of *Caluinus*. See **83**, 9–10 n.
3–4 *Pharisaei ... timent*: cf. especially *Matthew* 23:34.
4 *Adventumque*: the church season of Advent comes immediately before Christmas and is a preparation not only for the first, but also for the Second Coming of Christ in Judgement.
5–6 *parendum ... suum*: cf. **104**, 8–10 and n.
9 *nobis*: primarily Episcopalians.
10 *Cnoxiacis*: cf. **43**, 1 and n.
11 *Andream ... Jacobumque*: cf. **107**.

111

Notes. For George Heriot, see **43**. He was born in early June 1563. Annually, on the first Monday of the month ('June Day'), the Governors, staff and boys (now also girls) of the Hospital celebrate the memory of the pious Founder. By statute the Ministers of Edinburgh are Governors; one of them by rotation is required to deliver a sermon, for which he is paid. In the evening an elaborate dinner is held. By contrast Presbyterians did not observe Christmas as a festival, but rather as a fast (**110**, 1–2).

Robert Calder (1650?-1723), the speaker in 7–9, was the dispossessed Episcopalian minister of Elgin, afterwards incumbent at Toddrick's Wynd in Edinburgh. He is best known as the probable author of *Scotch Presbyterian Eloquence Display'd*

COMMENTARY

(1692; cf. **18**, introductory n.), but he also wrote, among much else, two works relevant to the present poem, *The Lawfulness and Expediency of Set Forms of Prayer* (1706), and *The Lawfulness and Necessitie of observing the Anniversary Fasts and Festivals of the Church* (1710). Pitcairne and he appear to have been friends.

As with **43**, the occasion for the poem was probably the dispute between the Governors of Heriot's Hospital and Dr George Mackenzie.

2 *Knoxiadae*: The Presbyterian ministers, 'sons of [John] Knox'. The form is patronymic. Cf. **43**, 1 and n., **110**, 10.
5 *nummos*: the fee paid for the sermon.
10 *pretium Caroli Martyris*: On 30 January 1647 the Presbyterian Scottish army abandoned Charles I to English forces at Newcastle, 'receiving shortly afterwards the first instalment due to them by England for their service' (*DNB*). Exactly two years later Charles was beheaded. Pitcairne, like many others, regarded the surrender as a Judas-like betrayal. There is also a reference to the Episcopalian cult of 'Charles King and Martyr'.

112

Notes. On the surface, an old man's longing in winter for summer, but with strong Jacobite overtones.

1 *Jane*: see **13**, 5n.
2 *Junius*: the Pretender had been born in June 1688.
4 *caedes*: the execution of Charles I.

113

Notes. 10 June is a figure for the Pretender. The identity of that date with 29 May is assumed; see **103**. Sacheverell (2) is the English High Church clergyman Henry Sacheverell (1674?-1724), tried before the House of Lords in 1710 for a sermon delivered at St Paul's in 1709, 'The Perils of False Brethren,' directed against the supposed threat of Whigs and Non-conformists to the Church of England as re-established by the return of Charles II. Tories and High Churchmen regarded the guilty verdict, accompanied as it was by a light sentence, as a triumph, which contributed to their success in the election of 1710.

Despite his opinions, Sacheverell does not seem to have been a Jacobite. Pitcairne urges him, in effect, to carry his doctrines one further step and accept the claims of the Pretender.

Pitcairne regarded the Ascension as a pattern for the return of the Pretender.

POEM 115

3   *Qui*: the masculine relative indicates that 10 June represents a man, the Pretender.
    memorem Maii faciet: because 10 June (NS) is the same as 29 May (OS); i.e., the Pretender and Charles II are, as it were, one and the same person.
4   *aurea Secla*: the Golden Age of a restored Charles II and a returned Astraea; cf. 2, 1n.
    Colophon. *Christi ... reditus*: implicit in the phrase is the idea that the Pretender also will ascend the throne in succession to Anne.

114

Notes. For St Margaret see **37**, introductory note. Pitcairne again plays with the identity of 29 May (OS) and 10 June (NS), in terms of which 29 May becomes the feast-day of St Margaret and the Pretender's birthday. He also weaves variations on the names of days of the week, Tuesday, Saturday and Wednesday, and on the words *Arbitra* and *Arbiter*.

1   *Marti*: 29 May (OS) was a Tuesday, *dies Martis*, in 1713.
    Caroloque: Charles II was born on 29 May 1630. The Restoration took place on his 30th birthday.
2   *Arbitraque ... Salus*: probably a reference to the Treaty of Utrecht, signed on 11 April 1713, a Wednesday, which Pitcairne seems to have regarded as a Tuesday.
2,6. *Arbitraque Europae*; *Arbiter, Europe*: cf. **97**, **98**, both, as here, referring to the negotiations leading to the Peace of Utrecht and the consequences.
3   *Saturnus*: the reign of Saturn was the Golden Age. He is also the god or planet of Saturday, *dies Saturni*. 10 June 1713 (NS) was a Saturday.
3–4 *Secla... Aurea*: cf. **2**, 1n.; **112**, 4 and n.
4   *Junius Ille meus*: the Pretender, born on 10 June 1688, the festival commemorating the Translation of the relics of St Margaret in 1250.
5   *Qui*: cf. **112**, 3n.
    Marti Mercurioque: Mars is god of war, Mercury of commerce. The accession of the Pretender, as a consequence of the Peace of Utrecht, will encourage the revival of trade throughout Europe. *Dies Mercurii* is Wednesday.

115

Notes. The feast of St Peter and St Paul is celebrated on 29 June. On that day in 1713 St Peter, Prince of the Apostles and first bishop, responds to the presbyters (Church of Scotland ministers) who have reminded him of his triple denial of Christ (Matthew 26:69–75; also in the other Gospels). Two of the corresponding

COMMENTARY

Presbyterian acts of denial are self-evident, the surrender of Charles I to the English army on 30 January 1647 and the acceptance of William as king in place of James VII on 4 April 1689. The third king mentioned may be the Pretender, but, if so, the precise occasion is less clear. If the date 29 June 1713 has any significance other than the one already mentioned, the reference may be to the narrow defeat on 2 June of a motion for the dissolution of the Union (in Scottish terms a motion favourable to the Pretender), proposed in the House of Lords by the well-known trimmer, James Ogilvy (1663–1730), 4th Earl of Findlater, and 1st Earl of Seafield who had been Scottish Chancellor, 1705–1708 and who was responding to a feeling widespread both in Scotland and in England (Ferguson, *Scotland 1689 to the Present*, 61). But the defeat can hardly be put to the account of Presbyterian ministers.

Dr Money has suggested to us that, if the term *regibus* is not necessarily used exclusively of males, the third may well be Mary Queen of Scots, forced by Presbyterians to abdicate on 24 July 1567. In classical Latin *reges* sometimes means 'a king and his queen'; cf. from the story of Servius Tullius in Livy, *Ab Urbe Condita*, 1, 39, 2: *plurimo igitur clamore inde ad tantae rei miraculum orto excitos reges, et cum quidam familiarium aquam ad restinguendum ferret, ab regina retentum ....* The *reges* are Tarquinius Priscus, fifth king of Rome, and his queen Tanaquil. Pitcairne may have known the usage and extended it.

In Pitcairne's view, the presbyters abjure God simply by being Presbyterians.

116

Notes. An expression of hope and warning for the Pretender. He must give up his Roman Catholicism and any concessions to the Presbyterian Calvinists.

Title 25 July is the feast of St James the Great, Apostle and Martyr, in whose name the Pretender was baptised; cf. **107, 109,** 11.

1 *gens Grampia*: i.e., the Scots, the people of the Grampian Mountains.
Sancte: a reference both to St James and to the Pretender, sanctified in terms of the doctrine of the Divine Right of Kings, summarised by Figgis (*Divine Right*, 5–6) under four headings: (1) Monarchy is a divinely ordained institution. (2) Heredity right is indefeasible. (3) Kings are accountable to God alone. (4) Non-resistance and passive obedience are enjoined by God. None of these doctrines was acceptable to Roman Catholics (*Romae ... fidem*, 2) or Calvinists (*Genevae ... Relligionis*, 3).

117

Notes. For Robert Calder, see **110**, introductory note. William Wishart (1660–1729), Presbyterian clergyman, was imprisoned 1684–1685 for denying the King's authority. He was ordained in 1688 and in 1692 became minister of South Leith, despite much active opposition from the Episcopalian community. He became Moderator of the General Assembly for the first time in 1706. In 1707 he became minister of the Tron Kirk in Edinburgh. In 1713 he again became Moderator – in all, he held the office five times. On 19 August 1713, together with John Dundas, he published *Seasonable Warning by the Commission of the General Assembly concerning the danger of popery*, a manifesto which included an attack on Episcopalians and Jacobites, and which may be the occasion of the present poem. The precise point however remains obscure.

If the poem is in fact Pitcairne's, it is the latest of his to survive.

2   *Normannumque*: not identified.
6   *Usinulca*: Calvin; see **83**, 9–10n., **109**, 2.

118

Notes. In 1700, Philip of Anjou (1683–1746), grandson of Louis XIV, succeeded Charles II (1662–1700) as Philip V, King of Spain. This upset the European balance of power and in an attempt to restore something like the *status quo* other European powers, including Austria, England, Holland, and some of the German states, took up arms to promote Charles (1685–1740; see **118**), second son of the Hapsburg emperor Leopold I as King of Spain. Thus began the War of the Spanish Succession (1701–1714). Jacobites naturally supported Philip, while Whigs were on the side of Charles, at least until in 1711 he succeeded his elder brother Joseph I (1678–1711) as Emperor.

Version (a) was written, perhaps on the occasion of Philip's first marriage in 1702 to Maria Louisa of Savoy (d. 1714). Maria eventually bore him a son, Louis (1707–1724), who, before his death, was briefly king, when his father had made an abdication, which proved temporary.

Version (b), dated 1710, seems intended as a compliment to Louis. It takes the form of a prophecy by Philip's great predecessor, the Emperor Charles V (1500–1558), King of Spain as Charles I, whose rule had extended over much of Europe, America, and even parts of North Africa.

Pitcairne makes no reference to Philip's Catholicism, but in the poem immediately following (**119**) he derides that of Philip's opponent Charles, later the Emperor Charles VI. This is consistent with the attitude implied, **30**, 5–6, **48**, 4. On the other hand, Pitcairne praises the Catholic Duchess of Gordon (**89**), and of course the Pretender himself was a Catholic. Only in **115** is there any suggestion that he should change his faith. Pitcairne's hostility to Catholicism is secondary to his Jacobitism.

(a)

1 *Austriacas ... Belgas*: the forces opposed to Philip and supporting the claim of Charles. By 'Saxon' Pitcairne probably intends English as well as German forces.
2 *Ammone*: Philip is compared to Philip of Macedon (359–336 BC), a distinguished soldier, father of the still more distinguished Alexander the Great (356–322 BC), who was also regarded as in some sense child of the Egyptian god Ammon.
3 *puellum*: a rare diminutive. Pitcairne may have had in mind the couplet *et multae steriles Hymenaeis ante fuerunt/ pluribus et nactae post sunt tamen unde puellos* (*Lucretius* 4, 1251–1252).
4–5 *Eoas ... Iberis*: the Spanish overseas empire.

(b)

1 *Caesaris*: the Emperor Joseph I.
2 *meo*: i.e., Charles V, who had a distinguished military record.

119

Notes. The poem is addressed to Charles, rival of Philip V for the throne of Spain (see **118**), probably when he became Emperor in 1711. We have not been able to trace the presentation to him by Queen Anne of an ornamental sword, which in 1708 he dedicated to the Black Virgin, *Nuestra Señora de Montserrat, Patrona de Cataluña*, in the monastery of Montserrat, NW of Barcelona – an obvious attempt to bolster his position in Spain. An inscription commemorating the event, preserved as *N(79)*, gives some help in the exposition of the poem:

INSCRIPTIO
Quum gladium gemmis auroque nitentem suspenderet magnae suae Caelorum Reginae MARIÆ *ab* ANNA *terrarum mariumque maxima Regina sibi donatum* CAROLUS *Hispaniae Rex, 1708.*
Ad aram Virginis MARIÆ,
Quæ in sacris paginis nigra dicitur,
Sed formosa;

Quæ mater est ejus per quem Reges regnant,
Humillime
Provolutus in genua,
In perpetuam memoriam Austriacæ devotionis,
Consecro & depono
Gladium lateri meo detractum;
Ut pro me
Ita exarmato
Fortioribus armis Cœlum militet,
Sub auspiciis
Magnæ hujus Cœlorum Reginæ,
Quam eligo & constituo
In bello ducem exercitus,
In pace custodem regnorum,
Ac advocatum
Ad Deum pro me
Maximo peccatorum,
Montiserati, VII Calendis Julii,
Ejusdem Virginis matris MARIÆ,
Cœli terræque
Dominæ
Infimus clientum, servus perpetuus,
CAROLUS.

1 *Fratris*: Joseph I (1678–1711), elder brother of Charles, Emperor from 1705. *Parentis*: Leopold I (1640–1705), Emperor from 1658.
2 *proavum*: the House of Habsburg.
3 *Finge ... amicam*: cf. the inscription quoted above.
 Dei Matrem: the Virgin, *mater ... ejus per quem Reges regnant*.
 si qua est: Pitcairne demonstrates characteristic Protestant hostility to the cult of the Virgin.
7 *Nil bello ... pacis iniquus*: cf. from the inscription *In bellum ducem exercitus,/ In pace custodem regnorum*.
8 *sociis*: his allies in the War of the Spanish Succession.
9 *Ganeo ... aude*: the reference is probably to the counsel given by Roman Catholic priests.
10 *Tu ... eris*: Although Joseph had two daughters, it was widely expected before his death, that he would die without male issue.

COMMENTARY

120

Notes. The career of the Swedish king, Charles XII (1682–1718), is well summarized by Johnson in *The Vanity of Human Wishes*:

> On what foundation stands the warrior's pride,
> How just his hopes, let Swedish Charles decide.
> A frame of adamant, a soul of fire,
> No dangers fright him, and no labours tire;
> O'er love, o'er fear, extends his wide domain,
> Unconquer'd lord of pleasure and of pain;
> No joys to him pacific sceptres yield,
> War sounds the trump, he rushes to the field.
> Behold surrounding kings their pow'rs combine,
> And one capitulate, and one resign:
> Peace courts his hand, but spreads her charms in vain;
> 'Think nothing gain'd,' he cries, 'till nought remain,
> On Moscow's walls till Gothic standards fly,
> And all be mine beneath the polar sky.'
> The march begins in military state,
> And nations on his eye suspended wait;
> Stern Famine guards the solitary coast,
> And Winter barricades the realms of Frost;
> He comes, nor want nor cold his course delay;–
> Hide, blushing glory, hide Pultowa's day:
> The vanquish'd hero leaves his broken bands,
> And shows his misery in distant lands;
> Condemn'd a needy supplicant to wait,
> While ladies interpose, and slaves debate ...   (191–214)

Pitcairne's poem was probably written during Charles' campaign against the Russians, but before his defeat at Poltava (Pultowa) in 1709. Pitcairne assumes that negotiations are under way for a marriage between Charles and the princess Louisa Maria Theresa, something for which we have found no confirmatory evidence. The prospect was more a Jacobite dream than a political reality. The theme continues in the following two poems.

(a)

1   *Gothorum*: the Swedes.
2   *solum ... parem*: the Pretender, an exile in France, *Gallia ... ora*.

444

POEM 121

4 *Sauromatum*: the Russians. The classical Sarmatians were Slavs, living between the Vistula and the Ukrainian Don.
dextro ... pede: cf. Juvenal, *Satire* 10, 5–6: *quid tam dextro pede concipis ut te/ conatus non paeniteat?*
5 *in tui ... reducent*: i.e., bring Charles back from Turkey to Sweden.
8 *Sic ... Tibi*: i.e., by marrying him.
Gallobritanna: Louisa had spent her entire life in France.

(b)

2 JACOBUS: the Pretender, regarded as a capable soldier.
Alaricus: Visigothic king, who captured Rome in 410, and died shortly afterwards. Pitcairne regards him as the most distinguished Goth before Charles XII.
8 *Di ... Tui*: the altered text suggests that this version was composed when the death of Louisa in 1712 meant that a marriage was no longer a possibility.
Soror: Ulrika, sister of Charles XII, the Alarica of the following poems, who governed Sweden during his absence. Her marriage to the Pretender will show that both she and the gods favour Charles.

121

Notes. The poem is a celebration of the 18th birthday, the coming-of-age, of the princess Louisa Maria Theresa (1692–1712), youngest daughter of James VII and sister to the Old Pretender. The title in SP gives her birthday date OS; in modern works of reference it is usually given as 28 June, NS.

Either version is a variant on the topos *taceat superata vetustas* (Curtius, *Latin Middle Ages*, 162–165).

(i)

1 *Fratre Tuo*: the Old Pretender.
Gradivum: a surname of Mars. The Old Pretender was considered a capable soldier.
4 *Virgo patroa*: here, apparently, the Sun; see Introduction, p. 44. Pitcairne seems to have obtained the adjective from a corrupt reading in Catullus, 1, 9: *qualecumque; quod, o patrona virgo*. The 'Printer's Address to the Reader', prefixed to *Epistola Archimedis ad Regem Gelonem*, ends by misquoting the final three lines of the poem: *Quare habe tibi quicquid hocce scripti &/ Qualecunque; quod, o patroa Virgo,/ Plus uno maneat perenne sæclo.* Pitcairne seems to have used the same text, providing his own explanation for *patroa*. If even *patrona virgo* is accurate, the reference is probably to the Muse; see Fordyce, *Catullus*, 86–87. In ii, the reference is different.

445

COMMENTARY

(ii)

1–2 *Risit ... viget*: the lines refer to the birth of the Pretender.
4   *Apollo*: the reference is more straightforward than that in i, but not, perhaps, entirely appropriate.

122

Notes. These poems were written after the death of Louisa on 18 August 1712. Both take the form of instructions sent by her in the afterlife to Ulrika (1688–1741), sister of Charles XII, on whose death she became Queen of Sweden (1718–1720). Her marriage to the Pretender, together with his restoration to the British throne, is assumed. Ulrika in fact married Frederick of Hesse-Kassel (1715), in whose favour she gave up the Swedish throne.

The first four words of each poem are identical, but the development is substantially different. They are best regarded as separate poems.

(a)

1 *Anna*: Queen Anne.
3 *Matrem Britannis*: both as Queen Consort and as mother to a royal heir.
5 *Soror*: of Charles XII.
6 *Magni ... tres*: Scots, English, and Irish.

(b)

1–2 *Juppiter ... meo*: a convoluted compliment. Jupiter has divorced Juno and taken Louisa as his wife, because Juno was of lesser rank than a member of the Stuart royal family.
2   REGI ... *meo*: the Pretender, regarded as *de jure* monarch of Britain, likely to become so *de facto* on the death of Queen Anne.

123

Metre. (Latin): 'Ad PHILOSOPHOS,' 'In REGINAM': elegiac couplet. '*In Oreadum Regem*': hexameter.
Notes. There is no certain evidence that the translation is Pitcairne's; in style and subject matter it differs from anything else in his *opus*. It seems unlikely however that Dennistoun was capable of so virtuoso a performance, or that anyone other than Pitcairne would have assigned credit for the work to him. It is probably because Watson, himself a friend of Pitcairne and printer of some of his undoubted works,

knew what the attribution implied, that he included text and translation in his *Choice Collection*. He wished to introduce something by so distinguished a figure as his friend. In what follows we shall assume that Pitcairne is the translator.

Pitcairne rendered one other poem from the vernacular, '*An Inscription on* JOHN BELL' (**123**), very different in style and subject-matter from ΜΟΡΜΟΝΟΣΤΟΛΙΣΜΟS, and equally different from Pitcairne's other Latin verse.

Such translations are not unknown in other Scottish neo-Latin poets; cf., e.g., Buchanan's *Somnium*, last item before the *Palinodia* in *Fratres Fraterrimi* (1568), which is a version of William Dunbar's 'This nycht befoir the dawing cleir' ('How Dumbar wes Desyrd to be ane Freir,' Priscilla Bawcutt, *The Poems of William Dunbar*, 2 vols., [Glasgow, 1998], i, 248–249; see too Philip J. Ford, *George Buchanan Prince of Poets* [Aberdeen, 1982], 49–54). Arthur Johnston (1587–1641) has three translations of English poems, most notably '*Ne rogites, roseum sol dum iubar explicat, auro*,' a rendering of 'Ask me no more where Jove bestows,' by Thomas Carew (?1598–?1639; see MLA, ii, 201–205; H.J.C. Grierson [ed.], *Metaphysical Lyrics & Poems of the Seventeenth Century* [Oxford, 1921], 38–39. Geddes fails to recognise the source.). Similar examples from the Continent are '*Indignatus Amor telis petiisse Rosinam*,' by Paulus Melissus (1539–1602), a translation of 'Amour estant marri qu'il avoit ses saigettes,' a sonnet from Ronsard's *Continuation des Amours*, and *De Tristitia spirituali*, a sonnet sequence by Jacques de Billy (1535–1581). This last is unusual in that the French and Latin poems are by the same author and 'Dates of publication strongly suggest that the Latin versions were written after the original French' (McFarlane, *Renaissance Latin Poetry*, 60–61, 98–99, 232, 237).

The most probable source for part at least of the English poem translated is the second section (pp. 1–3) of *A* DESCRIPTION *Of the King and Queene of Fayries, their habit, fare, their abode, pompe, and state, Being very delightful to the sense, and full of mirth* (London, 1634; Rosenbach Museum and Library, Philadelphia, STC2 21512.5, p. 1);

A Description of the King
of Fayries Clothes, brought to him
on New-yeares day in the
morning, 1626. by his
Queenes Chamber-
maids.

First a Cobweb-shirt, more thinne
Than ever Spider since could spin
Chang'd to the whitenesse of the snow,
By the stormie windes that blow
5   In the vast and frozen ayre,
No shirt halfe so fine, so faire.

A rich Wascoat they did bring,
Made of the Trout-flies gilded wing.
At which his Elveship gan to fret,
10 Swearing it would make him sweat
Euen with it weight: he needs would weare
A wascoat made of downie haire
New shaven of an Eunuchs chin,
That pleased him well, twas wondrous thin.

15 The out-side of his doublet was
Made of the foure leavd true lov's grasse,
Changed into so fine a glosse,
With the oyle of Crispie mosse:
It made a Rainbow in the night
20 Which gave a lustre passing light:
On every seame there was a lace
Drawne by the unctious Snails slow pace.
To which the finest purest silver thread
Compared, did looke like dull pale lead.

25 His breeches of the Fleece was wrought,
Which from Chalchos, Iason brought:
Spun into so fine a yarne,
No mortall wight might it discerne.
Weaved by Arachne on her lome,
30 Just before she had her doome.

A rich Mantle he did weare
Made of Tinsell Gosemeare.
Beflowred over with a few
Diamond starres of morning dew:
35 Dyed Crimson in a maydens blush,
Lined with humble Bees soft plush.

His Cap was all of Ladies love,
So wondrous light that it did move;
If any humming gnat or flie
40 Buzzed the ayre in passing by.

About his necke a wreathe of pearle
Dropt from the eyes of some poore girle
Pinched, because she had forgot
To leave cleane water in the pot.

448

A possible alternative is to be found in *Musarum Deliciæ: OR, THE MUSES RECREATION, Conteining severall select Pieces of sportive Wit. By Sr J.M and Ja: S*, (London, 1655), 32–34 (BL, *E.1672.[1]*; University of Leeds, Brotherton Collection, *Lt.d.Men.*). In the first, there is no indication of authorship, beyond the initials R.S. subscribed to the prefatory Address to the Reader. These might suggest Dr John Smith (1605–1677), co-editor with Sir John Mennie (1599–1671) of the collection which includes the later version. The text itself however is usually attributed to Sir Simeon Steward (d. 1629), a friend of the poet Robert Herrick (1591–1674) and of the historian and divine Thomas Fuller (1608–1661). It is sometimes attributed to Herrick himself.

The English poem also exists in a number of MS versions, listed, together with a transcript of BL, *MS.Add.22603*, in Wood, *Choice Collection*, ii, 92–95.

No earlier version has been found of the introductory stanza, 'To the **Virtuosi**,' or the later verses on the Queen of Fairy. Pitcairne may himself have composed the first; the second however is written in a style very unlike anything else of his. The extended title of the 1634 version, *A Description of the King and Queene of Fayries, their habit* ('fashion or mode of apparel, dress' – the earliest sense of the word in English; note the plural, 'their'), *fare, their abode, pompe, and state*, suggests that the original poem was more extensive than the surviving copies, and that the dress of the Fairy Queen, as well as the King's, may have formed a part. By comparison with the title, the poem as we have it seems oddly incomplete – the little volume contains *A Description of his* (i.e., the King's) *Dyet* (pp. 4–6), representing *fare*, and *The Fairies Fegaries* (pp. 8–10; 'fegaries' = 'vagaries'), perhaps representing *state*, but no more. The volume also contains a certain amount of more or less unrelated padding. In his 'To the Reader' (A3), the editor apologises for the 'brevity of so short a volume,' with perhaps a suggestion that something is missing.

No source is known for 'To the VIRTUOSI,' but the idea may have been derived from the opening lines of the unpaged prefatory verses of *A Description*:

> Deepe skild Geographers, whose art and skill
> Do traverse all the world, and with their quill
> Declare the strangenes of each severall clime,
> The nature, situation, and the time
> Of being inhabited, yet all their art
> And deepe informed skill could not impart
> In what set climate of this Orbe or Ile,
> The king of Fayries kept; whose honor'd stile
> Is here inclosd, with the sincere description
> Of his abode, his nature, and the region
> In which he rules. (1–11)

These verses, it may be noted, are misplaced in the second edition (London, 1635; Bodleian *Arch.A.f.83[3]*), following rather than preceding *A Description of the King of Fayries Clothes*.

Pitcairne, it seems most probable, used either the 1634 text, or another, closely related but fuller. Like Buchanan and Johnston, Pitcairne misses the concision and some of the metrical lightness of his original. Hexameter and elegiac couplet are better fitted for the sonnet than for more lyrical measures. Nonetheless, he achieves a considerable measure of success; *Quam rigidus gelidâ Boreas diffundit ab Arcto*, for instance, is an effective rendering of 'When the Northern Winds do blow,' as is *ut trepidaret ad auram, / Quam musca aut cynips prætervolitando feriret* for 'If any Gnat or Humming Fly/ But beat the Air in passing by.' Incidentally, the coinage, *prætervolitando*, is an improvement made by Pitcairne in the second (1691) edition of the poem; see below. Delicate too is the way in which he translates the slight impropriety of the penultimate stanza. His Latin vocabulary he occasionally taxes to the limit, once or twice even beyond it; see notes.

Title The initial word is a compound of Greek Μορμῶν, 'a hideous she-monster used by nurses to frighten children,' and στολισμός, 'equipping, dressing.' The Latin has much the same meaning; *Lamia*, 'a witch who was said to suck children's blood,' and *vestitus*, 'clothing.' Pitcairne tends to use children's bugaboo words to describe the fairies, probably with deliberate ironic intent.

'To the VIRTUOSI'

The word *Virtuosi* is used in the sense 'scholars, scientists, particularly the latter': 'As great wits, as it may be e're saw the Sun, such as Pythagoras, Des-Cartes, Copernicus, Galileo, More, Kepler, and generally the vertuosi of the awakened world' (Joseph Glanvill, *Scepsis Scientifica* (1665), xi, 58, quoted in OED).

2 *Natural causes ... find*: i.e., in the work of such bodies as the Royal Society of London, founded in 1662.

4 *leav't ... guess*: the discussion of the apparently supernatural in relation to the world of nature was a feature of late-seventeenth-century thought, often provoked by the opinions of Thomas Hobbes (1588–1679): 'From their ignorance of how to distinguish Dreams and other strong Fancies, from Vision and Sense, did arise the greatest part of the Religion of the Gentiles in time past, that worshipped Satyres, Fawnes, Nymphs, and the like; and nowadayes the opinion that rude people have of Fayries, Ghosts, and of the power of Witches' (*Leviathan*, 1, 2). Henry More, Glanvill himself, and others defended the existence of such supernatural beings and powers, as did the Gaelic-speaking Scot, Robert Kirk (1644–1692) in his treatise *The Secret Commonwealth* (1691; ed. Stewart Sanderson [Cambridge and Ipswich, 1972]). Pitcairne ironically suggests that the poem provides an opportunity for such studies. His own position was probably closer to Hobbes's.

POEM 123

'Ad philosophos'

1 *Naturæ, & rerum*: a reminiscence of *De rerum natura*, the title of Lucretius' philosophic and materialist poem.

3 *Lemurum*: the Lemures were ghosts of the departed. Fairies were sometimes so regarded.

'On the king of fairy'

Title (Latin): *Oreadum*: the Oreads were mountain nymphs.

1.1 (Latin): *Lamiæ*: see 'Ad philosophos,' 3n.
circumdata: cf. *Aeneid* 4, 137, *Sidoniam picto chlamydem circumdata limbo*.

2.3 (Latin): *insolata*: literally 'placed in the sun.' This rare word is most often found in Columella, *De re rustica*, usually with a different sense; e.g., *insolati dies*, 'sunny days' (11.3.51).

3.4 (Latin): *Hepiali*: apparently not otherwise recorded for Latin; perhaps from Greek ἠπιόλης or ἠπίολος 'moth.'

5.1 (Latin): *theristrum*: late and ecclesiastical Latin, from late Greek θέριστρον, 'light summer garment.'

3 (Latin): *malâ & lanugine*: hendiadys, *metri causa*.

6.1 (Latin): *capitis … galerus*: cf. *Aeneid* 7, 688–689, *galeros/ tegmen habent capiti*.

3–4 (Latin): *ut trepidaret … feriret*: see above, **Text**. The version in (b) represents a deliberate improvement on (a), avoiding the clumsy assonance of *sine fine* and *moveret, feriret. prætervolitando*, a coinage based on the attested *prætervolo*, has a better metrical movement than *prætereundo*.

4 (Latin): *cynips*: *Cynips* in classical Latin is a river in Libya; cf. Virgil, *Georgics* 3, 312; Claudian, *De Bello Gallico* 1, 9. OED has *cynips*, 'gall-fly,' a formation, it is suggested, coined by Linnaeus (1707–1778) from Greek κύων, genitive κυνός, 'dog,' and ἴψ, 'woodworm.' Obviously however the coinage is earlier, a fact which may make more attractive the alternative origin suggested, from ecclesiastical Latin *ciniphes* or *sciniphes*, Greek σκνίψ, plural σκνῖφες, 'an insect found under the bark of trees, eaten by the woodpecker.'

8.2 (Latin): *Lineolâ … campi*: i.e., the spiders' webs often found spun between adjacent plants.

'On the queen'

4.4 (Latin): *Chloridis*: the name Chloris is here used for Flora, goddess of flowers and the flowery Earth in spring. *Chloris eram, quae Flora vocor: corrupta Latino/ nominis est nostri littera Graeca sono* (Ovid, *Fasti* 5, 195–196).

5.1 (Latin): *Candidulumque … pallidulumque*: note the effective diminutives. *pallidula* is found in the Emperor Hadrian's address 'To his Soul' (OBLV, 349).

8.3 (Latin): *scommate*: late Latin adaptation of Greek σκῶμμα, 'taunt, jest.'

124

Metre (Latin). (a) hendecasyllable. (b) elegiac couplet.
Notes. The Bells formed one of the clans who during the fifteenth and sixteenth centuries were notorious for robbery and cattle-reiving on the Scots-English Borders. Before he is hanged, *Thift* (Theft) acknowledges them as kinsfolk in Lindsay's *Ane Satyre of the Thrie Estaitis*:

> Adew my brethren common theifis,
> That helpit me in my mischeifis.
> Adew Grosars, Nicksons, and *Bellis*,
> Oft haue we run out-thoart the fellis. (3998–4001)

John Bell belonged to the eastern part of Annandale, on the Scots side of the Debatable Land between the rivers Esk and Sark. He was buried in what is now Redkirk churchyard, to the west of Old Graitney and the Kirtle Water. We have not been able to recover any other specific details, but it is clear that Pitcairne regarded him as a successful Border reiver.

The inscription disguises Bell's activities by a series of euphemisms. The usual context of 'sturt and strife' is given in Burns' song, 'McPherson's Farewell,' with words supposedly by the cattle-thief, James Macpherson, hanged in the market-place of Banff in 1700: 'I've lived a life of sturt and strife:/ I die by treacherie.' The bland denial of such activities in 3 is not to be taken at face value. 'Man of my Meat' implies reiving as a main source of supply. Version (a) is a relatively close paraphrase of the Scots, but the combination (2) of Mercury, god of thieves, with the name Bell (*Beloque*, Latin, 2) hints at the intended meaning. Version (b) is more expansive and specific, culminating in the reference to Laverna, patron goddess of rogues and thieves; cf. Horace, *Epistles* 1, 57–62:

> *Vir bonus, omne forum quem spectat et omne tribunal,*
> *quandocumque deos vel porco vel bove placat,*
> *'Iane pater!' clare, clare cum dixit 'Apollo!'*
> *labra movet metuens audiri: 'pulchra Laverna,*
> *da mihi fallere, da iusto sanctoque videri,*
> *noctem peccatis et fraudibus obice nubem.'*

125

Notes. This poem is ascribed to Pitcairne in the Library Catalog of the University of Texas at Austin, probably under the assumption that, as some of Pitcairne's verses were certainly written under the name of Walter Dennistoun, any other such verses are likely to be his. A probable corollary is that 'Dennistoun' is simply to be regarded as a pseudonym, with no reference to any actual person.

Neither is necessary or even likely. Dennistoun is a reasonably well-documented individual, known to have had the education and training required for the composition of Latin verse. Other verse by him has survived. There is nothing inherently improbable in the assignment of the poem to the author named or indicated.

Stylistically it is notably inferior to Pitcairne's authentic work. The convoluted and clumsy opening four lines, for instance, seem to omit a century from the chronology. In line 4, *et* (*&*) is curiously placed, presumably *metri gratia*. In l. 10, *atque* is used for *ac* before a consonant, again, presumably, *metri gratia*. In l. 11, *blanditur amicè* is little more than a line-filler.

Line 17, *Cuique suum dabitur: terras Astræa reviset*, is the only possible hint that Pitcairne might be the author. The phraseology is Jacobite, unparalleled in verses certainly by Dennistoun, but found in Pitcairne's own verse, e.g., **108**, 8. King William's pronounced hostility to the Company of Scotland and the Darien scheme may have led Dennistoun into this muted display of political dissent.

The poem is a brief *carmen saeculare* welcoming the new century. The concluding song in Dryden's *Secular Masque* (also 1700) offers an English parallel:

> *All, all of a piece throughout*:
>   *Thy Chase had a beast in View*;
> *Thy Wars brought nothing about*;
>   *Thy Lovers were all untrue.*
> *'Tis well an Old Age is out,*
>   *And time to begin a New.* (92–97)

Dennistoun's verses, in particular the final couplet, are given a certain poignancy by the fact that he died later in the year for which he composed this welcome. Perhaps because he was the poorer man, they come closer than anything by Pitcairne to the realities and illusions of life as lived by the majority of people in late-seventeenth-century Scotland.

1–2 *Post … sæcula*: these lines seem to indicate a total of 1600 rather than 1700 years. Perhaps ll. 3–4 are intended to mark the passing of another century.
5 *Nunc … cœco*: cf. Isaiah, 61:1: 'to proclaim liberty to the captives and the opening of the prison to them that are bound'.
7–8 *Hactenus … frequens*: a reference to the Nine Years War (1689–1697) and to the series of disastrous years for agriculture which began in 1692 and continued to the end of the century. 'Grain was short in some counties in 1695; the harvest failed badly and universally in 1696, bringing death to many in the following spring; recovery from this was very incomplete when the crops failed again

in 1698 and again the next year in many areas in 1699. We shall never know how many people died: contemporaries spoke of a fifth, or a quarter, or a third or even more of the inhabitants having died or fled in some areas, and from what we know of similar disasters in other north-European countries in the seventeenth century, they could have been right' (Smout, *History of the Scottish People 1560–1830*, 242).

13–14 *Eque ... opes*: a hopeful reference to the success of the Darien expedition.
13 *Caledoniâ*: New Caledonia, the Scottish colony on the Darien isthmus.
17 *cuique ... reviset*: see introductory note.
18 *Lares*: the household gods, the tutelary deities of the house.
19–20 *Interea ... simul*: as noted above, Dennistoun died, not long after writing these verses.

126

Notes. This and the following set of verses Foxon confidently assigns to Pitcairne (Foxon, *Verse*, 1, 583, 578; P400, P305). His reasons for so doing are much the same as those quoted in the Notes for the previous poem, but under the additional assumption that Pitcairne was in the habit of writing, not merely under the name of Walter Dennistoun, but under that of several other persons.

Robert Hepburn of Bearford, East Lothian, was born c. 1690. He studied law at Leiden. In 1710 he returned to Edinburgh to pursue a legal career. He came to some prominence with the publication of *The Tatler. To be published weekly by Donald MacStaff of the North*, a satirical journal which appeared in forty numbers between January and May 1711. *An idea of the modern eloquence of the Bar. Together with a pleading out of every part of law ... Translated into English* was published anonymously in the same year; it is a translation of *Idea eloquentiæ forensis hodiernæ* (Edinburgh, 1681), by Sir George Mackenzie of Rosehaugh. Hepburn was admitted to the Faculty of Advocates on 15 June 1714, some six months after Pitcairne's death. On 3 February 1716 the Faculty appointed him as one of the 'privat examinators' for the year. He died a few months later (Geoffrey Carnall, 'Hepburn, Robert' in *OxfDNB, s.v.*).

He seems to have been personally acquainted with Pitcairne, of whose writings he published a brief account, *Dissertatio de scriptis Pitcarnianis*, in 1715. His other publications are *Libellus singularis quo demonstratur quod Deus sit* (Edinburgh, 1714) and *A discourse concerning the character of a man of genius. With a poem on the young-company of Archers by Mr. Boyde* (Edinburgh, 1715).

Internally there is much to show that Pitcairne was not the author. The Latinity is clumsier and less idiomatic. There is a good deal of padding. Hepburn found it difficult to reconcile his vocabulary with the rigours of metrical form. The comparative *sæpius*, for instant, occurs twice (ll. 6, 26), *metri causa*, in initial position, where the positive *sæpe* would have been more appropriate. The repetition is clumsy, as is that of the phrase *in annum* (ll. 15, 28). In l. 15, the elision of *-um* in *annum* before *et* (&) is unusual, even awkward. The words joined by *et*, *hunc in annum* and *plures*, are separated, again rather awkwardly, by *vivere*. Parallels in Horace for *et* or *ac* in final position with elision do exist (*Odes* 3, 8, 26, 27; 27, 22, 46), but in all instances the elision is more straightforward and the structure more direct.

In ll. 14–15, *atque nasci/ Pulchrius*, we have another example of the comparative used *metri causa*. The phrase itself is padding, a mere repetition of *Posse præclarum fieri* (l. 14). Contrast the elegance and accuracy of the Horatian original: *nulla placere diu nec vivere carmina possunt* (*Epistles* 1, 19, 2).

Classical reminiscences are introduced with less subtlety than is usual with Pitcairne. In short, the verses more resemble the exercise of a bright schoolboy than a skilled adult performance.

The *Dissertatio de scriptis Pitcarnianis*, already mentioned, provides additional evidence for Hepburn's authorship. This ends (pp. 23–24) with a version of the poem addressed, not to Steele, but to Pitcairne, and introduced by the words: *Adjicere placuit huic Dissertationi carmen Sapphicum, quod olim ad* ARCHIBALDUM PITCARNIUM *rei medicæ gloriâ Edini florentem misi.* This contains a few variants; line 1 reads: *Dive, dic, præsens, medicum virumve*; line 7 has *Deorum* for *adæquos*, line 9 *quædam Dea* for *certus Deus*, line 29 *Pitcarni* for *Ricardi*. Otherwise the two are identical. The version addressed to Pitcairne may be the earlier. Under any circumstances the author is obviously Hepburn.

Title Sir Richard Steele (1672–1729), in collaboration with Joseph Addison (1672–1719), produced a London periodical, *The Tatler*, to great acclaim between April 1709 and January 1711. This provided the model for Hepburn's publication and the occasion for the present poem.

1 *Heroem Sociumve*: i.e., wine, the subject of the ode, but not specifically mentioned until l. 9. Contrast the direct reference to Pitcairne in the alternative version.

2 *Libero Patri, Venerique*: Liber Pater was an old Italian deity, later identified with the Greek Dionysus or Bacchus, god of wine. Here, as later in the poem, Hepburn had in mind Horace, *Epistles* 1, 19, in particular ll. 3–4: *ut male sanos/ adscripsit Liber Satyris Faunisque poetas/ vina fere dulces oluerunt mane Camenae*.

The association of Liber Pater with Venus, wine with love, is proverbial; *sine Cerere et Libero friget Venus* (Terence, *Eunuchus*, 4,5,6).

17–20 *Laudibus ... Homerus*: cf. Horace, *ut cit.*, 6: *laudibus arguitur vini vinosus Homerus*.

21–22 *Ennius ... plectro*: cf. Horace, *ut cit.*, 7–8: *Ennius ipse pater numquam nisi potus ad arma/ presiluit dicenda*. Quintus Ennius (239–169 BC) was an early Roman poet, author of *Annales*, an epic on the early history of Rome.

24 *Jaccho*: Iacchus is an appellation of Bacchus; cf. Virgil, *Eclogue* 6, 15 (of Silenus): *inflatum hesterno venas, ut semper, Iaccho*.

COMMENTARY

25–26 *Ipsa ... Virtus*: cf. Horace, *Odes* 3, 21, 11–12: *narratur et prisci Catonis/ saepe mero caluisse virtus*. Cato is mentioned, although in a diifferent context, in *Epistles* 1, 19, 12–14.
27–28 *Romuli ... annum*: Cato became Censor in 184 BC.
29 *Ricardi*: i.e., Steele, addressed only here in the envoi and in the title.

127

Notes. The poem celebrates the publication in 1711 of Hepburn's *An idea of the modern eloquence of the Bar*, translated from Mackenzie's *Idea eloquentiæ forensis hodiernæ*. There is nothing in it to suggest an authorship other than that claimed in the title. The Latin is again distorted by metrical demands. In ll. 2–3, for instance, it is extremely stilted and in l. 3, the use of the present participle *abiens*, and indeed the choice of the verb *abire*, is strained. In l. 14, the extra syllable in *descriptas* allows it to replace the more accurate, but less metrically amenable, *scriptas*; for the same reason the comparative *brevioris* replaces *brevis*. In l. 16, *non bene notus* is English rather than Latin idiom.

Title for Sir George Mackenzie of Rosehaugh see **5, Notes**.
1 *Te*: Mackenzie.
  læta ... Juventa: Hepburn was 21 when he published his translation.
3–4 *abiens ... Belgum*: this seems to mean that he made the translation during his time as a student at Leiden.
5–8 *Ore ... Orco*: the particular reference is to Book 3 of Mackenzie's *Aretina or the Serious Romance* (1661), an allegory of events from the English Civil War and the execution of Charles I to the Restoration.
5 *Theopompus*: in the romance, Charles I.
5–6 *atras ... cædes*: his execution.
6–7 *simulata ... fabula*: i.e., the narrative is in allegorical form.
7–8 *magnos ... Orco*: a variation on Horace, *Odes* 3, 30, 6–7: *non omnis moriar: multaque pars mei/ vitabit Libitinam*.
7 *Juvenis*: Mackenzie was 25 when he published *Aretina*. *Juvenis* parallels *Juventa* in line 1, thus emphasising the parallel (as Hepburn sees it) between himself and Mackenzie.
9 *quater ... Satiras*: the forty numbers of *The Tatler. To be published weekly by Donald MacStaff of the North*. For the phraseology, cf. Horace, *Epistles* 1, 20, 27: *me quater undenos sciat implevisse Decembris*; *Aeneid* 10, 213: *proceres ter denis navibus ibant*.
10–12 *decoro ... Ludum*: an adipose version of Horace, *Odes* 4, 12, 28: *dulce est desipere in loco*.
14 *Brevioris Ævi*: for the idiom, cf. Horace, *Satires* 2, 6, 97: *vive memor, quam sis aevi brevis*.

14–15 *Brevioris ... est*: cf. Edmund Waller (1606–1687), 'Of English Verse', 13–16 (the whole quoted in Money, *English Horace*, 10):

> *Poets that lasting Marble seek*
> *Must carve in Latine or in Greek,*
> *We write in Sand, our Language grows,*
> *And like the Tide our work o'erflows.*

Hepburn extends the concept to writers of prose, adding that English is little-known abroad.

INDEX OF PRIMARY TITLES

(by number of poem in this edition)

Ad ✸✸✸, 6
Ad Andream Tenant, 59a
Ad Annam Britannam, 98
Ad Annam Pitcarniam, 23
Ad Annam R. Anno MDCCXI, 91
Ad Annam Sexto Februarij, Anni 1711, 69
Ad Archibaldum Reidium Joannis Reidij Typographi Optimi Filius, 71
Ad Bertramum Stotum Equitem Anglum, 60
Ad Carolum XII. *Suecorum Regem*, 120
Ad Carolum II, 11
Ad Comitem Cromarteum, 87
Ad Cyclopas Alpinos. Virgilius Aeneidos Libro Octavo, 86
Ad Dannistonum, 9
Ad D. Davidem Dalrymplium Equitem &c., 52
Ad Elisam Pitcarniam 10 Junii. 1710, 25
Ad Elisam Ramisaeam Archibaldi Stevensoni Medicorum Principis Conjugem Archibaldus Pitcarnius, 41
Ad eundem, 36b
Ad G.B., 75a
Ad Georgium Kirtonum, Proserpinæ a Potione, 36a
Ad Georgium Makenzium, Regium, olim, apud Scotos, Advocatum, Roberti Hepburnii Scoti, Carmen Sapphicum, 127
Ad Gilb. Burnet. Scotum, A.P. Scotus, 75b
Ad Greppam, 8
Ad Gul. Benedictum de Grubbet, Equitem ----- A.P., 66
Ad Gulielmum Benedictum Equitem Auratum Grubetii Agri Dominum, 65
Ad Gulielmum Carmichael, 54
Ad Gulielmum Kethum Magnum Scotiæ Mariscallum, Anno MDCCXII
Ad Haium Comitem Kinulium, 42
Ad Homerum, Catulli carmen ex Græco Sapphûs versum, & Albæ Græcæ repertum, Anno vulgaris Æræ 1711, 90
Ad Hugonem Dalrimplium Supremi Senatus Juridici in Scotia Præsulem, 53
Ad Jacobum Dromondum, Dominum Stobhallum, Archibaldus Pitcarnius Scotus, 102
Ad Jacobum Gallovidium Equitem Caledonium, 88
Ad Jacobum Magnum, 107
Ad Jacobum VII, 10
Ad Januarium Anni MDCCXIII, *Archibaldus Pitcarnius Anno Aetatis suae* LXI, 112

INDEX OF PRIMARY TITLES

Ad Janum, 28
Ad Janum. 1709, 15
Ad Jesum Christum Dei Filium Archibaldus Pitcarnius Scotus, 110
Ad Joanetam Pitcarniam Decimo Junii Natam, 26
Ad Jonathenem ------ Novembris Anni MDCCXII, 93
Ad Josephum Scaligerum 29 Maij 1710, 103
Ad Jovem, 61
Ad Junium, 105a
Ad Junium Anni MDCCXII, 105b
Ad Kirktonum Chirurgum, 35
Ad --------- Malavillam, 78
Ad Lodoicam Stuartam, Ipso suo natali die, Decimo septimo Junii 1710, 121c
Ad Marcum Lermontium, 7
Ad Margaritam Pitcarniam, 27
Ad Phoebum, 74
Ad Phoebum Apollinem, 33
Ad Robertum Lindesium, 45
Ad Rob. Lindesium. 1689, 1
Ad Robertum Morisonum.M.D. et Botanices Professorem Oxoniensem, 32
Ad Thomam Kinkadium, 59b
Ad Walterum Dennistonum Ludi Magistrum Mussilburgensem, 49
Andraeae Flechero Regulo Saltonio Archibaldus Pitcarnius S.D., 67
An Inscription on John Bell, 124
Annae Reginae Archibaldus Pitcarnius Scotus S.D., 100
Archibaldi Pitcarnii Scoti. Carmen. Anno Aetatis suae LX, 22
Archibaldo Pitcarnio Gualterus Dannistonus Ευχαίϱειν, 68d
Archibaldo Stevensono Equiti, Scotorum Archiatrorum Comiti, Socero suo, Archibaldus Pitcarnius S., 40c

Balfoureus moriens loquitur, 29

Calderus Visharto, qui se Moderatorem, hoc est, vel Deum aut Regem vocat: Sacerdos spurius ex infima Fanatiquaque Plebe, 117

Dannistonus Pitcarnio S.D., 68a
D. Atkins Episcopus Orcadensis, 48
David ad Venerem, 18
Davidi Dromondio Jurisconsulto Archibaldus Pitcarnius S., 64
Davidi Drummondo, Edinburgi, xxv Decembris MDCCXIII, 109b
Die xxx Novembris, Anni MDCCXII. *Ad Andream Christi Apostolum. Qui Scotis dedit esse Christianis. A.P.*, 108
Die xxv Decembris, Anni MDCCXII, 109

Elisae Havartae Principi Gordoniae A.P. Scotus S.D., 89

INDEX OF PRIMARY TITLES

Fabulæ 2. Lib. 1 Phædri Metaphrasis, 12

Georg: Ferquhard ad uxorem demortuam, 57
Gualteri Dannistoni ad Georgium Buchananum Epistola et Buchanani Responsum, 20
Gualteri Dannistoni Epistola ad Joannem Cuningamium Juris Antecessoris, ut maturet reditum ad Inferos, 85
Gualterus Danistonus Scotus Sannazario Veneto Propriam quietem Gratulatur, 50

Harlaio, 96
Heriotus Senatui a se constituto sapere, 43
Horatius ad Luciferum, 82

In Annum Millesimum Septingentesimum, 125
In Barbaram & Margaritam Caroli Stuarti Comitis Traquairij Filias Gemellas, 62
In Carolum Wilson, 56
In Davidem Drummondum in certamine Sagitarriorum Edinburgensi Victorem Anno ------, 63
In Davidem Haium Medicum, 34
In Geo. Locartum, 3
In Geo. Makinnium, 5
In Geo. Makinnium Georgii filium, 17
In Jacobum Principem Hamiltonium Virum Fortissimum, Parricidio Foedissimo trucidatum Londini Die quindecimo Novembris Anni MDCCXII, 94
In Jacobum II. *Britanniæ Regem*, 80
In Joannem Patersonum, 46
In Johannem Belhavenium, 16
In Maij vigesimam nonam, Anno MDCCXII, 104a
In Maij vigesimam nonam, Anno MDCCXII, 104c
In Maii XXIX, *Sive Juni* X, *Anni* MDCCXII, 104b
In Marchionem Montis Rosarum, 84
In mortem Gulielmi Aurasionensis, 81
In mortem Vicecomitis Taodunensis, 4
In Nuptias Comitis Levinii, 77
In obitum Alexandri Monteith Chirurgi, 44
In obitum Archibaldi Stevensoni, Medici Regii, 40b
In obitum Archibaldi Stevensoni, Medicorum sui seculi facile principis, 40a
In Robertum Sibaldum M.D., 30
In undecimum Martii, quo ante annos octaginta natus est Archibaldus Stevensonus Medicorum apud Scotos facile Princeps, 40d,1
In 30. Januarii 1708, 13
In 30 Januarii 1709, 14
In Uxorem suam, 24
IV. *Nov.* MDCC.XII, *Ad Calvini Discipulos*, 106

Jacobo Septimo Ejus Nominis, Scotiæ Regi, Die Octobris Decimo Quarto, 73

INDEX OF PRIMARY TITLES

Joanni Duci Roxburgi Archibaldus Pitcarnius S.D., 21

Lauderdaliæ Dux, 72
Lodoix Maria Stuarta, 121a

Maecenati Duplinio Robertus Fribarnus S.D., 68c
Margarita Regina et Diva Scotorum, Ad Maij Vigesimam Nonam Anni MDCCXIII, 114
Maria Lodoix Britanna ad Alaricam Suecam, 122a
Maria Lodoix Stuarta, ad Alaricam Suecam, 122b
Monopennius J.C., 55
ΜΟΡΜΟΝΟΣΤΟΛΙΣΜΟΣ *sive Lamiarum Vestitus*, 123

On the Chief Physitian Sir Archibald Stevenson, 40d,2

Pitcarnius Dannistono S.D., 68b
Poema Pitcarnii M.D., 19b
Presbyteri Scoti Petro, 115
Proceres Scotorum Anno MDCXC, 76
Pythagoras Samius et Isaacus Neutonus Anglus, 47

Q. Horatio Flacco Archibaldus Pitcarnius Caledonius, 31
IV. *Nov.* MDCC.XII *Ad Calvini Discipulos*, 106

Ricardio Stilio Anglo, Viro hujus Sæculi Maximo, Robertus Hepburnius Scotus S.D., 126
Roberto Fribarnio, Typographo Regio, Et in certamine Sagitarriorum Regiorum Victori, A.P. S.D., 70
Roberto Graio Scoto Londini Medicinam Profitenti Archibaldus Pitcarnius Scotus S., 39

Scotia Martio. 1689, 2

Thomæ Boero Scoto, Matheseos & Medicinæ Professori, Arch. Pitcarnius Scotus S., 58
Thomæ Kinkadio Chirurgo. Archibaldus Pitcarnius Chirurgus S.D., 38
To Mʳ. B. Stote concerning the Edenburgh Taverns, 19a

Vaticinium, 118a
Vaticinium in Sepulcro Caroli Quinti repertum 1710, 118b
Venus ad Davidem, 18
Vice-Comes de Stairs, 51
XXV *Julii* MDCCXIII, 116

INDEX OF FIRST LINES

(*by number of poem in this edition. Comm. = Commentary*)

Advena, qui nostros cupies cognoscere Divos, **19i**
Andraea, vixti *Jacobo* semper Amicus, **108**
Andrea, facetis grate sodalibus, **59a**
Anna Caledoniae quae nunc felicior orae, **100**
Anna mihi genuit te Margaris Haia, nulli, **23**
ANNA, *Sibyllino* Quam nos veneramur in Antro, **69**
ANNA *Stuartorum* Decus et Spes altera Regum, **98**
ARBITER *Europae*, mandato Brittonis ANNAE, **97**
ARBITER *Europae*, mandatu Brittonis ANNAE, **96**
Austriacas acies & fultos Saxone Belgas, **118a**

Barbarus exclusit tumulo te *Nassus* avito, **80**

CAROLE *Gothorum* Ductor fortissime, solus, **120b**
Carole *Gothorum* longe Fortissime Ductor, **120a**
Carole, si pratis iterum reddare paternis, **11**
Carole, si similis Fratris, similisve Parentis, **119**
Caroli festæ jubeant quid Horæ, **7**
Clarkius, & quæ te quondam lætata sodali, **36b**
Cnoxiaci nostram faedastis Fraudibus Aedem, **43**
Consultissime juris, atque rite, **53**
Credidimus terras *Hydram* liquisse *Britannas*, **91**
Cum despecta Fides scelerato excederet Orbe, **2**
Cum mihi difficili caussa licèt sis semper patronus, **52**
Cum victor Ludo, Scotis qui proprius, esset, **46**
Cur Tibi Natalem felix *Heriote* quotannis, **111**

Dannistone jubes me digno dicere versu, **68b**
Dannistone meæ Patrone Musæ, **9**
Dannistone, meæ quid turbas otia vitæ, **20iii**
Davidis fautor *Jonathan* fuisti, **93**
Deepe skild Geographers, whose art and skill, **123 Comm.**
Delphinis quanto Balaena *Britannica* fertur, **95**
Dennistone Deo nunquam non plene quis ausit, **49**
Dexteram invictam canimus Jovemque, **20i**
Dicite Heroem Sociumve, Musæ, **126**
Dic mihi qui Medicæ mortalibus Auctor es artis, **33**

INDEX OF FIRST LINES

Dis Genite et Geniture deos, tibi surget avita, **84**
Diva, que cellis habitas Avernis, **8**
Dive, dic vatem medicumve Phœbo, **31**
Dum cives servare studes, dum Grampia regna, **16**
Dum genera herbarum divinâ digeris arte, **32**
Dum moriens laetor redeuntis munere vitæ, **22**
Dum nimis indulges sævo Kirtone dolori, **35**
Dum Patriae servire studes Patriaeq[ue] Parenti, **94a,b**
Dum Tibi laudatur *Maij* Vigesima Nona, **113**

Ecce Mathematicum, Vatem, Medicumque Sophumque, **109b**
Ergo magna Tui tellurem liquit Imago, **10**
Ergo nefasta dies, & secli dedecus acti, **13**
Esse Deum postquam te mors infanda coegit, **3**
Esse Tibi notum *Christum* ter *Petre* negasti, **115**

Fancy the great Hippocrates's Art, **40d2**
Felix Dupplinio, nuruque felix, **68e**
Festo quid potius die, **77**
First a Cobweb-shirt, more thinne, **123 Comm**.
Fratre Tuo viso derisit Apollo Gradivum, **121i**

Godolphine Stygem potas et Averna fluenta, **92**

Hac Christus jussit se nostram sumere formam, **109a**
Hac Christus jussit se nostram sumere formam, **109b**
Hac CHRISTUS voluit patrio se reddere cœlo, **104a**
Hac CHRISTUS *voluit patrio se reddere cœlo*, **104b**
Hac CHRISTUS voluit patrio se reddere coelo, **104c**
Hac *Jovis Hammonis* cineres conduntur in urna, **83**
HÆc est illa dies quæ sacræ conscia cœdis, **14**
Hæc tua, Pitcarni, fidei Confessio Christi, **109b**
Haie cui primos pepererunt flagra triumphos, **34**
Hectoris exuvias indutum cernite *Mosen*, **79**
Hic Belus abscondor, caput objectare periclis, **124b**

HIC est Ille Tuus natalis, *Septime*, qui Te, **73**
Hoc saxum mihi filii induerunt, **124a**
Hunc, *Benedicte*, tuo cineri *Pitcarnus* honorem, **65**
Hunc, Benedicte, tuo meritum Pitcarnus honorem, **66**

I Jocky Bell o' Braiken-brow lyes under this Stane, **124**
Ille ego Lauderiæ Dux, hoc inclusa sepulchro, **72**
Ille qui terris latitat Britannis, **39**
In fertile Weems, that soul refreshing place, **77 Comm**.

INDEX OF FIRST LINES

I Salutatum properè virorum, 58

Jam te, Dive, tenent *Homius*, sapiensque *Stevinus*, 42
Jane, jam Menses abiere sacri, &, 15
Jane, Senex optat *Pitcarnius* esse velitis, 112
Jane, Tui sexto mihi Filia prodijt *Agnes*, 28
Juni, Te Regem jam mensibus esse fatetur, 105a
Juni, te regem nunc annis esse jubemus, 105b
Juppiter arripuit Sibi Me, *Fratremque* jubebit, 122a
Juppiter arripuit sibi me, JUNONE relicta, 122b
Juppiter est hominis facie te fallere passus, 75a

Kinkadi, jucunde comes Dromondi, 37

Lindesi, stygias jamdudum vecte per undas, 1
Linquis invitas, venerande, Terras, 40a,b
Lucifer, nam Te Docilis Magistro, 82
Lux optata nitet, quæ soles noctibus æquat, 40d1

MAEcenas volui grates tibi solvere, musa, 68c
Magnanimis *Scotisque* Atavis dignissima vixti, 41
Maximus Atkinsi pietate et maximus annis, 48
Me brevis mimum peragente vitæ, 64
Me vis Duplinii divinas dicere laudes, 68d
Militis infesti me vis urgebat inermem, 18b
MILITIS infesti me vis urgebat inermem, 18a
Monticolæ quondam Lamiæ circumdata amictu, 123a
Multa tulere sacræ, Te, Rex, absente columbae, 101

Natalis Christi lux felicissima mundo, 109b
Natali vestro, lacrymis jejunia pascunt, 110
Naturæ, & rerum veras expendere caussas, 123a
Non hic Cæsarei surgunt monumenta sepulcri, 5
Nuper *Hamiltonus* vacuæ pertœsus *Edinæ*, 36a

OCTAVUS Martis Te jussit, Filia, nasci, 27
Optime, quàm gratos mihi fundis ab æthere nimbos!, 61
O salutaris militiæ decus, 38

Pallidi vivis bene spretor Orci, 40c
Phœbe, genus dic atque virum cui nuper honores, 63
PHOEBE Pater, Manes non hic vexare sepultos, 74
Pitcarni quereris quod nullo carmine laudem, 68a
Post mille exactos à partu virginis annos, 125
Post tot demersos Lethæo gurgite cives, 78

INDEX OF FIRST LINES

Prisca pharetratis quae propria gloria Scotis, 70
Prisca redit virtus, Pietasque refulget avita, 81
Proclamas omnes *Papistas* esse *Fugandos*, 117
Prudentissime Fergusî Nepotum, 6
Pythagora jactet *Samius* se fundus alumno, 47

Quæ, Morisone, viro potuit contingere major, 32
Quam cito te nobis, Longe Gratissima Conjunx, 24
Qua mihi non vixit vexatior altera Conjux, 57
Quam pudet Clio memorare gentem?, 76a
Quam Te prisca cupit gens *Grampia*, Sancte, redire!, 116
Quamvis dura tulit me mors, oriente juventa, 17
Quantus erat *Mariae* vindex *Havartus*, *Elisae*, 89
Quarta dies abiit Te Salvo, **Magne**, *Novembris*, 107
Quem virum aut Heroa lyra vel acri, 76b
Qui mihi combibulus puer es cupis atque jocari, 19ii
Quis fuero, cum Tu *Jacobe* redibis in Urbem, 88
Quis magis aut sapere, aut vitæ plus optet habere, 29
Quod non quinta dies potuit patrare Novembris, 106
QUOD repetita sequi nollet *Proserpina* Matrem, 67

Ranarum proceres paludis hujus, 12
Regia deseritur Ditis, Proserpina Matrem, 20ii
Risit *Apollo* tuo felici sidere fratri, 121ii
Risus atq[ue] Joci Deorum Alumni, 55

Sacra Dies olim Marti *Caroloque* fuisti, 114
Salve, dignus Avis, exoptatusque *Dromondis*, 102
Sancte Cuningami, quæ nunc tibi causa morandi?, 85
Saxonas ac Anglos olim Germania fudit, 99
Scaliger, quo nil voluere Musæ, 103
Si Gulielme diem placido vis fallere risu, 54
Si potuit virtus, si numina juris et æqui, 51
Stote Tuæ mœrens astat *Pitcarnius* urnæ, 60
Studious the busy Moments to deceive, 22.1

Tandem regna mei pereuntia liquit imago, 21
Tellurem fecere Dii, sua littora *Belgæ*, 50
Te placidus vidit Sol nasci, Filia, luce, 26
Te poetarum coluere Regem, 90
Te quoque Grampicolæ viderunt cedere fatis, 30
Te quoque Kirktono comitem, Montethe, dederunt, 44
Te quoque Sol vidit nascentem, Filia, luce, 25
Tertia *Septembris* vos orbi misit ovanti, 62
Te sequor læta calidus Juventa, 127

Teutonicas Acies, postremaque Cæsaris Arma, **118b**
Thoma facetæ Militiæ decus, **59b**
Tollite cuncta ---- caeptosque auferte labores, **86**

Ultime Scotorum, potuit quo sospite solo, **4**
Upon a time the Fairy Elves, **123a**

Vejovis est hominis facie te fallere passus, **75b**
Vidimus hæc pueri, Juvenes hæc vidimus arva, **45**
Vivacissime Fergusi nepotum, **87**
Vive diu felix, et laetos redde Parentes, **71**
Vixisti Volusene tuis pergratus Amicis, **56**

When, in late times of sin, an angry crew, **18c**

Ye *Virtuosi* hav't to you assign'd, **123a**

INDEX OF POEMS REFERRED TO IN THE INTRODUCTION

1	35, 44	49	35
3	36	50	42
4	36	51	36, 41
5	35, 36	53	39
6	39, 44	54	41
7	37, 44	55	39, 41, 46
9	29, 35, 39, 44	56	36, 41
10	44	57	36, 37, 41
12	39, 45	58	38, 40
16	46	59	38
18	37, 40	64	38
19	29	67	36
19(a)	35	68	36
19(b)	35, 37, 46	68(e)	39, 43
20	24, 35, 43, 46	69	36, 41
22	31, 32, 37, 46	72	37
23	36, 41	76	38, 40
24	36, 41	77	38, 40
25–28	36	80	37, 42
29	36, 41	83	42
30	36, 41	85	36
31	38, 41	87	39
32	41	89	36
34	41	93	38
35	45	103	37, 40
36	45	104	42
37	37	104–116	29
38	38, 41	105	42
39	38	109(a)	30, 43
40	38, 45	109(b)	44
40(a)	46	111	37
40(c)	32	115	37
43	37	119	42
44	41	121	44
45	34	122	18, 37
47	36, 40	123	35
48	36		

INDEX

Achilles, 364
Act of Settlement (1701), 429
Addison, Joseph, 38, 394, 455
   Cato, 394
   Letter from Italy, 394
   (with Sir Richard Steele), *Spectator, The*
Address from the people of Scotland, 16
Advent, 437
Advocates' Library, 15, 311, 316, 393
Ægidius (Giles), 321
Aemilius Paullus, 409
Aeneas, 306, 312, 327, 329, 330, 334, 335, 338–340, 343, 401, 419, 428
Aeschylus, 370
   Prometheus Bound, 370
Aesculapius, 363, 373, 377
Agricultural Revolution, 395
Airds Moss, skirmish at, 3, 309
Aitken, James, Bishop of Galloway, 36, 384
Alcinous, 423
Alexander the Great, 442
Almeloveen, Theodoor Jansson van, 9
   Inventa novantiqua, 9
Alsop, Anthony, 344, 373
Alves, William, 372
Ammianus Marcellinus, 377
Ammon, 417, 442
Anchises, 329, 340
Ancients and Moderns, 9, 13, 35, 40, 41, 345, 363
Andrew, Saint, 435, 437
Angers, 365
Anglicanism, 385
Anna Perenna, 357, 424
Anna, sister of Dido, 310
Anne, Queen, 2, 4, 19, 317, 324, 325, 338, 341, 349, 351, 355, 357, 380, 381, 393, 421, 424–426, 428–431, 433, 439, 442, 446
Apollo Staticus, 13
Apollo, 313, 315, 323, 340, 342, 363, 365–367, 384, 387, 393, 404, 406
Apollonius of Perge, mathematician, 374
   Conics, 374
Aquino, Carolo de, 415
   Sacra exequialia in funere Jacobi II, 415
Aratus, 346, 348
   Phaenomena, 346, 348
Arbuthnot, Dr John, 13, 23, 44, 426
   Modest Examination, A, 13
Arbuthnot, Robert, 44
Arcadicus/ Arabicus, 340
Archimedes, 7, 30, 38, 374
Aristarchus, 27, 383
Aristotle, 383
Arius, heretical theologian, 30, 436
Arthur, Colin, 10, 359
Ascension Day, 432, 433, 438
Assembly, The, 305
Astræa, 305, 415, 435, 439
Astrucius Francus, 390
Athanasius, Bishop of Alexandria, 30
Aubrey, John, 366
Aughrim, battle of, 328
Augustus, Emperor, 312, 317, 332, 397, 403, 407, 433
Ausonius, 341
Avernus, 319, 343
Averroes, 367
   Liber Canonis, 367
Avicenna, 367
   Canon of Medicine, 367
Ayton, Sir Robert, 34

INDEX

Bacchus, 322, 330, 332, 342, 373, 384, 391, 406, 455
Bacon, Francis, 357
Balconquhall, Walter, 21, 379
Balfour, Sir Andrew, physician, 36, 359, 360, 362, 375
Bank of Scotland, 393
Bannockburn, battle of, 349, 350
Barberino, Cardinal Charles, 415
Barberino, Maffeo, Pope Urban VIII, 415
Barbour, John, 348, 349
Barclay, John, 34, 311, 416
   Argenis, 311, 416
Baronius, Cardinal Cesare, 371
Bateman, Dr John, 38, 363–365
Battle of the Books, 383
Belgae, 385
Bell, John, 452
Bellini, Lorenzo, physician, 38, 355, 394
Bennet, Sir William, of Grubbet and Wideopen, 394
Bennet, William, 394
Bennet, William, son of Sir William, 395
Billy, Jacques de, 447
'Bischoppis lyfe and testament, The', 352
Blenheim, battle, 17
Blind Harry, Harry the Minstrel, 348
Blois, 365
Bobart, Jacob, 365
Boerhaave, Hermann, 8
Book of Common Prayer, 328
Borelli, Giovanni Alfonso, physician, 38, 355, 394
Borthwick, William, surgeon, 381
Boswell, James, 354, 391
   Journal of a Tour to the Hebrides, 354
   Life of Johnson, 391
Bothwell Brig, battle, 3, 309, 334, 400, 406, 409
Bower, Dr Thomas, 20, 22, 32, 388, 390, 391, 396, 397, 401
Boyd, Margaret, 360
Boyd, Mark Alexander, 34, 361
Boyd, Robert, of Kipps, 360

Boyne, battle of the, 328
Brigantium, 315
British Library, 35
Britto, 413, 428
Browne, Sir Thomas, 354
   Religio Medici, 354
Bruce, Robert, King of Scotland, 312
Buchanan, George, 24, 33, 34, 41, 311, 333, 344–348, 351–353, 376, 383, 389, 447, 450
   De Regni Jure, 348
   Fratres Fraterrimi, 447
Burnet, Gilbert, Bishop of Salisbury, 7, 386, 402, 403
   History of His Own Times, 402
Burnet, Sir Thomas, 361
Burns, Robert, 336, 452
   'McPherson's Farewell', 452

Cabal, The, 399
Cæsalpinus, Andreas, botanist and physician, 28
Caesar, Julius, 356, 407, 431, 433
   Bellum Gallicum, 356
Calder, Robert, 30, 37, 44, 334, 437, 441
   Lawfulness and Necessitie of observing the Anniversary Fasts and Festivals of the Church, The, 438
   Lawfulness and Expediency of Set Forms of Prayer, The, 438
Calvin, John, 3, 342, 380, 416, 434, 441
Calvinism, 338, 362
Cambridge Platonists, 35
Cameronians, 309
Campbell, Archibald, 10th Earl and 1st Duke of Argyle, 19, 328
Campbell, Archibald, 9th Earl of Argyll, 406, 409
Campbell, John, of Glenorchy, 1st Earl of Breadalbane, 313
Campbell, Revd. Colin, of Ardchattan, 306, 355
Cannae, battle of, 409
Cannon, Colonel, 309, 326, 410

472

INDEX

Carew, Thomas, 447
Carmichael, Hon. William, of Skirling, 41, 388
Carmichael, John, 2nd Lord, 1st Earl of Hyndford, 388
Castor and Pollux, 343, 364, 365, 408
Catherine, of Braganza, Queen, 306
Catholicism, 13, 360–362, 424, 430, 440, 441
Cato the Censor, 344, 419, 456
Cato Uticensis, 324, 344, 407
Cato (Addison), 370
Catullus, 39, 41, 306, 314, 321, 323, 327, 340, 387–389, 398, 419, 422, 423, 445
Cavalier (Jacobite) party, 349, 375, 376, 417
Celsus, 364
Cerberus, 343
Ceres, 319, 330–332, 395
Charleroi, 316
Charles I, King, 2, 3, 34, 311, 316, 321, 328, 330, 332, 342, 359, 366, 377, 381, 401, 413, 417, 421, 425, 433, 437, 438, 440, 456
Charles II, King, 1, 2, 37, 40, 41, 304, 306, 311, 312, 316–319, 324, 326, 328, 335, 372, 375, 399–401, 404, 406, 407, 432, 433, 435, 438, 439
Charles Edward, Prince (Young Pretender), 4
Charles II, King of Spain, 17, 441
Charles V, Emperor, 442
Charles VI, Emperor, 17, 18, 441–443
Charles XII, King of Sweden, 18, 430, 444–446
Cheyne, Dr George, 19, 20, 390
Chiesley, John, of Dalry, 307, 308
Chiron, 363
Chloris (Flora), 451
Christ Church, Oxford, 25, 385
Christmas, 393, 400, 436, 437
Churchill, John, 5th Earl and 1st Duke of Marlborough, 4, 17, 18, 26, 316, 330, 401, 415, 416, 424, 425, 427

Cicero, 39, 314, 378, 385, 387, 397
  Familiares, 385
  Pro Roscio Amerino, 387
  Tusculan Disputations, 397
Cincinnatus, 411
Circe, 414
Civil War, 1642–1652, 317
Clark, Robert, 368
Claudian, 305, 307, 313, 320, 360, 383, 415, 451
  De Bello Gallico, 451
  De Bello Gothico, 307
  De Raptu Proserpinae, 320
  'De sene Veronensi', 307, 313, 360
  De Sexto Consulatu Honorii Augusti, 307
  In Rufinum, 305, 383, 415
Cleanthes, 346
  Hymn to Zeus, 346
Cleland, William, 409, 410
Cleopatra, 342, 408, 416
Clerk, Robert, 368–370, 381
Clerk, Sir John, 1st baronet of Penicuik, 368
Clerk, Sir John, 3rd baronet of Penicuik, 368
Cockburn, William, physician, 8, 22
College of Justice, 344
Columella, 451
  De re rustica, 451
Commonwealth (Cromwellian), 3, 311
Company of Scotland Trading to Africa and the Indies, 15, 16, 453
Connor, Bernard, 27
  Dissertationes medico–physicæ, 27
Constable, Archibald, publisher, 42, 45
Copernicus, 383
Country party, 349, 353, 354
Court of Session, 14, 386, 388
Covenanters, 3, 310, 326
Crete, 332, 370, 417, 430
Cromdale, Jacobite defeat at, 326
Cromwell, Oliver, Lord Protector, 2, 311, 330, 393, 411, 413, 433
Culloden, battle of, 431
Cuninghame, Hugh, 39, 320, 322

473

INDEX

Cunningham, John, 36, 418
  Discourse by Mr. John Cuninghame advocate, 418
  Joannis Cuningamii j. cti. oratio inauguralis, 418
Cunningham, Sir John, of Caprington, Bt., 418

Dalrymple, James, 1st Viscount Stair, 8, 36, 41, 386, 387, 388, 402
  Institutions of the Laws of Scotland, 386
Dalrymple, John, 1st Earl of Stair, 386
Dalrymple, Sir David, of Hailes, 386, 387
Dalrymple, Sir Hew, Lord North Berwick, 386, 388
Dalrymple, Sir James, 386
Dante, 39, 324
  Convito, 324
  De Monarchia, 39, 324
  Purgatorio, 324
Darien, 15, 39, 325–327, 333, 349, 391, 424, 453, 454
David and Bathsheba, 335, 340
David, King, 413, 426
Declaration of Arbroath, 310, 350
Defoe, Daniel, 333
Delitiae Poetarum Scotorum, 34
Dennistoun, Walter, 5, 24, 35, 36, 39, 42, 44, 46, 318, 320, 321, 344–347, 352–354, 374, 384, 385, 392, 396–398, 418, 446, 452, 454
Devereux, Robert, 2nd (Devereux) Earl of Essex, 422
Diana, 387, 406, 411
Dido, 310, 324, 335, 338, 359, 419
Dionysus, 455
Dis, 313, 321, 342, 358, 369, 370, 400, 403, 432
Disticha Catonis, 341, 344
Divine Right of Kings, 39, 319, 359, 440
Donatus, 400
Douglas, Gavin, Bishop of Dunkeld, 24, 348, 349, 396, 397
Douglas, James, 2nd Duke of Queensberry, 328, 349, 424

Douglas, James, 4th Duke of Hamilton, 26, 43, 328, 333, 349, 379, 381, 401, 426, 427, 428
Douglas, James, 6th Duke of Hamilton, 16
Douglas, Sir James, 349, 350
Druids, 356
Drumclog, skirmish at, 3, 309, 409
Drummond, David, 26, 38, 372, 393, 394, 399
Drummond, David, minister of Moneydie, 393
Drummond, Dr John, 11, 26, 32, 372, 393, 396, 401
Drummond, James, 6th Earl and 3rd titular Duke of Perth, 350, 430, 431
Drummond, John, titular Duke of Melfort, 350
Dryden, John, 25, 305, 309, 311, 335, 377, 400, 401, 435, 453
  Absalom and Achitophel, 335
  Astræa Redux, 305, 415, 435, 439
  Britannia Rediviva, 400
  Secular Masque, 453
du Bellay, Joachim, 362
Dunbar, battle of, 411
Dunbar, William, 447
Dundas, John, 441
Dunkeld, defence of, 409, 410

Edinburgh Musical Society, 342
Edinburgh University, see Tounis College (Edinburgh University)
Edmonstone, Patrick, of Newton, 420
Eizat, Sir Edward, 12
  Apollo Mathematicus, 12, 13, 24
Elissa, 359
Elizabeth I, Queen of England, 36, 422
Elliot, Robert, surgeon, 8
Elphinstone, Arthur, 6th Baron Balmerino, 351
Elphinstone, John, 4th Baron Balmerino, 351
Elysian Fields, 343, 344, 365, 396, 398, 418, 419

474

INDEX

Ennius, 312, 338, 362, 397, 455
Epicureanism, 355
Epicurus, 356, 388
Episcopalian system, 2
Episcopalianism, 4, 31, 39, 315, 359, 399
Equivalent, the, 390
Erebus, 322
Erskine, Alexander, 5th Earl of Kellie, 10, 358
Erskine, Thomas Alexander, 6th Earl of Kellie, 10, 358
Erskine, Andrew, poet, 10, 358
Erskine, John, 22nd Earl of Mar, 20, 21, 392
Erskine, John, 23rd Earl of Mar, 369
Estates, Convention of, 305, 307, 308, 333, 401, 409
Estienne, Henri, 376
Euclid, 38, 374
Europa, 430
Eurydice, 363

Fabricius, 410, 411
Faculty of Advocates, 15, 26, 311, 316, 321, 344, 387, 388, 393, 418, 421, 454
Farquhar (Ferchard), George, of Leith, 36, 389
Fawkes, Guy, 433
Fergus I, legendary King of Scotland, 308, 310–312
Fergus II, King of Scots, 310
Fergusson, Robert, 343
  'Caller Oysters', 343
Ficino, Marsilio, 35, 302
Fletcher, Andrew, of Saltoun, 36, 395, 396
Flora (Chloris), 451
'Formula Lauream Candidatis dandi in Collegio Buterensi', 341
Fortuna, 435
Fraser, James, of Brae, 410, 411
  Memoirs of the life of the very Reverend Mr James Fraser of Brea, 410
Fraser, Sir James, of Brae, 410
Frederick of Hesse–Kassel, 446

Freebairn, Robert, printer, 25, 36, 41, 372, 389, 396, 397, 399, 418
Freind, Dr John, 426

Gaidhil Glas, 306, 315
Galloway, 384, 420
Galt, John, 309
  Ringan Gilhaize, 309
Garden, George, 20
Garth, Sir Samuel, 364
  Dispensary, The, 364
Gassendi, Pierre, 355
General Assembly, 3, 7, 305, 403, 406, 407, 409, 410, 414, 441
George I, King, 4, 380, 405, 416
George III, King, 4
George IV, King, 415
Ghibellines, 39
Gigantomachia, 341
Giric or Gregorius, King of Scots, 374
Glanvill, Joseph, 450
  Scepsis Scientifica, 450
Glasgow University, 302, 386, 402
Glencoe, Massacre of, 351
Glenfruin, battle of, 374
Glorious Revolution, 7, 305, 312, 330, 370
Godolphin, Sidney, 1st Earl of Godolphin, 330, 424, 425
Golden Age, 305, 317, 324, 326, 327, 330, 332, 417, 435, 439
Golf, 371, 382
Gordon, George, 4th Marquess of Huntly, 1st Duke of Gordon, 421, 431
Gordon, George, 388, 390
Græmus, 310, 312, 348, 417
Graham, James, 5th Earl and 1st Marquess of Montrose, 310, 417
Graham, James, 4th Marquess and 1st Duke of Montrose, 417
Graham, John, of Claverhouse, 1st Viscount Dundee, 4, 36, 305, 308, 310, 312–314, 326, 401, 418
Graham, William de, 310
Grantham, 310

475

INDEX

Gray, Dr Robert, 6, 11, 16, 23, 24, 27, 29, 38, 45, 301, 326, 363–365, 367, 368, 373, 374
Great Northern War, 18
Greenshields, James, 428
Gregorian calendar, 37, 431
Gregorie, James, 6, 38, 374, 394
Gregory XIII, Pope, 431
Gregory, David, 6–8, 10, 19, 20, 27, 38, 46, 373–375, 383, 390, 393, 394
   Astronomiae Physicae et Geometricae Elementa, 374
Greping-office, 26, 28, 29, 36, 39, 318, 319, 321, 322, 341, 343, 398
Greppa, 39, 318–323, 341, 398
Greyfriars Churchyard, 311, 312, 384
Guelphs, 39
Gunpowder Plot, 433
Gyllenborg, Count, 18

Hadrian, Emperor, 451
Haliburton, Margaret, 311, 334
Halley, Edmund, astronomer, 38
Hamilton, James, 2nd Earl of Arran, 351
Hamilton, James, MD, 367–370
Hamilton, John, 2nd Baron Belhaven, 21, 46, 333, 334
Hamilton, John, Archbishop of St Andrews, 333, 346, 351, 352
Hamilton, Margaret, *neé* Leslie, Countess of Rothes, 404
Hamilton or Leslie, John, 9th Earl of Rothes, 349, 404
Hannibal, 30, 312, 409
Hanoverian Succession, 325, 369, 381, 393, 421, 428, 429
Harderwijk, University of, 9
Harley, Abigail, 396–398
Harley, Robert, 1st Earl of Oxford and Mortimer, 17, 18, 26, 330, 396, 425, 426, 428, 429
Harvey, William, 7, 348, 363, 365, 383
Hay, Anna, 301
Hay, Colonel James, of Pitfour, Aberdeenshire, 7, 349, 357

Hay, George Henry, Viscount Dupplin, 36, 396, 397
Hay, Jean, 317
Hay, John, 1st Marquess of Tweeddale, 349
Hay, Margaret, 7, 36, 349, 357
Hay, Sir David, 41, 366, 367
Hay, Sir Gilbert, of Errol, 349
Hay, Sir Patrick, of Pitfour, 301
Hay, Thomas, 7th Earl of Kinnoull, 396, 397
Hay, Thomas, of Alderston, 317
Hector, 414
Henderson, Mrs (Greppa), 318
Henryson, Robert, 427
   Fables, 427
Hepburn, George, 12, 13, 361
   Tarrugo unmasked, 12
Hepburn, Robert, 32, 454, 456
   An idea of the modern eloquence of the Bar, 454, 456
   Dissertatio de scriptis Pitcarnianis, 32, 454, 455
   The Tatler. To be published weekly by Donald MacStaff of the North, 454, 456
Hercules, 408, 415, 424
Heriot, George, 20, 21, 37, 375, 379, 437
Heriot's Hospital, 20, 375, 379, 438
Hippocrates of Cos, 9, 360, 362, 377, 383
Hippolytus, 377
Hobbes, Thomas, 432, 450
   Leviathan, 432, 450
Home, Alexander, 7th Earl of Home, 377
Home, Alexander, 376
Home, Charles, 5th Earl of Home, 349
Home, Charles, 6th Earl of Home, 375, 376, 378
Homer, 422
   Iliad, 347, 364, 414
   Odyssey, 341, 422, 423, 437
Hooke, Robert, 27
   (ed.) *Philosophical Collections* of the Royal Society, 27

INDEX

Horace, 37, 38, 41, 312, 313, 315, 317, 321–323, 338, 340, 342, 344, 352, 354, 357, 358, 363, 364, 374, 376, 384, 388–392, 396–398, 403, 404, 407, 411, 416, 452, 455, 456
  Ars Poetica, 352, 354, 374, 384
  Epistles, 354, 398, 452, 455, 456
  Epodes, 313, 357
  Odes, 37, 38, 312, 315, 317, 322, 323, 338, 340, 342, 357, 358, 363, 364, 376, 388, 390–392, 397, 403, 409, 411, 416, 455, 456
  Satires, 321, 323, 344, 354, 456
Howard, Henry, 6th (Howard) Earl of Norfolk, 421
Howard, Lady Elizabeth, Duchess of Gordon, 26, 36, 421, 422, 431, 441
Howard, Thomas, 4th (Howard) Duke of Norfolk, 422
Hume or Home, Sir David, 376
Hume, Patrick, 1st Earl of Marchmont, 19, 333, 381
Hyde, Anne, 325
Hydra, 415, 424
Hyginus, 315
  Fabulae, 315

Iacchus, 455
Incorporation (later Royal College) of Surgeons of Edinburgh, 15, 368, 369, 370, 371, 372, 373, 381
Institution and Progress of the Buttery College, 341
Ios, 401, 427
Irus, 437
Isidore, of Seville, 323
Islam, 339
Israel (Jacob), 426
Issachar, 379, 401

Jacob, 426
Jacobitism, 4, 15, 36, 38, 39, 46, 306, 316, 319, 323, 324, 326, 327, 330, 335, 350, 353, 384, 396, 442
James V, King of Scotland, 303
James VI and I, King, 2, 351, 379, 433
James VII and II, King, 2, 3, 4, 7, 19, 37, 44, 303, 304, 306–309, 311, 315–317, 319, 324–328, 331, 332, 334, 339, 343, 349–351, 359, 360, 366, 369–371, 375, 377, 379, 382, 384–386, 394, 400–403, 406, 407, 413, 415, 417–419, 421, 425, 430, 432, 437, 440, 445
James Francis, Prince (Old Pretender), 4, 7, 15, 19, 317, 319, 325, 328–332, 349, 358, 359, 366, 371, 372, 378, 394, 400, 419–423, 425–436, 438–441, 444–446
James, Apostle, 435, 437, 440
January 30, 316, 328, 334, 342, 359, 433, 438, 440
Janus, 329, 330, 434
Johnson, Dr Samuel, 4, 354, 391, 398, 444
  Vanity of Human Wishes, The, 444
Johnston, Arthur, 34, 35, 307, 341, 369, 447, 450
  Encomia Urbium, 35
  Epigrammata, 34
  Parerga, 34
Johnstone, William, 3rd Earl of Annandale, 350
Jonathan, 426
Joseph I, Emperor, 17, 441, 443
Julian calendar, 37, 431
June 10, 326, 328–331, 358, 371, 372, 400, 431–433, 435, 438, 439
Juno, 370, 435, 446
Jupiter, 325, 327, 332, 342, 343, 348, 366, 369, 370, 384, 385, 390, 392, 398, 401–405, 407, 408, 417, 430, 435, 446
Juvenal, 41, 329, 427, 445
  Satires, 329, 427, 445
Juvencus, 425
  Evangeliorum Libri Quattuor, 425

Keill, James, 22
Keill, John, 21, 22
Keith, George, 9th Earl Marischal, 379
Keith, Sir Robert, 349
Keith, William, 8th Earl Marischal, 16, 376, 378, 390

INDEX

Kellie, Egidia, 378
Kennedy, Hugh, 403, 407, 408
Kennedy, James, 306
   Aeneas Britannicus, 306, 307
Ker, John, 1st Duke of Roxburghe, 19, 42, 352
Kerr, Professor John, 41, 395
Key, 45, 46, 368
Killiecrankie, battle of, 4, 308, 314, 326, 405, 409
King Oak, 325
King's College, Aberdeen, 15, 20, 367, 388, 390, 396
Kinkaid, Thomas, surgeon, 41, 371–373, 391, 399
Kipps, 360, 361
Kirk, Robert, 450
   Secret Commonwealth, The, 450
Kirkton, George, 368–370, 374, 409
Kirkton, James, 338, 368, 408
   History of the Church of Scotland 1660–1679, A, 338, 368, 409
Knox, John, 321, 346, 352, 380, 421, 438

Laevius, 377
Laverna, 452
Learmonth, Mark, lawyer, 29, 37, 39, 316, 317, 320, 322, 368, 371, 374
Learmonth, Thomas, 316
Leda, 343, 408
Leiden, University of, 7, 9, 10, 354, 366, 375, 385, 386, 402, 406, 454
Leopold I, Emperor, 17, 441, 443
Lesbia, 423
Leslie, David, 5th Earl of Leven, 38
Leslie, John, 7th Earl and 1st Duke of Rothes, 404, 417
Lethe, 303, 418
Liber Pater, 455
Limerick, Treaty of, 328
Lindsay, David, Clerk to the Council, 302
Lindsay, James, 405
Lindsay, James, of the Mount, Fife, 5, 301
Lindsay, Robert, 5, 6, 34, 301, 303, 374, 382, 405

Lindsay, Sir David, of the Mount, 301, 303, 452
   Ane Satyre of the Thrie Estaitis, 303, 452
   Monarche, The, 303
Lindsay, William, 18th Earl of Crawford, 334, 403–405, 407, 414
Livy, 411, 440
Lockhart, George, of Carnwath, 307, 349, 351, 353, 376, 378, 387, 405, 417, 420
   Memoirs Concerning the Affairs of Scotland, 307, 387
Lockhart, Sir George, of Carnwath, 36, 305, 307, 311–313, 401, 419
Lockhart, Sir James, Lord Lee, 307
Lord Advocate, 307, 311, 387
Lord President, 307, 308, 386, 388
Louis XIV, King of France, 4, 17, 18, 316, 317, 325, 327, 329, 332, 343, 419, 423, 441
Louis de France, *Grand Dauphin*, 427
Louis duc de Bourgogne, 427
Louisa Maria Theresa, Princess, 18, 37, 44
Lucan, 309, 324, 328, 329
   Bellum Civile, 309, 324
Lucretius, 339, 357, 388, 413, 424, 442, 451
Lyon, John, 2nd Earl of Strathmore, 19

McKenzie, John, of Delvin, 355
mac Mhaighstir Alasdair, Alasdair, 330, 331
   'Oran a' Gheamhraidh', 331
   'Oran mu Bhliadhna Thearlaich', 330
Macartney, Colonel George, 426, 427
MacDiarmid, Hugh, 362
Macduff, Thane of Fife, 350, 413
Macduffs, Earls of Fife, 350
Machaon, 363, 373
Mackenzie, etymology of name, 312
Mackenzie, Dr George, 21, 311, 334, 375, 380, 381, 438
   Lives and Characters of the most Eminent Writers of the Scots Nation, 380
Mackenzie, Kenneth, 4th Earl of Seaforth, 326, 328

INDEX

Mackenzie, Sir George, of Rosehaugh, 25, 36, 305, 308, 311–313, 334, 400, 401, 418, 454, 456
   Aretina, 311, 456
   Defence of the Antiquity of the Royal Line of Scotland, 311, 312
   Idea eloquentiæ forensis hodiernæ, 454, 456
   Institutions of the Laws of Scotland, 311, 418
   Jus Regium, 311, 312
   Religio Stoici, 312
Mackenzie, Sir George, of Tarbat, 1st Earl of Cromarty, 313, 399, 419, 420
Macpherson, James, cattle thief, 452
Macrobius, 315, 403, 426
   In Somnium Scipionis, 426
   Saturnalia, 315, 403
Maecenas, 317, 396, 397
Main, James, 434
Maitland, John, 2nd Earl, 1st Duke of Lauderdale, 37, 308, 311, 399, 400
Malplaquet, battle, 17
Manius Curius Dentatus, 410, 411
Marcellus, 312, 317, 407, 432
Margaret, St., 37, 371, 372, 439
Maria Louisa of Savoy, 18, 441
Marischal College, Aberdeen, 373, 390, 402, 410
Mars, 439, 445
Martial, 35, 39, 41, 327–330, 383, 387, 437
   Liber Spectaculorum, 387
Mary I, Queen of Scots, 36, 303, 346, 351, 380, 422, 440
Mary II, Queen, 2, 303, 305, 324, 350, 378, 401, 402
Mary of Modena, Queen, 325, 331
Massacre of Glencoe, 314, 386
Massey, John, 384
Massie, Andrew, 384
Maxwell, John, Bishop of Ross, 381
May 29, 306, 316, 331, 372, 431–433, 438, 439
Mead, Richard, physician, 8, 19

Meikle, James, 395
Melissus, Paulus, 447
Melville or Leslie, David, 5th Earl of Leven and 2nd Earl of Melville, 404, 405, 411, 413, 414
Melville, Andrew, 34, 414
Melville, George, 1st Earl of Melville, 406
Mennie, Sir John, 449
   (with Dr John Smith) *Musarum Deliciæ*, 449
Menzies, Paul, of Pitfodel, 371
Mercury, 338, 353, 439, 452
Merton College, Oxford, 364
Middleton, Principal, 388, 390, 396
Milton, John, 311, 339, 366, 408, 421
   'On the new Forcers of Conscience under the Long Parliament', 408, 421
   Paradise Lost, 339
Minerva, 304, 391, 396, 398, 405
Minos, 324, 418, 419
Minute Book of the Faculty of Advocates, 317, 345
Moderator, 403, 407, 441
Mohun, Charles, 4th Baron, 333, 349, 426, 427
Moneypenny, Sir John, of Pitmilly, 388
Moneypenny, William, 388
Monro, Alexander, Principal, 306, 406
Monro, John, surgeon, 8
Monteith, James, of Auldcathie, 381
Monteith, Sir Alexander, 11, 381
Montgomerie, Sir James, of Skelmorlie, 350
More, Henry, 302
   Immortality of the Soul, 302
Morini, 306
Morison, Robert, 6, 14, 364, 365
   Plantarum Historiæ Pars Tertia, 14, 365
   Plantarum Historiæ Universalis Oxoniensis Pars Secunda, 365
   Præludia Botanica, 365
Mortonhall, Lady, 406
Moses, 414

National Covenant, 3

Navigation Acts, 15
Nennius, 413
  Historia Brittonum, 413
Neptune, 387, 411, 416
Nestor, 377, 398
New Caledonia, 454
New Style, 371
Newton, Sir Isaac, 1, 7, 8, 10, 27, 31, 36, 38, 40, 353, 373, 374, 383, 390, 391
  'De Natura Acidorum', 8
  Principia, 6, 373, 383
Nicolson, William, Bishop of Carlisle, 25, 26
Nine Years War, 37, 316, 332, 453
North Loch (Edinburgh), 322
'Note of School Authors', 42
Numa Pompilius, 406
Octupla, 344

'Of Tribute,', 357
Ogilvy, James, 4th Earl of Findlater and 1st Earl of Seafield, 440
Old Pretender, see James Francis, Prince (Old Pretender)
Old Style, 331, 371, 424
Oliphant, Elizabeth, 373
Orange–Nassau, House of, 304
Origin legend, Scottish, 306
Orpheus, 363, 374, 398, 404
Orrock, Alexander, 410
Oudenarde, battle, 17
Ovid, 310, 339, 340, 346, 348, 357, 374, 400–403, 451
  Amores, 334, 339, 340, 348, 400
  Ars Amatoria, 339
  Fasti, 310, 357, 402, 451
  Metamorphoses, 346, 357, 374, 425
  Tristia, 401

Paisley Missal, 352
Pallas Athena, 398
Pallas Athene, 391
Pappus, 27
Paris, 5, 6, 301–303, 324, 359, 365, 415, 427, 431

Paterson, Hugh, surgeon, 16
Paterson, John, Archbishop of Glasgow, 25, 302, 345, 346, 348, 351, 352
Paterson, John, Bishop of Ross, 302, 351
Paterson, Sir William, 302
Paterson, William, financier, 390
Patersone, John, 382
Paul, Saint, 438, 439
Peace of Utrecht, 18, 26
Pelion on Ossa, 342
Peter the Great, Czar of Russia, 18, 28
Peter, Saint, 439
Phaedrus, 39, 325, 328
  'Ranae Regem petierunt', 325
Phaethon, 366
Philip V, King of Spain, 17, 18, 441, 442
Philip of Macedon, 442
Philp or Philip, James, of Almerieclose, 309, 324
  Grameidos Libri Sex, 309, 324
Phœbus, 304, 345, 373, 387, 393
Phoenix, 435
Picts, 306, 370, 435
Pisistratus, 325
Pitcairne, Agnes, 10, 359
Pitcairne, Alexander, 5
Pitcairne, Andrew, 8, 10, 15
Pitcairne, Anne, 7, 357
Pitcairne, Archibald, 1, 2, 5, *et passim*
  Archibaldi Pitcarnii oratio, 8
  Archibaldi Pitcarnii, Scoto–Britanni, medici celeberrimi, Opera omnia, 43
  Archimedis Epistola ad Regem Gelonem, 422
  Assembly, The, 7, 40, 304, 305, 306, 319, 328, 334, 335, 340, 368, 403, 406, 409, 411, 414
  Babell, 11, 40, 54, 305, 335, 342, 403, 406, 411, 412, 414
  De circulatione sanguinis in animalibus genitis et non genitis, 33
  Disputatio de curatione Febrium, 12
  Dissertatio de Legibus Historiæ Naturalis, 12, 22, 361
  Dissertationes medicæ, 8, 26, 390

480

INDEX

Epistola Archimedis ad Regem Gelonem, 7, 30, 31, 445
Fabulæ 2 Lib. 1. Phædri Metaphrasis, 16, 39
Key, 44, 45, 301, 313, 316, 318, 320, 325, 367, 368
Poemata Selecta, 40, 43
Roberti Morisoni Vita, 365
'Roundel on Sir Robert Sibbald', 362
Selecta Poemata, 15, 41, 42
Solutio problematis de historicis, 7, 9, 383
Tollerators and Con–Tollerators, 19
Pitcairne, Elizabeth, 10, 358
Pitcairne, Jane or Janet, 10, 358
Pitcairne, Margaret, 10, 359
Plain of Truth, 382
Plato, 35, 302, 382
   Phaedrus, 302, 382
   Republic, 302, 387
Plautus, 391, 424
   Bacchides, 391
Pliny the Elder, 323
Pliny the Younger, 327
   Panegyric, 327
Pluto, 319, 358
Podalirius, 363, 373
Pollio, 317
Poltava (Pultowa), 18, 444
Potter, Walter, 368–370
Presbyterianism, 3, 361, 399, 407, 435
Priapea, 321
Prior, Matthew, 37, 38, 354–356, 374, 401, 402, 426, 429
   'Carmen Seculare for the year 1700', 402
   Poems on Several Occasions, 355
Privy Council, 302, 387, 388, 428
Propertius, 396, 401
Proserpine, 319–321, 332, 348, 369, 389, 395, 396, 418
Protesters, 3
Ptolemy, 27
Pythagoras, 36, 356, 357, 383

Quintilian, 314
Quintilius Varus, 323

Ramillies, battle, 17
Ramsay, Allan, 324, 342
   'Epistle to Robert Yarde of Devonshire Esquire', 343
   Gentle Shepherd, The, 324
   Poems, 342
Ramsay, Elizabeth, 375, 378
Ramsay, John, of Idington, 378
Ramsay, Robert, Provost and Rector, 428
Randolph, Thomas, 1st Earl of Moray, 350
Real Presence, doctrine of the, 30
Regulus, Marcus Atilius, 409
Regulus (Rule), St., 435
Reid, Archibald, printer, 399
Reid, John, junior, printer, 399
Reid, John, senior, printer, 399
Remonstrants, 3
Renwick, James, 334
Resolutioners, 3
Restoration, 3, 37, 40, 306, 307, 311, 316, 317, 319, 331, 365, 377, 386, 410, 421, 430–433, 435, 439, 456
Revenant, 303, 319, 324, 332
Rhadamanthus, 305, 418
Rheims, University of, 6
Rising (1708), 21, 329, 333, 351, 394, 395, 420, 430
Rising (1715), 4, 20
Rising (1745), 4
Robert I, Bruce, King of Scots, 348–350
Robertson, Alexander, of Struan, 305
Roman Catholicism, 3, 5
Romulus, 339, 406
Ronsard, Pierre de, 447
Rosa Ciphiana, 361, 362
Rose, Anne, 351
Rose, Arthur, Archbishop of St Andrews, 351, 410
Rose, Alexander, Bishop of Edinburgh, 342
Royal Botanic Garden, Edinburgh, 360
Royal College of Physicians, Edinburgh, 6, 10, 12, 21, 26, 40, 360, 363–366, 372, 373, 375, 376, 378

INDEX

Royal College of Physicians, London, 27, 364
Royal Company of Archers, 393, 399
Royal Oak, 326
Royal Society, 20, 27, 28, 353, 450
Ruddiman, Thomas, 15, 41, 42, 45
Rufinus, 415
Rule, Principal Gilbert, 306, 380, 406
Rullion Green, skirmish at, 3
Russell, James, in Kettle, 405
Rye House Plot, 406
Rymore, Henry, 410
'Ryot' in the College, 14
Ryswick, Peace of, 316, 327

Sacheverell, Henry, 26, 438
   'Perils of False Brethren, The', 26, 438
Samos, 340, 356, 383
Sancroft, William, Archbishop of Canterbury, 402, 403
Sannazaro, Jacopo, 41, 385
   De mirabile urbe Venetiis, 385
Sanquhar Declaration, 309
Sappho, 348, 422
Saturn, 327, 332, 369, 370, 407, 417, 439
Saturnalia, 320
Saul, 426
Scaliger, Joseph Justus, 40, 431, 432
   De emendatione temporum, 431, 432
Scaliger, Julius Caesar, 341
Schacht, Lucas, 7
Scotch Presbyterian Eloquence, 334, 335, 352, 409, 410, 437
Scott, James, Duke of Monmouth, 406
Scott, Sir John, of Scotstarvet, 34
Scott, Sir Walter, 309, 361, 404, 422
   'Wandering Willie's Tale', 404
   Antiquary, The, 361
   Heart of Midlothian, 422
   Old Mortality, 309
   Redgauntlet, 404
Scott, Sir William, of Thirlestane, 41, 395
Scottish Prayer Book, 380, 381
Secret Treaty, 316

Seneca, the Younger, 362, 394
   Epistulae, 394
   Naturales Quaestiones, 362
Servius, 338, 400
Seton, Alexander, 4th Earl of Dunfermline, 350
Seton, Archibald, of Touch, 420
Seton, Sir Alexander, 350
Shakespeare, William, 413
   King Lear, 417
   Macbeth, 413
Sharp, James, Archbishop of St Andrews, 405
Sibbald, Sir Robert, 12, 14, 22–26, 36, 41, 360–363, 366, 375, 396, 416
   Answer to the second letter, 26
   Letter from Sir R- S- to Dr Archibald Pitcairn, A, 22
   Memoirs, 416
   Nuncius Scoto–Brittanicus, 362, 363
   Scotia Illustrata, 12, 26, 360–362
   Vindiciæ Scotiæ Illustratæ, 22, 361
   Ode Parænetica, 23
Sibyl, 398
Silver Arrow of Musselburgh, 393, 399
Sinclair, Henry, 10th Lord Sinclair, 350
Sinclair, Henry, of Roslin, 350
Sinclair, John, styled 11th Lord Sinclair, 350
   Memoirs of the Rebellion, 350
Sinclair, Sir William, of Roslin, 350
Sinclair, William, Bishop of Dunkeld, 350
Sloane, Sir Hans, 28, 364
Smith, Dr John, 449
   (with Sir John Mennie) *Musarum Deliciæ*, 449
Socinus, theologian, 30, 436
Solemn League and Covenant, 3
Solomon, 335, 340, 426
Song of Songs, 340
Sophia, electress of Hanover, 405
Sozini, Francesco Maria, theologian (Socinus), 436
Sozzini, Fausto Paolo, theologian (Socinus), 30, 436

Squadrone Volante, 353
St Giles', Edinburgh, 12, 36, 322
St John, Henry, 1st Viscount Bolingbroke, 396
St. Clair or Sinclair, Matthew, 366
Stamfield, Anne, 26, 36, 41, 320, 322, 341, 343, 398
Statius, 39, 310, 320, 328, 329, 398
  Silvae, 39, 310, 320, 328, 329, 398
Steele, Sir Richard, 455, 456
  (with Joseph Addison) *Spectator, The*, 394
  Tatler, The, 455
Steill, John, 342
Stevenson, Elizabeth, 10, 358, 359, 375
Stevenson, Rev. Andro, 375
Stevenson, Sir Archibald, 10, 13, 14, 20, 24, 38, 46, 302, 329, 360, 375, 376, 378, 380
Steward, Sir Simeon, 449
  A DESCRIPTION *Of the King and Queene of Fayries*, 447
Stewart, Alexander, 20th Earl of Moray, 350
Stewart, Charles, 4th Earl of Traquair, 392
Stewart, Ladies Barbara and Margaret, 392
Stirling, Archibald, of Carden, 420
Stirling, Charles, of Kippendavie, 420
Stirling, James, of Keir, 420
Stott, Sir Bertram, 35, 38, 354, 391, 392
Stuart, Charles Edward, Prince (Young Pretender), 4, 421, 431
Stuart, Louisa Maria Theresa, Princess, 425, 444, 445, 446
Styx, 319, 322, 358, 403
Suetonius, 308, 392
  'Titus', 392
Swift, Jonathan, 13, 18, 38, 425, 426
  Conduct of the Allies, The, 425
  History of the Last Four years of Queen Anne, 425
Sydserf, Thomas, Bishop, 5
Sydserff, Janet, 5

Sylvius, Franciscus, 354, 355
Symson, Andrew, printer, 25, 26, 396
  Larger Description of Galloway, 26

taceat superata vetustas (topic), 383, 385, 445
Tacitus, 370
  Annals, 370
Tanaquil, 440
Tarquinius Priscus, 440
Tenant, Andrew, 391
Terence, 391
  Eunuchus, 455
  Phormio, 391
Thackeray, William Makepeace, 426
  Henry Esmond, 426
Theodosius the Great, Emperor, 415
Tibullus, 377
Tories, 4, 330, 417, 424, 427, 438
Toubacanti, 15
Tounis College (Edinburgh University), 5, 6, 34, 373, 375, 380, 384
Trinity, doctrine of, 30–31
Trojan War, 363, 364, 373
Trotter, Dr Robert, 13
Troy, 327, 414

Ulrika, sister of Charles XII, 18, 430, 445, 446
Union (1603), 379
Union (1707), 2, 16, 21, 25, 306, 307, 329, 330, 333, 334, 349, 351, 353, 377–379, 387, 390, 395, 417, 422, 428, 440
University College, Oxford, 311, 334
Unuist, King of the Picts, 435
Urry, John, 25, 26
Usinulca, 416, 437, 441
Utrecht, Peace of, 355, 396, 428, 429, 439

Vejovis, 402, 403, 427
Venus, 321, 330, 332, 336, 337, 338–340, 411, 430
Vespasian, 308

INDEX

Virgil, 41, 312, 322, 323, 327, 330, 332, 339, 340, 343, 346, 354, 357, 374, 396, 397, 400, 401, 408, 426, 434, 451, 455
  Aeneid, 24, 25, 35, 36, 303, 305, 306, 308, 309, 312, 313, 315, 317, 319, 322, 324, 327–330, 334, 338–343, 346–348, 352, 356, 357, 359, 362, 370, 372, 373, 376, 378, 385, 387, 389, 392, 396–398, 400, 401, 408, 414, 418, 419, 423, 426, 427, 432, 451, 456
  Eclogues, 327, 339, 340, 346, 354, 374, 434, 435, 455
  Georgics, 312, 332, 339, 342, 398, 451
Vulcan, 337, 340, 342, 419
Vulgate, 339, 347, 413, 436

Walkinshaw, Dr James, 21–23
  Letter from Dr James Walkinshaw to Sir Robert Sibbald, A, 22
Wallace, Sir William, 312, 379, 424
Waller, Edmund, 457
  'Of English Verse', 457
Wallis, John, mathematician, 5, 27, 373
  Opera Mathematica, 5, 27
War of the Spanish Succession, 17, 18, 332, 424, 425, 428, 429, 441, 443
Watson, James, printer, 16, 25, 46, 368, 418, 446
  Choice Collection, A, 341, 447
Watson, John, 21, 380
Wedderburn, David, 34
Wedderburn, James, Bishop of Dunblane, 381
Weir, Major Thomas, of Kirktown, diabolist, 409

Wemyss, John, Lord, of Elcho, 350
Wemyss, Lady Anne, 38, 404, 405, 411, 413, 414
Wemyss, Margaret, Countess of Wemyss, 419
Wemyss, Sir David, 350
Wild Geese, 328
William II and III, King (William of Orange-Nassau), 2, 3, 8, 15, 16, 19, 25, 34, 36, 40, 303–305, 307, 309, 310, 316, 319, 324–328, 330–333, 341, 349, 350, 359, 369, 370, 378, 386, 395, 400–402, 405, 407, 409, 415–419, 424, 429, 433, 434, 440, 453
Williamson, David, 37, 304, 334–336, 338–340, 406, 408, 411, 413
Wilmot, John, 2nd Earl of Rochester, 359
Wilson, Charles, 36, 389
Wilson, Florence (Florentius Volusenus), 389
  De Animi Tranquillitate, 389
Wishart, William, Moderator, 441
  Seasonable Warning by the Commission of the General Assembly, 441
Wodrow, Robert, 29, 302
  Analecta, 302
Worcester, battle of, 306, 326, 411, 433
World Upside Down (topic), 308, 381
Writers to the Signet, Society of, 345

Young Pretender, see Charles Edward, Prince (Young Pretender)
Young, John, 6, 373

Zeus, 370, 377, 398, 417, 426